The Rambl

Yearbook & Accomm

CW01551723

2001

EDITOR
Keith Marr

COVER DESIGN
Clare Warne, Venus, London

COVER PHOTOGRAPH
Phil Seale –
Members of Cumbernauld & Kilsyth RA
Group on Craig Rossie, in the Ochil Hills
near Auchterarder

PRINTING
Benham & Co Ltd, Colchester, Essex

TRADE DISTRIBUTION
W. Foulsham & Co Ltd
The Publishing House
Bennets Close
Cippenham, Berks SL1 5AP
☎ (01753) 526769

ACCOMMODATION ADVERTISING
The Editor
The Ramblers' Association
☎ 020 7339 8585
Email:
yearbook@london.ramblers.org.uk

COMMERCIAL ADVERTISING
Terry Lock Media Sales
☎/Fax (01372) 276233

PUBLISHED BY
The Ramblers' Association
2nd Floor, Camelford House
87-90 Albert Embankment
London SE1 7TW
☎ 020 7339 8500 • Fax: 020 7339 8501
Email: ramblers@london.ramblers.org.uk
Web: www.ramblers.org.uk

Scottish Office
Kingfisher House
Auld Mart Business Park
Milnathort, Kinross KY13 9DA
☎ 01577 861222 • Fax: 01577 861333.
Email:
enquiries@scotland.ramblers.org.uk
Web: www.ramblers.org.uk/scotland

Welsh Office
Ty'r Cerddwyr
High Street, Gresford
Wrexham LL12 8PT.
☎ 01978 855148 • Fax 01978 854445
Email: cerddwyr@wales.ramblers.org.uk
Web: www.ramblers.org.uk/wa

ISBN 1-901184-35-8

Published January 2001

Help keep her head above water...

Jasmine is an Indo-Chinese tiger. There are only 1,200 left in the wild.

The worldwide tiger population is in deep water as poaching and the illegal trade in tiger bones is on the increase. We are seeking foster parents for Jasmine. She was only a month old when rescued from smugglers who were intending to sell her. She was destined for the animal trade and was already suffering from rickets and malnutrition. We need the support of foster parents to help with her on-going care.

The money you give will help to provide her with the care she needs at her natural habitat enclosure in Cambodia and will provide funds for tiger conservation worldwide.

For £18.95 you will receive a gift pack which includes:
- A fostering certificate with a colour picture
- An exclusive tiger T-shirt
- A tiger fact sheet
- An update after six months
- A renewal request after twelve months

The pack is available individually (without a donation) for £4.95

**Care for the Wild International,
1 Ashfolds, Horsham Road, Rusper,
West Sussex, RH12 4QX.
Telephone (01293) 871596
Fax (01293) 871022
E-mail: info@careforthewild.com
Web: www.careforthewild.com
Registered charity no. 288802**

Yes! I would like to adopt Jasmine the orphan tiger:

RAMB00

Person making payment
Mr/Mrs/Miss/Ms _____
Address _____
_____
_____ Postcode _____

Foster parent
Mr/Mrs/Miss/Ms _____
Address _____
_____
_____ Postcode _____

Please send the initial gift pack to: The foster parent ☐   The person making payment ☐
I would like to receive a tiger T-shirt in size: Child ☐   Small ☐   Medium ☐   Large ☐   X-Large ☐
I enclose a cheque/postal order *(Payable to Care for the Wild International)* ☐   or debit my credit card ☐ for £ _____
Visa/Amex/MCard/Switch No. _____ / _____ / _____ / _____ Expiry Date _____
(If the person receiving the gift pack is abroad please add £3.00 Europe £5.00 elsewhere)
If you would like to receive further information about Care for the Wild International's other projects and fostering programmes please tick here ☐

2

CONTENTS

Foreword

elcome to the Rambler's Yearbook, which started life as the Catering Handbook in 1935 and, with the exception of some wartime years, has been published every year since. That's because it is THE accommodation guide for walkers and a bottomless pit of other information besides – gear shops, long distance paths, Ramblers groups, walking organisations in other countries, walks books, walking holidays in Britain and, for the first time, public transport provision in national parks.

Just before Christmas 2000, the Countryside and Rights of Way Bill received royal assent, which will give the British public freedom to roam responsibly over uncultivated land. The Ramblers' Association has been campaigning for this for 65 years. During 2001 we will be helping to make the legislation a reality and in this Yearbook we are at last able to tell you what your rights will be under the new laws – see page 37.

There are over 3,000 places where walkers are welcome – where you won't feel a stranger arriving in muddy boots or tucking into an enormous breakfast, many where wet clothes can be dried out properly overnight and where you'll find your hosts helpful and enthusiastic about your travels. There is a wide variety of prices and types of accommodation, too. Turn to page 126 for B&Bs, page 100 for self-catering accommodation, page 85 if you want to stay in a hostel or camping barn and page 91 if you're looking for somewhere big enough for a group.

If it's gear you're after, see the listing of shops starting on page 77 and if you want to find out about walking elsewhere in Europe or in North America or South Africa turn to page 40 for a list of contacts.

Whoever you are, wherever you live, enjoy your walking in 2001.

PS Members of the Ramblers' Association get this book free – see the cut price membership offer on page 15

The Ramblers' Association exists to facilitate, for the benefit of everyone, the enjoyment and discovery that walking outdoors can bring; and to promote respect for the life of the countryside.

The association encourages walking; protects rights of way; defends the beauty of the countryside; and has campaigned for many years for freedom to roam over uncultivated, open country.

The association is a democratic, voluntary organisation, registered as a charity (no.306089).

The Ramblers' Association

THE RAMBLERS' Association exists to facilitate, for the benefit of everyone, the enjoyment, discovery and health benefits of travelling on foot in Britain and to promote respect for the life of the countryside.

Since its beginnings in 1935, the work of the Ramblers has been in pursuit of its charitable aims: **to encourage walking in Britain; to protect public paths; to campaign for freedom to roam over uncultivated open country; and to defend the beauty of the countryside.** Members organise walking and campaigning events through the year in support of these aims.

SPECIAL EVENTS IN 2001

MARCH 3rd to JUNE 17th EUROWALKS
Walks along the Trans-Pennine Trail as part of a Europe-wide initiative to highlight issues surrounding walking throughout the continent.

JUNE 16th & 17th National Weekend of Walks walks all over Britain.

JULY 8th Footpaths Day
A day to highlight the massive problems on the nations rights of way network.

DECEMBER Festival of Winter Walks
A programme of walks over the Winter period.

For further details of these events, contact Ramblers Central Office on 020-339 8500 or see the website at **www.ramblers.org.uk**

The Ramblers' Association aims to bring a love and understanding of the countryside to the minority of the population who never walk there, either because they do not have the means, because their mobility is impaired by disability, or simply because they have not yet had the opportunity to discover the sense of liberation and enjoyment that walking for pleasure in the outdoors can bring. An estimated 95% of walking routes in Britain are impassable to wheelchairs and others who have mobility impairment. The Ramblers' Association seeks to open up the countryside for people with different physical abilities. It seeks to involve young people in its work and has a number of young people's walking groups across the country (see page 31). And it seeks to include people of all races and creeds in its work.

The work of the Association has brought many new freedoms to walkers since its inception in 1935. The year 2000 was an especially important one: at last, after 65 years of campaigning by the Ramblers and others, walkers in Britain will have freedom to roam in certain areas of open, uncultivated countryside. See page 36 for more information about the additional rights and responsibilities that will result from the new legislation. Page 32 answers your questions about using the public paths network of England and Wales and information about walking in Scotland is given on page 39.

As we enter 2001, membership of the Association has reached 130,000. Members may take part in organised walks, get involved in conservation work, help campaign for better access to the countryside, or just support the work of the Ramblers by paying their annual subscription. See page 15 for discount membership offer for one year, page 9 for how to get involved in Ramblers' work and page 13 for a list of member benefits.

The governing body of the Ramblers is its General Council, a democratic body which establishes the association's objectives. Welsh and Scottish Councils aim to further the objectives of the Ramblers in their countries. See page 10 for a diagram of the decision-making structure.

The association is not affiliated to any political party and is required by its national constitution to be non-sectarian.

The main office is in London and there are also offices in Wales and Scotland. See pages 10-11 for the list of staff and addresses of all offices.

Footpath Work

Thanks to Ramblers' volunteers, thousands of miles of paths are opened up and kept open for the public to enjoy. In recent years, there has been a dramatic improvement in the state of the paths in England and Wales. Many more are now open, signposted, and shown on the map thanks to volunteers' efforts, but there is still a long way to go. Some landowners abuse the network by blocking paths with crops and barbed wire, or by threatening people who use them. By law, highway authorities (county councils, unitary councils, and metropolitan authorities) must protect the public's right to walk footpaths and must remove obstructions, but many of them are doing a very poor job. Audit Commission figures published in March 2000 show that in England only 75% and in Wales only 48% of paths are easy to use.

In many parts of Britain, Ramblers volunteers have launched campaigns to persuade their tardy authorities to take action. They point out that walking is free, healthy, lucrative for local trade, and is everyone's right. They persist until the councillors take notice and do something to improve matters.

Members also go quietly about their work reporting path problems (see *Highway Authorities* p.41 and *Path Problem Report Form* on p.281), surveying, clearing, way-marking and building footbridges and stiles, and opposing path diversions which bring no benefit to the public. In Scotland, local groups also carry out valuable footpath work and press for new rights of way to be created.

The Association is recognised as a much-respected source of expertise. It seeks to have illegal obstructions on rights of way removed and, where necessary, prosecutes offenders. It urges farmers to obey the law on ploughing and rights of way and calls upon local authorities and the government to ensure that these and other laws are respected (see *Access to the Countryside*, page 32). The Ramblers seek restrictions on the grazing of dangerous animals such as bulls in fields containing pubic rights of way, and press for new rights of way to be created where necessary.

Part II of the Countryside and Rights of Way Bill introduces a number of significant changes to rights of way law. The Association has been closely involved, lobbying the Government, MPs and Peers to seek to ensure that those changes will not weaken the existing provisions protecting rights of way.

At local level voluntary footpath secretaries oppose public path closures and diversions if they are not in the public interest, and carry out research to add unrecorded public rights of way to definitive maps. If necessary such matters are pursued to public inquiry and if inquiry decisions appear contrary to the requirements of the law, the Association will consider High Court action.

Freedom to Roam

After more than a century of campaigning, we now have a new law in England and Wales which will secure greater public access to open countryside for generations to come. The new law provides a public right to walk on certain types of uncultivated land, measures to improve the footpath network and greater protection for wildlife and the countryside. The National Assembly for Wales will take forward the implementation of the legislation in Wales.

The Countryside and Rights of Way Bill was introduced by the Government in March 2000. Despite strong opposition from some quarters, the Bill completed its arduous journey through both Houses of Parliament to become an Act in December 2000. The passage of the Act is a time of celebration for the Ramblers' Association, the culmination of many years of hard work by volunteers and staff. However, the new right will not come into force immediately but only once the mapping process has been completed — this could take several years. There is still plenty of work for the Ramblers to do to ensure that the provisions of the Act are implemented as soon as possible and to the best advantage of walkers.

The Countryside Agency (CA) and the Countryside Council for Wales (CCW) are the agencies responsible for delivering the Countryside and Rights of Way Act in England and Wales. Over the next year the agencies will be producing various materials to inform the public of the new right of access as well as guides for farmers and landowners on managing public access. The Ramblers' Association hopes to play a major role in the provision of information to the public and will be working closely with the CA and CCW.

Under the Countryside and Rights of Way Act, the countryside agencies have a duty to prepare maps which show all open country and all registered common land, where the new right of access will apply. Pilot mapping projects are currently underway; however it is estimated that the mapping process will take three to four years to complete. It is hoped that the countryside agencies will begin mapping as soon as possible, for there will be no right of access until the maps are produced. The Ramblers will do everything possible to ensure that all areas of open country are properly mapped and that the public get to see the effects of the legislation on the ground as soon as possible.

The CA and CCW also have a duty under the Act to create a network of 'local countryside access fora' across England and Wales. These will become important advisory bodies and will influence how local authorities and the CA and CCW carry out the provisions of the Act. It is expected that the fora will be made up of representatives of users, landowners and managers, local authorities, local businesses and conservation interests. Outside the national parks and areas of outstanding natural beauty, it is likely that local access fora will be based on county or unitary authority territories. It will be vitally important for the Association to be represented on local access fora across England and Wales.

The National Parks (Scotland) Act 2000 received Royal Assent in August 2000, formally establishing a national parks system in Scotland. The Act is enabling legislation and the first national park (Loch Lomond and the Trossachs) will be established through further legislation in 2001. The Cairngorms will follow in 2002.

For more than 50 years, campaigners in Scotland have faced an uphill struggle against vested interests determined to prevent any change to land and their control of it. The establishment of the Scottish Parliament has provided the driving force for land reform and the Ramblers are delighted that national parks are at the forefront of this work and are arriving on the statute book within the Parliament's first year. Over time the Ramblers believe this will be recognised as landmark legislation.

Countryside work

Defending the beauty of the countryside is an integral part of the Association's work. Indeed it is a necessary part of ensuring that walkers can continue to enjoy their view from the footpath and that the open country over which the organisation has secured a legal right to roam is not despoiled.

The success of this work can be seen in recent moves taken by the Government to better protect the countryside, such as the introduction of a new quarry tax, assurance that Areas of Outstanding Natural Beauty will receive better management, and the progress of the designation of the New Forest and South Downs as new national parks. The Association works to ensure that all these moves are carried through — by influencing the policies made by local and central government planning authorities, and also the policies of other organisations that influence land use planning. Members also monitor and where appropriate make representations on individual planning applications that present a threat to the countryside and open spaces in urban areas. These may include proposals for quarrying, house building on greenfield sites, opencast coal extraction and new road schemes.

Another important part of Ramblers' work is campaigning to protect and improve public transport in rural areas. This is also a way to help those without private transport or keen to reduce their reliance on the car to explore the countryside on foot. You will find details of the enquiry line, and public transport provisions within our National Parks, in the *Public Transport* section of this book.

As devolution becomes more intrinsic to the planning system, the Association is working to set up regional working groups to get the voice of walkers heard at this increasingly important level of administration.

The Organisation

VOLUNTEERS

The Association relies on its hundreds of volunteers working in their neighbourhoods to reinforce and carry out its aims and policies. In many cases it is their diligence that sparks off major changes in legislation affecting walkers' rights. It is they who are walking, clearing and keeping open our wonderful network of footpaths, spreading a love of the countryside with walks programmes and newsletters and firing enthusiasm in local campaigns. There are 53 areas in England, Wales and Scotland (the organisation is not at present active in Northern Ireland) running 423 local groups.

Willing volunteers are always needed and appreciated, in particular for leading walks; helping working parties clear and waymark footpaths; launching footpath campaigns; helping members with special needs to go on walks; undertaking a variety of administration tasks; serving on local committees; and taking on key posts such as footpath secretary, publicity officer or countryside secretary, according to whichever skills, interests or ideas they may have. If you can help, contact your local area or group secretary, the development team at central office or staff at the Scottish or Welsh offices. All offers will be most gratefully received!

IF YOU NEED TO PHONE ANY AREA OR GROUP CONTACTS (PAGES 17–31) PLEASE REMEMBER THEY ARE VOLUNTEERS WORKING FROM HOME. PLEASE DON'T MAKE CALLS LATE IN THE EVENING.

The Ramblers' Association Structure

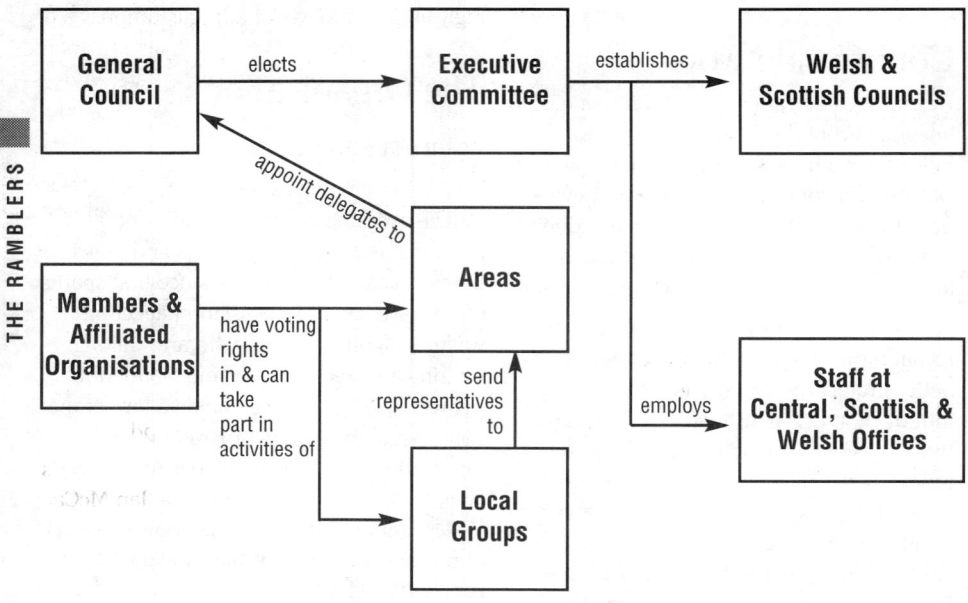

THE RA EXECUTIVE COMMITTEE, JANUARY 2001

Chairman	Cath MacKay
Vice Chairman	Brian Reader
Treasurer	David Hunt
Chairman, Scottish Council	John Holms
Chairman, Welsh Council	Terry Squires

Other members:

Kate Ashbrook, Peter Ayling, Jo Bird, Annette Cotter, Kevin Matthews, Alison Mitchell, Terry Pollard, Mavis Rear, Peter Skipp.

Observers:

Jerry Pearlman (Hon. Solicitor) and Geoff Eastwood (Ramblers' Association Services).

RAMBLERS MEMBERS ARE COVERED BY THE RA PUBLIC LIABILITY INSURANCE POLICY. FIND OUT MORE FROM THE CENTRAL OFFICE

MEMBERS OF STAFF, JANUARY 2001

The Association's staff give assistance to volunteers as well as co-ordinating campaigning work and disseminating information throughout the organisation and to the public. The staff are as follows:

RA CENTRAL OFFICE

2nd Floor, Camelford House, 87-90 Albert Embankment, London SE1 7TW
Tel: 020 7339 8500, Fax: 020 7339 8501
Email: ramblers@london.ramblers.org.uk
Web: www.ramblers.org.uk

Chief Executive's Office

Chief Executive	Nick Barrett
Senior Executive Officer	Janice Samuel
Executive Officer	Salli Carson

Communications

Publicity Officer	Rachael Bryett
Marketing & Publicity Assistant	Reena Chadha

Finance

The association's main source of income – over £1.75 million in 2000 – is the subscriptions of its members and affiliated bodies and the repayments of tax which the Association can recover on those subscriptions paid under Gift Aid. Part of this income is paid to areas for area and group finance. The rest is used at national level, although a good deal of this is used to support local campaigns and local Association work.

Another important source of income – £400,000 in 2000 – is a regular grant from the Ramblers' Association Trust. The Trust is financed by Ramblers' Association Services Ltd (RAS). This is a commercial company which (through its subsidiary, Ramblers Holidays) organises walking, mountaineering, trekking, skiing and sightseeing holidays at home and abroad. The main purpose of the Trust is to support the work of the Ramblers. Much of the Ramblers' Association's campaigning and other work at national level could not be carried out without this support.

Members will appreciate from this that it is of vital importance to the Association that Ramblers Holidays continues to be a flourishing and profitable organisation. Members are therefore encouraged to take their holidays with Ramblers Holidays whenever they can (see their listing in the *Useful Addresses* section of this book).

Ramblers members also give generous support to the organisation by donating money, buying raffle tickets and taking part in the affinity credit card scheme administrated by MBNA. These sources raise about £200,000 a year and fund many important activities. For more information about the MBNA card call 0800 776262.

Income from legacies is another very important source of funds (£250,000 in 2000). All members are urged to mention the Ramblers' Association in their wills. See page 4 for details of a new brochure explaining how to proceed.

Valuable financial support also comes from business sponsorship. We continue to strengthen our relationship with Millets, Britain's biggest outdoor retailer, and draw attention to their colour advertising at the end of the book. We are delighted that Ordnance Survey remain commited to sponsor the membership cards until June this year. Also, we thank Regatta for donating prizes for various competitions, and Hi-Tec for sponsoring the Festival of Winter Walks. Last, but by no means least, we thank Country Walking magazine for their subscription offer to members.

Expenditure on the Association's work was £3 million in 2000. Regular reports of this work appear in *The Rambler*, free to members.

A full copy of the current annual report and accounts can be supplied without charge to any member or affiliated organisation, on request to the Ramblers office in London.

Publications and Information service

The central office offers a comprehensive information service to anyone who wants to go walking in Britain. A range of publications and information sheets on various aspects of walking is available.

Of particular interest are:

- accommodation guides to most long distance walking routes;
- a collection of free factsheets covering:

  Walking in Britain (a general introduction)

  Maps and Navigation

  Equipment and Safety

  A Short Guide to the RA

  Walking Holidays in Britain

  Advice & Information for Leaders of Walks

  An Introduction to the Hadrian's Wall Path

  An Introduction to the Pennine Way

  An Introduction to the Coast to Coast Walk

  An Introduction to the Cotswold Way

  Rambling for People with Disabilities

  Walking Facts and Figures

  RA Policy on Mountain Bikes

  Footpath Erosion

Lyme Disease & Ticks

Walking: How to get Started

A Guide to Long-Distance Paths in Britain

Walking for Health

Freedom to Roam

Walking in France

- regional guides covering everywhere in England, Scotland and Wales, giving information about long-distance paths, maps, useful organisations and guides to short walks in each region;

- a series of walks guides published jointly with Harper Collins Publishers, each with 30 walks. Four were published in 2000: North Wales, Dartmoor, Ben Nevil & Glencoe and Peak District. During 2001, books on the Chilterns and Ridgeway; the Lake District; and the Yorkshire Dales will be completed.

For a full publications list please ask the London office, or see our website on www.ramblers.org.uk.

Walkers can also receive advice on walking gear through the information service.

For addresses of retail outlets see the *Equipment Directory* later in this book and for a listing of Milletts shops see the colour page at the back of the book.

RAMBLERS MERCHANDISE

White T-shirts with RA logo in green, sizes L and XL   £5

Green sweatshirts with RA logo in white, sizes L and XL   £10

Oval brass pin badge with RA logo (in 4 colours)   £1

RA cloth badge (free with orders over £20)   £1

Membership

See page 15 for current rates and special membership offer.

Members receive, as an entitlement of their membership, at no extra cost:

- an annual membership card;
- annual Yearbook & Accommodation Guide;
- quarterly colour magazine, *The Rambler*;
- up to four local/regional area newsletters a year where published;
- campaign information sheets on request.

Members can join a local group of their choice and take part in its programme of walks and social events. Members may also participate in events and walks run by any other group and can receive their programme by arrangement with that group. They can also borrow maps from the Association's map lending library at a nominal charge. (See *Maps* section).

Many outdoor equipment shops offer discounts to Ramblers members on production of their card, though this is at the shop's discretion.

On joining the Ramblers each member agrees "to respect the countryside, its beauty and wildlife and to promote access to it on foot." The association insists that those taking part in walks and other events respect the life of the countryside by leaving no litter, doing no unnecessary damage, keeping dogs under control, etc.

The Ramblers' Association, many of whose members live in or close to the countryside, is mindful of the needs and concerns of rural communities. It is keen to work with members of these communities – and in particular with farmers, farmworkers and landowners – to ensure that the social, economic and environmental well-being of rural areas is maintained and improved.

Over 50% of members pay their subscriptions by direct debit, which saves them trouble and greatly reduces the RA's administration costs and bank charges. Members are informed of the date and amount of each payment well in advance and can, of course, cancel the arrangement at any time.

The revisions to the Gift Aid scheme made in April 2000 mean it is now much simpler to make subscriptions to the RA tax effective. All that is needed is a simple declaration (form provided by the Ramblers) and all subsequent donations and subscriptions are increased in value because the Inland Revenue gives us a tax refund. Only those who pay income tax in the UK can make the declaration.

All Ramblers' Association members are entitled to attend and vote at the annual general meetings of their area and group. They can propose motions for debate at their annual meetings and they can stand for election to their area and group committees.

Through their areas, members may also seek election as delegates to General Council, where national policy is determined. Members of General Council may stand for election to the Executive Committee.

In Wales and Scotland, members can, through their areas and groups, seek election to the Welsh and Scottish Councils and their committees.

LEAVING A LEGACY TO THE RA

As someone who derives great pleasure and satisfaction from walking in our beautiful countryside, you will no doubt share the Association's wish that future generations may also enjoy that pleasure.

But our footpaths and countryside face many threats. More than ever, the vigilance of the Ramblers' Association is needed to save our heritage for walkers of the future.

The Ramblers' Association is constantly campaigning to keep footpaths open and ensure that freedom to roam across the hills, mountains and common land of Britain becomes a reality. And we are fighting to protect the natural beauty of the countryside—its hedgerows and woodlands, its heathlands and downs.

What we bequeath to our successors may depend on a bequest from you to the Ramblers. Income from legacies is of enormous importance in helping us to achieve the Association's objectives. May we therefore appeal to you to leave a legacy to the Ramblers' Association? In this regard we draw your attention to our advert on page 4.

A free leaflet on legacies and a booklet *Making and Updating my Will* are obtainable from the central office in London.

A walker's guide to freedom to roam legislation in England and Wales

A leaflet describing your rights and responsibilities under the new laws.

If you were a member of the Ramblers in January 2001, you will have received a copy with your Yearbook.

You can photocopy it or ask the central office to send you more.

Please leave them in public places and distribute them to newcomers on walks.

A Comfortable Choice

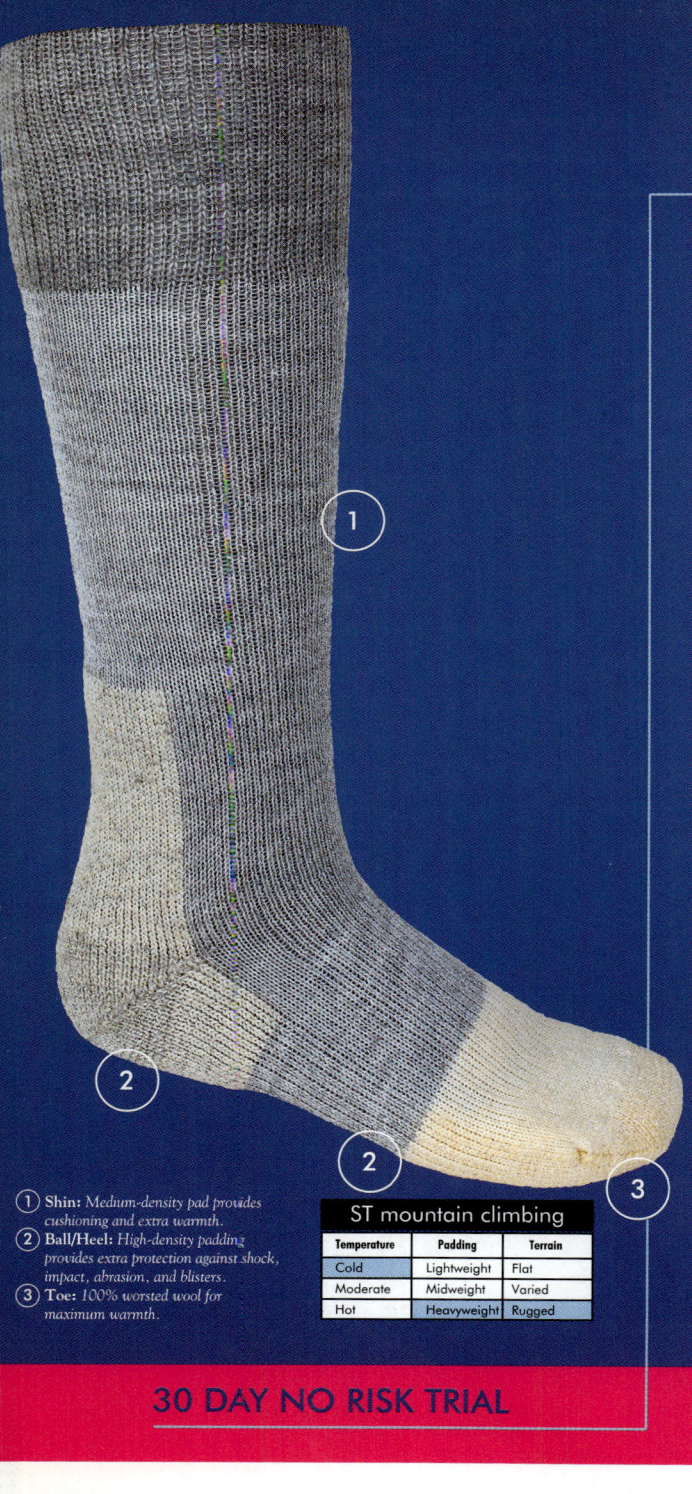

Thôrlos

COMFORT· SCIENCE™

Choosing the right sock is critical to help keep your feet cushioned, well protected, dry and warm when winter walking..

Unlike ordinary socks, Thôrlos® have been based on years of scientific and medical research. From this research, Thôrlo engineers have discovered that there are seven critical design elements, which when optimised, define what we refer to as COMFORT·SCIENCE™.

Using Comfort·Science™ as a design discipline, every pair of Thôrlos® are made in the USA using Thôrlo's patented construction process to cushion and protect your feet against impact. Thôrlo yarns wick moisture away from your feet and Thôrlo 'anti-friction zones' combat rubbing to protect against blisters and ensure your feet remain protected and comfortable mile after mile after mile.

If you want warm, comfortable and well protected feet this winter, then why not turn on to the latest Thôrlos® and step into our Comfort·Science™.

After all, we have so much confidence in our Comfort·Science™, that we guarantee your satisfaction with every pair.

Available from Britain's leading Mountain and Outdoor stores.

1. **Shin:** *Medium-density pad provides cushioning and extra warmth.*
2. **Ball/Heel:** *High-density padding provides extra protection against shock, impact, abrasion, and blisters.*
3. **Toe:** *100% worsted wool for maximum warmth.*

ST mountain climbing

Temperature	Padding	Terrain
Cold	Lightweight	Flat
Moderate	Midweight	Varied
Hot	Heavyweight	Rugged

30 DAY NO RISK TRIAL

The Mountain Boot Co. Ltd.,
Tel: 0191 296 0212
Fax: 0191 296 0213
Email: info@mountainboot.co.uk.
www.thorlo.com

Ramblers' Area and Group Contacts

The Association's groups throughout England, Wales and Scotland provide the essential voluntary help required of any good campaigning organisation. These groups carry out vital work in their localities — clearing and maintaining footpaths, organising walks programmes, giving publicity to rights of way and access issues and, of course, walking and socialising together. Members of the public are welcome to try out one or two walks to see if they are suitable before joining the Ramblers. Non-members can receive a copy of the walks programme by sending an sae to the group secretary. Some groups also publish details from a website, see www.ramblers.org.uk for links to them.

We list here the area and group secretaries. They give their time for no payment and many work from home. Some are happy to have their telephone numbers published; others are not. If you telephone, please do so at reasonable times.

The details are correct at 30 November 2000 but changes take place during the year in both officers and the groups themselves (i.e. some are disbanded, some formed).

Most groups are mixed but some specialise. The **Friends** group, based in Essex, is for people who want to walk shorter distances; and there are now a number of young people's groups. We have listed these within their areas and, additionally, in alphabetical order at the end of the section.

☎ ☎ ☎

IF YOU NEED TO PHONE ANYONE LISTED IN THIS SECTION PLEASE REMEMBER THEY ARE VOLUNTEERS WORKING FROM HOME. PLEASE DON'T MAKE CALLS LATE IN THE EVENING.

AVON

THE AUTHORITIES OF BATH & NORTH EAST SOMERSET; BRISTOL AND SOUTH GLOUCESTER

AREA SECRETARY
Ms S C Popham, 56 Falcon Drive, Stoke Dean, Patchway, Bristol, BS34 5RB

GROUP SECRETARIES
Bath Mr E McGaul, 24 Heathfield Close, Weston, Bath, BA1 4NW ☎ 01225 313126
Bristol Mr J A Grant, 103 Queensholm Crescent, Downend, Bristol, BS16 6LJ ☎ 0117 957 3450
Brunel Walking & Activity [20s/30s] Mr Colin Marshall ☎ 0117 946 6495
Chew Valley Mrs P Everett, 66 Bath Hill East, Keynsham, Bristol, BS31 1HH
Kingswood Mrs Dorothy Peddle, 14 Waters Road, Kingswood, Bristol, BS15 8EB ☎ 0117 967 9250
Norton Radstock Mrs S Haddon, 4 Dymboro Close, Midsomer Norton, Bath, BA3 2QS
Severnside Mr P J Smith, 7 Greville Road, Southville, Bristol, BS3 1LN ☎ 0117 953 2310
Southwold (Yate) Miss S S Naqui, 3 Brake Close, Sherbourne Park, Bradley Stoke, Bristol, BS32 8BA ☎ 0117 969 7246

BEDFORDSHIRE

AREA SECRETARY
Mike Clarke, 5 Tyrells End, Eversholt, Beds, MK17 9DS ☎ 01525 280547

GROUP SECRETARIES
Ivel Valley Ms Elizabeth Lambert, 9 Cotman Close, Manton Heights, Bedford, MK41 7NL
Lea & Icknield Mr M West, 515 Hitchin Road, Stopsley, Luton, Beds, LU2 7TT
Leighton Buzzard Mr J Duxbury, 8 Carlton Grove, Leighton Buzzard, Beds, LU7 8BJ ☎ 01525 383595
North Bedfordshire Mrs L J Tongue & Mr D Tongue, 25 Field Cottage Road, Eaton Socon, St Neots, Cambs, PE19 3HA ☎ 01480 350345
Ouse Valley Mrs Annabel Nelms, 45 Woodstock Road, Bedford, MK40 4JY

BERKSHIRE

AREA SECRETARY
Mr Cliff Lambert, 'Marandella', 73 Fifth Road, Newbury, Berkshire, RG14 6DT ☎ 01635 32842

AREA AND GROUP CONTACTS

GROUP SECRETARIES

Berkshire Walkers Caroline McDonagh, 2 Andrews Close, Theale, Reading, Berks, RG7 5BH

East Berkshire Mr Gerald Barnett, 9 Fremantle Road, High Wycombe, Bucks, HP13 7PQ ☎ 01494 522404

Great Park Miss J M Clark, 7 Dyson Close, Windsor, Berkshire, SL4 3LZ ☎ 01753 866 545

Loddon Valley Mr G G Fyffe, 19 Gingells Farm Road, Charvil, Twyford, Berkshire, RG10 9DJ
☎ 0118 934 2273

Mid Berkshire Ms E Cuff, Donkey Pound Cottage, Beech Hill, Reading, Berkshire, RG7 2AX
☎ 0118 988 2674

Pang Valley Mrs A M Hallam, 22 St Johns Road, Caversham, Reading, RG4 5AL ☎ 0118 946 3858

South East Berks Mr J Moules, 50 Qualitas, Roman Hill, Bracknell, Berks, RG12 7QG ☎ 01344 421002

West Berkshire Mrs J M Young, 10 Porchester Road, Newbury, Berks, RG14 7QJ ☎ 01635 42006

BUCKINGHAMSHIRE & W MIDDLESEX

BUCKINGHAMSHIRE PLUS THE LONDON BOROUGHS OF BRENT, EALING, HARROW, HILLINGDON AND HOUNSLOW

AREA SECRETARY
Mr D Bradnack, 47 Thame Road, Haddenham, Aylesbury, Bucks, HP17 8EP ☎ 01844 291069

GROUP SECRETARIES

Amersham & District Mrs E Hutt, 13 Manor Road, Ruislip, Middlesex, HA4 7LA ☎ 01895 634251

Aylesbury & District Mr M Roe, 47 Patrick Way, Aylesbury, Bucks, HP21 9XJ ☎ 01296 424 835

Chilterns 20s-30s Walking Group Sue McGuirk, 67a Herga Court, Harrow On The Hill, Middx, HA1 3RT
☎ 020 8426 5907

Hillingdon Mrs Sybil Denman, Chatsworth, 103 Hercies Road, Hillingdon, Middlesex, UB10 9LU
☎ 01895 234380

Milton Keynes & District Miss J Heywood, 38 Station Road, Winslow, Buckingham, MK18 3EH
☎ 01296 711126

North West London Miss H O Lee, 12b Wellesley Road, Harrow, Middlesex, HA1 1QN ☎ 020 8863 7628

West London Mr T Berry [acting], 128 Park Lane, South Harrow, Middlesex, HA2 8NL
☎ 020 8422 3284

Wycombe District Mr J L Esslemont, 4 Park Farm Way, Lane End, High Wycombe, Buckinghamshire, HP14 3EG ☎ 01494 881597

CAMBRIDGESHIRE

AREA SECRETARY
Mr G Smith, 74 Maitland Avenue, Cambridge, CB4 1TB ☎ 01223 510665

GROUP SECRETARIES

Cambridge Mrs A Webb, 26 Courtyards, Little Shelford, Cambs, CB2 5ER ☎ 01223 843 964

East Cambridgeshire Mr G Smith, 74 Maitland Avenue, Cambridge, CB4 1TB ☎ 01223 510665

Fenland Mrs S L Ledger, 18 Alexandra Road, Wisbech, Cambs, PE13 1HS ☎ 01945 587135

Huntingdonshire Mr R A Ostler, 3 Ouse Road, Eaton Ford, St Neots, Cambs, PE19 3AY

Peterborough Mr P Bennett, 93 Woodhurst Road, Stanground, Peterborough, Cambs, PE2 8PQ

CHESHIRE

SEE MERSEYSIDE & WEST CHESHIRE AREA; SOUTH & EAST CHESHIRE AREA; NORTH & MID CHESHIRE AREA

CORNWALL

AREA SECRETARY
Mrs C James, Chy-Vean, Tresillian, Truro, Cornwall, TR2 4BN ☎ 01872 520368

GROUP SECRETARIES

Bude/Stratton Mr P Judson, Meadowcroft, Bagbury Road, Bude, Cornwall, EX23 8QJ

Camel District (Wadebridge) Mr George Burke, 5 Sherwood Drive, Bodmin, Cornwall, PL31 2PR
☎ 01208 73489

Caradon Mr R L & Mrs C E Barrett, 13 Courtney Road, Liskeard, Cornwall, PL14 3NP
☎ 01579 344004

Carrick Mr J B Jennings, 7 Moresk Close, Truro, Cornwall, TR1 1DL ☎ 01872 278317

Newquay Mrs D Clarke, 2 Brewers Road, St Clement Vean, Truro, Cornwall, TR1 1AJ ☎ 01872 222 367

Restormel Mrs J C Sloan, Westering, Old Hill, Grampound, Truro, TR2 4RY

West Cornwall (Penwith & Kerrier) Mrs Marion Greenwood, Woodbine House, 17 Tredrea Lane, St Erth, Hayle, Cornwall, TR27 6JS ☎ 01736 755 153

DERBYSHIRE

WEST DERBYSHIRE, AMBER VALLEY, DERBY, SOUTH DERBYSHIRE AND EREWASH DISTRICTS OF DERBYSHIRE. SEE ALSO SOUTH YORKSHIRE & NORTH EAST DERBYSHIRE, AND MANCHESTER AREAS

AREA SECRETARY
Mr John Hayes, The Old Rectory, Old Brampton, Chesterfield, Derbyshire, S42 7JG ☎ 01246 567776

GROUP SECRETARIES

Amber Valley Ms M L Ayre, 66 Windmill Lane, Belper, DE56 1GP ☎ 01773 824605

Derby & S Derbyshire Mr D H G Varley, 27 Amber Road, Allestree, Derby, DE22 2QB ☎ 01332 551552

Derbyshire Dales Mrs Ann Wayne, Barnfield, 37 Yokecliffe Hill, Wirksworth, Derby, DE4 4PE
☎ 01629 822922

Erewash District Mr A Beardsley, 14 York Avenue, Sandiacre, Nottingham, NG10 5HB ☎ 01159 392554

DEVON

AREA SECRETARY
Mrs E Linfoot, 14 Blaydon Cottages, Blackborough, Cullompton, Devon, EX15 2HJ
☎ 01884 266435

GROUP SECRETARIES
Bovey Tracey Mr W H Wright, Hadlywood, Teign Village, Bovey Tracey, Devon, TQ13 9QJ
☎ 01626 853981
East Devon Mr R Cook, Overtoun, Hillside Road, Sidmouth, Devon, EX10 8JG ☎ 01395 579698
Exeter & District Mrs J W Mills, 1a Hampton Buildings, Blackboy Road, Exeter, Devon, EX4 6SR
☎ 01392 413073
Moorland Mr R Seidel, 'Alauna', 7 Rendells Meadow, Bovey Tracey, Newton Abbot, Devon, TQ13 9QW
☎ 01626 832955
North Devon Mrs Pauline Newbound, Mauretania, Burrington, Umberleigh, Devon, EX37 9LT
☎ 01769 520529
Plymouth Mr D Pawley, 35 Whiteford Road, Mannamead, Plymouth, Devon, PL3 5LU
☎ 01752 662350
South Devon Mr R A Woolcott, The Lodge, Manor Park, Seymour Drive, Watcombe Torquay, TQ2 8PY
☎ 01803 313430
South Hams Mr P Boult, Bridge Cottage, Frogmore, Kingsbridge, Devon, TQ7 2UN ☎ 01548 531701
Tavistock Mrs R Clarke, 39 Anderton Court, Whitchurch, Tavistock, Devon, PL19 9EX
☎ 01822 615564
Teignmouth & Dawlish Miss J Dawkins, 6 The Close, Windward Lane, Holcombe, Devon, EX7 0JH
☎ 01626 863724
Tiverton Mrs M A Cox, 18 Anstey Crescent, Tiverton, Devon, EX16 4JR ☎ 01884 256395
Totnes Mrs Thelma Bickford ☎ 01803 862829

DORSET

AREA SECRETARY
Mr A Brown, 2 Walkford Way, Walkford, Christchurch, Dorset, BH23 5LR ☎ 01425 272673

GROUP SECRETARIES
East Dorset Mr Andy Hopkinson, 32 Nugent Road, Hengistbury Head, Bournemouth, Dorset, BH6 4ET
☎ 01202 418955
North Dorset Mr A T Combridge, Green Bushes, North Rd, Sherborne, Dorset, DT9 3JN
☎ 01935 812809

South Dorset Mr Stan Faris, 4 Long Acre, New Street, Portland, Dorset, DT5 1HH ☎ 01305 820957
West Dorset Mrs K Barnard, 'Conoor', Watton, Bridport, Dorset, DT6 5JZ

COUNTY DURHAM

SEE NORTHUMBRIA, AND NORTH YORKSHIRE & SOUTH DURHAM AREAS

EAST YORKSHIRE & DERWENT

EAST RIDING OF YORKSHIRE, YORK AND THE OLD RURAL DISTRICTS AND TOWNS OF DERWENT, EASINGWOLD, FLAXTON, MALTON, NORTON, AND FILEY; PART OF SCARBOROUGH, RYDALE AND HAMBLETON

AREA SECRETARY
Mrs M A Cumberland, 33 Mill Lane, Acaster Malbis, York, YO23 2UJ ☎ 01904 708479

GROUP SECRETARIES
Beverley Mr J Roach, Hollins, The Park, Swanland, HU14 3LU ☎ 01482 632117
Driffield Mr J R Jefferson, Delamere, 2 Spellowgate, Driffield, YO25 5BB ☎ 01377 252412
Hull & Holderness Vacant
Ryedale John Williams, The Old School, Howsham, York, YO60 7PH ☎ 01653 618 583
Scarborough & District Mr & Mrs R A Johnson, 69 Newby Farm Road, Scarborough, North Yorkshire, YO12 6UJ ☎ 01723 364660
York Miss V Silberberg, 41 North Parade, Bootham, York, YO30 7AB ☎ 01904 628134

ESSEX

ESSEX PLUS LONDON BOROUGHS OF WALTHAM FOREST, REDBRIDGE, HAVERING, BARKING & DAGENHAM, AND NEWHAM

AREA SECRETARY
A Vincent-Jones, Flat 14, Nelmes Court, Hornchurch, Essex, RM11 2QL ☎ 01708 473253

GROUP SECRETARIES
Basildon Greenway Mr D J Tucker, 5 Mount Close, Wickford, Essex, SS11 8HF ☎ 01268 734932
[membs enqs Peggy Brown, 40 Selworthy Close Billericay CM11 2SL]
Brentwood Mr R V Carpenter, 43 Arnolds Avenue, Shenfield, Brentwood, Essex, CM13 1ET
☎ 01277 220781
Chelmer & Blackwater Mrs J E Murthy, 11 Pinecroft Gardens, Highwoods, Colchester, Essex, CO4 4TH
☎ 01206 531947
Colchester Mrs L K Sherman, 29 Chaplin Road, East Bergholt, Suffolk, CO7 6SR ☎ 01206 298930
Essex Young Ramblers Vacant
Friends Group Mrs Joyce Kelsey, 'Tregilders', High Easter, Nr. Chelmsford, Essex, CM1 4QL
[membs enqs ☎ 01245 420887]

LAKE DISTRICT

CUMBRIA PLUS LANCASTER DISTRICT OF LANCASHIRE

AREA SECRETARY
Mr Peter Jones, 44 High Fellside, Kendal, Cumbria,
LA9 4JG ☎ 01539 723705

GROUP SECRETARIES
Carlisle Miss A M Cole, 101 Etterby Lea Crescent,
Stanwix, Carlisle, Cumbria, CA3 9JR
☎ 01228 546544
Furness Mrs P Leverton, 6 Churchill Drive, Millom,
Cumbria, LA18 5DD ☎ 01229 772217
Grange over Sands Mrs Wendy Bowen, Hollyhow,
Hazelrigg Lane, Newby Bridge, Ulverston, Cumbria,
LA12 8NY ☎ 015395 31785
Kendal Mr T F Baynes, 5 Stainbank Green, Brigsteer
Road, Kendal, Cumbria, LA9 5RP ☎ 01539 740605
Lancaster Mrs J Gilligan, 22 Endsleigh Grove,
Lancaster, LA1 2TX ☎ 01524 68853
Penrith Mr Jim Burns, Gin Case Barn, Hill Houses,
Calthwaite, Penrith, Cumbria, CA11 9RY
☎ 01768 885125
West Cumbria Mr David Woodhead, Cropple How,
Birkby, Ravenglass, Cumbria, CA18 1RT
☎ 01229 717270

LANCASHIRE

SEE LAKE DISTRICT AREA; MID LANCASHIRE AREA; NORTH EAST
LANCASHIRE AREA

LEICESTERSHIRE & RUTLAND

AREA SECRETARY
Ms S Marlow, 47 Edward St, Anstey, Leicester, LE7
7DQ ☎ 0116 236 5789

GROUP SECRETARIES
Coalville Mrs Jackie Seager, 58 Bromleys Rd,
Coalville, Leicester, LE67 4DA ☎ 01530 452053
Hinckley Mrs B Elliston, 5 Sherbourne Road,
Burbage, Hinckley, Leics, LE10 2BE ☎ 01455
238881
Leicester Mr & Mrs R Phipps, 21 Piers Rd, Glenfield,
Leicester, LE3 8PB ☎ 0116 233 2613
Leicestershire & Rutland Walking Group Miss
Heather Davies, Newton House, Turville Road,
Gilmorton, Lutterworth, LE17 5LZ ☎ 01455 558389
Loughborough & District Mrs J Noon, 8 Ribble Drive,
Barrow-Upon-Soar, Loughborough, Leics, LE12 8LJ
Lutterworth Mrs A D Hutton, 6 The Square,
Frolesworth, Lutterworth, LE17 5EQ
☎ 01455 209932
Melton Mowbray Mr M Drake, 6 Ross Close, Thorpe
Park, Melton Mowbray, Leicestershire, LE13 1NG

Rutland Dr B Taylor, Hill House, 18 Teigh Road,
Market Overton, Oakham, Leics, LE15 7PW
☎ 01572 767337

LINCOLNSHIRE

AREA SECRETARY
Mr S W Parker, 129 Broughton Gardens, Brant Road,
Lincoln, LN5 8SR
☎ 01522 534655 (incl answerphone)

GROUP SECRETARIES
Boston Mrs Sheila Pratt, Capri, Whitehouse Lane,
Fishtoft Boston, Lincolnshire, PE21 0BH
Gainsborough Mrs P McClure, The Cottage, 52 Aisby,
Gainsborough, Lincs, DN21 5RF ☎ 01427 838789
Grantham Mr John Oldfield, 18 Welby Gardens,
Grantham, Lincs, NG31 8BN ☎ 01476 575483
Grimsby & Louth Mrs S C Lundie, 2 Carlton Close,
Cleethorpes, South Humberside, DN35 0NP
☎ 01472 816157
Horncastle Mr Michael Henden, Park House,
Aswardsby, Spilsby, Lincs, PE23 4JX
☎ 01790 754709
Lincoln Mrs Miriam Smith, 2 Belgravia Close, Forest
Park, Lincoln, LN6 0QJ ☎ 01522 682479
Scunthorpe Mrs V Bowser, 4 Orchid Rise, Church
Lane, Scunthorpe, North Lincs, DN15 7AB
Skegness Mrs G Malcolm, 10 Saxby Avenue,
Skegness, Lincs, PE25 3JZ ☎ 01754 764687
Sleaford Mrs A Grout, 12 Manor Road, Quarrington,
Sleaford, Lincs, NG34 8UJ ☎ 01529 414590
Spalding Mrs W A Hicks, 2 Jubilee Close, Spalding,
Lincolnshire, PE11 1YD ☎ 01775 725531
Stamford Mrs F M Jacklin, 15 Perth Road, Stamford,
Lincs, PE9 2TX ☎ 01780 752736

LONDON

FOR INNER LONDON BOROUGHS SEE INNER LONDON AREA, FOR
OUTER LONDON BOROUGHS SEE BUCKINGHAMSHIRE &
WEST MIDDLESEX AREA; ESSEX AREA; HERTFORDSHIRE & NORTH
MIDDLESEX AREA; KENT AREA; SURREY AREA

MANCHESTER

FORMER GREATER MANCHESTER PLUS HIGH PEAK DISTRICT OF
DERBYSHIRE

AREA SECRETARY
Mr T Perkins, 34 Grangethorpe Drive, Burnage,
Manchester, M19 2LG ☎ 0161 225 2650

GROUP SECRETARIES
Bolton Mrs H Brizland, 345 Bury Road, Turton,
Bolton, BL7 0BS ☎ 01204 853124
Bury Mrs E Marsden, 14 Jesmond Drive, Bury,
Lancs, BL8 1EE ☎ 0161 761 3040

AREA AND GROUP CONTACTS

New Mills Mr Allan Minchin, 1 Diglands Avenue, New Mills, Stockport, Cheshire, SK22 4JD ☎ 01663 743983

Oldham Janet Hewitt, 2 Hillside Avenue, Carrbrook, Stalybridge, Cheshire, SK15 3NE ☎ 01457 834769

Rochdale Mrs M J Marrion, 36 Plover Close, Bamford, Rochdale, Lancs, OL11 5PU ☎ 01706 355849

Stockport Mr P T Wild, 83 Cheadle Old Road, Edgeley, Stockport, SK3 9RH ☎ 07899 952903

Wigan & District Mr P Taylor, 11 Corfe Close, Aspull, Wigan, Lancs, WN2 1UW

MERSEYSIDE AND WEST CHESHIRE

MERSEYSIDE PLUS CHESTER AND ELLESMERE PORT DISTRICTS OF CHESHIRE, THE DISTRICT OF VALE ROYAL, THE WESTERN PART OF MACCLESFIELD DISTRICT AND HALTON AND WARRINGTON.

AREA SECRETARY
Miss G F Thayer, 53 Bramwell Avenue, Prenton, Wirral, CH43 0RQ ☎ 0151 608 9472

GROUP SECRETARIES
Cestrian (Chester) Ms F Parsons, 32 Wetherby Way, Little Sutton, South Wirral, CH66 4NY ☎ 0151 3391178

Liverpool Miss J Hughes, 34 Eton Court, Hornby Lane, Liverpool, L18 3HQ

Southport Mr D Wall, 22 Dunbar Crescent, Southport, Lancs, PR8 3AB

St Helens Mr W Walker, 3 Beech Avenue, Eccleston Park, Prescot, Merseyside, L34 2RL ☎ 0151 426 2445

Wirral Mr A Wall, 35 Mount Avenue, Bebington, Wirral, CH63 5QY ☎ 0151 608 0586

MID LANCASHIRE

LANCASHIRE; BLACKPOOL, FYLDE, PRESTON, SOUTH RIBBLE, CHORLEY, WEST LANCASHIRE AND WYRE BOROUGHS

AREA SECRETARY
Mr D Kelly, 4 Buttermere Close, Bamber Bridge, Preston, Lancs, PR5 4RT ☎ 01772 312027

GROUP SECRETARIES
Chorley Mrs J Tudor Williams, Oaklands, 5 The Bowers, Chorley, Lancs, PR7 3LA

Fylde Mr M J Bloomfield, 4 Rockingham Road, Bispham, Blackpool, Lancs, FY2 0LP

Garstang & District Mrs C Stenning, 20 Meadowcroft Avenue, Catterall, Garstang, Lancs, PR3 1ZH ☎ 01995 601478

Preston Mr A Manzie, 3 Ruthin Court, Dunbar Road, Ingol, Preston, Lancs, PR2 3YE ☎ 01772 736467

South Ribble Mr B A Kershaw, 2 Moss Way, New Longton, Preston, Lancs, PR4 4ZQ

West Lancashire Mr W G Wright, 49 Riverview, Tarleton, Preston, Lancs, PR4 6ED ☎ 01772 812034

NORFOLK

AREA SECRETARY
Mrs E K Harris, 7 Dyers Yard, Coslany Street, Norwich, NR3 3QY ☎ 01603 612644

GROUP SECRETARIES
Dereham Mrs Carol Jackson, Mandola, Mill Street, Elsing, Dereham, Norfolk, NR20 3EJ ☎ 01362 637752

Fakenham Mr R Smythe, Longview, Westgate, Gt. Walsingham, Norfolk, NR22 6DY ☎ 01328 820515

Great Yarmouth Mrs M Nicholls, Fircroft, Stepshort, Belton, Gt Yarmouth, NR31 9JS ☎ 01493 780341

King's Lynn Mr J Keenan, 15 Gaskell Way, King's Lynn, Norfolk, PE30 3SD ☎ 01553 674262

Norwich Mr D J Goddard, 49 Lindford Drive, Eaton, Norwich, Norfolk, NR4 6LR

Sheringham & District Mr Don Davenport, 'Malbank', 20 Newhaven Close, Cromer, Norfolk, NR27 0BD ☎ 01263 514955

Southern Norfolk Mr G H Head, 9 Henley Road, Norwich, NR2 3NL

Swaffham Mrs J Reader, Davisa, Birch Drive, Station Road, Roydon, Nr Kings Lynn, Norfolk, PE32 1AW

Wensum Mr Tony Smith, 3 Priors Drive, Old Catton, Norwich, NR6 7LJ ☎ 01603 423085

NORTH AND MID CHESHIRE

AREA SECRETARY
Mrs D Armitage, Birchtree Bungalow, Red Lane, Appleton, Warrington, WA4 5AB ☎ 01925 268540

GROUP SECRETARIES
Halton Mr K Doughty, 12 Oak Road, Penketh, Warrington, Cheshire, WA5 2LH

North & Mid Cheshire Under 40 Mr E W Thom, 42 Portola Close, Grappenhall, Warrington, WA4 2SW ☎ 01925 486837

Vale Royal and Knutsford Mrs D Armitage, Birchtree Bungalow, Red Lane, Appleton, Warrington, WA4 5AB

Warrington Mrs J Hood, 21 Belmont Crescent, Gt Sankey, Warrington, Cheshire, WA5 3DT

NORTH EAST LANCASHIRE

LANCASHIRE; RIBBLE VALLEY, PENDLE, BURNLEY, ROSSENDALE, BLACKBURN AND HYNDBURN DISTRICTS

AREA SECRETARY
Mrs S Baxendale, 101 Blackburn Road, Clayton-Le Moors, Accrington, Lancs, BB5 5JT ☎ 01254 235049

GROUP SECRETARIES

Blackburn & Darwen Miss M G Brindle, 103 School Lane, Guide, Blackburn, BB1 2LW ☎ 01254 671269

Burnley & Pendle Mrs J Kay, 19 Barrowford Road, Colne, Lancs, BB8 9QP ☎ 01282 866890

Clitheroe Mr B Brown, 2 Chorlton Terrace, Barrow, Whalley, Clitheroe, Lancs, BB7 9AR ☎ 01254 822851

Hyndburn Mr P J Bedson, 8 Mill Street, Church, Accrington, Lancs, BB5 4EJ ☎ 01254 399559

Rossendale Mr Alan Johnson, 10 Pendle Close, Bacup, Lancashire, OL13 9JT ☎ 01706 877521

NORTH YORKS & SOUTH DURHAM

CLEVELAND; CO. DURHAM EXCEPT DERWENTSIDE, DURHAM AND CHESTER-LE-STREET DISTRICTS; NORTH YORKSHIRE; PRESENT RICHMONDSHIRE DISTRICT AND THE FORMER URBAN AND RURAL DISTRICTS OF BEDALE, HELMSLEY, KIRKBYMOORSIDE, NORTHALLERTON, PICKERING, STOKESLEY, THIRSK, AND WHITBY NOW FORMING PART OF THE HAMBLETON AND RYDALE DISTRICT, SEE ALSO WEST RIDING AREA; EAST YORKSHIRE AREA

AREA SECRETARY

Mr A Patterson, 141 Castle Road, Redcar, Cleveland, TS10 2NF ☎ 01642 474864

GROUP SECRETARIES

Barnard Castle Mr T & Mrs J T Fenton, Garden House, Westholme, Winston, Darlington, Co Durham, DL2 3QL ☎ 01325 730895

Cleveland Mr A Patterson, 141 Castle Road, Redcar, Cleveland, TS10 2NF ☎ 01642 474864

Crook & Weardale Mrs K Berry, 11 Wood Square, Bishop Auckland, Co. Durham, DL14 6QQ ☎ 01388 608979

Darlington Mr Bryan Spark (acting), 3 Thirlmere Grove, West Auckland, Bishop Auckland, Co Durham, DL14 9LW ☎ 01388 834213

Northallerton Mr M F Kent, 131 Valley Road, Northallerton, North Yorkshire, DL6 1SN ☎ 01609 777618

Richmondshire Mrs B Forde, Hargill House, Gilling West, Richmond, North Yorkshire, DL10 5LJ ☎ 01748 824156

NORTHAMPTONSHIRE

AREA SECRETARY

Mr P Ellement, 5 Holdenby Close, Market Harborough, Leicestershire, LE16 8JE

GROUP SECRETARIES

Daventry Mrs J Smith, The Stables, Ashby, St Ledgers, Warwickshire, CV23 8UN

Kettering Miss E M Wildman, 36 Skeffington Close, Geddington, Northants, NN14 1BA

Northampton Mr P J Keeble, 58 Fishers Close, Little Billing, Northampton, NN3 9SR ☎ 01604 405527

Wellingborough & District Mr I S Lavender & Mrs C M Lavender, 77 Brickhill Road, Wellingbrough, Northamptonshire, NN8 3NU

NORTHUMBRIA

NORTHUMBERLAND; FORMER TYNE & WEAR, PLUS DERWENTSIDE, DURHAM AND CHESTER-LE-STREET DISTRICTS OF CO. DURHAM

AREA SECRETARY

Ms N S Wright, 3 Lily Crescent, Newcastle, Tyne & Wear, NE2 2SP ☎ 0191 2813578

GROUP SECRETARIES

Alnwick Mr J Sim, 18 Chapel Lands, Alnwick, Northumberland, NE66 1EL ☎ 01665 605212

Berwick Mr W D Gill, 3 Knowes Close, Hutton, Berwick Upon Tweed, TD15 1TS ☎ 01289 386791

Chester le Street Mr John Kay, 6 Briarhill, Hilda Park, Chester Le Street, Co Durham, DH2 2LL ☎ 0191 3883474

Derwentside Mrs J D Thomas, 48 Alderside Crescent, Lanchester, Durham, DH7 0PZ

Durham City Mr C Ludman, 5 Church Street, Durham, DH1 3DG ☎ 0191 386 6886

Gateshead Mrs M Watson, 48 Gleneagles Road, Low Fell, Gateshead, Tyne & Wear, NE9 6JS ☎ 0191 4825071

Hexham Mr Dennis Harrington, 9 Warden View, Wall Hexham, Northumberland, NE46 4DT ☎ 01434 681619

Morpeth Miss M Siggens, 17 Kingswell, Carlisle Lea, Morpeth, Northumberland, NE61 2TY ☎ 01670 518031

Northumbria Mr A Wright, 15 Ord Court, Fenham, Newcastle Upon Tyne, NE4 9YF ☎ 0191 274 5961

Ponteland Mr Colin Braithwaite, 105 Western Way, Ponteland, Newcastle Upon Tyne, NE20 9LY ☎ 01661 822929

Sunderland Miss J Middleton, 4 Kirknewton Close, The Grange, Houghton Le Spring, Co Durham, DH5 8EH

Tyneside Miss M E Ramsdale, 36 Frankland Drive, Whitley Bay, Tyne & Wear, NE25 9DS ☎ 0191 2521949

NORTHUMBERLAND

SEE NORTHUMBRIA AREA

NOTTINGHAMSHIRE

AREA SECRETARY

Mr A Beverley, 6 Hathersage Rise, Ravenshead, Nottingham, NG15 9DX ☎ 01623 483673

GROUP SECRETARIES

Broxtowe Dr A H Brittain, 23 Banks Road, Toton, Nottingham, NG9 6HE ☎ 0115 9720 258

Collingham Mr D H Moore MBE, 10 The Hemplands, Collingham, Newark, Notts, NG23 7PE
☎ 01636 892 950
Dukeries Mr A Gamble, 35 Greenwood Crescent, Boughton, Newark, Notts, NG22 9HX
☎ 01623 861376
Gedling Mrs J M Fillingham, 1 Albany Close, Arnold, Nottingham, NG5 6JP ☎ 0115 9204066
Hucknall Mrs Jenny Marriott, 6 Hartington Avenue, Hucknall, Nottingham, NG15 6TA ☎ 0115 9533020
Newark Mrs C Grant, 16 Elizabeth Road, Newark, Notts, NG24 4NP ☎ 01636 681994
Nottingham Mr S Brint, 23 Shipley Rise, Carlton, Nottingham, NG4 1BN ☎ 0115 955 4475
Notts Derby Group Sarah Rich, 10 Cartbridge, Cotgrave, Nottingham, NG12 3PF ☎ 0115 989 0302
Ravenshead Mr Allan Rogers, 63 Quarry Road, Ravenshead, Nottingham, NG15 9AP
☎ 01623 797321
Retford Mrs J Anson, Townrows Farm, High Street, Elkesley, Notts, DN22 8AJ ☎ 01777 838 763
Rushcliffe Mr R Parrey, 61 West Leake Road, Kingston On Soar, Notts, NG11 0DN
☎ 0115 9830730
Sherwood & Mansfield Vacant
Southwell Mrs A Oakes, 7 Monkton Drive, Southwell, Notts, NG25 0AW
Vale of Belvoir Mr M Brimble, 22 Fleming Avenue, Bottesford, Nottingham, NG13 0ED
☎ 01949 842 658
Worksop Ms S J McGuire, 44 Sandy Lane, Worksop, Notts, S80 1SW ☎ 01909 500278

OXFORDSHIRE

AREA SECRETARY
Ms P M P Kingsnorth, 4 Coombe Hill Crescent, Thame, Oxon, OX9 2EH ☎ 01844 212227

GROUP SECRETARIES
Bicester & Kidlington Mr C Edgar, 35 Fair Close, Buckingham Road, Bicester, Oxon, OX6 7YW
☎ 01869 244436
Cherwell Mrs Dianna Lathbury, 74 Valley Road, Brackley, Northants, NN13 7DQ ☎ 01280 704320
Didcot & Wallingford Miss J M Bird, Middle Garth, Stainton, Barnard Castle, DL12 8RD
☎ 01833 637756{from 22.9.00}
Henley & Goring Mrs J Boddington, 14 Western Road, Henley On Thames, Oxon, RG9 1JL
☎ 01491 579065
Oxford Mrs E M Steane, 36 Harpes Road, Summertown, Oxford, OX2 7QL ☎ 01865 552531
Oxon 20s&30s Walking Group Miss D M Glenister, 50 Laurel Drive, Southmoor, Abingdon, OX13 5DJ
☎ 01865 821756
Thame & Wheatley Mrs J E Noyce, 27 Worminghall Road, Ickford, Aylesbury, Bucks, HP18 9JB

☎ 01844 339376
Vale of White Horse Mr P Lonergan, 35 Cherwell Close, Abingdon, Oxon, OX14 3TD ☎ 01235 202784
West Oxfordshire Mrs J M Yates, 55 Begbroke Crescent, Begbroke, Oxon, OX5 1RW
☎ 01865 371357

SHROPSHIRE

AREA SECRETARY
Mrs M V Law, 3 Ainsdale Drive, Priorslee, Telford, Shropshire, TF2 9QJ ☎ 01952 299297

GROUP SECRETARIES
Broseley & Wenlock Mr R Jones, 2 St Nicholas Cres, Bridgnorth, Shropshire, WV15 5BN ☎ 01746 762876
East Shropshire Mr B J Williams, 17 Turnberry Close, Perton, Wolverhampton, WV6 7RE
Market Drayton Mrs J Hill, 93 Country Meadows, Market Drayton, Shropshire, TF9 3LP
Oswestry Mrs A Parker, 11 St Johns Hill, Ellesmere, Shropshire, SY12 0EY
Shrewsbury & Mid-Shropshire Mr Roy Powell, 6, Mobile Home Park, The Mount, Shrewsbury, Shropshire, SY3 8PE ☎ 01743 359797
South Shropshire Dr P Johnson, Pedlars Rest, Elsich Court, Seifton, Ludlow, Shropshire, SY8 2DL
☎ 01584 861487

SOMERSET

AREA SECRETARY
Mrs M Henry, 22 Linden Grove, Taunton, Somerset, TA1 1EF ☎ 01823 333369

GROUP SECRETARIES
Clevedon Mrs V Norman, 3 Princes Road, Clevedon, Avon, BS21 7SY ☎ 01275 874 124
Mendip Miss V White, 6 Jocelyn Drive, Wells, Somerset, BA5 2EW ☎ 01749 678710
Sedgemoor Mr M B Beveridge, 3 Broadway Avenue, Chilton Polden, Bridgwater, Somerset, TA7 9ER
☎ 01278 792034
South Somerset Mr I L Rendall, 3a Tintern, Abbey Manor Park, Yeovil, Somerset, BA21 3SJ
☎ 01935 421235
Taunton Deane Mr R A Faulkes, 31 The Oaks, Taunton, Somerset, TA1 2QX ☎ 01823 330 196
West Somerset Dr L A M Evans, Brook House, Huntscott, Wootton Courtenay, Minehead, Somerset, TA24 8RR ☎ 01643 841426
Woodspring Ms Julie Westgarth, 20 Ivybridge, Tavistock Road, Weston-Super-Mare, North Somerset, BS22 6LP

SOUTH & EAST CHESHIRE

CHESHIRE; CREWE & NANTWICH AND CONGELTON DISTRICTS PLUS
EASTERN SECTION OF MACCLESFIELD DISTRICT

AREA SECRETARY
Mrs June Mabon, 'Highwinds', 15 Churchfields,
Bowdon, Altrincham, Cheshire, WA14 3PL
☎ /fax 0161 928 3437

GROUP SECRETARIES
Congleton Mrs M E Baker, 2 Buckbean Way,
Goostrey, Crewe, Cheshire, CW4 8JJ
☎ 01477 534238
East Cheshire Dr F I Wasson, 69 Valley Road,
Bramhall, Stockport, SK7 2NJ ☎ 0161 440 0171
South Cheshire Mr John McCombie, 15 Shelburne
Drive, Haslington, Crewe, Cheshire, CW1 5QG
☎ 01270 581769

SOUTH YORKS & N.E.DERBYSHIRE

FORMER SOUTH YORKSHIRE PLUS NORTH EAST DERBYSHIRE;
CHESTERFIELD, AND BOLSOVER DISTRICTS OF DERBYSHIRE

AREA SECRETARY
Mr T M Howard, 334 Manchester Road, Crosspool,
Sheffield, S10 5DQ

GROUP SECRETARIES
Barnsley & Penistone Mr C P Cooper, 4 Colster
Close, Pogmoor, Barnsley, S75 2LR
Bolsover District Mrs Julie Portington, 106 Welbeck
Road, Bolsover, Derbyshire, S44 6DH
Chesterfield & North East Derbyshire Mr A Hunt,
17a Loads Road, Holymoorside, Chesterfield,
Derbyshire, S42 7ET
Dearne Valley Mrs Pauline Gibbons, 6 Ruskin
Avenue, Mexborough, South Yorkshire, S64 0AU
Doncaster Mrs M Thompson, 31 Broom Hill Drive,
Cantley 6, Doncaster, South Yorkshire, DN4 6QZ
☎ 01302 371093
Rotherham Metro District Patrick J Cook, 16 Sheep
Cote Road, Brecks, Rotherham, South Yorkshire, S60
4DA ☎ 01709 540201
Sheffield Mrs Pat Peters, 751 Gleadless Road,
Sheffield, S12 2QD ☎ 0114 239 8505

STAFFORDSHIRE

STAFFORDSHIRE PLUS DUDLEY, SANDWELL, WALSALL AND
WOLVERHAMPTON DISTRICTS OF FORMER WEST MIDLANDS

AREA SECRETARY
Geoff Budd, 6 Berry Gardens, Winshill, Burton-On-
Trent, Staffs, DE15 0EE ☎ 01283 561535

GROUP SECRETARIES
Biddulph Mr J Cockburn, 21 Colwyn Drive,
Knypersley, Stoke On Trent, ST8 7BJ
Bilston Ms E A Bayley, 9 Legge Street, Park Fields,
Wolverhampton, WV2 2DH ☎ 01902 671449
Chase & District Mr P Baker & Mrs J M Baker, 2
Anker Close, Burntwood, Staffordshire, WS7 9JW
☎ 01543 672983
East Staffordshire Mrs J King, 39 Faraday Avenue,
Stretton, Burton On Trent, Staffs, DE13 0FX
☎ 01283 543483
Leek Mrs Shirley Lunt, 17 Rennie Crescent,
Cheddleton, Leek, ST13 7HD ☎ 01538 360907
Lichfield Mrs Carole Cope, 15 Woodford Crescent,
Burntwood, Staffs, WS7 9AE ☎ 01543 675339
Mid Staffordshire Mrs V Wilkinson, 20 Princefield
Avenue, Penkridge, Stafford, ST19 5HG
☎ 01785 712068
Sandwell Mr Barry Hedley, 2 Blackberry Lane, Four
Oaks, Sutton Coldfield, West Midlands, B74 4JE
☎ 0121 308 3076
Stoke/Newcastle Mr Graham Evans, 65 Pacific Road,
Trentham, Stoke On Trent, Staffs, ST4 8RS ☎ 01782
642872 [membs enqs ☎ 01782 622344]
Stone Mrs Isabel Lowe, 11 Beechwood Drive,
Watton, Stone, Staffs, ST15 0EH ☎ 01785 286965
Stourbridge Mrs Joan Crowe, 29 Stennels Avenue,
Halesowen, West Midlands, B62 8QJ
☎ 0121 422 1698
Walsall Mrs Alice Harrison, 30 Clarendon Place,
Pelsall, Walsall, West Midlands, WS3 4NL
☎ 01922 683411
Wolverhampton Mr D Hellyar (acting), 123 Castlecroft
Road, Finchfield, Wolverhampton, WV3 8BY

SUFFOLK

AREA SECRETARY
Mr G C Pratt, 3 Sidegate Avenue, Ipswich, Suffolk,
IP4 4JJ ☎ 01473 724656

GROUP SECRETARIES
Alde Valley Mrs M Brown, 10 Orwell Avenue,
Saxmundham, Suffolk, IP17 1XY ☎ 01728 453378
Bury St Edmunds Mr H R Bowerman, 16 Sutton
Close, Bury St Edmunds, Suffolk, IP32 7EP
☎ 01284 762886
Ipswich & District Mrs Janet Johnson, Oakley, 63
Heath Road, Ipswich, Suffolk, IP4 5RY
☎ 01473 425393
Newmarket & District Mr N Atherton, 3 Bell Cottages,
52 Main Street, Hockwold, Norfolk, IP28 4NF
Stour Walking Group Andy Webb, 36 Hertford Road,
Clare, Sudbury, Suffolk, CO10 8QJ ☎ 01440 716208
Stowmarket Mrs B Peart, 5 Combs Green, Combs,
Stowmarket, Suffolk, IP14 2NP
Sudbury Mr A C O'Reilly, 18 Raven Way, Hadleigh,
Ipswich, Suffolk, IP7 5AX ☎ 01473 822304

Waveney Mr B Covey, 1 Moat Cottages, Ilketshall St Andrews, Beccles, Suffolk, NR34 8NR

SURREY

SURREY PLUS LONDON BOROUGHS OF RICHMOND, KINGSTON, MERTON, SUTTON AND CROYDON

AREA SECRETARY
Mr G Butler, 109 Selsdon Park Road, South Croydon, CR2 8JJ

GROUP SECRETARIES
Croydon Mrs L Serafino, 48 Priory Crescent, Beulah Hill, London, SE19 3EE
East Surrey Miss Y A Wood, 65 Mares Field, Chepstow Road, Croydon, Surrey, CR0 5UB ☎ 0208 680 3958
Epsom & Ewell Mr D J Newman, 56a Acacia Grove, New Malden, Surrey, KT3 3BU ☎ 0208 949 3471
Farnham & District Mrs R Soden, 11 Merryacres, Witley, Godalming, Surrey, GU8 5RG
Godalming & Haslemere Mr R K C Evans, 25 Oaklands, Tanners Lane, Haslemere, Surrey, GU27 3RD ☎ 01428 643 624
Guildford Mr G E Spencer, Clandon Cottage, The Street, West Clandon, Surrey, GU4 7ST ☎ 01483 222477
Kingston Mr M Lake, 87 Porchester Road, Kingston Upon Thames, Surrey, KT1 3PW ☎ 020 8541 3437 [membs enqs ☎ 020 8977 0817]
Mole Valley Mrs V R Hall, 3 Old School Court, Poplar Road, Leatherhead, Surrey, KT22 8SN ☎ 01372 361011 (membs enqs ☎ 01372 454012)
Reigate Mr Glyn Jones, 12 Briars Wood, Horley, Surrey, RH6 9UE ☎ 01293 773198
Richmond Miss G M Taylor, 58 Richmond Road, London, SW20 0PQ ☎ 0208 946 2604 [membs enqs Mrs Sharp ☎ 0208 748 0049]
Staines Mr E J Lucas, 64 Marriott Close, Bedfont, Middx, TW14 9PZ
Surrey Heath Mrs C Norris, 11 Warwick Close, Camberley, Surrey, GU15 1ES ☎ 01276 26821
Surrey Under 35s Mr Graham Wilson, 3 Nell Court, 32 Lovelace Road, Surbiton, Surrey, KT6 6LZ ☎ 0208 399 6119
Sutton/Wandle Valley Mr J C Parkin, 59 Beechwood Court, West Street Lane, Carshalton, Surrey, SM5 2QA ☎ 0208 773 0048
Woking & District Mrs A Brown, Beckdale House, White Hart Lane, Wood Street Village, Guildford, Surrey, GU3 3EA

SUSSEX

EAST AND WEST SUSSEX

AREA SECRETARY
Mrs Janet M Barber, 7 Stirling Way, Horsham, West Sussex, RH13 5RX ☎ 01403 263346

GROUP SECRETARIES
Arun-Adur Miss G M Agate, 136 Abbey Road, Sompting, Lancing, Sussex, BN15 0AD ☎ 01903 761352
Beachy Head Mrs. M Ferguson, 3 Milton Crescent, Eastbourne, E Sussex, BN21 1SP ☎ 01323 726 364
Brighton & Hove Mrs J Pool, 20 Nevill Road, Uckfield, East Sussex, TN22 1PF ☎ 01825 765111
Crawley & North Sussex Miss S M Darby, 14 Chevening Close, Broadfield, Crawley, RH11 9QU ☎ 01293 533242
Heathfield & District Mrs R Brown, Chant House, Eridge Lane, Rotherfield, Nr Crowborough, Sussex, TN6 3JU ☎ 0189 285 2153
High Weald Walkers Mrs N Etherton, Hazards, Blackness Rd, Crowborough, East Sussex, TN6 2NA ☎ 01892 654850
Horsham & Billinghurst Evelyn Hussey, 44 Forestfield, Horsham, Sussex, RH13 6DZ ☎ 01403 263726
Mid Sussex Mrs Celia Parrott, 27 Dale Avenue, Hassocks, West Sussex, BN6 8LP
Rother Mrs J Squibb, 15 The Close, Fairlight, Hastings, Sussex, TN35 4AQ ☎ 01424 813205
South West Sussex Miss J Russell-Smith, 19 Orchard Avenue, Chichester, West Sussex, PO19 3BG

WARWICKSHIRE

WARWICKSHIRE PLUS BIRMINGHAM, COVENTRY AND SOLIHULL DISTRICTS OF FORMER WEST MIDLANDS

AREA SECRETARY
Mr M Bird, 16 Melford Hall Road, Solihull, West Midlands, B91 2ES ☎ 0121 705 1118: 0121 414 4203 [w]

GROUP SECRETARIES
Castle Bromwich Mrs J Mackey, 84 Redstone Farm Road, Hall Green, B28 9NL ☎ 0121 749 4760
City of Birmingham Mr Phillip Barnes, 27 Hillcrest Road, Wylde Green, Sutton Coldfield, West Midlands, B72 1EG ☎ 0121 373 7105
Coventry Mrs Y Rouse, 11 Mylgrove, Finham, Coventry, West Midlands, CV3 6RE ☎ 024 76417457
Mid Warwickshire Mrs S M Coates, 40 Windy Arbour, Kenilworth, Warwickshire, CV8 2AS ☎ 01926 855123
Rugby Mr Jack Kelly, 220 Hillmorton Road, Rugby, Warks, CV22 5BB ☎ 01788 536732
Solihull Mrs S M Woolley, 36 Alderwood Place, Princes Way, Solihull, West Midlands, B91 3HX ☎ 0121 7055753
South Birmingham Miss C A Sumpter, 12 Henlow Road, Birmingham, B14 5DT ☎ 0121 471 2060
Southam Mr C Haywood, 44 Pendicke Street, Southam, Warks, CV47 1PF ☎ 01926 812820

Biggar Mrs M Gow, 14 Southcroft Road, Biggar, Lanarkshire, ML12 6AJ ☎ 01899 220 216

Clyde Valley Mrs P Whyte, 8 Garfield Avenue, Mossend, Bellshill, Lanarkshire, ML4 2NS

Cumbernauld & Kilsyth Mr Ian Jarvis, 89 Arden Grove, Kilsyth, G65 9LZ ☎ 01236 824592

Cunninghame Mrs M D Windsor, 1 Kildale Road, Kildale Court, Lochwinnoch, PA12 4DF ☎ 01505 843626

Dumfries & Galloway Marcia Foster, 2 Blackacre Cottages, Coyrance, Lockerbie, DG11 1TR

Eastwood Miss M R Hamilton, 5 Burnfield Gardens, Giffnock, Glasgow, G46 7EB ☎ 0141 620 1205

Glasgow Mr J Riddell, 61 Balcarres Avenue, Glasgow, G12 0QE ☎ 0141 334 5586

Helensburgh & W Dunbartonshire Una Campbell, 5 Dalmore House, Dalmore Crescent, Helensburgh, G84 8GP

Kilmarnock & Loudoun Mrs Isabel Ferguson, 15 Cuillin Place, Bellfield, Kilmarnock, Ayrshire, KA1 3UW

Monklands Ms C McMahon, 4 Blackmoor Place, New Stevenston, Motherwell, ML1 4JX ☎ 01698 833983

Paisley Miss E S Brownlie, 47 Cochran Street, Paisley, PA1 1JZ

South Ayrshire Mrs R Riddell, 3 Coats Place, Dundonald, Kilmarnock, Ayrshire, KA2 9DJ ☎ 01563 850406

Strathkelvin Mrs R R Scott, 10 Gray Street, Kirkintilloch, Glasgow, G66 3LL ☎ 0141 578 3166

Wales

DYFED

THE AUTHORITIES OF CARMARTHENSHIRE; CEREDIGION; AND PEM-BROKESHIRE

AREA SECRETARY
Mr G D Williams, Maesquarre, Bethlehem Road, Llandeilo, Carmarthenshire, SA19 6YA ☎ 01558 822960

GROUP SECRETARIES
Aberystwyth Mrs S A Kinghorn, 16 Bryn Glas, Llanbadarn, Aberystwyth, Dyfed, SY23 3QR ☎ 01970 624965

Cardigan & District Mrs Joy Evans, The Old Shed, Soar Hill, Cwm Yr Eglwys, Newport, Pembrokeshire, SA42 0SJ ☎ 01348 811374

Carmarthen & District Mrs B L Davies, 7 Gelli Ayr, Bronwydo, Carmarthen, Dyfed, SA33 6BE ☎ 01267 236997

Dinefwr Mr David Foot, Ty Isaf, Taliaris, Llandeilo, SA19 7DE ☎ 01550 777623

Lampeter Mr G D Jones, Talar Wen, Drefach, Llanybydder, Dyfed, SA40 9SX

Llanelli Mr I McConkey, 6 Railway Place, Llanelli, Carms, SA15 2PW ☎ 01554 759280

Pembrokeshire Mr Robert Godbehere, Trefonnen, Penffordd, Narberth, Pembrokeshire, SA66 7HX ☎ 01437 563144

GLAMORGAN

THE AUTHORITIES OF BRIDGEND; CARDIFF; RHONDDA, CYNON TAFF; SWANSEA; VALE OF GLAMORGAN; AND WEST GLAMORGAN

AREA SECRETARY
Mr Terry Squires, 7 Glan-Yr-Afon, Pontyclun, CF72 9BJ ☎ 01443 223526

GROUP SECRETARIES
Bridgend & District Mr John Sanders, 3 Bryn Rhedyn, Pencoed Bridgend, CF35 6TL ☎ 01656 861835

Cardiff Ms Diane Davies, 9 Cyncoed Rise, Cyncoed, Cardiff, CF23 6SF ☎ 029 2075 2464

Cynon Valley Mr Allan Harrison, 8 Stuart Street, Aberdare, Mid Glamorgan, CF44 7LY ☎ 01685 881824

Merthyr Valley Mr J E Thomas, Brynawel, 91 Clydach Road, Tony Pandy, Rhondda, CF40 2DG ☎ 01443 438719

Neath Port Talbot Ms C Coates, 4 Cerise Close, Port Talbot, SA12 7AY ☎ 01639 882773

Penarth & District Mrs L Davies, 3 Barrians Way, Barry, Vale Of Glamorgan, CF62 8JG

Taff Ely Mr J T Roszkowski, 18 Parc Y Coed, Creigiau, Nr Cardiff, CF15 9LX ☎ 02920 891455

Vale of Glamorgan Mr David Cobourne, 9 The Verlands, Cowbridge, Vale Of Glamorgan, CF71 7BY ☎ 01446 773301

West Glamorgan Ms A Sedge, 12 Bron Y Wawr, Pontardawe, Swansea, SA8 4FY ☎ 01792 864035

GREATER GWENT

THE AUTHORITIES OF BLAENAU GWENT; CARPHILLY; MON-MOUTHSHIRE; NEWPORT; AND TORFAEN

AREA SECRETARY
Keiron O'Hagan (acting), 45 John Street, Bargoed, Mid Glamorgan, CF81 8PH ☎ 01443 836257

GROUP SECRETARIES
Gelligaer Mrs D Price, 26 Tyn Y Coed, Ystrad Mynach, Caerphilly, CF82 7DD ☎ 01443 813220

Islwyn Mr M J Matthews, 77 Park Place, Risca, Newport, NP11 6BN ☎ 01633 615165

Lower Wye Mrs J M Jones, Swn Yr Afon, Tintern, Chepstow, Monmouthshire, NP16 6TH ☎ 01291 689550

North Gwent Mr A Nicholas, 31 Windsor Road, Brynmawr, Blaenau, Gwent, NP23 4HE ☎ 01495 311088

Pontypool Mrs Barbara Whitticase, Glantawell, Llanfihangel Talyllyn, Brecon, Powys, LD3 7TH ☎ 01874 658386
South Gwent Mr K Phillips, 39 Penylan Close, Bassaleg, Newport, Gwent, NP10 8NN ☎ 01633 894172

NORTH WALES

THE AUTHORITIES OF ISLE OF ANGLESEY; CONWY; DENBIGHSHIRE; FLINTSHIRE; GWYNEDD; AND WREXHAM

AREA SECRETARY
Mr P D Bland, 11 Endsleigh Close, Upton, Chester, CH2 1LX ☎ 01244 377024

GROUP SECRETARIES
Bangor-Bethesda Miss A G Penketh, 2 Sychnant View, Old Mill Road, Penmaenmawr, Gwynedd, LL34 6TN ☎ 01492 622887
Berwyn Mr J A & Mrs U Kay, Erw Fain, Llantysilio, Llangollen, Clwyd, LL20 8BU ☎ 01978 861 1793
Caernarfon Mrs Anita Thomas, 'Cae Goronwy', Fachwen, Llanberis, Gwynedd, LL55 3HA ☎ 01286 870979
Clwydian Mr William Wood, 4 Maes Cantaba, Ruthin, Denbighshire, LL15 1YP ☎ 01824 703509
Conwy Valley Mr D Cuthbert, 10 Bryn Celyn, Cadnant Park, Conwy, Gwynedd, LL32 8PW ☎ 01492 593 841
Deeside Mr Jim Irvine, 30 St Davids Drive, Connahs Quay, Flintshire, CH5 4SR ☎ 01244 818577
Meirionnydd Mr Geoff Elliott, Groes Lwyd, Harlech, Gwynedd, LL46 2TS ☎ 01766 780984
Vale of Clwyd Mrs P Phillips, , Tan Y Berllan, Deganwy, Conwy, LL31 9RD ☎ 01492 582635
Walking Group 18-40 Ms S L Troilett, The Flat At The Byre, Chester Road, Cheshire, CH3 6LB ☎ 01829 271332
Wrexham Mr Paul Davies, 5 Glyndwr Road, Wrexham, LL12 7TR ☎ 01978 362253
Ynys Mon Mr S Hughes, Glyn Pentraeth Road, Menai Bridge, Anglesey, Gwynedd, LL59 5HD ☎ 01248 712315

POWYS

AREA SECRETARY
Mr C J Playford, Hawthorn Villa, Cusop, Hay On Wye, Hereford, HR3 5QX ☎ 01497 820074

GROUP SECRETARIES
4 Wells Ms J M Annetts, 2 Brickfield Cottages, Brookland Road, Llandrindod Wells, Powys, LD1 6DE ☎ 01597 824866
Welshpool Mrs Gwen Evans, Moorwood, Leighton, Welshpool, Powys, SY21 8LW ☎ 01938 580352

YOUNG PEOPLE'S GROUPS

WE REPEAT THESE GROUPS HERE FOR YOUR CONVENIENCE, THIS LIST IS PART OF A DEVELOPMENT PROGRAMME AND THERE MAY ALREADY BE OTHERS. CHECK WITH MURRAY HATCHER AT CENTRAL OFFICE IF YOU FIND THERE IS NO GROUP NEAR YOU.

Berkshire Walkers (Berks) Caroline Mcdonagh, 2 Andrews Close, Theale, Reading, Berks, RG7 5BH
Brunel Walking & Activity [20s/30s] (Avon) Mr Colin Marshall ☎ 0117 9466495
Chilterns 20s-30s Walking Group (Bucks) Sue McGuirk, 67a Herga Court, Harrow On The Hill, Middx, HA1 3RT ☎ 020 8426 5907
Essex Young Ramblers No contact at present
Leicestershire & Rutland Walking Group Miss Heather Davies, Newton House, Turville Road, Gilmorton, Lutterworth, LE17 5LZ ☎ 01455 558389
North & Mid Cheshire Under 40 Mr E W Thom, 42 Portola Close, Grappenhall, Warrington, WA4 2SW ☎ 01925 486837
Northumbria Mr A Wright, 15 Ord Court, Fenham, Newcastle Upon Tyne, NE4 9YF ☎ 0191 274 5961
Notts Derby Group Sarah Rich, 10 Cartbridge, Cotgrave, Nottingham, NG12 3PF ☎ 0115 989 0302
Oxon 20s&30s Walking Group Miss D M Glenister, 50 Laurel Drive, Southmoor, Abingdon, OX13 5DJ ☎ 01865 821756
Stour Walking Group (Suffolk) Andy Webb, 36 Hertford Road, Clare, Sudbury, Suffolk, CO10 8QJ ☎ 01440 716208
Surrey Under 35s Mr Graham Wilson, 3 Nell Court, 32 Lovelace Road, Surbiton, Surrey, KT6 6LZ ☎ 0208 399 6119
Walking Group 18-40 (North Wales) Ms S L Troilett, The Flat At The Byre, Chester Road, Cheshire, CH3 6LB ☎ 01829 271332
West Kent Walking Group (20-35) Mr D R Noakes, The Willow House, 14 Knowsley Way, Hildenborough, Kent, TN11 9LG ☎ 01732 832 202
West Midlands Walking Group (Warwicks) Lindsay Cosgrove, 53 St Francis Avenue, Solihull, West Midlands, B91 1EB ☎ 0121 241 7923

☎ ☎ ☎
IF YOU NEED TO PHONE ANYONE LISTED IN THIS SECTION PLEASE REMEMBER THEY ARE VOLUNTEERS WORKING FROM HOME. PLEASE DON'T MAKE CALLS LATE IN THE EVENING.

Access to the Countryside

England & Wales: public rights of way

Below are answers to the questions people most often ask about rights of way.

1. WHAT IS A RIGHT OF WAY?

A right of way in the countryside is either a footpath, a bridleway or a byway. On footpaths the public has a right of way on foot only. On bridleways it also has a right of way on horseback and on a pedal cycle. Byways are open to all classes of traffic, including motor vehicles. Legally, a public right of way is part of the Queen's highway and subject to the same protection in law as all other highways.

2. WHAT ARE MY RIGHTS ON A PUBLIC RIGHT OF WAY?

The public's right is to pass and repass along the way. You may stop to rest or admire the view, or to consume refreshments, providing you stay on the path and do not cause an obstruction. You can also take with you a "natural accompaniment" which includes a pram or pushchair or a dog. However, you should ensure that dogs are under close control. Note that there is no requirement for stiles to be made suitable for use by accompanying dogs or pushchairs.

3. HOW DO I KNOW WHETHER A PATH IS A PUBLIC RIGHT OF WAY OR NOT?

The safest evidence is the definitive map of public rights of way. These are available at county, unitary, district and outer London borough council offices. Some are also available in libraries and some are sold by the councils concerned. In addition, public rights of way information derived from them, as amended by subsequent orders, is shown on Ordnance Survey Outdoor Leisure, Explorer and Pathfinder maps (1:25,000) and Landrangers (1:50,000). But note that many public rights of way are not yet shown on definitive maps and can quite properly be used, and that application may be made to surveying authorities (see Q6) for ways to be added to the definitive map.

4. HOW DOES A PATH BECOME PUBLIC?

In legal theory most paths become rights of way because the owner "dedicates" them to public use. In fact very few paths have been formally dedicated, but the law assumes that if the public uses a path without interference for upwards of 20 years then the owner intends dedication. Most public paths came about this way. But it is not true that a path can cease to be public if it is unused for 20 years (except in Scotland). The legal maxim is "once a highway, always a highway". Paths can also be created by agreement between local authorities and owners or by compulsory order, subject, in the case of objection, to the consent of the Secretary of State for the Environment, Transport and the Regions, or the National Assembly for Wales.

5. WHO OWNS THE PATHS?

The surface of the path is for most purposes considered to belong to the highway authority. What this means is that the authority owns the surface of the way and so much of the soil below and the air above as is necessary for the control, protection and maintenance of the highway. The rest normally belongs to the owner of the surrounding land.

6. WHICH COUNCILS DEAL WITH PATHS?

The councils to which duties have been given as highway and definitive map surveying authorities are the county, unitary, metropolitan district and London borough councils. Highway authorities have a general duty "to assert and protect the rights of the public to the use and enjoyment" of paths in their area and "to prevent as far as possible the stopping up or obstruction" of such paths. They should therefore deal with any deliberate obstruction such as a barbed wire fence or crops across a path. They are also legally responsible for maintaining the surface of the path (including bridges) and keeping it free of overgrowth. Shire district councils are entitled to take over the maintenance of public paths from the county councils if they wish and may by agreement take over other responsibilities. Parish councils and community councils also have the power to maintain paths (see the RA leaflet Paths for People - details below). Highway authorities have the power to require owners to cut back overhanging growth from the side of a path.

7. HOW WIDE SHOULD A PATH BE?

The path should be whatever width was dedicated for public use. This width may have arisen through usage or by formal agreement or by order eg if the path has been diverted. The width may be recorded in the statement accompanying the definitive map but in many cases the proper width will be a matter of what has been past practice on that particular path. (See also Q15 and Q17 below.) Note the width of the right of way may be greater, or sometimes less, than the width of any track or hard-surfaced strip along the route.

8. ARE HORSES ALLOWED ON PUBLIC PATHS?

Riders have a right to use bridleways, as the name implies. Riders have no right to use footpaths, but they often do. In doing so they are committing a trespass against the owner of the land, rather than a criminal offence. If use of a footpath by riders becomes a nuisance the highway authority can make a traffic regulation order forbidding riders to use that path.

9. IS IT ILLEGAL TO DRIVE CARS OR MOTOR CYCLES ON PUBLIC PATHS?

Anyone who drives a vehicle on a footpath or bridleway without permission is committing an offence. This does not apply if the driver stays within 15 yards of the road and only goes on the path to park. The owner of the land, however, can still order vehicles off even within 15 yards from the road. Races or speed trials on paths are forbidden. Permission for other types of trials on paths may be sought from the local authority, if the landowner consents.

10. WHAT IS A ROAD USED AS A PUBLIC PATH (RUPP)?

RUPPS, as they are commonly known, are a type of way shown on the definitive map which is usually unsurfaced and may or may not carry vehicular rights. This classification is now in process of abolition and all RUPPS will eventually be reclassified as either footpaths, bridleways or byways open to all traffic.

11. CAN A LANDOWNER PUT UP NEW GATES AND STILES WHERE NONE EXIST PRESENTLY?

No. Not without seeking and getting permission from the highway authority and then complying with any conditions to that permission.

12. WHO IS SUPPOSED TO LOOK AFTER STILES AND GATES ON A PATH?

Maintaining these is primarily the owner's responsibility, but the highway authority (or the district council if it is maintaining the path) must, in certain cases, contribute 25% of the cost if asked and may contribute more if it wishes. If the landowner fails to keep his stiles and gates in proper repair the authority can, after 14 days' notice, do the job itself and send the bill to the owner.

13. ARE ALL THE PATHS SUPPOSED TO BE SIGNPOSTED?

Highway authorities have a legal duty to put up signposts at all junctions of footpaths, bridleways and byways with metalled roads. Also parish and community councils can relieve authorities of the obligation for particular paths. Highway authorities also have a duty to waymark paths so far as they consider it appropriate.

14. WHAT IS WAYMARKING?

Waymarking is a means of indicating the line or direction of a path at points where it may be difficult to follow. The Countryside Agency recommends a standard system of coloured arrows for waymarking - yellow for footpaths, blue for bridleways and red for byways.

15. IS IT ILLEGAL TO PLOUGH UP OR DISTURB THE SURFACE OF A PATH SO AS TO MAKE IT INCONVE- NIENT TO USE?

No, if the path is a footpath or bridleway running across a field and it is not reasonably convenient to avoid disturbing it; yes, if the path is a byway, or any other footpath or bridleway. However, in the former case, the farmer must make good the surface within 24 hours of the disturbance (two weeks if the disturbance is the first one for a particular

crop). A path so restored must be reasonably convenient to use, must have a minimum width of one metre for a footpath and two metres for a bridleway (or the legal width if known), and its line must be clearly apparent on the ground.

16. WHAT HAPPENS IF A PATH SURFACE HAS BEEN DISTURBED BUT NOT RESTORED?

A highway authority may serve notice on the occupier and, if necessary, then restore the path itself and send the bill to the occupier. The authority may also prosecute the person responsible for the disturbance.

17. WHAT ABOUT CROPS GROWING ON OR OVER A PATH?

The farmer has a duty to prevent a crop (other than grass) from making the path difficult to find or follow. The minimum widths given in Q15 apply here also, but if the path is a field-edge path they are increased to 1fi metres for a footpath, three metres for a bridleway. You have every right to walk through crops growing on or over a path, but stick as close as you can to its correct line. Report the problem to the highway authority: it has power to prosecute the farmer or cut the crop and send him the bill.

18. WHAT IS AN OBSTRUCTION ON A PATH?

Anything which interferes with your right to proceed along it, e.g. a barbed wire fence across the path or a heap of manure dumped on it. Dense undergrowth is not normally treated as an obstruction but is dealt with under path maintenance.

19. CAN I REMOVE AN OBSTRUC- TION TO GET BY?

Yes, provided that (a) you are a bona fide traveller on the path and have not gone out for the specific purpose of moving the obstruction, and (b) you remove only as much as is necessary to get through. If you can easily go round the obstruction without causing any damage, then you should do so. But report the obstruction to the highway authority and/or the RA: see details of our Reporting Path Problems leaflet below.

20. CAN A FARMER KEEP A BULL IN A FIELD CROSSED BY A PUBLIC PATH?

A bull of up to ten months old, yes. Bulls over ten months of a recognised dairy breed (Ayrshire, British Friesian, British Holstein, Dairy Shorthorn, Guernsey, Jersey and Kerry) are banned from fields crossed by public paths under all circumstances. All other bulls over ten months are banned unless accompanied by cows or heifers. If any bulls act in a way which endangers the public, an offence may be committed under health and safety legislation.

21. CAN A LANDOWNER CLOSE OR DIVERT A PATH?

No. Closure and diversion (i.e. change of a path's route) can only be carried out by local authorities or central government. Under the commonest procedure for closure an authority is empowered to make an order to close a path if it considers it is no longer needed for public use. A notice that the council has made an order must be published in a local paper and also placed at both ends of the path. It must allow at least 28 days for objections. These must be heard at a public inquiry taken by an inspector from the DETR (or the National Assembly for Wales), or by private hearing, or they may be considered in writing if the objectors agree.

Path diversions may not take place if the new path will be substantially less convenient to the public than the existing one, and account must also be taken of the effect the diversion will have on public enjoyment of the way as a whole. Paths may also be closed or diverted under the Town and Country Planning Act 1990 "in order to enable development to be carried out in accordance with planning permission". The procedure for these orders, and for diversion orders under the Highways Act, is the same as for closure orders. There are also provisions for highway authorities to apply to magistrates courts for closure or diversion of paths, and for closure and diversion orders to be made in other circumstances, e.g. construction of new roads, railways and reservoirs, both on a permanent and temporary basis. If you have any doubts about the legality of a change to a path, contact the highway authority.

22. WHAT IS A MISLEADING NOTICE?

A misleading notice is one calculated to deter you from using a public right of way, for example, a notice saying PRIVATE at the point where a public footpath enters a park. Such notices should be reported immediately to the highway authority. They are illegal on paths shown on the definitive map.

23. WHAT IS TRESPASS?

The civil tort of trespass arises from the bare fact of unauthorised entry. A person who strays from a right of way, or uses it other than for passing and repassing (see Q1) commits trespass against the landowner. A landowner may use "reasonable force" to compel a trespasser to leave, but not more than is reasonably necessary. Unless injury to the property can be proven, a landowner could probably only recover nominal damages by suing for trespass. But of course you might have to meet the landowner's legal costs. Thus a notice saying "Trespassers will be Prosecuted", aimed for instance at keeping you off a private drive, is usually meaningless. Prosecution could only arise if you trespass and damage property. However, under public order law, trespassing with an intention to reside may be a criminal offence under some circumstances. It is an offence to trespass on railway land and also sometimes on military training land.

24. HOW CAN I HELP THE RA DEAL WITH PATH PROBLEMS?

Sadly, one in four public paths are blocked. To help tackle path problems, you can:

(a) Send full details to the highway authority (see the list starting on page 41), and to the RA (see the path problem report form on page 282 or on our website or ask for one from central office).

(b) Ask the farmer or landowner concerned to clear the obstruction.

(c) Take part in RA footpath clearance working parties.

(d) If the problems persist, write to your local councillors about them.

(e) Send letters to local newspapers seeking support for any representations you may be making.

(f) If the authority fails to take action, consider complaining to the local ombudsman.

The more path users show their concern for the state of the rights of way network, by complaining about trouble spots, the better.

Please note that the provisions of the Countryside and Rights of Way Act will make changes to rights of way law. Please contact the rights of way policy team at central office, or visit our website, for the latest information.

> HIRING MAPS FROM THE RA MAP LIBRARY?
> **GIVE PLENTY OF NOTICE** – MAPS OF
> POPULAR AREAS RUN OUT IN HIGH SEASON

Publications

RA PUBLICATIONS ON RIGHTS OF WAY AND ACCESS

Footpath Worker, a bulletin containing matters of interest to those concerned with public paths is available from the RA, price £7 for a volume of 4 issues.

Ramblers' Atlas of Public Forests (2nd edition), showing land in England, Scotland and Wales held by the Forestry Commission. Free A4 booklet.

FREE RA LEAFLETS

Available from RA central office. Please enclose s.a.e.
Defending Public Paths – a leaflet on the RA's work protecting paths.
Paths for People – a leaflet on rights of way law for parish, community and town councillors. (Welsh version available.)
Planning for Public Paths – a leaflet for developers and planning authorities aimed at preventing the obstruction of rights of way by new buildings.
Ploughed and Cropped Paths – a leaflet explaining the law on ploughing and cropping of public paths.
Reporting Path Problems – a leaflet incorporating a path problem report form.
Please note that these publications are relevant to England and Wales only.

OTHER USEFUL PUBLICATIONS

There are some useful Countryside Agency publications on rights of way and access to the countryside in England:
Out in the Country - where you can go and what you can do;
A Guide to Definitive Map Procedures;
Waymarking Public Paths;
A Guide to Procedures for Public Path Orders;
Managing Public Access.
These booklets are available from Countryside Agency Postal Sales. (Tel 01604) 781848.
The Countryside Council for Wales has produced Welsh versions of *Out in the Country* and *Managing Public Access*. Available free of charge from CCW, Tel. (01284) 370444

ACCESS TO THE COUNTRYSIDE

England & Wales: Freedom to Roam

WHAT DOES THE NEW "RIGHT TO ROAM" LAW SAY?

The Countryside and Rights of Way Act creates a new legal right of access on foot to some, but not all, areas of open, uncultivated countryside. The law will allow walkers to explore away from paths on approximately four million acres of mountain, moor, heath, down, and common land in England and Wales. It also includes safeguards to protect the environment and landowners' interests. It does NOT allow people to walk through back gardens, or over crops. The Act also grants the Secretary of State and the National Assembly for Wales powers to extend a right of access to coastal land, subject to a full impact assessment, in the future.

WILL THE NEW LAW APPLY DIFFERENTLY IN ENGLAND AND WALES?

The Ramblers' Association will work to ensure that the new access is consistently applied in England and Wales, but variations may occur where the Welsh Assembly and the Department for the Environment, Transport and Regions so choose.

WHEN WILL THE LAW COME INTO EFFECT?

The Countryside and Rights of Way Act is now on the statue books, but we shall not be able to enjoy the new right fully for several years. The Countryside Agency (CA) and the Countryside Council for Wales (CCW) will draw up maps showing where the new right of access will apply. The mapping of open countryside areas will take 3-4 years to complete and until these maps are published, there is no general right to roam over areas of open, uncultivated countryside (see below). There must also be time for landowners and farmers to apply for closures and restrictions where necessary.

DO I HAVE ANY RIGHT OF ACCESS TO OPEN COUNTRY BEFORE THE MAPS ARE PRODUCED?

The current situation will persist until the access maps are produced. In general, there is no freedom to roam and in most areas of open country, you are a trespasser. However, there are some places where walkers may currently enjoy a freedom to wander.

Some places, such as town parks, country parks and village greens are intended for public use and so are open to the public. Most of the 1.37 million acres of common land in England and Wales are privately owned. The public has a legal right of access to only about one-fifth of this land although there is de facto access to many areas of common land.

The National Trust owns common land and other open country, and it is Trust policy to allow the public onto their land. Most Forestry Commission woodlands and plantations are also open to the public.

Areas of land where access agreements apply or where access is tolerated by the landowner may remain open to walkers, although in the latter case the landowner could turn people off at any time, making the walker a trespasser.

Some moorland water-gathering grounds are open to people on foot by virtue of special nineteenth-century legislation and although they are privately owned like other types of land, the public usually enjoys access to beaches. There is, however, no right to cross private land in order to reach a beach.

Government cash for access programmes such as Countryside Stewardship and agri-environment schemes including Tir Gofal are also set to continue.

Finally, 'fast track access' may be granted to certain types of land (common land and land over 600m) which are defined as open country under the Act and can already be identified on existing maps.

WHAT RESPONSIBILITIES COME WITH THE NEW RIGHT OF ACCESS?

Anyone who drops litter, lights fires, wilfully damages walls, plant or animal life, leaves gates open or commits a criminal offence will be treated as a trespasser and barred from entering the land for the next 72 hours. The Countryside Agency and the Countryside Council for Wales are preparing guidance and formal codes of practice for land users, owners and managers to explain the new rights and responsibilities. Until these guidelines are published, walkers should follow the country code.

HOW WILL I KNOW WHERE TO FIND ACCESS LAND?

In addition to new Ordnance Survey maps showing access land, the Countryside Agency and the Countryside Council for Wales will produce information on access opportunities and restrictions. This information will be published and distributed nationally in various guides, booklets, leaflets, and over the internet. Access information will also be available locally through tourist information offices, the local media, pubs, shops and at information points near access land.

WHAT CAN I DO ON ACCESS LAND?

The new law provides a right of access for walkers only. It does not confer any additional rights for cyclists or horse riders. Dogs are permitted on some areas of open country, but must be kept on short fixed leads on access land between 1 March and 31 July and at any time in the vicinity of livestock. Furthermore, dogs may be banned temporarily or permanently from some areas of land. Camping and organised games are prohibited except with the permission of the landowner. Access at night is permitted but may be subject to local restrictions. Walkers are responsible for their own safety at all times.

HOW WILL ACCESS BE MANAGED LOCALLY?

Local countryside access fora, made up of landowners, users and others with an interest in the land, will be established to advise the countryside agencies and national park authorities on restrictions and how the new law will be applied generally on a local basis. Specific access needs and concerns can be addressed through local countryside access fora or bylaws. Local authorities, including National Parks, have the power to enact and enforce bylaws which will apply to open access land in their jurisdiction subject to consultation with the relevant local access forum and countryside body.

HOW WILL I FIND OUT ABOUT LOCAL CLOSURES AND RESTRICTIONS?

Information on local closures and restrictions will be obtainable from the relevant local authority. If bylaws apply, notices may be displayed at information points near the relevant area of access land. Information about local regulations will also be made available by the countryside agencies through tourist information offices, the local media, pubs, shops and at information points near access land.

WILL LANDOWNERS BE ABLE TO CLOSE THEIR LAND FOR ANY REASON?

The Act allows landowners to close their land for up to 28 days a year (including some

ACCESS TO THE COUNTRYSIDE

Saturdays and Sundays) for any reason. The countryside agencies should be informed of these closures and can pass the information on to the public. Landowners may also apply to the Countryside Agency and the Countryside Council for Wales for further closures or restrictions, on a temporary or permanent basis, to protect wildlife or areas of historic interest, for health and safety, military purposes, or for land management.

WILL LANDOWNERS AND FARMERS BENEFIT FROM THIS LEGISLATION?

Landowners will benefit from this legislation in several ways. The new law allows landowners to close or restrict access to their land for up to 28 days per year. Restrictions can be put in place should any conflict arise. Occupier's liability towards walkers on access land has been lowered significantly. Landowners may also benefit from wardening services, and the practical costs resulting from the Act - for example, the erection of signs - will be met by the countryside agencies. Finally, the benefits from tourism could be enormous for rural areas. It is likely that the new Act will encourage more people to visit the countryside for day trips or holidays, therefore bringing more revenue into rural areas and helping to create jobs.

WILL A FREEDOM TO ROAM DAMAGE THE ENVIRONMENT?

In general there is no irreconcilable conflict between a freedom to roam and wildlife. The new Act allows land to be closed to protect wildlife habitats, flora and fauna, or for conservation reasons. The Act includes measures to protect wildlife and the environment, and in particular Sites of Special Scientific Interest and Areas of Outstanding Natural Beauty. Furthermore, allowing access will encourage people to learn to enjoy, respect, and therefore protect the environment.

DON'T FOOTPATHS PROVIDE ENOUGH PLACES TO WALK?

Freedom to roam is different from walking on public paths. A freedom to roam will provide the public with the opportunity to wander, responsibly, away from paths without being accused of trespass, and to see and visit particular views or special features. For many people, the pleasure of walking is to get away from the beaten track and enjoy the delights of the open countryside. And in many places, there are no paths to take us over open country.

Access to Scotland's countryside

There is a long-established *de facto* right to roam in the Scottish hills which has a strong legal basis. It is expected that the Scottish Parliament will shortly enshrine this tradition in new access legislation. This will guarantee freedom of access for informal recreation to most of Scotland's countryside, providing this is exercised responsibly, taking due account of conservation and management needs.

Freedom of access should be exercised with care. When crossing cultivated land, try to use paths or tracks or field margins. Use gates whenever possible but where walls or fences have to be crossed, do so carefully to avoid damage to the structure.

Further guidance on using the countryside responsibly should be available in the Scottish Outdoor Access Code. This is expected to accompany the right of access when it is approved by the Scottish Parliament. The aim of the proposed Code is to show how recreational users, land managers and public bodies can help each other to make sure the right of access works well on the ground.

Highway Authorities

The Ramblers' Association is constantly working towards keeping our many miles of footpaths open and free from obstruction. You can help by reporting any problems you encounter. You can send your report either to the Ramblers' Association in the area concerned (in which case the local footpath officer will take the matter up with the local authority) or direct to the local authority. **If you choose the latter, please send a copy to the local RA local contact as well.** (See list starting on page 17).

The following listing is of the authorities in England, Wales and Scotland as at August 2000. Each county or unitary authority has its own department for dealing with rights of way. The inner London boroughs, rightful members of this listing, have not been included due to lack of space. We hope to do so in future editions.

In England and Wales, your report should be addressed to the Public Rights of Way Officer of the appropriate authority unless we have given the title of a different officer in the listing (for example, the Countryside Officer). In Scotland you should write to the Director of Planning. If the problem is within a National Park, the report should be made to the National Park Authority. (See *Useful Addresses and Websites* in this book).

If you find it helpful, use the Path Problem Report form later in this book to describe the nature of the obstruction. Make sure you report **what** the problem is, **where** it is and **when** it was you noticed it. Further forms are available from RA offices.

Abbreviations used:

CC County Council

UA Unitary Authority

MB Metropolitan Borough

England

Barnsley (MB) Countryside Officer, Leisure & Amenities Dept, Phase III Court House Site, County Way, Barnsley S70 2TL.

Bath & North East Somerset (UA) The Guildhall, Bath BA1 5AW.

Bedfordshire (CC) Countryside Manager, Leisure Services Dept, County Hall, Cauldwell Street, Bedford MK42 9AP.

Berkshire (CC) Babtie Public Services, Shire Hall, Shinfield Park, Reading RG2 9XG.

Birmingham City Council (MB), City Engineers & Highways Information, 1 Lancaster Circus, Queensway, Birmingham B4 7DQ.

Blackburn with Darwen (UA), Town Hall, Blackburn BB1 2LX.

Blackpool (UA), Municipal Buildlings, PO Box 77, Town Hall, Blackpool FY1 1AD.

Bolton (MB), Group Engineer, Planning & Eng Serv Dept, The Wellsprings, Bolton BL1 1US.

Bournemouth (UA) Town Hall, Bourne Avenue, Bournemouth BH2 6DY

Bracknell Forest (UA), Leisure Services, Edward Elgar House, Skimped Hill Lane, Bracknell RG12 1LR.

Bradford (MB), Holycroft, Goulbourne Street, Keighley, W. Yorkshire BD1 1PY.

Brighton & Hove (UA) Town Hall, Bartholomew Sq, Brighton BN1 1JA

Bristol (UA) City & County of Bristol, The Council House, College Green, Bristol BS1 5TR.

Buckinghamshire (CC), Wycombe Area Office, Easton Street, High Wycombe HP11 1NH.

Bury (MB) Maintenance Section, Lester House, 21 Broad Street, Bury BL9 0A.

Calderdale (MB), Highways & Technical Services, Northgate House, Halifax HX1 1UN.

Cambridgeshire (CC) Access & Recreation Manager, Property Dept, Shire Hall, Castle Hill, Cambridge CB3 0AP.

Cheshire (CC), Countryside Access Manager, Rights of Way Unit, Goldsmith House, Hamilton Place, Chester CH1 1SE.

Cornwall (CC), Countryside Access Manager, Western Group Centre, Radnor Road, Scorrier, Redruth TR16 5EH

Coventry CC, Strategic & Local Plans, Council House, Earl Street, Coventry CV1 5RR.

Cumbria (CC), Highways & Engineering, Viaduct Estate, Carlisle CA2 5BN.

Darlington Town Hall, Darlington, DL1 5QT

Derby (UA) The Council House, Corporation Street, Derby DE1 2FS

Derbyshire (CC), County Planning & Highways, County Offices, Matlock DE4 3AG.

Devon (CC) Public Rights Of Way Manager, Lucombe House, Topsham Road, Exeter EX2 4QW.

Doncaster (MB), Public Works Directorate, Scarborough House, 25 Chequer Road, Doncaster DN1 2DB.

Dorset (CC) Rights Of Way Section, Transport & Engineering, County Hall, Dorchester DT1 1XJ.

Dudley (MB) Senior Engineer, Public Works Dept, Mary Stevens Park, Stourbridge, DY8 2AA.

Durham (CC) Environment Dept, County Hall, Durham DH1 5UQ.

Essex (CC), Planning Office, County Hall, Chelmsford CM1 1NF.

Gateshead (MB) Planning Dept, Civic Centre, Regent Street, Gateshead NE8 1HH.

Gloucestershire (CC), Public Rights of Way & DC Manager, Environment Services, Shire Hall, Gloucester, GL1 2TH.

Gloucestershire (South) (UA) The Council Offices, Castle Street, Bristol BS12 1HF.

Halton (UA), Municipal Building, Kingsway, Widnes, WA8 7QF.

Hampshire (CC), Countryside Services, Basing House, Redbridge Lane, Basingstoke RG24 7HB.

Hartlepool (UA) Civic Centre, Hartlepool TS24 8AY.

Herefordshire (UA), PO Box 185, Hereford Educ. & Conf. Centre, Blackfriars Street, Hereford HR4 9ZF.

Hertfordshire (CC), Countryside Access Manager, Planning & Environment Dept, County Hall, Hertford SG13 8DN.

Isle of Wight (UA) Council, Rights Of Way Manager, Engineering & Technical Services, County Hall, Newport PO30 1UD.

Kent (CC) Director of Highways and Transportation, Sandling Block, Springfield, Maidstone ME14 2LQ.

Kingston upon Hull (UA) Guildhall, Alfred Gelder Street, Hull HU1 2AA.

Kirklees (MB), Highway Services, 2 Oldgate, Huddersfield HD1 6QQ.

Knowsley (MB), Dept of Planning & Devlopment, PO Box 26 Muncipal Buildings, Archway Road, Huyton L36 9FB.

Lancashire (CC) County Hall, PO Box 9, Guild House, Cross Street, Preston PR1 8RD

Leeds (UA), Leisure Services Dept, 19 Wellington Street, Leeds LS1 4DG

Leicester (UA) New Walk Centre, Welford Place, Leicester LE1 6ZG

Leicestershire (CC) County Hall, Planning & Transportation, Glenfield, Leicester LE3 8RJ

Lincolnshire (CC) Countryside Manager, Recreation Services Dept, County Offices, Newland, Lincoln LN11 OEL.

Lincolnshire (North) (UA) Environment Team Leader, 18 Bigby Street, Brigg

Lincolnshire (North East) (UA) Muncipal Offices, Grimsby DN31 1HU.

Liverpool (MB) Development & Environmental Services Directorate, Millenium House, 60 Victoria Street, Liverpool L1 6JH.

London Boroughs (outer boroughs only)

Barking & Dagenham Civic Centre, Dagenham RM10 7BN.

Barnet Barnet House, Whetstone, N20 0EJ.

Bexley Civic Offices, Broadway, Bexleyheath DA6 7LB.

Brent Town Hall, Forty Lane, Wembley HA9 9EZ.

Bromley Civic Centre, Stockwell Close, Bromley BR1 3UH.

Croydon Crosfield, Mint House, Croydon CR0 3HH.

Ealing Town Hall, New Broadway, Ealing W5 2BY.

Enfield Civic Centre, Silver Street, Enfield EN1 3XA.

Haringey Civic Centre, PO Box 264, High Road N22 4LE.

Harrow Civic Centre, Harrow, Middx HA1 2UW.

Havering Mercury House, Mercury Gardens, Romford RM1 3DS.

Hillingdon Civic Centre, Uxbridge UB8 1UW.

Hounslow Civic Centre, Lampton Road, Hounslow TW3 4DN.

Kingston upon Thames Guildhall, Kingston upon Thames KT1 1EU.

Merton Civic Centre, London Road, Morden SM4 5DX.

Newham Town Hall, East Ham E6 2RP.

Redbridge Town Hall, High Road, Ilford IG1 1DD.

Richmond upon Thames Civic Centre, 44 York Street, Twickenham TW1 3BZ.

Sutton Civic Offices, 24 Denmark Hill, Carshalton SM1 1EA.

Waltham Forest Town Hall, Forest Road, Walthamstow E17 4JF.

Luton (UA) Town Hall, Luton LU1 2BQ

Manchester (MB) City Eng & Surv Dept, PO Box 488, Town Hall, Albert Sq, Manchester M60 2JT

Medway Towns (UA), Civic Centre, Strood, Rochester ME2 4AU.

Middlesbrough (UA), Municipal Buildings, Middlesbrough TS1 2QQ.

Milton Keynes (UA) Civic Offices, 1 Saxon Gate, Milton Keynes MK9 3HG

Newcastle upon Tyne (MB) Eng, Environment & Protection, Civic Centre, Barras Bridge, Newcastle-upon-Tyne NE1 8PD.

Norfolk (CC) Access Development Officer, Norfolk (CC),

Northamptonshire (CC), Planning & Transportation, PO Box 221, John Dryden House, 8-10 The Lakes, Northampton NN4 7DE.

Northumberland (CC) Countryside Team Leader, County Hall, Morpeth NE61 2EF.

Nottinghamshire (CC) County Hall, Planning & Economic Development, Trent Bridge House, West Bridgford, Nottingham NG2 6BJ.

Oldham (MB), Technical Services Department, Henshaw House, Cheapside, Oldham OL1 1NY.

Oxfordshire (CC), Countryside Section, Department of Cultural Services, Holton, Oxford OX33 1QQ.

Peterborough City (UA), Town Hall, Bridge Street, Peterborough PE1 1HG.

Plymouth (UA), Civic Centre, Plymouth PL1 2EW.

Poole (UA) Borough and County of the Town of Poole, Poole BH15 2RU

Portsmouth (UA) Civic Offices, Guildhall Square, Portsmouth PO1 2AL.

Reading (UA), Civic Centre, Reading RG1 7TD.

Redcar & Cleveland (UA) Langbaurgh Town Hall, Fabian Road, PO Box 8, South Bank, Middlesborough TS6 9AR.

Rochdale (MB), Public Footpaths Officer, Support Services Dept, Electric House, Smith Street, Rochdale OL16 1YP.

Rotherham (MB), Dept. of Engineering, Bailey House Rawmarsh Road, Rotherham S60 1TD.

Rutland (UA) Catmose, Oakham, Rutland LE15 6HP

Salford (CC), Assistant Engineer, 11th Floor, Peel House, Albert Street, Eccles, Salford M30 0LA.

Sandwell (MB), Tech & Devlopement Services, PO Box 42, Wigmore, Pennyhill Lane, West Bromwich B71 3RZ.

Sefton (MB), Traffic Services, Eng & Surveying, Balliol House, Stanley Precint, Bootle L20 3NJ

Sheffield (CC), Highway & Traffic Division, Desighn & Building Services, 2-10 Carbrook Hall Road, Sheffield S9 2DB.

Shropshire (CC) Head of Countryside Service, The Shire Hall, Abbey Foregate, Shrewsbury SY2 6NW.

Slough (UA), Development & Consumer Protection Services, Wellington House, High Street, Slough SL1 1FA.

Solihull (MB), Technical Services, PO Box 19, Council House, Solihull B91 2QT.

Somerset (CC), Environment Dept, County Hall, Taunton TA1 4DY.

Somerset (North) (UA) North Somerset Council, Avon House North, St James Barton, Bristol

Southampton (UA) City Council, Southampton LE15 6HP

Southend-on-Sea (UA), Civic Centre, Southend-on-Sea SS2 6ER.

St Helens (MB), Engineers Division, Wesley House, Corporation Street, St Helens WA10 1HF.

Staffordshire (CC), County Countryside Officer, Cultural & Recreational Services, Shire Hall, Market Street, Stafford ST16 2LQ

Stockport (MB), Works Division, Petersgate House, St Petersgate, Stockport SK1 1HU.

Stockton-on-Tees (UA) Municipal Buildings, Church Road, Stockton-on-Tees TS18 1LD.

Stoke-on-Trent (UA) PO Box 636 Civic Centre, Glebe Street, Stoke-on-Trent ST14 1RN

Suffolk (CC), Highways Dept, County Hall, St Helens Street, Ipswich IP4 1LZ.

Sunderland (MB) Environmental Dept, Civic Centre, Sunderland SR2 7DN.

Surrey (CC), County Hall, Kingston upon Thames KT1 2DY, for all areas except the following:

Runneymede Borough Council, Civic Offices, Station Road, Addleston KT15 2AH

Spelthorne Borough Council, Council Offices. Knowle Green, Staines TW18 1XB

Surrey Heath Borough Council, Surrey Heath House, Knoll Road, Camberley GU15 3HD

Sussex (East) (CC), Highways Dept, Sackville House, Brooks Close, Lewes BN7 1UE.

Sussex (West) (CC) County Hall, Countryside Management Unit, Chichester PO19 1RH.

Swindon (UA) Civic Offices, Swindon SN1 2JH

Tameside (MB), Council Offices, Wellington Road, Ashton-under-Lyne, Tameside OL6 6DL.

Telford and Wrekin (UA), Civic Offices, Telford TF3 4LD.

Thurrock (UA), Civic Offices, New Road, Grays RN17 6SL.

Torbay (UA), Civic Offices, Torquay TQ1 3DR.

Trafford (MB), Engineering & Planning, Trafford Town Hall, Talbot, Stretford M32 0YX.

Tyneside (North) (MB) Environment Function, Graham House, Whitley Road, Benton, Newcastle-upon-Tyne NE12 9TQ.

Tyneside (South) (MB), Directorate of Dev Services, Town Hall & Civic Offices, Westoe Road, South Shields NE33 2RL.

Wakefield (MB), Regeneration Department, Newton Bar, Wakefield WF1 2TX.

Walsall (MB), Technical Administration, Eng & Town Planning Dept, Civic Centre, Darwall Street, Walsall WS1 1DG.

Warrington (UA), Town Hall, Warrington WA1 1UH.

Warwickshire (CC), Countryside Access Officer, Planning & Transport Dept, PO Box 43,Shire Hall, Warwick CV34 4SX.

West Berkshire (UA), Babtie Group, School Green, Shinfield, Reading RG2 9HL.

Windsor and Maidenhead (UA), Babtie Group, School Green, Shinfield, Reading RG2 9HL.

Wigan (MB), Tech Services Dept, Civic Centre, Hillgate, Wigan WN1 1YD.

Wiltshire (CC) Environmental Service Department, County Hall, Trowbridge BA14 8JD.

Wirral (MB), Local Paths Liaison Officer, Borough Engineer's Dept, Town Hall, Bebington L63 7PT.

Wokingham (UA), Environmental Services Department, Engineering Services, PO Box 153, Shute End, Wokingham RG40 1WL.

Wolverhampton BC, Tech Services Dept, Civic Centre, St Peters Square, Wolverhampton WV1 1RP.

Worcestershire (CC), County Hall, Spetchley Road, Worcester WR5 2NP.

York (City of) (UA) The Guildhall, 9 St Leonard's Place, York YO1 1QN.

Yorkshire (East Riding of) (CC) County Hall, Beverley, HU17 8HL.

Yorkshire (North) (CC) County Hall, Highways & Transportation Dept, Northallerton DL7 8AH .

Scotland

Aberdeen (UA) Town House, Broad Street, Aberdeen AB9 1AQ.

Aberdeenshire (UA) Woodhill House, Westburn Road, Aberdeen AB16 5GB.

Angus (UA) County Buildings, Market Street, Forfar DD8 1BX.

Argyll & Bute (UA) Kilmory Castle, Lochgilphead, Argyll PA31 8RT.

Ayrshire (East) (UA) Council Offices, London Road Centre, London Road, Kilmarnock KA3 7DG.

Ayrshire (North) (UA) Cunninghame House, Friar's Croft, Irvine KA12 8EE.

Ayrshire (South) (UA) Council Offices, Wellington Square, Ayr KA7 1DR.

Clackmannanshire (UA) Council Offices, Greenfield, Alloa FK10 2AD.

Dumfries & Galloway (UA) Council Offices, English Street, Dumfries DG1 2DD.

Dunbartonshire (East) (UA) Council Offices, Tom Johnston House, Civic Way, Kirkintilloch G66 4TJ.

Dunbartonshire (West) (UA) Council Offices, Garshake Road, Dunbarton G82 3PU.

Dundee (UA) Council Offices, 21 City Square, Dundee DD1 3BY.

Edinburgh (UA) City of Edinbrugh Council, George IV Bridge, Edinburgh EH1 1UQ.

Falkirk (UA) Municipal Buildings, Falkirk FK1 5RS.

Fife (UA) Fife House, North Street, Glenrothes, Fife KY7 5LT.

Glasgow (UA) City Chambers, George Square, Glasgow G2 1DU.

Highland (UA) Highland Council, Glenurquhart Road, Inverness IV3 5NX.

Inverclyde (UA) Municipal Buildings, Clyde Square, Greenock PA15 1LX.

Lanarkshire (North) (UA) Civic Centre, Motherwell ML1 1TW.

Lanarkshire (South) (UA) Council Offices, Almada Street, Hamilton ML3 0AA.

Lothian (East) (UA) Council Buildings, Haddington, East Lothian EH41 3HA.

Lothian (West) (UA) West Lothian House, Almondvale North, Livingstone EH54 6QG.

Midlothian (UA) Midlothian House, 40 Buccleuch Street, Dalkeith EH22 1DJ.

Moray (UA) Council Offices, High Street, Elgin IV30 1BX.

Orkney Islands (UA) Council Offices, School Place, Kirkwall, Orkney KW15 1NY.

Perth & Kinross (UA) Council Offices, 2 High Street, Perth PH1 5PH.

Renfrewshire (UA) Municipal Buildings, Cotton Street, Paisley PA1 1BU.

Renfrewshire (East) (UA) Council Offices, Eastwood Park, Rouken Glen Road, Giffnock G46 6UG.

Shetland Islands (UA) Town Hall, Lerwick ZE1 0HB.

Scottish Borders (UA) Council Headquarters, Newtown St Boswells, Melrose TD6 0SA.

Stirling (UA) Council Offices, Viewforth, Stirling FK8 2ET.

Western Isles (UA) Council Offices, Sandwick Road, Stornoway, Isle of Lewis PA87 2BW.

Wales

Blaenau Gwent (UA) Cwmbran, Blaenau Gwent

Bridgend (UA) Civic Offices, Angel Street, Bridgend CF31 1LX

Caerphilly (UA) Council Offfices, Nelson Road, Tredomen, Ystrad Mynach CF82 7WF

Cardiff (UA) County Hall, Atlantic Wharf, Cardiff CF10 4UW

Carmarthenshire (UA) Old Llansteffan Road, Johnstown, Carmarthen SA31 3LZ

Ceredigion (UA) Town Hall, Pen Morfa, Aberystwyth SY23 1QA

Conwy (UA) Conwy Road, Mochdre, Colwyn Bay LL28 5AX

Denbighshire (UA) Dept of Technical Services, County Hall, Mold CH7 6GU

Flintshire (UA) County Hall, Mold CH7 6NB

Gwynedd (UA) Senior Engineer, Cae Penarlag, Dolgellau LL40 2YB

Merthyr Tydfil (UA) Civic Centre, Castle Street, Merthyr Tydfil CF47 8AN

Monmouthshire (UA) County Hall, Cwmbran NP44 2XH

Neath Port Talbot (UA) Countryside Officer, Civic Centre, Neath SA13 1PJ

Newport, Civic Centre, Newport NP20 4UR

Pembrokeshire (UA) County Hall, Haverfordwest, Pembrokeshire SA61 1TP

Powys (UA) St John's Offices, Fiveways, Llandrindod Wells, Powys LD1 5ES

Rhondda, Cynon, Taff (UA) Rhondda The Pavillions, Clydach Vale, Rhondda

Swansea (UA) Guild Hall, Swansea SA1 4PH

Torfaen (UA) Pontypool NP4 6YB

Vale of Glamorgan (UA) Dock Offices, Barry Docks, Barry CF63 4RT

Wrexham (UA) Wrexham LL11 1WF

Ynys Mon (UA) Swyddfa'r Sir, Llangefni, Ynys Mon LL77 7TW

Do you know your rights when you're out walking in the countryside?
See pages 32–39

Also worth a mention here are their Long Distance Path route guides, which cover the West Highland Way, St Cuthbert's Way, South Downs Way, The Ridgeway, Cumbria Way, Speyside Way and Cotswold Way. These excellent waterproof guides include the full route on one sheet, including accommodation, camping, food, banks, tourist information, directions to the start, Ranger Service contact numbers, enlargements of towns/villages and other facilities available – everything a walker might need on one map. For those without internet access the contact details are: Harveys Maps, 12-16 Main St, Doune, FK16 6BJ, ☎ 01786 841098

THE RA AND ORDNANCE SURVEY

The Ramblers' Association works very closely with Ordnance Survey to ensure that walkers' needs are taken care of in the maps produced. Most recently, the Ordnance Survey has announced it will be showing previously unpublished public rights of way (white roads) as well as National Trust and Forest Enterprise Access land on all 1:50,000 and 1:25,000 maps. The RA has played a big part in this development.

At the time of going to press the Ordnance Survey continues to adapt itself to technological developments, and there are many interesting products and services now available on their website, which can be found at www.ordsvy.gov.uk.

THE MAPS IN THIS YEARBOOK

These were created using the PAF (Postal Address File) database. The grid reference of the first entry in any place is taken as the grid reference for that place for the creation of the maps. This grid reference is derived from the PAF which calculates grid references from postcodes. For these reasons the places as seen on our maps are not always precise, but are intended to be a useful guide to the geographical distribution of accommodation listed.

LEARNING ABOUT MAPS

Some organisations which run courses on navigation skills are listed in the Ramblers' Association Fact Sheet No 2 *Maps and Navigation*, available from RA central office free of charge.

During 2001 the RA will be running three training days for those wishing to organise courses in walk planning, leading and navigation in their areas: 28th April in Somerset, 26th May in Derbyshire and 2nd June in Hertfordshire. Contact Salli Carson at central office for further details.

THE RA MAP LIBRARY

The library at RA national office stocks the Landranger 1:50,000 maps, the Outdoor Leisure 1:25,000 maps, and Explorer maps as they become available. All these are available on loan to RA members only for a small fee plus the cost of post and packing (Pathfinder 1:25,000 maps are NOT stocked.) No more than 10 maps may be borrowed at any one time.

To order maps, telephone or write at least five days in advance to the Map Library Service at central office stating the number(s) of the map(s) required, the date you want them and your membership number. Please do not send any money with your order, as an invoice will be sent with the maps.

For further information call the Ordnance Survey's customer information helpline
☎ **08456 050505**

MAPS

Useful Addresses and Websites

We list a number of addresses we hope will be of use to you, together with some websites at the end of the section for all you surfing ramblers.

ACTION WITH COMMUNITIES IN RURAL ENGLAND (ACRE)
Somerford Court, Somerford Road, Cirencester, Glos GL7 1TW. ☎ (01285) 653477
www.acreciro.demon.co.uk
IDENTIFIES RURAL PROBLEMS, ENCOURAGES SELF-HELP AND ADVISES ON RURAL POLICIES.

ANGLERS' CONSERVATION ASSOCIATION
Shalford Dairy, Aldermaston, Reading, Berks RG7 4NB. ☎ 0118-971 4770
ALSO INCORPORATES THE PURE RIVERS SOCIETY.

ASSOCIATION FOR THE PROTECTION OF RURAL SCOTLAND
Gladstone's Land, 483 Lawnmarket, Edinburgh EH1 2NT. ☎ 0131-225 7012   www.aprs.org.uk
GIVES ADVICE AND INFORMATION ON MATTERS AFFECTING RURAL AREAS IN SCOTLAND. ENCOURAGES APPROPRIATE DEVELOPMENT.

BACKPACKERS CLUB
Pete Macguire, 29 Lynton Drive, High Lane, Stockport SK6 8JE.
www.catan.demon.co.uk/backpackers
A CLUB FOR LIGHT WEIGHT CAMPERS INCLUDING AN ADVISORY AND INFORMATION SERVICE ON LIGHT WEIGHT EQUIPMENT.

BACKPACKERS PRESS
Sam Dalley, 2 Rockview Cottages, Matlock Bath, DE4 3PG ☎ 01629 580427.
PUBLISHER OF A SERIES OF GUIDES FOR OUTDOOR ENTHUSIASTS AND BUDGET TRAVELLERS, INCLUDING THE EXCELLENT INDEPENDENT HOSTEL GUIDE.

THE BLACK ENVIRONMENT NETWORK
9 Llainwen Uchf, Llanberis, Gwynedd LL55 4LL.
BEN IS ESTABLISHED TO PROMOTE EQUALITY OF OPPORTUNITIES WITHIN THE ETHNIC COMMUNITIES IN THE PROTECTION, PRESERVATION AND DEVELOPMENT OF THE ENVIRONMENT.

BRITISH HORSE SOCIETY
British Equestrian Centre, Stoneleigh, Nr Kenilworth, Warks CV8 2XZ. ☎ (01926) 707700
www.bhs.org.uk
PROMOTES THE UPKEEP OF BRIDLEWAYS AND ENCOURAGES SAFETY AND TRAINING OF HORSES AND RIDERS.

BRITISH MOUNTAINEERING COUNCIL
177-179 Burton Road, Manchester M20 2BB.
☎ 0161-445 4747.   www.thebmc.org.uk
PROMOTES THE INTERESTS OF BRITISH MOUNTAINEERS IN THE UK AND OVERSEAS.

BRITISH ORIENTEERING FEDERATION
Riversdale, Dale Road North, Darley Dale, Matlock, Derbys DE4 2HX. ☎ (01629) 734042
www.cix.co.uk/bof

BRITISH TRUST FOR CONSERVATION VOLUNTEERS (BTCV)
36 St Mary's Street, Wallingford, Oxon OX10 0EU.
☎ (01491) 839766   www.btcv.org
INVOLVES VOLUNTEERS IN PRACTICAL CONSERVATION WORK TO PROTECT AND IMPROVE THE ENVIRONMENT. AFFILIATED GROUPS NATIONWIDE. RUNS NATURAL BREAK WORKING HOLIDAYS.

BRITISH UPLAND FOOTPATH TRUST
PO Box 96, Manchester M20 2FU.
☎ 0161-445 4747.
http://freespace.virgin.net/andy.carling/buft
AIMS TO IMPROVE THE QUALITY AND STANDARD OF FOOTPATH WORKS AND DEAL WITH EROSION PROBLEMS.

BRITISH WATERWAYS
Willow Grange, Church Road, Watford WD1 3QA.
☎ (01923) 226422.   www.british-waterways.org
RESPONSIBLE FOR THE MAINTENANCE & SAFETY OF 2,000 MILES OF CANALS AND RIVERS.

BYWAYS & BRIDLEWAYS TRUST
PO Box 117, Newcastle-upon-Tyne NE3 5YT.
☎/Fax 0191-236 4086
AIMS TO PROTECT AND DEVELOP BYWAYS, BRIDLEWAYS AND PUBLIC RIGHTS OF WAY IN GENERAL BY PUBLISHING INFORMATION AND HOLDING TRAINING COURSES.

CAMPAIGN FOR THE PROTECTION OF RURAL WALES (Ymgyrch Diogelu Cymru Wledig)
Ty Gwyn, 31 High Street, Welshpool, Powys SY21 7YD. ☎ (01938) 552525/556212
www.cprw.org.uk
13 BRANCHES IN WALES. SIMILAR AIMS TO THOSE OF CPRE.

CAMPING & CARAVANNING CLUB LTD
Greenfields House, Westwood Way, Coventry CV4 8JH. ☎ (01203) 694995
www.campingandcaravanningclub.co.uk/core.htm

CIVIC TRUST
17 Carlton House Terrace, London, SW1Y 5AW.
☎ 020 7930 0914   www.civictrust.org.uk
AIMS TO STIMULATE INTEREST IN, AND ACTION FOR, THE IMPROVEMENT OF THE ENVIRONMENT THROUGHOUT THE UK.

CIVIC TRUST FOR WALES
(Treftadaeth Cymru)
4th Floor, Empire House, Mount Stuart Square, Cardiff CF1 6DN. ☎ (01222) 484606
www.civictrustwales.demon.co.uk

COMMON GROUND
Seven Dials Warehouse, 44 Earlham Street, London WC2H 9LA. ☎ 020 7379 3109
www.commonground.org.uk
PROMOTES CONSERVATION BY ENCOURAGING LOCAL ACTION. MAKES PRACTICAL LINKS WITH ALL BRANCHES OF THE ARTS.

CONSERVATION FOUNDATION
1 Kensington Gore, London SW7 2AR.
☎ 020 7591 3111.
www.conservationfoundation.co.uk
ORGANISATION DISSEMINATING NEWS ABOUT ENVIRONMENTAL
AND CONSERVATION MATTERS.

COUNCIL FOR NATIONAL PARKS (CNP)
246 Lavender Hill, London SW11 1LJ.
☎ 020 7924 4077
www.councilfornationalparks.freeserve.co.uk
WORKS TO PROTECT BRITAIN'S NATIONAL PARKS AND PROVIDES A
FORUM FOR DISCUSSION AMONG INTERESTED ORGANISATIONS.

COUNCIL FOR THE PROTECTION OF RURAL ENGLAND (CPRE)
Warwick House, 25 Buckingham Palace Road,
London SW1W 0PP. ☎ 020 7976 6433
www.greenchannel.com/cpre
CONCERNED WITH THE PROTECTION OF THE COUNTRYSIDE.
CAMPAIGNS FOR THE CAUSE OF CONSERVATION.

COUNTRYGOER PROJECT
15 Station Road, Knowle, Solihull, West Midlands
B93 0HL. ☎ (01564) 778323.
PROMOTES THE USE OF PUBLIC TRANSPORT TO GAIN ACCESS TO
THE COUNTRYSIDE AND PUBLISHES INFORMATION ABOUT
SERVICES AND ROUTES.

COUNTRY LANDOWNERS' ASSOCIATION (CLA)
16 Belgrave Square, London SW1X 8PQ.
☎ 020 7235 0511   www.cla.org.uk
PROMOTES AND PROTECTS THE INTERESTS OF RURAL AND AGRI-
CULTURAL LANDOWNERS.

COUNTRYSIDE AGENCY
John Dower House, Crescent Place, Cheltenham,
Glos GL50 3RA. ☎ (01242) 521381
www.countryside.gov.uk
OFFICIAL GOVERNMENT BODY. ADVISES AND SUPPORTS CONSER-
VATION AND COUNTRYSIDE RECREATION POLICY AND PRACTICE.

COUNTRYSIDE AGENCY PUBLICATIONS
PO Box 125, Wetherby, West Yorkshire LS23 7EP.
☎ 0870 120 6466

COUNTRYSIDE COUNCIL FOR WALES
(Cyngor Cefn Gwlad Cymru)
Plas Penrhos, Penrhos Road, Bangor, Gwynedd LL57
2LQ. ☎ (01248) 370444   www.ccw.gov.uk
STATUTORY BODY RESPONSIBLE FOR THE PROTECTION OF NATURE
AND THE COUNTRYSIDE IN WALES.

COUNTRYWIDE HOLIDAYS
Miry Lane, Wigan, Lancs WN3 4AG.
☎ 0161-446 2226.   http://countrywide-walking.org
ORGANISES WALKING HOLIDAYS FROM 8 CENTRES IN BRITAIN.

CYCLISTS' TOURING CLUB
Cotterell House, 69 Meadrow, Godalming, Surrey
GU7 3HS. ☎ (01483) 417217   www.ctc.org.uk
REPRESENTS CYCLISTS IN MATTERS AFFECTING USE OF ROADS,
ACCESS TO THE COUNTRYSIDE. CLUB ACTIVITIES.

DARTMOOR PRESERVATION SOCIETY
Old Duchy Hotel, Princetown, Yelverton PL20 6QF
☎ 01822 890646
office@dartmoor-preservation-assoc.org.uk
www.dartmoor-preservation-assoc.org.uk

DEPARTMENT OF THE ENVIRONMENT, TRANSPORT & THE REGIONS
Eland House, Bressenden Place, London SW1E 5DU.
☎ 020 7890 3000   www.detr.gov.uk

DISABLED RAMBLERS
Dr M Bruton, 14 Belmont Park Road, Maidenhead
SL6 6HT. ☎ 01628 621414
AIMS TO IMPROVE ACCESS FOR DISABLED PEOPLE

ECOLOGY BUILDING SOCIETY
18 Station Road, Cross Hills, near Keighley, W Yorks
BD20 7EH ☎ (01535) 635933
www.inaise.org/INAISE/Members/Profiles/ecology
SPECIALISES IN MAKING ADVANCES FOR PROPERTIES USING MOST
ECOLOGICALLY EFFICIENT USE OF LAND.

ENGLISH HERITAGE
23 Savile Row, London W1X 1AB.
☎ 020 7973 3000   www.english-heritage.org.uk
CARES FOR OVER 350 PROPERTIES OPEN TO THE PUBLIC;
PROMOTES THE CONSERVATION OF ENGLAND'S HISTORIC BUILT
HERITAGE.

ENGLISH NATURE
Northminster House, Northminster Road,
Peterborough PE1 1UA. ☎ (01733) 455000
www.english-nature.org.uk
STATUTORY BODY RESPONSIBLE FOR ADVISING GOVERNMENT AND
OTHERS ON NATURE CONSERVATION IN ENGLAND.

ENGLISH TOURIST COUNCIL
Thames Tower, Blacks Road, Hammersmith, London
W6 9EL. ☎ 020 8846
9000.   www.travelengland.co.uk

ENVIRONMENT AGENCY
Rio House, Waterside Drive, Aztec West,
Almondsbury, Bristol BS12 4UD. ☎ (01454) 624400.
www.environment-agency.gov.uk
 General enquiries ☎ (0645) 333111
GOVERNMENT AGENCY SET UP TO PROTECT AND ENHANCE THE
ENVIRONMENT.

THE ENVIRONMENT COUNCIL
212 High Holborn, London WC1V 7VW
☎ 020 7836 2626   www.greenchannel.com/tec

ENVIRONMENT WALES
4th Floor, Empire House, Mount Stuart Square,
Cardiff CF1 6DN. ☎ (01222) 471121
www.environmental-agency.wales.gov.uk

EUROPEAN PARLIAMENT UK OFFICE
2 Queen Anne's Gate, London SW1H 9AA
☎ 020 7227 4300

EUROPEAN RAMBLING ASSOCIATION
Europäische Wandervereinigung e.V., Wilhelmshöher Allee 157-159, D-34121 Kassel, Germany
www.gorp.com/gorp/activity/europe/ERA
AIMS TO FURTHER WALKING AND CLIMBING, CARE FOR AND PROTECT THE COUNTRYSIDE, AND CREATE EUROPEAN LONG DISTANCE PATHS. SEE ALSO EUROPE SECTION OF THIS YEARBOOK.

FARM HOLIDAY BUREAU
National Agricultural Centre, Stoneleigh Park, Warks CV8 2LZ. ☎ (01203) 696909
www.farm-holiday.co.uk
NETWORK OF FARMING FAMILIES OFFERING COUNTRY HOLIDAYS.

FARMING & WILDLIFE ADVISORY GROUP
National Agricultural Centre, Stoneleigh, Kenilworth, Warks CV8 2RX. ☎ (01203) 696699
CONCERNED WITH COUNTRYSIDE AND CONSERVATION OF WILDLIFE IN THE CONTEXT OF PRACTICAL FARMING.

FIELDFARE TRUST
67a The Wicker, Sheffield S3 8HT.
☎ 0114-270 1668   www.fieldfare.org.uk
SUPPORTS INITIATIVES WHICH ENABLE PEOPLE WITH SPECIAL NEEDS TO ENJOY THE COUNTRYSIDE

FIELD STUDIES COUNCIL
Preston Montford, Montford Bridge, Shrewsbury, Shrops SY4 1HW. ☎ (01743) 850674
www.field-studies-council.org
ENCOURAGES FIELD WORK AND RESEARCH THROUGH ITS FIELD CENTRES. RUNS COURSES.

FORESTRY COMMISSION
231 Corstorphine Road, Edinburgh EH12 7AT.
☎ 0131-334 0303   www.forestry.gov.uk
GOVERNMENT DEPARTMENT. RESPONSIBLE FOR ESTABLISHING AND MANAGING FORESTS IN GB FOR A VARIETY OF USES.

FRIENDS OF THE EARTH (FOE)
26/28 Underwood Street, London N1 7JQ.
☎ 020 7490 1555   www.foe.co.uk
and:

FRIENDS OF THE EARTH (SCOTLAND)
Bonnington Mill, 72 Newhaven Road, Edinburgh EH6. 5QG ☎ 0131-554 9977   www.foe-scotland.org.uk
ENVIRONMENTAL CAMPAIGNING ORGANISATION.

FRIENDS OF THE LAKE DISTRICT
The Secretary, No 3, Yard 77, Highgate, Kendal, Cumbria LA9 4ED. ☎ (01539) 720788
www.uk-charities.org/lake
WORKS TO PROTECT AND ENHANCE THE COUNTRYSIDE OF THE LAKE DISTRICT. REPRESENTS THE CPRE WITHIN CUMBRIA.

GAY OUTDOOR CLUB (G.O.C.)
c/o Jonathan at GOC, PO Box 16124, Glasgow G12 9YT. ☎ 0141-334 0812   www.bi.org/goc
MIXED CLUB ORGANISES WALKS, CYCLING, SWIMMING, MOUNTAINEERING, OVERSEAS HOLIDAYS ON A REGIONAL GROUP BASIS.

GLENMORE LODGE
Aviemore, Inverness-shire PH22 1QU.
☎ (01479) 861276
www.glenmorelodge.org.uk/enter
SCOTTISH NATIONAL SPORTS CENTRE. ORGANISES COURSES ON MOUNTAIN ACTIVITIES, CLIMBING, AND WINTER SKILLS.

GREENPEACE LIMITED
Greenpeace House, Canonbury Villas, London N1 2PN. ☎ 020 7865 8100   www.greenpeace.org
PROMOTES PEACEFUL BUT UNCOMPROMISING ACTION IN DEFENCE OF THE ENVIRONMENT.

HEALTH AND SAFETY EXECUTIVE
Public Information Line ☎ 0114-289 2345 (Fax 2333)   www.open.gov.uk/hse/hsehome

HF HOLIDAYS LTD
Imperial House, Edgware Road, London NW9 5AL. ☎ 020 8905 9556   www.hfholidays.co.uk
ORGANISES WALKING HOLIDAYS IN BRITAIN FROM 19 CENTRES

INLAND WATERWAYS ASSOCIATION
P.O. Box 114, Rickmansworth, Herts. WD3 1ZY ☎ 01923 711114   www.waterway.demon.co.uk
PROMOTES RESTORATION AND DEVELOPMENT OF INLAND WATERWAYS FOR TRADE AND RECREATION.

INSTITUTE OF PUBLIC RIGHTS OF WAY OFFICERS
PO Box 78, Skipton BD23 4UP.
☎ 07000 782318

THE LAND IS OURS
Box E, 111 Magdalen Road, Oxford OX4 1RQ.
☎ (01865) 722016   www.oneworld.org/tlio
A LANDRIGHTS CAMPAIGN FOR BRITAIN

JOHN MUIR TRUST
13 Wellington Place, Leith, Edinburgh EH6 7JD.
www.jmt.org
PROMOTES THE CARE OF WILD PLACES THROUGH RAISING FUNDS TO PURCHASE THREATENED AREAS.

LONDON GREEN BELT COUNCIL
13 Oakleigh Park Avenue, Chislehurst, Kent BR7 5PB ☎ 020 8467 5346
www.homepages.tesco.net/bobcatuk/LGBC
VOLUNTARY BODY MADE UP OF NATIONAL, REGIONAL AND LOCAL ORGANISATIONS CONCERNED WITH THE PROTECTION OF LONDON'S GREEN BELT.

LONDON WALKING FORUM
3rd Floor, 31-33 Bondway, London SW8 1SJ.
info@londonwalking.com   www.londonwalking.com
☎ 020 7993 1116 or 020 7582 4071.
LINKING UP LONDON'S OPEN SPACES INTO A WALKS NETWORK.

LONG DISTANCE WALKERS ASSOCIATION
Tom Sinclair, Bank House, High Street, Wrotham, Sevenoaks TN15 7AE. ☎ (01732) 883705
www.ldwa.org.uk
AIMS TO FURTHER THE INTERESTS OF THOSE WHO ENJOY LONG DISTANCE WALKING.

MARINE CONSERVATION SOCIETY
9 Gloucester Road, Ross-on-Wye, HR9 5BU.
☎ (01989) 566017.   www.mcsuk.mcmail.com
AIMS TO PROTECT THE BEACHES AND SEAS AROUND OUR COASTS.

MILITARY RANGES

THESE NUMBERS CAN BE USED FOR OBTAINING INFORMATION ON TIMES AND DATES WHEN FIRING WILL BE TAKING PLACE.

Castle Martin, Dyfed	☎ (01874) 636361 x3417
Dartmoor	☎ (01837) 52939
Lulworth, Dorset	☎ (01929) 462721 x4819
Otterburn, Northumberland	☎ 0191-239 4201
Salisbury Plain, Wiltshire	☎ (01980) 674695

MOUNTAINEERING COUNCIL OF SCOTLAND

The Old Granary, West Mill Street, Perth PH1 5QP
☎ (01738) 638227   www.themcofs.org.uk
AIMS TO PROMOTE MOUNTAINEERING IN SCOTLAND. GOVERNING BODY FOR THE SPORT IN SCOTLAND.

NATIONAL FARMERS' UNION

164 Shaftesbury Avenue, London WC2H 8HL.
☎ 020 7331 7200   www.nfu.org.uk
REPRESENTS THE INTERESTS OF FARMERS AND GROWERS.

NATIONAL FARMERS' UNION SCOTLAND

The Rural Centre, West Mains, Inglestone, Newbridge, Mid-Lothian EH28 8LT. ☎ 0131-472 4000

NATIONAL FARMERS' UNION WALES

24 Tawe Business Village, Phoenix Way, Swansea Enterprise Park, Swansea SA7 9LB.
☎ (01792) 774848

NATIONAL PARKS

THE MAIN OFFICES OF THE NATIONAL PARKS ARE LISTED BELOW. IN MOST INSTANCES THERE WILL BE AN INFORMATION OFFICER WHO CAN ANSWER QUESTIONS OR SEND LEAFLETS. ALL THE NATIONAL PARKS RUN INFORMATION CENTRES WHERE YOU CAN OBTAIN BOOKS, MAPS, WALKS INFORMATION ETC. SOME OF THESE ARE ONLY OPEN IN SUMMER.

National Park Offices:
Brecon Beacons National Park Office, 7 Glamorgan Street, Brecon, Powys LD3 7DP. ☎ (01874) 624437
The Broads Authority Thomas Harvey House, 18 Colegate, Norwich NR3 1BQ. ☎ (01603) 610734
Dartmoor National Park Authority, Parke, Haytor Road, Bovey Tracey, Newton Abbot, Devon TQ13 9JQ. ☎ (01626) 832093
Exmoor Exmoor House, Dulverton, Somerset TA22 9HL. ☎ (01398) 323665
Lake District National Park Office, Murley Moss, Oxenholme Road, Kendal, Cumbria LA9 7RL.
☎ (01539) 724555
Northumberland National Park, Eastburn, South Park, Hexham, Northumberland NE46 1BS.
☎ (01434) 605555
North York Moors National Park Office, The Old Vicarage, Bondgate, Helmsley, N Yorks YO6 5BP.
☎ (01439) 770657
Peak District National Park Office, Baslow Road, Bakewell, Derbyshire DE45 1AE. ☎ (01629) 816200
Pembrokeshire Coast National Park, County Offices, Winch Lane, Haverfordwest, Pembrokeshire, SA61 1PY. ☎ (01437) 764636

Snowdonia National Park Office, Penrhyndeudraeth, Gwynedd LL48 6LS. ☎ (01766) 770274/770701
Yorkshire Dales National Park, Hebden Road, Grassington, Skipton, N Yorks BD23 5LB.
☎ (01756) 752748

NATIONAL TRUST

36 Queen Anne's Gate, London SW1H 9AS.
☎ 020 7222 9251   www.nationaltrust.org.uk
PROTECTS, THROUGH OWNERSHIP, COUNTRYSIDE, COASTLAND AND MANY HISTORIC BUILDINGS IN ENGLAND.

NATIONAL TRUST (NORTHERN IRELAND)

Rowallane House, Saintfield, Co Down BT24 7LH.
☎ Saintfield 028 9751 0721
www.nationaltrust.org.uk

NATIONAL TRUST FOR SCOTLAND

5 Charlotte Square, Edinburgh EH2 4DU.
☎ 0131-226 5922   www.nts.org.uk

NORTHERN IRELAND TOURIST BOARD

St Anne's Court, 59 North Street, Belfast BT1 1NB.
☎ 028 9024 6609   www.ni-tourism.com

NORTH YORK MOORS ASSOCIATION

Peter Woods, Rosedale Intake, Denby, Whitby YO21 2LX ☎ 01287 660602

OPEN SPACES SOCIETY

25a Bell Street, Henley-on-Thames, Oxon RG9 2BA.
☎ (01491) 573535   www.oss.org.uk
AIMS TO PROTECT COMMON LAND, OPEN SPACES AND FOOTPATHS.

ORDNANCE SURVEY

Romsey Road, Maybush, Southampton, Hants SO16 4GU. ☎ (01703) 792000   www.ordsvy.gov.uk
NATIONAL MAPPING AGENCY OF GREAT BRITAIN.

ORDNANCE SURVEY OF NORTHERN IRELAND

Colby House, Stranmillis Court, Belfast BT9 8BJ.
☎ Belfast. 028 9025 5755

OUTDOOR INDUSTRIES ASSOCIATION (previously COLA)

Morrit House, Station Approach, South Ruislip HA4 6SA. ☎ 020 8842 1111.
colassoc@compuserve.com   www.cola.org.uk
ORGANISE TRADE EXHIBITITIONS FOR THE OUTDOOR LEISURE INDUSTRY

OUTDOOR WRITERS GUILD

PO Box 520, Bamber Bridge, Preston PR5 8LF.
☎ (01772) 696732
ASSOCIATION OF PROFESSIONALS INVOLVED IN OUTDOOR WRITING AND PHOTOGRAPHY.

PEAK & NORTHERN FOOTPATHS SOCIETY

23 Turncroft Lane, Stockport SK1 4AB.
☎ 0161 480 3565 (Fax 0161 429 7279)
AIMS TO PRESERVE THE RIGHTS OF THE PUBLIC TO USE THE PUBLIC HIGHWAYS IN THE EIGHT NORTHERN COUNTIES.

PEDESTRIANS ASSOCIATION

3rd Floor, 313/33 Bondway, London SW8 1SJ.
☎ 020 7820 1010   www.pedestrians.org.uk

PLANTLIFE
21 Elizabeth Street, London SW1W 9RP
☎ 020 7800 0100 (Fax 020 7730 8377)
enquiries@plantlife.org.uk

PLAS-Y-BRENIN
Capel Curig, Conwy LL24 0ET.
☎ (01690) 720214   www.pyb.co.uk
NATIONAL MOUNTAIN CENTRE. ORGANISES COURSES ON
MOUNTAIN WALKING AND LEADERSHIP, NAVIGATION & CLIMBING

RAIL USERS CONSULTATIVE COMMITTEE
Crescent House, 46 Priest Gate, Peterborough PE1
1LF. ☎ (01733) 312188
www.rail-reg.gov.uk/rucc/index
STATUTORY CONSUMER COMMITTEES COVERING THE VARIOUS
REGIONS OF BRITAIN. THEY MONITOR THE QUALITY OF RAIL
SERVICES AND PURSUE RAIL USERS' UNRESOLVED COMPLAINTS.

RAILWAY DEVELOPMENT SOCIETY
2 Clematis Cottages, Hopton Bank, Cleobury
Mortimer, Kidderminster DY14 0HF.
☎ (01584) 890807
www.rail-reg.gov.uk/docs/48/4rds
VOLUNTARY NATIONAL PRESSURE GROUP FOR THE RETENTION
AND MODERNISATION OF RAILWAY SERVICES.

RAILWAY RAMBLERS
12 Harefield Gardens, Middleton-on-Sea, Bognor
Regis PO22 6EQ. ☎ (01243) 582242
www.jeffvinter.freeserve.co.uk/railramb
PROMOTES THE PRESERVATION OF DISUSED RAILWAY LINES FOR
WALKING AND CYCLING.

RAMBLERS' ASSOCIATION SCOTLAND
Kingfisher House, Auld Mart Business Park,
Milnathorpe, Kinross KY13 9DA. ☎ (01577) 861222
www.ramblers.org.uk/scotland

RAMBLERS' ASSOCIATION WALES
Ty'r Cerddwyr, High Street, Gresford,
Wrexham LL12 8PT. ☎ (01978) 855148
www.ramblers.org.uk/wa

RAMBLERS HOLIDAYS LTD
Box 43, Welwyn Garden City, Herts AL8 6PQ.
☎ (01707) 331133   www.ramblers.org.uk/holiday
GUIDED WALKING, SKIING AND SIGHTSEEING HOLIDAYS ABROAD.
GUIDED WALKING HOLIDAYS IN THE LAKE DISTRICT.

RED ROPE
Malcolm Doune, 70 Weston Road, Olney, Bucks
MK46 5BBQ   ☎ 01234 711175
www.gn.ape.org/redrope
OUTDOOR ASSOCIATION FOR SOCIALISTS

ROYAL SOCIETY FOR THE PROTECTION OF BIRDS (RSPB)
The Lodge, Sandy, Beds SG19 2DL.
☎ (01767) 680551   www.rspb.org.uk

ROYAL WELSH AGRICULTURAL SOCIETY
Llanelewedd, Builth Wells LD2 3SY.
☎ (01982) 553683   www.rwas.co.uk

SCOTTISH COUNTRYSIDE ACTIVITIES COUNCIL
c/o Hon. Sec. Mr Harold Wilkinson, 23 Lochardil
Place, Inverness IV2 4LN. ☎ (01463) 235720.
AN UMBRELLA GROUP OF ORGANISATIONS WITH INTERESTS IN
COUNTRYSIDE RECREATION IN SCOTLAND.

SCOTTISH FIELD STUDIES ASSOCIATION
Kindrogan Field Centre, Enochdhu, Blairgowrie,
Perthshire PH10 7PG. ☎ (01250) 881286
RUNS RESIDENTIAL COURSES ON ALL ASPECTS OF NATURAL
HISTORY AND THE COUNTRYSIDE, INCLUDING WALKING.

SCOTTISH NATURAL HERITAGE
12 Hope Terrace Edinburgh EH9 2AS.
☎ 0131-447 4784.   www.snh.org.uk
BODY FORMED BY THE MERGER OF THE COUNTRYSIDE
COMMISSION FOR SCOTLAND AND THE NATURE CONSERVANCY
COUNCIL FOR SCOTLAND.

SCOTTISH OFFICE
Old St Andrew's House, Regent Road, Edinburgh
EH1 3DG. ☎ 0131-556 8400   www.scotland.gov.uk
THE PRINCIPAL GOVERNMENT DEPARTMENTS THAT DEAL WITH
COUNTRYSIDE AND ACCESS MATTERS.

SCOTTISH RIGHTS OF WAY SOCIETY
24 Annandale Street, Edinburgh EH7 4AN.
☎ 0131 558 1222   www.scotways.demon.co.uk
PRESERVES, DEFENDS AND SEEKS TO ESTABLISH PUBLIC RIGHTS
OF WAY IN SCOTLAND.

SCOTTISH SPORTS COUNCIL
Caledonia House, South Gyle
Edinburgh EH12 9DQ. ☎ 0131-317 7200
www.scotsport.co.uk

SCOTTISH TOURIST BOARD
23 Ravelston Terrace, Edinburgh EH4 3EU.
☎ 0131-332 2433   www.holiday.scotland.net

SCOTTISH WILDLIFE TRUST
Cramond House, Kirk Cramond, Cramond Glebe
Road, Edinburgh EH4 6NS ☎ 0131-312 7765
www.wildlifetrust.org.uk/scottish
VOLUNTARY ORGANISATION FOR THE CONSERVATION OF ALL
FORMS OF WILDLIFE AND THEIR HABITATS IN SCOTLAND.

SCOTTISH YOUTH HOSTELS ASSOCIATION
7 Glebe Crescent, Stirling FK8 2JA.
☎ (01786) 451181   www.syha.org.uk

SHELL BETTER BRITAIN CAMPAIGN
Victoria Works, 21a Graham Street, Hockley,
Birmingham B1 3JR. ☎ 0121-212 9221.
www.shell-betterbritain.org/welcome
HELPS VOLUNTARY GROUPS UNDERTAKING COMMUNITY ENVI-
RONMENTAL PROJECTS.

SOCIETY OF SUSSEX DOWNSMEN
10 The Drive, Hove, East Sussex BN3 3JA.
☎ (01273) 771906
AIMS TO PRESERVE AND PROTECT THE SOUTH DOWNS.

SNOWDONIA SOCIETY
Tŷ Hyll, Capel Curig, Betws-y-Coed,
Gwynedd LL24 0DS. ☎ 01690 720247
PRESERVATION AND PROTECTION OF SNOWDONIA.

USEFUL ADDRESSES & WEBSITES

SUSTRANS
35 King Street, Bristol BS1 4DZ
☎ 0117 929 0888   www.sustrans.org.uk
SUSTainable TRANSport – DESIGNING AND BUILDING A NATIONWIDE
NETWORK OF ROUTES FOR CYCLISTS AND WALKERS

ENGLISH SPORTS COUNCIL
16 Upper Woburn Place, London WC1H 0QP.
☎ 020 7273 1500   www.english.sports.gov.uk
AIMS TO FOSTER THE PRACTICE OF SPORT AND RECREATION
AMONG THE PUBLIC AT LARGE.

WELSH INSTITUTE OF SPORTS
National Sports Centre for Wales, Sophia Gardens,
Cardiff CF1 9SW. ☎ (01222) 300500
www.tigerbay.com/newcity/SportsCentre

TOWN & COUNTRY PLANNING ASSOCIATION
17 Carlton House Terrace, London SW1Y 5AS.
☎ 020 7930 8903
AIMS TO IMPROVE THE ENVIRONMENT THROUGH EFFECTIVE PLAN-
NING, PUBLIC PARTICIPATION AND SUSTAINABLE DEVELOPMENT.

TRANSPORT 2000
Walkden House, 10 Melton Street, London NW1 2EJ.
☎ 020 7388 8386   www.transport2000
CAMPAIGNS FOR TRANSPORT POLICIES THAT WILL NOT HARM THE
ENVIRONMENT AND WILL MOST BENEFIT THE PUBLIC.

ULSTER FEDERATION OF RAMBLING CLUBS
Paddy McAteer, 12B Breda House, Drumart Drive,
Belfast BT8 7EU. ☎ 028 9064 8041
AIMS TO PROTECT AND PROMOTE THE COUNTRYSIDE AND
WALKING.

WALES TOURIST BOARD (Bwrdd Croeso Cymru)
Brunel House, 2 Fitzalan Road, Cardiff CF2 1UY.
☎ (01222) 499909   www.tourism.wales.gov.uk

WALES COUNCIL FOR VOLUNTARY ACTION (WCVA)
(Cyngor Gweithredu Gwirfoddol Cymru)
North Wales Office, Tyldesley House, Clarence Road,
Craig y Don, Llandudno LL30 1DT.
☎ (01492) 862100   www.wcva.org.uk

WELSH LOCAL GOVERNMENT ASSOCIATION
10/11 Raleigh Walk, Atlantic Wharf, Cardiff CF1 5LN.
☎ (01222) 468600

WELSH OFFICE
Gwydyr House, Whitehall, London SW1A 2ER.
☎ 020 7270 3000.   www.welsh-ofce.gov.uk

WILDLIFE & COUNTRYSIDE LINK
1st Floor, Camelford House, 87-90 Albert
Embankment, London SE1 7TP ☎ 020 7820 8600
enquiry@wcl.org.uk   www.wcl.org.uk

THE WILDLIFE TRUSTS
The Kiln, Waterside, Mater Road, Newark NG24 1WT.
☎ 01636 677711 (Fax 670001)
info@wildlife-trusts.cix.co.uk
www.wildlifetrust.org.uk
DEALS WITH ALL ASPECTS OF WILDLIFE PROTECTION. NATIONAL
ORGANISATION OF THE 47 WILDLIFE TRUSTS AND WATCH, THE
JUNIOR CLUB FOR YOUNG ENVIRONMENTALISTS.

THE WOODCRAFT FOLK
13 Ritherdon Road, London SW17 8QE.
☎ 020 8672 6031   www.poptel.org.uk/woodcraft

WOODLAND TRUST
Autumn Park, Dysart Road, Grantham, Lincs NG31
6LL. ☎ (01476) 581111.
www.woodland-trust.org.uk
AQUIRES WOODS THROUGHOUT BRITAIN TO SAFEGUARD THEIR
AMENITY, WILDLIFE AND LANDSCAPE VALUE.

WWF - WORLD WIDE FUND FOR NATURE (UK)
Panda House, Weyside Park, Godalming, Surrey GU7
1XR. ☎ (01483) 426444
www.panda.org/home.cfm
MAJOR ENVIRONMENTAL CAMPAIGNING AND FUND-RAISING BODY:
PART OF A WORLD-WIDE NETWORK.

YORKSHIRE DALES SOCIETY
Otley Civic Centre, Cross Green, Otley, W Yorks
LS21 1HD. ☎ (01943) 607868/461938)
www.users.globalnet.co.uk/Salaam/
AIMS TO ADVANCE PUBLIC KNOWLEDGE AND TO PRESERVE THE
LANDSCAPE AND NATURAL BEAUTY OF THE DALES.

YOUTH HOSTELS ASSOCIATION
Trevelyan House, 8 St Stephen's Hill, St Albans, Herts
AL1 2DY. ☎ (01727) 855215   www.yha.org.uk
AIMS TO HELP ALL PEOPLE OF LIMITED MEANS TO A GREATER
KNOWLEDGE, LOVE AND CARE OF THE COUNTRYSIDE, BY PROVID-
ING YOUTH HOSTEL AND CAMPING BARN ACCOMMODATION, AND A
WIDE RANGE OF OUTDOOR RECREATION, LEISURE AND ENVIRON-
MENTAL EDUCATION PROGRAMMES.

YOUTH HOSTELS ASSOCIATION OF NORTHERN IRELAND
22 Donegall Road, Belfast BT12 5JN.
☎ 028 9032 4733   www.irelandyha.org

**Do you know your rights when you're out walking in the countryside?
See pages 32-39**

Ramblers' Area and Group Publications

The following list of books and pamphlets are researched, written and published by Ramblers areas and groups. All publications listed here are currently available at the prices stated. Some of these have become the definitive guide to a certain long-distance path founded by the area or group, others are books of short walks in a particular locality.

If you're planning a walking break it is well worth ordering books from the addresses shown. Many of these publications are only available in local shops which means it's often hard to buy your holiday walking guide beforehand.

For a list of publications available from central office please call, asking for the sales list, or look at the publications page on our website, www.ramblers.org.uk.

AVON

Severnside Group
Walk West. £6.99, plus 80p p&p .
Order from: Severnside Ramblers, 12 Gadshill Drive, Stoke Gifford, Bristol BS34 8UX.

BEDFORDSHIRE

Leighton Buzzard Group
Leighton Buzzard Millenium Walks. 50p p&p.
Order from: John Duxbury, Group Secretary, 8 Carlton Grove, Leighton Buzzard, LU7 8BJ.

BERKSHIRE

East Berkshire Group
Footpath maps:
Parish of Bray. 30p.
Cookham & District. 50p
Hurley & District. 50p
Twyford & District. 50p
Wargrave & District. 30p.

Windsor & The Great Park. 50p.
Walk Guides: Rambling for Pleasure series:
Along the Thames. £2.95.
Around Reading – 1st series. £2.95.
Around Reading – 2nd series. £2.95 (New Issue)
Kennet Valley & Watership Down. £2.95.
Thames Valley & The Chilterns. £2.95.
The Three Castles Path. £2.95.
In East Berkshire. £2.95 (Spring 2001). (New Walks)
Plus 50p p&p per guide, 30p per map.
Order from: East Berks RA Group, PO Box 1357, Maidenhead SL6 7FP. Cheques to 'RA East Berks'.

West Berkshire Group
21 Walks for the 21st Century. £6.00, plus £1.00 p&p
Order from: West Berkshire Ramblers, 38 Kipling Close, Thatcham RG18 3AY.
Cheques to 'West Berks Ramblers'.

BUCKINGHAMSHIRE & WEST MIDDLESEX

Best Walks in Buckinghamshire by Bus and Train. £5 plus 65p p&p
Order from: Barry Totterdell, 15 Bowlers Orchard, Chalfont St Giles HP8 4LB

West London Group
17 Walks in South Bucks. £1 plus 50p p&p
Order from: Tom Berry, 128 Park Lane, Harrow, Middlesex, HA2 8NL.

CAMBRIDGESHIRE

Cambridge Group
Walks in South Cambridgeshire
Walks in East Cambridgeshire
Walks on the South Cambridgeshire Borders
All are £4.50, including p&p, order from: Mr John Hunter, 61 Netherhall Way, Cambridge CB1 8NU

CORNWALL

Six North Cornwall Walks Book 1
Six North Cornwall Walks Book 2
Six Walks from Truro.
Rambles in the Roseland

Six Walks around Falmouth I
Six Walks around Falmouth II
Wendron's Church and Chapels Walks
Six Coastal Walks with Inland Returns in or on The Lizard.
Six Circular Coast and Country Walks on the Lizard.
Six Coastal Walks with Inland Returns in Penwith No 1.
Six Coastal Walks with Inland Returns in Penwith No 2.
All the above titles are £1.00 or £1.20 plus SAE.
Order all from: Publicity Officer: Miss M Weston, 2 Lanaton Road, Penryn TR10 8RB, ☎ 01326 372462.

DEVON

Plymouth & District Group
Roundabout Family Rambling - Western Fringe Of Dartmoor. £2 plus 50p p&p.
Order from: Jenny Adamson, 29 Armada Street, North Hill, Plymouth, Devon

DORSET
The Dorset Jubilee Trail Guide. £4.50 plus 50p p&p
Order from: Jubilee Trail Contact, 19 Shaston Crescent, Dorchester DT1 2EB.
Cheques payable to *Ramblers Association, Dorset Area*

EAST YORKSHIRE & DERWENT
Minster Way £4.00 + 50p p&p.
Chalkland Way (leaflet). Send SAE.
Order both from: Mr Ray Wallis, 75 Ancaster Avenue, Kingston upon Hull HU5 4QR. Cheques payable to 'Ray Wallis', all income to Ramblers' Association.
Wolds Way Accommodation Guide. 95p + SAE.
Order from:
Mrs S M Smith, 65 Ormonde Avenue, Beverley High Road, Kingston upon Hull HU6 7LT.

ESSEX
15 Walks in South East Essex for all the Family. £2.25 post free
17 More Walks in South East Essex. PoA
Order from: P. A. Hayes, 29 Keswick Close, Rayleigh, Essex SS6 8LG

GLOUCESTERSHIRE

Gloucestershire Area
The Cotswold Way Handbook & Accommodation List 2000. £2.00 plus 50p p&p.
The North Cotswold Diamond Way. £3.50 plus 50p p&p
The Glevum Way. 50p plus 30p p&p.
The Forest of Dean East. 40p plus 30p p&p.
Cheques payable to *RA, Gloucestershire Area.* Order from: Mail Order Secretary, Tudor Cottage, Berrow, Malvern, Worcs., WR13 6JJ. ☎ 01531 650349.

Cirencester Group
The Cirencester Circuit. £1 plus 40p p&p.
Walks Around Cirencester. 80p plus 40p p&p.
Order from: Mr W Irving, 80 Melmore Gardens, Cirencester GL7 1NS.

South Cotswold Group
More Favourite Walks in the South Cotswolds. £3.95 + 50p p&p (post free to members).
Order from: South Cotswold Ramblers, Southcot, The Headlands, North Woodchester, Stroud GL5 5PS. Tel. 01453 873625.
Yellow Arrow Route (East Dene) Walks Leaflet. 40p + 30p p&p.
Order from: Mrs S Wall, 17 Octavia Place, Roman Park. Lydney, Glos., GL15 5NX.

HAMPSHIRE

Winchester Group
12 Walks in and Around Winchester. £1.50 (50p p&p)
Order from: Mr Alan Charles, 50 Tower Street, Winchester SO23 8TA.

New Forest Group
More Walks around the New Forest. £3.50 + 44p sae.
Order from: 9 Pine Close, Dibden Purlieu, Southampton SO45 4AT.

Alton Group
Walks From Alton. £3.50
Order from; Mrs D Longley, Cross Trees, New Farm Road, Alresford SO24 9QS, tel. 01962 732330

HEREFORD & WORCESTER
Our Favourite Herefordshire Walks £4.
Order from Liz Andrews, Gawsworth, North Road, Kingsland, Leominster HR6 9RU.

Leisure Walks from Worcester Bridge. £3.95
Order from: Patrick Bradley, 9 Cherry Street, Worcester WR5 3EB

Vale Of Evesham Group

Walks in the Vale of Evesham. £2 plus A5 1st class SAE.

Order from: Diana Harwood, 12 Queens Road, Evesham WR11 4JN

HERTFORDSHIRE & NORTH MIDDLESEX

North Herts Group

Ten Walks in North Herts. £1.50 plus 50p p&p

Order from: Robin Parker, 21 Bedford Road, Hitchin, Herts SG5 2TP

ISLE OF WIGHT

12 Favourite Walks. £2 plus 30p p&p.

12 More Favourite Walks (New Issue). Price as above

12 Walks from Towns. £2 plus 30p p&p.

Order from Mrs J. Deacon, Dibs, Main Road, Rookley, Ventnor PO38 3NQ.

Vectis Trail. £1.75 plus 30p p&p.

Order from Mrs B. Aze, Shalimar, Upper Hyde Farm Lane, Shanklin PO37 7PS.

LAKE DISTRICT

Carlisle & North Cumbria Group

Walks Around Carlisle & North Cumbria. £3.25 post free to members

Order from:
Jo Leighton, 24 Currock Mount, Carlisle CA2 4RF

Furness Group

Park Your Car and Take a Walk, £1.50 post free

Inns and Outs in South Lakeland, £1.20 post free

Order from: Walter Scott, 55 Ainslie Street, Barrow-in-Furness LA14 5AY

Kendal Group

Walks in the Kendal Area, Series 3. 2nd Edition £2.95 post free

Order from: Mr & Mrs Adams, 6 Riverbank Road, Kendal LA9 5JS

Lancaster Group

Walks from the Limestone Link. £2.95 plus 33p p&p

Walks in North-West Lancashire. £2.95 plus 33p p&p

Order from: Mrs Jean Gilligan, 22 Endsleigh Grove, Lancaster LA1 2TX.

Penrith Group

Walks in the Penrith Area Book 1.
£1.50 plus 25p p&p.

Walks in the Penrith Area Book 2.
£1.75 plus 25p p&p.

Order from:
R Burgin, St Andrews Place, Penrith CA71 7AR

KENT

Maidstone Circular Walk, Part 1. £1.80 + 38p p&p.

Maidstone Circular Walk, Part 2. £1.80 + 38p p&p.

Order from: Tony Smith, Little Preston Lodge, Coldharbour Lane, Aylesford, Kent ME20 7NS.

MID LANCASHIRE

Preston Group

The Round Preston Walk. £1.80 post free

Ten Rambles around Preston. £2.30 post free

Order both from: Mr A Manzie, 3 Ruthin Court, Dunbar Road, Ingol, Preston PR2 3YE.

LINCOLNSHIRE

The Plogsland Round. £4.90 plus 60p p&p.

Order from Major H B Collier, Chloris House, 208 Nettleham Road, Lincoln LN2 4DH

NORFOLK

The Angles Way. £2.70 plus 30p p&p

The Iceni Way. £2.10 plus 30p p&p

Norfolk Heritage Walks. £2.10 plus 40p p&p

Peddars Way, Angles Way & Iceni Way (if ordered together). £7.50 p&p free

Order from: Sheila Smith, Caldcleugh, Cake Street, Old Buckenham, Attleborough NR17 1RU

Peddars Way & Norfolk Coast Path Guide & Accommodation List. £2.70 plus 40p p&p

Order from: John Kent, Knights Cottage, The Old School, Honing, North Walsham NR28 9TR

NORTHUMBRIA AREA

Walking the Tyne from Mouth to Source . £4 plus £1 p&p. To be published during 2001.

Order from Mrs A Key, 22 Highbury, Jesmond, Newcastle-upon-Tyne NE2 3DY.

SOMERSET

Rambling for Pleasure – Exploring the hidden countryside in and around Taunton Deane.
£1.50 plus 30p p&p

Order from: Mr M Emmett, Fairacre, West Hatch, Taunton TA3 5RJ. Cheques to *Mr F M Emmett*

Channel to Channel (Seaton – Watchet). £2 plus 50p p&p.

Order from: Mr Ken Young, 14 Wilton Orchard, Taunton TA1 3SA.

Cheques payable to *Mr Ken Young*

SOUTH YORKSHIRE & NE DERBYSHIRE

In Praise of Rambling. £3.00 + 50p p&p.

Easy Going Trails. £2.50 + 50p p&p.

Order from: Mrs Y P B Peters, 751 Gleadless Road, Sheffield S12 2QD.

Seven Walks in the Dearne Valley. £1.30 incl. p&p

Order from: P & E Gibbons, 6 Ruskin Avenue, Mexborough S64 0AU

STAFFORDSHIRE

Walking in & around the Staffordshire Way. £5.95

Order from: Mr G Loodwick, 19 Glebefields, Woodseaves, Stafford ST20 0LA

Mid Staffs Group

Our Favourite Walks. £2.95 plus 45p p&p (A5 SAE)

Order from Mr D Cashmore, 46 Grange Crescent, Penkridge, Stafford ST19 5LU

Stourbridge Group

Walks Around Stourbridge. £4.50 inc p&p

Order from Mrs J Crowe (Secretary), 29 Stennels Avenue, Halesowen B62 8QJ

Cheques payable to *Ramblers Association - Stourbridge Group.*

SUFFOLK

Waveney Group

Rural Rambles Round Lowestoft. £1.80 plus 35p p&p

Rural Rambles Round Southwold.
£1.80 plus 35p p&p

Rural Rambles Round Beccles. £1.80 plus 35p p&p

The Waveney Way. £2.10 plus 35p p&p

Order from Miss B Le Grys, Waveney Ramblers, 1 Church Close, Reddenhall IP20 9QS

Seven walks starting from Thorpeness. £1.50 plus 35p p&p

Order from J. L Hardy, 24 Meadow Gardens, Beccles, Suffolk NR34 9PA

SHROPSHIRE

Ramblers Guide to the Shropshire Way
£5.99 plus £1 p&p

Order from Powneys Bookshop, 4-5 St Alkmunds Place, Shrewsbury SY1 1UJ, tel 01743 369165

SURREY

Four Stations Way £2

Order from Kate Colley, 6 Hill Court, Haslemere GU27 2BD

Twenty-five Favourite Walks in West Surrey & Sussex. £4.75 inc p&p.

Order from: Mrs Rosemary Bryant, Kinfauns Cottage, Petworth Road, Witley, Godalming GU8 5QW.
☎ 01483 421612

SUSSEX

Sussex Diamond Way (Midhurst to Heathfield).
£3.50 post free

Order from: Rambler's Association (Sussex Area), 11 Old London Road, Brighton BN1 8XR.

Heathfield & District RA

Walks to Interesting Places (Sussex & Kent). £3.95 post free

Order from: Mrs V Treacher, Cobbetts, Burnt Oak Road, High Hurstwood TN22 4AE

WARWICKSHIRE

City of Birmingham Group

Waterside Walks in the Midlands.
£4.95 plus 75p p&p.

More Waterside Walks in the Midlands.
£5.95 plus £1 p&p.

The Birmingham Greenway. £4.95 plus £1 p&p

Order from: Meridian Books, 40 Hadzor Road, Oldbury B68 9LA.

Warwick District Walks. £2.00 post free.

Order from: Mr P Heelas, 7 Almond Grove, Warwick CV34 5TB.

WEST RIDING

The Brontë Way. £4.50 & £1 p&p
Ramblers' Bradford, Volume 1. £4.95 & £1 p&p
The Airedale Way. £4.50 & £1 p&p
Country Walks in and around Mirfield, Emley, Thornhill & Denby Dale. Published Easter 2001. Ask for price.
Ramblers' Leeds, Volume 1 East of Leeds. £4.95 & £1 p&p
Ramblers' Leeds, Vol 2 West of Leeds. £5.95 plus £1 p&p
Ramblers' Wakefield. £5.50 plus £1 p&p
KiddiWalks. £4.50 plus £1 p&p.
Order from: Douglas Cossar, West Riding Area Publications, 27 Cookridge Avenue, Leeds LS16 7NA

Ripon Group

Rambles Around Ripon. £3.60 plus 50p p&p
The Ripon Rowell Walk. £4.95 plus 50p p&p
Order from: Peter Sleightholm (Secretary), 9 Melrose Road, Bishop Monkton, Harrogate HG3 3RH.

Huddersfield Group

Walks In and Around Kirklees. £2.40 plus £1 p&p
More Walks In and Around Kirklees. £2.40 plus £1 p&p
Order from: J M Lieberg, 11 Woodroyd Avenue, Hunley, Huddersfield, W Yorks HD7 2LG.

Harrogate Group

Popular Walks Around Harrogate. £3.50 plus 50p p&p
Order from: Mr & Mrs J Taylor, 171 Otley Road, Harrogate HG2 0DA.
Harrogate Ringway. 30p plus SAE
Knaresborough Round. 30p plus SAE
Harrogate Dalesway. 30p plus SAE
Order from: Mrs J Clack, 40 Woodlands Grove, Harrogate HG2 7BG

WILTSHIRE

Mid-Wiltshire Group

Ten Walks Around Devizes. £1.50 plus 25p p&p from Mr McClennand, 1 Coppings Close, Devizes SN10 4SQ

North East Wiltshire Group

Nine Downland Walks between Swindon and Marlborough. £1.30 inc p&p
Twelve Walks around Marlborough. £1.50 inc p&p

Eleven Half-day Walks in N.E. Wiltshire. £1.80 inc p&p
20 Walks around Swindon. £2.50 inc p&p
Order all from Mrs P Crabb, Frenshams, Turnball, Chiseldon, Swindon SN4 0LJ.

South Wiltshire Group

Eight Easy Walks in the Salisbury Area.
Ten Shorter Walks in the Salisbury Area.
Ten Longer Walks in the Salisbury Area.
All the above are £2.50 post free.
The Sarum Way. £2.50 + 50p p&p.
Order all from Mrs S Brown, 32 Hill Top Way, Salisbury SP1 3QY

West Wiltshire Group

Walking in West Wiltshire - Books 2 & 3
Each book is £1.25.
Order from John Rowe, Southview, 86 High Street, Littleton Panell, Devizes SN10 4EU

Wales

DYFED

Lampeter Group

Lampeter Walks. £4.45 inc. p&p from Lampeter Bookshop, 21 Bridge Street, Lampeter SA48 7AA.

GLAMORGAN

West Glamorgan Group

Walking Around Gower. £7.50 post free.
Order from Peter Beck, 24 Hazelmere Road, Sketty, Swansea SA2 0SN

NORTH WALES

The Clwydian Way. £5.95 plus £1 p&p
Order from Dave Hollett, 69 Wethersfield Road, Prenton, Wirral CH43 9YF

POWYS

Walks You Will Enjoy (East Radnorshire). £3.50 plus 25p p&p
Order from ER Publications, 'Bala', Presteigne Road, Knighton, Powys LD7 1HY

Long Distance Paths

This year we have added the London LOOP (London Outer Orbital Path) and the Chiltern Way to this section, re-instated the Dyfi Valley Way and made the Mendip Way whole by adding the East Mendip Way.

In the B&B accommodation section you will find cross-referencing of any paths listed here (except those under the heading *Other Paths with Guidebooks Published Recently*). Any B&B place within two miles (3.2 km) of these paths has the path's name printed below it.

Map numbers refer to the Ordnance Survey 1:50 000 Landranger series unless stated. Although larger scale (Explorer) maps exist for many routes, Landrangers are often the most convenient for long-distance paths as they cover a wider area.

The 6th edition of the *Long Distance Walkers Handbook* is available at RA central office, price £11.99 plus £1.50 p&p. This gives details of many more paths than we have room for here. See also the *Long Distance Path Chart* published by Harveys and the LDWA, available from outdoor shops or from Tim Glenn, 2 Sandy Lane, Beeston, Nottingham NG9 3GS at £7.95.

Regular readers will notice that the RA is now THE retail outlet for accommodation guides for long distance paths, most of them being available from the central office.

Symbols used in this section:

♟ Path designated a National Trail.

✪ Official long distance path in Scotland.

✷ Path added to the section this year.

(M) Publication includes detailed maps.

(A) Publication includes places to stay.

ANGLES WAY

Great Yarmouth to Knettishall Heath
77 miles (123 km)

An easy meander along the Norfolk/Suffolk border, following the Waveney and Little Ouse rivers.

Maps 134, 144, 156

Publications
THE ANGLES WAY (MA)
BY NORFOLK AND SUFFOLK RA AREAS. £2.70. AVAILABLE PLUS
70P POSTAGE FROM RA CENTRAL OFFICE.
LANGTON'S GUIDE TO THE WEAVERS WAY AND ANGLES WAY (MA).
LANGTON'S GUIDES. £6.95.

CALDERDALE WAY

Circular from Clay House, Greetland
50 miles (80 km)

Follows old packhorse routes and moorland paths, circling high up around the Calder Valley in West Yorkshire, close to Halifax, Todmorden and Hebden Bridge.

Maps 103, 104, 110

Publications
THE CALDERDALE WAY (M) BY CALDERDALE WAY ASSOCIATION.
£6 INC. P&P. FROM HEBDEN BRIDGE TIC.

CAMBRIAN WAY

Cardiff to Conwy: 274 miles (440 km)

Tony Drake's spectacular but demanding coast to coast route through Wales, via the Brecon Beacons, Cader Idris and Snowdonia. For experienced hill-walkers only.

Maps 115, 124, 135, 146/147, 160, 161, 171

The Cambrian Way Walkers Association is at Llanerchindda Farm, Cynghordy, Llandovery SA20 0NB. Tel (01550) 750274.

Publications
CAMBRIAN WAY: THE MOUNTAIN CONNOISSEURS WALK (MA)
BY A. J. DRAKE - AUTHOR, PUBLISHER AND ENQUIRIES.
AVAILABLE FROM RA CENTRAL OFFICE £5.50 PLUS £1 P&P

CHESHIRE RING CANAL WALK

Circular: 97 miles (155 km)

Easy and interesting towpath walk via Greater Manchester and rural Cheshire, linking six historic canals, including the Macclesfield, Peak Forest and Trent & Mersey. A varied walk in town and country.

Maps 108, 109, 117, 118

Luggage carrier Byways Bike Breaks 0151-722 8050

Publications
WALKING THE CHESHIRE RING (M) (GUIDEBOOK STARTING AT
DUNKENFIELD)
BY JOHN MERRILL. £4.95 FROM HAPPY WALKING INTERNATIONAL

CHILTERN WAY ✳

Circular from Hemel Hempstead: 133 miles (200 km)

Meandering trail through Bedfordshire, Berkshire,
Herts and Oxfordshire taking in many beautiful parts
of the Chilterns. Connects with parts of the Thames
Path, The Ridgeway, Oxfordshire Way and Icknield
Way.

Maps 166, 176, 165, 175

Publication
THE CHILTERN WAY BY NICK MOON (M).
£8.85 INC P&P FROM THE CHILTERN SOCIETY

CLEVELAND WAY

Helmsley to Filey Brigg: 110 miles (177 km)

Horseshoe-shaped National Trail around the northern
edge of the North York Moors to Saltburn, then
coastal tracks south via Whitby and Scarborough.
The whole route is accessible by public transport.

Maps 93, 94, 99, 100, 101 (and most of route shown
on Outdoor Leisure 26 and 27)

Luggage carrier Sherpa Van, tel. 020 8569 4101

Publications
CLEVELAND WAY (NATIONAL TRAIL GUIDE) (M)
BY IAN SAMPSON. AURUM PRESS £10.99.
CLEVELAND WAY ACCOMMODATION GUIDE (A)
NORTH YORK MOORS NAT PARK (SEE USEFUL ADDRESSES) FREE.
ALSO AVAILABLE FROM RA CENTRAL OFFICE.
CLEVELAND WAY COMPANION (M)
BY PAUL HANNON. HILLSIDE PUBLICATIONS £6.50 PLUS 50P P&P.
WALKING THE CLEVELAND WAY AND THE MISSING LINK
BY MALCOLM BOYES. CICERONE PRESS £5.99 PLUS £1 P&P.
THE CLEVELAND WAY
BY JOHN MERRILL. HAPPY WALKING INTERNATIONAL £4.95

COAST TO COAST WALK

St Bees to Robin Hoods Bay: 190 miles (304 km)

Scenic if over-popular Wainwright trail across
northern England, via the Lakes, Yorkshire Dales and
North York Moors. Includes some fairly demanding
upland stretches.

Maps See Outdoor Leisure Coast to Coast strip maps
33 (St Bees to Keld) & 34 (Keld to Robin Hoods Bay)

YHA Coast to Coast Accommodation Booking Bureau:
YHA Northern Region, PO Box 11, Matlock, Derbys
DE4 2XA (large SAE), tel 01426 939215 (24 hours).

Luggage carrier Coast to Coast Baggage Service, tel
(01642) 489173 and Sherpa Van, tel. 020 8569 4101.

Publications
A COAST TO COAST WALK (M)

BY A WAINWRIGHT. MICHAEL JOSEPH £11.99. ALSO AVAILABLE
PLUS £1.50 P&P FROM RA CENTRAL OFFICE
COAST TO COAST BY RONALD TURNBULL (INCLUDES SOME INFO
ABOUT WALKING EAST TO WEST). DALESMAN PUBLISHING £4.99
COAST TO COAST WALK (M)
BY PAUL HANNON. HILLSIDE PUBLICATIONS £8.99 PLUS 50P P&P.
THE COAST TO COAST WALK ACCOMMODATION LIST (A)
£3.95 PLUS 70P P&P FROM RA CENTRAL OFFICE
FREE FACTSHEET FROM RA CENTRAL OFFICE

COTSWOLD WAY

Chipping Campden to Bath: 100 miles (161 km)

Now awarded National Trail status, the idea of a path
along the handsome Cotswold escarpment was originally suggested by RA Gloucestershire Area in the
early 1950s.

Maps 150, 151, 162, 163, 172

Luggage carrier Compass Holidays 01242 250642

Publications
THE COTSWOLD WAY (M) BY MARK RICHARDS.
£3.95 PLUS £1 P&P FROM RA CENTRAL OFFICE
THE COTSWOLD WAY HANDBOOK (A) BY GLOUCESTERSHIRE AREA
RA £2 PLUS 70P P&P FROM RA CENTRAL OFFICE
THE COTSWOLD WAY (M)
BY ANTHONY BURTON. AURUM PRESS £10.99

CUMBRIA WAY

Ulverston to Carlisle: 70 miles (112 km)

Mostly low-level route through the heart of the Lake
District National Park, via Langdale and Borrowdale,
Coniston, Derwent Water and Caldbeck with plenty of
scope for high-level detours.

Maps 85, 90, 97 (and part of route shown on
Outdoor Leisure 4, 6 and 7) and see Harvey's route
map of the Cumbria Way.

YHA Cumbria Way Booking Bureau - see YHA
Northern Region address under Coast to Coast Walk.

Luggage carrier Sherpa Van, tel. 020 8569 4101.

Publications
THE CUMBRIA WAY (MA)
BY ANTHONY BURTON. AURUM PRESS £12.99
GUIDE TO THE CUMBRIA WAY (MA) BY PHILLIP DUBOCK. MIWAY
PUBLISHING £5.95 PLUS 60P P&P (PLUS ACCOMMODATION GUIDE,
FREE WITH BOOK, £1 PLUS SAE WITHOUT)
HARVEY'S CUMBRIA WAY WATEPROOF MAP £7.95

DALES WAY

Ilkley to Bowness-on-Windemere: 81 miles (130 km)

Inspired by members of RA West Riding Area, this
fairly easy, largely riverside trail through the
Yorkshire Dales ends in the southern Lakes. Three
'extensions' lead to the Way: the Leeds-Dales Way,
the Shipley-Dales Way and the Harrogate-Dales Way.

Maps 97, 98 104 (and part of route shown on
Outdoor Leisure 2, 7, 10 and 30)

Luggage carrier Sherpa Van, tel. 020 8569 4101.

Publications
DALES WAY ROUTE GUIDE BY ARTHUR GEMMELL & COLIN
SPEAKMAN. STILE PUBLICATIONS £4 PLUS 60P P&P.
THE DALES WAY (M) BY ANTHONY BURTON. AURUM PRESS £12.99.
THE DALES WAY HANDBOOK (A) BY WEST RIDING RAMBLERS £1.50
PLUS 70P P&P FROM RA CENTRAL OFFICE.
DALES WAY (M)
BY PAUL HANNON. HILLSIDE PUBLICATIONS £5.99 PLUS 60P P&P.
THE DALES WAY (A)
BY TERRY MARSH. CICERONE PRESS £6.99 PLUS £1 P&P.

The Dales Way Association is c/o David Smith
Dalegarth, Moorfield Road, Ilkley LS29 8BL.

DYFI VALLEY WAY

Aberdyfi to Borth: 108 miles (172 km)

From the mouth to the source of the beautiful Afon
Dyfi, traditionally the frontier between North and
South Wales, then back down the other side via
Machynlleth.

Maps 124, 125, 135, 136

Publications
THE DYFI VALLEY WAY BY LAURENCE MAIN (M) BY AND FROM
LAURENCE MAIN. £7.95 POST FREE.

ESSEX WAY

Epping Station to Harwich Quay: 81 miles (130 km)

Pioneered by RA and CPRE members, the trails
leaves north-east London across quiet countryside
via Dedham Vale and Constable country to finish at
the Stour estuary. Links with the Stour Valley Path at
Manningtree.

Maps 167, 168, 169

Publications
THE ESSEX WAY (MA)
BY AND FROM ESSEX COUNTY COUNCIL. £3.

GLYNDWR'S WAY

Knighton to Welshpool: 128 miles (206 km)

Linking with Offa's Dyke at either end, this scenic
route through central Wales visits many sites associ-
ated with the 15th century hero Owain Glyndwr. A
proposed National Trail.

Maps 125, 126, 135, 136, 148

Luggage carrier Pack-horse Services 01938 590536

Publications
THE GLYNDWR'S WAY (M)
SERIES OF 16 ROUTE LEAFLETS, 25P EACH OR £4 THE SET.
GLYNDWR'S WAY GENERAL LEAFLET
GLYNDWR'S WAY ACCOMMODATION LIST (A).
ALL BY POWYS COUNTY COUNCIL AND AVAILABLE FROM
NEWTOWN TIC (10P/SAE FOR LEAFLETS).

GRAND UNION CANAL WALK

Paddington, London to Gas Street Basin, Birmingham
145 miles (234 km)

Lengthy towpath walk connecting the two city
centres, via Tring, Braunston, Warwick and much
peaceful countryside. Mostly a towpath route.

Maps 139, 151, 152, 165, 176

Publications
THE GRAND UNION CANAL WALK (M)
BY ANTHONY BURTON AND NEIL CURTIS. AURUM PRESS. £9.99.

GREENSAND WAY

Haslemere to Ham Street, near Ashford
105 miles (169 km)

Another attractive RA-inspired walking route, this
time along the undulating Greensand ridge of Surrey
and Kent, crossing Ide Hill and Toy's Hill, orchards
and hop fields. Parts of the route were devastated by
the 1987 storm. The guide published in 1998 covers
both the Kent and Surrey sections for the first time.

Maps 186, 187, 188, 189

Publications
ALONG AND AROUND THE GREENSAND WAY (MA)
BY AND FROM SURREY AND KENT COUNTY COUNCILS. £7.95.
AVAILABLE PLUS £1 P&P FROM RA CENTRAL OFFICE

HEART OF ENGLAND WAY

Cannock Chase to Bourton-on-the-Water
100 miles (161 km)

Wandering green route taking in Cannock Chase,
Lichfield, the Avon Valley and northern Cotswolds.

Maps 127, 128, 139, 140, 150, 151, 163

Publications
THE HEART OF ENGLAND WAY
BY RICHARD SALE (M). AURUM PRESS £12.99
THE HEART OF ENGLAND WAY WALKERS GUIDE (M)
BY JOHN ROBERTS. WALKWAYS £6.95 PLUS ACCOMMODATIOIN
LIST (FREE/SAE)
HEART OF ENGLAND WAY (AND ACCOMMODATION LEAFLET)
BY HEART OF ENGLAND WAY ASSOCIATION, FREE.
ALSO AVAILABLE FROM RA CENTRAL OFFICE.

The Heart of England Way Association is at 20
Throckmorton Road, Alcester B49 6QA, tel: (01789)
762840.

ICKNIELD WAY

Ivinghoe Beacon to Knettishall Heath
105 miles (169 km)

Follows course of prehistoric trackway from the
Chilterns into East Anglia, passing many sites of
archaeological interest and ending at the start of the
Peddars Way. An optional loop avoids Luton and
Dunstable.

Maps 144, 154, 155, 165, 166

Publications

THE ICKNIELD WAY PATH - A WALKERS GUIDE (M)
BY ICKNIELD WAY ASSOCIATION. £4.50
AVAILABLE PLUS £1 P&P FROM RA CENTRAL OFFICE.
ICKNIELD WAY ACCOMMODATION LIST (A)
ICKNIELD WAY ASSOCIATION £1 PLUS SAE

The Icknield Way Association is c/o Mrs.Chris James, 56 Back Street, Ashwell, Baldock SG7 5PE, tel. (01462) 742684.

ISLE OF MAN COASTAL PATH

Circular from Douglas: 75 miles (121 km)

Known in Manx as the Gulls Road, the scenically varied but often rugged path encircles the whole island close to the shore and is waymarked by a herring gull symbol. Fantastic cliff-top views.

Maps 95

Publications

ISLE OF MAN COASTAL PATH
BY AILEEN EVANS. CICERONE PRESS £7.99 PLUS £1 P&P
WALKING THE ISLE OF MAN COAST PATH
BY JOHN MERRILL. HAPPY WALKING INTERNATIONAL £4.25

ISLE OF WIGHT COASTAL PATH

Circular from Ryde: 65 miles (105 km)

Another attractive island circuit, via chines, salt-marshes, cliffs and holiday resorts. Plenty of accommodation and good public transport links.

Maps 196

Publications

THE COMPLETE ISLE OF WIGHT COASTAL FOOTPATH (M)
BY B G SMAILES. AVAILABLE FROM ISLE OF WIGHT TOURISM £3.50
PLUS 50P P&P.
THE ISLE OF WIGHT COAST PATH
BY JOHN MERRILL. HAPPY WALKING INTERNATIONAL £4.95

JURASSIC WAY

Banbury to Stamford: 88 miles (142 km)

Recently-opened route along the Jurassic Limestone ridge across northern Northants. Via the Oxford Canal and Braunston.

Maps 141, 151, 152

Publication

THE JURASSIC WAY (M)
SERIES OF 3 LEAFLETS BY AND FROM NORTHAMPTONSHIRE
COUNTY COUNCIL. 85P EACH OR £2.25 FOR SET INC POSTAGE

KERRY WAY

Circular from Killarney: 135 miles (215 km)

Mostly low-level route through Killarney National Park and around the Iveragh Peninsula in south west Ireland.

Maps OS (Eire) Discovery series (1:50 000) 78, 83, 84, 85

Publications

THE KERRY WAY MAP GUIDE (M) CORDEE. £2.50 PLUS 50P P&P.

LANDSKER BORDERLANDS TRAIL

Circular from Canaston Bridge, Dyfed 60 miles (96 km)

Winding trail through the Pembrokeshire/ Carmarthenshire borderland, east of the Cleddau estuary. Links with the South of Landsker Trail which runs from Narberth to Pembroke.

Maps 158

Luggage carrier Landsker Countryside Holidays (also accommodation booking service)

Publications

THE LANDSKER BORDERLANDS AREA GUIDE (M) (FREE)
BY AND FROM LANDSKER COUNTRYSIDE HOLIDAYS.

LONDON LOOP ✶

Circular around London: 150 miles (241 km)

The LOOP is London's premier orbital footpath. The circuit takes full advantage of the pretty and pleasantly varied countryside which lines the capital's fringe. It passes several villages and is an ideal way to sample London's countryside, and yet still be in reach of the city centre.

Maps 176, 177, 187

Publications

THE LONDON LOOP. AURUM PRESS £12.99 (PUBL FEBRUARY 2001)
LOOP WALKS: SOUTH LONDON. (PACK OF LEAFLETS 1 TO 8)
FROM DOWNLANDS PROJECT £6 PLUS 61P P&P (CHEQUE TO
SURREY COUNTY COUNCIL, POST TO DOWNLANDS PROJECT)

MACMILLAN WAY

Boston, Lincs to Abbotsbury, Dorset
290 miles (467 km)

Magnificent coast-to-coast route running diagonally accross England now fully waymarked and documented in both directions. Some steep climbs but largely great tracts of rolling pastoral countryside. In April 2001 Macmillan Way West opens. This runs 100 miles from Castle Cary to Barnstaple, across the Somerset Levels, the Quantocks and Exmoor.

Maps 130, 131, 141, 151, 152, 162, 163, 172, 180, 181, 183, 193, 194

Publications

THE MACMILLAN WAY: BOSTON TO ABBOTSBURY. £9
MACMILLAN WAY WEST: CASTLE CARY TO BARNSTAPLE £6.25.
THE MACMILLAN WAY SOUTH-NORTH SUPPLEMENT. £4.50
THE MACMILLAN WAY PLANNER (A) (OFT-UPDATED INFORMATION
BOOKLET) £2.75
ALL AVAILABLE POST FREE FROM MACMILLAN WAY ASSOCIATION

The Association is at St Mary's Barn, Pillerton Priors, Warwick CV35 0PG, tel. (01789) 740852

LONG DISTANCE PATHS

MENDIP WAY

Uphill, near Weston-super-Mare, to Frome

50 miles (80 km)

Borne of the combination of the routes east and west of Wells, the Mendip Way is a pleasant route across the whole length of the Mendip Hills, including the broad vale of the Western Mendips, the high plateau of the central part and the wooded valleys of the eastern end. Includes some steep climbs.

Maps 182, 183

Luggage carrier Mendip Walks (01934) 418784

Publications
WEST MENDIP WAY (M) BY ANDREW EDDY £3.50 PLUS 50P P&P FROM WESTON HERITAGE CENTRE.
UPHILL TO FROME: A GUIDE TO THE MENDIP WAY BY DAVID WRIGHT. £8 INC. P&P FROM DAVID WRIGHT

THE NIDDERDALE WAY

Circular from Hampsthwaite, near Harrogate

53 miles (85km)

Waymarked walk around the valley of the River Nidd in North Yorkshire, featuring gritstone outcrops and rough, open moorland.

Maps 99, 104

Publications
THE NIDDERDALE WAY
BY PAUL HANNON. HILLSIDE PUBLICATIONS £3.50 PLUS 40P P&P.
THE NIDDERDALE WAY (M) A5 CARDS IN FOLDER
BY KEN PIGGIN. YORKSHIRE FOOTPATH TRUST £2.95 PLUS 50P P&P

NORTH COTSWOLD DIAMOND WAY

Circular (diamond!) from Moreton-in-Marsh

60 miles (96 km)

Imaginative and scenic route through rural Gloucestershire, created by the RA's North Cotswold Group to celebrate the 60th Jubilee in 1995. Stretches from Northleach in the south to near Chipping Campden in the north, Guiting Power in the west to near Bourton-on-the-Water in the east.

Maps 151, 163

Publications
THE NORTH COTSWOLD DIAMOND WAY (M) BY NORTH COTSWOLD RA. £3.50 PLUS 50P P&P FROM GLOUCESTERSHIRE AREA RA

NORTH DOWNS WAY

Farnham to Dover 141 miles (227 km)

Along the attractive wooded downland of Surrey into Kent, with an optional loop via Canterbury.

Maps 178, 179, 186, 187, 188, 189

Publications
NORTH DOWNS WAY - NATIONAL TRAIL GUIDE
BY NEIL CURTIS AND JIM WALKER. AURUM PRESS £10.99
THE NORTH DOWNS WAY PRACTICAL HANDBOOK (MA)
BY AND FROM KENT COUNTY COUNCIL £2.95
ALSO AVAILABLE FROM RA CENTRAL OFFICE PLUS 70P P&P.

GUIDE TO THE PILGRIMS' WAY AND NORTH DOWNS WAY BY C J WRIGHT. CONSTABLE £10.95

OFFA'S DYKE PATH

Chepstow to Prestatyn 168 miles (270 km)

Fascinating if sometimes challenging path along the English/Welsh border via Hay, Knighton and Llangollen. Passes 60 miles of the 8th century dyke and is rich in scenic variety and historic interest.

Maps 116, 117, 126, 137, 148, 161, 162 (and part of route shown on Outdoor Leisure 13 and 14)

Luggage carrier Byways Bike Breaks 0151-722 8050

Publications
OFFA'S DYKE PATH NORTH AND OFFA'S DYKE PATH SOUTH - NATIONAL TRAIL GUIDES BY ERNIE & KATHY KAY AND MARK RICHARDS. AURUM PRESS £10.99 EACH. ALSO AVAILABLE PLUS £1.50 P&P FROM RA CENTRAL OFFICE
OFFA'S DYKE ACCOMMODATION LISTS (A) BY AND FROM OFFA'S DYKE ASSOCIATION. £3 PLUS 70P P&P FROM RA CENTRAL OFFICE.
OFFA'S DYKE NORTH TO SOUTH AND OFFA'S DYKE SOUTH TO NORTH (FOLDERS) £2 PLUS 30P P&P AND STRIP MAPS £5 EACH FROM OFFA'S DYKE ASSOCIATION.
LANGTON'S GUIDE TO THE OFFA'S DYKE
BY ANDREW DURHAM. £12.99 LANGTON'S GUIDES
WALKING OFFA'S DYKE
BY DAVID HUNTER. CICERONE PRESS £8.99 PLUS £1 P&P

The Association is at Offas Dyke Centre, West Street, Knighton, Powys LD7 1EW, tel. (01547) 528753.

OXFORDSHIRE WAY

Bourton-on-the-Water to Henley-on-Thames

65 miles (105 km)

Easy lowland path to the north of Oxford linking the Heart of England Way with the Thames Path via the Cotswolds to the Chilterns.

Maps 163, 164, 165, 175

Publications
OXFORDSHIRE WAY (M) BY ALISON KEMP. FROM OXFORDSHIRE COUNTY COUNCIL. £5.99 PLUS 80P P&P (INCLUDES PUBLIC TRANS-PORT AND ACCOMMODATION LISTINGS).

PEDDARS WAY AND NORFOLK COAST PATH

Knettishall Heath, near Thetford, to Cromer

94 miles (138 km)

Roman road through the Norfolk countryside to near Hunstanton, then east along the coast via Sheringham. Joins up with the Weavers Way and Angles Way to make a circuit of eastern Norfolk.

Maps 132, 133, 144

Luggage carrier Walkfree, tel. (01760) 724295.

Publications
NATIONAL TRAIL GUIDE: PEDDARS WAY & NORFOLK COAST PATH - NATIONAL TRAIL GUIDE(M)
BY BRUCE ROBINSON. AURUM PRESS. £10.99.
LANGTON'S GUIDE TO THE PEDDARS WAY & NORFOLK COAST PATH (MA) BY ANDREW DURHAM. LANGTON'S GUIDES. £6.95.
WALKING THE PEDDARS WAY & NORFOLK COAST PATH WITH THE WEAVERS WAY (MA).

BY AND FROM NORFOLK AREA RA, KNIGHTS COTTAGE, THE OLD
SCHOOL, HONING, NORFOLK NR28 9TR. £2.70 PLUS 40P P&P.

PEMBROKESHIRE COAST PATH

Amroth to Cardigan: 186 miles (299 km)

Dramatic and sometimes stern cliff and bay walking
via Tenby, Pembroke and Fishguard.

Maps 145, 157, 158 (but route now fully shown on
Outdoor Leisure 35 and 36)

Luggage carrier Pembrokeshire Discovery, tel.
(01437) 710720.

Publications
PEMBROKESHIRE COAST PATH - NATIONAL TRAIL GUIDE: (M)
BY BRIAN JOHN, AURUM PRESS. £10.99
THE PEMBROKESHIRE COASTAL PATH (MA)
BY DENNIS KELSALL. CICERONE PRESS. £9.99 PLUS £1 P&P.
ACCOMMODATION GUIDE (A) £2.50 AND MILEAGE CHART 20P PLUS
38P P&P FROM PEMBROKESHIRE COAST NATIONAL PARK OFFICE
(SEE USEFUL ADDRESSES).

PENNINE WAY

Edale to Kirk Yetholm: 256 miles (412 km)

Tom Stephenson's grand but demanding trail along
the high, open backbone of England into Scotland is
for experienced hill walkers with a lot of stamina.

Maps 74, 80, 86, 87, 91, 92, 98, 103, 109, 110

YHA Pennine Way Booking Bureau - see YHA
Northern Region address under Coast to Coast Walk

Luggage carrier Sherpa Van, tel. 020 8569 4101.

Publications
THE PENNINE WAY ACCOMMODATION & CAMPING GUIDE (A)
BY THE PENNINE WAY ASSOCIATION. £1.50 PLUS 70P P&P
FROM RA CENTRAL OFFICE
PENNINE WAY NORTH AND PENNINE WAY SOUTH BY TONY
HOPKINS - NATIONAL TRAIL GUIDES. AURUM PRESS £10.99 EACH.
ALSO AVAILABLE PLUS £1.50 P&P FROM RA CENTRAL OFFICE
PENNINE WAY BY TERRY MARSH. DALESMAN PUBLISHING £4.99

The Pennine Way Association is at 29 Springfield
Park Avenue, Chelmsford, Essex CM2 6EL, tel.
(01245) 256772

RIBBLE WAY

Dolphin Inn, Longton to Gayle Moor, near Hawes
72 miles (118 km)

A mouth to source walk along this attractive
Lancashire river, via Preston, Clitheroe and Settle.

Maps 98, 102, 103

Publications
THE RIBBLE WAY (M)
BY GLADYS SELLERS. CICERONE PRESS. £5.99 PLUS £1 P&P.

THE RIDGEWAY

Overton Hill, near Avebury to Ivinghoe Beacon
85 miles (137 km)

Via the ancient hillforts of the North Wessex Downs
and the wooded Chilterns, via Streatley and
Wendover. Connects with Icknield Way and Wessex
Ridgeway to form a continuous path along the chalk
ridge.

Maps 165, 173, 174, 175 and see Harvey's route
map of the Ridgeway

Publications
THE RIDGEWAY - NATIONAL TRAIL GUIDE (M)
BY NEIL CURTIS. AURUM PRESS. £10.99
THE RIDGEWAY COMPANION ((A) AND TRANSPORT) £3.95 FROM RA
CENTRAL OFFICE
HARVEY'S RIDGEWAY WATEPROOF MAP £7.95

Friends of the Ridgeway is c/o Peter Gould at 18
Hampton Park, Bristol BS6 6LH

ROBIN HOOD WAY

Starts at Nottingham Castle, ends at various places
105 miles (165 km)

Containing a number of circular offshoots, this trail
winds its way through Sherwood Forest and the
Dukeries.

Maps 120, 129

Publications
THE ROBIN HOOD WALKS (M)
BY NOTTINGHAM WAYFARERS. CORDEE. £4.95.

SAINTS WAY

Padstow to Fowey: 37 miles (59 km)

Short coast to coast route across Cornwall, following
a route possibly taken by the Celtic saints.

Maps 200, 204

Publications
TRAIL GUIDE TO THE SAINTS WAY (M) FOLDER OF CARDS BY AND
FROM CORNWALL COUNTY COUNCIL. £4.50 INC. POSTAGE.

SAXON SHORE WAY

Gravesend to Hastings: 163 miles (261 km)

Interesting walk around the South East coastline (or
at least its former position in Roman times), via
Rochester, Herne Bay and Dover. Connects with 1066
Country Walk at Rye, the Greensand Way and Royal
Military Canal Path.

Maps 177, 178, 179, 189, 199

Publications
SAXON SHORE WAY (M) BY BEA COWAN. AURUM PRESS. £10.99.
SAXON SHORE WAY WALKS (M): SHORNE AND HIGHAM MARSHES;
BROCKHILL COUNTRY PARK; SWALE HERITAGE TRAIL.
BY AND FROM KENT COUNTY COUNCIL £1.95 EACH.

SEVERN WAY

Near Plynlimon, Powys, to Severn Beach, near Bristol
210 miles (338 km)

A long and exciting source to sea walk, from the wild

mid-Wales hills via Welshpool, Shrewsbury, Worcester and Gloucester to a finish near Bristol.

Maps 126, 127, 136, 138, 150, 162, 172

Publications
THE SEVERN WAY (M)
BY AND FROM THE ENVIRONMENT AGENCY. £6.95

SHROPSHIRE WAY

Circular from Wem: 125 miles (201 km)

Large wriggling tour of the county via Shrewsbury, Ludlow, Clee Hills, Wenlock Edge and the Wrekin.

Maps 117, 126, 127, 137, 138

Publications
RAMBLERS GUIDE TO THE SHROPSHIRE WAY
BY SHROPSHIRE AREA RA. AVAILABLE FORM POWNEYS BOOKSHOP
(SEE PUBLISHERS ADDRESSES). £5.99 PLUS £1 POSTAGE.
THE SHROPSHIRE WAY
BY TERRY MARSH AND JULIE MEECH. CICERONE £9.99

SOUTH DOWNS WAY

Eastbourne to Winchester:106 miles (171 km)
Exhilarating bridleway route along the rolling chalk downs of Sussex and Hampshire. Connects with the North Downs Way via the Downs Link at Shoreham-by-Sea and with the 1066 Country Walk at Alfriston.

Maps 185, 197, 198, 199 and see Harveys route map of the South Downs Way.

Publications
SOUTH DOWNS WAY - NATIONAL TRAIL GUIDE
BY PAUL MILLMORE. AURUM PRESS £10.99
ALONG THE SOUTH DOWNS WAY TO WINCHESTER (MA)
BY THE SOCIETY OF SUSSEX DOWNSMEN (£5). AVAILABLE PLUS £1
POSTAGE FROM RA CENTRAL OFFICE.
ACCOMMODATION GUIDE TO THE SOUTH DOWNS WAY
FROM RA CENTRAL OFFICE £2.50 PUS 70P P&P

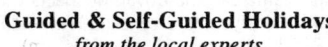
SOUTH WEST COAST PATH

Minehead to Poole: Approx 600 miles (965 km)

An awesome, continuous path around the whole of Devon and Cornwall, and much of Dorset and Somerset. Spectacular and sometimes arduous, usually approached in week or weekend chunks!

Maps 180, 181, 190, 192, 193, 194, 195, 200, 201, 202, 203, 204

Publications
THE SOUTH WEST COAST PATH GUIDE (A)
BY SOUTH WEST COAST PATH ASSOCIATION. £6 PLUS £1 POSTAGE.
FROM RA CENTRAL OFFICE.
THE SOUTH WEST COAST PATH, THE NATIONAL TRAIL GUIDE
PUBLISHED IN 4 VOLUMES, EACH £10.99, BY AURUM PRESS
THE SOUTH WEST WAY BY MARTIN COLLINS. PUBLISHED IN TWO
VOLUMES BY CICERONE PRESS AT £8.99 EACH PLUS £1 P&P.

The South West Coast Path Association is at Windlestraw, Penquit, Ermington, Ivybridge, Devon PL21 0LU.

SOUTHERN UPLAND WAY

Portpatrick to Cockburnspath: 212 miles (341 km)

Scenic but often remote coast to coast route across southern Scotland via Sanquhar, Moffatt and Melrose. Can be linked with St Cuthbert's Way at Melrose.

Maps 67, 73, 74, 77, 78, 79, 82 (official guide includes two 1:50 000 strip maps of route)

Publications
THE SOUTHERN UPLAND WAY
BY ANTHONY BURTON. AURUM PRESS £12.99
THE SOUTHERN UPLAND WAY (M)
BY ROGER SMITH. MERCAT PRESS £14.99.
SOUTHERN UPLAND WAY INFORMATION & ACCOMMODATION LEA-
FLET (A). FROM SOUTHERN UPLAND WAY OFFICE,. FREE/SAE
ALSO AVAILABLE FROM RA CENTRAL OFFICE.

SPEYSIDE WAY

Buckie to Aviemore: 90 miles (145 km)

From the coast near Buckie, the route heads south by the River Spey along footpaths, forest rides and an old railway track. The River Spey is said to be the fastest flowing and cleanest river in Britain.

Maps 28, 36 (and Harvey's map of the Way)

Publications
THE SPEYSIDE WAY (M) ROUTE GUIDE BY AND FROM MORAY
DISTRICT COUNCIL £7.95 (INC HARVEY'S MAP)
INFORMATION AND ACCOMMODATION LEAFLET (A) FROM SPEYSIDE
WAY RANGER'S OFFICE (FREE/SAE) OR FROM RA CENTRAL OFFICE.

STAFFORDSHIRE WAY

Mow Cop Castle to Kinver Edge: 93 miles (148 km)

Varied trail through the county via Leek, Uttoxeter and Penkridge, including the Caldon Canal towpath, Cannock Chase and grounds of Shugborough Hall.

Maps 118, 127, 128, 138

Luggage carrier Old Furnace Walking Holidays, tel. (01538)703331

Publications
WALKING ON AND AROUND THE STAFFORDSHIRE WAY

LONG DISTANCE PATHS

BY GEOFF LOADWICK. SIGMA LEISURE £5.95
THE STAFFORDSHIRE WAY (M)
BY AND FROM STAFFS COUNTY COUNCIL (A). £5.50 PLUS 40P P&P
WHERE TO STAY ALONG THE STAFFORDSHIRE WAY (A)
BY STAFFS AREA RA FROM RA CENTRAL OFFICE. FREE/SAE.

ST CUTHBERT'S WAY

Melrose, Scottish Borders to Lindisfarne, Northumberland: 62 miles (100km)

A pilgrimage path, linking the places where St Cuthbert started and finished his ministry in the 7th century. It covers a variety of terrain including the Eildon Hills, the river Tweed, the Roman Dere Street, the foothills of the Cheviots and Northumberland National Park. A mostly easy walk but beware the remote upland stretch between Kirk Yetholm and Wooler.

Maps 73, 74, 75. See also Harveys map of St Cuthberts Way

Luggage carrier Carry-Lite, tel. 01670 774455 and Sherpa Van, tel. 020 8569 4101

Publications
ST CUTHBERT'S WAY BY ROGER SMITH AND RON SHAW. MERCAT PRESS £9.99 (INCLUDES HARVEYS MAP)
ST CUTHBERT'S WAY - A PILGRIM'S COMPANION
BY MARY LOW. WILD GOOSE PUBLICATIONS £9.99
COMPLETE GUIDE TO ST CUTHBERT'S WAY (MA) BY ROGER NOYCE. SIGMA LEISURE £4.95
ST CUTHBERT'S WAY ACCOMMODATION AND FACILITIES BOOKLET FREE FROM JEDBURGH TOURIST INFORMATION CENTRE
ALSO AVAILABLE FROM RA CENTRAL OFFICE PLUS.

STOUR VALLEY PATH

60 miles (96 km)

Newmarket to Cattawade, near Manningtree

Easy, picturesque path along the valley of the East Anglian Stour, mostly following the Suffolk/Essex border via Sudbury. Passes through Constable country and links with Icknield Way and Essex Way.

Maps 154, 155, 168, 169

Publications
THE STOUR VALLEY PATH (MA)
BY AND FROM SUFFOLK COUNTY COUNCIL. £3.50.

TAFF TRAIL

Cardiff to Brecon: 55 miles (88 km)

Walking/cycling route along the Taff valley, linking Cardiff Bay to the Brecon Beacons via Llandaff, Pontypridd and Merthyr Tydfil.

Maps 160, 161, 170, 171

Publications
THE TAFF TRAIL (M)
BY JEFF VINTER AVAILABLE FROM THE TAFF TRAIL PROJECT £10.99.

TARKA TRAIL

Usually started at Barnstaple: 180 miles (288 km)

Unusual and massive figure of eight around the Devon countryside, including a stretch of the North Devon coast, but also and rather oddly involving a long section by railway.

Maps 180, 190, 191 (and part of route shown on Outdoor Leisure 9)

Publications
THE TARKA TRAIL: A WALKER'S GUIDE (M)
BY THE TARKA PROJECT. DEVON COUNTY COUNCIL £4.95

THAMES PATH

Thames Head, Glos, to Thames Barrier, London 180 miles (288 km)

Splendid riverside trail pioneered by David Sharp and the RA. Leads from the Cotswolds to the capital, passing through a wealth of fascinating places, such as Oxford, Henley and Windsor.

Maps 163, 164, 174, 175, 176

Publications
THE THAMES PATH - NATIONAL TRAIL GUIDE (FROM SOURCE TO BARRAGE) (M) BY DAVID SHARP. AURUM PRESS. £12.99. ALSO AVAILABLE PLUS £1.50 POSTAGE FROM RA CENTRAL OFFICE.
THE THAMES PATH (FROM BARRAGE TO SOURCE)
BY LEIGH HATTS. CICERONE £7.99.
THE THAMES PATH NATIONAL TRAIL COMPANION ((A) AND TRANSPORT) AVAILABLE FROM RA CENTRAL OFFICE £4.95 PLUS £1 P&P.

THREE CASTLES PATH

Windsor to Winchester: 60 miles (96 km)

Gentle route through the Berkshire and Hampshire countryside, following the 13th century journeys of King John.

Maps 175, 176, 185, 186

Publications
THREE CASTLES PATH (M) BY EAST BERKS RA. £2.50. AVAILABLE PLUS 70P POSTAGE FROM RA CENTRAL OFFICE.
ACCOMMODATION LIST (A).FREE/9" X 4" SAE FROM BRACKNELL TIC ALSO AVAILABLE FROM RA CENTRAL OFFICE.

TWO MOORS WAY

Ivybridge to Lynmouth: 103 miles (166 km)

Appealing south-north route through Devon, linking Dartmoor to Exmoor and the north coast. Unwaymarked across the moors. Links to Tarka Trail.

Maps 180, 181, 191, 202 (and much of route shown on Outdoor Leisure 9 and 28)

Luggage carrier Organised by B&B proprietors who are identified in accommodation guide — see below.

Publications
THE TWO MOORS WAY (M)
BY TWO MOORS WAY ASSOCIATION. £3 PLUS 70P P&P AVAILABLE FROM RA CENTRAL OFFICE.

LONG DISTANCE PATHS

THE TWO MOORS WAY BY JOHN MACADAM. AURUM PRESS £12.99.
ACCOMMODATION LEAFLET (A) 50P PLUS 9" X 4" SAE FROM THE
TWO MOORS WAY ASSOCIATION (ADDRESS BELOW)
ALSO AVAILABLE FROM RA CENTRAL OFFICE .
THE TWO MOORS WAY (M)
BY JAMES ROBERTS. CICERONE PRESS. £5.99 PLUS £1 P&P.

The Two Moors Way Association is at Coppins, The
Poplars, Pinhoe, Exeter, Devon EX4 9HH.

ULSTER WAY

Circular from Belfast anti-clockwise: 666 miles (920 km)

Encircling most of Northern Ireland, via the
Causeway and Antrim coasts, Fermanagh lakes,
Sperrins and Mournes. Passes through most of
Ulster's AONBs. It is a fully waymarked and much
enjoyed route in its entirety or short walks.

Maps 20 Discovery maps (1:50 000) cover the route.
Details from Ordnance Survey of Northern Ireland
(see Useful Addresses).

Publications
THE ULSTER WAY BY PADDY DILLON. O'BRIEN PRESS. £9.99.
WALKING THE ULSTER WAY
BY ALAN WARNER. APPLETREE PRESS. £6.99.
AN INFORMATION GUIDE TO WALKING (14 CIRCULAR WALKS ON
THE ULSTER WAY) (M) AND ACCOMMODATION LEAFLET (A) FREE
FROM NORTHERN IRELAND TOURIST BOARD, ALSO AVAILABLE
FROM RA CENTRAL OFFICE.

VANGUARD WAY

Croydon to Newhaven: 66 miles (107 km)

A pleasant ramble from the suburbs to the sea, via
Crockham Hill and Forest Row to Seaford, and with a
new extension to Newhaven.

Maps 187, 188, 198, 199

Publications
THE VANGUARD WAY (MA)
BY AND FROM VANGUARDS RAMBLING CLUB £2.95. ALSO AVAIL-
ABLE PLUS 70P P&P FROM RA CENTRAL OFFICE.
WEALDWAY AND THE VANGUARD WAY
BY KEV REYNOLDS. CICERONE PRESS £4.99 PLUS £1 P&P.

VIKING WAY

Barton-upon-Humber to Oakham
140 miles (225 km)

From the Humber Bridge this gentle route heads
south along the Lincs Wolds to Horncastle and
Lincoln, to finish near Rutland Water.

Maps 112, 113, 121, 122, 130, 141

Publications
THE VIKING WAY (MA)
BY AND FROM LINCS COUNTY COUNCIL. £4.95 PLUS £1 P&P
VIKING WAY BY JOHN STEAD. CICERONE £5.99 PLUS £1 P&P.

WEALDWAY

Gravesend to Eastbourne: 80 miles (129 km)

From the mouth of the Thames to the south coast, via

Ashdown Forest and the Weald of Kent and Sussex.

Maps 117, 188, 198, 199

Publications
THE WEALDWAY (M) BY KENT & EAST SUSSEX. COUNTY COUNCILS.
£10.95 FROM KENT COUNTY COUNCIL.
WEALDWAY ACCOMMODATION LEAFLET (A). £1 PLUS SAE FROM
SUSSEX RAMBLERS, ALSO AVAILABLE FROM RA CENTRAL OFFICE.
THE WEALDWAY AND THE VANGUARD WAY (M)
BY KEV REYNOLDS. CICERONE PRESS. £4.99 PLUS £1 P&P.

WEAVERS WAY

Cromer to Great Yarmouth: 56 miles (90 km)

Easy trail through the Norfolk Broads via Aylsham
and North Walsham.

Maps 133, 134

Publications
LANGTON'S GUIDE TO THE WEAVERS WAY AND THE ANGLES WAY
(MA). LANGTON'S GUIDE. £6.95.
WALKING THE PEDDARS WAY & NORFOLK COAST PATH WITH THE
WEAVERS WAY (MA)
BY AND FROM NORFOLK AREA RA, KNIGHTS COTTAGE, THE OLD
SCHOOL, HONING, NORFOLK NR28 9TR. £2.70 PLUS 40P P&P.

WESSEX RIDGEWAY

Marlborough to Lyme Regis: 136 miles (219 km)

Starting from near the beginning of the Ridgeway
National Trail, the path goes as near as possible to
what is believed to be the final part of the ancient
Ridgeway route from East Anglia to the sea. From
deepest Wiltshire via the edge of Salisbury Plain and
Cranborne Chase to the Dorset coast.

Maps 173, 183, 184, 193, 194, 195

Publications
WALK THE WESSEX RIDGEWAY IN DORSET (MA)
BY PRISCILLA HOUSTOUN. DORSET PUBLISHING COMPANY. £5.95.
WALK THE WESSEX RIDGEWAY IN WILTSHIRE (M)
BY BRIAN PANTON. RAMBLERS' ASSOCIATION. £4.50. AVAILABLE
PLUS £1 P&P FROM RA CENTRAL OFFICE.

WEST HIGHLAND WAY ❀

Milngavie, Glasgow, to Fort William
95 miles (153 km)

Handsome trail via Loch Lomond and Rannoch Moor,
ending at the foot of Ben Nevis. Busy in the summer,
potentially tricky in the winter at northern end.

Maps Official guide includes 1:50 000 strip map of
route; whole route also covered by Outdoor Leisure
38 and 39; and see Harveys route map of the West
Highland Way.

Luggage carrier Travel-Lite, tel. 0141-956 7890
(April to September) and Sherpa Van, tel. 020 8569
4101

Publications
THE WEST HIGHLAND WAY OFFICIAL GUIDE BY BOB AITKEN AND
ROGER SMITH. MERCAT PRESS £14.99
THE WEST HIGHLAND WAY

BY TERRY MARSH. CICERONE PRESS £6.99 PLUS £1 P&P
THE WEST HIGHLAND WAY INFORMATION & ACCOMMODATION
LEAFLET (A) FROM THE WEST HIGHLAND WAY PATH MANAGER
(SOUTH). FREE/SAE. ALSO AVAILABLE FROM RA CENTRAL OFFICE.
ACCOMMODATION GUIDE (A) £2.50 FROM STUART MACPHERSON,
24 ATHERTON DRIVE, HOUGHTON LE SPRING DH4 6TA

WHITE PEAK WAY

Circular from Bakewell: 80 miles (130 km)

Circuit of the southern Peak District, via the lovely
limestone scenery around Bakewell and Hartington,
and designed in seven stages that all finish at youth
hostels.

YHA White Peak Way Booking Bureau - see YHA
Northern Region address under Coast to Coast Walk

Maps 110, 119

Publications
WHITE PEAK WAY (M)
BY ROBERT HASLAM. CICERONE PRESS £4.99 PLUS £1 P&P.

WICKLOW WAY

Marlay Park, south of Dublin, to Clonegal
82 miles (132 km)

The first of Ireland's officially waymarked long-
distance trails. Heads through the Dublin and
Wicklow Mountains to end in County Carlow.

Maps OS (Eire) Discovery series (1:50 000) 50, 56,
62

Publications
THE COMPLETE WICKLOW WAY (M)
BY J. B. MALONE. O'BRIEN PRESS £5.95.
THE WICKLOW WAY MAP GUIDE (INCLUDES 1:50 000 ROUTE MAP)
FROM EASTWEST MAPPING £4.50 PLUS 65P P&P.

WOLDS WAY 🔒

Filey to Hessle, Kingston upon Hull 79 miles (127 km)

A curving route around and across the Yorkshire
Wolds via Market Weighton, linking the North Sea to
the Humber. Joins the Cleveland Way at Filey. In
1999 the route of the way was altered to pass
through the fascinating ruins of Wharram Percy.

Maps 100, 101, 106, 107

Publications
WOLDS WAY - NATIONAL TRAIL GUIDE (M)
BY ROGER RATCLIFFE. AURUM PRESS £9.99.
WOLDS WAY ACCOMMODATION AND INFORMATION GUIDE (A).
95P PLUS 40P P&P FROM MALTON TIC.

WYE VALLEY WALK

Chepstow to Rhayader: 107 miles (172 km)

Follows the course of the River Wye, via Monmouth,
Hereford and Builth Wells.

Maps 136, 146, 147, 148, 149, 160, 161, 162, 172.

Publications
THE WYE VALLEY WALK BY ANTHONY BURTON. AURUM £12.99
WYE VALLEY WALK (MA)

BY HEREFORD & WORCESTER, MONMOUTH, AND POWYS COUNTY
COUNCILS. £3.95 (FROM POWYS COUNTY COUNCIL).
WYE VALLEY WALK - ACCOMMODATION AND TRANSPORT GUIDE
POWYS COUNTY COUNCIL FREE PLUS 30P P&P
ALSO AVAILABLE FROM RA CENTRAL OFFICE.

OTHER PATHS WITH GUIDEBOOKS PUBLISHED RECENTLY

Channel to Channel 50 miles across the southwest
peninsula at its narrowest point (Seaton to Watchet).
Guidebook by Ken Young for Somerset Ramblers from
the author at 14 Wilton Orchard, Taunton TA1 3SA, £2
plus 50p p&p.

The Clwydian Way circular from Prestatyn, 122 miles.
Devised by Dave Hollett for North Wales Area RA.
Guidebook available from the author at 69 Wethersfield
Road, Prenton, Wirral CH43 9YF, £5.95 plus £1 p&p.

The D'Arcy Dalton Way an Oxfordshire path from Near
Banbury to the Ridgeway at Wayland's Smithy.
Guidebook by Nick Moon for the Oxford Fieldpath
Society published by the Book Castle at £6.99 (ISBN 1
871 199 34 4)

Dorset Jubilee Trail a 90-mile walk across Dorset
devised by Dorset Ramblers. Guidebook available from
Jubilee Trail Contact, 19 Shaston Crescent, Dorchester
DT1 2EB, £4.50 plus 50p p&p (ISBN 1 901184 04 8).

The Elan Valley Way 128 miles from Elan Valley to
Birmingham. Guidebook by David Milton available from
Meridian Books £7.95 (ISBN 1 869922 39 5).

North to the Cape a 21-day walk for experienced
walkers from Fort William to Cape Wrath. Guidebook by
Denis Brook and Phil Hinchcliffe published by Cicerone
at £10.99 (ISBN 1 85284 285 7)

The Rutland Round 65 miles around Rutland.
Guidebook by John Williams available from Rutland
Water TIC, Sykes Lane, Empingham, Oakham LE15 8PX,
£5.60.

The Scottish Coast to Coast 128 miles from Oban to St
Andrews. Guidebook by Brian Smailes published by
Challenge Publications at £6.50 (ISBN 095269008X).

The Socratic Trail 47 miles from Croydon to Brighton.
Guide booklet by Maurice Hencke available from the
author at 25 Placehouse Lane, Old Coulsdon CR5 1LA,
£1.50 plus large sae.

The Trans-Pennine Way a 100 mile walk across the
Pennines, from the Forest of Bowland to Fountains
Abbey. Guidebook by Paul Hannon available from
Hillside Publications, see publishers' addresses below,
£6.99 plus 50p p&p.

PUBLISHERS' ADDRESSES

APPLETREE PRESS, 19-21 ALFRED STREET, BELFAST BT2 8DL, TEL
028 90 243074
AURUM PRESS, 25 BEDFORD AVENUE, LONDON WC1B 3AT, TEL 020
7637 3225
BRACKNELL TIC, THE LOOK OUT, NINE MILE RIDE, BRACKNELL RG12
7QW, TEL 01344 868196
THE CHILTERN SOCIETY, MAIL ORDER BOOKSHOP, 20 THE
RIDGEWAY, WATFORD WD17 4TN

LONG DISTANCE PATHS

CICERONE PRESS, 2 POLICE SQUARE, MILNTHORPE, CUMBRIA LA7 7PY, TEL 015395 62069

CONSTABLE, 3 THE LANCHESTERS, 162 FULHAM PALACE ROAD, LONDON W6 9ER, TEL 020 8741 3663

CORDEE, 3A DE MONTFORT STREET, LEICESTER LE1 7HD, TEL 0116 254 3579

CORNWALL COUNTY COUNCIL, TRANSPORTATION & ESTATES, CASTLE CANYKE ROAD, BODMIN PL31 1DZ, TEL 01872 322000

COUNTRYSIDE BOOKS, HIGHFIELD HOUSE, 2 HIGHFIELD AVENUE, NEWBURY, BERKS RG14 5DS, TEL 01635 43816

DALESMAN PUBLISHING, CLAPHAM, VIA LANCASTER LA2 8EB, TEL 015242 51225

DEVON COUNTY COUNCIL, TOURIST INFORMATION CENTRE, EXETER MOTORWAY SERVICES AREA (M5), SIDMOUTH ROAD, EXETER EX2 7HF. TEL 0870 608 5531

DORSET PUBLISHING COMPANY (SEE HALSGROVE)

DOWNLANDS PROJECT, HIGHWAY HOUSE, 21 CHESSINGTON ROAD, WEST EWELL, SURREY KT17 1TT

A.J. DRAKE, 2 BEECH LODGE, 67 THE PARK, CHELTENHAM GL50 2RX. TEL 01242 232131EAST YORKS & DERWENT RAMBLERS, C/O SHEILA SMITH, 65 ORMONDE AVENUE, BERESFORD AVENUE, BEVERLEY HIGH ROAD, HULL HU6 7LT.

EASTWEST MAPPING, BALLYREDMOND, CLONEGAL, ENNISCORTHY, CO WEXFORD, IRELAND, TEL 00353 54 77835

ELLENBANK PRESS, PARK HILL SOUTH, CAMP ROAD, MARYPORT, CUMBRIA CA15 6JW, TEL 01900 817773

ENVIRONMENT AGENCY, HAFREN HOUSE, WELSHFPOOL ROAD, SHELTON, SHREWSBURY SY3 8BB, TEL 01743 272828.

ESSEX COUNTY COUNCIL, WAYS THROUGH ESSEX, TOPS, COUNTY HALL, CHELMSFORD, ESSEX CM1 1QH, TEL 01245 437647

GLOUCESTERSHIRE AREA RA, MAIL ORDER SECRETARY, 1 SOVER-EIGN CHASE, STAUNTON, GLOUCESTER GL19 3NW. TEL 01452 840172

GLOUCESTERSHIRE C C, RIGHTS OF WAY SECTION, ENVIRONMENT DEPT, BEARLAND, GLOUCESTER GL1 2TH, TEL 01452 425000

HALSGROVE, HALSGROVE HOUSE, LOWER MOOR WAY, TIVERTON BUSINESS PARK, TIVERTON, DEVON EX16 6SS, TEL 01884 243242

HAPPY WALKING INTERNATIONAL, UNIT 1, MOLYNEUX BUSINESS PARK, WHITWORTH ROAD, DARLEY DALE, MATLOCK DE4 2HJ, TEL 01629 735911

HARVEYS, 12-16 MAIN ST, DOUNE, FK16 6BJ, TEL 01786 841098

HEBDEN BRIDGE TOURIST INFORMATION CENTRE, 1 BRIDGE GATE, HEBDEN BRIDGE, WEST YORKSHIRE HX7 8EX, TEL 01422 843831

HILLSIDE PUBLICATIONS, 12 BROADLANDS, SHANN PARK, KEIGHLEY BD20 6HX. TEL 01535 681505

ISLE OF WIGHT TOURISM, WESTRIDGE CENTRE, BRADING ROAD, RYDE PO33 1QS, TEL 01983 813800

JEDBURGH TIC, MURRAY'S GREEN, JEDBURGH TD8 6BE, TEL 01835 863435

KENT COUNTY COUNCIL,COUNTRYSIDE DEPT, ENVIRONMENT MAN-AGEMENT, INVICTA HOUSE, COUNTY HALL, MAIDSTONE ME14 1XX TEL 01622 221526

LANDSKER COUNTRYSIDE HOLIDAYS, THE OLD SCHOOL, STATION ROAD, NARBERTH, SA67 8DU TEL 01834 860965

LANGTON'S GUIDES, ASHLEIGH, RADLEY ROAD, HALAM, NEWARK NG 22 8AQ. BOOKS DISTRIBUTED BY CORDEE, SEE ABOVE

LINCOLNSHIRE COUNTY COUNCIL, EDUCATION & CULTRAL SERVICES, COUNTY OFFICES, NEWLAND, LINCOLN LN1 TEL 01522 453234

MACMILLAN WAY ASSOCIATION, ST MARY'S BARN, PILLERTON PRIORS, WARWICK CV35 0PG, TEL 01789 740852

LAURENCE MAIN, 9 MAWDDWY COTTAGES, MINLYN, DINAS MALTON TIC, , 58 MARKET PLACE, MALTON YO17 7LW MAWDDWY, MACHYNLLETH SY20 9LW

MERCAT PRESS, TEL 0131-622 8222

MIWAY PUBLISHING, P O BOX 2, KESWICK CA12 4GA

MORAY DISTRICT COUNCIL, HIGH STREET, ELGIN, MORAYSHIRE IV30 1BX, TEL 01343 563486

NATIONAL TRAILS OFFICE, COUNTRYSIDE SERVICE, CULTURAL SERVICES, HOLTON, OXFORD OX33 1QQ, TEL 01865 810224

NEWTOWN TIC, TEL. 01686 625580

NORTHAMPTONSHIRE C C,P O BOX 163, COUNTY HALL, NORTHAMPTON NN1 1AX, TEL 01604 237227

NORTHERN IRELAND TOURIST BOARD, 24 HAYMARKET, LONDON SW1Y 4DG, TEL 020 7766 9920

O'BRIEN PRESS, 20 VICTORIA ROAD, DUBLIN 6, IRELAND. TEL 00353 149233 33

OXFORDSHIRE COUNTY COUNCIL, COUNTRYSIDE SERVICE, CULTURAL SERVICES, HOLTON, OXFORD, OX33 1QQ, TEL 01865 810226

POWNEYS BOOKSHOP, 4-5 ST ALKMUNDS PLACE, SHREWSBURY SY1 1UJ, TEL 01743 369165

POWYS C C, RIGHTS OF WAY SECTION, PLANNING & ECONOMIC DEVELOPMENT, COUNTY HALL, LLANDRINDOD WELLS, LD1 5LE, TEL 01597 827500

SIGMA LEISURE, 1 SOUTH OAK LANE, WILMSLOW SK9 6AR, TEL (01625) 531035

SOUTH DOWNS WAY OFFICER, SUSSEX DOWNS CONSERVATION BOARD, CHANCTONBURY HOUSE, CHURCH ST, STORRINGTON RH 20 4LT

SOUTHERN UPLAND WAY OFFICER, PLANNING & ENVIRONMENT CONSERVATION GROUP, DUMFRIES & GALLOWAY CC, RAY STREET, DUMFRIES DG1 1LW, TEL 01387 260184

SPEYSIDE WAY RANGER'S OFFICE, BOAT OF FIDDICH, CRAIGELLACHIE, BANFFSHIRE AB38 9RQ, TEL. 01340 881266

STAFFORDSHIRE C C, CULTURAL & CORPORATE SERVICES DEPT, SHIRE HALL, MARKET ST, STAFFORD ST16 2LQ, TEL 01785 223121

THE STATIONERY OFFICE, PO BOX 276, LONDON SW8 5DT, TEL 0870 600 5522

STILE PUBLICATIONS, 16 DENTON ROAD, MIDDLETON, ILKLEY LS29 0AA, TEL 01943 601572

SUFFOLK COUNTY COUNCIL, DEDHAM VALE & STOUR VALLEY PROJECT, ENVIRONMENT & TRANSPORTATION DEPT, ST EDMUNDS HOUSE, ROPE WALK, IPSWICH IP4 1LZ, TEL 01473 583176

SURREY C C, INFORMATION CENTRE, PLANNING DEPT, COUNTY HALL, KINGSTON-UPON-THAMES, KT1 2DT, TEL 020 8541 8800

SUSSEX RAMBLERS, 11 OLD LONDON ROAD, BRIGHTON BN1 8XR

TAFF TRAIL PROJECT, C/O GROUNDWORK MERTHYR & RHONDDA-CYNON-TAFF, FEDW HIR LLWYD COED, ABERDARE CF44 0DX, TEL. 01685 883880

VANGUARDS RAMBLING CLUB, 109 SELSDON PARK ROAD, SOUTH CROYDON, SURREY CR2 8JJ

WALKWAYS, 67 CLIFFE WAY, WARWICK CV34 5JG, TEL 01926 776363

WEST HIGHLAND WAY PATH MANAGER (SOUTH), BALLOCH CASTLE, BALLOCH PARK, BALLOCH, G83 8LX, TEL 01389 758216

WESTERN MAIL, HAVELOCK STREET, CARDIFF CF1 1XR, TEL 029 258 3441

WESTON-HERITAGE CENTRE, 3-6 WADHAM STREET, WESTON-SUPER-MARE BS23 1JY, TEL 01934 412144

WILDGOOSE PUBLICATIONS, C/O ST ANDREW PRESS, 121 GEORGE STREET, EDINBURGH EH2 4YN, TEL. 0131-225 5722

DAVID WRIGHT, INGLENOOK COTTAGE, RUDGE, FROME BA11 2QG, TEL. 01373 830795

YORKSHIRE FOOTPATH TRUST, 37, HAZEL GARTH, STOCKTON LANE, YORK YO31 1HR, TEL 01904 412917

Walking Holidays and Courses in Britain

Some of these companies offer activities over the whole country and others cover a small area or particular paths. Many take the form of a group with a leader but some are unescorted, providing itineraries, maps and advice. Some provide luggage transportation, one or two offer training in mountaineering or navigation skills and yet others offer a range of outdoor activities.

Those listed here have chosen to advertise with us and their inclusion should not imply any recommendation by the RA.

For a fuller list of tour operators and their activites ask for *Factsheet No. 5 Walking Holidays in Britain* available from RA central office. You can also access our factsheets on our website.

Great Britain

AVALON TREKKING

40 Waverley Gardens, Etching Hill, Rugeley, Staffs WS15 2YE. ☎/Fax 01889 575646.
http://www.avalontrekking.co.uk
Email: hames@avalontrekking.co.uk
UK & Madeira. Guided and self-guided supported walks in LDPs. Comfortable accommodation.
Free brochure available.

INSTEP LINEAR WALKING HOLIDAYS (Including White Knight Services)

35 Cokeham Road, Lancing, W Sussex BN15 0AE. ☎/Fax (01903) 766475.
http://www.instephols.co.uk
EMail: walking@instephols.co.uk
Unescorted walking holidays, national trails • AW's Coast to Coast a speciality • Luggage service.

PACK AND GO

Alan Windebank, 58 Northcroft, Slough, SL2 1HR. ☎/Fax: (01753) 647371.
http://www.pack-and-go/co/uk
EMail: walks@pack-and-go.co.uk • England and Wales • Services for he rambler: accommodation booking, luggage transfer, walking holidays.

WALKING WITH WATER

HEHNB, Basingstoke Canal Centre, Mytchett Place Road, Mytchett, Surrey GU16 6DD.
http://www.hotelboats.co.uk
EMail: daviddare@hotelboats.co.uk
☎ (01252) 3786779. Fax (01252) 371758.
Semi-guided walking/cruising along Britain's canals aboard en-suite hotelboats.

England

BATH & WEST COUNTRY WALKS

Osmington, Brewery Lane, Holcombe, Bath BA3 5EG.
☎ 01761 233807. Email: info@bathwestwalks.com
Website: www.bathwestwalks.com
Guided and self-guided walks through the beautiful
Somerset countryside • Selected accommodation and
luggage transportation.

BYWAYS 1

25 Mayville Road, Liverpool L18 0HG.
☎/Fax 0151 722 8050.
Email: info@byways-breaks.co.uk
Website: byways-breaks.co.uk
Shropshire, Cheshire & Peaks • Gentle cycling and
walking holidays. Luggage transported.

CHICHESTER INTEREST HOLIDAYS

14 Bay View Terrace, Newquay, Cornwall TR7 2LR.
☎/Fax (01637) 874216.
EMail:sheila.harper@virgin.net
Cornwall • Spring & Autumn guided walking holidays
in Cornwall. 20th year.

CURLEW GUIDED WALKING

26 De Vitre Cottages, Ashton Road, Lancaster LA1
5AN. ☎ 01524 35601.
Email: curlewgw@globalnet.co.uk
Website: www.users.globalnet.co.uk/~curlewgw
England (North) Lake District, Yorkshire Dales, Eden,
Hadrians Wall, Bowland, Howgills • Quality
holidays/breaks.

DISCOVERY TRAVEL

12 Towthorpe Road, Haxby, York YO32 3ND.
☎/Fax 01904 766564.
Lakes, Yorks Dales and Moors • Self-guided walking
holidays including Coast to Coast.

LIGHTFOOT WALKING HOLIDAYS

Nanquitho, Calloose Lane, Leedstown, Hayle,
Cornwall TR27 5ET. ☎ (01736) 850715.
Cornish Coastal Path • Unescorted • Carefully
selected accommodation • Luggage transported.

MENDIP WALKS

51 Thornbury Road, Uphill, Weston-Super-Mare,
Somerset BS23 4YG. ☎ (01934) 418784.
Email: mendips@80days.com
Guided walks along West Mendip Way with transport
and accommodation options.

NEW FOREST WALKING CO LTD

2 Northover Road, Pennington, nr Lymington, Hants
SO41 8GW. ☎ (01590) 672938.
Email: david@newforestwalking.freeserve.co.uk
New Forest • Informative guided walks, treasure
hunts • Forest and Coast • Accommodation arranged.

THE OLD FURNACE WALKING HOLIDAYS

Greendale, Oakamoor, Staffs Moorlands ST10 3AP.
☎ (01538) 703331. http://www.oldfurnace.co.uk.
Singles guided weekends and breaks in
Staffordshire Moorlands/Derbyshire Dales.

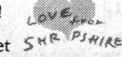
WALKING HOLIDAYS

ORCHARD TRAILS

5 Orchard Way, Horsmonden, Tonbridge,
Kent TN12 8JX. ☎/Fax (01892) 722680.
http://www.btinternet.com/~orchard.trails
Email: grabham@btinternet.com
Unescorted walking/cycling holidays. Kent and East
Sussex • Luggage transported.

RAMBLING ROADS

60 High Street South, London E6 6ET.
☎ (07944) 947764.
http://www.rambling-roads.co.uk
Email: info@rambling-roads.co.uk
England • Inclusive walking and activity breaks for all
ages and abilities.

STEP BY STEP WALKING HOLIDAYS

c/o Hambledon Hotel, Queens Road, Shanklin, Isle of
Wight PO37 6AW. ☎ (01983) 862403. Fax (01983)
863651. Isle of Wight • Guided and unescorted
walking holidays • Island coastal path •
Holiday specialists.

WALKING BREAKS

Bradfield Hall Barn, Alder Carr Farm, PO Box 82,
Needham Market IP6 8BW.
☎ 01449 721555. Fax: 01449 721707.
http://www.walkingbreaks.co.uk
Constable Country and the Suffolk coast • Self-
guided, luggage transferred, wonderful
accommodation beautiful routes.

WALKING WOMEN HOLIDAYS

22 Duke Street, Leamington, CV32 4TR.
☎/Fax: 01926 313321.
http://www.walkingwomen.com
Email: queries@walkingwomen.com
Lake District • Women's guided holidays. Small
friendly groups. All levels.

WESTCOUNTRY WALKING HOLIDAYS
(formerly A Step Ahead)

55 The Quay, Clovelly, Bideford EX39 5TF.
☎ (01237) 431436. Fax: (01237) 431919.
http://www.westcountry-walking-holidays.com
Email: mick@westcountry-walking-holidays.com
South West Coast Path, Two Moor Ways, Lundy
Island • Walking holiday packages, Luggage transport, Packed lunches. Discounts for parties of 4+

WALKING HOLIDAYS

Scotland

HIGHLAND ADVENTURE

Highland Adventure Residential and Multi-Activity Centre, Knockshannoch, Glenisla by Alyth, Perthshire PH11 8PE. ☎ (01575) 582238.
E-mail jbsmuir@highlandadventure.co.uk
http://www.highlandadventure.co.uk • Angus, Perthshire • Walking, cycling, canoeing, climbing/abseilling, nordic skiing, archerty, assault course.

MOUNTAIN INNOVATIONS

Fraoch Lodge, Deshar Road, Boat of Garten PH24 3BN. ☎/Fax (01479) 831331.
Higlands of Scotland, Cairngorms our speciality • Easy day walks to challenging expeditions • Courses • Guided independent and flight link packages • 4000ers The Big 3, Munros etc.

NORTH-WEST FRONTIERS

18a Braes, Ullapool, Ross-shire IV26 2SZ.
☎/Fax (01854) 612628.
E-mail: NWF@compuserve.com
http://www.nwfrontiers.com
Highlands & Islands • Seven day holidays at three grades • Centres include Ullapool, Skye, Torridon, Harris, Gairloch, Glen Affric • Coastal walks to mountain ridges • Established 1986.

WILD EXPOSURE GUIDED WALKS

Harbour View B&B, Badachro, Gairloch, Ross-shire IV21 2AA. ☎ (01445) 741717 Fax: (01445) 741316.
NW Highlands of Scotland inc. Torridon mountains • Day walks, expeditions, holidays, personal guiding service, all qualified guides.

Wales

Celtic Trails

Abercelyn, Llanycil, Bala LL23 7YF.
☎ (01678) 520556.
http://www.walking-wales.com
Email: walking@celtrail.com
Wales • Quality walking holidays with luggage transfer. • Offa's Dyke Path • Wye Valley Walk • Glyndwr's Way • Pembrokeshire Coast Path • Snowdonia Trail.

HILLSCAPE WALKING HOLIDAYS

Blaen-Y-Ddôl, Pontrhdygroes, Ystrad Meurig SY25 6DS. ☎ (01974) 282640
http://www.wales-walking.co.uk
Mid Wales • The specialists in self-guided walking holidays. ★★★ guesthouse accommodation.

MARCHES WALKS

Footsteps, Cwmbach, Glasbury on Wye, Powys HR3 5LT. ☎ 01497 847149.
E-mail: ryb@marches-walks.co.uk
A holiday to remember, with friendly and homely accommodation, transportation, guided/unguided walks, incorporating the Black Mountains, Brecon Beacons, Offa's Dyke Path and the Wye Valley Walk. Brochure available.

WELSH WAYFARING HOLIDAYS

Neuadd Arms Hotel, Llanwrtyd Wells LD54 4RB.
℅ (01591) 610236. • Mid Wales • Guided and Self-guided walking in Welsh Lake District. Ensuite accommodation in family run hotel (see also display adverts in B&B and Group sections).

WYSK WALKS

Church Farm, Mitchell Troy, Monmouth, Gwent NP25 4HZ. ☎ (01600) 712176.
Guided and self-guided walkers • Wye Valley, Black Mountains, Offa's Dyke Path and Wye Valley Walk • Character accommodation. See also B&B section.

Ireland

WALKING HOLIDAYS

Public Transport

The Ramblers' Association enthusiastically supports initiatives which facilitate the use of public transport in the countryside and which help people from towns and cities to reach the countryside, particularly in the very popular walking areas.

In previous years we have used these pages to publish the enquiry lines for each local authority but this system has now been changed to that of a **national enquiry line**. This is available from 0700–2000 daily and the number is **0870 6082608** (charged at national rate). You'll get the call centre nearest to where you are phoning from, but you can be put through on request to the area in which you require information is further afield.

The **Countrygoer** project, which formerly published an annual travel guide and newsletters for its subscribers, is now providing information from its website only. The sites address is www.countrygoer.org and there are no plans at present for further editions on paper.

Another good source of information is *Doe's Directory of Bus and Train Timetables* and *The Great Britain Bus Timetable*.

Train Bus and Coach Hotline gives timetable information on all trains, express coaches and local bus services throughout Great Britain. Call 0906 5500000 between 0700–2200 daily.

There is a lot of useful of public transport information on the Internet, quite an amount of which has been gathered in the form of links onto a website named http://website.lineone.net/~travelinfo one of the links being the UK Public Transport Information site. If you want to access this directly call them up on www.pti.org.uk.

National Parks

Below is a summary of the present arrangements in the National Parks of England and Wales. Funding for these schemes is variable and details may well alter, information is correct as at 1st October 2000.

The contact details for each park are listed in the *Useful Addresses* section of this book.

All 11 National Parks can be easily accessed by public transport – some very well served, others requiring more careful planning. For more details see the Countrygoer website (qv).

BRECON BEACONS

The town of Brecon is the centre for bus services. Abergavenny is the best centre for access by rail.

On Sundays and Bank Holidays there is the Beacons Bus network throughout the Park, and the Beacons Bike Bus from Cardiff operates parallel to the Taff Trail up to Brecon. Special tickets are available with integrated rail services to and from Cardiff.

More details
Park and Visitor Information: 01874 623156.
Public Transport Information: 01597 526643 (Powys) and 01495 355444 (Blaenau Gwent).
Best centres without a car: Brecon, Abergavenny.

THE BROADS

Most easily accessed by rail from Norwich to Lowestoft and Great Yarmouth. There is a basic bus service out to the villages and nearby market towns from these centres. Beccles is another option for rail access.

More details
Broads Authority Information: 01603 610734.
Public Transport Information: 0845 300 6116 (Norfolk) and 0845 958 3358 (Suffolk).
Best centres without a car: Norwich, Lowestoft, Great Yarmouth.

DARTMOOR

Rail links from the Great Western Lines by the Tamar Valley line from Plymouth to Gunnislake, and by the Dartmoor Line (weekends in summer only) between Exeter, Crediton and Okehampton.

Devonbus 82 (Transmoor Link) goes through the Park from Plymouth to Exeter, and Devonbus 86 skirts the northern perimeter. Also there is the Dartmoor Sunday Rover service connecting with trains to Okehampton and Gunnislake, going into the Park.

More details

Park and Visitor Information: 01822 890414.

Public Transport Information: 01392 382800.

Best centres without a car: Okehampton, Tavistock, Moretonhampstead.

EXMOOR

Rail access is by Great Western main line to the south, the Barnstaple-Exeter (Tarka Trail) line to the west, and West Somerset Railway (Bishop's Lydeard-Minehead) to the east. These link with the Barnstaple-Lynton (13) bus which covers the Park area.

More details

Park and Visitor Information: 01598 741321.

Public Transport Information: 01392 382800.

Best centres without a car: Lynton, Lynmouth, Minehead, Ilfracombe.

LAKE DISTRICT

There is an extensive network of bus, rail and boat services, the main link through the Park being the 555 service, which links Lancaster, Kendal, Ambleside, Grasmere and Keswick with Windermere rail station, for access to the west coast main line.

More details

Park and Visitor Information: 01539 724555.

Public Transport Information: 01228 606000.

Best centres without a car: Ambleside, Windermere, Bowness, Keswick.

NORTHUMBERLAND

Although relatively underpopulated, there is a good service to the south of the Park by Tyne Valley rail and bus 685 from Newcastle to Carlisle. There is also a Hadrian's Wall Bus daily through the summer.

Less extensive but still quite good are services to Rothbury and Thropton, linking to the East Coast main line at Morpeth; and Wooler, accessible from Berwick, but careful planning is needed.

More details

Park and Visitor Information: 01434 605555.

Public Transport Information: 0870 608 2608.

Best centres without a car: Hexham, Haltwhistle, Rothbury.

NORTH YORK MOORS

All year round there are regular seven-day train and bus services in the North and East from Teesside, York and Scarborough, and rather less frequent, weekdays only services in the South and West.

In addition during spring and summer there is the Moorbus service (unlimited travel tickets available) to areas not normally serviced by public transport. Moorsbus operates Sundays and Bank Holidays from April to October with a seven-day service during the school holidays.

More details

Park and Visitor Information: 01439 770657.

Public Transport Information: Moorsbus 01439 770657, general timetables from TICs and Park Centres.

Best centres without a car: Whitby, Scarborough, Helmsley, Pickering.

PEAK DISTRICT

For the busiest of the National Parks the key rail service is the Hope Valley Line (Manchester-Sheffield via Edale) with other services from Manchester to Glossop in the north of the Park, Buxton (centre) and Matlock (south).

Extensive bus services cover the area: Trans-Peak services (Manchester-Buxton-Derby-Nottingham via Bakewell).

PUBLIC TRANSPORT

X23 Peak Express (Stoke on Trent-Sheffield via Axe Edge, Buxton and Bakewell).
X1 (Manchester-Derby via Leek) serves the Manifold Valley.
57/58 goes over the Cat & Fiddle Pass from Macclesfield to Buxton.
173 (Bakewell, Monsall Head, Castleton).
442 (Buxton-Hartington via Manifold Valley, Dovedale and the High Peak cycleway).

Additional to these all-year routes on summer Sundays and Bank Holidays the Park Authority promote several leisure routes, from neighbouring town and cities such as Sheffield, Barnsley, Huddersfield, Derby and Manchester, into the Park.

More details
Park and Visitor Information: 01629 813227.
Public Transport Information: 01298 23098.
Best centres without a car: Buxton, Bakewell, Castleton, Matlock.

PEMBROKESHIRE COAST
Easily accessed by the West Wales railway line from Swansea and Carmarthen to Pembroke (via Tenby) and Milford Haven.

There is a bus service to the south-eastern corner of the Park but west of Pembroke is less well served.

Bus service 411 links Haverfordwest with St David's, but careful planning is needed as some services in this area don't run on Sundays. The walking and cycling areas around Narberth and Cleddau area are served by a Greenways project run by the South Pembrokeshire Action for Rural Communities Project (SPARC ☎ 01834 860965) which links local bus and train services.

More details
Park and Visitor Information: 01437 764636.
Public Transport Information: 01437 775227.
Best centres without a car: Tenby, Pembroke, St David's, Narberth (see SPARC details above).

SNOWDONIA
Best access is by rail from the North Wales Coast line from Crewe and Manchester (via Chester for trains from London) to Llandudno to meet the Conwy Valley Line to Blaenau Ffestiniog. In summer this meets the Festiniog narrow gauge railway.

Bus links are extensive and very good into the northern part of the Park around Snowdon itself, from Llandudno, Betwys y Coed, Bangor, and Caernarvon, and from Porthmadog to Llanberis. All these use the Snowdon Sherpa service.

The southern part of the Park is served by rail from Birmingham and Shrewsbury via the Cambrian Coast Line. The 94 bus from Wrexham to Barmouth via Llangollen, Bala and Dolgellau being the main road option.

More details
Park and Visitor Information: 01690 710426.
Public Transport Information: 01286 679535 (Gwynedd), 01492 574000 (Conwy).
Best centres without a car: Llanberis, Betwys y Coed, Bedgellert, Llanwrst, Porthmadog, Barmouth, Llandudno.

YORKSHIRE DALES
Excellent rail services from the south serve the two main start points to this Park, Ilkley and Skipton. There is also the Leeds-Carlisle line via Settle, Horton, Ribblehead, Dent, Garsdale, and Kirkby Stephen. There are also less frequent minibus links from Garsdale to Hawes, Dent to Dentdale, and Sedbergh and the Howgills (summer only). During spring and summer there are regular weekday buses form Skipton and Ilkley into Upper Wharfedale, and from Lancaster to Ingleton – the Dalesbus network cover most of the area. Peak summer also have direct buses from Manchester, Teesside and County Durham. The winter months have very irregular services and careful planning is needed.

More details
Park and Visitor Information: 01756 752774.
Public Transport Information: 0870 608 2608 (NYorks), 0113 245 7676 (WYorks), 01228 606000 (Cumbria).
Best centres without a car: Grassington, Settle, Hawes.

Equipment Directory

An alphabetical listing by town of as many shops as we could find space for. Please note that any discount offered is at the retailer's discretion and is not a membership entitlement.
For a list of MILLETT'S stores see the two-sided colour advert at the end of this book.

Marshall Ltd, 186 George Street, **Aberdeen**
☎ 01224 636952

Graham Tiso, 26 Netherkirkgate, **Aberdeen**
☎ 01224 634934

Badlands, 40c Great Darkgate Street, **Aberystwyth**
☎ 01970 625453

Walkabout, 3 East St. Helens Street, **Abingdon**, Oxon
☎ 01235 527704

H M Supplies, 27 Grosvenor Road, **Aldershot**
☎ 01252 342788

Wild Spirit, Greenwell Road, **Alnwick**,
Northumberland ☎ 01665 604961

The Climbers Shop, Compston Corner, **Ambleside**
☎ 015394 32297

Cunningham Stewart, 1-2 Rydal Road, **Ambleside**
☎ 015394 32636

Gaynor Sports, Market Cross, **Ambleside**
☎ 015394 33305

Hawkshead, 10 Market Cross, **Ambleside**
☎ 015394 31054, Direct orders ☎ 0990 434000

Fox's, 1 London Road, **Amersham**, Bucks
☎ 01494 431431

Amersham Outdoor Sports, 11 Hill Avenue,
Amersham, Bucks ☎ 01494 722574

Peglers, 69 Tarrant Street, **Arundel**, W Sussex
☎ 01903 883375

Track & Trail, 30-32 St John St, **Ashbourne**
☎ 01335 346403

Outdoor Action, 214 Stamford St, **Ashton under Lyne**
☎ 0161-343 2151

Frasers of Ayr,47 Burns Statue Square, **Ayr**,
Strathclyde ☎ 01292 266029

Track Trail, Gramby Croft, **Bakewell**, Derbys
☎ 01629 815483

Mid Antrim Camping, 20 Broughshane Street,
Ballymena, Co Antrim ☎ 01266 47187

Hitch 'n' Hike, High Peak Garden Centre, **Bamford**,
Hope Valley, Derbys ☎ 01433 651013

Four Seasons, 44 The Bank, **Barnard Castle**, Co
Durham ☎ 01833 637829

John Pollock, 67 High Street, **Barnet**, Herts
☎ 020 8440 3994

Barnsley Outdoor Centre, 35 Peel Parade, **Barnsley**,
W Yorks ☎ 01226 200120

The Outdoor Centre, Gisburn Road, **Barrowford**,
Lancs ☎ 01282 611129

B C H Camping & Leisure, 30 Southgate, **Bath**
☎ 01225 460200

Itchy Feet, 4 Bartlett Street, **Bath**
☎ 01225 337987

Rickards of Bath, 11 Northumberland Place, **Bath**
☎ 01225 464107

Oswald Bailey, 8 The Mall, Southgate, **Bath**
☎ 01225 463202

Two Seasons, 42 Harpur St, **Bedford**
☎ 01234 350720

Home Stores, 433 Lisburn Road, **Belfast**
☎ 028 9038 1284

Beverley Walking Centre, 2 Butcher Row, **Beverley**,
Humberside ☎ 01482 861908

BJ Camping & Clothing, High Street, **Billericay**,
Essex ☎ 01277 624372

Taunton Leisure, 1045 Stratford Road, Hall Green,
Birmingham ☎ 0121-777 3337

Camping & Outdoor Centre, 62 New Street,
Birmingham ☎ 0121-643 0885

Snow & Rock, 14 Priory Queensway, **Birmingham**
☎ 0121-236 8280

YHA Adventure Shops, 90-98 Corporation Street,
Birmingham ☎ 0121-236 7799

Windrow Sports, 5-7 Fore Bondgate, **Bishop
Auckland**, Durham ☎ 01388 603759

Outdoor Action, 26 King Street, **Blackburn**, Lancs
☎ 01254 671945

Odlo, Ardblair Sports Importers, Yard Road,
Blairgowrie, Perthshire ☎ 01250 873863

Polaris, Bolsover Business Park, **Bolsover**,
☎ 01246 240218

Outdoor World, 79-83 Rimrose Road, **Bootle**
☎ 0151-944 2202

Camping & Outdoor Centre, 7 Gervis Place,
Bournemouth ☎ 01202 558797

Allan Austin, Jacob Street Mills, Manchester Road,
Bradford ☎ 01274 728674

Out and About, 2 Elcho Street, **Brae,** Peebles
☎ 01721 723590

Jons Work & Leisure Store, 11 Sandpit Lane,
Braintree, Essex ☎ 01376 320436

Field & Trek, 23-25 & 41 Kings Road, **Brentwood**
☎ 01277 222230 and mail order ☎ 01277 494444

Camping & Outdoor Centre, 24 St James's Street,
Brighton ☎ 01273 684281

YHA Adventure Shops, 126-127 Queen's Road,
Brighton 01273 821554

YHA Adventure Shops, 10-12 Fairfax Street, **Bristol**
☎ 0117-929 7141

Oswald Bailey, 61 Horsefair, **Bristol**
☎ 0117-929 3523

Taunton Leisure, 72 Bedminster Parade, **Bristol**
☎ 0117-963 7640

Camping & Outdoor Centre, 9-10 Transom House,
Victoria Street, **Bristol** ☎ 0117-926 4892

Kingswood Caravan & Camping Centre, 137-145 High
Street, Kingswood, **Bristol** ☎ 0117-960 0205

Marcruss Stores, 181 Hotwells Road, **Bristol**
☎ 0117-929 7427
Landmark, 45 High Street, **Broadway**, Worcs ☎
01386 854995
Oswald Bailey, High Street, **Bromsgrove,** Hereford &
Worcester ☎ 01527 871562
Stepping Out, 55 St John's Street, **Bury St Edmunds,**
Suffolk ☎ 01284 763150
H M Supplies, 157-159 London Road, **Camberley,**
Surrey ☎ 01276 20550
Hughes, 92 Mill Road, **Cambridge** ☎ 01223 576611
Open Air Cambridge Ltd, 29 Green Street, **Cambridge**
☎ 01223 324666
YHA Adventure Shops, 6-7 Bridge Street, **Cambridge**
☎ 01223 353956
Field & Trek, 3 Palace Street, **Canterbury,** Kent
☎ 01227 470023
Camping & General, Charlfleets, **Canvey Island,**
Essex ☎ 01268 692141
Up & Under, 490 Cowbridge Road East, Victoria Park,
Cardiff CF5 1BL ☎ 029 2057 8579
YHA Adventure Shops,13 Castle Street, **Cardiff**
☎ 029 2039 9178
Cardiff Sportsgear, 81 Whitchurch Road, **Cardiff**
☎ 029 2062 1757
Camping & Outdoor Centre, 10 Duke Street, **Cardiff**
☎ 029 2039 0887
The Old Barn, Market place, **Castleton,** Sheffield
☎ 01433 620528
Bowden James & Sons, 50-54 The Square, **Chagford,**
Devon ☎ 01647 433271
Kent Camping, 39-41 High Street, **Chatham,** Kent
☎ 01634 402255
Outdoor Pursuits Centre, 38-40 High Street,
Chatham, Kent ☎ 01634 826582
The Gorge Outdoors, Hanlith House, **Cheddar**
☎ 01934 742688
Ski Plus, Navigation Road, **Chelmsford,** Essex
☎ 01245 264143
Backpackers, 44 Winchcombe St, **Cheltenham** ☎
01242 242200
Snow & Rock, 99 Fordwater Road, **Chertsey,** Surrey
☎ 01932 566886
Camp & Climb, 95-97 Brook Street, **Chester**
☎ 01244 311174
Yeomans Army Stores Head Office, The Warehouse,
Markham Road, **Chesterfield** ☎ 01246 232419
Nevisport, 26-28 Park Road, **Chesterfield,**
☎ 01246 201437
Rohan, 1 Priory Lane Shopping Centre, Northgate,
Chichester, W Sussex ☎ 01243 787214
Oswald Bailey, 2 Saxon Square, **Christchurch,** Dorset
☎ 01202 483043
Tent Direct UK Ltd, 23a Castle St, **Cirencester,** Glos
☎ ☎ 01285 641401
Outdoor World, Kingsway Sports, 139 Grimsby Road,
Cleethorpes, Humberside ☎ 01472 601616
Ken Varey, 4 New Market Street, **Clitheroe,** Lancs
☎ 01200 23267

Outdoors, 16 Short Wyre Street, **Colchester,** Essex
☎ 01206 577040
Hawkshead, 5 Yewdale Road, **Coniston**
☎ 01539 441822, Direct orders ☎ 0990 434000
Conwy Outdoor Shop, 9 Castle Street, **Conwy,**
Gwynedd ☎ 01492 593390
Kit Bag, 121 Far Gosford Street, **Coventry,** Warks
☎ 024 7622 2624
Jacksons of Old Arley, Unit 8 Springhill Industrial
Estate, Arley, **Coventry,** Warks ☎ 01676 540878
OBI Camping Centre, 5 Westgate Street, **Cowbridge,**
S Glamorgan ☎ 01446 772498
Camping & Outdoor Centre, 37-39 George's Walk,
Croydon ☎ 020 8688 1730
Field & Trek, 32 Church Street, **Croydon,** Surrey
☎ 020 8680 8798
Sgt. Pepper, 27 Bonnygate, **Cupar,** Fife
☎ 01334 654862
Simpsons Sports, Post House Wynd, **Darlington**
☎ 01325 381068
Tracks, 47 Queen Street, **Derby**
☎ 01332 342245
Birds of Dereham, 4-8A Norwich Street, **Dereham,**
Norfolk ☎ 01362 692941

Don Valley, Littleworth Lane, Old Rossington, Nr
Doncaster, S Yorks ☎ 01302 868408
Great Western Camping, 35 Great Western Road,
Dorchester ☎ 01305 266800
Dorchester Rambler, 40 Trinity Street, **Dorchester**
☎ 01305 251411
Pattie's of Dumfries, 109 Queensberry Street,
Dumfries ☎ 01387 252891
The Great Escape, 80/90 Friars Vennel, **Dumfries**
☎ 01387 267327
Munros Specialist Outdoor Shop, 14 Bank Street,
Aberfeldy, **Dundee** ☎ 01887 820008
Summits Ltd, 5 Bridge Street, **Dunfermline,** Fife
☎ 01383 730181
The North Sea Outlet, 53 The Plaza, **East Kilbride**
☎ 013552 38383
Oswald Bailey, 15 Market Street, **Eastleigh,** Hants
☎ 023 8061 3238
Nevisport Ltd, 81 Shandwick Place, **Edinburgh**
☎ 0131-229 1197

Camping & Outdoor Centre, 77 Southbridge, **Edinburgh** ☎ 0131-225 3339
One Step Ahead, 177 Morningside Road, **Edinburgh** ☎ 0131-447 0999
The Outdoor Trading Co, 73 South Clark Street, **Edinburgh**.☎ 0131-662.8057
Leith Army Stores, 7-10 Brunswick Place, **Edinburgh** ☎ 0131-556 2337
Graham Tiso, Rose Street Precinct, **Edinburgh** ☎ 0131-225 9486
BAC Outdoor Leisure, Central Hall, Coronation St, **Elland**, W Yorks ☎ 01422 371146
Taunton Leisure, 110 Fore Street, **Exeter** ☎ 01392 410534
Challenge Sports, 25 Bank Street, **Falkirk** ☎ 01324 612328
Cornish Rambler, 11 Arwenack Street, **Falmouth**, Cornwall ☎ 01326 314760
Breaking Free, 6 Town Hall Building, The Borough, **Farnham** ☎ 01252 724347
Boots & Saddle Wear, 175 Fleet Road, **Fleet**, Hants ☎ 01252 616889
S B & S Camping, The Square, **Forest Row**, E Sussex ☎ 01342 822740
The Outdoor Store, 97 High Street, **Forfar**, Tayside ☎ 01307 465471
Leisure Time, 10 The Esplanade, **Fowey**, Cornwall ☎ 01726 832207
Barrets of Feckenham, Selby Road, **Garforth**, LS25 2AQ ☎ 0113 286 7976
Camping International Superstore, Clock Tower House, Watling Street, **Gillingham** ☎ 01634 577326
Outside Now, 316 Byres Road, **Glasgow** ☎ 0141-339 2202
Graham Tiso, 129 Buchanan Street, **Glasgow** ☎ 0141-248 4877
Adventure 1, 38 Dundas Street, **Glasgow** G1 ☎ 0141-353 3788
New Heights, 200 Great Western Road, **Glasgow** G4 ☎ 0141-332 5533
Catstycam, The Outdoor Shop, **Glenridding**, Cumbria ☎ 017684 82351
Field & Trek, 74 Westgate Street, **Gloucester** ☎ 01452 416549
Oswald Bailey, 24 The Oxebode, **Gloucester** ☎ 01452 305555
SK Camping, Eastbourne Road, South **Godstone**, Surrey RH9 8JG ☎ 01342 893881
Outdoor World, G.O. Red Lion Square, **Grasmere**, Cumbria ☎ 015394 35614
Vango, Kilburn Business Park, Port Glasgow, **Greenock**, Strathclyde ☎ 01475 744122
The Outdoor Scene, 4-6 Regent Arcade, Old Market Place, **Grimsby** ☎ 01472 240763 Mail order also
Rock Bottom, 19C Crown Street, Hebden Bridge, **Halifax**, W Yorks ☎ 01422 844500
Springfield Camping, Denholme Road, Burnley Rd, Luddenden Foot, **Halifax**, W Yorks ☎ 01422 883164

Cotswold, 8-10 West Park, **Harrogate** ☎ 01423 701100
Out and About, 18 Bower Road, **Harrogate** ☎ 01423 561592
Nevisport, 71 Station Parade, **Harrogate** ☎ 01423 562874
Outdoors, 324a Station Road, **Harrow**, Middx ☎ 020 8427 3809
Outdoor Trading Post, Unit 51, The Galleria, Comet Way, **Hatfield**, Herts ☎ 0800 413650
Outside Ltd, Main Road, **Hathersage**, Derbys ☎ 01433 651936 and

Outside — BRITAIN'S BEST MOUNTAIN SHOPS

Walking Boots ✔	Rucksacks	✔
Waterproofs ✔	Walking Poles	✔
Fleece Jkts ✔	Socks, Gloves etc..	✔
Lt/wt Clothing ✔	Compasses	✔
Thermals ✔	Maps & Guides	✔

EXCELLENT RANGE OF WOMEN'S EQUIPMENT

PEAK DISTRICT	SNOWDONIA	SHEFFIELD
Main Road	High Street	45 Mowbray St
Hathersage	Llanberis	Sheffield
S32 1BB	LL55 4EN	S3 8EN
01433 651936	01286 871534	0114 2797427

Filarinskis of Havant, 26-28 East Street, **Havant**, Hants ☎ 023 9249 9599
Hawkshead, Main Street, **Hawkshead**, LA22 0SW ☎ 01539 436633, Direct orders ☎ 0990 434000
Trail Traders, 17 Sussex Road, **Haywards Heath**, W Sussex ☎ 01444 452824
Footloose, Borogate, **Helmsley**, N Yorks ☎ 01439 770886
Discount Outdoors, 1 Marlowes, **Hemel Hempstead**, Herts ☎ 01442 214631
The Complete Outdoors, London Road, Bourne End, **Hemel Hempstead**, Herts ☎ 01442 873133
Campestral, Wargrave Road, **Henley on Thames**, Oxon ☎ 01491 575829
Out & About, 11 King St, **Hereford** ☎ 01432 274084
Bartletts of Hillingdon, 1-2 Rosslyn Parade, Uxbridge Road, **Hillingdon**, Middx ☎ 020 8573 2076

EQUIPMENT SHOPS

79

J & R Camping & Leisure, Eggington Road, **Hilton**, Derbys ☎ 01283 733525

Eskdale Outdoor Shop, Eskdale Green, **Holmrook**, Cumbria ☎ 019467 23229

Mountain Trail, 49 High Street, **Holywood**, N Ireland ☎ 028 9042 8529

The Outdoor Store, 10 Bishopric, **Horsham** RH12 1QR ☎ 01403 754027

Blackburns Outdoor Pursuits, 303 Old Wakefield Road, Mold Green, **Huddersfield**, W Yorks ☎ 01484 531561

Wet & Wild Adventure Sports, 619 Anlaby Road, **Hull** ☎ 01482 354076

Broadman Ltd, Wiltshire Road, **Hull** ☎ 01482 561181

Mountain Equipment, Redfern, Dawson Street, **Hyde**, Cheshire ☎ 0161 366 5020

Sports & Fashions, 51 High Street, **Huntingdon, Cambs** ☎ 01480 454541

Ilkeston Camping & Leisure, 138 Nottingham Road, **Ilkeston**, Derbys ☎ 0115-930 9457

Graham Tiso, 41 High Street, **Inverness** ☎ 01463 716617

W D Macpherson & Sons, 34 Church Street, **Inverness** ☎ 01463 711427

Craigdon Sports, Craigdon House, High Street, **Inverurie**, Grampian ☎ 01467 625855

Action Outdoors, 10 Gt Colman Street, **Ipswich**, Suffolk ☎ 01473 211647

Speaks Of Keighley Field & Fell, 3-11 Lawkholme Cres, **Keighley**, W Yorks ☎ 01535 603979

Lowe Alpine, Ann Street, **Kendal**, Cumbria ☎ 01539 740840

Kentdale Rambler, 34 Market Place, **Kendal**, Cumbria ☎ 01539 729188

Kendal Survival Shop, 1 Kent View, **Kendal**, Cumbria ☎ 01539 729699

George Fisher, 2 Borrowdale Road, **Keswick** ☎ 017687 72178

Keswick Army Supplies, Tithebarn Street, **Keswick**

Head for the Hills, 40 High Street, **Kingston-upon-Thames**, Surrey ☎ 020 8974 8882

Lang & Hunter, 12 Thames Street, **Kingston-upon-Thames**, Surrey ☎ 020 8546 5427

Ultimate Outdoors,17 New Street, **Lancaster** ☎ 01524 66610

Lockwoods, 125-129 Rugby Road, **Leamington Spa**, Warks ☎ 01926 339388

Maughans, 20 The Parade, **Leamington Spa**, Warks ☎ 01926 428685

Kathmandu Trekking, 5 Crabtree Lane, Great Bookham, **Leatherhead**, Surrey ☎ 01372 454773

Nevisport, 34 Woodhouse Lane, **Leeds** ☎ 0113-244 4715

Outdoors, 110 Albion Street, **Leeds** ☎ 0113-245 7273

YHA Adventure Shops, 119-121 Vicar Lane, **Leeds** 0113-246 5339

Centresport, 57-59 New Briggate, **Leeds**, W Yorks ☎ 0113-245 2917

The Great Outdoors, 1 Ivegate, Yeadon, **Leeds** ☎ 0113-250 4686

J & R Camping & Leisure, Byron St, Off Lee Circle, **Leicester** ☎ 0116-255 1595

Roger Turner, 52a London Road, **Leicester** ☎ 0116-255 1952

City Surplus, 79 Granby St, **Leicester** ☎ 0116-255 0208

Tracks, 22/24 Halford, **Leicester** ☎ 0116-251 7040

Canyon Mountain Sports, 92 Granby St, **Leicester** ☎ 0116-255 7957

Graham Tiso, 41 Commercial Street, **Leith** ☎ 0131-554 0804 Mailorder ☎ 01202 747096

BaseCamp One, 12/14 The Arcade, **Letchworth** ☎ 01462 486794

Sheppards Stores, Upperhill, **Leominster** ☎ 01568 720262

Ski Force Outdoor Leisure, 38 Tamworth St, **Lichfield** ☎ 01543 411422

Linsports Outdoor Centre, 21 Silver St, **Lincoln** ☎ 01522 524674

The Base Camp, 54 High Street, **Littlehampton**, W Sussex ☎ 01903 723853

Camp 'A' Tent, 92 St John's Road, Crosby, **Liverpool** L22 9QQ ☎ 0151-920 9535

YHA Adventure Shops, 25 Bold Street, **Liverpool** ☎ 0151-709 8063

Outside, Old Baptist Chapel, High Street, **Llanberis,** Gwynedd ☎ 01286 871534

Wayfarers Outdoor Leisure, Station Crescent, **Llandrindod Wells**, Powys ☎ 01597 825100

Ben Nevis Clothing,237 Royal College Street, **London** NW1 ☎ 020 7485 9989

Outdoors, 44 Birchington Road, **London** ☎ 020 7328 2166

Camping & Outdoor Centre, 41 Ludgate Hill, **London** EC4 ☎ 020 7329 8757

Joe's Outdoor Centre, 26 Station Road, **London** NW10 ☎ 020 8961 8300

Snow & Rock, 150 Holborn, **London** EC1 ☎ 020 7831 6900

Camping & Outdoor Centre, 27 Buckingham Palace Road, **London** SW1 ☎ 020 7834 6007

Decathlon, West Building, Canada Water Retail Park, Surrey Quays Rd, **London** SE16 2XU ☎ 020 7394 2000

Field & Trek, 105 Baker Street, **London** W1 ☎ 020 7224 0049

Snow & Rock, 188 Kensington High Street, **London** W8 ☎ 020 7937 0872

B T Cullum, 199 Wandsworth High Street, **London** SW18 ☎ 020 8874 2346

Tarpaulin & Tent Co, 101-103 Brixton Hill, **London** SW2 ☎ 020 86740121

Ray Ward Gunsmith, 12 Cadogan Place, **London** SW1X ☎ 01737 766715

YHA Adventure Shops, 14 Southampton Street, Covent Garden, **London** WC2 ☎ 020 7836 8541

YHA Adventure Shops, 120 Victoria Street, Victoria, **London** SW1 ☎ 020 7233 6500

Bob's Surplus Stores, 2 Rupert Road, Chiswick, **London** W4 1LX ☎ 020 8994 8665

YHA Adventure Shops, 174 Kensington High Street, **London** W8 ☎ 020 7938 2948
Crystal Palace Camping, 15-17 Central Hill, **London** ☎ 020 8766 6060
Arnolds Leisure, 154-156 Broadway, West Ealing, **London** ☎ 020 8840 7383
Backpacker, 136 Charing Cross Road, **London**, WC2 ☎ 020 7836 1160
McLains Outdoor Wear, 161 Holloway Road, **London** N7 ☎ 020 7607 8413
John Pollock, 157 High Road, **Loughton**, Essex ☎ 020 8508 6626
Mullen Marine, Kinnego Marina, **Lurgan** ☎ 01762 343911
Leisure Fayre, 60 High Street, **Lyndhurst**, Devon ☎ 023 8028 3445
Compass Point, 10 Market Square, **Lytham**, Lancs ☎ 01253 795597
Greenstiles, 4 Maen Gwyn Street, **Machynlleth** ☎ 01654 703543
Outdoors, 2-4 Granada House, Gabriels Hill, **Maidstone**, Kent ☎ 01622 763008
Cave & Crag, Cove Centre, **Malham**, N Yorks ☎ 01729 830432
Robinelt Shoes, 7 Church St, **Malvern** ☎ 01684 573904
YHA Adventure Shops, 201 Deansgate, **Manchester** ☎ 0161-834 7119
Camping & Outdoor Centre, 7 Oldham Street, **Manchester** ☎ 0161-835 1016
Jack Wolfskin, Brochure Centre, PO Box 30, **Manchester** M20 4BQ
First Ascent, Units 3-5, Limetree Business Park, **Matlock** ☎ 01629 580484
Newisport, 100 Newport Road, **Middlesbrough**, Cleveland ☎ 01642 248916
Walkmoors, 18b Park St, **Minehead**, Somerset ☎ 01643 707192
Northumbria Mountain Sports,The Chantrey, **Morpeth**, Northumberland ☎ 01670 513276
TAM Leisure, 180-186 Kingston Road, **New Malden**, Surrey ☎ 020 8949 5435
New Forest Army & Navy Stores, 62 Lymington Road, **New Milton**, Hants ☎ 01425 638220
Metro Angling Centre, 14 Garden Walk, Metro Centre, **Newcastle-upon-Tyne** ☎ 0191-460 8733
Freemans Campingr Centre, 1 Bigg Market, **Newcastle-upon-Tyne** ☎ 0191-232 1646
M L Great Outdoors, 89/98 Grainger Market, **Newcastle-upon-Tyne** ☎ 0191-261 8371
Traveller, 1st Floor 55 Grey St, **Newcastle-upon-Tyne** ☎ 0191-261 5622
Nevisport, 100-104 Grainger Street, **Newcastle-upon-Tyne** ☎ 0191-232 4941
White & Bishop Ltd, 13-17 Bridge Street, **Northampton** NN1 1NL ☎ 01604 230901.
Gilroy Wilson Shoes, 7 Market Street, **Northwich**, Cheshire ☎ 01606 42577
Outdoors, Boston House, 5 Orford Hill, **Norwich** ☎ 01603 625645

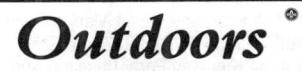

Norwich Camping Company, 56 Magdalen Street, **Norwich** ☎ 01603 615525

Venturesport, 17 Westlegate, **Norwich** ☎ 01603 613378

Outdoors, 3-7 St James's Street, **Nottingham** ☎ 0115-948 4571

Castle Mountain & Moor, 40-44 Maid Marian St, **Nottingham** ☎ 0115-941 4059

Kit Bag, 22 Pool Bank Street, **Nuneaton**, Warks ☎ 024 7664 1033

Nancy Black, 18-19, Argyll Square, **Oban**, Strathclyde ☎ 01631 562550

Caseys, Stephen Smith's Garden Centre, Pool Rd, **Otley**, W Yorks ☎ 01943 465462

Chevin Trek, 34 Gay Lane, **Otley** ☎ 01943 851166

Camping & Outdoor Centre, 17 Turl Street, **Oxford** ☎ 01865 247110

YHA Adventure Shops, 9-10 St Clements (The Plain), **Oxford** ☎ 01865 247948

Touchwood Sports, 107 St Aldates, **Oxford** ☎ 01865 725220

Touchwood Sports, 426 Abingdon Road, **Oxford** ☎ 01865 246551

Summits Outdoor Gear, 36 Moor Street, **Paisley**, Strathclyde ☎ 0141-887 5536

The Castle Warehouse, 1 Greenside, 4 Upland Way **Peebles**, EH45 8JA ☎ 01721 723636

Penrith Survival Equipment, The Square, **Penrith**, Cumbria ☎ 01931 714444

Outdoor Adventure, 6 Hereward Cross, Broadway, **Peterborough**, Cambs ☎ 01733 341381

Wright Outdoors, 5-7 Lincoln Road, **Peterborough**, Cambs ☎ 01733 312184

Camping & Outdoor Centre, 4-6 Royal Parade, **Plymouth** ☎ 01752 662614

YHA Adventure Shops, 105 New George Street, **Plymouth** ☎ 01752 665615

Tordoff, Jubilee Way, **Pontefract**, W Yorks ☎ 01977 702002

Outdoor Adventure, 34 Station Road, Lower Parkstone, **Poole**, Dorset ☎ 01202 735639

Oswald Bailey, 31-33 Kingland Crescent, **Poole**, Dorset ☎ 01202 675495

Wolfpack Trading Post, 52 Commercial Road, **Poole**

Gelert, Bryncir Products, Gelert House, Unit 2, Penamser Industrial Estate, **Porthmadog**, Gwynedd ☎ 01766 512412

Jansport, Wentworth Street, **Portree**, Isle of Skye ☎ 01478 612559

Mountain Top Products, 48 St Mary's Road, **Portsmouth**, Hants ☎ 023 9273 0667

Safari, Unit 44 Kingwell Path, Cascade Shopping Centre, **Portsmouth** ☎ 023 9282 9410

Out 'n' About, 25 Breck Road, **Poulton-le-Fylde**, Lancs ☎ 01253 892445

Leisure Croft, 279 Victoria Road, **Prestatyn** ☎ 01745 853646

Outdoors, 23 Miller Arcade, **Preston**, Lancs ☎ 01772 250242

Outdoor Action, 132 Church St, **Preston**, Lancs ☎ 01772 561970

Grips, 58 Eastwood Road, **Rayleigh**, Essex ☎ 01268 776661

Alt Berg, 14 Finkle Street, **Richmond**, North Yorkshire ☎ 01748 826922

Milletts Camping & Countrywear, Unit 7 The Furlong Centre, **Ringwood**, Hants ☎ 01425 480047

Royston Outdoor, 13 Kneesworth Street, **Royston**, Herts ☎ 01763 243195

White & Bishop, 29-31 Clifton Road, **Rugby**, Warks ☎ 01604 230901

Backpack Caravan, 13 Hill St, **Saffron Walden**, Essex ☎ 01799 525639

Outdoor Gear Ltd, 17 Cross Keys, Chequer, **Salisbury** ☎ 01722 331290

Edlas, 16 Winchester Street, **Salisbury** ☎ 01722 327316

Oswald Bailey, Old George Mall, **Salisbury** ☎ 01722 328689

YHA Adventure Shops, 9 Priory Square, The Maltings, **Salisbury** ☎ 01722 422122

Crag & Moor, 38 Victoria Rd, **Scarborough**, N Yorks ☎ 01723 368777

Lyon Equipment, Dent, **Sedbergh**, Cumbria ☎ 015396 25493

Castleberg Sports, Cheapside, **Settle**, N Yorks ☎ 01729 823751

Cave & Crag, Market Place, **Settle**, N Yorks ☎ 01729 823877

Godfreys, Otford Road, **Sevenoaks**, Kent ☎ 01732 741177

Foothills, 11 Edgedale Rd, **Sheffield** ☎ 0114-258 6228

Outside, Mowbray Street, **Sheffield** ☎ 0114-279 7427

Camping & Outdoors, 13 Castle Foregate, **Shrewsbury** ☎ 01743 355168

Hawkshead, 15 Craven Court, **Skipton** ☎ 01756 700319, Direct orders ☎ 0990 434000

Craven Rambler, 19 Coach St, **Skipton**, N Yorks ☎ 01756 796166

Sleat Trading, Armadale Pier, **Sleat**, Isle of Skye ☎ 01471 844265

Field & Trek, 313 High Street, **Slough**, Bucks ☎ 01753 554252

Four Points, 12-13 The Village Shopping Centre, High Street, **Slough**, Bucks ☎ 01753 691027

Oswald Bailey, 48 Station Road, **Solihull** ☎ 0121-705 3226

McRed's Ramble In, 74 Dean Road, **South Shields** ☎ 0191-456 6402

Camping & Outdoor Centre, 9 East Street, **Southampton** ☎ 023 8033 4462

Oswald Bailey, 109 Above Bar Street, **Southampton** ☎ 023 8033 3687

YHA Adventure Shops, 14 High Street, **Southampton** ☎ 023 8023 5847

Hill & Dale, 39 Burnley Rd, **Sowerby Bridge** ☎ 01422 833360

Breaking Away, 36 London Road, **St Albans**, Herts ☎ 01727 833586

Day & Night Stores, 140-142 St Albans Road, **St Annes,** Blackpool ☎ 01253 726800

EQUIPMENT SHOPS

County Wise, 6 Victoria Place, **St Austell**, Cornwall
☎ 01726 70780

Weathergear & Cornish Industrial Supplies, 42
Polkyth Road, **St Austell**, Cornwall ☎ 01726 66183

YHA Adventure Shops, 133 High Street, **Staines**,
Middx ☎ 01784 452987

County Hardware Ltd, Unit 6, Ind Estate, **St Columb
Major**, Cornwall ☎ 01637 881275

Countryside Ski & Climb, 118 High St, **Stevenage**,
Herts ☎ 0800 353086

Alpenstock, 35 St Petersgate, **Stockport**
☎ 0161-480 3660

Blake Maurice Ltd, 12 Mill Road, **Stokenchurch**,
Bucks ☎ 01494 483971

Hi-Peak Leisure Ltd, Stafford House, Clouth St,
Hanley, **Stoke-on-Trent**, Staffs ☎ 01782 268102

The Outdoor Shop, 27-31 High St, **Stony Stratford**,
Bucks ☎ 01908 568913

Stowmarket Caravan & Leisure Centre, Bury Road,
Stowmarket, Suffolk ☎ 01449 612677

Geoff Turner, Outdoor People, Unit 11, Charles Ind.
Estate, Stowupland Road, **Stowmarket**, Suffolk
☎ 01449 675511

Hawkshead, 6/7 High Street, **Stratford-upon-Avon**
☎ 01789 267004, Direct orders ☎ 0990 434000

Rohan Designs, 23-24 Wood St, **Stratford-upon-
Avon**, Warks ☎ 01789 414498

M L Great Outdoors,9 The Bridges, **Sunderland**, Tyne
& Wear ☎ 0191-567 2727

Reynolds Outdoor Centre, 6 Derwent Street,
Sunderland, Tyne & Wear ☎ 0191-565 7945

Ranger, 10 Central Parade, St Marks Hill, **Surbiton**,
Surrey ☎ 020 8399 9995

SSS Camping Centre, 9 Market St, Huthwaite, **Sutton
in Ashfield**, Notts ☎ 01623 511181

Midwest Camping, Wyndley Garden Centre, Lichfield
Road, **Sutton Coldfield** ☎ 0121-308 7279

Taunton Leisure, 206 High St, **Swansea**
☎ 01792 476515

Leisure Quest, Parc Tawe, The Piazza, Oasis Park,
Swansea ☎ 01792 646647

Taunton Leisure, 40 East Reach, **Taunton**
☎ 01823 332987

Somerset Camping & Caravan, 38 Bridgwater Road,
Walford Cross, **Taunton**, Somerset ☎ 01823 413333

The Wearhouse, 32 North Street, **Taunton**
☎ 01823 333291

Country Kit, 22-23 West Street, **Tavistock,** Devon
☎ 01822 613089

Supersales of Totnes, 90 High Street, **Totnes**, Devon
☎ 01803 862737

Elements Outdoor Leisure, 71 High Street, **Totnes**,
Devon ☎ 01803 862255

BCH Camping & Leisure, 8-12 Islington, **Trowbridge**,
Wilts ☎ 01225 764977

Rohan Travel & Leisure, Town Quay, **Truro**, Cornwall
☎ 01872 260042

Country Trails, 39 Mount Pleasant, **Tunbridge Wells**,
Kent ☎ 01892 539002

Adventure Shop, 83 Clayton St, **Tyneside**
☎ 0191-233 1572

Countrywise, 27 Molesworth Street, **Wadebridge**,
Cornwall ☎ 01208 812423

Outdoor Focus at Rentatent, Twitch Hill, Horbury,
Wakefield ☎ 01924 275131

Mitchells, Hostingley Lane, Middlestown, **Wakefield**
☎ 01924 272877

Kenmar Camping & Leisure, Spring Green Nurseries,
Pontefract Road, Sharleston, **Wakefield**
☎ 01924 864494

White Mountain, 31a Stafford Street, **Walsall**, W
Mids ☎ 01922 722422

Whites, 147 Warrington Market, **Warrington**
☎ 01925 631531

Outdoor World, Mersey Building, Winwick Road,
Warrington, Cheshire ☎ 01925 634794

Adventure Centre, Evans House, Orford Lane,
Warrington, Cheshire ☎ 01925 411385

Cheshire Leisure, 30-42 Knutsford Road, **Warrington**,
Cheshire ☎ 01925 630554

Escape Two, 29 Emscote Road, **Warwick**
☎ 01926 493929

Waterlooville Camping & Angling, 157a London
Road, Waterlooville, Hants ☎ 02392 250699.

Tradewinds, 4 Park Road, **Wellingborough**,
Northants ☎ 01933 276632

W Alexander Ltd, 29 Broad St, **Welshpool**
☎ 01938 552329

Marcruss Stores, 52 Meadow Street, **Weston-super-
Mare**, Avon ☎ 01934 415041

Outdoor World, 49 Ilfracombe Gardens, **Whitley Bay**,
Tyne & Wear ☎ 0191-251 4388

Hugh Lewis & Sons, 29-31 Moor Lane, **Widnes**,
Cheshire ☎ 0151-424 7316

Active Leisure (Standish), Cannells Garden Centre,
Back Lane, Appley Bridge, **Wigan**, Lancs
☎ 01257 422945

Oswald Bailey, 5 Crown Mead Centre, **Wimborne**,
Dorset ☎ 01202 880366

Up & Away of **Winchester**

Hawkshead, King Edward Court, **Windsor**
☎ 01753 831036, Direct orders ☎ 0990 434000

CTC (Whitney), 89-91 Corn St, **Witney**
☎ 01993 771080

Midwest Camping, Codsall Garden Centre, Codsall,
Wolverhampton ☎ 01902 845404

White Mountain, 22 Worcester Street,
Wolverhampton, W Mids ☎ 01902 773395

Hillfolk, 28-32 High Street, **Wooler**, Northumberland
☎ 01668 281735

The Wearhouse, 21 The Cross, **Worcester**
☎ 01905 617727

Camping & Outdoor Centre, 20 Brighton Road,
Worthing, Sussex ☎ 01903 232028

The Wearhouse, 84 Middle Street, **Yeovil**, Somerset
☎ 01935 71260

Nevisport, 8 St.Sampsons Square, **York**
☎ 01904 679263

Camping & Outdoor Centre, 3 Queen's House, Mickle
Gate, **York** ☎ 01904 653567

The Accommodation Guide

There are four parts to the Guide.

Hostels and Bunkhouses;

Accommodation Suitable for Groups;

Self-catering Accommodation;

Bed & Breakfast.

These are followed by the *Accommodation Index* which we hope will help you find accommodation in a particular place rather than of a certain sort.

On pages 289–304 you will find the maps section. These maps show the location of all accommodation except that of the Self-catering section. The self-catering locations are omitted because they can often be quite approximately stated due to being remote from a centre of population. It just makes it too complicated.

The listings in the guide are organised by country, then county order. Sometimes we have banded together authorities which are small in size or where there are fewer listings — in particular, central Scotland, north east Scotland, north east Wales and south Wales. The same method is used for all the accommodation sections. We hope you can find your way around.

Tourist Board classifications are given for those establishments who have applied for and been awarded them. This year the English Tourist Board became the English Tourism Council. They have agreed a common standard with the AA and RAC. This means that, in England, some of the establishments may have the AA or RAC rating given instead. This only applies to England. Some establishments still list awards from an older system, using Crowns, because they had not been inspected by the time we required their information. Next year all establishments should be using the new system. The system is 1–5 stars for hotels and 1–5 diamonds for smaller guest accommodation. Self-catering establishments in England still use the keys system, 1–4 keys, with commended and highly commended. In addition there are Silver and Gold awards for excellence. In Scotland and Wales the 1–5 Stars system is still in use for all serviced accommodation. Additionally, in Wales, either Grades (1, 2, 3 etc.) or Dragons are used for self-catering. In Ireland establishments are graded by Stars. Other Tourist Board awards are for holiday parks and these are Rose (England), Thistle (Scotland) and Ticks (Wales). Both the Scottish and Welsh tourist boards have Welcome Cyclists and Walkers schemes.

We hope that one day the system will be less complex and more consistent nationwide. In the meantime for a fuller explanation of the classifications, consult your local Tourist Information Centre. As always we explain the abbreviations used within our guide at the back of the book, just before the location maps.

Some accommodation providers are not part of the Tourism Council scheme and this in no way reflects the service they give.

To find your way around the guide, use the side tabs on the outside edge of each page. They show you which section you are in and which county.

Please keep sending recommendations to the Editor. It is the best way we have of keeping high standards in the Yearbook.

> **Members of the Ramblers'
> Association get this book FREE plus
> 4 magazines a year—Join by using the
> discount form on page 15**

Hostels, Bunkhouses and Camping

This section lists accommodation of many kinds. There are campsites, stone tents, "luxury" hostels with en suite rooms and hot showers, and a wide variety in between. Some centres listed here are primarily for groups, but they should all be open to individuals as well. If you have to book, this is stated. Any centres catering solely for groups are now in the *Accommodation Suitable for Groups* section, beginning on page 91.

In each case we state prices per night, whether or not meals and/or self-catering facilities are available, long-distance paths nearby, times of year the hostel or barn is closed and items of special interest such as wheelchair access. If no months of closure are given, the establishment is open all year. Prices given are for adults. Many hostels accept children at a reduced rate. A 6-figure map reference has been given in most cases together with the sheet number of the appropriate Ordnance Survey 1:50,000 Landranger map.

Any walking routes mentioned in the entries are as supplied by the organisers and are not checked.

Categories of establishments are:

BB = Bunkhouse Barn A converted farm building, better equipped than the camping barn. Stoves and cooking facilities provided. Toilets may be chemical. Separate sleeping areas for males and females but little privacy. Bunk beds are provided.

B = Bunkhouse Other kinds of converted buildings, simply but comfortably furnished. They can be run by hotels, sporting estates or individuals. Cooking facilities and utensils provided. Separate sleeping areas for males and females with beds or bunks. Showers and drying facilities provided.

C = Campsite May be for tents only, plus tourers, or have hook-up facilities for caravans. Some sites have static caravans available. Usually self-catering, but may provide meals on-site.

CB = Camping Barn A redundant farm building converted to provide basic shelter. Little or no privacy. Limited facilities. Toilets may be chemical. Sleeping areas are usually not divided between the sexes and there are wooden sleeping platforms. Camping barns are often described as stone tents.

IH = Independent Hostel A privately run hostel. The standards and conditions will vary from hostel to hostel. Some provide meals but majority are self-catering. Sheet sleeping bag liners usually required.

OC = Outdoor Centre Often available to groups only. See also *Accommodation Suitable for Groups* section in this Yearbook.

YHA = Youth Hostel A hostel which is a member of the Youth Hostel Association. For more information about YHA hostels call 01727 855215.

England

CORNWALL

KELYNACK CARAVAN & CAMPING PARK (B/IH/C)
St Just, Penzance TR19
☎ (01736) 787633. Map 203/373301.
Bednight £7 Camping £3 • SC only • South West Coast Path.

THE OLD CHAPEL BACKPACKERS HOSTEL (C/IH)
Zennor, St Ives, TR26 3BY
☎ (01736) 798307 • Bednight £10 • Meals available. South West Coast Path.

PENZANCE BACKPACKERS (IH) The Blue Dolphin,
Alexandra Road, Penzance TR18 4LZ
☎ (01736) 363836. Map 203/467299. Bednight £9 (£10 July-Aug) closed Dec • SC • South West Coast Path.

☆ **RIVER VALLEY HOLIDAY PARK (C)** London Apprentice, St Austell PL26 7AP ☎ (01726) 73533. Bednight £8–£12 • SC • South West Coast Path.

River Valley Holiday Park
London Apprentice
St Austell   01726 73533

A small family park set in the Pentewan Valley an ideal base for walking-cycling-relaxing.
Open April–October • Large flat camping pitches • Caravans for hire daily or weekly • Indoor heated swimming pool • Adjoins Pentewan Valley cycle trail • Peace and tranquility prevails
Visit our web page river-valley.co.uk

ST IVES BACKPACKERS (IH) Lower Stennack, St Ives ☎ (01736) 799444. 1-12 NX
www.backpackers.co.uk • Bednight from £8 • SC • South West Coast Path.

CUMBRIA

COWPERTHWAITE FARM (B) Lowgill, Kendal LA8 9BZ ☎ (01539) 824240. Bednight £8 • SC, foodstuffs available at farmhouse • Dales Way.

DERWENT HILL (C/B/OC) Portinscale, Keswick CA12 5RD. • ☎ (017687) 72005. Map 89, 90/254236 Bednight £27.50 full board (OC) • SC (B) • Closed Xmas. • Cumbria Way, Allerdale Ramble.

GILLSIDE FARM CARAVAN & CAMPING SITE & BUNKHOUSE (C/B) Gillside Farm, Glenridding, Penrith CA11 0QC. ☎ (017684) 82346. Map 90/378167 • Bednight £4 (camping), £6 (bunkhouse), no camping Nov-Feb • SC • Coast to Coast.

GRASMERE HOSTEL (B/IH) Broadrayne Farm, Grasmere LA22 9RU. • ☎ (015394) 35733/35055. Bednight £9.50–£14.50 in separate rooms • SC • Coast to Coast.

THE HAYLOFT BUNKHOUSE B&B (B) Langwathby Hall, Langwathby, Penrith CA10 1LW. ☎ (01768) 881771 • Map 90/568338 • Book through Eden Ostrich World, Langwathby • B&B £14 • No SC, meals possible • Closed Dec-Jan.

MAGGS HOWE CAMPING BARN (CB) Maggs Howe, Kentmere, Kendal LA8 9JP • ☎ (01539) 821689. www.smoothhound.co.uk/hotels/maggs.html Map 90/462041 • Bednight £6 • SC, Breakfast/EM available • Group bookings accepted • Fully equipped except for bedrolls/sleeping bags• Lakeland-Lindisfarne walk nearby.

ROOKHOW CENTRE (B/BB/IH/OC) Rusland in Grizedale LA12 8LA. ☎ (01229) 860231. rookhaw@tesco.net • Map 97/332896. • Bednight £8.50 • SC, no meals. Set in 13 acres of woodland.

STICKLEBARN TAVERN BUNKHOUSE (BB) Great Langdale LA22 9JU. ☎ (015394) 37356. Map 90/325057 • Bednight £10 • EM • Cumbria Way.

WHERNSIDE MANOR (B) Dent LA10 5RE. ☎ (01539) 625213. Map 98/725858 • Bednight £5 • SC only, breakfasts available • Dales Way/Craven Way • Local pick-up and drop-off by arrangement.

DERBYSHIRE

NEW BUILDINGS FARM BUNK BARN (B) New Buildings Farm, Ashleyhay, Wirksworth, Matlock DE4 4AH.
☎ (01629) 823191. Map 119/296518. Bednight £8 • Sole use £80 • SC only • Closed Xmas/New Year • Sleeps 12/14 • Showers, heating • Mid-Shires Way, High Peak Trail.

THE OLD RECKONING HOUSE (CB) Mandale Farm, Haddon Grove, Bakewell DE45 1JF
☎ (01629) 812416 • Bednight £4.50 • Sole use £54 • Limestone Way. Sleeps 12 in two separate rooms.

DEVON

CREACOMBE PARSONAGE CAMPING BARN (CB) Creacombe Parsonage Farm, Rackenford, Tiverton EX16 8EL. Email: creaky.parson@dial.pipex.com ☎ (01884) 881441. Fax: (01884) 881551. Map 181/820185 • Bednight £4.75 or sole use £65 • Meals £7.50 (book first), breakfast £4.50, or SC • Two Moors Way • Poss OK for wheelchair users • B&B & camping also.

GLOBE BACKPACKERS (IH) 71 Holloway Street, Exeter EX2 4JD. ☎ (01392) 215521. Map 192/920921. Bednight £11 (1st night, subsequent nights £10) • SC • No disabled access. No curfew. Social areas open 24hrs.

ILFRACOMBE YOUTH HOSTEL (YHA) Ashmore House, Hillsborough Terrace, Ilfracombe EX34 9NR ☎ (01271) 865337. Map 180/524476 • Bednight £10 • EM and SC • South West Coast Path, Tarka Trail.

LOPWELL CAMPING BARN (CB) Lopwell Dam, Lopwell, Nr Roborough PL6 7BZ.
Map 201/475650. Book through Camping Barns Reservation Office, 16 Shaw Bridge Street, Clitheroe, Lancs BB7 1LZ. ☎ (01200) 420102. Closed Dec-Jan • West Devon Way, Tamar Discovery Trail.

POWDER MILLS BUNKHOUSE (B) Powder Mills, Princetown, Yelverton, PL20 6SP. ☎ (01822) 880277. Bednight £7.50 • Sole use £140 (26 beds) • Dartmoor Lych Way and Two Moors Way.

TORQUAY BACKPACKERS (IH) 119 Abbey Road, Torquay, Devon. ☎ (01803) 299924. Bednight £7 • SC only • South West Coast Path.

WATERCOMBE BUNKBARN (YHA/CB) Watercombe Farm, Cornwood, Ivybridge. ☎ (01752) 668846. Map 202/625613 • Book through YHA Camping Barns, 6 King Street, Clitheroe, BB7 2EP. ☎ (01200) 420102. Bednight £3.80 • Open Apr-Sept • SC • Two Moors Way. Ramps for mobility impaired to en-suite family room for 5 people.

COUNTY DURHAM

THE HUDEWAY CENTRE (IH) Stacks Lane, Middleton-in-Teesdale, Barnard Castle DL12 0QR. ☎ (01833) 640012. Fax (01833) 641044. Map 92/943257
Bednight £12 B&B, group discounts also • Meals or SC • Pennine Way.

NORFOLK

DEEPDALE GRANARY (IH) Deepdale Farm, Burnham Deepdale PE31 8DD. ☎ (01485) 210256. www.deepdalegranary.co.uk
Email: info@deepdalegranary.co.uk
Map 132/803443. Bednight £9.50 • SC only • Norfolk Coast Path.

NORTHUMBERLAND

BARRASFORD ARMS BUNKHOUSE (CB) Barrasford, Hexham NE48 4AA.
☎ (01434) 681237. Map 87/919733.
Bednight £5 • Meals available, no SC • Near Hadrian's Wall • Lakeland to Lindisfarne walk • B&B and SC property also. Two bunkhouses, each sleeping 8.

BORDER FOREST CARAVAN PARK BUNKHOUSE (B) Cottonshopeburnfoot, Nr Otterburn NE19 1TF. ☎ (01830) 520259. Map 80/779014. Bednight £7.25 • SC only • Pennine Way • B&B also.

HADRIAN'S WALL BACKPACKERS (IH) Hadrian's Lodge, Hindshield Moss, North Road, Hadrian's Wall NE47 6NF. ☎ (01434) 688688, Fax (01434) 684867. Map 87/830675. • www.hadrianswall.co.uk
Email: hadrianlodge@hadrianswall.co.uk
• Bednight £10 • SC or meals • Hadrians Wall Path • Disabled toilets and ground floor accommodation • Licensed bar, fishing available.

NOTTINGHAMSHIRE

IGLOO TOURIST HOTEL (IH) 110 Mansfield Road, Nottingham NG1 3HL.
Email: reception@igloohostel.co.uk
www.igloohostel.co.uk ☎ (0115) 947 5250.
Map 129/725827. • Bednight £10 • SC only • Robin Hood's Way, Trent Valley Way.

SHROPSHIRE

THE ENGINE HOUSE HOSTEL (B/IH/OC) Nantmawr Quarry, Oswestry SY10 9HL. ☎ (01691) 659358. Map 126/249244. • Bednight £12.50 • SC only • Offa's Dyke; Shropshire Way; Glyndwr's Way.

STOKES BARN (BB) Newtown House Farm, Much Wenlock TF13 6DB. ☎ (01952) 727293.
Email: stokesbarn@hotmail.com
Map 69/609999. • Bednight £8 • Meals available • Shropshire Way • Family rooms • Campsite also • Situated on Wenlock Edge.

NORTH YORKSHIRE

AIRTON QUAKER HOSTEL (IH) Airton, nr Skipton BD23 4AE. Book through Mr & Mrs G Parker, The Nook, Airton, Nr Skipton BD23 4AE.
☎ (01729) 830263. Map 103/904592.
Bednight £5 • SC only • Pennine Way.

BARDEN BUNK BARN (BB) Barden, Nr Skipton BD23 6AP • ☎ (01756) 720330 • Map 103/050571. Bednight £7.50 • SC only • Dalesway • Groups (20–25 people) pre-booked £100–£150 pn at weekends only • Closed Jan.

CLIFF FARM (CB) Sinnington, York YO62 6SS. ☎ (01751) 473792. Map 94/752849. Bookings to 6 King Street, Clitheroe BB7 2EP. ☎ (01200) 420102. Bednight £4 • SC • Wheelchair access.

HARBOUR GRANGE (B) Spital Bridge, Whitby YO22 4EF. ☎ (01947) 600817. Map 94/901104.
Email: backpackers@harbourgrange.co.uk • Sleeps 24 • Bednight from £9 • Groups £170 • Cleveland Way, Coast to Coast Walk. Family rooms available.

HOOK'S HOUSE FARM CAMPSITE (C) Whitby Road, Robin Hood's Bay YO22 4PE. ☎ (01947) 880283. Map 94/946058 • Bednight £3.50 • Meals available at local pubs or SC • Lyke Wake Walk, Cleveland Way, Coast to Coast • Small, friendly campsite with self-catering accommodation on working farm. Panoramic views.

ENGLAND

HOSTELS, BUNKHOUSES AND CAMPING

MIDDLEWOOD FARM HOLIDAY PARK (C) Robin Hood's Bay YO22 4UF. ☎ (01947) 880414. Map 94/945045 • Bednight £5 (camping), from £27 (static caravans) • SC • Camping mid March-Oct, caravans March-Dec • Coast to Coast, Cleveland Way, Lyke Wake Walk • 5mins to pub/food/shops, 10mins to beach • Walker's paradise!

NORTHCLIFFE HOLIDAY PARK (C) Bottoms Lane, High Hawsker, nr Whitby YO22 4LL. ☎ (01947) 880477. • Bednight from £3 • Meals available • Mid March-Oct • Coast to Coast, Cleveland Way.

RICHMOND EQUESTRIAN CENTRE (B) Breckenborough Farm, Brough Park, Richmond DL10 7PL. ☎ (01748) 811829. Map 99/208969 • SC • Riding school. 2 rooms, 8 bunks/4 doubles per room, disabled shower room, disabled facilities.

SKIRFARE BRIDGE DALES BARN (BB) Kilnsey, Skipton BD23 5PT. ☎ Grassington (01756) 752465. Map 98/973688. • Bednight £8 • SC or meals by arrangement • Sleeps 25 • Heated • Groups only weekends • Dalesway.

USHA GAP CARAVAN & CAMPSITE (C) Usha Gap, Muker in Swaledale, Richmond DL11 6DW. ☎ (01748) 886214. Map 98/902979. • Bednight £3 • Pennine Way, Coast to Coast.

WEST END OUTDOOR CENTRE (B) Whitmoor Farm, West End, Summerbridge, Harrogate HG3 4BA. ☎ (01943) 880207. Email: m.verity@virgin.net Website: www.yorkshirenet.co.uk/accgde/westend Map 104/146575.Bednight £5–£7 • 30 people in 9 bedrooms • SC only • Family room available • Dalesway Link & Nidderdale Way.

WOODSIDE FARM CARAVAN & CAMPING PARK (C) Woodhouse Farm, Winksley, Ripon HG4 3PG. ☎ (01765) 658309. Map 99/241715 • Mar-Oct.

WEST YORKSHIRE

☆ **WESTFIELD LODGE MOORSIDE BUNKHOUSES (B)** Upper Marsh, Oxenhope, nr Keighley, BD22 9RH. ☎ (01535) 646900 • SC, EM • Pennine Way, Brontë Way • Large function/SC complex.

Scotland

DUMFRIES & GALLOWAY

GALLOWAY SAILING CENTRE (B/IH/OC) Parton, Loch Ken, Castle Douglas DG7 3NQ. ☎ (01644) 420626. Map 77, 84/657735. www.lochken.co.uk, email: gsc@lochken.co.uk • EM £5.50 on request, SC also • Southern Upland Way.

WANLOCKHEAD OUTDOOR COMMUNITY CENTRE (OC) Wanlockhead, Lanarkshire. Bookings to Sanquhar Community Centre, Station Road, Sanghuar DG4 6QL ☎ 01659 50426. • SC • Disabled access. Mattress only provided.

HIGHLAND

AITE CRUINNICHIDH (IH) 1 Achluachrach, By Roy Bridge, Nr Fort William, Inverness-shire PH31 4AW. ☎ (01397) 712315. Map 41/301811. • Bednight £8 • SC only • Sauna, meeting room, garden • Nr Ben Nevis.

BADENOCH CHRISTIAN CENTRE (IH) Kincraig by Aviemore, Inverness-shire PH21 1QD. Email: badenoch@dial.pipex.com www.kincraig.com/bcc.htm ☎ (01540) 651373. Map 35/833057. Bednight £9.50 • SC • Disabled access • Cairngorms, Sustrans cycle route 7.

CROFT HOLIDAYS (IH) Strone Road, Newtonmore, Inverness-shire PH20 1BA ☎ (01540) 673504 Email: crofthols@newtonmore.com • Map 35/720001. • Bednight: £9 • SC • Speyside Way extension • Meals nearby • Disabled access.

☆ **FARR COTTAGE LODGE & ACTIVITY CENTRE (IH)** Farr Cottage, Corpach, Fort William PH33 7LR ☎ (01397) 772315, Fax: (01397) 772247 • Map 41/097768. • Bednight: £8–£11 • SC, EM • Great Glen Way • Theme nights, ensuite rooms.

GERRY'S ACHNASHELLACH HOSTEL (IH) Craig, Achnashellach, Strathcarron, Wester-Ross IV54 8YU. www.gerryshostel-achnashellach.co.uk
☎ (01520) 766232. Map 25/037493.
Bednight £9 • SC only • No smoking • Family rooms • Coulin Pass, Corrie Lair, Glen Uig routes.

GLENFESHIE HOSTEL (IH) Balachcroick House, Glenfeshie, Kincraig, Inverness-shire PH21 1NH.
Email: glenfeshiehostel@totalise.co.uk
☎ (01540) 651323. Map 33, 36/850009.
Bednight £8 inc. porridge • SC and evening meals • Mountaineering centre also.

KIRKBEAG HOSTEL (IH) Kirkbeag, Kincraig, Kingussie, Inverness-shire PH21 1ND.
Email: kirkbeag@kincraig.com • www.kincraig.com
☎ (01540) 651298. Map 35/840068.
Bednight £9 • SC only • Breakfast by arrangement • B&B also.

LOCH NESS BACKPACKERS LODGE (IH/B) Coiltie Farmhouse, East Lewiston, Drumnadrochit IV63 6UJ.
(01456) 450807. Map 26/2951.
www.lochness-backpackers.com
Email: hostel@lochness-backpackers.com
Bednight £9–£9.50 • Meals nearby • B&B or SC • Well-equipped kitchens • Heated • Great Glen Way.

NEWTONMORE HOSTEL (IH) Craigellachie House, Main Street, Newtonmore, Inverness-shire PH20 1DA. ☎ (01540) 673360. Map 35/713990.
www.highlandhostel.co.uk
Email: info@highlandhostel.co.uk
Bednight £9 (reductions for groups) • SC • Meals nearby • Breakfast by arrangement • No smoking • Speyside Way Ext., National Cycle Route 7.

OSSIAN'S HOSTEL (B) Hig Street, Fort William PH33 6DH. ☎ (01397) 700857. Map 41/102739. • Bednight £12 • EM available • West Highland Way.

☆ **RED SQUIRREL CAMPSITE (C/CB/B/IH)**
Leacantuim Farm Bunkhouses, Glencoe, Argyll PA39 4HX. • ☎ (01855) 811256. • Map 19/116577 • 1-12 • SC only Bednight £6-£7.50 Camping £4.50 (under 12s 50p) • River and Mountain walks.

SAIL MHOR CROFT HOSTEL (IH) Camusnagaul, Dundonnell, Ross-shire IV23 2QT.
☎ (01854) 633224. Email: sailmhor@btinternet.com

www.sailmhor.co.uk • Map 19/064893. • Bednight £9 • SC and meals • Closed Xmas/New Year • Anti-midge screens on bedroom windows • An Teallach Ridge route.

SPEYSIDE BACKPACKERS (IH) The Stopover, 16 The Square, Grantown-on-Spey, Morayshire PH26 3HG.
☎ (01479) 87351. • www.scotpackers-hostels.co.uk • Bednight £9.50–£11.50 • SC • Speyside Way • Disabled access and bathroom on ground floor.

STATION LODGE (IH) Tulloch, Roy Bridge, Inverness-shire PH31 4AR. ☎ (01397) 732333.
Email: info@stationlodge.co.uk
www.stationlodge.co.uk • Map 41/355802 • Bednight £10–£11 • EM, SC • Disabled toilets and access.

ULLAPOOL TOURIST HOSTEL (IH) West House, West Argyle Street, Ullapool IV26 2TY.
☎ (01854) 613126. Map 19/126939 • SC • Cape Wrath Trail • Bike hire and minibus service available.

ISLE OF EIGG

THE GLEBE BARN (IH) PH42 4RL.
☎ (01687) 482417. SC • April-Oct. See also entry in *Accommodation Suitable for Groups* section.

ISLE OF MULL

ARLE FARM LODGE (IH) Arle, Aros PA72 6JS.
☎ (01680) 300343. Map 48/551483.
Bednight £12 • SC only • Twin & Family rooms graded ★★★.

PERTH & KINROSS

CAIRNWELL MOUNTAIN SPORTS (OC/IH) Gulabin Lodge, Spittal of Glenshee, Perthshire PH10 7QE.
☎ (0870) 443 0254, Office: ☎ /Fax: (0870) 443 0253 • www. carnwellmountainsports.co.uk •
Email: cairnwell.h@virgin.net
Map 43/109703. Bednight £10–£15 • B&B or SC • Kirkmichael to Spittal of Glenshee path.

STIRLING

WILLY WALLACE HOSTEL (IH) 77 Murray Place, Stirling FK8 1AU ☎ (01786) 446773 • SC • City centre location. 2 mins walk to rail/bus. Good base to explore Trossachs & Highlands.

For further information about
YHA Hostels call 01727 855215.

WESTERN ISLES

AM BOTHAN (C/B/IH) Ferry Road, Leverburgh, Isle of Harris HS5 3UA. ☎/Fax(01859) 520251. www.ambothan.com • Bednight £12 • SC • Disabled access.

GALSON FARM BUNKHOUSE (B) South Galson, Isle of Lewis HS2 0SH. ☎ (01851) 850492. Map 8/437592 • Bednight £9 • SC and meals.

Wales

CONWY

THE EAGLES HOTEL (B/IH) Penmachno, nr Betws-y-Coed, Conwy LL24 0UG. ☎ (01690) 760177. Map 115/790506. Bednight from £10–£12, breakfast £4 • EM • Groups welcome.

GWYNEDD

☆ **HENDRE MYNACH TOURING CARAVAN AND CAMPING PARK (C)** Llanaber, Barmouth LL42 1YR. ☎ (01341) 280262. Map 124/608168 • Cambrian Way • Open Mar-Dec • Site shop/takeway.cafe, 15mins walk to Barmouth centre.

HENDRE MYNACH
Touring Caravan and Camping Park
Barmouth
★★★★★ Park, all modern amenities
Near mountains, estuary and sandy beach. Pets welcome. Excellent base for walking, cycling and touring north/mid-Wales.
Special rates off-season
Open 1st March–9th January
Phone for brochure 01341 280262
email mynach@online.net

PEMBROKESHIRE

TYCANOL FARM CAMP SITE (B) Newport SA42 0ST. ☎ (01239) 820264. Map 157, 145/043396. Bednight £6 • SC only • Pembrokeshire Coast Path, Nature Trail on-site.

POWYS

CANAL BARN (YSGUBOR CAMLAS) (B/IH) Ty Camlas, Canal Bank, Brecon LD3 7HH. ☎ (01874) 625361. Map 160/052279. • Bednight from £8.75. • SC. Meals by arrangement • Disabled access • No smoking • Taff Trail, Sustrans route 8.

LLYSDINAM FIELD CENTRE (OC) Newbridge on Wye, Llandrindod Wells, Powys, LD1 6NB. ☎ (01597) 860308. Fax (01597) 860381. Map 147/008587 • Bednight £7.50 + VAT, groups only • SC only • Wye Valley Walk

STONECROFT HOSTEL (IH) Dolecoed Road, Llanwrtyd Wells LD5 4RA. ☎ (01591) 610327. Email: party@stonecroft.co.uk • Map 147/878468 • Bednight £12.50 • EM (adjoining pub), SC • No bunks, full c/h, bed linen provided.

TRERICKET MILL BUNKHOUSE (B/IH) Erwood, Builth Wells LD2 3TQ. • www.treiricket.co.uk ☎ (01982) 560312. Map 148, 161/112415. Bednight £8.50 • SC • Meals available • Pub nearby • Camping & B&B also • On Wye Valley Walk • SSSI.

UPPER CANTREF FARM (B/BB) Cantref, Brecon LD3 8LR. www.btinternet.com/~cantref/breconbeacons • ☎ (01874) 665223. • Map 160/057258. Bednight £9.50 • SC, B&B also • Wheelchair facilities.

Ireland

COUNTY KERRY

FÁILTE HOSTEL (IH) Shelbourne Street, Kenmare, Co Kerry ☎ 00 353 64 42333. Bednight £8.50 • SC, Aga cooker • Free hot showers • Private rooms (ensuite) • Bike hire.

INDEPENDENT HOLIDAY HOSTELS OF IRELAND 57 Lower Gardiner Street, Dublin 1. ☎ Int. 00 353 1 836 4700. Fax 00 353 1 836 4710. www.hostels-ireland.com • Email: ihh@iol.ie Free, comprehensive list of 145 hostels in Ireland. Dorm beds from £7.50 per night. Meals, private/family rooms and camping available at many hostels.

Do you know your rights when you're out walking in the countryside? See pages 32-39

Accommodation Suitable for Groups

Accommodation listed here includes many places tried and tested by RA groups and recommended to us. There is a variety of types, standards, prices, facilities and sizes. Some self-catering, others providing meals, yet others doing some of each. There are hotels, hostels, university halls of residence, cabins in the woods, farmhouses, hopefully something for everyone.

When making a booking for a group, it's worth remembering that a discount can sometimes be negotiated for factors such as size of group, time of year, mid-week bookings or number of nights stay.

Note that not all accommodation for groups is listed here – many places able to take large numbers appear in the other three accommodation sections.

See page 84 for tourist board details.

England

CORNWALL

☆ **Bossiney House Hotel**, Tintagel PL34 0AX • ☎ (01840) 770240 • Ian & Heather Graham • Map 200/066887 • 2-11 • B&B £22 • Max 40 • D9 T9 F1 • P B D S ★★ • Guided walks also • South West coast Path. Special Group rates.

The Countryman Hotel, 7 Victoria Road, Camelford PL32 9XA • ☎ (01840) 212250 • Deborah Reeve • Map 200/108839 • 1-12 • B&B £15–£25 • Max 20 • S2 D4 T2 F3 • P B D S • Guided and self-guided walks also.

St Ives Backpackers, Stennack, St Ives • ☎ (01736) 799444 • Ray Smith, bookings to Newquay Backpackers, Tower Rd, Newquay • ☎ (01637) 879366 • 1-12 NX • SC from £8 • Max 79 • D2 T2 Dorm (11) • D S R • Over 16s only.

CUMBRIA

Bassenthwaite Parish Room, Bassenthwaite Village, Nr Keswick • ☎ (017687) 76393 • Mrs A M Trafford • SC only • Max 50 • Min charge £72 for 2 nights • Heated hall, similar to camping barn with good kitchen, 2 showers • Near Cumbria Way.

BOSSINEY HOUSE HOTEL
TINTAGEL, CORNWALL
AA★★ ETC ★★

Ideal base from which to explore this scenic and wonderful part of North Cornwall. At side of coastal path with many inland walks, the hotel is family run and offers excellent food, hospitality and facilities. Escorted walks/excursions a speciality. 19 double and twin rooms sleeping 40. Heated indoor pool. Large Car Park

Tel. 01840 770240   Fax. 01840 770501

☆ **Derwent Hill**, Portinscale. Keswick CA12 5RD • ☎ (017687) 72005, Fax: (017687) 75422 Email: derwenthill@enterprise.net • Alastair Kellas • Map 89, 90/254236 • Full board + P £27.50–£42.50 • Groups 20–85 • S3 T16 F8 • 1-12 NX • P B D S • Varies from dormitories to single or twin ensuite.

DERWENT HILL OUTDOOR CENTRE Established 1962

THE LAKE DISTRICT
Explore the most beautiful area of England from our superb house and estate overlooking Derwentwater.
Fully catered - excellent food!
Group bookings only.
Call 017687 72005 or email derwenthill@enterprise.net

☆ **Glaramara House**, Borrowdale CA12 5XQ • David Oglethorpe or Trevor Keough • Map 90/247138 • ☎ (017687) 77222 Bookings to Markholme, Keswick CA12 5PW or Brundholme, Keswick CA12 5ER • 1-12 • £18 B&B £30 full board inc packed lunch • Max 50 • S22 T14 • P D S • See display ad on next page.
☆ **The Inn on the Lake**, Glenridding CA11 0PE • Beverley Kelso • ☎ (017684) 82444 • 1-12 • from £37 B&B • Max 20 • S6 D12 T20 F6 • P B D • See display ad on next page.

Low Gillerthwaite Field Centre, Ennerdale, Cleator CA23 3AX • ☎ (01946) 861229. Email: warden@lgfc.org.uk • The Warden • Map 89/139141 • SC £7.50 (£5.50 student) • Max 40 • 5 Dorms (2 x 4-, 8-, 10- and 14-bed), SC £7.65 (£5.60 student) • D S • AALA licensed & MLTB/BCU qualified instructor available for hire on site.

Rookhow Centre, Rusland, Nr Grizedale LA12 8LA • ☎ (01229) 860231. Email: rookhow@tesco.net • Robert & Lesley Straughton • Map 96, 97/332896 • 1-12 • SC £85 • Max 30 • F3 • D S • 13 acres of woodland, meeting/seminar space also. See SC & Hostels entries too.

☆ **Smallwood House Hotel**, Compston Road, Ambleside LA22 9DJ • ☎ (015394) 32330 • Anthony Harrison • 1-12 • B&B £24.50 • Max 30 • S2 D11 T7 F3 • P B D S • 3Cr/Comm • Homely atmosphere, private car park.

☆ **St Martin's College**, Scale How, Ambleside LA22 9BB. Accommodation at Lancaster ☎ (01524) 384460 (Sarah Fisher) and Ambleside ☎ (015394)

30217 (Kath Teasdale) • Easter/Summer Breaks only B&B, SC • Max 150 Ambleside, 450 Lancaster • P B S (R Lancaster). See display ad on facing page.

Whernside Manor, Dent, Sedburgh LA10 5RE. ☎ (01539) 625213 • Elaine Johnson • Map 98/725858 • 1-12 • B&B £18, SC also • Max 12 • P B S House of historic interest. Local pick-up and drop-off by arrangement.

DERBYSHIRE

Hope Valley, 18 Castleton Road, Hope S33 6RD • ☎ (01433) 621407 • Judith Lane • 1-12 NX • B&B £22.50 • Max 12 • D1 T4 F1 • P B D S R

DEVON

Braddon, Ashwater, Beaworthy EX21 5EP • ☎/Fax 01409 211350 • George Ridge • Map 190/397984 • 1-12 • Max 60 • SC (special rates based on numbers) • D10 T15 F1 • B D S • 4KComm.

Kerslake Farm, Meldon, Okehampton EX20 4LU • ☎/Fax 01837 54892 • Lizzie St George • Map 191/559923 • 1-12 • Min 4, max 11 • B&B £18, SC £150-£500 pw (£80-£150 3 day break), EM option • D2 T2 F1 • P B D S R

Ilfracombe Youth Hostel, Ashmoor House, 1 Hillsborough Terrace, Ilfracombe EX34 9NR. ☎ 01271 865337 • John Hextall & Lisa Sture • Map 180/524476 • 1-12 • Max 50 • Bednight £22 (under 18s £18), SC £375 out of season or £10 pppn (under

18s £6.90) • T3 F10 (1 x 3, 6 x 4, 2 x 6, 1 x 8) • P
D R • Details of local walks available.

Imagine ...
walking from the front door of your accommodation, into the heart of the

English Lakes

or travelling 5 minutes into the peaceful

Lancashire countryside

Imagine ...
returning to the warmest of welcomes, delicious food and comfortable
accommodation

✳ ✳ ✳

You can when you stay at ...

St Martin's College

in **Ambleside** or **Lancaster**

Our rural campuses provide superb value
for money accommodation at Easter and
the summer, with the choice of self-
catering, full board or B&B. The ideal
choice for families, individuals and groups.

Contact:
Kath Teasdale at Ambleside
015394 30217
Sarah Fisher at Lancaster
01524 384460

☆ **Royal York & Faulkner Hotel**, Esplanade,
Sidmouth EX10 8AZ • ☎ (Freephone) 0800 220714 •
Peter Hook • 2-12 • Min 25, max 110 • DB&B • S22
D9 T30 F7 • P B D S • 4Cr/Comm.

Wild Pear Centre, King Street, Combe Martin, EX34
0AG • ☎ (01271) 883086 • Book through Juliana
Brown, 36 Womersley Road, Crouch End, London N8
9AN • ☎ 020 8341 7226 • 1-12 • SC £15, Bednight
£30 (incl Tea/Coffee) • Min 6, max 25 • D2 T/S3 F3-4
• P D S • South West Coast Path/Exmoor.

DORSET

☆ **Churchview Guesthouse**, Winterbourne Abbas,
Dorchester DT2 9LS • ☎ (01305) 889296 • Michael
& Jane Deller • 1-12 • Map 194/618905 • B&B
£21–£29, DB&B £35-£43 • Min 6, max 18 • S1 D4 T3
F1• P B D S ◆◆◆ • Can take 8 more by
arrangement with B&Bs, meals taken together.

THE ROYAL YORK & FAULKNER HOTEL
Esplanade Sidmouth South Devon

**Charming Regency hotel on the centre
of Sidmouth's delightful Esplanade.
Long-established family run hotel with emphasis
on personal efficient service, coupled with all
amenities and excellent indoor leisure facilities.**

*Ideally situated for walking the superb coastal
paths and inland walks offering stunning flora,
fauna and views.*

Regular host to Rambling Clubs
Special group rates available. For full information
pack containing a series of guided walks and maps.

FREEPHONE: 0800 220714
Website: www.royal-york-hotel.co.uk

The Crown Hotel, 51-53 St Thomas Street,
Weymouth DT4 8EQ • ☎ (01305) 760100 • Mr K
Thwaite • Bookings: King & Partners, 12 The
Esplanade, Weymouth DT4 8EB • ☎ (01305) 760800
• 1-12 • Max 150 • DB&B £26 • S18 D19 T34 F15 • P
B D S T ★★ • Heritage Walks. See B&B section.

Eypes Mouth Country Hotel, Eype, nr Bridport DT6
6AL • ☎ (01308) 423300 • Elizabeth Tye •
Email: eypehotel@aol.com • 1-12 • Max 34 • B&B
£24.50 • S2 D13 T3 F2 • P B D S 🐾 ★★ •
Heritage Coastline Walks.

Churchview Guest House
Winterbourne Abbas. Dorchester DT2 9LS

ETC
◆◆◆

Our beautiful 17C Guest House is ideal for groups
wishing to explore West Dorset. We cater for up to 18
(more by arrangement with local B&Bs).
Delicious evening meals. Two lounges and bar.
Call Michael and Jane Deller ☎ **01305 889296**
stay@churchview.co.uk   www.churchview.co.uk

☆ **Hardy Cottage**, Manor Farm, Dorchester Road,
Frampton DT2 9ND • ☎ (01300) 320197 • Jackie &
Bill Kind • 1-12 • 12 cottages SC various prices • Min
6, max 40 • D R ★★★★ • See display ad next page.

The Kingcombe Centre, Toller Porcorum •
☎ (01300) 320684, Fax: (01300) 321409 • Nigel
Spring • 1-12 • Min 8, max 35 • DB&B £30 (inc P) •
S5 D2 T5 F4 • P D S • ◆◆ • See B&B entry, SC
for individuals also.

ACCOMMODATION SUITABLE FOR GROUPS

ACCOMMODATION SUITABLE FOR GROUPS

GLOUCESTERSHIRE

☆ **Littledean House Hotel**, Littledean, Cinderford GL14 3JT • ☎ (01594) 822106 • Map 162/668136 • 4-1 • B&B £20 • Min 10, max 60 • S15 D2 T17 F11 • P B D • .

HAMPSHIRE

☆ **The Wessex Centre**, Sparsholt College, Sparsholt, Winchester SO21 2NF • ☎ (01962) 797259 • Map 185/424320 • 4, 6-9 • B&B £23.50 DB&B £33.50, P £5.50 • Min 10, max 170 • S295 D1 T20 • P B D S T V • Farm tours by request.

HEREFORD & WORCESTER

Park View Hotel, Waterside, Evesham WR11 6BS • ☎ (01386) 442639 • Mrs M C Spires • 1-12 NX • Map 150/038433 • B&B £20 • Max 40 • S10 D5 T11 • P D S R • ♦♦♦

☆ **Thornbury House Hotel**, 16 Avenue Road, Great Malvern WR14 3AR • ☎ (01684) 572278 • Marian E Humm • Map 150/781457 • £48.50 • Min 10, max 29 • S5 D8 T3 F1 • P B D S R • ★★

LANCASHIRE

☆ **University of Central Lancashire Hospitality Services**, Foster Building, Preston PR1 2HE • ☎ (01772) 892650 • Maria Dominguez • June-Sept • Map 102/534303 • SC from £12.75 per night, from £82 per week • Min 1-7, max 1500 • S1500 • P B S R

Discover Lancashire and Beyond

Base yourself at the University and explore! Situated near the centre of Preston, we are within easy reach of areas of outstanding natural beauty such as the Lake District, Yorkshire Dales, Forest of Bowland and Ribble Valley.

- *Budget self-catering accommodation*
- *Available June - mid September*
- *1500 rooms some with ensuite facilities*
- *Groups, families and individuals welcome*
- *Sport and leisure facilities*
- *Easily accessible by road and rail*

Contact:
Hospitality Services Office,
Tel: **01772 892650**
Fax: **01772 892977**
Email: hospitality.services@uclan.ac.uk
Website: www.uclan.ac/trading/index.htm

UNIVERSITY OF CENTRAL LANCASHIRE

LINCOLNSHIRE

Woodhall Spa, 9/11 Witham Road, Woodhall Spa LN10 6RW • ☎ (01526) 352000 • Mrs C Brennan • 1-12 • B&B £15 • Max 12 • S3 D2 T1 F4 • Ⓟ Ⓑ Ⓓ Ⓢ ◆◆ • Viking Way.

ISLE OF WIGHT

Farringford Hotel, Bedbury Lane, Freshwater IoW • ☎ (01983) 752500 • Lisa Hollyhead • 1-12 • B&B £35, DB&B £50, SC £270-£630 per building (29 SC units) • Max 150 • S3 D6 T6 F4 SC29 (2 beds in each) • Ⓟ Ⓑ Ⓓ ★★★ • Set in 33 acres parkland, surrounded by 1000 acres NT downland.

NORFOLK

Deepdale Farm, Burnham Deepdale, PE31 8DD • ☎ (01485) 210256 • Jason Borthwick • 1-12 • Max 18 • Map 132/803443 • SC night £9.50, £121.50 all 18 places (Sun-Thurs) • T1 F3 (1 x 4, 2 x 6) • Ⓓ Ⓢ • Discounts for local activities and eating.

The Friars Quire, 5 High Street, Little Walsingham NR22 6BY • Map 132/832422 • Miss Ann Ryan • Bookings to 10 Radnor Walk, London SW3 4BN, ☎ 020 7352 1210 • 1-12 • Max 10 • SC £7.50 pppn • F2 (x 5 bed) • Ramps for access, wall handles to toilets, non-pedestal washbasins

☆ See Display Advertisement

 University of East Anglia

Just 2 miles from historic Norwich city centre, On a rural campus. UEA is an ideal base for coastal walking & exploring the broads. Individuals, groups & families welcome. En suite rooms available all year round.
Budget accommodation available June-September. Closed at Xmas
Tel: 01603 593271   Fax: 01603 250585

☆ **University of East Anglia**, Earlham Road, Norwich NR4 7TJ • ☎ (01603) 593271 • Anna Jarratt • 1-12 NX • SC per week in summer only £180 (2 person flats) – £900 (10 person houses) enquire for further details, B&B £18 summer, £30.50 otherwise • S56 (100 during summer) D4 T6 • Ⓟ Ⓑ

NORTHUMBERLAND

Hadrian Lodge, Hindshield Moss, North Road, Hadrians Wall NE47 6NF • ☎ (01434) 688688, Fax (01434) 684867 • www.hadrianswall.co.uk Email: hadrianlodge@hadrianswall.co.uk • Lyn Murray • 1-12 • Max 50 • B&B from £13, SC from £8 • S2 D3 T2 F4 and 2 dormitories, SC cottages also • Ⓟ Ⓑ Ⓓ Ⓡ • SC 3k/Comm • Pub onsite, 18 acre grounds.

SHROPSHIRE

Belvedere Guest House, Burway Road, Church Stretton SY6 6DP • ☎ (01694) 722232 • Mr D Rogers • 1-12 NX • Map 137/451941 • B&B £25 • Max 24 • S3 D4 T3 F2 • Ⓟ Ⓑ Ⓓ Ⓢ Ⓡ • ◆◆◆◆

Hesterworth, Hopesay, Craven Arms SY7 8EX • ☎ (01588) 660487 • Roger & Sheila Davies • Map 137/391817 • 1-12 • B&B from £22, SC PoA • Max 45 • S3 D6 T10 F2 • Ⓟ Ⓑ Ⓓ Ⓡ • ★★–★★★ • On the Shropshire Way • See also B&B and SC sections.

Longmynd Hotel, Cunnery Road, Church Stretton • ☎ (01694) 722244 • Lee Chapman • 1-12 • DB&B £31 • Min 20 • S6 D22 T13 F9 • Ⓟ Ⓑ Ⓓ Ⓢ Ⓡ • ★★★

SOMERSET

Baymead Hotel, Longton Grove Road, Weston-Super-Mare BS23 1LS • ☎ (01934) 622951, Fax: (01934) 628110 • Justin Taylor • 3-12 • Map 182/320618 • DB&B from £22.50 • Max 55 • S11 D8 T11 F3 • Ⓟ Ⓑ Ⓢ Ⓡ • 3Cr/Comm.

Exton House Hotel, Exton, Dulverton TA22 9JT • ☎ (01643) 851365, Fax: (01643) 851213 • Martin Glaister • 1-12 • Map 181/926336 • DB&B from £37 • Min 5, max 26 • 9 rooms (flexible use) S1-5 D3-6

T2-5 F4 + local holiday cottages • P B D S
◆◆◆◆ • Access to Exmoor from the door.

☆ **Yarn Market Hotel**, 25–31 High Street, Dunster
TA24 6SF • ☎ (01643) 821425 • Antony Brunt • 1-12
• Map 181/993437 • B&B from £25, EM available •
Min 10, max 40 • S3 D10 T5 F4 • P B D S R •
★★★ • within Exmoor National Park • Dogs welcome.

SUSSEX

Dower Cottage, Underhill Lane, Clayton, Hassocks •
☎ (01273) 843363 • Christine & Andy Bailey • Map
198/309136 • B&B and SC • B&B £20 • Min 2, max 6
• 1 bunk room sleeping 6 • P D S R • 10 mins
South Downs Way.

Moat House, Moat Road, East Grinstead RH19 3HZ •
☎ (01342) 326785 • Mr & Mrs Ian Forbes • 1-12 NX
• B&B £22, EM by request • Max 15 • S1 D2 T3 F1
(sleeps 4) • P B D S R T

Stafford House, 91 Keymer Road, Hassocks BN6 8QJ
☎/Fax (01273) 845530 • Barbara Lees • B&B and SC
• Full board £39.13, SC £11.34 per nt • Min 15, max
45, • S31 T6 • P D S R • No Dogs.

WILTSHIRE

Mayfield House Hotel, Crudwell, Malmesbury SN16
9EW • ☎ (01666) 577409 • Mr Chris Marston • 1-12
NX • DB&B from £32 • Max 45 • S3 D10 T6 F5 • P B
D S • ★★ • Quality restaurant food. See B&B entry.

NORTH YORKSHIRE

☆ **Bowerley Country Hotel**, Langcliffe-Settle BD24
9LY • ☎ (01729) 823811 • Peter Wales • 1-12 • B&B
£27.50, DB&B £37.50 • Max 40 • S2 D6 T8 F2 • P
B S R • ★★ • Spacious bar restaurant. Set in 3
acres.

☆ **Cober Hill**, Newlands Road, Cloughton,
Scarborough YO13 0AR • ☎ (01723) 870310 • Carol
Webster • 1-12 • Map 101/010948 • DB&B and lunch
or P £35 • Min 15, max 140 • S21 D11 T28 F10 • P
B D S

The Firs, 26 Hinderwell Lane, Runswick Bay, nr
Whitby • ☎ (01947) 840433 • www.the-firs.co.uk •
Mandy Shackleton • 1-12 • B&B £22.50 • Max 24 •
S1 D4 T2 F4 • P B D S • Dogs welcome. Family
room discounts.

Keld Held Farm Cottages, Keld Head, Pickering •
☎ (01751) 473974 • www.keldheadcottages.com •
Penny & Julian Fearn • 1-12 • SC £185-£635 pw •
Max 35 • D7 T5 F3 • P D • ★★★★, Access Cat 3.

Miresfield Farm, Malham, Skipton BD23 4DA •
☎ (01729) 830414 • Map 98/901628 • Vera Sharp •
1-12 NX • B&B £22 • Min 10, max 30 • S1 D6 T6 F2 •
P B D S • 3Cr/Comm • 3 ground floor rooms
suitable for people with walking difficulties.

WEST YORKSHIRE

☆ **Stones Centre**, Rochdale Road, Ripponden •
☎ (01422) 824030 • P A Smith • Map 110/031189 •
SC £4.50 pppn • Min 20, max 42 • 2 dorms + F4 • D

Scotland

HIGHLAND

Ardenbeg, Grant Road, Grantown-on-Spey PH26 3LD
• ☎ (01479) 872824 • Book through Tim & Rebecca
Bird, 8 St Andrews Close, Ashchurch, GL20 8LE •
☎ (01684) 294405 • 1-12 • Map 36/030278 • SC
£7.50 • Max 24 • F4 • Ⓑ Ⓓ Ⓢ • Snow/Ice gear for
hire • Near local facilities.

☆ **Farr Cottage Lodge & Activity Centre**, Corpach,
Fort William PH33 7LR, ☎ (01397) 772315 • Paula
Vincent/Pru Luker/Stuart Nicol • 1-12 • Map
41/097768 • £11-£15, EM • Max 40 • Ⓟ Ⓑ Ⓓ Ⓢ Ⓡ

Kyle Hotel, Main Street, Kyle of Lochalsh IV40 8AB •
☎ (01599) 534204 • Susan Waugh • 1-12 •
Map 33/761273 • B&B from £30 • Min 20, max 50 •
S8 D5 T16 • Ⓟ Ⓑ Ⓓ Ⓢ Ⓡ • ★★★ • See B&B ad.
Ossian's Hotel, High Street, Fort William PH33 6DH •
☎ (01397) 700857 • Janice Wallace • 1-12 • B&B

£16-£25 • Max 55 • S5 D10 T10 F4 + 6 bunkrooms •
Ⓟ Ⓑ Ⓓ Ⓡ • Bar (meals), pool table • See entries
in B&B and Hostel sections also.
Speyside Backpackers, 15/16 The Square,
Grantown-on-Speyside PH26 3HG • ☎ (01479)
873513 • Margaret Dingwall • 1-12 • SC £10 • Max 30
• D1 T3 F5 • Ⓓ Ⓢ • Central heating. Good base for
Winter sports areas (Lecht and Cairngorm) • See
entry in Hostel section also.
Torren Cottages, Glencoe PH49 4HX • ☎ (01855)
811295 • Victoria Sutherland, bookings ☎ (01855)
811207 • 1-12 • SC £425-£575 pw • Min 8, max 22 •
D3 T4 F2 • Ⓓ • ★★★ • Recreation room, bike/canoe
store • See also SC section. Discounts av. booking
more than one cottage.
Ullapool Tourist Hostel, West House, West Argyle
Street, Ullapool IV26 2TY • ☎ (01854) 613126 •
Richard or Stewart • 1-12 • SC £10 • Max 22 • F5 • Ⓑ
Ⓓ Ⓢ • Bike hire. Minibus service • See entry in
Hostel section also.

ISLE OF EIGG

☆ **The Glebe Barn**, Isle of Eigg PH42 4RL •
☎ (01687) 4824176 • 1-12 • Min 14 (or min charge
£120), Max 24 • B&B PoA, SC (weekend) £9.50 pppn
or £240, parties over 140 £8.50 pppn • T3 F3 •
Ⓟ Ⓓ Ⓢ Ⓡ

ISLE OF TIREE

☆ **The Hebridean Trust**, Hynish , Isle of Tiree, Argyll
PA77 6UG • ☎ (01879) 220726 • Book through Ian
Rees, North Parade Chambers, 75A Banbury Road,
Oxford OX2 6PE • ☎ (01865) 311468 • 1-12 • Fullbd
£22, SC PoA • Min 10, max 32 • T8 F4 • Ⓟ Ⓑ Ⓓ
Ⓢ See display ad on next page.

PERTH & KINROSS

☆ **YMCA Bonskeid House**, Pitlochry PH16 5NP
• ☎ (01796) 473208. Email: bonskeid@aol.com •
Hilary Pratt • Map 43/894612 • B&B £18.50, DB&B
£26.50 • Max 100 • S7 D4 T18 F13 • Ⓟ Ⓓ Ⓢ • ★ •
Pets welcome. Special rates for OAPs. See display ad
on next page.

to Craighall, Blairgowrie. Perthshire PH10 1JB • 1-12 • B&B £11.40, SC rates PoA • Max 54 • D1 T1 F7 • D S R • ★★ • Left luggage facility, free tea/coffee, discounts av. • Good base for Trossachs/Highlands • See Hostel section.

Wales

ANGLESEY

Outdoor Alternative, Cerrig-yr-Adar, Rhoscolyn, Holyhead LL65 2NQ • ☎ (01407) 860469 • Ian Wright • Map 114/278752 • Fllbd £34.55 (inc. EM, tea/coffee and P), SC £11.50 pppn, min £140 per day Min 12, max 36 • T2 F7 • P B D S Coast Path 300m.

GWYNEDD

Dwy Olwyn, Coed-y-Fronallt, Dollgellau • ☎ (01341) 422822 • Mrs Norma Jones • 2-11 • B&B £15-£18 • Max 10 • T1 F2 • P D S • ★★★ • Peaceful location, 10 mins walk to town.

MONMOUTHSHIRE

☆ **Ty'r Morwydd House**, Pen-y-Pound, Abergavenny NP7 5UD • ☎ (01873) 855959 • Map 161/297147 • 1-12 NX • B&B £16.50 • Min 10, max 72 • S30 T18 F2 • P D S R • ★★★ See display ad facing page.

NORTH EAST WALES

Tyddyn Bychan, Cefn Brith, Cerrig y drudion, Corwen LL21 9TS • Email: tyddyn.bychan@tesco.net • ☎ (01490) 420680 • Map 116/931504 • 1-12 • B&B £12, EM £8.50, SC £9 pppn • Max 24 • 3 rooms, sleeping 4, 8 & 10 • P B D S • ★★ • Off road parking, bedding & heating inc.

SCOTTISH BORDERS

Bailey Mill, Bailey, Newcastleton, Roxburghshire TD9 0TR • ☎ (016977) 48617 • Mrs P Copeland • 1-12 • B&B and SC • B&B £20, SC cottage £58-£128 (w/end), £98-£478 (week) • Max 46 • S6 D8 T4 F2 • P B D • 3k/Comm • Bar, Sauna, Jacuzzi & mountain bike hire on site plus pony trekking.

STIRLING

☆ **Glengarry House**, Tyndrum FK20 8RY • ☎ (01830) 400224 • Jim & Diane Mailer • 1-12 • B&B/SC • Min 2, max 12 • D2 T2 F1 • P B D S R • ★-★★ • All inclusive West Highland Way packages. Home cooking. Vehicle back-up.

Willy Wallace Hostel, 77 Murray Place, Stirling FK8 1AU • ☎ (01786) 446773 • Louise Ramsay, bookings

Liverpool House, East Street, Rhayader LD6 5EA • ☎ (01597) 810706 • Mrs Ann Griffiths • 1-12 • Map 147, 136/972681 • B&B £16 • Max 18 • S1 D5 F2 • P B D S

Stonecroft Inn, Dolecoed Road, Llanwrtyd Wells LD5 4RA • ☎ (01591) 610327 • Diane Lutman • Email: party@stonecroft.co.uk • 1-12 • Max 59 • S2 D7 T2 F16 • P D S R • ★★ • Linen inc.

PEMBROKESHIRE

☆ **Lochmeyler**, Llandeloy, Penycwm, Nr Solva, St David's SA62 6LL • ☎ (01348) 837724 • Mrs M Jones • 1-12 • Map 157/855275 • B&B from £20, EM from £12.50 • Max 40 • S2 D5 T5 F4 • P B D S • ★★★★ • Coastal path 2.5 miles. National Park Pack in each room with all walks in Pembs.

Nolton Haven Farmhouse, Nolton Haven, Haverfordwest SA62 7NH • ☎ (01437) 710263 • Jim & Joyce Canton • Map 157/860187 • B&B £15, SC £125-£460, w/es (Nov-Mar) £75 • Min 6, max 60 • B&B: S1 D2 T1 F3. SC: D1 T6 F5 • P B D • ★-★★ • Beach 50yds, Pub 50yds, Pembs Coast Path 35 yds.

St Davids • ☎ 0118 926 6094 • Thelma Hardman • Map 175/740731 • SC £95-£950 • Min 2, max 18 • S R • ★★★★★ • See SC entry also.

POWYS

☆ **Belle Vue Hotel**, Llanwrtyd Wells LD5 4RE • ☎ (01591) 610237 • Eileen & Bernie Dodd • Full board £28 • Min 10, max 30 • 1-12 • S4 D4 T7 F2 • P B D R • Walk guide available. See B&B entry also.

Elan Valley Hotel, Rhayader LD6 5HN • ☎ (01597) 810748 • Pippa Boss, bookings to 2 Nantmadog, Elan Valley, Rhayader LD6 5HN ☎ (01597) 810783 • 1-12 • Min 8, max 24 • B&B • S2 D4 T2 F3 • P B D S • ★★ • Speciality weekends, raptor rambles, biking breaks, fungi forays.

☆ **Elan Valley Lodge**, Rhayader LD6 5HN • ☎ (01597) 811143 • Roy Davies • 1-12 • Map 147/933648 • Min 10, max 36 • £47.50, full board • S12 T12 • P B D S V ★★ • Walking weekends available.

ACCOMMODATION SUITABLE FOR GROUPS

Self-catering Accommodation

Prices for self-catering accommodation vary considerably by season, peak times normally being school summer holidays, Christmas and the late May Bank Holiday. We give the lowest and highest cost, usually per week. Where a proprietor lets more than one property, the price of the cheapest in low season and the most expensive in high season are given.

You are advised to make full enquiries before booking. You might want to know how many bedrooms and bathrooms there are, what the views are like, if there's a garden or how far away the pub is.

Location of some properties being rather approximate, it becomes too complicated to show the location of property in this section on maps at the end of the book.

Where there is more than one property, the conditions might be different in each. For example, you might be able to take your dog to one but not another. Tourist board awards may be different for each property let also — in these cases we give the range of classifications awarded.

There is a guide to the symbols used in the entries at the end of the book, just prior to the maps, and for an explanation of the tourist board classifications see page 84.

England

CHESHIRE

Bosley, Macclesfield • cottage • Sleeps 8 • £200-£400 • 3k/Comm • Old Beamed Shippon with modern facilities • Dorothy Gilman ☎ (01260) 273650 • Category 3 disabled; B&B also

CORNWALL

Boscastle • 3 bungalows, 1 cottage • Sleeps 2-8 • £95-£650 • SW coastpath, offpeak breaks from £70 • Mrs G Congdon ☎ /fax (01840) 250233 • Ⓢ 🐾

Bude • Caravans • Sleeps 2-6 • £70-260 • Closed Nov-Easter • List/App • Tourers, campers, walking groups - transport arranged • Mr & Mrs Woods ☎ (01288) 361380 • 🐾

Cape Cornwall, St Just • Cottage • Sleeps 4 • £120-£350 • Closed Jan-Feb • 100 yds SW Coast Path • Mrs Jo Hill ☎ (01736) 788458 • Ⓢ 🐾 • B&B also

Carnon Downs, nr Truro • 1 cottage • Sleeps 5 + cots • £210-475 • C.H. Log fire; beautiful garden • Martin & Anne Hughes ☎ (01872) 862917 • Ⓢ Ⓡ

☆ **Fal Estuary** • 25 cottages • Sleeps 2-8 • £140-£925 • ★★★★ • www.specialplacescornwall.co.uk • Margie Lumby ☎ (01872) 864400 • Ⓢ Ⓡ 🐾

Fowey • 10 cottages & flats • Sleeps 2-6 • £100-£750 • ★-★★★ • On Cornish coast path & Saints way • Fowey Harbour Cottages ☎ (01726) 832211 • 🐾

Helford River • 6 waterside cottages • Sleeps 2-9 • £135-725 • Enchanting creekside cottages on coastal footpath • Pam Royall ☎ 01326 231666 • 🐾 • B&B

Lamorna • 3 cottages • Sleeps 2-4 • £150-420 • Top quality cottages on 'The Cornish Way'. • Rachel Hood ☎ (01736) 731969 • Ⓢ 🐾

Lanivet • 2 cottages • Sleeps 4-6 • £130-305 • Middle Saints Way, Nr Cornish Way & Camel Trail • Betty & Peter Fuller ☎ (01208) 831650 • Ⓢ 🐾

Lanreath by Looe • 2 cottages • Sleeps 2-6 • £125-£460 • Barn conversion; winter short breaks available • Mr T E Gamble ☎ (01503) 220289 • 🐾 • B&B also

Lizard Point • Clifftop Chalet • Sleeps 2-3 • £160-£220 • Closed 11-3 • On coastal path, magnificent sea views • Mr G Sowden ☎ (01326) 290300 • Ⓢ • B&B also

SELF-CATERING ACCOMMODATION CHESHIRE – CORNWALL

☆ **Lostwithiel** • 3 houses, 5 cottages, 3 flats • Sleeps 2-6 • £140-£650 • ★★★-★★★★ • Waterside; Eden project; excellent walking; cycling • Mr H F Edward-Collins ☎ (01208) 872444 • ® 🐾 • Short breaks av.

☆ **Lostwithiel (near)** • 9 cottages • Sleeps 2-6 • £150-745 • ★★★★ • Excellent walks from front door • Tim & Nicky Reed ☎ (01208) 873618 • ⑤ ® 🐾

Mullion Cove • 25 timber lodges • Sleeps 2-6 • £137-£545 • ★★★★ • 200 yds coastal footpath, 1 mile village • Mike & Jackie Bolton ☎ (01326) 240496 • 🐾 • B&B also

Mullion, Lizard • cottage • Sleeps 6 • £160-£360 • SW coastal path & sea • Barbara Downing ☎ (01326) 290443 • 🐾

Newlyn, Penzance • 1 cottage • Sleeps 1-5 • £150-400 • Quiet terrace 25 metres from coastpath • Victoria Howard ☎ (01736) 810961 • ⑤ ® 🐾

Pendeen • Annexe • Sleeps 4 • £80-£280 • www.carminowefarm.cwc.net • Mr J A Beasley ☎ (01736) 788587

Polperro • 2 cottages • Sleeps 2-4 • £100-£380 • ★★★★ • Secluded gardens, balcony, panoramic views • Mrs S E Julian ☎ (01503) 272089 • ⑤

Polperro • 2 cottages • Sleeps 2-4 • £150-300 • Harbourside views • Martin Friend ☎ (01206) 734555 • ⑤

☆ **Port Isaac/Pencarrow** • 1 house, 1 bungalow • Sleeps 5 • £150-£400 • Ideal for coastal path and Bodmin Moor • Mrs J Baldock ☎ (01840) 213542 • 🐾

Porthleven • 1 Cottage • Sleeps 2 • £140-170 • Electricity & bedding included • Mrs C Cookson ☎ (01326) 574493 • 🐾

Rock (nr) • 10 cottages, 1 bungalow • Sleeps 2-8 • £95-£825 • www.polzeath.com • James Bloye ☎ (01208) 862359 • ⑤ 🐾 • Groups also

☆ **St Agnes & Perrancombe** • 7 cottages • Sleeps 2-5 • £125-475 • www.rosemundy.clara.net • Jenny & Martin Butterworth ☎ (01872) 552293 • ⑤ 🐾

☆ **St Austell** • 7 cottages • Sleeps 2-6+cot • £180-£725 • ★★★★ • www.cornwall-holidays.co.uk • Judith Clemo ☎ 01726 68202 • ® 🐾 • See display advert on next page.

☆ See Display Advertisement

CORNWALL

SELF-CATERING ACCOMMODATION

Tregongeeves Farm Cottages
St Austell   01726 73533

Set in mid Cornwall, seven character cottages around a flower-filled courtyard.
Open all year • Indoor heated swimming pool • All weather professional tennis court • Adjoining 18-hole golf course • Surrounding 22 acres of farmland • Log burners • Accommodation for 2–6 persons plus cots

Visit our web page cornwall-holidays.co.uk

☆ **St Breward** • 3 cottages • Sleeps 2-6 • £105-425 • 4k/Comm • www.chycor.co.uk/cottages/darrynane • Angela Clark ☎ 012 0885 0885 • Ⓢ 🐾

DARRYNANE COTTAGES
Darrynane St. Breward Cornwall PL30 4LZ
Ph/Fx 01208 850885
Bodmin Moor
Absolutely fabulous detached cottages
Private gardens, waterfalls, woods, river
Unique moorland valley setting
Excellent walking. Camel trail close-by
Ideal touring centre. Dogs welcome
Non-smoking available
Open All Year
e-mail alegna@eclipse.co.uk
http://www.chycor.co.uk/cottages/darrynane

St Ives • Barn conversions • Sleeps 2-10 • £150-£475 • Near coastal path, guided walks available • Mrs J Harling ☎ 01736 795132 • Ⓢ Ⓡ 🐾 • Groups also

☆ **St Mawgan** • 1 cottage, 6 bungalows • Sleeps 1-5 • £110-360 • Closed Feb (bungalows) • ★-★★ • Mrs J Bertoli ☎ (01637) 860460 • 🐾

ST MAWGAN RETORRICK MILL

Stone cottage and six holiday bungalows set in nine acres in quiet wooded valley. Footpath to large sandy beach (1 mile) and coastal walks. Newquay six miles, Padstow nine miles. Tourist board Approved. Short breaks. Cottage open all year.
Tel. (01637) 860460

St. Wenn, Bodmin • 3 converted barns • Sleeps 2-8 • £140-515 • Clothes drying facilities. Saints Way • Mrs Marilyn Hawkey ☎ (01208) 812154 • 🐾 • B&B

Stithians • 10 cottages • Sleeps 2-8 • £100-£595 • 2-4k/Comm • Converted farmstead; close to North and South coasts • Peter Stokes ☎ (01209) 860863 • 🐾

Tregony, Roseland Peninsula • C18th cottage • Sleeps 2 • £165-350 • ★★★★ • Quiet; parking; garden; near coastal path • B F Hunt ☎ (01202) 693817 • Ⓢ

Widemouth Bay, Bude • 5 linked bungalows • Sleeps 4-7 • £100-750 • Closed Jan/Feb • www.atlanticview.co.uk • Chris Raven ☎ (01288) 361716

Zennor • Cottage • Sleeps 4 • £180-£350 • Walks leaflets, organic garden, sea sunsets • Dr E Gynn ☎ (01736) 794183 • Ⓢ • B&B also

CUMBRIA

Ambleside • 7 lodges • Sleeps 4-6 • £145-£355 • Closed Dec-Feb • ★-★★ • Secluded woodland setting in central Lakeland • Gareth Evans ☎ (015394) 36583

Ambleside • Flat • Sleeps 4 • £100-£200 • Closed 11-12 • Opens onto garden; private parking • P F Quarmby ☎ (015394) 32326 • Ⓢ

Ambleside • 4 cottages • Sleeps 4-6 • £195-£360 • twosparrows@havengreen.fsbusiness.co.uk • Fiona Sparrow ☎ (015394) 32441 • 🐾

Bassenthwaite Village • 3 cottages, 1 studio • Sleeps 2-20 • £100-£695 • www.s-h-systems.co.uk • Mrs Alison Trafford ☎ (017687) 76393 • 🐾 • B&B also

Borrowdale • Detached bungalow • Sleeps 4 • £108-294 • Idyllic walking location. Parking. Relaxing conservatory • Mrs K Readett ☎ (01204) 852546 • Ⓢ

Borrowdale • 2 cottages • Sleeps 2-4 • £200-£450 • 2-4k • B&B also • Jean Wood ☎ 017687 77215 • 🐾

Bouth/Satterthwaite/Rusland • Cottage • Sleeps 3/4 • £150-£300 • 3-4k/Comm-HC • Ideal for walking; quiet location; views • Mrs Haddow ☎ (015394) 36280/46534 • Ⓢ 🐾

Bowness-on-Windermere • Flat • Sleeps 4 • £175-£230 • Closed Nov-Mar • Modern, central, lake view, no children under 10 • Mrs J Kay ☎ (01925) 755612 • Ⓢ Ⓡ

☆ **Bowness-on-Windermere** • 1 cottage, 5 flats • Sleeps 2-6 • £130-430 • Closed Jan-Feb • ★★★ • Edwardian mansion, Sylvan setting, secluded walks • Mrs P Fanstone ☎ (015394) 45557 • Ⓡ

Deloraine
istinctive holiday homes
Helm Road, Bowness-on-Windermere

NEAR BOWNESS BAY BOATS, RIDING, SHOPS, DALES WAY. FREE SWIMMING/ SAUNA. LAUNDRY FACILITIES
TEL 015394 45557
gordon@deloraine.demon.co.uk

Bowness-on-Windermere • Flat • Sleeps 2-4 • £100-£220 • Lake views, central situation; well-equipped • Mr & Mrs E Jones ☎ 0151-228 5799 • Ⓢ Ⓡ

Burton-in-Kendal • 1 cottage • Sleeps 4 • £120-270 • Well equipped cottage. Historic village. Local fells • Mrs Frances M Roberts ☎ (0161) 432 3408 • S 🐾

☆ **Buttermere Valley** • One house, 3 cottages • Sleeps 1-10 • £195-1095 • ★★★★-★★★★★ • Peace, unsurpassed views, variety walks, spotless • Mrs C Thompson ☎ (01900) 85637 • 🐾

Crummock Water Holiday Cottages
Buttermere Valley
(Grid NY142216)

Foulsyke House and Barn Cottages are all Grade II listed properties, set in idyllic, peaceful position with unrivalled views down the Buttermere Valley and Crummock Water. Maintained to the highest standadrs for total enjoyment. Pets welcome. Good eating nearby. Walks from the door.

Tel 01900 85637

★★★★★ up to 5 Stars ★★★★★

☆ **Caldbeck** • 9 Cottages • Sleeps 2-12+2 • £230-1565 • ★★★★-★★★★★ • www.monkhousehill.co.uk • Jennifer or Andy Collard ☎ (016974) 76254 • 🐾

MONKHOUSE HiLL
Cottages

Discover the difference – Unique cottage holidays at an imaginatively converted Cumbria hill farm nestling in the unspoilt splendour of Northern Lakeland.

ETC 4-5 Stars
Colour brochure

Tel. 016974 76254
www.monkhousehill.co.uk

Caldbeck (near) • 2 cottages • Sleeps 4-6 • £190-385 • ★★★ • Remote setting in northern Lake District • Fran and Robin Jacobs ☎ (016974) 78430 • 🐾

Cartmel Fell • 3 Cottages • Sleeps 4 + cot • £240-495 • Tranquil lakeland vicarage • David Hoyle ☎ (01663) 762634 • 🐾

Chapel Stile/Great Langdale • 1 cottage • Sleeps 4 • £170-270 • CH; peaceful location; walks from the door. • Mrs D C Taylor ☎ (015396) 25385 • S 🐾

Coniston • Flats • Sleeps 2-6 • £72-£245 • 3k/App • Private parking, village location, owner maintained • Mr & Mrs A Jefferson ☎ (01204) 419261 • 🐾

Coniston • Flat • Sleeps 2 • £120-150 • Available for weekend or midweek breaks • M Nicholson ☎ (015394) 41415 • 🐾

Coniston • 2 chalet bungalows • Sleeps 2-6 (11 altogether) • £170-325 • Closed Dec-Feb • Quiet location overlooking lake; owner-maintained • Mrs Anne Hall ☎ (015394) 41558 • 🐾

Coniston • 2 Cottages • Sleeps 6 • £230-395 • ★★-★★★ • www.bigwig.net/high-arnside • Jan Meredith ☎ (01539) 432261 • 🐾

☆ **Crook** • 5 apartments • Sleeps 2-8 • £160-£515 • ★★★★ • Open fires; short breaks off season • Kath Wharram ☎ (01539) 720010 • R 🐾

Plumgarths
Crook, South Lakes

17th C. Lakeland house converted into 5 comfortable apartments sleeping 2-8. Open fires. Large gardens. Dogs by arrangement. Short breaks off season. 4 keys Highly Commended

Tel: (01539) 720010

☆ **Crosby Garrett, Nr Kirkby Stephen** • 1 flat • Sleeps 2 • £155-210 • Short breaks available. Converted Victorian listed building • Mrs Clare Hallam ☎ (017683) 71149 • 🐾

Crosby Garrett, Cumbria
4 miles from Kirkby Stephen

Quiet fellside village in conservation are. Excellent centre for walking. Two miles from Coast to Coast route, near the Pennine Way. Superb Victorian schoolroom conversion with log fire, central heating, sleeps 2. Prices fully inclusive. Use of owners tennis court. Dogs welcome.

Telephone 017683 71149

Dent • Cottage • Sleeps 6-8 • £130-£350 • Mrs Marlene Williamson ☎ (01539) 625353 • 🐾

Dufton • 1 flat • Sleeps 4 • £120-250 • o_halloran@hotmail.com • Liam & Sue O'Halloran ☎ (017683) 51296 • S 🐾

Ennerdale Valley • Farmhouse, cottage & barn conversion • Sleeps 2-8 • £130-£480 • 2k/Comm • Set in seven acres; open fires • Norman Stanfield ☎ (01946) 861249 • 🐾 • B&B also

Eskdale • 1 Cottage, 1 house • Sleeps 1-8, 1-16 • £270-£1500 • 4-5k/HC • Peaceful location amid spectacular scenery • Mrs D M Postlethwaite ☎ (019467) 23235 • S R

Eskdale • House • Sleeps 8 + Cot • £255-565 • ★★★★ • Jacuzzi, drying room, log fire, brochure. • Mrs C Carter ☎ (019467) 23201 • R 🐾 • B&B also

Eskdale Green • house • Sleeps 2-8 • £275-£515 • 4k/Comm • Well-appointed home in secluded location • Jenny Prestwood ☎ 019467 23217 • S R

Grasmere • 3 flats + 1 cottage • Sleeps 2-5 • £150-£310 • ★★-★★★ • www.meadowbrow.com • Wendy & Tony Wade ☎ (015394) 35275 • B&B also

☆ See Display Advertisement

☆ **Grasmere** • 5 apartments + 7 extra bedrooms for groups • Sleeps 2-4 or groups • £165-£343 • 3k/Comm • Free membership of local health club • Grasmere Lodge ☎ 015394 35250 • Ⓢ 🐾 • Groups also

☆ **Grasmere** • 3 cottages • Sleeps 2-6 • £200-400 • www.come.to/glenthorne • Phil Mitchell ☎ (015394) 35389 • Ⓢ 🐾

BREAKS IN THE LAKES Grasmere

Friendly guest house, full board accommodation, double, family and single rooms (no supplement). All H&C. Good home cooking, including packing lunches. B&B from £21.00. Bargain midweek breaks Spring/Autumn. Families and Groups welcome. Also self-catering flat for two or 4/5.

Glenthorne Country Guest House
Tel: 015394 35389   gthorn@globalnet.co.uk

Grasmere • cottages • Sleeps 2-5 • £165-£537 • 4-5k/Comm-HC • Dramatic views, quiet location, colour brochure • Mrs Jo Dennison Drake ☎ (015394) 35733/35055 • Ⓢ 🐾 • Bunkhouse also

Grasmere • 4 cottages • Sleeps 2-6 • £190-600 • 4-5k/Comm • www.grasmerecottages.co.uk • Martin Wood ☎ (015394) 35395 • Ⓢ

☆ **Grizedale Forest** • Converted 17thC barn • Sleeps 2-6 • £174-£478 • 3-4k/up to HC • peterbrown@highdalepark.demon.co.uk • Mr P Brown ☎ (01229) 860226 • Ⓢ 🐾

GRASMERE LODGE
Self Catering Apartments
Forest Side, Grasmere
ETB 3 keys Commended

Converted coach house providing five one-bedroomed apartments sleeping 2/4 persons, with ancilliary bedrooms providing additional sleeping accommodation for the larger groups. Mountain bike hire. Free membership of Health and Fitness club (2 per apt). Free linen, towels.
Full weeks £165-£343.
Telephone: 015394 35250
e-mail: hotel@forestsidehotel.com
Web site: www.forestsidehotel.com

☆ **Grasmere** • 5 apartments • Sleeps 2-6 (+2) • £130-535 • Richard Fowler ☎ (015394) 35417 • Ⓢ 🐾

Beck Steps
Self-Catering Apartments
IN THE CENTRE OF GRASMERE
OVERLOOKING THE VILLAGE GREEN

Five self-contained apartments with parking, designed, furnished and equipped to a high standard, on the banks of the River Rothay – providing an excellent centre for walks and drives to all parts of the National Park.
For brochures or enquiries
Tel 015394 35417

GRIZEDALE FOREST
HIGH DALE PARK BARN
3/4 KEYS up to Highly Commended

Newly converted 17th C barn. Two centrally heated units sleeping six and two, or ten altogether. Glorious position, secluded valley, superb wildlife and walking. Situated well within the National Park in an extremely quiet and peaceful location.
Open all year.
£174 - £478 per week.
Short breaks available.
Tel: (01229) 860226

Hawkshead • cottage & flat • Sleeps 4-5 • £145-£295 • In village; early home of Wordsworth • Mrs L R Walton ☎ (015394) 36405 • 🐾 • B&B also

SELF-CATERING ACCOMMODATION   ENGLAND   CUMBRIA

SELF-CATERING ACCOMMODATION ENGLAND CUMBRIA

Motherby • Cottage • Sleeps 4-6 • £150-245 • Closed Xmas • Converted coach house • Mrs Jacquie Freeborn ☎ (017684) 83368 • 🐾 • B&B also

Mungrisdale • 3 Cottages & house • Sleeps 4-7 • £180-£490 • Up to 4k/HC • Northern Lakes; please send for brochure • Christine Weightman ☎ (017687) 79678 • Ⓢ • B&B also

Newbiggin (Stainton) • 3 cottages • Sleeps 2-3 • £200-310 • ★★★ • Panoramic views • Gill Harrington ☎ (01768) 866383 • Ⓢ

Newlands Valley, Keswick • 1 Cottage • Sleeps 2-4 • £160-£270 • 3k/Comm • Extremely pleasantly situated amongst Cumbrian mountains • Mrs Beaty ☎ (017687) 78278 • Ⓢ • B&B also

Nr Keswick • 10 caravans, 1 bunkhouse, 3 apartments • Sleeps 2-6 • £160-600 • Closed Vans Nov-March • 4k/HC • www.almondirtonhousefarm.com • Mrs J Almond ☎ (017687) 76380 • Ⓢ 🐾

Patterdale • 1 cottage • Sleeps 4 • £220-350 • ★★★ • www.deepdalehall.co.uk • Sue Wheeler ☎ (017684) 82369 • Ⓢ

Patterdale, nr Ullswater • 1 ground floor apt. • Sleeps 2-5 • £165-375 • ★★★ • www.coast2coast.co.uk/grisedalelodge • Mrs Joan Martin ☎ (017684) 82084

Portinscale, Keswick • 1 Cottage • Sleeps 5 + cot • £230-360 • ★★★ • 3 bedrooms, open fire, parking • Mr & Mrs Pope ☎ (017687) 75161 • Ⓢ 🐾

Ravenstonedale • Cottage • Sleeps 6 • £300-£400 • 4k/HC • Walkers luxury paradise, Howgills, Eden Valley • Sally Cannon ☎ (015396) 23230 • Ⓢ 🐾

St Bees • 1 Cottage • Sleeps 1-6 • £180-225 • Closed Xmas & New Year • Sea view, excellent walking area. • Mrs Karen Greene ☎ (01946) 824302 • Ⓢ Ⓡ 🐾

St Johns in the Vale • Apartments • Sleeps 2-4 • £120-270 • ★★★★ • Stunning views; handsomely furnished; rural retreat • Mr N Green ☎ (017687) 79666 • Ⓢ • See also Brigham Farm, Keswick

Ullswater • 17 properties - cottages, lodges, coach houses, chalets • Sleeps 2-6 • £129-£440 • 1-4k/Comm • Private 300 acre estate below Helvellyn • Stephen Foxall ☎ (017684) 82308 • 🐾 • Accessibility grade 3

Ullswater • 4 log cabins • Sleeps 2-4 • £207-399 • 2-3k/Comm • Peaceful 7 acre grounds, 2 ponds • Barbara Holmes ☎ (017684) 86438 • 🐾 • B&B also

☆ **Wasdale Valley** • 1 Cottage & 1 Flat • Sleeps 2-4 • £140-340 • ★★★-★★★★ • pauline@corleyp.freeserve.co.uk • Pauline Corley ☎ (019467) 26285 • Ⓢ 🐾

☆ **Wastwater Lake** • 1 apartment • Sleeps 4 • £190-£295 • 3k/Comm • Near Wastwater Lake, 8 miles to coast • Mrs J Burnett ☎ (019467) 26243 • 🐾

Windermere • Ground floor flat • Sleeps 2-3 • £150-£200 • Close to walks, shops and restaurants • Mrs Sanderson ☎ (015394) 46295 • Ⓡ 🐾 • B&B also

Windermere • Bungalow • Sleeps 4 • £195-295 • Overlooks lake, peaceful setting, comfortable & well equipped • Mrs K McGinnes ☎ (01274) 592610 • Ⓡ 🐾

DERBYSHIRE

☆ **Alstonefield** • 1 cottages, 2 apartments • Sleeps 2-6 • £95-£295 • 3k/Comm • Trails, hills & dales from your door • Mr & Mrs J M Allen ☎ (01335) 310201 • 🐾

Ashleyhay, Wirksworth • Farm cottage • Sleeps 2-6 • £140-£340 • Closed Xmas/NY • Good walking, wildlife; short breaks available • Mr & Mrs Wiltshire ☎ (01629) 823191 • Bunkhouse also

Bakewell • 8 cottages • Sleeps 2-8 • £200-610 • 4k/C-HC • EMTB award winners; brochure bolehill-farmcottages.co.uk • Jan & Tony Staley ☎ (01629) 812359 •

Bamford, Hope Valley • 3 cottages • Sleeps 4-6 • £190-400 • ★★★★ • Laundry; hard tennis court; farm walks • Mrs A H Kellie ☎ (01433) 620635 • S R

Bamford, Hope Valley • 3 cottages • Sleeps 4-6 • £200-400 • ★★★★ • Gardens, farm walks, tennis court, laundry, trout lake • Mrs A H Kellie ☎ (01433) 620635 • S R • Groups also

Belper • £220-280 • www.derbyhill.co.uk • Jane Grant ☎ 01773 550489

Birchover • Cottage • Sleeps 5 • £180-£210 • ★★★★ • www.cressbrook.co.uk/youlgve/eagle/ • Mrs Mary Prince ☎ (01629) 650634

Carsington • cottage • Sleeps 8 • £350-£800 • 3Cr/Comm • Farmhouse on working farm • Peter Oldfield ☎ (01629) 540570 •

☆ **Chelmorton** • Farmhouse • Sleeps 6 • £220-£320 • Closed Oct-Mar • 3k/Comm • Historic farmhouse, high in the White Peak • Mrs Lucilla Marsden ☎ 01298 85249

The Hall, Town End Farm
Chelmorton, Nr. Buxton

Two-storey section of historic grade II listed farmhouse in the picturesque village of Chelmorton in the Peak District National Park. Buxton 5 miles, Bakewell 7 miles. Pub meals 10 mins walk. Ideal for exploring the Derbyshire Dales and Peaks. Maximum number of tenants 6 adults/children plus baby. No dogs. Rents include electricity and fuel.

Bookings start Sat. 16.00hrs and end Sat. 10.00hrs
Available: April-September • ☎ 01298 85249

Cromford • Cottage • Sleeps 11 • £280-325 • Converted historical building - village conservation area • Jeremy Beckett ☎ (01629) 822659 • S R

Edale • 2 cottages • Sleeps 2-4 • £170-£210 • ★★★ • 2 cottages on working hill farm • Mrs Sally Gee ☎ (01433) 670273 • R • B&B also

☆ **Eyam** • 3 cottages • Sleeps 2-6 • £150-£400 • 4-5k/HC • Unique village square setting & private parking • Mrs Dorothy Neary ☎ (01433) 620214 •

Historic Eyam

A fine house; a delightful old barn & a cosy cottage. Just-renovated yet retaining a singular character – Three stone cottages overlooking Derbyshire's most historic village square. Exceptional decor, lovely furnishings. Courtyard garden and private parking. Cottages sleep 2-6 £150–£380 pw (breaks from £65)

Tel. Mrs Neary 01433 620214 for brochure
www.laneside.fsbusiness.co.uk

Flash • Flats in converted barn • Sleeps ★★-★★★ • £85-360 • 3k/Comm • Superb views, excellent walking centre • Mrs E Andrews ☎ (01298) 22543 •

☆ **Great Longstone** • cottage • Sleeps 4 • £198-£355 • ★★★★ • Owner provides folder of local walks • Mike Scawen ☎ (01629) 640593 • S • B&B also

---

Applehoe Cottage
Great Longstone, Nr Bakewell

Beamed cottage in quiet village. Centrally-heated & fully equipped to ETB 4 Stars. Folder of local walks provided. non-smoking. Pets welcome.

Tel: 01629 640593

Hartington • 2 cottages • Sleeps 2-4 • £160-£380 • 4k/HC • Exposed beams, log fire, glorious location • Mrs F Skemp ☎ (01298) 84447 • S

Hayfield • Cottage • Sleeps 2 • £190-£240 • Beautiful, comfortable 17th Cent. beamed cottage • Jan & Tom Abbotts ☎ (01663) 745090 • S

☆ **Hope** • 4 cottages • Sleeps 2-6 • £160-£375 • ★★★★ • Superb location for walking • Mrs P M Mason ☎ (01433) 620291 • R

CRABTREE COTTAGES
HOPE, HOPE VALLEY S33 6SA

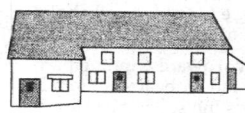

Four well-equipped warm cottages in a garden setting. CH, fuel, linen and use of laundry included in rent. Ample parking but car not essential. Short breaks in winter from £60 for 2. Ideal location for walking.

TEL/FAX: HOPE VALLEY 01433 620291
crabtree@prime.net   www.prima.net/crabtree

Hope Valley • 3 cottages • Sleeps 2-7 • £175-450 • 4k/HC • www.farfield.gemsoft.co.uk • Mrs Gill Elliott ☎ /fax 01433 620640 • R

Hope • Cottage • Sleeps 2 • £165-255 • Closed Nov-Apr • ★★★ • Walkers paradise; peaceful location • Mrs Julie Hadfield ☎ (01433) 621955 • R

☆ **Hope** • 3 cottages • Sleeps 2-6 • £150-£400 • 4k/Comm • Delightful riverside setting bordering Hope village • Mrs Dorothy Neary ☎ (01433) 620214 • R • See display box at start of next page.

Ramblers' Association members are covered by a public liability insurance policy. Further details from central office

---

☆ See Display Advertisement

Ilam • 2 farmhouses, 1 cottage • Sleeps 7-12 • £200-£650 • ★★★-★★★★ • throwleyhall@talk21.com • Mrs Muriel Richardson ☎ (01538) 308202 • 🐾 • B&B also

☆ **Matlock** • 79 Pine Lodges • Sleeps 2-8 • £215-£820 • ★★★★ • www.darwinforest.co.uk • Joanne Fern ☎ 01629 732428 • 🐾

Set in 44 acres of woodland in the heart of the Peak District, our luxury natural pine lodges provide the ideal base for your family holiday, short break or weekend away.

This environmental award winning park includes; a superb indoor heated swimming pool, the Forester's Inn serving bar meals, childrens' playground, tennis courts, mini-golf and games room.

For a free colour brochure contactt

Darwin Forest Country Park
Two Dales, Matlock, Derbyshire
Telephone: 01629 732428
Website: www.darwinforest.co.uk
Email: info@darwinforest.co.uk

Matlock • Cottage • Sleeps 8 • £512-£988 • ★★★★ • Refurbished single story cottage, park facilities. • Joanne Fern ☎ 01629 732428 • Ⓡ • Touring caravans

The symbols used in the Accommodation Guide are explained on page 287

☆ **Matlock** • 1 flat • Sleeps 6 • £250-350 • ★★★★ • Mrs Anna Baker ☎ (01629) 760615 • Ⓢ Ⓡ

DEVON

Chagford, Dartmoor • annexe • Sleeps 2 • £130-£250 • www.jackspatchhouse.co.uk • Mrs Margaret Marsh ☎ (01647) 433225 • Ⓢ • Self-contained, beautiful views, excellent walking

Challacombe • 4 Cottages • Sleeps 2-7 • £105-£460 • Closed Jan • 4k/Comm • www.holidayexmoor.co.uk • Mark Ravencroft ☎ (01598) 763283 • 🐾 • B&B also

Dartmoor • Converted water tower • Sleeps 6/7 • £220-£540 • Stylish accomodation, fabulous views, excellent walking • Toad Hall Cottages ☎ 01548 853089 (24 hrs) • Ⓢ

Dartmoor • 3 Cottages • Sleeps 2-4 • £150-255 • bucknall@hookner.freeserve.co.uk • Mrs H S Bucknall ☎ (01647) 221385 • 🐾

Dartmoor Chagford • self-contained unit in house • Sleeps 2-4 • £160-320 • Closed Xmas & New Year • Stunning location, panoramic views. Also B&B • Pauline & Jim Hamer ☎ (01647) 432005 • Ⓢ 🐾

Dartmoor, Throwleigh • 1 cottage • Sleeps 2 • £110-195 • Near Chagford & Two Moors Way • Mr & Mrs Paget ☎ (01647) 231213 • Ⓢ 🐾

☆ **Dawlish** • 2 cottages, 4 apartments • Sleeps 2-10 • £150-1,000 • shellcovehouse@btclick.com • Miss Linda Jameson ☎ (01626) 862523 • Ⓢ Ⓡ 🐾

☆ See Display Advertisement

Dunsford, Teign Valley • 2 cottages • Sleeps 2-5 • £130-280 • Peaceful farmland; lovely views; woodland walks • Mrs Jean May ☎ (01647) 252784 • Ⓢ
Hope Cove • Bungalow & luxury apartment • Sleeps 2-10 + cot • £200-900 • Central heating, good parking, porches, gardens • Mrs Jenifer Jones ☎ /Fax (01926) 402107 • 🐾
Hope Cove • 1 cottage • Sleeps 8 • £350-750 • All mod cons, on SW Coast Path • Mr Noel Cleave ☎ (01666) 577411
Meldon Village • 1 cottage • Sleeps 2-7 • £150-500 • lizzie@cantabds.demon.co.uk • Lizzie St.George ☎ (01837) 54892 • Ⓢ 🐾
☆ **Modbury** • Cottages • Sleeps 2-6 • £149-448 • ★★★★ • Working farm; short breaks; beautiful countryside • Cathy Evans ☎ (01548) 830842 • 🐾 • Dogs low/mid-season only

---

OLDAPORT FARM COTTAGES
Modbury, Ivybridge, Devon
Four Comfortable Cottages on Small Historic Sheep Farm & Miniature Shetland Pony Stud. Peaceful Location — South Coastal Footpath Nearby, Dartmoor 8 Miles — Open all Year
For Brochure or enquires
Tel: 01548 830842   Fax 01548 830998
email: cathy.evans@dial.pipex.com
English Tourism Council ★★★★

☆ **Moretonhampstead** • 7 barn conversions - cottages & flats • Sleeps 2-6 • £110-£395 • 2-3k/Comm • www.members.aol.com/farmleigh • Judith Harvey ☎ (01647) 440835 • 🐾 • Camping also

---

Budleigh Farm,
Moretonhampstead, Devon
(in the Dartmoor National Park)

Walk the Dartmoor Way, follow local trails or stride out on the moors. Granite barns converted with flair into 7 self-catering properties, warm & comfortable all year. Pretty gardens, outdoor heated pool. Safe parking for cars and cycles.
☎ 01647 440835
farmleigh@aol.com

Newton Ferrers • 5 Cottages • Sleeps 4-12 • £190-1400 • ★★★ • Many coastal walks. Close to Dartmoor. • Anne Edwards ☎ (01752) 872235 • Ⓢ 🐾
Noss Mayo • Barn conversion • Sleeps 4-6 • £190-440 • Headland location, coastal walks, tennis court • J & H Darbyshire ☎ (01730) 821207 • Ⓢ 🐾
Okehampton • 2 cottages • Sleeps 2-6 • £100-200 • Dartmoor. Heart of Devon. Tarka Trail. • Mrs M E Stevens ☎ (01837) 52305 • Ⓡ 🐾
☆ **Paignton** • 36 studio apartments & 6 family suites • Sleeps 2-7 • £210-546 • ★-★★ • www.thm.co.uk • Mr Booth ☎ (01803) 558226 • 🐾

☆ **Parracombe, Exmoor** • 2 cottages - barn conversion • Sleeps 6 • £180-465 • 4k/HC • Secluded; on footpath; woodburner; short breaks • Judith Killen ☎ (01598) 763315

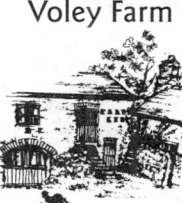
☆ **Parracombe, Exmoor** • Cottage • Sleeps 8 • £150-£200 • Open fire in sitting room • Rosemary Lewis ☎ 020 8688 7078 • Ⓢ 🐾

☆ See Display Advertisement

SELF-CATERING ACCOMMODATION   ENGLAND   DEVON

☆ **Plymouth** • 3 cottages • Sleeps 1-7 • £150-445 • ★★★★ • Accessibility scheme category 2. Short breaks. • Mrs S Rowland ☎ (01752) 862264 • 🐾

Traine Farm Cottages
Wembury, nr Plymouth

Beautifully converted barns on working farm, rolling countryside, stunning views. 1 mile from beach and coastal path. Open all year. Pets welcome

Tel/Fax 01752 862264

rowland.trainefarm@eclipse.co.uk

Poundsgate, Dartmoor • Lodge • Sleeps 2-6 • £80-£500 • Closed Jan-Feb • ★★★ • Lovely walking area. • Mrs Margaret Phipps ☎ 01364 631421 • ⑤

Sidmouth • 1 cottage, 4 bungalows • Sleeps 2-4 • £135-410 • ★★★ • Farm near coastal path - excellent walking • Geoff & Gill Davis ☎ (01395) 516065 • 🐾

☆ **Sidmouth** • 3 flats, 12 cottages • Sleeps 2-8 • £160-585 • ★★★★ • www.drupefarm.co.uk • Miss Gill Elliott ☎ (01395) 568838 • 🐾

Drupe Farm

Delightful very well equipped farm conversions around pretty courtyard in Otter Valley near Heritage Coast, river estuary, acres of commons, excellent bird watching. Village pub and shop, own footpath for dogs. Perfect holidays/short breaks.

Ring 01395 568838 for detailed colour brochure

WCTB ★★★★

Sidmouth • Regency house • Sleeps 7 • £200-£500 • Closed Oct-Mar • Adjacent beach; on coast path • Peter Wilton ☎ 01628 781901 • 🐾 • Bus service from Honiton

Torquay • Chalet • Sleeps 1-5 • £160-250 • Closed 11-2 • Parking; own garden; blissfully quiet location • Mr Russell Davies ☎ (01803) 215564 • ⑧ 🐾 • B&B also

North Devon

3 miles coastal footpath, close Exmoor. Quiet village with shop, pub, known for foot-paths. Cottage equipped to high standard, central heating. Three bedrooms, bathroom, shower. ETB ★★★★ Swimming pool.

Tel 01271 865222 Fax 0870 130 2133
Mrs T E Buchan
The Old Vicarage, West Down, Ilfracombe
Devon EX34 8NF

Torrington • 6 cottages • Sleeps 4-6 • £185-470 • ★★★ • www.stowford.dial.pipex.com • Mrs S Milsom ☎ (01805) 601540 • 🐾

☆ **West Down, Ilfracombe** • 1 cottage • Sleeps 5 + cot • £150-500 • ★★★★ • wm.te.buchan@lineone.net • Toni Buchan ☎ (01271) 865222 • ⑤

Whimple, Nr Exeter • 3 cottages, 1 flat • Sleeps 4-6 • £129-327 • ★★★ • Comfortable accommodation in delightful rural situation • Pat Penfold ☎ (01404) 822989 • 🐾

Widecombe-in-the-Moor, Dartmoor • Farmhouse & cottages • Sleeps 2-12 • £140-870 • ★★★ • Beautiful quiet location; CH; well equipped • Mrs Angela Bell ☎/Fax (01364) 621391 • 🐾 • Disabled category 2 in two units

DORSET

Abbotsbury • Cottages • Sleeps 2-8 • £190=700 • 4k/HC • Coastal path/Macmillan Way. Disabled access • Mrs J M Pengelly ☎ (01305) 871401 • ⑤ 🐾

Beaminster • 1 converted barn apartment • Sleeps 2-4 • £200-380 • dillonclarke@virgin.net • Mrs L D Clarke ☎ (01308) 863395 • ⑤ 🐾

Bridport • Caravans & touring pitches • Telephone for brochure • Closed Dec-Feb • 5 ticks • www.wdlh.co.uk • Martin Cox ☎ (01308) 422139 • 🐾

Eype, Nr Bridport • Annexe • Sleeps 2 • £150-£200 • Sue Boize ☎ (01308) 425600 • ⑤ 🐾

Frampton • 12 cottages • Sleeps 2-6 • £171-619 • ★★★-★★★★ • manorfarmholcott@aol.com • Jackie & Bill Kind ☎ (01300) 320197 • Ⓡ 🐾

Lulworth Cove • Flat • Sleeps 2 • £185min • Closed Nov-Mar • Near Dorset Coastal Path • J M Palmer ☎ (01929) 400235 • ⑤ 🐾

Milborne St Andrew • Semi-detached cottage • Sleeps 6 • £150-420 • ★★★ • Peaceful location ideal for exploring Dorset • Charlotte Martin ☎ 01258 837195 • ⑤

☆ **Milton Abbas** • Cottage • Sleeps 4-6 • £195-£425 • ★★★ • G D Garvey ☎ (01300) 341352 • ⑤ 🐾

Primrose Cottage
Milton Abbas

Thatched cob cottage, which sleeps four to six, with everything you would expect from a Grade II listed building. The beamed sitting-room, of course, has an inglenook fireplace with wood stove. Really it's a cottage in which romantics can relax. ☎ **01300 341352**

Pallington • stable conversion • Sleeps 2 • £210-340 • Closed 1-2 • ★★★★ • Rural location. Hardy Way. Forest walks • Mrs E J Peckover ☎ (01305) 849344 • 🏠

West Lulworth • Cottage • Sleeps 4 + 2 children • £185-430 • Log fire; centre village; 3 days min. • A Cake ☎ (01202) 741938 • 🏠

Weymouth • Flats • Sleeps 4-6 • £170-475 • ★★★ • Georgian house with panoramic sea views • Mrs Veronica Brown ☎ (01305) 814152 • Ⓡ 🏠

Winterborne Kingston • 2 bungalows • Sleeps 4-6 • £160-410 • Quiet situation surrounded by fields • Mr & Mrs Jenkins ☎ (01929) 471293 • Ⓢ 🏠

COUNTY DURHAM

☆ **Barnard Castle** • 6 cottages • Sleeps 2-6 • £114-382 • Closed Jan • ★★★★ • www.eastbriscoe.co.uk • Peter Wilson ☎ (01833) 650087 • 🏠

Cotherstone, Nr Barnard Castle • 2 cottages • Sleeps 2-8 + cot • £225-650 • Barn conversion; oak floor boards & beams • ☎ (01833) 650822 • Ⓢ 🏠

Sedgefield • 1 cottage • Sleeps 4 • £155-295 • EdgooseJ@aol.com • Sam & Judith Edgoose ☎ (01740) 620244 • Ⓢ

Wolsingham • cottage • Sleeps 7 • £183-397 • ★★★ • Listed building located in conservation area • Mrs M E Shepheard ☎ 01388 527466 • 🏠

Wolsingham, Weardale • 4 cottages • Sleeps 2-5 • £145-£350 • ★★★ • Short breaks; working farm • Judith Stephenson ☎ (01388) 527285 • 🏠 • caravan park also

Wolsingham-in-Weardale • Terraced cottage • Sleeps 4 • £120-£198 • 2k/Comm • Cosy cottage; excellent walking area • Mrs M Gardiner ☎ (01388) 527538 • 🏠

GLOUCESTERSHIRE

Chipping Campden • Coach house flat & cottage • Sleeps 2-4 • £150-£475 • Closed Jan-Feb • 4k/C • Magnificently situated on Cotswold Way • Mrs J Whitehouse ☎ (01386) 840835 • 🏠 • B&B also

Coberley, Nr Cheltenham • self-contained wing • Sleeps 4 • £190-£275 • ★★★ • Delightful setting amidst beautiful walking country • Anne Allen ☎ (01242) 870306

Cotswolds • 1 flat • Sleeps 2 • £195 • Stunning rural location, many walks • Kate Beim ☎ (01285) 821102 • 🏠

Cotswolds, Orchard & Tewkesbury • 2 cottages • Sleeps 4 • £180-325 • ★★★ • Wychavon & Cotswold Ways; Orchard; Flocks • Mrs L T C Rolt ☎ (01242) 602594 • Ⓢ 🏠

Daglingworth, Cirencester • Cottage • Sleeps 2 • £190 • ★★★★ • Cosy cottage. Tariff all inclusive • Mrs V M Bartlett ☎ (01285) 653478 • Ⓢ

Doynton • 3 converted stable blocks • Sleeps 2-4 • £186-286 • www.country-retreats.co./wilkesfarm • Mrs K Dinham ☎ 0117 937 2381 • Ⓢ 🏠

Elkstone, Cotswolds • 1 duplex apartment - part of country house • Sleeps 2 • £145-225 • Charming comfortable accomodation, very walker friendly • Mrs Lois Eyre ☎ (01242) 870375 • Ⓢ 🏠

Lechlade-on-Thames • 2 barn conversions • Sleeps 6-8 • £100-275 • Closed Nov-Feb • Cherry Mace ☎ (01367) 253821

Stanton • 2 cottages • Sleeps 2-6 • £150-400 • 3k/Comm • www.myrtle-cottage.co.uk/ryland.html • Mrs V Ryland ☎ (01386) 584339/584270 • 🏠

Staunton, Coleford • Cottage • Sleeps 6 • £150-£450 • 3k/HC • Woodland walks direct from cottage • Mrs Ann Richards ☎ (01594) 833122/0467 425755 • Ⓢ 🏠

☆ **Stow on the Wold** • 6 converted Cotswoldstone barns • Sleeps 2-16 • £220-1650 • www.cotswold-farmhouse.com • Ann Whitney ☎ (01451) 832215 • 🏠

Uley, Dursley • Flat • Sleeps 2 • £120-£140 • Rural; Cotswold Way; beautiful views; quiet • G & N Kent ☎ (01453) 860267 • ⑤

Upper Cam • Terraced cottage • Sleeps 4 • £126-£207 • 3k/Comm • Tranquil village setting near Cotswold Way • Mrs F A Jones ☎ (01453) 543047 • ⑤ ⑧

☆ **Whitecroft** • 1 house • Sleeps 6 • £200-300 • ★★★ • Well equipped; 2 mins from woodland walks • Val Long ☎ (01600) 714464 • ⑤ 🐾

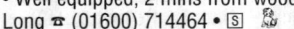

☆ **Woodchester** • cottage • Sleeps 6 • £200-£450 • 4k/HC • Open fires, converted stone coach house • Carol & Gerry Walsh ☎ (01453) 873088 • ⑤ ⑧ 🐾 • B&B in main house

HAMPSHIRE

Lockerley • Thatched cottage • Sleeps 5 • £150-250 • Bed linen supplied • Mrs R J Crane ☎ (01794) 340460 • ⑧ 🐾

Milford-on-Sea • Wing of Listed building • Sleeps 2-6 • £130-£270 • Coastal & inland footpaths: Lovely garden • Mrs J M Halliday ☎ (01590) 642077 • 🐾

Sway, New Forest • 1 cottage, 2 flats • Sleeps 2-6, 17 altogether • £140-320 • Comfortable accommodation in excellent walking area • Mrs Helen Beale ☎ (01590) 682049 • ⑧ 🐾

HEREFORD & WORCESTER

Broadway • 17th Cent. listed cottage • Sleeps 2 • £150-£200 inc. services • 3k/Comm • Cosy cottage; private courtyard; Cotswold walks • Liz Dungate ☎ (01895) 834357 • 🐾

Goodrich, Ross-on-Wye • 6 farm cottages • Sleeps 2-7 • £170-£650 • 3-4k/HC • In 80 acres beside River Wye • Mrs P Unwin ☎ (01531) 650448 • 🐾

Malvern (West) • Garden flat • Sleeps 2-4 • £125-195 • ★★★ • Conservatory, use of garden, drying room • Mrs S Matthews ☎ (01684) 567328 • ⑧ 🐾

Malvern Hills • cottage • Sleeps 6 • £195-325 • 3k/Comm • Ideal for walking; near all facilities. • Mrs P M Longmire ☎ 01684 566689 • ⑤ ⑧ 🐾

Malvern Wells • Self contained annexe • Sleeps 2 + 1 Child • £170-200 • Mrs Gwyn Sloan ☎ (016894) 561074 • ⑤

☆ **Much Cowarne** • 5 cottages • Sleeps 2-8 • £120-£420 • ★★★-★★★★ • Malvern Hills/Wye Valley - free maps & guides • Mr R M Bradbury ☎ (01432) 820317 • 🐾

Ross on Wye • 1 flat • Sleeps 2 • £120-180 • http://freespace.virgin.net/river.wye-view • Jane Roberts ☎ (01989) 563299 (07931) 561553 • ⑤

Whitbourne • 19th-cent. Farmhouse • Sleeps 11+cot • £265-525 • ★★★ • Access Cat 3. Spacious personally maintained 5 bedrooms • Mrs Anne Evans ☎ (01886) 821534 • ⑤ 🐾

ISLE OF WIGHT

Bonchurch • 5 wooden lodges • Sleeps 2-4 • £145-450 • ★★ • Linen, central heating, launderette, coastal/countryside walks • Mrs Jan Maclean ☎ (01983) 852268 • ⑤ 🐾

Collwell Bay • 10 bungalows • Sleeps 2-10 • £90-£590 • ★-★★★ • Centrally heated. 100 yards from beach • Rod Hopkins ☎ 01983 752511 • ⑧ 🐾

Freshwater Bay • 24 cottages • Sleeps 4-6 • £270-630 • www.farringford.co.uk • Lisa Hollyhead ☎ (01983) 752500 • 🐾 • B&B also

Godshill • cottages, conv. hayloft & milk parlour • Sleeps 3-6 • £150-£500 • Closed Nov-Jan • ★★★ • Nicely converted stone farm cottages • Mrs P R Lazenby ☎ 01983 840536 • ⑤ 🏠

☆ **Isle of Wight** • 35 cottages • Sleeps 1 up to 14 • £117-£950 • ★-★★★★★ • www.islandcottageholi-days.com • Honor Vass ☎ (01929) 480080 • ⑤ ® 🏠

Ryde • Bungalow • Sleeps 2 • £150-£180 • Closed Nov-Feb • Peaceful location; 500 miles of sign posted walks • Mrs Jan Brading ☎ (01983) 565909 • ⑤ ®

Yarmouth • cottage • Sleeps 4 • £100-£250 • Closed Nov-Feb • Near Bus & Ferry on coastal path • Mrs J Manfield ☎ 01983 760814 • 🏠

KENT

☆ **Charcott, nr Tonbridge** • 2 Cottages • Sleeps 2-4 • £258-£480 • 4k/HC • Hamper, log stoves, very high standard • Sandra Bell ☎ (01892) 870138 • ® 🏠

Crundale, Canterbury • Half of large C16th Farmhouse • Sleeps 2-5 • £180-£360 • Closed Jan-Feb • Working organic farm overlooking North Downs • Maggie Baur ☎ 01227 730748 • ⑤

East Peckham • 3 cottages • Sleeps 4-5 • £250-490 • ★★★★ • 10% discount to RA members. wagonlodge@lineone.com • Esther McClelland ☎ (01622) 873230 • ⑤

Pluckley • Apartment • Sleeps 2 • £105-£120 • Closed Dec • Off-road parking, Channel Tunnel 35 mins • Jean Johnson ☎ 01233 840683 • ⑤ ® 🏠

☆ See Display Advertisement

LANCASHIRE

Chipping, Forest of Bowland • Coach-house • Sleeps 2 • £145-£190 • ★★★★ • joanporter@ukonline.co.uk • Mrs J Porter ☎ (01995) 61160 • ⑤ 🏠

Chipping, Nr Clitheroe • 4-part barn conversion • Sleeps 2-21 • £75-479 • ★★★-★★★★ • CH; woodburners; meals; laundry; panoramic views • Mrs Pat Gifford ☎ (01995) 61332 • 🏠 • B&B also

Longridge Fell, Nr Chipping • 2 cottages which can be linked in barn conversion • Sleeps 4-10 + 2 cots • £180-£280 • AONB; panoramic views; laundry; CH • Ness & Oliver Starkey ☎ (01995) 61476 • ⑤ 🏠

Ribble Valley • 2 apartments in converted stable • Sleeps 4-6 • £200-300 • ★★★★ • pilko@madasafish.com • Mrs Freda M Pilkington ☎ (01200) 445370 • ⑤

Rossendale Valley • 1 farmhouse • Sleeps 6-8 • £200-275 • Excellent walks, woodburner, views, parking, peaceful • Wendy Davison ☎ (01706) 224741 • ⑤ 🏠

☆ **Slaidburn** • 2 Semi-detached cottages • Sleeps 2-5 • £140-£165 • Farmhouse close by; convenient for shop and inn • Mrs S Parker ☎ (01200) 446288

Todmordern • semi-detached cottage • Sleeps 4 • £120-£170 • 3k/Comm • Comfortable accommodation. Pennine/Calderdale Way • Mr & Mrs A Bentham ☎ 01706 815265 • ⑤ ®

LEICESTERSHIRE & RUTLAND

Belton-in-Rutland • Cottage • Sleeps 2-3 • £120-£185 (short breaks av.) • Closed Xmas • Rambler's/birdwatcher paradise; idyllic position • Mrs Patricia L Brown ☎ (01572) 717440 • ⑤ 🏠 • B&B also

Belton-in-Rutland • 2 apartments • Sleeps 2-5 • £150-260 • 3k/Comm • Conservation village; Macmillan Way/Leicestershire Round • Richard & Vanessa Peach ☎ (01572) 717279 • ⑤ 🏠 • B&B also; Caravan/Camping also

☆ **Edith Weston** • 3 cottages • Sleeps 4-8 • £385-£525 • 4k/HC • www.rutnet.co.uk • J Barber ☎ 01780 720081 • 🏠

Rutland Water

Three period stone cottages located in the pretty village of Edith Weston (South Shore) & Rutland conservation village of Morcott

ɪ ɪ ɪ ɪ They comprise of 2, 3, & 4 bedroom cottages all with private gardens. All have log burning fires or stoves and are located in quiet cul-de-sacs, just minutes from the village pub.

Rutland is an ideal area for walking and Birdwatching

Tel 01780 720081 (w/e) or 0115 9373201 (week)

Sibbertoft, Market Harborough • 3 chalets • Sleeps 3-6 • £140-£420 • ★★★-★★★★ • Peaceful lakeside setting. Jurassic Way 1 mile • Mary & Jasper Hart ☎ (01858) 880886 • 🏠 • B&B also; Caravan/camping also

LINCOLNSHIRE

Dunholme, Lincoln • 1 cottage • Sleeps 3 • £120-160 • david@remy.freeserve.co.uk • Mrs D Pymer ☎ (01673) 860134 • Ⓢ

Louth • 1 cottage, 1 flat, 3 log cabins • Sleeps 2-6 • £180-380 • 3-4k/HC • Includes use of private health club. www.ashwaterhouse.co.uk • Mrs H Mapletoft ☎ (01507) 609295 • Ⓢ 🏠

GREATER MANCHESTER

Delph • 1 converted barn • Sleeps 2 • £130-250 • Closed Xmas • Overlooks reservoirs; Nr Pennine Way • Beverley Johnson ☎ (01457) 875886 • 🏠

MERSEYSIDE

Canning • 5 rooms, 42 dorm beds • Sleeps 4-20 • £12.50-81.50 • www.embassie.com • Kevin Murphy Ⓢ

NORFOLK

Alby, nr Aylsham • cottage • Sleeps 2 • £150-£225 • Unspoilt countryside • Mr & Mrs Parry ☎ 01263 768606/733843 • Ⓢ • B&B also

Aylsham • Barn conversion • Sleeps 3 • £170-£240 • Sunny rural situation near Weavers Way • Dick Applin ☎ (01263) 733626 • Ⓢ Ⓡ

Blakeney • 6 cottages/flats • Sleeps 2-7 • £199-399 • veronicaalvarez@compuserve.com blakeneycottages.co.uk • Veronica Alvarez ☎ (01462) 768627 • 🏠

Brancaster • 11 cottages • Sleeps 2-10 • £230-825 • ★★★ • www.brancaster.com • Mrs S Lane ☎ 07885 269538 • 🏠

Brancaster Staithe • 2 cottages • Sleeps 2-6 • £180-600 • up to 4k/Comm • Open fires, superb views, short breaks • Gloria Smith ☎ (01328) 738380 • 🏠

Burnham Market • cottage • Sleeps 5+3+cot • £140-£453 • ★★ • Weekly short breaks available. Parking • Enid & Bert Poll ☎ (01328) 738840 • 🏠

Castle Acre • cottage • Sleeps 6 • £150-£250 • Closed Oct-Mar • 3k/Comm • Delightful village on Peddars Way • Mrs A C C Swindell ☎ (01534) 727480 • Ⓢ 🏠

☆ **Cley-next-the-Sea** • cottage • Sleeps 2-7 • £150-360 • 3k/Comm • Character cottage, comfortable and well-equipped • Mrs V Jackson ☎ (01992) 511303 • Ⓢ 🏠

Cromer • 6 cottages • Sleeps 2-6 • £135-540 • 3-4k com • www.smoothound.co.uk/hotels/grovebed.html • John Graveling ☎ (01263) 512412 • Ⓢ Ⓡ 🏠

Foxley, Dereham • 8 converted stables, 2 cottages • Sleeps 3-7 • £160-£390 • ★★★ • 365 acres mature woodland; ideal for ramblers • Mr P Davis ☎ (01362) 688523 • 🏠

☆ **Holt** • 8 cottages • Sleeps 2-6 • £150-£550 • 4k/Comm-HC • Surrounded by fields and trees • Diana Elsby ☎ /Fax 01263 587347 • Ⓢ 🏠

☆ **Norwich** • flats & houses on campus • Sleeps 2-10 • £72.50-92.50 • Closed late Sept- early Jun • Sports centre • Anna Jarrett, Conference Office ☎ 01603 593271 • B&B also; groups also

University of East Anglia

Just 2 miles from historic Norwich city centre, On a rural campus. UEA is an ideal base for coastal walking & exploring the broads. Individuals, groups & families welcome. En suite rooms available all year round.
Budget accommodation available June-September. Closed at Xmas
Tel: 01603 593271   Fax: 01603 250585

Wells-next-the-Sea • Cottage • Sleeps 2 • £190-£285 (Xmas/NY extra) • Traditional flint cottage by salt-marshes • Lesley Whitby ☎ 020 7485 0573/020 7679 9477 • ⑤

Weybourne • 5 Cottages • Sleeps 2-7 • £120-425 • ★★★ • Outdoor pool, games room, laundry, parking • Sally Middleton ☎ (01263) 588334

NORTHAMPTONSHIRE

Sibbertoft, Market Harborough • 3 chalets • Sleeps 3-6 • £140-£420 • ★★★-★★★★ • www.brook-meadow.co.uk • Mary & Jasper Hart ☎ (01858) 880886 • 🛁 • B&B, Caravan/camping also

NORTHUMBERLAND

Barrasford, Hadrian's Wall • Cottage • Sleeps 6 • £220-280 • ★★ • www.smoothhound.co.uk/hotels/barrasfd.html • Joyce Milburn ☎ (01434) 681237 • 🛁 • B&B and bunkhouse also

Cheviot Hills, Wooler • Farm cottage • Sleeps 7 • £150-350 • 3K • www.kimmerston.com • Dickie & Jane Jeffreys ☎ (01668) 216283 • ⑤ 🛁

Corbridge • 3 + cottage • Sleeps 3+cot • £100-£260 • 3k/Comm • Comfortable, convenient cottage near Roman Wall • Mrs V Robson ☎ /fax 01661 871135 • Ⓡ

Embleton • 7 cottages • Sleeps 2-7 • £225-£495 • 3-4k/Comm-HC • www.doxfordfarm.co.uk • Sarah Shell ☎ (01665) 579348 • ⑤ 🛁

Hadrian's Wall • 5 cottages • Sleeps 2-6 • £190-£300 • 3k/Comm • Pub nearby. cottages@hadrianswall.co.uk • Mrs Lyn Murray ☎ (01434) 688688 • Ⓡ 🛁 • B&B, groups and hostel also

Hadrian's Wall, Haltwhistle • 3 farm cottages • Sleeps 2-6 • £155-£410 • ★★★ • www.old-white-craig-farm.co.uk • Mrs I Laidlow ☎ 01434 320565 • ⑤ Ⓡ 🛁 • B&B also

☆ **Morpeth** • 2 cottages • Sleeps 4-6 • £210-400 • 5k/HC • Mr & Mrs Coatsworth ☎ (01661) 881241 • ⑤

Gallowhill Farm
Whalton, Morpeth, Northumberland NE61 3TX

Two spacious, comfortable tastefully decorated fully equipped cottages. Set in rural countryside with wonder-sul views and walks. Sorry no pets.
Brochure 01661 881241

☆ **Rothbury** • 1 cottage • Sleeps 2 • £150-250 • 4k/Comm • sarah@chisolm5.fsnet.co.uk • Mrs Sarah Chisholm ☎ (01665) 570661 • ⑤

Cartwheel Cottage
Northumberland

Cottage on working farm sleeps 2, twin or double. Quiet walking area in the Coquet Valley. Open all year.
Enquiries Mrs S Chisholm 01665 570661

Seahouses • cottage • Sleeps 4-5 • £170-330 • ★★★ • Comfortable cottage, Cheviot and coastal walks • Mrs A K Riley ☎ 01665 720325 • ⑤

Sharperton • 1 cottage • Sleeps 8 • £320-690 • ★★★★★ • www.charityhallfarm.com • Mandy Lance ☎ (01669) 650219

Slaley Nr Hexham • 1 cottage • Sleeps 4-5+cot • £180-300 • ★★★★ • www.moorgair.co.uk • Mrs Vicki Ridley ☎ (01434) 673473 • ⑤

Thropton, Morpeth • 2 Cottages • Sleeps 2-5 • £140-£325 • ★★★ • Quiet & rural • Mrs H Farr ☎ (01665) 574672 • B&B also

Wooler • 1 cottage • Sleeps 4 • £190-340 • Beautiful cottage in National Park • Mrs Jean Alexander ☎ (01668) 216077 • ⑤

OXFORDSHIRE

The Mill at Burford • 1 cottage, 4 apartments • Sleeps 2-5 • £190-492 • 3-4k • themillatburford.co.uk • Pat Waddell ☎ (01993) 822379 • 🛁

☆ See Display Advertisement

115

SHROPSHIRE

Bishop's Castle • 3 cottages • Sleeps 2-6 • £120-£300 • ★★★ • www.go2.co.uk/claremont • Mrs Audrey Price ☎ (01588) 638170 • 🐾

Bishop's Castle • Cottage • Sleeps 4-6 • £100-£240 • Victorian, Grade II Listed; open fire • Mrs Pamela Towlson ☎ (01588) 620422 • Ⓢ 🐾

Church Stretton • Bungalow • Sleeps 6 + cot • £180-£300 • ★★★★ • Beautiful views. Homely. Free Central Heating • R E & L J Powell ☎ 01694 723159 • Ⓡ 🐾

☆ **Clun** • 1 cottage • Sleeps 2 • £130-250 • G Davies ☎ (01588) 640835 • 🐾

Clun, South Shropshire

Cottage in village centre
with pubs & shops.
S/C sleeps 2, C/H, linen included.
Smokers/pets welcome.

Offa's Dyke, Stretton Hills,
Local walks.

01588 640 835/490

Clun Valley • 11 cottages & flats • Sleeps 2-8 & groups • £103-367 • ★★-★★★ • Beautiful area, caring owners, short breaks • Roger & Sheila Davies ☎ /Fax (01588) 660487 • Ⓡ 🐾 • B&B, groups also

Clun, Nr Biston • 1 cottage • Sleeps 4 • £225-385 • ★★★★ • G Della Casa & Andrew Farmer ☎ (01588) 640409 • Ⓢ

Colebatch • Bungalow • Sleeps 2-4 • £140-£230 • ★★★ • Overlooks open countryside, own garden, CH • Maureen Thuraisingham ☎ 01588 638560 • 🐾

☆ **Diddlebury, Nr Ludlow** • 3 cottages • Sleeps 4-6 • £190-410 • sally@goosefoot.freeserve.co.uk • Mrs S Loft ☎ (01584) 861326 • Ⓢ 🐾

Goosefoot Barn Cottages

Pinstones, Diddlebury, near Ludlow

Converted in 2000 from stone and timbered barns, the three cottages are equipped to the highest standards. Each cottage has ensuite facilities and private garden or seating area. Situated in a secluded valley with walks from the doorstep through beautiful Corvedale. Pets welcome. Short breaks.

Telephone 01584 861326

☆ **Eudon Burnell, Bridgnorth** • 3 cottages • Sleeps 4-5+baby • £190-£310 • 4-5k/Comm • Lovely rural area. Well-equipped & comfortable • Margaret Crawford Clarke ☎ 01746 789235 • 🐾

Eudon Burnell Cottages,
Nr. Bridgnorth, Shropshire

1 at 4 Keys Commended   2 at 5 Keys Commended
3 Bedroomed cottages on working dairy/arable farm. Own attractive gardens, centrally heated well equipped & comfortable. A peaceful situation with lovely views of Shropshire Hills and surrounding countryside.
Tel:01746 789235   Fax:01746 789550
www.stargate-uk.co.uk/eudon-burnell-cottages
email: Eudon-Burnell@talk21.com

Leintwardine • 1 cottage • Sleeps 4 • £180-300 • ★★★ • Near to Offas Dyke & Mortimers Way • Deanna Jones ☎ (01547) 540670 • Ⓢ 🐾

Ludlow • 6 cottages • Sleeps 2-6 • £195-460 • ★★★★ • www.go2.co.uk/suttoncourtfarm • Jane Cronin ☎ 01584 861305 • 🐾

Much Wenlock • Cottage • Sleeps 5-6 • £180-250 • Closed Oct-Mar • 3k/C • stokesbarn@hotmail.com • Mrs Suzanne Hill ☎ (01952) 727293 • Ⓢ 🐾 • Bunkbarn also

Priest Weston • 1 cottage • Sleeps 2-4 • £125-250 • Between Stiperstones & Offas Dyke. Pub nearby • Mr R Edwards ☎ (01588) 620090

Stiperstones • Cottage • Sleeps 2+2+cot • £100-£180 • 2k/Comm • Breathtaking scenery; shop and inn nearby • Mrs Penelope Thornton ☎ (01743) 791401 • 🐾

Stiperstones • 1 studio, 1 caravan • Sleeps 2-4 • £100-£150 • Closed Dec/Jan • 3k/Comm • Wonderfull views; footpath to the Stiperstones • Marlene Rowson ☎ (01743) 791219 • 🐾

Stiperstones • 1 cottage • Sleeps 3-5 • £100-200 • Charming cottage; scenery; short breaks • Alison Symons ☎ (07855) 109538 • Ⓢ 🐾

Woolston • Cottage • Sleeps 2 • £120-140 • Map 137/423872; near Longmynd and Wenlock Edge • Mrs Carol Morris ☎ (01694) 781427 • 🐾

SOMERSET

Barton, nr Cheddar • 5 converted barns • Sleeps 2-6 • £190-£340 • }}}}S • www.homefarmcottages.co.uk • Christine Marlow ☎ 01934 842078 • Ⓢ 🐾

SPRING COTTAGES, CHEDDAR

ETC ★★★

Converted Barn for all seasons with Parking/ Gardens/Drying room. Dogs welcome. No smoking. Mendips/Somerset Levels offer varied walking.
Tel/Fax 01934 742493
www.springcottages.co.uk
email: buckland@springcottages.co.uk

Burrowbridge • bungalow annexe • Sleeps 2 • £130-£165 • 3k/Comm • Fully equipped; central heating; rural location • Mrs Ros Griffiths ☎ (01823) 698308 • ⑤ 🐾

☆ **Cheddar** • 3 cottages • Sleeps 2-3 • £170-£260 • ★★★ • See display ad for website/email • Mrs Jennifer Buckland ☎ (01934) 742493 • ⑤ 🐾

☆ **Exmoor** • Bungalow • Sleeps 2-3 • £125-£195 • 3k/App • Mrs Hudson ☎ (01643) 831223/487 • 🐾

EXMOOR NATIONAL PARK
on Two Moors Way

Two bedroom, centrally heated bungalow sleeps 3. Quiet isolated moorland farm.

Fantastic waymarked walks
Private river fishing
Good birdwatching
Brochure available

☎ **01643 831223/487**

☆ **Exmoor National Park** • 4 barn-conversion cottages • Sleeps 2-7 • £95-£415 • ★★★★ • Peaceful location beside River Exe • Leone & Brian Martin ☎ (01643) 831480 • 🐾

Exmoor National Park

Riscombe Farm Holiday Cottages

✦ Four charming self-catering stone cottages converted from barns surrounding an attractive courtyard
✦ Very comfortable, with log fires and equipped to a high standard, sleeping 2-7
✦ Peaceful, relaxing location beside the River Exe in the centre of Exmoor National Park
✦ Excellent walking country in the valleys, across the moors or along the spectacular coast
✦ One and a half miles from Exford village
✦ Dogs welcome. Open all year.
✦ ETC ★★★★

Brochure from the resident owners
Leone & Brian Martin, Riscombe Farm, Exford,
Minehead, Somerset TA24 7NH
Tel/Fax (01643) 831480
website: www.riscombe.co.uk

☆ **Exmoor** • cottages • Sleeps 2-5 • £500-700 • 4K • www.hindon.co.uk • Penny Webber ☎ (01643) 705244 • ⑤ Ⓡ 🐾

☆ **Exmoor, nr Dulverton** • Castle • Sleeps 2-5 • £300-700 • "Another world; another time; another place!" • Mrs Judy Dale ☎ (01398) 341615 • ⑤ 🐾

☆ **Roadwater** • 1 cottage • Joan Facey-Middleton ☎ 020 8310 1450 • ⑤ 🐾

Simonsbath, Exmoor • 5 cottages • Sleeps 1-6 • £165-540 • 4k/HC • Ideal base for a walking holiday • Jane Styles ☎ (01643) 831222 • 🐾

☆ See Display Advertisement

SOMERSET ENGLAND SELF-CATERING ACCOMMODATION

☆ **Timberscombe, Nr Dunster** • 1 house, 9 cottages & 2 flats • Sleeps 2-12 • £175-1510 • 3-4k/HC • Richard@Duddings.freeserve.co.uk • Richard Tilke

Duddings Country Cottages

Exmoor National Park, Dunster

★ Thatched Longhouse and eleven cottages for 2–12 persons, beautifully converted from old stone barns and stables.

★ Excellent base from which to explore National Park, 2 miles from Dunster.

★ Facilities include heated indoor pool, hard tennis court, putting, pool & table tennis.

★ Dogs welcome.

Open all year. Short breaks available.
ETC 3–4 keys highly commended
**Colour brochure from resident owners
Richard & Julie Tilke
Duddings, Timberscombe, nr Dunster
Tel 01643 841123   Fax: 01643 841165**

STAFFORDSHIRE

Kingsley • Cottage • Sleeps 2-5 • £165-£220 • 3k/App • Cosy, all-inclusive rambler's rest • Linda Salmon ☎ (01538) 754762 •

SUFFOLK

Darsham • Converted 17thC granary • Sleeps 4 • £135-£325 • ★★★ • Out of season wk/ends £35 per night • Mrs Bloomfield ☎ (01728) 668459 • Ⓢ Ⓡ • B&B also

Haughley, Stowmarket • Cottage • Sleeps 2/4 • £180-£210 • ★★★ • Comfortable cottage; rural area • Mrs Mary Noy ☎ (01449) 673323 • Ⓢ • B&B also

Orford • cottage • Sleeps 4 • £236-£363 • ★★★ • kaysorford@compuserve.com • Penny Kay ☎ 01394 450652 • Ⓢ

SURREY

Holmbury St Mary • 2 units • Sleeps 2-4 • £180-330 • ★★★ • Converted farm buildings on Greensand Way • Gill Hill ☎ (01306) 730210 • • Category 3 accessibility. B&B also

EAST SUSSEX

Alfriston • 1 cottage • Sleeps 4 • £170-365 • 4K • Charming village location. South Downs Way. • Mrs L Carwood ☎ (01273) 477044 •

Alfriston • 1 annex to house • Sleeps 2-small family • £210 • South Downs Way, excellent views • Fay Smith ☎ (01323) 870407 • Ⓢ

Nutley • 1 converted coach house • Sleeps 2 • £260-300 • chris@courthousecottage.fsnet.co.uk • Mrs C Hornett ☎ (01825) 713854 • Ⓢ

Pevensey Levels, Hailsham • 1 Eco-Building • Sleeps 4 • £250-375 • ★★★★ • kathryn.webster@which.net • Kathryn Webster ☎ (01323) 844690 • Ⓢ

☆ **Rye** • 5 cottages • Sleeps 2 • £150-395 • Newly converted. Full GCH. Linen included. • Jane Apperly ☎ (01797) 225426 • Ⓢ Ⓡ

CADBOROURGH FARM

Udimore Road, Rye, East Sussex TN31 6AA
Tel: 01797 225426 Fax: 01797 224097
E-Mail: cadfarm@marcomm.co.uk
Web: www.marcomm.co.uk/cadborough
5 Newly converted individual farm cottages.
Each sleeps 2 with own courtyards. Direct access to 1066 country walks and cliff track with sea views to Rye (1 mile). Full Gas c/h. Pets welcome.

Telscombe Village, Nr Lewes • Converted coach house • Sleeps 4 • £230-550 • 4K • Exquisite cottage on South Downs Way • Mrs Elizabeth Hollington ☎ (01273) 301844 • Ⓡ

WEST SUSSEX

Compton, nr Chichester • Flat • Sleeps 2 • £120-£195 • 4k/Comm • Ideal for walking South Downs • Mr J Buchanan ☎ 023 9232 4555 day/023 9263 1248 eve •

Henfield • 1 cottage, 1 flat • Sleeps 4-9 • £150-305 • ★★★ • On footpath close to South Downs • Mrs M W Carreck ☎ (01273) 492546 •

Slindon • 2 Flats • Sleeps 4 • £140-£350 • 3k/Comm • In NT village; views to coast • Peter & Sarah Fuente ☎ (01243) 814440 • • B&B also

FOUND A GOOD B&B THAT'S NOT IN THE YEARBOOK?
Send us recommendations for future editions

Steyning • bungalows • Sleeps 2-4 • £135-£235 • ★★ • www.wappingthorn.demon.co.uk • Mrs A Shapland ☎ 01903 813236 • B&B also

WILTSHIRE

Heddington • Barn conversion and bungalow • Sleeps 2-5 • £150-£395 • 4k/Comm • Roman Road, Wansdyke & downland walks from farm • Mrs Janet Tyler ☎ (01380) 850523 • ⑤

Manningford Abbotts, Pewsey Vale • 1 apartment in converted barn • Sleeps 2-4 • £200-270 • Well appointed apartment on ground level • Mrs Margot Andrews ☎ (01672) 563663 • ⑤ ⑱ 🐾

EAST YORKSHIRE

Beverley (nr) • 12 cottages • Sleeps 1-6 • £190-500 • ★★★★ • www.rudstone-walk.co.uk • Mrs Laura Greenwood ☎ (01430) 422230 • ⑤ 🐾 • B&B also

NORTH YORKSHIRE

Ampleforth/North York Moors • 2 cottages • Sleeps 2-6 • £180-440 • ★★★★ • www.highwoodsfarm.demon.co.uk • P & C Rowe ☎ (01347) 868188 • ⑤

Askrigg • Cottage • Sleeps 6 • £130-£325 • ★★★ • www.derbyhill.co.uk • Jane Grant ☎ (01773) 550489 • 🐾

Askrigg • Cottage • Sleeps 4 • £200 • Lounge with open fire • Mrs B Bowe ☎ (01969) 650535 • 🐾 • B&B also

☆ **Aysgarth Falls** • Cottage • Sleeps 5 • £152-284 • ★★★ • Wensleydale; unspoiled village; centre National Park • M C Mason ☎ (01792) 371602 • ⑤ 🐾

NEAR AYSGARTH FALLS

🍴🍴🍴🍴
Commended

MEADOWCROFT, THORALBY
Converted barn in quiet Dales village •
Superb walking • Sleeps 5 • Brochure •
Tel/Fax 01792 371602

☆ **Barningham, Teesdale** • Cottage • Sleeps 2-6 • £120-£300 • 3k/Comm • Wonderful walks, moors, dales, log fires • S M Catton ☎ (01833) 621374 • Transport from station

Burtersett, Wensleydale • Cottage • Sleeps 6 • £115-265 • Idyllic; walking, biking, secure storage, telephone • Steve Birkin ☎ (01959) 523071 • ⑤ 🐾

Clapham • 2 caravans • Sleeps 1-4 • £135-170 • Closed Dec-Jan • Modern caravans, Yorkshire Dales, Brochure available • Mrs Joan Close ☎ (015242) 51277 • ⑤ ⑱

☆ **Cloughton, Scarborough** • 4 cottages • Sleeps 2-7 • £105-£450 • ★★★★ • Quiet, peaceful, beautiful views, good walking • Mr D P Martin ☎ (01723) 870924 • B&B also

Ebberston • 2 apts & 6 cottages • Sleeps 2-6 • £200-750 • ★★★-★★★★ • cliffhouseebberston@btinterent.com • Simon Morris ☎ (01723) 859440

Egton Bridge, Whitby • Cottage • Sleeps 4 • £195-£220 • welcome@broomhouseegtonbridge.freeserve.co.uk • Mrs M White ☎ (01947) 895279 • ⑤ ⑱ 🐾 • B&B also

Goathland, North York Moors • Stone Cottage • Sleeps 2-10 • £300-750 • rhollingsb@aol.com • Jan Hollingsbee ☎ (01621) 742100 • ⑱ 🐾

Grassington • Apartment • Sleeps 2-4 • £115-£230 • ★★★ • Large, comfortable accommodation, over-looking village square • Ann Wadsworth ☎ (01253) 404726 • 🐾

Hawes, Askrigg, Muker • 5 Cottages • Sleeps 2-6 • £150-£450 • ★★★-★★★★ • www.askrigg.yorks.net • Kate Empsall ☎ /Fax (01969) 650565 • ⑤ 🐾 • B&B also

☆ See Display Advertisement

☆ **Hebden, nr Grassington** • 3 cottages, 1 bungalow, 3 flats • Sleeps 2-9 • £90-£350 • Secluded wooded valley, near Dales Way • Judith Joy ☎ (01756) 752369 • 🏕 • Camping also (field, no facilities)

Jerry and Ben's Holiday Cottages

7 properties near Grassington, Yorkshire Dales National Park. Open all year, sleep 2–9, £90 to £350.

Brochure available:

Mrs J Joy, Jerry and Ben's, Hebden, Skipton, N. Yorks BD23 5DL. Tel: 01756 752369. (Fax: 753370). Email: dawjoy@aol.com

Family run business for 30 years

Helmsley • Cottage • Sleeps 6 • £90-210 • Peaceful farm; walks galore; log fire • Mrs Isabelle Rickatson ☎ (01439) 748238 • Ⓢ 🏕 • Caravan site for members

Horton-in-Ribblesdale • Cottage & Barn Conversion • Sleeps 2-6 • £110-350 • ★★★ • Three Peaks; linen/towels inc. • Mrs S E Lambert ☎ (01729) 860367

Leyburn in Wensleydale • 2 cottages and 3 apartments • Sleeps 3-6 • £125-£230 • ★★ • Secluded courtyard off marketplace. Ideal centre • Mr Chilton ☎ 01969 623707/622808 • 🏕

Low Row, Richmond • Cottage • Sleeps 6 • £235-410 • 3k/Comm • Superb walking & touring; secluded; spectacular views • Kathleen Hird ☎ (01748) 886243

Malham • 3 Cottages, 1 flat • Sleeps 2-6 • £150-300 • Centre of village amidst limestone scenery • Mrs G Boocock ☎ (01729) 830317 • B&B also

☆ **Masham** • 2 cottages • Sleeps 5 • £100-£250 • HC • Double glazed, built in Yorkshire stone • J & V McCourt ☎ (01765) 689477 • Camping also - 4 ticks

FOUND A GOOD B&B THAT'S NOT IN THE YEARBOOK? Send us recommendations for future editions

North Yorks • 2 converted barn cottages • Sleeps 4-6 • £120-380 • ★★★ • Wonderful walks; Moors; Cleveland Way; Coasts • Mrs Nealia Pattinson ☎ (01947) 880243

North Yorks Moors • 1 Cottage & 1 House • Sleeps 5-7 + cots • £160-415 • ★★★ • Mrs Heather Eddon ☎ (01751) 460281 • www.cottageguide.co.uk/lilac-farm • Ⓡ 🏕

☆ **Pateley Bridge** • 4 lodges, 2 cottages • Sleeps 2-10 • £185-630 • ★★★★ • www.oldspringwoodlodges.co.uk • Rosemary Helme ☎ (01423) 780279 • 🏕

Old Spring Wood Lodges

& Cottages

Walk the Nidderdale Way through the Dales & Moors

Exclusive Scandinavian Lodges in natural woodland overlooking the Nidd valley. Excellently equipped. Cosy local pubs and eating places. Welcome Host Award. Pets welcome.

Contact: Rosemary Helme: 01423 780279

info@oldspringwoodlodges.co.uk www.oldspringwoodlodges.co.uk

☆ **Pickering, Ryedale** • 7 cottages (1 & 2 storey) • Sleeps 2-6 • £185-635 • ★★★★ Accessible Cat 3 • www.keldheadcottages.com • Penny & Julian Fearn ☎ (01751) 473974

Sedbusk, Hawes, and West Burton • 3 cottages • Sleeps 4-7 • PoA • 4k/HC • Lovely character old Dales stone cottages • Anne Fawcett ☎ (01969) 667481 • Ⓢ 🏕

Skipton • House • Sleeps 2-5 • £130-£270 • ★★★ • Panoramic moorland views, close Skipton centre • Ann Wadsworth ☎ 01253 404726 • Ⓡ 🏕

Sutton Bank, Thirsk • 1 Cottage • Sleeps 6-7 • £185-£330 • 4k/Comm • Fully equipped, including dishwasher, games room • Mrs Jean Jeffray ☎ (01845) 597363 • B&B also

Thormanby • 2 cottages • Sleeps 2-6 • £140-£310 • CH; open fires; quiet lane • Rachel Ritchie ☎ (01845) 501417 • 🏕 • B&B also

ETC ✓✓✓ ## Black Swan Holiday Park

Masham

Luxury caravans for hire, tourers and tents welcome. The park is in an area of outstanding natural beauty designated by the Countryside Agency as ideal for walking.

www.geocities.com/theblackswan_uk/ blackswanholidaypark@fsmail.net Tel/Fax 01765 689477

Gateway to the North Yorkshire Moors
Keld Head Farm Cottages
Pickering, North Yorkshire

★★★★ English Tourism Council ★★★★

Seven character stone cottages one and two storey, set around a secluded courtyard, each with open beamed ceilings and stone fire places. Superbly equipped, CH, double glazed, private parking, landscaped gardens and children's play area. Sleeps two to six. All cottages have linen, towels, TV, radio, microwave, toaster, coffee maker etc. provided. Open all year. Off peak senior citizen discount. Short breaks.
DISABLED ACCESS CAT. 3
Contact Penny & Julian Fearn.
Tel: 01751 473974 post code YO18 8LL

Whitby • 3 holiday apartments • Sleeps 1-4 • £195-450 • Closed Dec • ★★★★ A non-smoking establishment. Short breaks welcome • Mrs Pauline Moore ☎ (01947) 604813 • ⑤ ®

York • 14 lodges, 2 cottages • Sleeps 2-7 • £195-660 • ★★★★-★★★★★ • www.yorklakesidelodges.co.uk • Mr R N Manasir ☎ (01904) 702346 • ® 🐕

WEST YORKSHIRE

Haworth • 7 cottages • Sleeps 2-6 • £90-420 • ★★★★ • www.brontecountrycottages.co.uk • Mrs C Pickles ☎ (01535) 644568 • ® 🐕

Scotland

ARGYLL & BUTE

Isle of Luing, nr Oban • 6 caravans • Sleeps 2-8 • £100-£250 • Closed Nov-Mar • Waterside, wildlife, spectacular location. • Pat Moffat ☎ 01852 314274 • 🐕 • Groups also

Kilmelford • 1 cottage • Sleeps 1-5 • £177-321 • Closed Nov-March • ★★ • Great walking among hills & forests • Mrs G H Dalton ☎ (01866) 844212

Rambler's Association members are covered by a public liability insurance policy further details from central office

CENTRAL BELT

AYRSHIRE (E, N & S), CLACKMANNANSHIRE, DUMBARTONSHIRE (E & W), DUNDEE, EDINBURGH, FALKIRK, FIFE, GLASGOW, INVER-CLYDE, LANARKSHIRE (N & S), LOTHIAN (E & W), MIDLOTHIAN, RENFFREWSHIRE & EAST RENFREWSHIRE

Edinburgh • Flat • Sleeps 5 • £300-£475 • ★★ • Unrestricted parking; first floor; residential area • Jim Donaldson ☎ 0131-337 1066 • ⑤ ® • B&B also

DUMFRIES & GALLOWAY

Garlieston, Wigtownshire • Cottage • Sleeps 2-6 • £180 • Sea view. Forest & hill walking nearby • J & P Bainbridge ☎ 01400 230396 • 🐕

☆ **Laurieston** • House • Sleeps 6 • £230-320 • Galloway Hills & Southern Upland Way • Miss A C Paterson ☎ (01224) 595561

HIGHLAND

☆ **Arinacrinachd, Wester Ross** • 1 converted byre • Sleeps 4 • £12.50 per person per night • school-house@balnacra.com • M Buchanan ☎ (01520) 755231 • ⑤

Diabaig, Ross & Cromarty • Caravan • Sleeps 4 • £28-£40 • Closed Dec-Feb • Harbour nearby, hill walker's paradise • Mrs I Ross ☎ (01445) 790268 • 🐕 • B&B also

☆ See Display Advertisement

SELF-CATERING ACCOMMODATION ENGLAND – SCOTLAND

Diabaig, Torridon • Caravan • Sleeps 4 • £75-130 • Private location, fully equipped, walkers paradise • Ms Anne Ross ☎ (01445) 790240 • 🏠

☆ **Fort William** • 8 chalets, 3 Bdm Log House • Sleeps 4-7 • £275-£700 • Closed Nov • 2 Cr • Spectacular Mountain Views; Quiet rural location • Chris Carver ☎ (01397) 703015 • 🏠

☆ **Glencoe Village** • 3 cottages • Sleeps 6-8 • £425-£575 • ★★★ • www.aboutscotland.com./glencoe/torren • Victoria Sutherland ☎ 01855 811207 • 🏠 • Groups also

Glenelg, nr Shiel Bridge • 1 bungalow, 6 chalets, 1 caravan • Sleeps 1-6 • £100-£320 • ★★★ • Laundry, indoor games room, payphone, parking • M & E Lamont ☎ (01599) 522231 • 🏠

Grantown-on-Spey • Flat/Bunkhouse • Sleeps 24 • £7.50 pppn • Groups over 6 - Leaders stay free • Tim & Rebecca Bird ☎ (01479) 872824 • Ⓢ 🏠

Inveralligin, Torridon • Cottage • Sleeps 2-6 • £180-£280 • Ideally situated for climbing and walking • Mrs Mary Mackay ☎ (01445) 791333 • Ⓢ • B&B also

Invergarry • Cottage, flat, house • Sleeps 2-12 • £150-£1200 • B&B also • Miss J Ellice ☎ (01809) 501287/501373 • 🏠

Invergarry • 3 cottages • Sleeps 4-6 • £160-400 • www.ardochy.ukgateway.net • Mr C L G Sangster ☎ (01809) 511292 • Ⓢ 🏠

☆ **Lochaber, Nr Fort William** • 2 farmhouses • Sleeps 6-9 • £500-800 • germanribon@postmaster.co.uk • Marilyn German-Ribon ☎ 020-7736-4684 • 🏠

Nethy Bridge • 2 chalets • Sleeps 4-7 • £95-255 • Closed Nov • Adjacent Speyside Way; Owners both mountaineers. • David Mordaunt ☎ /fax (01479) 821062 • 🏠 • BB also

Nethy Bridge • 6 studios, 2 cottages & 3 bungalows • Sleeps 2-9 • £120-680 • ★★★-★★★★ • speyside@enterprise.net • Brian Patrick ☎ (01309) 672505 • 🏠

Newtonmore • 4 cottages • Sleeps 4-18 • £140 upwards • ★★★W • Cairngorms, Monadhliaths, way-marked walks, drying room • Croft Holidays ☎ (01540) 673504 • Ⓡ 🏠 • Hostel also

☆ **Northern Cairngorms** • 3 log chalets • Sleeps 6-12 • £420-£1680 • 1 Cr • Bar, Pool, Gym, Climbing Wall, sauna. • Tim Walker ☎ (01479) 861256 • Ⓢ 🏠 • B&B and groups also

☆ **Ullapool, Ross-shire** • 2 cottages • Sleeps 2-6 • £180-£300 • Closed 11-3 • ★★ • Quiet conservation area, close to shops, harbour • Mrs P Campbell ☎ (01854) 612107 • Ⓢ 🏠

ISLE OF ARRAN

Blackwaterfoot • 2 cottages • Sleeps 2-6 • £175-£330 • Centrally heated, near beach & village, Aga • Mrs M Bannatyne ☎ (01770) 860276 • 🏠 • B&B also

ISLE OF EIGG

• Croft house • Sleeps 7 • £120-£260 • Beautiful Hebridean island, views of Skye/Rum • Peter Wade-Martins ☎ (01362) 668435 • 🏠

ISLE OF MULL

Salen, Argyll • 5 cottages • Sleeps 4-7 • £215-360 • ★★ • www.glenaros.co.uk • Sarah Scott ☎ (01631) 770369 • 🏠

ISLE OF SKYE

Glen Eynort, nr Glenbrittle • Cottage • Sleeps 6-8 • £300-£450 • ★★ • Walks start from doorstep; private location • R Van Der Vliet ☎ (01478) 640320 • 🏠 • B&B also

Isle of Skye • 3 chalets, conv. black house, cottage • Sleeps 4/5 • £110-£375 • chalets ★ • Quiet scenic locations. Paradise for walkers • Alistair & Helen Danter ☎ 01470 582221 • Ⓢ 🏠

Kildonan, nr Edinbane • Upper level flat • Sleeps 4 • £165-£245 • Closed Nov-Mar • Superb sunsets, loch & mountain views. • Mrs Barbara Herbert ☎ (01470) 582285 • 🏠

NORTH EAST SCOTLAND

ABERDEEN, ABERDEENSHIRE, ANGUS AND MORAY

Braemar, Aberdeenshire • 1 cottage, 1 chalet • Sleeps 2-5 • £200-320 • ★★★-★★★★ • www.hotel-braemar.co.uk • M Franklin ☎ (013397) 41275 • Ⓢ 🏠 • B&B also

☆ **Kintore, Inverurie** • cottage • Sleeps 4+cot • £225-£350 • Closed Dec-Feb • ★★★W • kfield@clara.net • Mrs J Lumsden ☎ (01467) 632366 • Ⓡ

Strathdon, Aberdeenshire • 2 cottages, 1 house • Sleeps 2-8 • £200-£310 • ★★ • Hill & woodland walks from accomodation • Mrs Elizabeth Ogg ☎ (019756) 51238 • 🏠 • B&B also

SCOTTISH BORDERS

Carlisle/Newcastleton • 4/5 cottages/flats • Sleeps 2-9 per cottage • £98-508 • 3k/Comm • Pony trekking, leisure suite, bar, meals • Mrs P Copeland ☎ (016977) 48617 • 🏠 • Groups also

STIRLING

Tyndrum • 1 chalet • Sleeps 4-6 • £180-200 • ★ • www.glengarryhouse.co.uk • Jim & Diane Mailer ☎ (01838) 400224 • Ⓡ 🏠

Wales

CARMARTHENSHIRE

Bethlehem, Llandeilo • Barn cottage • Sleeps 2-6 • £9 pppn • Historic farmhouse. Brecon Beacons National Park • Dick Walden-Jones ☎ (01558) 823465 • 🏠

CEREDIGION

Aberporth • 2 cottages, 1 caravan • Sleeps 2-5 • £130-350 • Closed Xmas • Peaceful sea/country views. Coastal walks • Christine Morgan ☎ (01239) 811506 • Ⓢ 🏠

Rhydlewis • 1 cottage • Sleeps 5/7 • £200-450 • ★★★★ • www.terradat.co.uk/rhydlewis • Judith Russill ☎ (01239) 851748 • Ⓢ

CONWY

Llansannan • 3 cottages • Sleeps 2-6 • £99-£256 • Off beaten track. Idyllic. Beams. CH • Mrs C Johnson ☎ (01745) 870426 • 🏠

☆ See Display Advertisement

GWYNEDD

☆ **Aberdovey** • 20 cottages & apartments • Sleeps 4-8 • £140-720 • ★★★★-★★★★★ • info@aberdoveyhillsidevillage.co.uk • Mary Robinson ☎ (01654) 767522 • Ⓡ 🐾

Aberdovey Hillside Village

Aberwynolwyn • Bungalow • Sleeps 4-5 • £150-175 • Closed Oct-April • Quiet location, Snowdonia National Park. • R Greenhalgh ☎ (01244) 679340 • Ⓢ Ⓡ

Beddgelert • House • Sleeps 6 • £65-285 • Snowdon path and inn nearby; views • Michael & Sue Davies ☎ 020 8670 2756

Bontddu • caravan • Sleeps 6 • £140-170 • Closed Nov-Feb • Working farm, estuary views, countryside walks • Mrs O Williams ☎ (01341) 430277 • 🐾

Criccieth, Snowdonia • 2 cottages • Sleeps 2-6 • £170-600 • ★★★★★ • www.rhos-cottages.co.uk • Mrs Anwen Jones ☎ (01758) 720047 • 🐾

Dolgellau • 2 cottages, 2 parts country house • Sleeps 2-21 • £121-602 • Walk guidesheets provided; Large bird-rich garden. • Gilbert & Pamela Gauntlett ☎ (01341) 423481 • 🐾

Dyffryn Ardudwy • cottage • Sleeps 2 • £125-£225 • Closed Jan • Delightfully rural. Sea/mountain views. Peaceful • Val & Tom Bethel ☎ 01341 247033 • Ⓢ Ⓡ 🐾

Llanuwchllyn • Cottage • Sleeps 2-8 • £180 • Isolated; mountain views; wood stove; no TV; telephone • J H Gervis ☎ (01992) 892331 • 🐾

Lleyn Peninsula • Farmhouse and caravan • Sleeps 6 • £85-£170 • Closed Oct-May (house) • Comfortable, clean accommodation; situated on B4417 • Mrs J M Roberts ☎ (01758) 770261 • 🐾

Nant Gwynant • House • Sleeps 2-12 • £330-675 • Unique situation, 14 acres, garden, lake • Harvey Lloyd ☎ 0118-948 2226 • Ⓢ 🐾 • Courses also

☆ **Pwllheli** • 9 cottages on farm • Sleeps 1-12 • £140-515 • 5 dragons • www.gwynfrynfarm.co.uk • Mrs R A Ellis ☎ (01758) 612536 • Ⓢ Ⓡ 🐾 • B&B also

Snowdonia • Cottage • Sleeps 6 • £179-£360 • ★★★ • www.mtn.co.uk/bobcole • Ann & Bob Cole ☎ (01766) 831356 • Ⓢ Ⓡ 🐾 • B&B also

Snowdonia • 5 Barn conversions, 2 Farmhouses • Sleeps 2-8 • £160-750 • 5 dragons • www.ystumgwern.co.uk • Jane Williams ☎ (01341) 247249 • Ⓢ Ⓡ 🐾

Tywyn • Cottage • Sleeps 2-5 • £285-£475 • ★★★★★ http://beganif.gwynedd.net/croeso.cader.idris/hendy.htm • Anne Lloyd-Jones ☎ (01654) 710457 • Ⓢ 🐾 • B&B also

MONMOUTHSHIRE

Tintern, Nr Chepstow • Apartment • Sleeps 3 + child • £169-300 • www.tinternoldirectory.co.uk • Wendy Taylor ☎ (01291) 689519 • Ⓢ 🐾

PEMBROKESHIRE

Broad & Little Haven • 4 cottages • Sleeps 2-9 • £95-£385 • welshhaven@aol.com • R Llewellin ☎ (01437) 781386 • 🐾 • B&B also

Manorbier • 2 Cottages • Sleeps 4-6 • £200-550 • 4 dragons • Pembs Coast Path. oldvic@manorbiertenby.fsnet.co.uk • Jill McHugh ☎ 01834 871452 • Ⓢ Ⓡ • B&B also

Newport • Farmhouse & 4 cottages • Sleeps 2-17 • £80-£620 • 4-5 dragons • Sea/mountain views; near Coastal path • Ann Evans ☎ (01239) 820733 • 🐾

Nolton Haven • 6 Cottages • Sleeps 4-6 • £125-460 • ★★ • www.noltonhaven.com • Jim Canton ☎ (01437) 710263 • 🐾

Penally, Tenby • Caravan • Sleeps 6-8 • £130-£160 • Shower, toilet, heating, close coastal path • Judy Williams ☎ (01834) 844467 • Ⓡ 🐾

Porthgain, St Davids • 3 stone cottages, 9 cedar lodges • Sleeps 1-9 • £130-£550 • 3 dragons • Peaceful location, overlooking sea, spectacular walking • Steve Craft ☎ (01348) 831220 • 🐾 • Groups also

St Davids • 4 cottages • Sleeps 2-18 • £95-£950 • ★★★★★ • Beautiful location, near coast. Groups also. • Thelma M Hardman ☎ (0118) 9266094 • Ⓢ Ⓡ 🐾

POWYS

Border country • Cottage • Sleeps 7-8 + cot • £160-£260 • Near Offa's Dyke; log fire • Mrs J E Pinches ☎ (01544) 370219

Brecon Beacons • 1 bungalow + 1 apartment • Sleeps 2-10 • PoA • 4-5 dragons • Walk direct from accommodation onto mountains • Ann Phillips ☎ (01874) 665329 • 🐾

Brecon Beacons • 3 cottages • Sleeps 4-6 • £190-£350 • ★★★★★ • http://selfcateringcottagesinwales.co.uk • Chris Benson ☎ 01685 383358 • Ⓢ 🐾

Crickhowell • 1 ground floor flat • Sleeps 2-3 • £90-125 • Closed Open Frid-Mon only • ★★★ • Laura Kostoris ☎ (01874) 676498 • Ⓢ 🐾

Llanwrtyd Wells • 2 large houses • Sleeps 28-31 • £1095 • ★★ • www.stonecroft.co.uk • Diane Lutman ☎ (01591) 610332 • Ⓢ Ⓡ

Ireland

COUNTY CORK

Glenduff, North Cork • 1 thatched farmhouse • Sleeps 5 • £125-280 • peterhouse@unisonfree.net • Peter Household ☎ (01904) 797972

COUNTY DONEGAL

The Rosses • Converted barn • Sleeps 2 + children • £165-220 • Baby sitting & evening meal by arrangement • Richard Cannon & Agnes Lynch ☎ 00 353 75 43146 • 🐾 • B&B also

COUNTY KERRY

Annascaul, Dingle Peninsula • Bungalow • Sleeps 4 • £130-300 • ★★ • Lake, sea, mountains; near Annascaul village • Kathleen O'Connor ☎ 00 353 66 9157168 • Ⓢ 🐾 • B&B also

Brandon Bay • 2 cottages • Sleeps 2-10 • £125-£225 • Close Brandon mountain, Dingle Way, beaches • Mrs G Pring ☎ 00 353 66 71 38305 • Ⓢ 🐾

Lauragh (Healy Pass Road) • Cottage • Sleeps 5-6 • £120-270 • 2 stars • Magnificent view of sea & countryside • Mrs Mary Moriarty ☎ 00 353 64 83131 • 🐾

COUNTY MEATH

Julianstown • 1 cottage • Sleeps 4-6 • up to £400 • Nr Newgrange, beaches & golf course. • Linda Scanlan ☎ /Fax (01799) 599616 • Ⓢ 🐾

France

NORMANDY

Putanges-Pont-Ecrepin • 1 converted barn • Sleeps 6 + cot • £200-275 • Closed Nov-Easter • Mr J Higgs normandie@tinyonline.co.uk • ☎ (01255) 860340

ORIENTALE

French Pyrenees • villa • Sleeps 2-6 • £80-£320 • Beautiful views, comfortable villa & mountain walking • Charley Symes ☎ 020 7733 1626 • 🐾

PAS DE CALAIS

Raye-sur-Authie • Old presbytery • Sleeps 2-15 • £300-1000 • sallelec@compuserve.com Boulogne/Calais 1 hour • Mike Potter ☎ 0033 (0) 321 86 32 25/(01227) 720464 • B&B also

Italy

TUSCANY

☆ **Fivizzano** • 2 apartments • Sleeps 4-8 • £1.200.000-2.000.000 Lira • Help with food preparation on request • Christina Meager ☎ /Fax 00 39 0585 926794

Portugal

ALGARVE

Lagoa, Porches, Algarve • 2 studio apts • Sleeps 2 • £100-125pw • Carol Brownson ☎ +351 282 449 921 Ⓡ

Porches, Lagoa • 1 studio chalet • Sleeps 2 • £175-350 • Margaret Reed ☎ +351 289 561 820 • Ⓢ

Spain

CANARY ISLANDS

☆ **Chirche, Tenerife** • 2 cottages • Sleeps 4-6 • £350-£400 • fellsandra@hotmail.com • Sandra Fell ☎ 01282 815798

The B&B Accommodation Guide

The entries are listed in order of country— England, Isle of Man, Scotland, Wales, Ireland and France in that order; then in alphabetical order of county (departments in France) or unitary authority, and then by place. The place might be a village or town or even a hamlet and the choice is determined by a number of elements—proximity to one of the long distance paths we feature on page 58; its ease of access to a resort or walking centre; or on occasion, the request of an advertiser. It is not possible to standardise this procedure and it is done by consulting maps and guides. If the place is within two miles of one of the long distance paths, the name of that path is given after the place name. As some "places" are sprawling, it is always best to check the location on a map.

Many of the entries in this guide come from readers' recommendations. As we are not able to vet the establishments, this is a most valuable resource. Please keep your recommendations coming in, by letter, telephone or email, or by using the recommendation form at the end of the book.

Six-figure grid references are given for each entry and the maps referred to are the Ordnance Survey Landranger series, scale 1:50,000, or the Discovery series in Ireland. These are generated using the postcode and can be innaccurate in some sparsely populated areas.

Finally—a disclaimer. Information in this guide is based on details received during 2000. The Ramblers' Association cannot be held responsible for errors or omissions.

For an explanation of the symbols used in this guide see back of book

England

BEDFORDSHIRE

■ **THORNCOTE GREEN (Sandy)**
GREENSAND WAY

Anne Franklin, Village Farm, SG19 1PU. ☎ (01767) 627345 • Map 153/152478 • BB **C** • EM book first £7, 7.30pm • S1 D1 T1 F1 • 1-11 • Ⓥ Ⓑ Ⓓ Ⓢ Ⓡ Ⓟ Ⓣ 🐾 • ◆◆ • On Greensand Ridge Walk.

BERKSHIRE

■ **COMPTON (Newbury)**
RIDGEWAY

☆ Garry Mitchell FBII, Compton Swan Hotel, High Street, RG20 6NJ. ☎ (01635) 578269 • Map 174/520799 • BB **D** • EM £7, 7-9.30pm • D1 T3 F1 • 1-12 • Ⓥ Ⓑ Ⓓ Ⓢ Ⓟ Ⓣ 🐾 • List • Caravan also • garry@comptonswan.freeserve.co.uk

■ **COOKHAM (Maidenhead)**
THAMES PATH

Cynthia Crowe, Wylie Cottage, School Lane, SL6 9QJ. ☎ (01628) 520106 • Map 175/895851 • BB **D** • D1 T1 • 1-12 NX • Ⓓ Ⓢ Ⓡ Ⓣ 🐾 • ◆◆◆ • crowegc@cwcom.net

■ **HUNGERFORD**

Liz & Gabriel Cave, Beacon House, Bell Lane, Upper Green, Inkpen, RG17 9QJ. ☎ (01488) 668640 • Map 174/369634 • BB **C** • EM book first £10, 6-9pm • S2 T1 • 1-12 • Ⓥ Ⓓ Ⓢ Ⓟ Ⓣ 🐾 • ◆◆◆ • l.g.cave@classicfm.net

Mr & Mrs Colin Honeybone, "Alderborne", 33 Bourne Vale, RG17 0LL. ☎ (01488) 683228 • Map 174/333682 • BB **B** • S1 T2 • 1-12 NX • Ⓑ Ⓓ Ⓢ Ⓡ Ⓟ Ⓣ Ⓜ • ◆◆◆◆ • Guided walks • honeybones@hungerford.co.uk

■ MAIDENHEAD
THAMES PATH

R J Street, Sheephouse Manor Guest House, Sheephouse Road, SL6 8HJ. ☎ (01628) 776902 • Map 175/898831 • BB **E** • S3 D1 T1 • 1-12 NX • Ⓑ Ⓓ Ⓢ Ⓟ Ⓣ ⛛ • ◆◆◆ • SC also

Mrs B Fox, 48 Birdwood Road, SL6 5AP. ☎ (01628) 670198 • Map 175/865809 • BB **C** • T2 • 1-12 NX • Ⓑ Ⓓ Ⓢ Ⓡ Ⓣ

■ READING
THAMES PATH

Mrs Hubbard, 24 Castle Crescent, RG1 6AG. ☎ 0118 961 0329 • Map 175/708727 • BB **C** • D1 F3 • 1-12 • Ⓓ Ⓢ Ⓡ Ⓣ ⛛ • Food nearby

■ STREATLEY (Reading)
RIDGEWAY & THAMES PATH & CHILTERN WAY

Mr & Mrs Vanstone, Pennyfield, The Coombe, RG8 9QT. ☎ (01491) 872048 • Map 174/587807 • BB **D** • D2 T1 • 1-10 • Ⓑ Ⓓ Ⓢ Ⓡ Ⓟ Ⓣ • ◆◆◆◆ • Oxon/Berks border • mandrvanstone@hotmail.com

■ WARGRAVE (Reading)
THAMES PATH

Heather Carver, Windy Brow, 204 Victoria Road, RG10 8AJ. ☎ 0118-940 3336 • Map 175/794788 • BB **E** • S2 D1 T1 • 1-12 NX • Ⓑ Ⓓ Ⓢ Ⓡ Ⓣ ⛛ Ⓜ • ◆◆◆◆ • House is on opposite side from path • heathcar@aol.com

■ WINDSOR
THAMES PATH & THREE CASTLES WALK

Mrs Joyce, "The Laurells", 22 Dedworth Road, SL4 5AY. ☎ (01753) 855821 • Map 175,176/952765 • BB **C** • S1 T2 • 1-12 NX • Ⓑ Ⓓ Ⓢ Ⓡ Ⓣ ⛛

BUCKINGHAMSHIRE

■ BLEDLOW
RIDGEWAY & CHILTERN WAY

Ronald Coulter, Cross Lanes Cottage, HP27 9PF. ☎ (01844) 345339 • Map 165/774024 • BB **D** • D2 T1 • 1-12 • Ⓑ Ⓓ Ⓢ Ⓡ Ⓟ

■ EDLESBOROUGH (Dunstable, Beds)
RIDGEWAY & ICKNIELD WAY

Mr & Mrs Lloyd, Ridgeway End, 5 Ivinghoe Way, LU6 2EL. ☎ (01525) 220405 • Map 165/974183 • BB **C** • S1 D1 T1 F1 • 1-11 • Ⓑ Ⓓ Ⓢ Ⓟ Ⓣ

■ GREAT KINGSHILL (High Wycombe)

Mrs M A Davies, Hatches Farm, Hatches Lane, HP15 6DS. ☎ (01494) 713125 • Map 165/873980 • BB **B** • D1 T1 • 1-12 NX • Ⓓ • ◆◆

■ GREAT MISSENDEN

Patchwicks, The Lee, HP16 9LZ. ☎ (01494) 837596 • Map 165/899043 • BB **C** • EM book first £9-11, 7.30pm • D1 T1 • 1-12 NX • Ⓥ Ⓑ Ⓓ Ⓢ Ⓟ • Food nearby

■ MARLOW
THAMES PATH & CHILTERN WAY

Mr & Mrs B Wells, Merrie Hollow, Seymour Court Hill, Marlow Road, SL7 3DE. ☎ (01628) 485663 • Map 175/837889 • BB **D** • EM book first £9, 7-8pm • D1 T1 • 1-12 • Ⓥ Ⓓ Ⓢ Ⓡ Ⓟ Ⓣ ⛛ • ◆◆◆

Mrs Mary Cowling, Acha Pani, Bovingdon Green, SL7 2JL. ☎ (01628) 483435 & fax • Map 175/834869 • BB **B** • EM book first £7 • S1 D1 T1 • 1-12 • Ⓥ Ⓑ Ⓓ Ⓡ Ⓟ Ⓣ ⛛ • ◆◆

■ NAPHILL (High Wycombe)

Sally Woodbridge, Woodside, Forge Road, HP14 4ST. ☎ (01494) 562281 • Map 165/840975 • BB **C** • T2 • 1-12 NX • Ⓑ Ⓓ Ⓢ Ⓟ Ⓣ

■ SAUNDERTON (High Wycombe)
RIDGEWAY

Mrs Anne Dykes, Hunters Gate, Deanfield, HP14 4JR. ☎ (01494) 481718 • Map 165/809975 • BB **D/E** • D2 T1 • 1-12 • Ⓑ Ⓓ Ⓢ Ⓡ Ⓟ Ⓣ ⛛ Ⓜ • dadykes@ibm.net

■ WENDOVER (Aylesbury)
RIDGEWAY & GRAND UNION CANAL WALK

Mrs E C Condie, 26 Chiltern Road, HP22 6DB. ☎ (01296) 622351 • Map 165/865082 • BB **B** • S1 T/F1 • 1-12 NX • Ⓓ Ⓢ Ⓡ Ⓣ ⛛ Ⓜ • App • SC also

☆ The Red Lion Hotel, 9 High Street, HP22 6DU. ☎ (01296) 622266 • Map 165/868078 • BB **E** • EM book first £7-12, 6-10pm, 7-9.30pm Sun • S2 D11 T4 F4 • 1-12 • Ⓥ Ⓑ Ⓓ Ⓡ Ⓟ • ★★

■ WEST WYCOMBE (High Wycombe)
The Swan Inn, HP14 3AE. ☎ (01494) 527031 • Map 175/829945 • BB **D** • S1 D2 T1 F1 • 1-12 NX • Ⓢ Ⓡ Ⓣ

☆ See Display Advertisement

127

BERKSHIRE – BUCKINGHAMSHIRE

ENGLAND

B&B ACCOMMODATION

CAMBRIDGESHIRE

■ CALDECOTE (Cambridge)

☆ Margaret & George Baigent, Avondale, 35 Highfield Road, CB3 7NX. ☎ (01954) 210746 • Map 154/358590 • BB **C** • D1 T1 F1 • 1-12 NX • Ⓑ Ⓓ Ⓢ Ⓣ 🛠

■ CAMBRIDGE

Mrs M Sanders, 145 Gwydir Street, CB1 2LJ. ☎ (01223) 356615 • Map 154/462579 • BB **C** • T1 • 1-12 NX • Ⓓ Ⓢ Ⓡ Ⓟ Ⓣ • marysan@waitrose.com

Mrs D J Wyatt, The Willows, 102 High Street, Landbeach, CB4 8DT. ☎ (01223) 860332 • Map 154/477650 • BB **B** • S2 D1 T1 • 1-12 • Ⓓ Ⓢ Ⓡ Ⓣ 🛠

Dykelands Guest House, 157 Mowbray Road, CB1 7SP. ☎ (01223) 244300 • Map 154/471561 • BB **C** • S1 D2 T3 F3 • 1-12 • Ⓑ Ⓓ Ⓢ Ⓡ Ⓣ 🛠 • ◆◆◆ • www.dykelands.com

■ HEMINGFORD GREY (Huntingdon)

Willow Guest House, 45 High Street, PE18 9BJ. ☎ (01480) 494748 • Map 153/295706 • BB **C** • S2 D2 T1 F2 • 1-12 • Ⓑ Ⓓ Ⓢ Ⓟ Ⓣ

■ KIRTLING (Newmarket, Suffolk)

☆ Mrs Ann Bailey, Hill Farm, CB8 9HQ. ☎ (01638) 730253 • Map 154/682583 • BB **C/D** • EM book first £12.50, 7-9.30pm • S1 D1 T1 • 1-12 NX • Ⓥ Ⓑ Ⓓ Ⓟ Ⓣ 🛠 • ◆◆◆

■ LINTON
ICKNIELD WAY

Mrs M Clarkson, Cantilena, 4 Harefield Rise, CB1 6LS. ☎ 01223 892988 • Map 154/571466 • BB **B** • D1 T1 F1 • 1-12 • Ⓓ Ⓢ Ⓣ • Situated in a quiet road

■ WISBECH

P J Parish, Ravenscourt Guest House, 138 Lynn Road, PE13 3DP. ☎ (01945) 585052 • Map 131,143/466102 • BB **B** • D2 T1 F1 • 1-12 NX • Ⓑ Ⓓ Ⓢ Ⓣ • www.placetostay-uk.com

■ WITCHFORD (Ely)

Rosendale Lodge, 223 Main Street, CB6 2HT. ☎ 01353 667700 • Map 143/493788 • BB **C** • EM book first £10, 7-8pm • S1 D3 T3 F1 • 1-12 • Ⓥ Ⓑ Ⓓ Ⓢ Ⓟ Ⓣ • ◆◆◆◆◆ Ⓢ

CHESHIRE

■ ALTRINCHAM

Oasis Hotel, 46-48 Barrington Road, WA14 1HN. ☎ (0161) 928 4523 • Map 109/769885 • BB **C/D/E** • EM £10, 5.30-10.30pm • S10 D11 T9 F3 • 1-12 • Ⓥ Ⓑ Ⓓ Ⓡ Ⓟ Ⓣ • ★★ • www.oasishotel.co.uk

■ CHURCH MINSHULL (Crewe)

Mrs A M Charlesworth, Higher Elms Farm, Cross Lane, Minshull Vernon, CW1 4RG. ☎ (01270) 522252 • Map 118/669607 • BB **C** • S1 D1 T1 F1 • 1-12 • Ⓑ Ⓓ Ⓢ Ⓟ Ⓣ 🛠 • ◆◆ • Food nearby www.guestaccom.co.uk/468.htm

■ CONGLETON
STAFFORDSHIRE WAY & CHESHIRE RING CANAL

Mrs Sheila Kidd, Yew Tree Farm, North Rode, CW12 2PF. ☎ (01260) 223569 • Map 118/890665 • BB **B/C** • EM book first £10, 6.30pm • D1 T2 • 1-12 NX • Ⓥ Ⓑ Ⓓ Ⓢ Ⓟ Ⓣ • ◆◆◆◆ • Beautiful views. • kiddyewtreefarm@netscapeonline.co.uk

■ HARGRAVE (Chester)

Deborah & Peter Newman, Greenlooms Cottage, Martins Lane, CH3 7RX. ☎ (01829) 781475 • Map 117/476633 • BB **C** • EM book first £12.50, 7.30pm • D1 T1 • 1-12 • Ⓥ Ⓑ Ⓓ Ⓢ Ⓟ Ⓣ 🛠 • greenlooms@talk21.com

■ NORTHWICH
CHESHIRE RING CANAL

Mrs S M Schofield, Ash House Farm, Chapel Lane, Acton Bridge, CW8 3QS. ☎ (01606) 852717 • Map 117/587755 • BB **C** • EM book first £10, 7.00pm • S1 D1 T1 F1 • 1-12 • Ⓥ Ⓑ Ⓓ Ⓢ Ⓡ Ⓟ 🛠 • ◆◆◆ • sue_schofield40@hotmail.com

☆ Mrs Terri Campbell, Manor Farm, Cliff Road, Acton Bridge, Weaverham, CW8 3QP. ☎ (01606) 853181 • Map 117/587767 • BB **C** • S1 D1 T1 F1 • 1-12 NX • Ⓑ Ⓓ Ⓢ Ⓡ Ⓟ Ⓣ♿ • ◆◆◆◆ • terri.mac.manorfarm@care4free.net

■ TIMBERSBROOK (Congleton)
STAFFORDSHIRE WAY & CHESHIRE RING CANAL

Pedley House Farm, CW12 3QD. ☎ (01260) 273650 • Map 118/897637 • BB **B** • EM book first £10, 6.30pm • D/T1 F1 • 1-12 NX • Ⓥ Ⓓ Ⓟ • SC also

■ WINCLE (Macclesfield)

Mrs Susan Brocklehurst, Hill Top Farm, SK11 0QH. ☎ (01260) 227257 • Map 118/965661 • BB **C** • EM book first £9, 6-6.30pm • D1 T2 • 3-11 • Ⓥ Ⓑ Ⓓ Ⓢ Ⓟ Ⓣ♿

■ WYBUNBURY (Nantwich)

☆ Mrs Jean Callwood, Lea Farm, CW5 7NS. ☎ (01270) 841429 • Map 118/716489 • BB **B/C** • EM book first £11, 7pm • D1 T1 F1 • 1-12 NX • Ⓑ Ⓓ Ⓢ Ⓟ Ⓣ♿ • ◆◆◆

CORNWALL

■ BOSCASTLE
SOUTH WEST COAST PATH

The Old Coach House, Tintagel Road, PL35 0AS. ☎ (01840) 250398 • Map 190/098906 • BB **B/C** • D4 T1 F3 • 1-12 NX • Ⓑ Ⓓ Ⓢ Ⓟ Ⓣ♿ • ◆◆◆◆ • www.old-coach.co.uk

Trerosewill Farmhouse, Paradise, PL35 0DL. ☎ (01840) 250545 • Map 190/094906 • BB **C** • D3 T1 F2 • 1-12 NX • Ⓑ Ⓓ Ⓢ Ⓟ Ⓣ • ◆◆◆◆Ⓢ • nicholls@trerosewill.telme.com

☆ Mr & Mrs A & R Watson, St Christopher's Hotel, High Street, PL35 0BD. ☎ (01840) 250412 • Map 190/099906 • BB **C** • EM £11.50, 7-8pm • S1 D5 T2 • 2-12 • Ⓥ Ⓑ Ⓓ Ⓢ Ⓟ Ⓣ♿

Julie & Jean, Lower Meadows House, Penally Hill, PL35 0HF. ☎ (01840) 250570 • Map 190/100913 • BB **C** • D2 T1 F1 • 1-12 • Ⓑ Ⓓ Ⓢ Ⓟ Ⓣ • www.north-cornwall.co.uk/client/lower-meadows-house

■ BOTALLACK (St. Just)
SOUTH WEST COAST PATH

Reg Blackwell, The Black Well, TR19 7QH. ☎ (01736) 787461 • Map 203/368329 • BB **B/C** • S1 D2 T2 F2 • 1-12 NX • Ⓑ Ⓓ Ⓣ♿

■ BUDE
SOUTH WEST COAST PATH

M & E Payne, Pencarrol Guest House, 21 Downs View, EX23 8RF. ☎ (01288) 352478 • Map 190/207071 • BB **B/C** • S2 D3 F2 • 1-11 • Ⓑ Ⓓ Ⓢ Ⓟ Ⓣ • ◆◆◆

Sally-Ann Trewin, Lower Northcott Farm, Poughill, EX23 9EQ. ☎ (01288) 352350 • Map 190/223077 • BB **C** • EM from £8, 6.30pm • S1 D1 T1 F2 • 1-12 • Ⓥ Ⓑ Ⓓ Ⓢ♿ • ★★★ www.coast_countryside.co.uk

☆ See Display Advertisement

■ **BUDE (continued)**
SOUTH WEST COAST PATH

Mike & Ruth Curtis, Atlantic Calm, 30 Downs View, EX23 8RG. ☎ 01288 359165 • Map 190/206071 • BB B/C • EM book first £12, 6.30pm • S2 D4 T2 F2 • 1-12 • Ⓥ Ⓑ Ⓓ Ⓢ Ⓟ Ⓣ 🛁 Ⓜ • ◆◆◆ • www.atlantic-calm.bude-cornwall.co.uk

■ **CAMELFORD**

Mrs Deborah Reeve, The Countryman Hotel, Victoria Road, PL32 9XA. ☎ (01840) 212250 • Map 200/108839 • BB B/C • EM book first £10, 7-8.30pm • S2 D3 T2 F3 • 1-12 • Ⓥ Ⓑ Ⓓ Ⓢ Ⓟ Ⓣ 🛁 • Guided walks • www.cornwall-online.co.uk/countryman

■ **COVERACK (Helston)**
SOUTH WEST COAST PATH

Mrs Muriel Fairhurst, Mellan House, TR12 6TH. ☎ 01326 280482 • Map 204/780186 • BB A • S1 D1 T1 • 1-12 NX • Ⓑ Ⓓ Ⓢ Ⓟ Ⓣ 🛁

■ **CURY (nr Mullion)**
SOUTH WEST COAST PATH

☆ Mrs Hilary Lugg, Cobblers Cottage, Nantithet, TR12 7RB. ☎ (01326) 241342 • Map 203/681223 • BB C • EM book first £12, 6.30pm • D2 T1 • 1-12 NX • Ⓑ Ⓓ Ⓢ Ⓟ Ⓣ • ◆◆◆Ⓢ

Near Mullion
South Cornwall

Situated just 2½ miles from the coastal path at Poldhu Cove this picturesque 17th century cottage set in an acre of beautiful gardens with meandering stream. Oak beams, log fires. All bedrooms ensuite. Evening dinner optional
ETC 4 diamonds Silver Award.
Colour brochure from Mrs H Lugg, Cobblers Cottage, Cury, Helston, Cornwall TR12 7RB • Tel/Fax 01326 241342

■ **FALMOUTH**
SOUTH WEST COAST PATH

☆ The Grove Hotel, Grove Place, TR11 4AU. ☎ (01326) 319577 • Map 204/794323 • BB C/D • EM £9, 7-9pm • S2 D3 T6 F4 • 1-12 • Ⓥ Ⓑ Ⓓ Ⓢ Ⓡ Ⓟ Ⓣ 🛁 • ◆◆ • grovehotel.falmouth@virgin.net

☆ Ann Picken, Lerryn Hotel, De Pass Road, TR11 4BJ. ☎ (01326) 312489 • Map 204/813319 • BB D • EM book first £12, 6.30-8pm • S3 D7 T8 F2 • 1-12 • Ⓥ Ⓑ Ⓓ Ⓢ Ⓡ Ⓟ Ⓣ 🛁 • www.thelerrynhotel.co.uk

☆ Falmouth Beach Resort Hotel, Gyllyngvase Beach, Seafront, TR11 4NA. ☎ (01326) 312999 • Map 204/816320 • BB E • EM £15, 7-10pm • S16 D47 T47 F13 • 1-12 • Ⓥ Ⓑ Ⓓ Ⓢ Ⓡ Ⓟ Ⓣ 🛁 • ★★★ • £5 for dogs, food extra. www.falmouthbeachhotel.co.uk

■ **FOWEY**
SOUTH WEST COAST PATH & SAINTS WAY

John & Carol Eardley, 4 Daglands Road, PL23 1JL. ☎ (01726) 833164 • Map 200/123518 • BB C • D2 2-11 • Ⓑ Ⓓ Ⓢ Ⓟ Ⓣ 🛁 Ⓜ • carol@stkevernel.fsnet.co.uk

Hazel Smith, Seahorses, 14 St Fimbarrus Road, PL23 1JJ. ☎ (01726) 833148 • Map 200/122514 • BB B/C • S0 D1 T1 • 3-10 • Ⓑ Ⓓ Ⓢ Ⓣ • www.users.globalnet.co.uk/~jandh/fowey.htm

■ **GORRAN HAVEN (St Austell)**
SOUTH WEST COAST PATH

Llawnroc Inn, PL26 6NU. ☎ (01726) 843461 • Map 204/010416 • BB **B/C** • EM £5, 7-9pm • D3 T3 F1 • 1-12 • Ⓥ Ⓑ Ⓓ Ⓢ 🐾 • 3Cr/HC

■ **HAYLE**
SOUTH WEST COAST PATH

Mrs Anne Cooper, 54 Penpol Terrace, TR27 4BQ. ☎ (01736) 752855 • Map 203/558378 • BB **B** • S1 D1 T1 • 1-11 • Ⓓ Ⓢ Ⓡ Ⓟ Ⓣ

■ **HELFORD (Helston)**
SOUTH WEST COAST PATH

Pam Royall, Point, TR12 6JY. ☎ 01326 231666 • Map 204/758262 • BB **C/D** • T1 • 1-12 • Ⓑ Ⓓ Ⓢ Ⓣ • SC also • Food nearby • info@helfordcottages.co.uk

■ **HELSTON**
SOUTH WEST COAST PATH

T Tucker, Lyndale Guest House, 4 Greenbank, Meneage Road, TR13 8JA. ☎ (01326) 561082 • Map 203/663267 • BB **B** • EM £14.50, 7pm • S1 D4 T1 F1 • 1-12 • Ⓥ Ⓑ Ⓓ Ⓟ Ⓣ • ◆◆◆ • www.lyndale1.freeserve.co.uk

■ **LANIVET (Bodmin)**
SAINTS WAY

Margaret Oliver, Tremeere Manor, PL30 5BG. ☎ (01208) 831513 • Map 200/046642 • BB **B** • D2 T1 • 3-11 • Ⓥ Ⓑ Ⓓ Ⓢ Ⓟ Ⓣ • SC also • oliver.tremeere.manor@farming.co.uk

Annie & George Miles, Willowbrook, Old Coach Road, Lamorick, PL30 5HB. ☎ 01208 831670 • Map 200/037646 • BB **C** • EM book first £10, 7-8pm • S1 D2 T1 • 1-12 NX • Ⓥ Ⓑ Ⓓ Ⓢ Ⓟ Ⓣ • ◆◆◆◆ • miles.willowbrook@talk21.com

Mrs J Austin, Lilac Cottage B&B, 5 Church Road, PL30 5EZ. ☎ 01208 832083 • Map 200/039641 • BB **C** • D1 T1 F1 • 1-12 NX • Ⓑ Ⓓ Ⓢ Ⓟ Ⓣ • www.cornwall-online.co.uk/lilaccottage

■ **LANREATH (Looe)**

Mrs B C Gamble, Rowan Lodge, PL13 2NX. ☎ (01503) 220289 • Map 201/181568 • BB **B** • S1 D2 • 1-12 NX • Ⓑ Ⓓ Ⓟ Ⓣ 🐾 • SC also

■ **LISKEARD**

Mr & Mrs B J Slocombe, Elnor Guest House, 1 Russell Street, PL14 4BP. ☎ (01579) 342472 • Map 201/250642 • BB **B/C** • S4 D3 T1 F1 • 1-12 NX • Ⓥ Ⓑ Ⓓ Ⓢ Ⓡ • 2Cr/C • b_slocombe@talk21.com

Georgina Kelly, Brook House, Tremar Coombe, PL14 5HF. ☎ (01579) 348000 • Map 201/254687 • BB **A/B** • EM book first £5, 7pm • D2 T1 • 1-12 NX • Ⓥ Ⓓ Ⓢ Ⓟ Ⓣ 🐾

☆ Mrs S Demmer, Hyvue House, Barras Cross, PL14 6BN. ☎ (01579) 348175 • Map 201/250649 • BB **B** • D2 T1 • 1-12 • Ⓑ Ⓓ Ⓢ Ⓡ Ⓟ Ⓣ • ◆◆◆

■ **LOOE**
SOUTH WEST COAST PATH

☆ Marwinthy Guest House, East Cliff, East Looe, PL13 1DE. ☎ (01503) 264382 • Map 201/257532 • BB **B/C** • D3 T1 F1 • 1-12 • Ⓑ Ⓓ Ⓢ Ⓡ Ⓣ 🐾 Ⓜ • eddie_mawby@tinyonline.co.uk

Schooner Point Guest House, 1 Trelawney Terrace, Polperro Road, PL13 2AG. ☎ (01503) 262670 • Map 201/252537 • BB **B/C** • S2 D3 F1 • 1-12 NX • Ⓑ Ⓓ Ⓢ Ⓡ Ⓟ • melv-neaves@tinyworld.co.uk

☆ Tim & Susan Langdon, The Beach House, Marine Drive, PL13 2DH. ☎ (01503) 262598 • Map 201/257527 • BB **C/D** • D3 T2 • 3-1 NX • Ⓑ Ⓓ Ⓢ Ⓡ Ⓟ Ⓣ • www.thebeachhouse.uk.com

☆ See Display Advertisement

■ **MARAZION (Penzance)**
SOUTH WEST COAST PATH

Pete & Hazelmary Bell, The Chymorvah Private Hotel, TR17 0DQ. ☎ (01736) 710497 • Map 203/526305 • BB **D/E** • EM book first £12, 6.30-7.30pm • S1 D4 T1 F3 • 1-12 NX • Ⓥ Ⓑ Ⓓ Ⓢ Ⓟ Ⓣ ⌘ • ◆◆◆

■ **MAWGAN PORTH (Newquay)**
SOUTH WEST COAST PATH

Trevarrian Lodge, Trevarrian, TR8 4AQ. ☎ (01637) 860156 • Map 200/851661 • BB **B/C/D** • EM book first £10, 6.30pm • S3 D3 T1 F1 • 1-12 • Ⓑ Ⓓ Ⓢ Ⓟ Ⓣ • 3Cr • www.trevarrian-lodge.co.uk

■ **MEVAGISSEY (St Austell)**
SOUTH WEST COAST PATH

Tremarne Hotel, Polkirt, PL26 6UY. ☎ (01726) 842213 • Map 204/017442 • BB **C/E** • EM book first £12-16, 7.15+ • S4 D6 T3 F2 • 1-12 • Ⓥ Ⓑ Ⓓ Ⓢ Ⓟ Ⓣ ⌘ • ★★ • www.tremarne-hotel.co.uk

Mr & Mrs Schofield, The Spa Hotel, Polkirt Hill, PL26 6UY. ☎ (01726) 842244 • Map 204/015443 • BB **C/D** • EM £12, 7-7.30pm • S2 D4 T2 F3 • 3-10 • Ⓥ Ⓓ Ⓢ Ⓟ Ⓣ ⌘ • ★★ • alan@the-spa-hotel.fsnet.co.uk

Pat & Dermot Lee, The Anchorage, Portmellon Rd, PL26 6PH. ☎ (01726) 844412 • Map 204/016441 • BB **C** • D3 • 1-12 NX • Ⓑ Ⓢ Ⓟ Ⓣ • theanchorage@community-care.net

■ **MORWENSTOW (Bude)**
SOUTH WEST COAST PATH

Monica Heywood, Cornakey Farm, EX23 9SS. ☎ (01288) 331260 • Map 190/208157 • BB **B** • EM book first £9, 6.30pm • D1 T1 F1 • 1-11 NX • Ⓥ Ⓑ Ⓓ Ⓢ Ⓟ Ⓣ • ◆◆◆

■ **MULLION (Helston)**
SOUTH WEST COAST PATH

Mrs J Tyler Street, Trenance Farmhouse, TR12 7HB. ☎ (01326) 240639 • Map 203/673184 • BB **C** • D2 T1 • 3-10 • Ⓑ Ⓓ Ⓢ Ⓟ Ⓣ ⌘ • ◆◆◆◆ • SC also www.cornwall-online.co.uk/trenance-farm/

Joan Hyde, Campden House, The Commons, TR12 7HZ. ☎ (01326) 240365 • Map 203/677194 • BB **B** • EM £7, 6.30pm • S2 D3 T1 F2 • 1-12 NX • Ⓥ Ⓑ Ⓓ Ⓢ Ⓟ Ⓣ

Mike & Jackie Bolton, Criggan Mill, Mullian Cove, TR12 7EU. ☎ (01326) 240496 • Map 203/667180 • BB **B/C** • EM book first £9 • S4 D4 T4 F4 • 4-10 • Ⓥ Ⓑ Ⓓ Ⓟ Ⓣ ⌘ • ★★★★ • SC timber lodges also www.crigganmill.co.uk

FOUND A GOOD B&B THAT'S NOT IN THE YEARBOOK?
Send us recommendations for future editions

☆ June Lugg, Tregaddra Farm, Cury Cross Lanes, TR12 7BB. ☎ (01326) 240235 • Map 203/701219 • BB **C/D** • EM book first £11, 6.30pm • D4 T1 F2 • 1-12 NX • Ⓥ Ⓑ Ⓓ Ⓢ Ⓟ Ⓣ • ◆◆◆◆Ⓢ • Groups also www.tregaddra.freeserve.co.uk

■ **NEWQUAY**
SOUTH WEST COAST PATH

☆ S R Harper, Chichester, 14 Bay View Terrace, TR7 2LR. ☎ (01637) 874216 • Map 200/813614 • BB **B** • EM book first £5, 6.30pm • S2 D2 T2 F1 • 3-11 • Ⓥ Ⓑ Ⓓ Ⓢ Ⓡ Ⓟ Ⓣ Ⓜ • ◆◆◆ • Organised walking weeks. sheila.harper@virgin.net

Dave & Terri Clark, Trewerry Mill, Trerice, St Newlyn East, TR8 5GS. ☎ (01872) 510345 • Map 200/837580 • BB **B/C** • S2 D2 T1 F1 • 2-11 • Ⓑ Ⓓ Ⓢ Ⓡ Ⓟ Ⓣ ⌘ • www.connexions.co.uk/trewerry.mill

Mrs P Williams, Roma Guest House, 1 Atlantic Road, TR1 1QJ. ☎ (01637) 875085 • Map 200/803616 • BB **A/B** • EM book first £6-£7, 6pm • S1 D4 T1 F1 • 1-12 NX • Ⓥ Ⓑ Ⓓ Ⓢ Ⓡ Ⓟ Ⓣ • Credit Cards taken

Mrs T Smith, Kendra, 20 Arundel Way, TR7 3BB. ☎ 01637 878935 • Map 200/826621 • BB **B** • D3 T1 • 4-10 • Ⓑ Ⓓ Ⓢ Ⓡ Ⓟ Ⓣ🐾

Barrowfield Hotel, Hilgrove Road, TR7 2QY. ☎ (01637) 878878 • Map 200/820620 • BB **E** • EM £16, 7-8.30pm • S6 D43 T12 F22 • 1-12 • Ⓥ Ⓑ Ⓢ Ⓡ Ⓟ Ⓣ🐾 • ★★★★ • booking@barrowfield.prestel.co.uk

Greg & Fiona Dolan, The Three Tees Hotel, 21 Carminow Way, TR7 3AY. ☎ (01637) 872055 • Map 200/823622 • BB **B/C** • EM book first £8, 6pm • S1 D2 T1 F6 • 1-12 NX • Ⓥ Ⓑ Ⓓ Ⓢ Ⓡ Ⓟ Ⓣ🐾 • www.3teeshotel.fsnet.co.uk

■ PADSTOW
SOUTH WEST COAST PATH & SAINTS WAY

Mr & Mrs Champion, 8 Treverbyn Road, PL28 8DW. ☎ (01841) 532551 • Map 200/921749 • BB **C** • S1 D2 T1 • 1-12 NX • Ⓑ Ⓓ Ⓢ Ⓣ🐾

☆ Mr & Mrs B Mealing, Trevorrick Farm, St Issey, PL27 7QH. ☎ (01841) 540574 • Map 200/921732 • BB **C** • D1 T1 F1 • 1-12 NX • Ⓥ Ⓑ Ⓓ Ⓢ🐾 • 2Cr • SC also

Peter Tamblin, Hemingford House, 21 Grenville Road, PL28 8EX. ☎ (01841) 532806 • Map 200/912752 • BB **C** • D1 T1 • 1-12 • Ⓑ Ⓓ Ⓢ Ⓟ Ⓣ🐾 • Buses to Bodmin rail • peter@ptamblin.freeserve.co.uk

■ PENDEEN (Penzance)
SOUTH WEST COAST PATH

Christine & Martin, Trewellard Arms Hotel, TR19 7TA. ☎ (01736) 788634 • Map 203/383344 • BB **B** • EM £7, 7-9pm • S1 D2 • 1-12 NX • Ⓥ Ⓑ Ⓓ Ⓢ Ⓟ Ⓣ🐾 • 3Cr

■ PENZANCE
SOUTH WEST COAST PATH

☆ Mrs G Ash, Torre Vene, Lescudjack Terrace, TR18 3AE. ☎ (01736) 364103 • Map 203/475308 • BB **B** • EM book first £8.50, 6.30pm • S2 D4 T4 F4 • 1-12 • Ⓥ Ⓓ Ⓟ Ⓣ

"Penalva", Alexandra Road, TR18 4LZ. ☎ (01736) 369060 • Map 203/466301 • BB **B/C** • S2 D3 T1 F1 • 1-12 • Ⓑ Ⓓ Ⓢ Ⓡ Ⓣ • ◆◆◆

John & Cherry Hopkins, Woodstock Guest House, 29 Morrab Road, TR18 4EZ. ☎ (01736) 369049 • Map 203/472300 • BB **B** • S2 D2 T2 F2 • 1-12 • Ⓑ Ⓢ Ⓡ Ⓟ Ⓣ🐾 • ◆◆◆ • woodstocp@aol.com

Teresa & Roy Stacey, Lynwood Guest House, 41 Morrab Road, TR18 4EX. ☎ (01736) 365871 • Map 203/472300 • BB **B** • S1 D2 T2 F2 • 1-12 • Ⓑ Ⓓ Ⓢ Ⓡ Ⓟ Ⓣ🐾 • ◆◆◆ • Food nearby • lynwood@aol.com

☆ Shan & Dave Glenn, Trewella Guest House, 18 Mennaye Road, TR18 4NG. ☎ (01736) 363818 • Map 203/469298 • BB **B** • S2 D4 F2 • 3-10 • Ⓑ Ⓢ Ⓡ Ⓣ

Pauline & Barry Schofield, Chy An Gof Guest House, 10 Regent Terrace, TR18 4DW. ☎ (01736) 332361 • Map 203/474299 • BB **C** • S2 T2 • 1-12 NX • Ⓑ Ⓓ Ⓡ Ⓟ Ⓣ • scholfield@callnetuk.com

Jeff Maddern, The Tarbert Hotel & Resturant, 11/12 Clarence St, TR18 2NU. ☎ (01736) 363758 • Map 203/471304 • BB **E** • EM £18.50, 7-8.30pm • S2 D7 T1 F2 • 2-12 NX • Ⓥ Ⓑ Ⓓ Ⓢ Ⓡ Ⓟ Ⓣ • ★★ • reception@tabert-hotel.co.uk

■ PERRANPORTH
SOUTH WEST COAST PATH

W Woodcock, Chy An Kerensa, Cliff Road, TR6 0DR. ☎ (01872) 572470 • Map 200,203/754543 • BB **B/C** • S2 D2 T2 F3 • 1-12 • Ⓑ Ⓓ Ⓢ Ⓟ Ⓣ🐾 • ◆◆◆

■ POLZEATH (Nr Wadebridge)
SOUTH WEST COAST PATH

Paul & Julie Duffield, Seascape Hotel, PL27 6SX. ☎ (01208) 863638 • Map 200/939789 • BB **D/E** • EM £12, 7.30-8pm • D11 T4 • 4-10+X • Ⓥ Ⓑ Ⓓ Ⓢ Ⓟ Ⓣ🐾 • ★★ • information@seascapehotel.co.uk

☆ See Display Advertisement

B&B ACCOMMODATION   ENGLAND   CORNWALL

CORNWALL ENGLAND B&B ACCOMMODATION *(side margin)*

■ **PORT ISAAC**
SOUTH WEST COAST PATH

☆ Colin & Maxine Durston, Anchorage, The Terrace, PL29 3SG. ☎ (01208) 880629 • Map 200/999807 • BB **B** • EM book first £8, 7pm • S2 D2 T1 F2 • 2-12 NX • Ⓥ Ⓑ Ⓓ Ⓟ 🐾

Anchorage Guest House
STUNNING SEA VIEWS
PERFECTLY SITUATED ON THE NORTH
CORNISH COASTAL PATH
Colin & Maxine Durston
The Terrace, Port Isaac PL29 3SG
01208 880629

George & Barbara Oxley, Corestin Christian Guest House, 11 The Terrace, PL29 3SG. ☎ (01208) 880267 • Map 200/999807 • BB **B** • EM £7-£9, 7pm • S1 D2 T2 F4 • 1-12 • Ⓥ Ⓓ Ⓢ Ⓟ Ⓣ

■ **PORTH (Newquay)**
SOUTH WEST COAST PATH

"Sea Drift", 79 Penhallow Road, TR7 3BZ. ☎ (01637) 872311 • Map 200/831620 • BB **B** • EM book first £6, 6pm • D2 T1 F1 • 1-12 NX • Ⓥ Ⓑ Ⓢ Ⓡ Ⓟ Ⓣ 🐾 • www.seadrift.co.uk

■ **PORTHCURNO (Penzance)**
SOUTH WEST COAST PATH

Susan Davis, Sea View House, The Valley, TR19 6JX. ☎ (01736) 810638 • Map 203/383227 • BB **C** • EM £8.50, 5-7.30pm • S1 D3 T2 • 1-12 • Ⓥ Ⓑ Ⓓ Ⓢ Ⓟ Ⓣ 🐾 • seaview.porthcurno@tinyworld.co.uk • Phone bookings Oct-April

Porthcurno Hotel, The Valley, TR19 6JX. ☎ 01736 810119 • Map 203/383227 • BB **B/C/D** • EM £12-£15, 5PM • S1 D5 T5 F1 • 1-12 • Ⓥ Ⓑ Ⓓ Ⓟ Ⓣ 🐾 • ◆◆◆◆ • porthcurnohotel.co.uk

■ **PORTLOE (Truro)**
SOUTH WEST COAST PATH

Mrs Clare Holdsworth, Tregain Licensed Restaurant & Tea Room, TR2 5QU. ☎ (01872) 501252 • Map 204/935395 • BB **C** • EM book first £10-30.00, 7-8.30pm • S1 T1 • 3-10 • Ⓥ Ⓓ Ⓢ Ⓟ🐾

■ **PORTSCATHO (Truro)**
SOUTH WEST COAST PATH

Sally Hart, Hillside House, 8 The Square, TR2 5HW. ☎ (01872) 580526 • Map 204/876354 • BB **B** • S2 D3 T1 F1 • 1-12 NX • Ⓑ Ⓓ Ⓢ Ⓟ Ⓣ🐾 • Food nearby

Ramblers' Association members are covered by a public liability insurance policy further details from central office

■ **ROCK (Wadebridge)**
SOUTH WEST COAST PATH

Mrs Barbara Martin, Silvermead, PL27 6LB. ☎ (01208) 862425 • Map 200/933757 • BB **C** • EM book first £10, 6-7.30pm • S2 D3 T2 F2 • 1-12 • Ⓥ Ⓑ Ⓓ Ⓢ Ⓟ Ⓣ🐾 • ◆◆◆ • barbara@silvermead.freeserve.co.uk

■ **RUAN-HIGH-LANES (Truro)**
SOUTH WEST COAST PATH

☆ Mrs R Dingle, Treburthes, TR2 5JP. ☎ (01872) 501345 • Map 204/905398 • BB **B** • D1 • 4-9 • Ⓑ Ⓓ Ⓢ Ⓟ Ⓣ🐾

Treburthes Farm
Ruan High Lanes, Truro, Cornwall TR2 5JP

Stay at our comfortable farmhouse in the beautiful Roseland. Wonderful coastal walks and NT gardens within the local area. Also, Lost Gardens of Heligan and Eden Project. En-suite rooms, traditional farmhouse fare.
B&B band B

Mrs R Dingle ☎ **01872 501345**

■ **SEATON (Torpoint)**
SOUTH WEST COAST PATH

Pat Rowlandson, Blue Haven Hotel, Looe Hill, PL11 3JQ. ☎ (01503) 250310 • Map 201/262551 • BB **C** • EM book first £10, 7.30pm • D3 T1 F1 • 1-12 NX • Ⓥ Ⓑ Ⓓ Ⓢ Ⓟ Ⓣ🐾 • ◆◆◆ • www.smoothhound.co.uk/hotels/bluehave.html

■ **ST AGNES**
SOUTH WEST COAST PATH

☆ Mrs Gill-Carey, Penkerris, Penwinnick Road, TR5 0PA. ☎ (01872) 552262 • Map 204/720501 • BB **B** • EM book first £8.50-10, 6.30pm • S2 D2 T2 F2 • 1-12 • Ⓥ Ⓑ Ⓓ Ⓟ Ⓣ🐾 • 2Cr • Single lets available.

Dorothy Gill-Carey   Tel: 01872 552262
PENKERRIS AA RAC 🏵🏵 QQ
Penwinnick Road B3277
St. Agnes, Cornwall TR5 0PA
Enchanting Edwardian residence with own grounds in unspoilt Cornish village. Beautiful rooms. Log fires in winter. Superb home cooking with fresh local produce. Licensed. Dramatic cliff walks, St Agnes Beacon and beaches nearby. Prices from £15 pppn.

■ **ST AUSTELL**
SOUTH WEST COAST PATH

Shirley Mathieson, Coastguard House, 11 Coastguard Terrace , PL25 3NJ. ☎ (01726) 72828 • Map 204, 200/039515 • BB **A** • D1 T1 • 1-12 NX • Ⓓ Ⓢ Ⓡ Ⓟ Ⓣ🐾 Ⓜ • Guest rooms have sea views

Mrs Mcguffie, Spindrift, London Apprentice, PL26 7AR. ☎ (01726) 69316 • Map 204/007501 • BB **B** • D1 F1 • 1-12 NX • Ⓥ Ⓑ Ⓢ Ⓣ 🛇 • SC also mcguffspindrift@hotmail.com

■ ST ISSEY (Wadebridge)
SOUTH WEST COAST PATH & SAINTS WAY

Penny Sander, Menhinick House, PL27 7QA. ☎ (01841) 541210 • Map 200/928718 • BB **B** • T3 • 1-12 NX • Ⓓ Ⓟ Ⓣ

■ ST IVES
SOUTH WEST COAST PATH

Mrs M E McPherson, Ren-roy Guest House, 2 Ventnor Terrace, TR26 1DY. ☎ (01736) 796971 • Map 203/515405 • BB **B** • S2 D1 T1 F1 • 1-12 NX • Ⓑ Ⓓ Ⓡ Ⓟ Ⓣ Ⓜ • List

☆ David Watson, Chy-an-Dour Hotel, Trelyon Avenue, TR26 2AD. ☎ (01736) 796436 • Map 203/524398 • BB **E** • EM £17, 7-8pm • D11 T9 F3 • 1-12 NX • Ⓥ Ⓑ Ⓓ Ⓢ Ⓡ Ⓟ Ⓣ • ★★ • chyndour@aol.com

William Stirling, The Toby Jug Guest House, 1 Park Avenue, TR26 2DN. ☎ (01736) 794250 • Map 203/515403 • BB **B** • EM £7-£8, 5.30-7.30pm • S3 D4 T3 F3 • 1-12 • Ⓥ Ⓑ Ⓓ Ⓡ Ⓟ Ⓣ Ⓜ

☆ Rachael & Chris Manns, Chineside Guest House, St Ives Road, Carbis Bay, TR26 2JS. ☎ (01736) 795659 • Map 203/525385 • BB **B/C** • EM book first £14, 7-8.30pm • S1 D5 T1 F1 • 1-12 • Ⓥ Ⓑ Ⓓ Ⓢ Ⓡ Ⓟ Ⓣ 🛇 • www.chineside.co.uk

Audrey & Bill Clark, Primavera Private Hotel, 14 Draycott Terrace, TR26 2EF. ☎ (01736) 795595 • Map 203/520399 • BB **C** • EM £8.50, 6.30-9.30pm • S2 D1 T1 F1 • 1-12 NX • Ⓥ Ⓑ Ⓓ Ⓢ Ⓡ Ⓟ Ⓣ • ◆◆◆ • clarkprima@aol.com

☆ The Porthmeor Hotel, Godrevy Terrace, TR26 1JA. ☎ (01736) 796712 • Map 203/516407 • BB **C/D/E** • D8 T2 F2 • 2-11 • Ⓑ Ⓓ Ⓢ Ⓡ Ⓟ Ⓣ 🛇 • ◆◆◆ • www.porthmeor.com

■ ST JUST (Penzance)
SOUTH WEST COAST PATH

Ms T Griffiths & Mr N Nathan, Boswedden House, Cape Cornwall, TR19 7NJ. ☎ /Fax 01736 788733 • Map 203/359319 • BB **C** • S2 D2 T3 F1 • 1-12 • Ⓑ Ⓓ Ⓢ Ⓟ Ⓣ 🛇 • ◆◆◆ • relax@boswedden.org.uk

☆ Colin Lilley, Bosavern House, TR19 7RD. ☎ (01736) 788301 • Map 203/370304 • BB **B/C/D** • S1 D2 T2 F3 • 1-12 NX • Ⓑ Ⓓ Ⓢ Ⓟ Ⓣ 🛇 • ◆◆◆ • www.bosavern.u-net.com

☆ See Display Advertisement

Mrs Jo Hill, The Farmhouse, Bollowal, TR19 7NP. ☎ (01736) 788458 • Map 203/359314 • BB **A** • D1 • 3-12 NX • Ⓢ Ⓣ • SC also • 100 yds off Coast Path

Fi Kilpatrick, Copperhouse, 31 Fore Street, TR19 7LJ. ☎ (01736) 787342 • Map 203/371314 • BB **B** • D2 T1 • 1-12 • Ⓓ Ⓟ Ⓣ • www.copperhouse.co.uk

■ ST WENN (Bodmin)
SAINTS WAY

Mrs Marilyn Hawkey, Tregolls Farm, PL30 5PG. ☎ (01208) 812154 • Map 200/983661 • BB **A/B** • EM book first £8.75, 7pm • S1 D2 T1 • 1-12 NX • Ⓥ Ⓑ Ⓓ Ⓢ Ⓟ Ⓣ • ◆◆◆ • SC also • Saints Way

■ THE LIZARD (Helston, Cornwall)
SOUTH WEST COAST PATH

Linda & Peter Brookes, Parc Brawse House Hotel, Penmenner Road, TR12 7NR. ☎ (01326) 290466 • Map 203/701120 • BB **B/C** • EM book first £10, 6.30-8pm • S1 D3 T2 F1 • 1-12 • Ⓥ Ⓑ Ⓓ Ⓢ Ⓟ Ⓣ🛁 • ◆◆◆◆ • lindabrookes@cwcom.net

Mrs G Rowe, Trethvas Farm, TR12 7AR. ☎ (01326) 290720 • Map 203/709136 • BB **B/C** • D1 T1 F/D1 • 4-10 • Ⓑ Ⓓ Ⓢ Ⓟ Ⓣ🛁 • ◆◆◆

■ TINTAGEL
SOUTH WEST COAST PATH

☆ Ian & Heather Graham, Bossiney House Hotel, PL34 0AX. ☎ (01840) 770240 • Map 200/066887 • BB **C/E** • EM £14, 7-8pm • D9 T9 F1 • 2-11 NX • Ⓥ Ⓑ Ⓓ Ⓢ Ⓟ Ⓣ🛁 • ★★ • Groups also • guided walks

■ TORPOINT
SOUTH WEST COAST PATH

☆ Finnygook Inn, Crafthole, PL11 3BQ. ☎ (01503) 230338 • Map 201/366544 • BB **D** • EM £7.50, 6.30-9pm • T5 • 1-12 • Ⓥ Ⓑ Ⓟ Ⓣ🛁 • ★

☆ Whitsand Bay Hotel, Portwrinkle, PL11 3BY. ☎ (01503) 230276 • Map 201/354542 • BB **E** • EM £19.50, 7.30-9pm • S5 D10 T10 F20 • 1-12 • Ⓥ Ⓑ Ⓓ Ⓢ Ⓟ Ⓣ🛁 • 3 Cr • www.cornish-golf-hotels.co.uk

■ TREEN, ST LEVAN, PORTHCURNO (Penzance)
SOUTH WEST COAST PATH

Mrs A Jilbert, Penver House Farm, TR19 6LG. ☎ (01736) 810778 • Map 203/394231 • BB **B** • S/T1 D1 • 3-10 NX • Ⓑ Ⓓ Ⓢ Ⓟ🛁

■ TRURO

Bridget Dymond, Trevispian Vean Farm Guest House, St Erme, TR4 9BL. ☎ (01872) 279514 • Map 204/850502 • BB **C** • EM book first £10, 6.30pm • D4 T3 F2 • 2-11 • Ⓥ Ⓑ Ⓓ Ⓢ Ⓣ • ◆◆◆◆ • Groups also www.guesthousestruro.com

■ WHITSAND BAY
SOUTH WEST COAST PATH

Kathy Ridpath, Fir Cottage, Lower Tregantle, Antony, PL11 3AL. ☎ (01752) 822626 • Map 201/391537 • BB **B** • EM £6, 6-7pm • S1 F2 • 1-12 NX • Ⓥ Ⓓ Ⓟ🛁

■ ZENNOR (St Ives)
SOUTH WEST COAST PATH

Mrs N I Mann, Trewey Farm, TR26 3DA. ☎ (01736) 796936 • Map 203/454384 • BB **B/C** • S1 D2 T1 F2 • 2-10 • Ⓥ Ⓓ Ⓢ Ⓟ Ⓣ🛁

Dr E Gynn, Boswednack Manor, TR26 3DD. ☎ (01736) 794183 • Map 203/442378 • BB **B/C** • S1 D2 T1 F1 • 4-10 • Ⓥ Ⓑ Ⓓ Ⓢ Ⓟ Ⓣ • SC also

CUMBRIA

■ AINSTABLE (Penrith)
Mary Robinson, Bell House, CA4 9RE. ☎ (01768) 896255 • Map 86/526467 • BB **C** • D1 • 1-12 NX • Ⓑ Ⓓ Ⓢ Ⓡ Ⓣ🛁 • 4Cr • mrobinson@bellhouse.fsbusiness.co.uk

■ ALSTON
PENNINE WAY

Mrs P M Dent, Greycroft, The Raise, CA9 3AR. ☎ (01434) 381383 • Map 86,87/706465 • BB **B/C** • EM book first £11, 6.00pm • D1 T/F1 • 1-3 & 5-12 NX • Ⓥ Ⓑ Ⓓ Ⓢ Ⓟ Ⓣ • ◆◆◆Ⓢ • Transport av.

Mrs Jean Best, Chapel House, CA9 3SH. ☎ (01434) 381112 • Map 86,87/721464 • BB **B** • EM book first £8, 7pm • S1 D1 F1 • 1-12 • Ⓥ Ⓑ Ⓓ Ⓢ Ⓟ Ⓣ • ◆◆◆

Mrs Celia Pattison, High Field, Bruntley Meadows, CA9 3UX. ☎ (01434) 382182 • Map 87/720461 • BB **A/B** • EM £7, 7-9pm • S1 D1 T1 F1 • 1-12 NX • Ⓥ Ⓑ Ⓓ Ⓢ Ⓟ Ⓣ • Guided walks • remedial massage av.

Albert House Guesthouse, Townhead, CA9 3SL. ☎ (01434) 381793 • Map 86/720462 • BB **C** • EM £6 to £12, 7.30pm • D3 T3 F1 • 1-12 NX • Ⓥ Ⓑ Ⓓ Ⓢ Ⓟ Ⓣ ☙ • ◆◆◆ • Camping also • Near bus service

The Mogford Family, Nent Hall Country House Hotel, CA9 3LQ. ☎ 01434 381584 • Map 86,87/758457 • BB **E** • D/S10 T/S5 F/S2 • 1-12 NX • Ⓥ Ⓑ Ⓓ Ⓢ Ⓟ Ⓣ ☙ • ★★Ⓢ • info@nenthallhotel.com

■ AMBLESIDE

The Rysdale Hotel, Rothay Road, LA22 0EE. ☎ (015394) 32140 • Map 90/374043 • BB **C/D** • S3 D4 T1 F1 • 1-12 NX • Ⓑ Ⓓ Ⓢ Ⓟ Ⓣ ☙ • ◆◆◆

Alan & Sue Clarke, Broadview Guest House, Low Fold, Lake Road, LA22 0DN. ☎ (015394) 32431 • Map 90/377036 • BB **B/C** • D3 T1 F2 • 1-12 • Ⓑ Ⓓ Ⓢ Ⓟ Ⓣ • ◆◆◆ • enquiries@broadview-guesthouse.co.uk

Mr & Mrs Doano, Thorneyfield Guest House, Compston Road, LA22 9DJ. ☎ (015394) 32464 • Map 90/375044 • BB **B/C** • D3 T1 F3 • 1-12 • Ⓑ Ⓓ Ⓢ Ⓣ • ◆◆◆◆ • Groups also • www.thorneyfield.co.uk

Chris & Jane, Brantfell, Rothay Road, LA22 0EE. ☎ (015394) 32239/34124 • Map 90/374043 • BB **C/D** • S2 D4 T3 F3 • 1-12 • Ⓑ Ⓓ Ⓢ Ⓣ ☙ • ◆◆◆ • brantfell@kencomp.net

☆ Rothay Garth Hotel, Rothay Road, LA22 0EE. ☎ (015394) 32217 • Map 90/374043 • BB **E** • EM book first £ inc. in tariff, 7-8pm • S2 D9 T2 F3 • 1-12 • Ⓥ Ⓑ Ⓓ Ⓢ Ⓟ Ⓣ ☙ • 4Cr/C • Guided walks • www.rothay-garth.co.uk

Mrs K Siddall, Cross Parrock, 5 Waterhead Terrace, LA22 0HA. ☎ (015394) 32372 • Map 90/377030 • BB **B** • EM book first £11, 6.30pm • D2 T1 • 2-10 • Ⓥ Ⓓ Ⓢ Ⓟ Ⓣ ☙

☆ The Old Vicarage, Vicarage Road, LA22 9DH. ☎ (015394) 33364 • Map 90/373044 • BB **D** • S2 D8 T2 F2 • 1-12 • Ⓑ Ⓓ Ⓢ Ⓟ Ⓣ ☙ • ◆◆◆ • the.old.vicarage@kencomp.net

☆ Helen Green, Lyndhurst Hotel, Wansfell Road, LA22 0EG. ☎ (015394) 32421 • Map 90/375040 • BB **C/D** • EM £15, 6pm • D5 T1 • 1-12 • Ⓥ Ⓑ Ⓓ Ⓢ Ⓟ Ⓣ ☙ Ⓜ • 2Cr/C • lyndhurst@amblesidehotels.co.uk

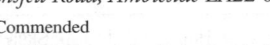
☆ Liz & Tim Melling, Nab Cottage, Rydal, LA22 9SD. ☎ (015394) 35311 • Map 90/355064 • BB **C** • EM £12, 7pm • S1 D2 T2 F2 • 10-6 • Ⓥ Ⓑ Ⓓ Ⓢ Ⓟ Ⓣ ☙ • www.kencomp.net/homepages/ell/nab

B&B ACCOMMODATION ENGLAND CUMBRIA

☆ See Display Advertisement

☆ Smallwood House Hotel, Compston Road, LA22 9DJ. ☎ (015394) 32330 • Map 90/375044 • BB **D** • EM £13, 6-8pm • S2 D11 T7 F3 • 1-12 • Ⓥ Ⓑ Ⓓ Ⓟ Ⓣ 🛁 • ★★ • www.smallwoodhotel.co.uk

☆ Judith Ireton, Holmeshead Farm, Skelwith Fold, LA22 0NU. ☎ 015394 33048 • Map 96,97/352982 • BB **C** • EM book first £12, 7pm • D1 T1 F1 • 1-12 • Ⓥ Ⓑ Ⓓ Ⓢ Ⓟ Ⓣ 🛁 • ◆◆◆◆ • www.amblesideonline.co.uk

☆ Mr & Mrs K Morgan, Norwood House, Church Street, LA22 0BT. ☎ (015394) 33349 • Map 90/375043 • BB **B/C** • S2 D4 T2 F2 • 1-12 NX • Ⓑ Ⓓ Ⓢ Ⓟ Ⓣ • www.norwoodhouse69.freeserve.co.uk

Gavin Lobb, Lyndale Guest House, Lake Road, LA22 0DN. ☎ (01539) 434244 • Map 90/377036 • BB **C** • S2 D2 F2 • 1-12 • Ⓑ Ⓓ Ⓢ Ⓟ Ⓣ 🛁 • gavin-lobb@lyndale.totalserve.co.uk

Lake Road, LA22 9BX. ☎ (01539 4) 32244 • Map 90/377044 • BB **E** • EM £19, 7-9pm • S3 D27 T8 F4 • 1-12 • Ⓥ Ⓑ Ⓓ Ⓢ Ⓟ Ⓣ 🛁 • ★★★ • enquiries@hotelambleside.uk.com

■ APPLEBY-IN-WESTMORLAND

Mrs K M Coward, Limnerslease, Bongate, CA16 6UE. ☎ (017683) 51578 • Map 91/689200 • BB **B** • D2 T1 • 2-10 • Ⓓ Ⓢ Ⓡ Ⓟ Ⓣ 🛁

☆ Anne & Malcolm Dayson, Bongate House, CA16 6UE. ☎ (017683) 51245 • Map 91/689200 • BB **B/C** • EM £9.50, 7pm • S1 D3 T2 F2 • 3-10 • Ⓥ Ⓑ Ⓓ Ⓡ Ⓟ Ⓣ 🛁 • ◆◆◆◆ • Groups also

Appleby Manor Ctry House Hotel, Roman Road, CA16 6JB. ☎ (017683) 51571 • Map 91/693205 • BB **E** • EM £22, 7-9pm • D13 T8 F9 • 1-12 NX • Ⓥ Ⓑ Ⓓ Ⓢ Ⓡ Ⓟ Ⓣ 🛁 Ⓜ • ★★★Ⓢ • www.appleby.co.uk

Susan Hirst, Wemyss House, 48 Boroughgate, CA16 6XG. ☎ (017683) 51494 • Map 91/684201 • BB **B** • S1 D1 T1 • 4-10 NX • Ⓓ Ⓡ Ⓟ Ⓣ Ⓜ • Georgian house • nickhirst@aol.com

■ ARNSIDE (Carnforth, Lancashire)

Janet & Ian Kerr, Willowfield Hotel, The Promenade, LA5 0AD. ☎ (01524) 761354 • Map 97/456788 • BB **D** • EM book first £14, 7pm • S2 D3 T3 F2 • 1-12 • Ⓥ Ⓑ Ⓓ Ⓢ Ⓡ Ⓟ Ⓣ 🐾 • ◆◆◆◆ • kerr@willowfield.net1.co.uk

■ BAMPTON GRANGE (Penrith)
COAST TO COAST WALK

Wendy Frith, Crown & Mitre Hotel, CA10 2QR. ☎ (01931) 713225 • Map 90/520179 • BB **B** • EM £4.85-7.90, 7-8.30pm • S2 D5 T3 F2 • 1-12 • Ⓥ Ⓓ Ⓟ Ⓣ 🐾

■ BASSENTHWAITE (nr Keswick)
CUMBRIA WAY

Mrs Alison Trafford, Bassenthwaite Hall Farm, CA12 4QP. ☎ (017687) 76393 • Map 89,90/230322 • BB **C** • S1 D1 T1 • 2-10 • Ⓓ Ⓢ Ⓟ Ⓣ • www.s-h-systems.co.uk

■ BLAWITH (Ulverston)
CUMBRIA WAY

Water Yeat Country Guest House, Water Yeat, LA12 8DJ. ☎ (01229) 885306 • Map 96,97/288892 • BB **D** • EM book first £17.50 (not Sun), 7.30pm • D1 T3 F1 • 2-12 NX • Ⓥ Ⓑ Ⓓ Ⓢ Ⓟ Ⓣ

■ BOOT (Eskdale)

John & Leigh Gray, The Post Office, Dale View, CA19 1TG. ☎ (019467) 23236 • Map 89,90/176010 • BB **B** • S1 D2 T1 • 1-12 NX • Ⓓ Ⓢ Ⓡ Ⓟ Ⓣ • daleview@booteskdale.fsnet.co.uk

■ BORROWDALE (Keswick)
COAST TO COAST WALK & CUMBRIA WAY

Mr & Mrs T Lopez, Derwent House, CA12 5UY. ☎ (017687) 77658 • Map 89, 90/257177 • BB **C** • EM book first £15, 7pm • S1 D5 T3 F1 • 2-12 NX • Ⓥ Ⓑ Ⓓ Ⓢ Ⓟ Ⓣ • ◆◆◆◆ • derwenthse@aol.com

Greenbank Country House Hotel, CA12 5UY. ☎ (017687) 77215 • Map 89,90/259180 • BB **E** • EM book first £14, 7pm • S1 D5 T2 F1 • 2-12 NX • Ⓥ Ⓑ Ⓓ Ⓢ Ⓟ Ⓣ • ◆◆◆◆Ⓢ

■ BOWNESS-ON-WINDERMERE
DALES WAY

☆ Mr R I Atkinson, Lingwood, Birkett Hill, LA23 3EZ. ☎ (015394) 44680 • Map 96,97/402963 • BB **C/D** • D3 T1 F2 • 1-12 • Ⓑ Ⓓ Ⓢ Ⓡ Ⓣ • ◆◆◆ • www.lingwood-guesthouse.co.uk/
Mrs J Gibson, Elim House, Biskey Howe Road, LA23 2JP. ☎ (015394) 42021 • Map 96,97/406971 • BB **B/C/D/E** • S4 D11 T2 F2 • 1-12 • Ⓑ Ⓡ Ⓟ Ⓣ 🐾 • ◆◆◆ • www.elimhouse.freeserve.co.uk

■ BRAMPTON

Una Armstrong, Town Head Farm, Walton, CA8 2DJ. ☎ (016977) 2730 • Map 86/520644 • BB **B** • EM book first £9, 6.30pm • D1 T1 • 1-12 NX • Ⓓ Ⓢ Ⓟ Ⓣ • ◆◆◆

■ BROUGHTON-IN-FURNESS

David & Sarah Hartley, Middlesyke, Church Street, LA20 6ER. ☎ (01229) 716549 • Map 96/208876 • BB **C** • D3 • 1-12 NX • Ⓑ Ⓓ Ⓢ Ⓡ Ⓟ Ⓣ Ⓜ • ◆◆◆◆

■ BURNESIDE (Kendal)
DALES WAY

Mrs J Ellis, Gateside Farm, LA9 5SE. ☎ (01539) 722036 • Map 97/496954 • BB **B** • EM book first £9.50, 6.30pm • D3 T1 F1 • 1-12 NX • Ⓥ Ⓑ Ⓓ Ⓡ • ◆◆◆ • gatesidefarm@aol.com

■ BUTTERMERE
COAST TO COAST WALK

Mrs Chris Knight, "Trevene", CA13 9XA. ☎ (017687) 70210 • Map 89/174172 • BB **B** • D1 T1 F1 • 1-12 NX • Ⓓ Ⓢ Ⓟ Ⓣ 🐾 Ⓜ • www.trevene.fsbusiness.co.uk

☆ Ramblers Holidays, Dalegarth, CA13 9XA. ☎ (017687) 70233 • Map 89,90/186160 • BB **B** • D4 T5 • 4-10 • Ⓑ Ⓓ Ⓜ

☆ Bridge Hotel, CA13 9UZ. ☎ (017687) 70252 • Map 89,90/175169 • BB **E** • EM from £5.20, 6-9.30pm • S2 D8 T12 • 1-12 • Ⓥ Ⓑ Ⓓ Ⓢ Ⓟ Ⓣ 🐾 • ★★★ • www.bridge-hotel.com • See next page for display box advertisement.

☆ See Display Advertisement

CUMBRIA   ENGLAND   ACCOMMODATION   B&B

BUTTERMERE VALLEY
★★ 2 star hotel

THE BRIDGE HOTEL is situated in an unrivalled position between two lakes – Buttermere and Crummock Water – and overlooked by famous mountains such as Haystacks, High Stile and Red Pike. Superb unrestricted walking country in an Area of Outstanding Natural Beauty. Good food, wines and real ales served in comfortable surroundings. Traditional Lakeland afternoon teas. **Dogs welcome. Self-catering available.** Special breaks all Year.
**BRIDGE HOTEL, BUTTERMERE, LAKE DISTRICT, CUMBRIA CA13 9UZ
TEL 017687 70252**
www.bridge-hotel.com

■ CALDBECK (Wigton)
CUMBRIA WAY

☆ Dorothy H Coulthard, The Briars, Friar Row, CA7 8DS. ☎ (016974) 78633 • Map 90/325399 • BB **C** • S1 D1 T1 • 1-12 NX • B D S 🖬 • ◆◆◆

THE BRIARS
Caldbeck
Situated in Caldbeck village, overlooking Caldbeck Fells. Ideal for touring Lake District, Scottish Borders and Roman Wall. We are right on the Cumbrian Way route. Tea-making facilities. Rooms en-suite with televisions. 2 mins walk to village inn. B&B band B.
Tel. 016974 78633

SWALEDALE WATCH
Whelpo, Caldbeck, Wigton, Cumbria CA7 8HQ
Enjoy comfort, fine food, beautiful surroundings and peaceful countryside on our farm. Central for touring or walking the rolling Northern fells. A warm welcome awaits you. Ideal for Cumbrian Way walkers. All rooms have private facilities. B&B £18-£24. EM (Tue, Wed, Thu, Sat) £12. Packed lunches by prior arrangement.
**Mrs Nan Savage
Caldbeck (Phone/Fax) 016974 78409
nan.savage@talk21.com**

☆ Mr & Mrs Savage, Swaledale Watch, Whelpo, CA7 8HQ. ☎ (016974) 78409 • Map 90/309396 • BB **B/C** • EM book first £12.00 Tue-Th & Sat only, 7pm • D2 T1 F1 • 1-12 NX • V B D S P 🖬 • ◆◆◆◆ • nan.savage@talk21.com

Mrs M Patterson, Gate House, CA7 8EL. ☎ (01697) 478092 • Map 90/324398 • BB **B/C** • D2 T1 • 3-10 • B D P 🖬 • ray@caldbeckgatehouse.co.uk

■ CARLISLE
CUMBRIA WAY

Angus Hotel & Almonds Bistro, 14 Scotland Road, Stanwix, CA3 9DG. ☎ (01228) 523546 • Map 85/400571 • BB **C/D** • EM £15, 7-9.30pm • S3 D3 T4 F4 • 1-12 NX • V B D S R P 🖬 • ◆◆◆◆ • angus@hadrians-wall.fsnet.co.uk

☆ Michael & Angela Hayes, Avondale, 3 St Aidan's Road, CA1 1LT. ☎ (01228) 523012(& Fax) • Map 85/410559 • BB **C** • EM book first £9.50, 6.30pm • D1 T2 • 1-12 NX • V B D S R P 🖬 • ◆◆◆◆ • beeanbee@hotmail.com

AVONDALE
3 St Aidan's Road, Carlisle
Our quiet, comfortable Edwardian house offers a friendly welcome, a room with its own bathroom, and an excellent breakfast. All rooms have central heating, TV, radio and tea-making facilities. Close to centre.
Michael & Angela Hayes ☎/Fax 01228 523012
Email beeanbee@hotmail.com
English Tourist Council ◆◆◆◆

Chatsworth Guest House, 22 Chatsworth Square, CA1 1HF. ☎ (01228) 524023 • Map 85/406560 • BB **B** • S1 D1 T2 F1 • 1-12 NX • V B S R P 🖬 • ◆◆◆

Robert Hendrie, Howard Lodge Guest House, 90 Warwick Road, CA1 1JU. ☎ (01228) 529842 • Map 85/406559 • BB **B/D** • EM book first £10, 6-9pm • S1 D1 T2 F2 • 1-12 • B S R P 🖬 • ◆◆◆◆

Mrs Pam Smith, Craighead, 6 Hartington Place, CA1 1HL. ☎ 01228 596767 • Map 85/406559 • BB **B** • S1 D2 T1 F1 • 1-12 NX • B D S R P 🖬 • ◆◆◆

Mrs M Irving, 'Dalrco', 411 Warwick Road, CA1 2RZ. ☎ (01228) 542805 • Map 85/421559 • BB **B** • EM book first £7, 6pm • S1 D1 T1 • 1-12 NX • V D S R P 🖬 • ★★★

■ CARTMEL (Grange-over-Sands)

Mrs P C Lawson, Bank Court Cottage, The Square, LA11 6QB. ☎ (015395) 36593 • Map 96,97/378787 • BB **B** • EM book first £12.50, 7pm • D1 T1 • 1-12 NX • Ⓥ Ⓓ Ⓢ Ⓡ Ⓟ Ⓣ ☃ • 1Cr/C

■ CARTMEL FEL (Kendal)

☆ Mrs Evelyn Cervetti, Lightwood Farmhouse Country Guest House, LA11 6NP. ☎ (015395) 31454 • Map 96,97/408890 • BB **D** • EM book first £14, 7pm • D2 T2 F2 • 2-11 • Ⓥ Ⓑ Ⓓ Ⓢ Ⓟ Ⓣ ☃ • ◆◆◆

■ COCKERMOUTH

Mrs D Richardson, Fellbarrow Pardshaw Hall, CA13 0SP. ☎ (01900) 822607 • Map 89/103254 • BB **B** • S2 D1 T/F1 • 1-12 NX • Ⓑ Ⓓ Ⓟ Ⓣ ☃ • Reduced rates for weekly bookings.

Mrs V A Waters, The Rook Guest House, 9 Castlegate, CA13 9EU. ☎ (01900) 828496 • Map 89/122307 • BB **B/C** • D2 T1 • 1-12 NX • Ⓑ Ⓓ Ⓢ Ⓟ Ⓣ

■ CONISTON

CUMBRIA WAY

☆ Beech Tree, Yewdale Road, LA21 8DX. ☎ (015394) 41717 • Map 96/302976 • BB **C** • D6 T2 • 1-12 NX • Ⓥ Ⓑ Ⓓ Ⓢ Ⓟ Ⓣ • ◆◆◆◆

☆ Lillian Grant, Cruachan, Collingwood Close, LA21 8DZ. ☎ (015394) 41628 • Map 96/303977 • BB **D** • D2 T1 • 2-11 • Ⓑ Ⓓ Ⓢ Ⓟ Ⓣ • ◆◆◆◆ • cruachan21@lineone.net

Lakeland House Guest House, and Licensed Tea Rooms, Tilberthwaite Avenue, LA21 8ED. ☎ (015394) 41303 • Map 96,97/304976 • BB **B/C** • EM book first £5-10 • S1 D2 T1 F3 • 1-12 NX • Ⓥ Ⓑ Ⓓ Ⓢ Ⓟ Ⓣ ☃ • ◆◆◆ • Groups also

☆ Kirkbeck House, Lake Road, LA21 8EW. ☎ (015394) 41358 • Map 96,97/301973 • BB **B** • D1 T1 F1 • 1-12 NX • Ⓓ Ⓟ ☃ • www.kirbeck.co.uk

Jenny Graham, Waverley, Lake Road, LA21 8EW. ☎ (015394) 41127 • Map 96,97/302974 • BB **A/B** • D1 T1 F1 • 1-12 NX • Ⓑ Ⓓ Ⓢ Ⓟ Ⓣ ☃

Crown Hotel, LA21 8EA. ☎ 015894 41243 • Map 96,97/302976 • BB **D** • EM £8, 9pm • D6 T4 F2 • 1-12 NX • Ⓥ Ⓑ Ⓓ Ⓢ Ⓟ Ⓣ • ◆◆ • enntiid45@crownhotel.freeserve.co.uk

☆ See Display Advertisement

☆ Marguerite & Graham Aldridge, Thwaite Cottage, Waterhead, LA21 8AJ. ☎ (015394) 41367 • Map 96/311977 • BB **C** • D2 T1 • 1-12 NX • B D S T • ◆◆◆ • thwaitcot.freeserve.co.uk

THWAITE COTTAGE — CONISTON

A beautiful C17th cottage in a peaceful wooded garden, close to village and lake. Central heating, log fires, beamed ceilings. Bathrooms private or en-suite. Leisure club membership included.

Non Smoking

☎ 015394 41367

■ COWGILL (Nr Dent)
DALES WAY

Mrs Ferguson, Scow Cottage, LA10 5RN. ☎ (015396) 25445 • Map 98/774852 • BB **B** • EM book first £12, 6.30pm • D1 T1 • 1-12 NX • V D S R P • ◆◆◆

Mr & Mrs Playfoot, River View, Lea Yeat, LA10 5RF. ☎ (015396) 25592 • Map 98/760870 • BB **B** • EM book first £8-10, 7pm • D1 T1 • 1-12 NX • V B D S R P T • www.dedicate.co.uk./river_view

■ DALTON-IN-FURNESS

Black Dog Inn, Holmes Green, Broughton Road, LA15 8JP. ☎ (01229) 462561 • Map 96/233761 • BB **B/C** • EM £5, until 9pm • S3 D3 • 1-12 • V B D S R P T • ◆◆

■ DENDRON (Ulverston)

Gill & Bill Whaley, Nuthatch, LA12 0QN. ☎ (01229) 869490 • Map 96/247705 • BB **C** • EM book first £8.50, 6.30-7.30pm • S0 D1 T1 • 1-12 • B D S P T Ⓜ • Transport av. bg.nuthatch@care4free.net

■ DENT (Sedbergh)
DALES WAY

Mrs A E Hunter, Rash House, Dent Foot, LA10 5SU. ☎ (015396) 20113 • Map 98/667897 • BB **B** • EM book first £10, 6.30pm • D1 F1 • 1-12 NX • V D P T

Kay Rushton, Stone Close Tea Shop, Main Street, LA10 5QL. ☎ (015396) 25231 • Map 98/705870 • BB **C** • EM book first £8.50, 7.30pm • S1 D2 F1 • 2-12 • V B D S P T • ◆◆◆ • free night in 5 nights+ • www.stoneclose.co.uk

Rita Smith, Garda View Guest House, Main Street, LA10 5QL. ☎ (015396) 25209 • Map 98/705870 • BB **B** • D2 T1 • 1-12 NX • D P T

Rambler's Association members are covered by a public liability insurance policy further details from central office

■ DUFTON (Appleby)
PENNINE WAY

Mrs M Hullock, Ghyll View, CA16 6DB. ☎ (017683) 51855 • Map 91/691250 • BB **B** • EM book first £8, 7pm • S2 D1 T2 • 3-10 • V B D S P

Sue O'Halloran, Sycamore House, CA16 6DB. ☎ (01768) 351296 • Map 91/689253 • BB **B** • EM book first £10, 7.30+ • S2 D1 T1 • 4-10 • V B D S P • o_halloran@hotmail.com

■ EAMONT BRIDGE (Penrith)

Mrs C O'Neil, River View, 6 Lowther Glen, CA10 2BP. ☎ (01768) 864405 • Map 90/524285 • BB **C** • S2 D2 T2 • 1-11 • B D S R P T

■ ELTERWATER (Ambleside)
CUMBRIA WAY

The Britannia Inn, LA22 9HP. ☎ (015394) 37210 • Map 90/327047 • BB **E** • EM £10.50, 6.30-9.30pm • S1 D9 T3 • 1-12 NX • V B D S P T • ★ • SC also • info@britinn.co.uk

■ ENNERDALE BRIDGE (Cleator)
COAST TO COAST WALK

Mrs Lake, The Old Vicarage, CA23 3AG. ☎ (01946) 861107 • Map 89/065156 • BB **B** • S1 D2 T1 F1 • 1-12 NX • D S P T Ⓜ • Food nearby

The Shepherd's Arms Hotel, CA23 3AR. ☎ (01946) 861249 • Map 89/069158 • BB **D** • EM £5-£15.50, 6.30-9.15pm • S1 D3 T4 F1 • 1-12 • V B D S P T • ★★ • enquiries@shepherdsarmshotel.co.uk

■ ESKDALE (Holmrook)

☆ Neil & Christine Carter, Forest How Guest House, CA19 1TR. ☎ (019467) 23201 • Map 96/136999 • BB **B/C** • EM book first £16, 7pm • S1 D3 T3 F1 • 1-12 NX • V B D R P T • ◆◆◆ • SC also fcarter@easynet.co.uk

FOREST HOW, ESKDALE, CA19 1TR

◆◆◆

Secluded, warm, comfortable guest house. Excellent home cooking. Delightful gardens with spectacular views. TVs, H&C, beverage trays. Some ensuite. Parking. Friendly informal atmosphere. Brochure.

☎ 019467 23201

■ ESKDALE GREEN

John & Jenny Prestwood, The Ferns, CA19 1UA. ☎ (019467) 23217 • Map 89/142000 • BB **B/C** • D2 T1 • 1-12 • B D S R P T • SC also

■ **GARRIGILL (Alston)**
PENNINE WAY

Mrs Laurie Humble, Ivy House, CA9 3DU. ☎ (01434) 382501 • Map 86,87/744414 • BB **B** • EM book first £12 • D1 T1 F1 • 1-12 • Ⓥ Ⓑ Ⓓ Ⓢ Ⓟ Ⓣ 🛆 • ◆◆◆◆ • www.garrigill.com

■ **GILSLAND (Brampton)**
PENNINE WAY

☆ Paul & Judith Barton, Bush Nook, Upper Denton, CA8 7AF. ☎ 016977 47194 • Map 86/622652 • BB **C** • EM book first £12.50, 7pm • S1 D2 T1 F0 • 1-12 • Ⓥ Ⓑ Ⓓ Ⓢ Ⓟ Ⓣ • PaulAlBarton@bushnook.freeserve

■ **GLENRIDDING (Penrith)**
COAST TO COAST WALK

☆ Mr & Mrs J S Lake, Moss Crag Guest House, CA11 0PA. ☎ (017684) 82500 • Map 90/385170 • BB **B/C/D** • EM book first £15, 7.30 summer 6.30 winter • D4 T2 • 1-11 • Ⓥ Ⓑ Ⓓ Ⓢ Ⓟ Ⓣ • ◆◆◆ • mosscrag@talk21.com

■ **GRANGE-OVER-SANDS**

Prospect House Hotel, Kents Bank Road, LA11 7DJ. ☎ (015395) 32116 • Map 96, 97/403773 • BB **C/D** • EM book first £12.50, 7pm • S1 D3 T2 F1 • 1-12 NX • Ⓥ Ⓑ Ⓓ Ⓢ Ⓡ Ⓟ Ⓣ 🛆

■ **GRASMERE (Ambleside)**
COAST TO COAST WALK

Mrs Alison Dixon, Oak Lodge, Easedale Road, LA22 9QJ. ☎ (015394) 35527 • Map 90/331081 • BB **C/D** • D2 T1 • 2-12 NX • Ⓑ Ⓓ Ⓢ Ⓟ Ⓣ

☆ Trevor & Lesley Bulcock, Dunmail House, Keswick Road, LA22 9RE. ☎ (015394) 35256 • Map 90/339084 • BB **C** • S1 D3 T1 F0 • 1-12 NX • Ⓑ Ⓓ Ⓢ Ⓟ Ⓣ • ◆◆◆◆ • enquiries@dunmailhouse.freeserve.co.uk

Wendy & Tony Wade, Meadow Brow, LA22 9RR. ☎ (015394) 35275 • Map 90/336090 • BB **C/D** • D2 • 4-10 • Ⓑ Ⓓ Ⓢ Ⓣ • SC also www.meadowbrow.com

☆ Glenthorne Country Guesthouse, Easedale Rd, LA22 9QH. ☎ (015394) 35389 • Map 90/335078 • BB **C** • EM £11.50, 7pm • S11 D3 T14 F3 • 2-11 • Ⓥ Ⓑ Ⓓ Ⓢ Ⓟ Ⓣ • gthorn@globalnet.co.uk

Grasmere Red Lion Hotel, Red Lion Square, LA22 9SS. ☎ (015394) 35456 • Map 90/336075 • BB **E** • EM £20, 7-9pm • S3 D28 T12 F4 • 1-12 • Ⓥ Ⓑ Ⓓ Ⓢ Ⓟ Ⓣ 🛆 • ★★★★ • enquiries@hotelgrasmere.uk.com

Geraldine & Bob Hamilton, Woodland Crag, How Head Lane, Town End, LA22 9SG. ☎ (015394) 35351 • Map 90/334073 • BB **D** • S2 D2 T1 • 1-12 NX • Ⓑ Ⓓ Ⓢ Ⓟ Ⓣ • ◆◆◆◆ • woodlandcrag@aol.com

☆ Glenthorne Country Guest House, Easedale Rd, LA22 9QH. ☎ (015394) 35389 • Map 90/335078 • BB **C** • EM £11.50, 7pm • S11 D3 T14 F3 • 2-11 • Ⓥ Ⓑ Ⓓ Ⓢ Ⓟ Ⓣ • gthorn@globalnet.co.uk • See display advert at start of next page.

☆ See Display Advertisement

BREAKS IN THE LAKES Grasmere

Friendly guest house, full board accommodation, double, family and single rooms (no supplement). All H&C. Good home cooking, including packing lunches. B&B from £21.00. Bargain midweek breaks Spring/Autumn. Families and Groups welcome. Also self-catering flat for two or 4/5.

Glenthorne Country Guest House
Tel: 015394 35389   gthorn@globalnet.co.uk

CUMBRIA (KESWICK) ENGLAND B&B ACCOMMODATION

■ GRAYRIGG (Kendal)
DALES WAY

Mrs J Bindloss, Grayrigg Hall Farm, LA8 9BU. ☎ (01539) 824689 • Map 97/579975 • BB **B** • EM book first £10, 6.30-7pm • S1 D/T2 F/T1 • 3-10 • Ⓥ Ⓓ Ⓟ Ⓣ ♨ • List/C

Mrs D Johnson, Punchbowl House, LA8 9BU. ☎ (01539) 824345 • Map 97/580972 • BB **C** • EM book first £14.75, 7.30pm • D2 T1 • 3-12 • Ⓥ Ⓑ Ⓓ Ⓢ Ⓟ Ⓣ • ♦♦♦♦Ⓢ • punchbowl.house@kencomp.net

■ HAWKSHEAD (Ambleside)

Ann Tyson's Guest House, Wordsworth Street, LA22 0PA. ☎ (015394) 36405 • Map 96,97/351981 • BB **C** • D2 T1 • 1-12 • Ⓑ Ⓓ Ⓢ Ⓣ ♨ • SC also • food nearby

■ HELTON (Penrith)

Mrs Lesley White, Beckfoot Country House, Guest Accommodation, CA10 2QB. ☎ (01931) 713241 • Map 90/500210 • BB **E** • EM book first £15(not w/e), 7-7.30pm • S1 D2 T2 F1 • 3-11 • Ⓥ Ⓑ Ⓓ Ⓢ Ⓟ Ⓣ ♨ • ♦♦♦♦ • Licensed. Lakes Paragliding Centre. bookings@beckfoot.co.uk

■ HESKET NEW-MARKET (Caldbeck, Wigton)
CUMBRIA WAY

Mrs Dorothy Studholme, Newlands Grange, CA7 8HP. ☎ (016974) 78676 • Map 90/350394 • BB **B** • EM book first £7.50, 6.30pm • S1 D1 T1 F2 • 1-12 NX • Ⓑ Ⓓ Ⓢ Ⓟ ♨

■ HIGH WRAY (Ambleside)
CUMBRIA WAY

Clare Irvine, Tock How Farm, LA22 0JF. ☎ (015394) 36106 • Map 96,97/351999 • BB **B/C** • D2 F1 • 1-12 • Ⓑ Ⓓ Ⓢ Ⓟ Ⓣ ♨

■ KENDAL (New Hutton)
DALES WAY

Mr & Mrs C Wilkinson, Sonata, 19 Burneside Road, LA9 4RL. ☎ (01539) 732290 • Map 97/513933 • BB **C** • EM book first £10.00, 6-7.30pm • D2 T1 F1 • 1-12 • Ⓥ Ⓑ Ⓓ Ⓢ Ⓡ Ⓟ Ⓣ ♨ • ♦♦♦ • Close to town centre • chris@sonataguesthouse.freeserve.co.uk

Mrs Brenda Denison, Hillside Guest House, 4 Beast Banks, LA9 4JW. ☎ (01539) 722836 • Map 97/513925 • BB **B** • S3 D3 T1 • 3-11 • Ⓑ Ⓓ Ⓢ Ⓡ Ⓣ ♨ • ♦♦♦ • Food nearby

Sue & Graeme Richardson, Sundial House, 51 Milnthorpe Road, LA9 5QG. ☎ (01539) 724468 • Map 97/516916 • BB **B** • EM book first £6-8, by arrangement • S1 D2 T1 F/D/T1 • 1-12 • Ⓑ Ⓓ Ⓢ Ⓡ Ⓟ Ⓣ ♨ • 1Cr/App • Evening meal by arrangement

Chris Green, The Glen, Oxenholme, LA9 7RF. ☎ (01539) 726386 • Map 97/534900 • BB **C** • EM book first £12, 6-6.30pm • D2 T1 F1 • 1-12 NX • Ⓢ Ⓡ Ⓟ Ⓣ ♨ • ♦♦♦ • www.smoothhound.co.uk/hotels/glen2.html

Mrs Gillian Wray, 1 Ashes Barn, New Hutton, LA8 0AS. ☎ 01539 729215 • Map 97/562910 • BB **B/C** • EM book first £8, 7.30pm • D1 T/S1 F/D1 • 1-12 • Ⓥ Ⓓ Ⓢ Ⓡ ♨ • mgswray@aol.com

Mr & Mrs Whitelock, Heaves Hotel, LA8 8EF. ☎ (015395) 60396 • Map 97/496866 • BB **D/E** • EM £13.50, 7-8pm • S1 D5 T6 F1 • 1-12 NX • Ⓥ Ⓑ Ⓓ Ⓢ Ⓟ Ⓣ ♨ • ★★ • hotel@heaves.freeserve.co.uk

■ KENTMERE (Kendal)

Mrs Christine Hevey, Maggs Howe, LA8 9JP. ☎ (01539) 821689 • Map 90/462041 • BB **B** • EM book first £10, 7pm • D1 T1 F1 • 1-12 NX • Ⓥ Ⓑ Ⓓ Ⓢ Ⓟ Ⓣ ♨ • ♦♦♦ • www.smoothhound.co.uk/hotels/maggs

■ KESWICK
CUMBRIA WAY

☆ Highfield Hotel, The Heads, CA12 5ER. ☎ (017687) 72508 • Map 89,90/264232 • BB **E** • EM £18, 6.30-8.30pm • S2 D11 T5 • 2-11+X • Ⓥ Ⓑ Ⓓ Ⓢ Ⓟ Ⓣ • ★★Ⓢ

★★ Silver Award
HIGHFIELD HOTEL
The Heads, Keswick

Small, friendly, family-run hotel, with superb views in quiet situation, 5 mins from town and lakeside. Walkers most welcome. We provide packed lunches, drying facilities, very good food in our award-winning restaurant. All bedrooms ensuite and non-smoking. Car park. Brochure from Derek or Celia Kitchingman.

Tel. 017687 72508
AA** red rosette   RAC**

☆ Mr K Pechartscheck, Chaucer House Hotel, Derwentwater Place, CA12 4DR. ☎ (017687) 72318/73223 • Map 89,90/268232 • BB **E** • EM £15, 6.30-8.30pm • S9 D13 T10 F3 • 2-11 • Ⓥ Ⓑ Ⓓ Ⓢ Ⓟ Ⓣ ♨ • chaucer-house.co.uk • See facing page for display box advert.

144

☆ Mrs Jean McNichol, Glendene, 8 Southey Street, CA12 4EF. ☎ (017687) 73548 • Map 89,90/268233 • BB **B** • EM book first £9, 6pm • D2 T1 F1 • 2-11 NX • Ⓓ Ⓢ Ⓣ

☆ Foye House, 23 Eskin Street, CA12 4DQ. ☎ (017687) 73288 • Map 89,90/270232 • BB **B/C** • S2 D3 T2 F1 • 1-12 • Ⓥ Ⓑ Ⓓ Ⓢ Ⓟ Ⓣ • ◆◆◆ • foye_house@keswick98.freeserve.co.uk

Dave & Vicky Wright, Kylesku Guest House, 22 Skiddaw Street, CA12 4BY. ☎ (017687) 72184 • Map 89,90/271233 • BB **B** • EM book first £10.00, 6.30pm • S2 D1 T1 F1 • 2-10 NX • Ⓥ Ⓓ Ⓢ Ⓟ Ⓣ

☆ Richmond House, 37/39 Eskin Street, CA12 4DG. ☎ (017687) 73965 • Map 89,90/270232 • BB **C** • EM book first £11.50, 7pm • S3 D6 T1 F1 • 1-12 NX • Ⓥ Ⓑ Ⓓ Ⓢ Ⓟ Ⓣ • ◆◆◆ • Groups welcome

☆ Mrs J Welch, Braemar, 21 Eskin Street, CA12 4DQ. ☎ (017687) 73743 • Map 89,90/270232 • BB **B/C** • S2 D3 T1 • 1-12 NX • Ⓑ Ⓓ Ⓢ Ⓟ Ⓣ • ◆◆◆◆ • www.braemar-guesthouse.co.uk

☆ Mr Rushton, Seven Oaks Guest House, Acorn Street, CA12 4EA. ☎ (017687) 72088 • Map 89,90/269232 • BB **B/C** • EM book first £11, 6.30pm • S3 D5 T3 F3 • 12 • Ⓥ Ⓓ Ⓢ Ⓟ Ⓣ ⬙ • p.rushtie@aol.com

☆ See Display Advertisement

B&B ACCOMMODATION ENGLAND CUMBRIA (KESWICK)

145

☆ Nel & Keith Nicholls, Hedgehog Hill, 18 Blencathra Street, CA12 4HP. ☎ (017687) 74386 • Map 89,90/269233 • BB **B/C** • S2 D3 T1 • 1-12 NX • Ⓑ Ⓓ Ⓢ Ⓟ Ⓣ • ◆◆◆ • hedhil@fsbdial.co.uk

Hedgehog Hill
18 Blencathra Street
Keswick CA12 4HP
(017687) 74386

Wet clothes and boots welcome in our friendly Victorian guesthouse near town centre, fells and lake. Freshly prepared large breakfasts with choice. Packed lunches available. All rooms with colour TV, tea/coffee making facilities, c/h, most en-suite. Mountain views. Non-smoking. A warm reception awaits you.

☆ Easedale Hotel, Southey Street, CA12 4EG. ☎ (017687) 72710 • Map 89,90/268233 • BB **C** • EM book first £12.50, 6.00-7.00pm • S2 D4 T2 F3 • 1-12 • Ⓥ Ⓑ Ⓓ Ⓢ Ⓟ Ⓣ • ◆◆◆ • Groups also easedaleh@aol.com

The Easedale Hotel

SOUTHEY STREET,
KESWICK-ON-DERWENTWATER
CUMBRIA CA12 4EG
Tel. 017-687-72710   Fax. 017-687-71127
Email:-easedalehotel@btinternet.com

With easy access to local felltops, but close to the Lake and Town Centre, this Hotel makes an ideal base for walking or touring holidays.

Several rooms have en-suite facilities, all have Colour TV, Clock/radio, tea/coffee making sets.

Excellent home cooking. Packed lunches on request. Delightful lounge with books/games. Drying room and secure cycle storage facilities. Fully licenced. Non-smoking.

Groups welcome.
Reduced rates from November–March

See us (photo, tarrif etc) on the wwweb!

http://www.milford.co.uk/go/easedale.html

MELBREAK HOUSE
29 Church Street, Keswick
ETC ◆◆◆
☎/Fax 017687 73398
www.melbreakhouse.co.uk
John, Jen & Carol welcome you to Melbreak House • Traditional home cooking • We are licensed • Attractive rates for everyone including groups • Evening meals available for large parties and packed lunches available upon arrangement • Children and dogs welcome • Non-smoking • Open all year.

☆ John, Jen & Carol Hardman, Melbreak House, 29 Church Street, CA12 4DX. ☎ (017687) 73398 • Map 89,90/269232 • BB **C** • EM book first £11.50, 6.30pm • D6 F4 • 1-12 • Ⓥ Ⓓ Ⓢ Ⓟ Ⓣ ♨ • ◆◆◆ • www.melbreakhouse.co.uk

Bill & Elizabeth Riding, Derwentdale Guest House, 8 Blencathra St, CA12 4HP. ☎ (017687) 74187 • Map 89,90/269233 • BB **B/C** • S2 D3 T1 • 1-12 • Ⓑ Ⓢ Ⓟ Ⓣ • ◆◆◆

☆ Ann & Tony Atkin, Glencoe Guest House, 21 Helvellyn, CA12 4EN. ☎ (017687) 71016 • Map 89,90/269233 • BB **B/C** • S1 D3 T2 • 1-12 NX • Ⓑ Ⓓ Ⓢ Ⓣ • ◆◆◆◆ • www.glencoeguesthouse.co.uk

Glencoe Guest House
Keswick
Double, single and twin rooms available, both en-suite and shared facilities, all with colour TV, radio alarm, quality fittings and hospitality tray. Only 5 min stroll from Keswick centre and amenities. Victorian home retaining much of its original character. Warm friendly atmosphere.
B&B from £18.00. Non Smoking.
Tel: 017687 71016
www.glencoeguesthouse.co.uk

☆ Mrs M Illman, Beckstones Farm, Thornthwaite, CA12 5SQ. ☎ (017687) 78510 • Map 89,90/221264 • BB **C** • S1 D5 T2 F1 • 1-12 NX • Ⓑ Ⓢ Ⓟ Ⓣ ♨ • ◆◆◆ • website.lineone.net/~beckstones

Beckstones Farm
Thornthwaite, Keswick CA12 5SQ
Converted Georgian farmhouse offering quality en-suite B&B, peaceful location. Magnificent views to Skiddaw and Helvellyn Range. TV lounge. Substantial breakfast. Ideal walking and touring base.
Brochure ☎ 017687 78510

Ann & Kevin Gladas, The Cartwheel, 5 Blencathra Street, CA12 4HW. ☎ (017687) 73182 • Map 89,90/269234 • BB **B** • S1 D4 T1 • 1-12 • Ⓥ Ⓑ Ⓓ Ⓢ Ⓟ Ⓣ • ◆◆◆ • www.thecartwheel.co.uk

☆ Barry & Cathy Colam, Cumbria House, 1 Derwentwater Place, Ambleside Road, CA12 4DR. ☎ (017687) 73171 • Map 89,90/268232 • BB **B/C** • EM book first £10 (groups 6+ only), 6.45pm • S3 D2 T3 F1 • 2-11 • Ⓥ Ⓑ Ⓓ Ⓢ Ⓟ Ⓣ Ⓜ • ◆◆◆◆ • www.cumbriahouse.co.uk • See display on next page.

Please mention the Rambler's Yearbook when booking your accommodation

Cumbria House

Ambleside Road,
Keswick
Cumbria CA12 4DR
Tel/Fax: 017687 73171
e-mail: rambler@cumbriahouse.co.uk
www.cumbriahouse.co.uk
Your Hosts: Barry & Cathy Colam

Everything for the hill walker

We can't guarantee the weather – but at least we have an efficient drying room and give you a local weather forecast twice a day.

Hearty, freshly-cooked breakfast with plenty of choice along with home made rolls and marmalade. Comfortable lounge with library of walking books. As experienced hill walkers we are happy to help with your route planning, and will even take a day off work to accompany you on the fells!

ETC
♦♦♦♦

PRIVATE CAR PARK

☆ Liz & Albert Johnson, Anworth House, 27 Eskin Street, CA12 4DQ. ☎ (017687) 72923 • Map 89,90/270232 • BB **C** • D3 T1 F1 • 1-12 NX • Ⓑ Ⓓ Ⓢ Ⓟ Ⓣ • ♦♦♦♦

Anworth House

27 Eskin Street
Keswick, Cumbria, CA12 4DQ

Small friendly Victorian guest house, offering all en-suite accommodation. A relaxed atmosphere and excellent food. Quiet location and ideally situated for town centre and fells.

Non –smoking   ETC
Tel 017687-72923   ♦♦♦♦

Ian Picken, Lynwood House, 35 Helvellyn Street, CA12 4EP. ☎ (017687) 72398 • Map 89,90/270233 • BB **B** • S1 D2 T1 F1 • 1-12 NX • Ⓑ Ⓓ Ⓢ Ⓟ Ⓣ • ♦♦♦♦ • lynwoodh@aol.com

☆ David & Valerie Fisher, Howe Keld Lakeland Hotel, 5/7 The Heads, CA12 5ES. ☎ (017687) 72417 • Map 89/264232 • BB **D** • EM book first £12.75, 6.30pm • S3 D7 T2 F3 • 1-12 NX • Ⓥ Ⓑ Ⓓ Ⓢ Ⓣ ♿ • ♦♦♦♦ • Groups also • david@howekeld.co.uk

HOWE KELD
LAKELAND HOTEL
5-7 THE HEADS, KESWICK CA12 5ES

• Delightful hotel in superb convenient location between town and lake
• Suitable for groups — 15 en-suite bedrooms
• Vegetarian specialities
• Excellent choice at breakfast
• CAR PARK • DRYING FACILITIES • EN-SUITE ROOMS

www.howekeld.co.uk
email david @howekeld.co.uk

AA
♦♦♦♦   **Tel. 017687 72417**   ETC ♦♦♦♦

☆ Joy & Colin Harrison, Swan Hotel, Thornthwaite, CA12 5SQ. ☎ (017687) 78256 • Map 89,90/221264 • BB **D** • EM £12, 6-9pm • S2 D10 T7 F2 • 2-12NX • Ⓥ Ⓑ Ⓓ Ⓟ Ⓣ ♿ • 3Cr/App • Groups also

The Swan Hotel & Country Inn
Thornthwaite, Keswick
 Commended

A family run 17th Century former coaching inn set in idyllic surroundings twixt lake and mountain. For a true sense of beauty, history and relaxation, cossetted by polite friendly staff catering for your every need. Enjoy an open fire, lake walks, imaginative home cooking and real ales.

SUMMER PRICES: £29 pp/nt, £45 DBB, 3 nts DBB £130. Children and pets welcome, open all year. Winter breaks Nov-March. Spring breaks April-May. Excellent restaurant and bar food. Groups up to 35 welcome. Please call Colin or Joy Harrison for a brochure.

Telephone 017687 78256
www.swan-hotel-keswick.co.uk

CUMBRIA (KESWICK)   ENGLAND

B&B ACCOMMODATION

☆ See Display Advertisement

☆ Robert & Janet Jones, Greystones, Ambleside Road, CA12 4DP. ☎ (017687) 73108 • Map 89/268232 • BB **C** • S1 D5 T2 • 1-10 • Ⓑ Ⓓ Ⓢ Ⓣ • ◆◆◆◆ • greystones@keslakes.freeserve.co.uk

☆ Carole & John Fullagar, West View Guest House, The Heads, CA12 5ES. ☎ (017687) 73638 • Map 89,90/264232 • BB **D** • D6 T1 • 1-12 NX • Ⓑ Ⓓ Ⓢ Ⓣ Ⓜ • ◆◆◆◆ • All rooms en-suite

☆ Irene Godfrey, Badgers Wood, 30 Stanger Street, CA12 5JU. ☎ (017687) 72621 • Map 89,90/265235 • BB **B/C** • S2 D4 T1 • 1-12 NX • Ⓑ Ⓓ Ⓢ Ⓣ • ◆◆◆◆ • enquiries@badgers-wood.co.uk

☆ Ray & Sally Newton, Sunnyside Guest House, 25 Southey Street, CA12 4EF. ☎ (017687) 72446 • Map 89,90/269233 • BB **C** • S1 D3 T1 F2 • 1-12 NX • Ⓑ Ⓓ Ⓢ Ⓟ Ⓣ Ⓜ • ◆◆◆◆ • www.survey.u-net.com

Louise Ellerton, Grassmoor Guest House, 10 Blencathra Street, CA12 4HP. ☎ (017687) 74008 • Map 89,90/269233 • BB **B** • S1 D2 T1 F1 • 1-12 NX • Ⓑ Ⓓ Ⓢ Ⓟ Ⓣ

☆ Gerry & Elsie Empson, Lynwood, 12 Ambleside Road, CA12 4DL. ☎ 017687 72081 • Map 89,90/266234 • BB **C** • EM book first £12, 6.30pm • S2 D3 T3 F1 • 1-12 • Ⓥ Ⓑ Ⓓ Ⓢ Ⓟ Ⓣ • ◆◆◆ • Cycle storage av. lynwood.keswick@virgin.net

☆ Mr & Mrs Lankester, Glendale Guest House, 7 Eskin Street, CA12 4DH. ☎ 017687 73562 • Map 89,90/269231 • BB **B** • EM book first £10, 6.30pm • S1 D2 T1 F2 • 1-12 NX • Ⓥ Ⓑ Ⓢ Ⓟ Ⓣ • glendale.guesthouse@talk21.com

Mrs K Wells, Ivy Lodge, 32 Penrith Road, CA12 4HA. ☎ 017687 75747 • Map 89,90/271235 • BB **B/C** • EM book first £10, 6.30pm • S2 D2 T2 F2 • 1-12 • Ⓑ Ⓓ Ⓢ Ⓟ Ⓣ • peter@ivy-lodge.freeserve.co.uk

☆ Hazeldene Hotel, The Heads, CA12 5ER. ☎ (01768) 772106 • Map 89,90/264232 • BB **D/E** • EM book first £16, 6.30-7pm • S2 D10 T4 F2 • 1-10 • Ⓥ Ⓑ Ⓓ Ⓢ Ⓟ Ⓣ • ★ • www.hazeldene-hotel.co.uk

Mr & Mrs G Osborn, Dolly Waggon, 17 Helvellyn Street, CA12 4EN. ☎ (017687) 73593 • Map 89,90/269235 • BB **B/C** • S/D1 D3 T/S1 F/T/D1 • 1-12 NX • [B] [D] [S] [P] [T] • ◆◆◆ • gjosborn@aol.com

Diane & Ian McConnell, 'Hawcliffe House', 30 Eskin Street, CA12 4DG. ☎ (017687) 73250 • Map 89,90/270232 • BB **B** • S2 D2 T1 • 1-12 • [D] [S] [P] [T] 🐾

■ KIRKBY STEPHEN
COAST TO COAST WALK

☆ Mrs C J Prime, Redmayne House, Silver Street, CA17 4RB. ☎ (017683) 71441 • Map 91/774088 • BB **B** • S1 D1 T1 F1 • 1-12 NX • [D] [S] [R] [P] [T] 🐾

Redmayne House
Kirkby Stephen
Cumbria

A spacious and attractive Georgian home set in a large garden.
Home made bread and preserves, walkers' breakfasts, private sitting room, parking. £17.50.
Mrs C J Prime   Tel. 017683 71441

Mrs M E Graham, "Lockholme", 48 South Road, CA17 4SN. ☎ (017683) 71321 • Map 91/772079 • BB **B** • S1 D1 T1 F1 • 1-12 NX • [B] [D] [S] [R] [P] [T] 🐾

■ LOWESWATER (Cockermouth)

Mrs M Vickers, Askhill Farm, CA13 0SU. ☎ (01946) 861640 • Map 89/110227 • BB **B/C** • EM book first £11, 6.30pm • D1 F1 • 4-10 • [V] [D] [S] [P] [T] 🐾 • ◆◆ • SC also

■ LOWICK (Ulverston)
CUMBRIA WAY

Everard Lodge, LA12 8ER. ☎ (01229) 885245 • Map 96,97/285863 • BB **B** • D1 T1 F1 • 1-12 • [B] [D] [S] [P] 🐾 • ◆◆◆ • Furness Way also • ali@elodge.fsnet.co.uk

Jenny Wickens, Garth Row, Lowick Green, LA12 8EB. ☎ (01229) 885633 • Map 96,97/289856 • BB **B** • D1 F1 • 1-12 NX • [D] [S] [P] [T] 🐾 [M] • ◆◆◆ • Baggage transfer av. B&B@garthrow.freeserve.co.uk

■ MALLERSTANG (Kirkby Stephen)
ALTERNATIVE PENNINE WAY

Val & John Porter, Faraday Cottage, Outhgill, CA17 4JU. ☎ (017683) 72351 • Map 91/784015 • BB **B** • EM book first £7 • D1 T1 • 1-12 NX • [V] [D] [S] [P] [T] 🐾

■ MOTHERBY (Penrith)

☆ Jacquie Freeborn, Motherby House, CA11 0RJ. ☎ (017684) 83368 • Map 90/429285 • BB **B** • EM book first £10.50, 7pm • F4 • 1-12 NX • [V] [B] [D] [S] [P] [T] • SC also www.motherbyhouse.co.uk

■ MUNGRISDALE (Penrith)

☆ Colin & Lesley Smith, Mosedale House, Mosedale, CA11 0XQ. ☎ (017687) 79371 • Map 90/356322 • BB **C/D** • EM book first £13.75, 7pm • S2 D3 T2 F1 • 1-12 NX • [V] [B] [D] [S] [P] [T] 🐾 • ◆◆◆◆ • Disabled person's room • SC also • colin.smith@ukonline.co.uk

C A Weightman, Near Howe Hotel, CA11 0SH. ☎ (017687) 79678 • Map 90/378286 • BB **C** • EM book first £11, 7pm • D3 T1 F3 • 1-12 NX • [V] [B] [D] [S] [P] [T] 🐾 • ◆◆◆ • SC also

C & P Bambrough, The Old Vicarage, CA11 0XR. ☎ (017687) 79274 • Map 90/363302 • BB **C** • S1 D1 T1 F1 • 1-12 NX • [D] [S] [P] [T] • oldvic@mungo33.freeserve.uk

■ NEWBIGGIN ON LUNE (Kirkby Stephen)
COAST TO COAST WALK

Brenda Boustead, Tranna Hill, CA17 4NY. ☎ (01536) 23227 • Map 91/702055 • BB **B** • EM book first £9, 6pm • D1 T1 • 3-10 • [V] [B] [D] [S] [P] [T] • ◆◆◆ • trannahill@hotmail.com

■ NEWLANDS (Keswick)
CUMBRIA WAY

M Beaty, Birkrigg Farm, Newlands Valley, CA12 5TS. ☎ (017687) 78278 • Map 89,90/214194 • BB **B** • S2 D2 T1 F1 • 3-11 • [D] [S] [P] • ◆◆ • SC also

Mrs Ann Grave, Low Skelgill, CA12 5UE. ☎ (017687) 78453 • Map 89,90/243208 • BB **B** • D2 T1 • 3-10 • [D] [S] [P] [T] 🐾 • ◆◆

☆ See Display Advertisement

■ PATTERDALE (Penrith)
COAST TO COAST WALK

Mrs Anne-Marie Knight, Fellside, Hartsop, CA11 0NZ. ☎ (017684) 82532 • Map 90/408132 • BB **B** • T2 • 1-12 NX • Ⓓ Ⓢ Ⓟ Ⓣ ♨ Ⓜ • List/App • SC also

Mrs Joan Barker-Martin, Grisedale Lodge, Grisedale Bridge, CA11 0PJ. ☎ (017684) 82084 • Map 90/391162 • BB **B** • D1 T2 • 1-12 NX • Ⓓ Ⓢ Ⓟ Ⓣ ♨ • SC also • coast2coast.co.uk/grisedalelodge

Sue Wheeler, Deepdale Hall, CA11 0NR. ☎ (01768) 482369 • Map 90/395142 • BB **C** • D1 F1 • 3-11 • Ⓑ Ⓓ Ⓢ Ⓟ Ⓣ • ◆◆◆◆ • www.deepdalehall.co.uk

■ PENRITH

Miss D Robinson, Corner House, 36 Victoria Road, CA11 8HR. ☎ (01768) 863566 • Map 90/518297 • BB **B/C** • EM book first £9, from 6pm • D2 T2 F0 • 2-11 • Ⓥ Ⓑ Ⓓ Ⓡ Ⓟ Ⓣ ♨

Newton Rigg Campus, University of Central Lancashire, CA11 0AH. ☎ 01768 863791 • Map 90/491312 • BB **B/C** • EM £7.25, 5.30-7.30pm • S245 D2 T20 • 4-9 • Ⓥ Ⓑ Ⓓ Ⓢ Ⓡ Ⓟ Ⓣ • info@newtonrigg.ac.uk

■ POOLEY BRIDGE (Penrith)

Mrs Kate Winter, Elm House, CA10 2NH. ☎ (017684) 86334 • Map 90/472244 • BB **C** • D4 T1 • 1-12 NX • Ⓑ Ⓓ Ⓢ Ⓟ Ⓣ ♨ • ◆◆◆◆ • elmhouse.demon.co.uk

■ PORTINSCALE (Keswick)
CUMBRIA WAY

☆ Janette Downer, Skiddaw Croft, CA12 5RD. ☎ (017687) 72321 • Map 89,90/254236 • BB **C** • S2 D2 T1 F2 • 1-12 • Ⓑ Ⓓ Ⓢ Ⓟ Ⓣ ♨ Ⓜ • skiddawcroft@amserve.net

■ RAVENGLASS

☆ "Rosegarth", Main Street, CA18 1SQ. ☎ (01229) 717275 • Map 96/084964 • BB **B** • EM book first £7.50, 5-7pm • S1 D3 T1 F1 • 1-12 NX • Ⓥ Ⓓ Ⓢ Ⓡ Ⓟ Ⓣ ♨

Holly House Hotel, Main Street, CA18 1SQ. ☎ (01229) 717230 • Map 96/084964 • BB **B** • EM £3.95-£7.50, until 9pm • S2 D2 T1 F1 • 1-12 • Ⓥ Ⓑ Ⓓ Ⓡ Ⓟ ♨

■ RAVENSTONEDALE (Kirkby Stephen)
COAST TO COAST WALK

Mr & Mrs C Irwin, The Book House, Grey Garth, CA17 4NQ. ☎ (015396) 23634 • Map 91/723041 • BB **B** • S1 T1 F1 • 1-12 NX • Ⓓ Ⓢ Ⓟ Ⓣ ♨ • ◆◆ • mail@thebookhouse.co.uk

C Hamer, Bowber Head, CA17 4NL. ☎ (01539) 623254 • Map 91/741032 • BB **B/C** • EM book first £12-15 • T1 F1 • 1-12 NX • Ⓥ Ⓑ Ⓓ Ⓢ Ⓟ Ⓣ ♨ • www.bowber.freeseve.co.uk

■ ROSTHWAITE (Borrowdale, Keswick)
COAST TO COAST WALK & CUMBRIA WAY

Royal Oak Hotel, CA12 5XB. ☎ (017687) 77214 • Map 89/258148 • BB **D** • EM £13, 7pm • S3 D5 T2 F5 • 1-12 NX • Ⓥ Ⓑ Ⓓ Ⓢ Ⓟ Ⓣ ♨ • ★ • Bookings pref to include EM. www.royaloakhotel.co.uk

Martin & Yvonne Crofts, Yew Craggs, CA12 5XB. ☎ (017687) 77260 • Map 89,90/256147 • BB **B/C** • D3 F2 • 3-11 • Ⓓ Ⓢ Ⓟ • List/C • yewcraggs@aol.com

■ SEDBERGH
DALES WAY

Mrs S Sharrocks, Holmecroft, Station Road, LA10 5DW. ☎ (015396) 20754 • Map 97/650919 • BB **B** • S1 D1 T1 • 1-12 NX • Ⓓ Ⓢ Ⓟ • ◆◆◆ • ssharrocks@breathemail.net

Miss M Thurlby, Stable Antiques, 15 Back Lane, LA10 5AQ. ☎ (015396) 20251 • Map 97/659921 • BB **B** • D1 T1 • 1-12 • Ⓓ Ⓢ Ⓟ Ⓣ ♨ • ◆◆

Pat & Paul Ramsden, Sun Lea, Joss Lane, LA10 5AS. ☎ (015396) 20828 • Map 97/658922 • BB **B** • D2 T1 • 1-12 NX • Ⓓ Ⓢ Ⓟ • pat@josslane.freeserve.co.uk

Mrs Anne Jones, Yew Tree Cottage, 35 Loftus Hill, LA10 5SQ. ☎ (015396) 21600 • Map 97/658917 • BB **B** • D1 T1 • 1-12 NX • Ⓓ Ⓢ Ⓟ Ⓣ ♨ • ◆◆◆

Joyce Cox, Bridge House, Brigflatts, LA10 5HN. ☎ (015396) 21820 • Map 97/640911 • BB **B/C** • EM book first £10.50, 7pm • D1 T1 • 1-12 • Ⓥ Ⓓ Ⓢ Ⓟ Ⓣ • ◆◆◆◆

☆ Mrs Jill Jarvis, The Moss House, Garsdale Road, LA10 5JL. ☎ (015396) 20940 • Map 98/670917 • BB **B** • EM • D1 F1 • 3-11 • Ⓑ Ⓓ Ⓢ Ⓟ Ⓣ

THE MOSS HOUSE

GARSDALE ROAD, SEDBERGH

Situated just outside the small market town of
Sedbergh on the A684 in the Yorkshire Dales
National Park • Just off the Dales Way and the
Howgills • Ideal centre for walking and touring •
Our accommodation offers a high standard of
comfort and friendliness, home cooking, and
optional evening meal and packed lunch • H/C in
all rooms • Full central heating • TV lounge •
Tea/coffee available • Drying room.

☎ 015396 20940

☆ Mrs Barbara Wilson, St Mark's, Cautley, LA10 5LZ.
☎ (015396) 20287 • Map 98/690944 • BB **C** • EM
book first £10, 7-7.30pm • S1 T3 F1 • 1-12 NX • Ⓥ
Ⓑ Ⓓ Ⓢ Ⓟ Ⓣ ♨ • ◆◆◆◆ • Groups also •
stmarks@talk21.com

ST. MARK'S
CAUTLEY, SEDBERGH LA10 5LZ

Treat yourself to the
tranquility of the Howgill
Fells and Western Dales.
Outstanding setting,
National Park, comfort-
able en-suite rooms,
Grade II listed, open fires, home cooking. Also
courses—guided walks, calligraphy, needlecrafts.
☎ **Barbara Wilson 015396 20287**

Mrs Anne Cooke, The Lodge, 10 Loftus Manor , LA10
5SQ. ☎ (015396) 21855 • Map 97/659916 • BB **B** •
EM book first £11.50 • D1 T1 • 1-12 • Ⓥ Ⓓ Ⓢ Ⓟ
Ⓣ ♨ • ◆◆◆ • anne.thelodge@talk21.com

■ SHAP (Penrith)
COAST TO COAST WALK

John & Carole Smith, Fell House, CA10 3NY. ☎
(01931) 716343 • BB **B/C** • D2 T1
F3 • 1-12 NX • Ⓑ Ⓓ Ⓢ Ⓟ Ⓣ ♨ • Food nearby
johnsmith@fellhouse.freeserve.co.uk

Mrs Margaret Brunskill, "Brookfield", CA10 3PZ. ☎
(01931) 716397 • Map 90/565144 • BB **B/C** • EM
book first £, 7.30-8.00pm • S1 D4 T3 F2 • 1-12 NX •
Ⓥ Ⓑ Ⓓ Ⓢ Ⓟ Ⓣ • ◆◆◆◆ • Home cooking

Shap Wells Hotel, CA10 3QU. ☎ (01931) 716628 •
Map 91/579095 • BB **E** • EM £15, 6.45-8.30pm • S14
D38 T36 F10 • 3-12 NX • Ⓥ Ⓑ Ⓓ Ⓟ Ⓣ ♨ •
★★★ • manager@shapwells.com

■ ST BEES
COAST TO COAST WALK

☆ Ms C M Smith, Stonehouse Farm, Main Street, CA27
0DE. ☎ (01946) 822224 • Map 89/971119 • BB **C** • S1
D3 T2 F3 • 1-12 NX • Ⓑ Ⓓ Ⓡ Ⓟ Ⓣ ♨ • ◆◆◆

STONEHOUSE FARM
Main Street
St Bees, Cumbria
(two mins railway station)
Comfortable modernised Georgian farmhouse, all
amenities. CH, CTV, B&B band B. Warm
welcome. Coast to Coast route, near shops and
beach, ideal walking area, golf, fishing. Car park.
Centre of village.
Tel. Ms C M Smith
Egremont (01946) 822224

☆ Mr & Mrs Whitehead, 1 Tomlin House, Beach
Road, CA27 0EN. ☎ (01946) 822284 • Map
89/963118 • BB **B** • D1 T2 F1 • 1-12 NX • Ⓑ Ⓓ Ⓢ
Ⓡ Ⓟ Ⓣ ♨ • id.whitehead@which.net

TOMLIN GUEST HOUSE
ST BEES, CUMBRIA
Close to the sea, near Lake District,
Sellafield Visitors Centre, St Bees head,
RSPB bird sanctuary. Start/finish point of
Wainwright's Coast to Coast Walk.
Irene and David Whitehead
☎ 01946 822284
Fax 01946 824243
Email id.whitehead@which.net

Susan & John Carr, Fairladies Barn Guest House, Main
Street, CA27 0AD. ☎ (01946) 822718 • Map 89/970114
• BB **B** • S1 D5 T2 • 1-12 • Ⓑ Ⓓ Ⓢ Ⓡ Ⓟ Ⓣ

QUEEN'S HOTEL
ST BEES
Start of Coast-to-Coast Walk and ideal for western
fells. Seventeenth-century freehouse, cosy atmosphere specialising in local ales and malt whiskies.
No games or machines. All rooms ensuite and
recently refurbished. Excellent, home-cooked food
can be taken in non-smoking conservatory and
extensive beer garden.
☎ 01946 822287

☆ See Display Advertisement

☆ Geoff Steele, Queens Hotel, CA27 0DE. ☎ (01946) 822287 • Map 89/971118 • BB **D** • EM £6.50, 6-9.30pm • S4 D7 T3 • 1-12 NX • Ⓥ Ⓑ Ⓓ Ⓢ Ⓡ Ⓟ Ⓣ 🐾 • ◆◆◆ • www.coast2coast.co.uk/queens-hotel • See display box on previous page.

■ STAVELEY (Kendal)
DALES WAY

Mrs Betty Fishwick, Stock Bridge Farm, LA8 9LP. ☎ (01539) 821580 • Map 97/475977 • BB **B** • S1 D4 F1 • 3-10 NX • Ⓓ Ⓡ Ⓟ 🐾

■ TEBAY (Penrith)
☆ Cross Keys Inn, CA10 3UY. ☎ (01539) 624240 • Map 91/616043 • BB **B** • EM £5.25, 6-9pm • D4 T2 • 1-12 • Ⓥ Ⓑ Ⓓ Ⓢ Ⓟ Ⓣ • ◆◆◆

THE CROSS KEYS INN
TEBAY PENRITH
CUMBRIA CA10 3UY

A 500 year old coaching inn nestled in the centre of Tebay village, surrounded by the Howgill Fells. A little gem of a pub ideally situated for those wishing to explore the Lake district, Yorkshire Dales and the Eden Valley. En-suite rooms, good food and real ale. Just off junction 38 on the M6.
Telephone 015396 24240

■ TROUTBECK (PENRITH)
Maureen Dix, Greenah Crag, CA11 0SQ. ☎ (01768) 483233 • Map 90/396283 • BB **B/C** • D2 T1 • 2-11 • Ⓑ Ⓓ Ⓢ Ⓟ Ⓣ

■ TROUTBECK (WINDERMERE)
☆ The Mortal Man Inn, LA23 1PL. ☎ (015394) 33193 • Map 90/410034 • BB **D/E** • EM £8, 7-9.30pm • D6 T6 • 1-12 • Ⓥ Ⓑ Ⓓ Ⓢ Ⓡ Ⓟ Ⓣ 🐾 • ★★ • the-mortalman@btinternet.co.uk

THE MORTAL MAN
ESTABLISHED 1689
Troutbeck, Windermere, Cumbria
Tel 015394 33193

Set in the foothills of Wansfell Pike, in the hear of the Troutbeck valley, we offer a relaxed, friendly, comfortable atmosphere in which to unwind. Bars, restaurant, beer garden, car park and spectacular views. B&B or DB&B rates. Ideal centre for walking. Scrumptious food and quaffable ale.
Website www.mortal-man-inns.co.uk
'First choice inn in North England' *Sunday Telegraph*
Call now for details and see Cumbria at it's best

■ ULPHA (Broughton-in-Furness)
Ray & Susan Batten, Oakbank, Ulpha, Duddon Valley, LA20 6DZ. ☎ (01229) 716393 • Map 96/201938 • BB **C** • EM book first £9, 7pm • D1 T2 • 1-12 NX • Ⓥ Ⓓ Ⓟ Ⓣ 🐾 • ◆◆

■ ULVERSTON
CUMBRIA WAY

Mike & Pat Ramsay, "Rock House", 1 Alexander Road, LA12 0DE. ☎ (01229) 586879 • Map 96,97/287779 • BB **C** • S1 F/D/T3 • 3-10 • Ⓓ Ⓢ Ⓡ Ⓟ Ⓣ • ◆◆◆◆

Jean Povey, The Walkers Hostel, Oubas Hill, LA12 7LB. ☎ (01229) 585588 • Map 96,97/296787 • BB **A** • EM £6, 7pm • T/D/F7 • 1-12 NX • Ⓥ Ⓓ Ⓢ Ⓡ Ⓟ Ⓣ Ⓜ • povey@walkershostel.freeserve.co.uk

■ UNDERBARROW (Kendal)
Mrs Cicely Simpson, High Gregg Hall, LA8 8BL. ☎ 015395 68318 • Map 97/464915 • BB **B** • D1 T1 • 5-10 • Ⓓ Ⓟ Ⓣ • ◆◆

■ WASDALE HEAD (Gosforth)
COAST TO COAST WALK & CUMBRIA WAY

Mrs A Buchanan, Burnthwaite Farm, Seascale, CA20 1EX. ☎ (019467) 26242 • Map 89/193091 • BB **D** • EM book first £from £15, 7pm • S2 D4 T2 • 3-10 NX • Ⓥ Ⓑ Ⓓ Ⓟ Ⓣ

■ WATERMILLOCK (Ullswater)
☆ Geoff & Steph Mason, Knotts Mill Country Lodge, CA11 0JN. ☎ (017684) 86699 • Map 90/437215 • BB **C/D** • EM book first £11.95, 7pm+ • D3 T2 F3 • 1-12 NX • Ⓥ Ⓑ Ⓓ Ⓢ Ⓡ Ⓟ Ⓣ 🐾 • ◆◆◆ • www.knottsmill.cwc.net

KNOTTS MILL COUNTRY LODGE
English Tourism Council
◆◆◆

Exceptional walking in Lake District by magical Ullswater overlooked by mighty Hellvelyn. Good food, licenced, comfortable, quality ensuite accommodation. Own grounds, drying room, maps and guides. M6 10 minutes.

Tel 017684 86699   www.knottsmill.cwc.net

■ WINDERMERE
DALES WAY

Cynthia & Tony Roberts, Kenilworth Guest House, Holly Road, LA23 2AF. ☎ (015394) 44004 • Map 96,97/413981 • BB **B** • S1 D2 T2 F1 • 1-12 • Ⓑ Ⓢ Ⓡ Ⓟ Ⓣ 🐾 • Transport av.

☆ Mr & Mrs A S Priestley, Holly Lodge, 6 College Road, LA23 1BX. ☎ (015394) 43873 • Map 96,97/411985 • BB **B/C** • S1 D5 T2 F3 • 1-12 NX • Ⓑ Ⓓ Ⓢ Ⓡ Ⓟ Ⓣ • ◆◆◆ • See display opposite.

Tony & Rhoda Graham, Gillthwaite Rigg, Heathwaite Manor, Lickbarrow Road, LA23 2NQ. ☎ (015394) 46212 • Map 97/419969 • BB **C** • D1 T1 • 1-12 NX • Ⓑ Ⓓ Ⓢ Ⓡ Ⓟ Ⓣ 🐾 • Free parking. • tony_rhodagraham@hotmail.com

HOLLY LODGE GUEST HOUSE

6 College Rd,
Windermere,
Cumbria,
LA23 1BX

Quietly situated in the village close to shops,
restaurants, buses and trains. Family run.
Friendly atmosphere. Good English breakfast.

Tel/Fax: 015394 43873

Mrs E Wood, The Haven, 10 Birch Street, LA23 1EG.
☎ (015394) 44017 • Map 96,97/413984 • BB **C** • D1
F2 • 1-12 NX • [V] [B] [D] [S] [R] [P] [T] 🐾 • ◆◆◆

☆ Mrs F Holcroft, Lynwood, Broad Street, LA23 2AB.
☎ (015394) 42550 • Map 96,97/413982 • BB **B/C** •
S1 D4 T1 F3 • 1-12 NX • [B] [D] [S] [R] [P] [T] •
◆◆◆ • Groups also

LYNWOOD

Broad Street, Windermere LA23 2AB

Relax in our elegant Victorian house in the heart of
Windermere. Each bedroom is individually furnished
and smoke-free with en-suite shower and wc, colour
TV, hairdryer & beverages. Convenient for bus and
train stations and close to parking. From £30 per night
for a double room with reductions for families.

Tel (015394) 42550   AA ◆◆◆   ETB ◆◆◆

☆ Roger & Carole Vernon, Thornbank House,
Thornbarrow Road, LA23 2EW. ☎ (015394) 43724 •
Map 96,97/409975 • BB **C** • EM book first £15.00, 7pm
• D3 T1 F1 • 2-11 • [V] [B] [D] [S] [R] [P] [T] • ◆◆◆

THORNBANK HOUSE

Thornbarrow Road, Windermere, Cumbria LA23 2EW

Small, family-run guest
house situated in a
quiet residential area
close to all amenities.
Comfortable rooms, all
ensuite. Ample car
parking. Free use of
leisure club facilities. Bargain breaks. B&B or D,B&B
available. Residential licence.

ETC ◆◆◆

Tel/Fax Windermere (015394) 43724

Sandra & Tim Shaw, Meadfoot Guest House, New
Road, LA23 2LA. ☎ (015394) 42610 • Map
96,97/411981 • BB **C/D** • S1 D3 T2 F1 • 2-11 • [B] [D]
[S] [R] [T] 🐾 • ◆◆◆◆

You'll find more accommodation in the *Hostels &
Bunkhouses, Self-catering* and *Groups* sections

DERBYSHIRE

■ ALSTONEFIELD (Ashbourne)
WHITE PEAK WAY

Mrs H Leason, Overdale, DE6 2FZ. ☎ (01335)
310206 • Map 119/135556 • BB **C** • S1 D5 T1 F2 • 1-
12 NX • [D]

■ ASHBOURNE

Angus & Vicki Haddon, Mercaston Hall, Mercaston,
DE6 3BL. ☎ (01335) 360263 • Map 119, 128/279419
• BB **D** • D2 T1 • 1-12 NX • [B] [D] [S] [P] [T] 🐾 •
◆◆◆◆ • mercastonhall@btinternet.com

☆ Compton House, 27-31 Compton, DE6 1BX. ☎
01335 343100 • Map 128,119/180463 • BB **C** • EM
book first £10-12, 7-8pm • D3 T1 F1 • 1-12 • [V] [B]
[D] [S] [P] [T] 🐾 • ◆◆◆ •
www.comptonhouse.co.uk

COMPTON HOUSE

27-31 Compton Ashbourne

Centrally placed in historic market town of
Ashbourne - Originally three terraced
cottages now converted into one rather
individual house offering high standard of
comfort and friendliness - en-suite rooms -
suppers/early breakfasts if needed - packed
lunches - clothes dried - flasks filled

Tel: 01335 343100
Fax: 01335 348100

■ BAKEWELL
WHITE PEAK WAY

☆ Mr & Mrs P Atkinson, Bourne House, The Park,
Haddon Road, DE45 1ET. ☎ (01629) 813274 • Map
119/219684 • BB **C** • D2 T1 • 1-12 NX • [B] [D] [S] [P]
[T] • ◆◆◆◆ •

BOURNE HOUSE

The Park, Haddon Road, Bakewell

Friendly and comfortable accommodation in
former manse overlooking Bakewell's park.
A short, riverside stroll to town centre restaurants and pubs. All rooms en-suite with TV, radio
and tea/coffee. Private off-road car park.
Separate guests' entrance.

Mrs Sue Atkinson
☎ **01629 813274**
atkinson@bakewellpark.freeserve.co.uk

atkinson@bakewellpark.freeserve.co.uk

Mrs J Finney, Mandale House, Haddon Grove Farm,
nr Over Haddon, DE45 1JF. ☎ (01629) 812416 • Map
119/184664 • BB **C** • D2 T1 • 3-11 NX • [B] [D] [S] [P]
[T] • ◆◆◆◆ • www.mandalehouse.co.uk

☆ See Display Advertisement

☆ Fieldsview, Station Road, Great Longstone, DE45 1TS. ☎ (01629) 640593 • Map 119/198714 • BB **B** • EM £8.50, 7pm • D2 T1 • 1-12 NX • Ⓥ Ⓓ Ⓢ Ⓟ Ⓣ • ◆◆◆◆ • SC also. Folder of local walks provided

■ BAMFORD (Hope Valley)
WHITE PEAK WAY

☆ Janet Treacher, Pioneer House, Station Road, S33 0BN. ☎ (01433) 650638 • Map 110/207825 • BB **C** • D2 T1 • 1-12 • Ⓑ Ⓓ Ⓢ Ⓡ Ⓟ ⓉⓂ • ◆◆◆◆ • pioneerhouse@yahoo.co.uk

Janet Wood, Crookhill Farm, Derwent, S33 0AG. ☎ (01433) 651184 • Map 110/187868 • BB **B** • D3 T1 • 1-12 NX • Ⓑ Ⓓ Ⓢ Ⓟ Ⓣ • Transport from railway

■ BIGGIN-BY-HARTINGTON

☆ Biggin Hall Hotel, SK17 0DH. ☎ (01298) 84451 • Map 119/153594 • BB **D** • EM book first £14.50, 7pm • D7 T8 F4 • 1-12 • Ⓥ Ⓑ Ⓓ Ⓢ Ⓟ Ⓣ🐾Ⓜ • ★★ • Groups also www.bigginhall.co.uk

■ BRADWELL (Hope Valley)
WHITE PEAK WAY

Marion Allcroft, Eden Tree House, S33 9JT. ☎ (01433) 621448 • Map 110/174818 • BB **B** • D1 T2 • 1-12 NX • Ⓑ Ⓓ Ⓢ Ⓡ Ⓟ Ⓣ

■ BUXTON

☆ Mrs S Pritchard, Devonshire Lodge Guest House, 2 Manchester Road, SK17 6SB. ☎ (01298) 71487 • Map 119/055738 • BB **B** • D2 T1 • 1-12 NX • Ⓑ Ⓓ Ⓢ Ⓡ Ⓣ🐾 • ◆◆◆◆

☆ Val & Roger Broad, Buxton View Guest House, 74 Corbar Road, SK17 6RJ. ☎ (01298) 79222 • Map 119/056742 • BB **C** • EM book first £10, 7pm • S1 D2 T1 F1 • 1-12 • Ⓥ Ⓑ Ⓓ Ⓢ Ⓡ Ⓟ Ⓣ🐾 • ◆◆◆◆ • See next page for display box advert.

Mrs H R Taylor, "Hilldene", 97 Dale Road, SK17 6PD. ☎ (01298) 23015 • Map 119/061731 • BB **B** • S1 T1 F1 • 1-12 NX • Ⓑ Ⓓ Ⓡ🐾 • 2Cr/C

BUXTON VIEW
VAL & ROGER BROAD
74 CORBAR ROAD, BUXTON SK17 6RJ
Wonderful walking through High Peak or Derbyshire Dales make this superbly comfortable guesthouse, with its relaxed atmosphere, a venue for a delightful holiday. All rooms have own bath (shower) WC facilities, colour TV, courtesy trays, heating. Payphone, parking. No effort spared.

ETC ♦♦♦♦ **Tel. (01298) 79222** AA ♦♦♦♦

☆ M A Roberts, Ford Side House, 125 Lightwood Road, SK17 6RW. ☎ (01298) 72842 • Map 119/059743 • BB **B** • D3 T1 • 4-10 NX • Ⓥ Ⓑ Ⓓ Ⓢ Ⓡ Ⓟ Ⓣ ♨ • ♦♦♦♦Ⓢ • fordside.house@ukgateway.net

FORD SIDE HOUSE
125 Lightwood Road
Buxton, Derbyshire SK17 6RW

Peaceful elegant Edwardian house for non-smokers, situated in a premier residential area, yet very close to town attractions, Peaks and Dales.
All guest rooms are en-suite with full amenities. Drying facilities for walkers.
Private parking. Full Fire Certificate.
B&B from £19 sharing (held for a further year).
Short Break, Long Stay and Low Season Discounts. Brochure Available.
Proprietors John & Margaret Roberts

Tel 01298 72842

ETC ♦♦♦♦ Silver Award

☆ Mrs Hilary Parker, Grendon, Bishops Lane, SK17 6UN. ☎ (01298) 78831 • Map 119/044731 • BB **C/D** • EM book first £12, 6-8pm • D2 T1 • 1-12 • Ⓑ Ⓓ Ⓢ Ⓡ Ⓣ ♨ • ♦♦♦♦Ⓢ • cressbrook.co.uk/buxton/grendon

GRENDON GUEST HOUSE
Bishops Lane, Burbage, Buxton SK17 6UN
Tel. 01298 78831 Fax 01298 79257
Welcoming, warm and spacious luxury ensuite accommodation adjacent to Goyt Valley and town centre, with outstanding views. Superbly situated for the area's many attractions. Delicious food and real log fire. B&B £23–£30 (for 4 poster honeymoon suite). Winter log warmer special (for 2, not incl Fri/Sat) – stay 2+ nights and eat dinner free.

AA ♦♦♦♦♦ Visit our extensive website www.cressbrook.co.uk/buxton/grendon ETC ♦♦♦♦

☆ Christine Green, All Season Guest House, 4 Wye Grove, SK17 9AJ. ☎ (01298) 74628 • Map 119/053730 • BB **C** • EM £10, 6pm • D2 T1 • 1-12 • Ⓥ Ⓑ Ⓓ Ⓢ Ⓡ Ⓟ Ⓣ • www.allseasonsguesthouse.fsnet.co.uk

All Seasons Guest House
Buxton
Warm friendly family run with good home cooking. Ideal base for some of the most beautiful walks in the White and Dark Peak. Open all year.

Ring Russ or Chris 01298 74628
www.allseasonsguesthouse.fsnet.co.uk

☆ T W & P A Cotton, The Old Manse, 6 Clifton Road, Silverlands, SK17 6QL. ☎ (01298) 25638 • Map 119/063734 • BB **B/C** • EM £9, 6.30pm • S2 D4 F2 • 1-12 • Ⓥ Ⓑ Ⓓ Ⓢ Ⓡ Ⓟ Ⓣ ♨ • ♦♦♦ • www.oldmanse.co.uk

The Old Manse
Private Hotel
6 Clifton Road, Buxton, SK17 6QL
Tele (01298) 25638
BB fr £18 www.oldmanse.com D,BB fr £27
A warm welcome, En-Suite rooms, Good home cooking, Excellent Walking, Clothes dried, Secure Bike storage, Packed Lunch, Flasks Filled, Ideal for the Goyt Valley, Millers Dale, Monsall Dale and Castleton

---

☆ Brian & Linda Millner, St Johns Road, SK17 6XQ. ☎ (01298) 22462 • Map 119/049733 • BB **C** • EM £12, 6.45-9pm • S5 D10 T5 F2 • 1-12 • Ⓥ Ⓓ Ⓢ Ⓡ Ⓟ Ⓣ ♨ • www.highpeak.co.uk/portlandhotel

32 St John's Road, Buxton, Derbyshire SK17 6XQ
Telephone (01298) 22462/71493
Facsimile (01298) 27464
www.highpeak.co.uk/portland
Situated in the heart of the Peak district or family run hotel offers warm, comfortable en-suite rooms with complimentary beverage facilities. Unwind in the Linden Bar before enjoying a hearty meal. Brian and Linda are waiting to welcome you.

☆ See Display Advertisement

B&B ACCOMMODATION ENGLAND DERBYSHIRE

■ **CALVER (Hope Valley)**
WHITE PEAK WAY

Dianne Payne, Pear Tree Cottage, Main Street, S32 3XR. ☎ (01433) 631243 • Map 119/238745 • BB **B** • EM book first £8, 6-7.30pm • S2 D1 • 1-12 NX • Ⓥ Ⓑ Ⓓ Ⓢ Ⓡ Ⓟ Ⓣ • Nr Chatsworth House, local Pubs.

Sue Stone, Valley View, Smithy Knoll Road, S32 3XW. ☎ (01433) 631407 • BB **C** • D2 T1 F1 • 1-12 • Ⓥ Ⓑ Ⓓ Ⓢ Ⓡ Ⓟ Ⓣ ♿ • ◆◆◆◆ • www.a-place-2-stay.co.uk Food nearby

■ **CASTLETON (Hope Valley)**
WHITE PEAK WAY

☆ Mary Gillott, Rambler's Rest, Mill Bridge, S33 8WR. ☎ (01433) 620125 • Map 110/150831 • BB **B/C/D** • S2 D5 T2 F1 • 1-12 NX • Ⓑ Ⓓ Ⓡ Ⓟ Ⓣ ♿ • ◆◆

RAMBLER'S REST

Mill Bridge, Castleton, Derbyshire

A 17thC guesthouse in the picturesque village of Castleton. The house is pleasant and olde worlde with 5 bedrooms, 3 en suite. All have central heating, colour TV, tea-making. Own car park. Mary and Peter Gillott.

Tel. Hope Valley (01433) 620125

Mr & Mrs T Skelton, Cryer House, S33 8WG. ☎ (01433) 620244 • Map 110/149829 • BB **C** • D2 F1 • 1-12 NX • Ⓑ Ⓓ Ⓢ Ⓡ Ⓟ Ⓣ ♿ • ◆◆◆• Teashop/garden w/e & hols fleeskel@aol.com

Janet Glennerster, Dunscar Farm, S33 8WA. ☎ (01433) 620483 • Map 110/143835 • BB **C** • D3 T2 • 1-12 NX • Ⓑ Ⓓ Ⓢ Ⓡ Ⓣ • ◆◆◆◆ • Grnd Flr rooms av.

Ivy Cottage, Pindale Road, S33 8WU. ☎ (01433) 620829 • Map 110/151826 • BB **C** • D3 • 1-12 • Ⓑ Ⓓ Ⓢ Ⓡ Ⓟ Ⓣ ♿

■ **CHELMORTON (Buxton)**
WHITE PEAK WAY

DITCH HOUSE CHELMORTON Nr BUXTON DERBYSHIRE SK17 9SG 01298 85719

Comfortable & spacious en-suite rooms in newly restored cottage with superb views. Good walking area, in Peak National Park. Packed lunches available.

☆ Trish Simmonds, Ditch House, SK17 9SG. ☎ 01298 85719 • Map 119/107697 • BB **C/D** • D1 T1 • 1-12 • Ⓑ Ⓓ Ⓢ Ⓟ Ⓣ • ◆◆◆◆

■ **CRICH**

Janice Lester, Clovelly Guest House, Roe's Lane, DE4 5DH. ☎ (01773) 852295 • Map 119/352545 • BB **B** • EM book first £5, 6pm • S1 D2 • 1-12 • Ⓥ Ⓓ Ⓢ Ⓡ Ⓟ Ⓣ • ◆◆

■ **CURBAR (Bakewell)**
WHITE PEAK WAY

C A & M J Payne, Breeze Hill, The Green, S32 3XH. ☎ (01433) 630046 • Map 119/239748 • BB **C** • EM £12.50, 7-9pm • S1 D1 • 1-12 NX • Ⓥ Ⓑ Ⓓ Ⓢ Ⓟ Ⓣ ♿ • mcpayne67@aol.com

■ **EDALE (Hope Valley)**
PENNINE WAY & WHITE PEAK WAY

J E Chapman, Brookfield, S33 7ZL. ☎ (01433) 670227 • Map 110/113847 • BB **B** • D1 T1 • 4-10 • Ⓓ Ⓢ Ⓡ Ⓟ Ⓣ • ★★

Mrs J Beney, The Old Parsonage, Grindsbrook, S33 7ZD. ☎ (01433) 670232 • Map 110/122860 • BB **B** • S0 D1 T1 • 3-10 • Ⓓ Ⓢ Ⓡ Ⓟ

Julia Reid, Stonecroft, S30 2ZA. ☎ (01433) 670262 • Map 110/122854 • BB **D** • EM book first £10-£20 NX, 7.30pm • D2 • 1-12 NX • Ⓥ Ⓑ Ⓓ Ⓢ Ⓡ Ⓟ Ⓣ • ◆◆◆◆Ⓢ • www.cressbrook.co.uk/edale/stonecroft

Mrs Sally Gee, Cotefield Farm, Ollerbrook, S33 7ZG. ☎ (01433) 670273 • Map 110/129858 • BB **C** • S1 D2 T1 F1 • 1-12 NX • Ⓑ Ⓓ Ⓢ Ⓡ Ⓟ Ⓣ • SC also

Caroline Jackson, Mam Tor House, S33 7ZA. ☎ (01433) 670253 • Map 110/123858 • BB **B** • T2 F1 • 1-12 NX • Ⓓ Ⓡ Ⓟ Ⓣ ♿

■ **ELTON (Matlock)**
WHITE PEAK WAY

☆ J Hirst, Elton Guest House, Moor Lane, DE4 2DA. ☎ (01629) 650217 • Map 119/221608 • BB **C** • D2 T1 F1 • 1-12 NX • Ⓑ Ⓓ Ⓢ Ⓟ Ⓣ • SC also

---

ELTON GUEST HOUSE

Elton, Near Matlock

Beautiful house in peaceful village convenient for all attractions and Alton Towers. Antique 4-poster beds, holiday cottage also available. Winter breaks in spacious rooms with 4 poster beds or in cottage. Private parking. House and cottage featured in TV series *Peak Practice*

Tel. Chris & Jenny Hirst for colour brochure Winster (01629) 650217

■ **FROGGATT (Calver, Hope Valley)**
WHITE PEAK WAY

Mrs Jean Agg, Old Orchard, The Green, S32 3ZA. ☎ (01433) 630659 • Map 119/245763 • BB **B** • S1 D1 T2 • 2-10 • Ⓑ Ⓓ Ⓢ Ⓡ Ⓟ Ⓣ • jeanagg@waitrose.com

■ GLOSSOP
PENNINE WAY

Margaret Child, Rock Farm, Monks Road, SK13 6JZ.
☎ (01457) 861086 • Map 110/027914 • BB **B** • D1 T1
• 1-12 NX • D S P T 🛁 • ◆◆◆◆ •
www.rockfarm99.freeserve.co.uk

■ HARTINGTON (Buxton)
WHITE PEAK WAY

Mrs H Harrison, Bank House, Market Place, SK17
0AL. ☎ (01298) 84465 • Map 119/128604 • BB **C** •
EM book first £7-£11.50, 6.30pm • S1 D4 T3 F2 • 1-
12 NX • V B D S P T • ◆◆

The Devonshire Arms, Market Place, SK17 0AW. ☎
(01298) 84232 • Map 119/131605 • BB **B** • EM book
first £6.50, 9.30pm • S1 D2 T2 • 1-12 NX • V P T

■ HATHERSAGE (Hope Valley)
WHITE PEAK WAY

Mrs J Wilcockson, Hillfoot Farm, Castleton Rd, S32
1EG. ☎ (01433) 651673 • Map 110/219818 • BB **C** •
S1 D3 T2 • 1-12 • B D S R P T • ◆◆◆◆ •
lorna@wilcockson.fsnet.co.uk

Mrs Nora Hickey, York Villa, Station Road, S32 1DD.
☎ (01433) 650339 • Map 110/230813 • BB **B** • D1 T2
• 1-12 • D S R T 🛁

☆ Barrie Walker, Highlow Hall, S32 1AX. ☎ (01433)
650393 • Map 110/218801 • BB **E** • D2 T1 F1 • 1-12
NX • B D S R P T 🛁

Highlow Hall
Hathersage

Sixteenth century manor house set in the
heart of the Peak District National Park, com-
manding excellent views over the
surrounding moorland. Accommodation
available includes ensuite and four-poster.

Attractions such as Hathersage, Chatsworth,
Haddon Hall, Castleton caves are all nearby.

Tel/Fax 01433 650393

Gill Wain, Highlow Farm, S32 1AX. ☎ (01433)
650907 • Map 110/218801 • BB **C** • EM book first
£7.50, 7pm • D1 • 1-12 • V B D R P T 🛁

Mrs S Oates, Cannon Croft, Cannonfields, S32 1AG.
☎ (01433) 650005 • Map 110/226815 • BB **C** • D3 T2
• B D S R T • ◆◆◆◆Ⓢ • www.cannon-
croft.fsbusiness.co.uk

■ HOPE (Hope Valley)
WHITE PEAK WAY

The Woodroffe Arms Hotel, 1 Castleton Road, S30
2RD. ☎ (01433) 620351 • Map 110/172835 • BB **D** •
EM £7, 6-10pm • D2 T1 • 1-12 • V B D S R
P • 3Cr/C • www.woodruffearms.co.uk

☆ Mill Farm, Edale Road, S33 6ZF. ☎ (01433)
621181 • Map 110/171838 • BB **C** • D1 T2 • 1-12 • D
S R P T • ◆◆◆ •
wilson@millfarm-hope.freeserve.co.uk

Mrs Dorothy Vernon, Chapman Farm, Dale Rd, S33
6ZF. ☎ (01433) 620297 • Map 110/172836 • BB **C** •
D2 • 1-12 • D S R P T • Single bookings taken.

■ LITTON (Buxton)

Annette Scott, Hall Farm House, SK17 8QP. ☎ 01298
872172 • Map 119/165750 • BB **C** • EM book first £8-
10, 7-7.30pm • D/F1 T/F1 • 1-11 • V B D S P
T 🛁 • ◆◆◆◆

■ MATLOCK

Mrs S Elliott, Glendon, Knowleston Place, DE4 3BU.
☎ (01629) 584732 • Map 119/301598 • BB **B/C** • D2
T2 F1 • 1-12 NX • B D S R P T • ◆◆◆◆ •
Fire certificate - car park

☆ Mrs K M Potter, Woodside, Stanton Lees, DE4
2LQ. ☎ (01629) 734320 • Map 119/254632 • BB **B** •
EM book first £12, from 7pm • D2 T1 • 1-12 • V B
D S T • ◆◆◆◆ •
kathpotter@stantonlees.freeserve.co.uk

DERBYSHIRE ENGLAND B&B ACCOMMODATION

■ **MATLOCK (continued)**

Riverbank House, Derwent Avenue, DE4 3LX.
☎ 01629 582593 • Map 119/299599 • BB **C** • EM
book first £9, 6.30-7.30pm • D3 T1 F2 • 1-12 NX • Ⓥ
Ⓑ Ⓓ Ⓢ Ⓡ Ⓟ Ⓣ Ⓜ • ◆◆◆◆ •
bookings@riverbankhouse.co.uk

■ **MATLOCK BATH (Matlock)**

Bernhard Trotman, The Firs, 180 Dale Road, DE4
3PS. ☎ (01629) 582426 • Map 119/295594 • BB **C** •
D1 T/D2 • 1-12 • Ⓥ Ⓑ Ⓓ Ⓡ Ⓟ Ⓣ 🐾 • ◆◆◆

■ **MIDDLETON-BY-YOULGREAVE (Bakewell)**
WHITE PEAK WAY

Mrs G F Butterworth, Castle Farm, DE45 1LS.
☎ (01629) 636746 • Map 119/192631 • BB **B/C** • T1
F1 • 1-12 NX • Ⓑ Ⓓ Ⓢ Ⓟ Ⓣ🐾 • ◆◆◆◆ •
Camping barn also. Caravan club site.

■ **MILLER'S DALE (Buxton)**
WHITE PEAK WAY

Mrs B McAuliffe, Dale Cottage, SK17 8SN.
☎ (01298) 872400 • Map 119/140734 • BB **C** • S1
D1 T1 F1 • 1-12 NX • Ⓥ Ⓑ Ⓓ Ⓢ Ⓟ Ⓣ • ◆◆◆ •
mik@dalecottage.freeserve.co.uk

■ **MONSAL HEAD (Bakewell)**

☆ Mrs J Mantell, Castle Cliffe, DE45 1NL. ☎ (01629)
640258 • Map 119/185519 • BB **C/D** • D2 T1 F2 • 1-
12 • Ⓥ Ⓑ Ⓓ Ⓢ Ⓟ Ⓣ🐾 • ◆◆◆

■ **MONYASH (Bakewell)**

Mr & Mrs R H Tyler, Sheldon House, Chapel Street,
DE45 1JJ. ☎ (01629) 813067 • Map 119/150666 •
BB **C** • D3 • 1-12 NX • Ⓑ Ⓓ Ⓢ Ⓟ Ⓣ • ◆◆◆◆ • SC
also • tyler.family@linone.net

Eileen Slater, Sunnyside, Handley Lane, Off Chapel
St, DE45 1JJ. ☎ (01629) 813981 • Map 119/150666
• BB **C** • D1 • 1-12 NX • Ⓑ Ⓓ Ⓢ Ⓟ Ⓣ🐾

■ **OVER HADDON (Bakewell)**

Mr & Mrs M Martin, Manor Cottage, DE45 1HZ.
☎ (01629) 812878 • Map 119/204665 • BB **C** • D1 T1
• 1-12 NX • Ⓓ Ⓢ Ⓣ • ◆◆◆

■ **ROWSLEY (Matlock)**
PEDDARS WAY & NORFOLK COAST PATH

Eastfield, Chatsworth Road, DE4 2EH. ☎ (01629)
734427 • Map 119/260662 • BB **B** • D1 T2 • 1-12 NX
• Ⓓ Ⓢ Ⓟ Ⓣ Ⓜ • bob@opsl.demon.co.uk

■ **SHATTON (Bamford, Hope Valley)**

Fiona Middleton, The White House, S33 0BG.
☎ (01433) 651487 • Map 110/200818 • BB **B** • S2
D1 T1 • 1-12 • Ⓓ Ⓢ Ⓡ Ⓟ Ⓣ🐾 • ◆◆◆

■ **THORPE (Ashbourne)**
WHITE PEAK WAY

Mrs B Challinor, The Old Orchard, Stoney Lane, DE6
2AW. ☎ (01335) 350410 • Map 119/157503 • BB **B** •
S2 D2 • 3-10 • Ⓑ Ⓓ Ⓢ Ⓟ Ⓣ🐾 • ◆◆◆

☆ Mr F Gould, St Leonard's Cottage, DE6 2AW. ☎
(01335) 350224 • Map 119/155504 • BB **C** • S1 D2
T1 • 1-12 NX • Ⓑ Ⓓ Ⓢ

Mrs M Moffett, Thorpe Cottage, DE6 2AW.
☎ (01335) 350466 • Map 119/155504 • BB **C** • EM
book first £14.50, 7.30pm • S1 D2 T1 F1 • 1-12 • Ⓥ
Ⓑ Ⓓ Ⓢ Ⓟ Ⓣ🐾 • 4K • SC also •
www.peakdistrict-band6.com

☆ Margaret Sutton, Hillcrest House, Dovedale, DE6
2AW. ☎ (01335) 350436 • Map 119/152505 • BB
B/C/D/E • EM book first £ • S1 D4 T1 F1 • 1-12 NX •
Ⓥ Ⓑ Ⓓ Ⓢ Ⓟ Ⓣ • ◆◆◆ •
hillcresthouse@freenet.co.uk

■ TIDESWELL (Buxton)
WHITE PEAK WAY

☆ Bernie & Naomi Harold, Rockingham Lodge, Market Square, SK17 8LQ. ☎ (01298) 871684 • Map 119/151758 • BB **C** • D2 T2 • 1-12 NX • Ⓑ Ⓓ Ⓢ Ⓟ Ⓣ Ⓜ • SC also

■ WARSLOW (Buxton)

The Greyhound Inn, SK17 0JN. ☎ (01298) 84249 • Map 119/087586 • BB **B** • EM £6.50, 7-9pm • S2 D2 • 1-12 NX • Ⓥ Ⓟ Ⓣ • Live band Sat. nights

■ WHATSTANDWELL (Matlock)

Mrs V A Durbridge, Riverdale, Middle Lane, DE4 5EG. ☎ 01773 853905 • Map 119/336542 • BB **C** • EM £9, 7pm • D2 • 1-12 • Ⓥ Ⓑ Ⓓ Ⓢ Ⓡ Ⓟ Ⓣ Ⓜ • ◆◆◆◆

■ YOULGREAVE (Bakewell)
WHITE PEAK WAY

Anne Croasdell, The Old Bakery, DE45 1UR. ☎ (01629) 636887 • Map 119/210643 • BB **B/C** • D2/T1 T1 • 1-12 • Ⓑ Ⓓ Ⓢ Ⓟ Ⓣs ◆◆◆

DEVON

■ ASHBURTON (Newton Abbot)

Chris & Annie Moore, Gages Mill, Buckfastleigh Road, TQ13 7JW. ☎ (01364) 652391 • Map 202/747688 • BB **D** • EM book first £13.50, 7pm • S1 D6 T1 • 3-10 • Ⓥ Ⓑ Ⓓ Ⓢ Ⓟ Ⓣ • ◆◆◆◆ • www.gagesmill.co.uk

■ AXMOUTH (Seaton)
SOUTH WEST COAST PATH

Stepps House, Stepps Lane, EX12 4AR. ☎ /Fax (01297) 20679 • Map 192,193/262909 • BB **C** • D1 T1 • 4-9 • Ⓓ Ⓢ Ⓟ • Food nearby.

■ BARNSTAPLE

Roy & Wynn Tyson, Crossways, Braunton Road, EX31 1GA. ☎ (01271) 379120 • Map 180/553337 • BB **B/C** • D2 T2 F1 • 1-12 • Ⓑ Ⓓ Ⓢ Ⓡ Ⓟ Ⓣ

■ BEER
SOUTH WEST COAST PATH

Mr & Mrs R Oswald, Bay View Guest House, Fore Street, EX12 3EE. ☎ (01297) 20489 • Map 192/230891 • BB **B/C** • S2 D6 T1 F1 • 4-11 • Ⓑ Ⓓ Ⓟ

■ BELSTONE (Okehampton)
TARKA TRAIL

Moorlands House, EX20 1QZ. ☎ (01837) 840549 • Map 191/620935 • BB **B/C** • D2 T1 • 1-12 • Ⓑ Ⓓ Ⓟ Ⓣ • Food nearby

Mrs Dawn Wood, Moor Hall, EX20 1QZ. ☎ (01837) 840604 • Map 191/619934 • BB **B** • D2 T1 • 1-12 • Ⓑ Ⓓ Ⓢ Ⓟ • Food nearby moorhallbelstone@hotmail.com

■ BIDEFORD
SOUTH WEST COAST PATH & TARKA TRAIL

☆ Heath & Andrew Laugharne, The Mount, Northdown Road, EX39 3LP. ☎ (01237) 473748 • Map 190/449269 • BB **D** • S2 D3 T1 F1 • 1-12 NX • Ⓑ Ⓒ Ⓢ Ⓟ Ⓣ • ◆◆◆◆

■ BLACKAWTON (Kingsbridge, Dartmouth)

Mrs S Edmonds, Ruby Farm, TQ9 7BN. ☎ (01803) 712424 • Map 202/806509 • BB **B** • D1 T2 • 1-12 • Ⓑ Ⓓ Ⓟ Ⓣ

John & Sue Hadow, Washwalk Farm, TQ9 7AD. ☎ (01548) 521204 • Map 202/784504 • T2 • 1-12 NX • Ⓑ Ⓓ Ⓢ Ⓟ Ⓣ

■ BRANSCOMBE (Seaton)
SOUTH WEST COAST PATH

Amanda Hart, Hole Mill, EX12 3BX. ☎ (01297) 680314 • Map 192/195885 • BB **B** • D2 T1 • 1-12 • Ⓓ Ⓢ • www.users.globalnet.co.uk/~branscombe/hole1.htm

■ BRAUNTON
SOUTH WEST COAST PATH & TARKA TRAIL

Mrs Jean Watkins, North Cottage, 14 North Street, EX33 1AJ. ☎ (01271) 812703 • Map 180/485367 • BB **B** • EM book first £8, 6-7pm • S2 D1 T1 F1 • 1-12 • Ⓥ Ⓑ Ⓓ Ⓟ Ⓣ Ⓜ

☆ See Display Advertisement

Audrey Issac, Crowborough, EX33 1JZ. ☎ (01271) 891005 • Map 180/467396 • BB **C** • D2 T1 • 1-12 • Ⓑ Ⓓ Ⓢ Ⓟ Ⓣ • members.aol.com/amisaac/index.htm

■ **BRIXHAM**
SOUTH WEST COAST PATH

Ian & Carol Hayhurst, Richmond House, Higher Manor Road, TQ5 8HA. ☎ (01803) 882391 • Map 202/921560 • BB **C** • D4 F2 • 2-12 NX • Ⓑ Ⓓ Ⓢ Ⓟ Ⓣ 🛏 • ◆◆◆

Martyn & Carol Bishop, Tor Haven Hotel, 97 King Street, TQ5 9TH. ☎ (01803) 882281 • Map 202/926561 • BB **C** • EM book first £9 • S2 D5 T1 F1 • 1-12 NX • Ⓥ Ⓑ Ⓓ Ⓢ Ⓟ Ⓣ 🛏 • ◆◆◆ • torhavenhotel@netscapeonline.co.uk

■ **CHAGFORD (Newton Abbot)**
TWO MOORS WAY

☆ Glendarah House, TQ13 8BZ. ☎ (01647) 433270 • Map 191/702879 • BB **D** • S1 D3 T3 F0 • 1-12 NX • Ⓑ Ⓓ Ⓢ Ⓟ Ⓣ 🛏 • ◆◆◆◆Ⓢ • glendarah-house.co.uk

■ **CLOVELLY (Bideford)**
SOUTH WEST COAST PATH

Mrs D Vanstone, The Old Smithy, Slerra Hill, EX39 5ST. ☎ (01237) 431202 • Map 190/312243 • BB **B/C** • D1 T1 F2 • 1-12 NX • Ⓑ Ⓓ Ⓢ Ⓟ Ⓣ

Mrs S Curtis, Fuchsia Cottage, Burscott Lane, EX39 5RR. ☎ (01237) 431398 • Map 190/314242 • BB **B** • S2 D1 F1 • 1-12 NX • Ⓑ Ⓓ Ⓢ Ⓟ Ⓣ 🛏 • ◆◆◆ • tomsuecurtis.fushsiacot@currantbun.com

■ **COLEBROOKE (Crediton)**

Pearl Hockridge, The Oyster, EX17 5JQ. ☎ (01363) 84576 • Map 191/770008 • BB **B** • D2 T1 • 1-12 • Ⓑ Ⓓ Ⓡ Ⓟ Ⓣ 🛏

■ **COLEFORD (Crediton)**
TWO MOORS WAY

Mrs D M Hockridge, Butsford Barton, EX17 5DH. ☎ (01363) 84353 • Map 191/764004 • BB **B** • S1 D1 T/F1 • EASTER-10 • Ⓓ Ⓢ Ⓡ Ⓟ Ⓣ

■ **COMBE MARTIN (Ilfracombe)**
SOUTH WEST COAST PATH & TARKA TRAIL

Mrs A Waldon, Idle Hour, Borough Road, EX34 0AN. ☎ (01271) 883217 • Map 180/577471 • BB **A** • S1 D2 T1 • 3-10 • Ⓓ 🛏

☆ Saffron House Hotel, King Street, EX34 0BX. ☎ (01271) 883521 • Map 180/581469 • BB **C** • EM book first £9, 6.45pm • D4 T1 F4 • 2-10 • Ⓥ Ⓑ Ⓓ Ⓢ Ⓟ Ⓣ 🛏 • 3Cr/C

Hillview Guest House, Woodlands, EX34 0AT. ☎ (01271) 882331 • Map 180/575469 • BB **B** • S1 D2 T1 • 4-10 • Ⓑ Ⓓ Ⓢ Ⓟ Ⓣ • hillviewgh@appleonline.net

Valetta Barry, Glendower, King Street, EX34 0AL. ☎ (01271) 883449 • Map 180/578472 • BB **A/B** • S1 D2 T2 • 1-12 • Ⓑ Ⓓ Ⓟ Ⓣ 🛏 • frankjbarry@netscapeonline.co.uk

Wild Pear Centre, King Street, EX34 0AG. ☎ 01271 883086/882579 • Map 180/581470 • BB **A** • D2 T/S3 F3-4 • 1-12 • Ⓓ Ⓢ Ⓣ • Groups also

Julie Lines, Cobblestones, Wood Lane, EX34 0NE. ☎ 01271 882050 • Map 180/597457 • BB **B** • EM book first £7.50 • S1 D1 F1 • 1-12 NX • Ⓥ Ⓓ Ⓢ Ⓟ Ⓣ 🛏

■ **COUNTISBURY (Lynton)**
SOUTH WEST COAST PATH & TARKA TRAIL

R S & S M Pile, Coombe Farm, EX35 6NF. ☎ (01598) 741236 • Map 180/766488 • BB **C** • D2 T1 F2 • 3-11 • Ⓑ Ⓓ Ⓢ Ⓟ Ⓣ 🛏 • ◆◆◆ • nr Two Moors Way

■ **CROYDE (Braunton)**
SOUTH WEST COAST PATH & TARKA TRAIL

Mrs Gwen Adams, Combas Farm, Putsborough, EX33 1PH. ☎ (01271) 890398 • Map 180/449396 • BB **C** • EM book first £10, 6.30pm • S1 D2 F/T2 • 3-12 NX • Ⓥ Ⓑ Ⓓ Ⓢ Ⓟ • ◆◆◆

■ **DARTMOUTH**
SOUTH WEST COAST PATH

Mrs K Greeno, The Cedars, 79 Victoria Road, TQ6 9RX. ☎ (01803) 834421 • Map 202/872513 • BB **B** • S1 D3 T2 F2 • 1-12 NX • Ⓓ Ⓡ Ⓟ Ⓣ 🛏

■ **DODDISCOMBSLEIGH (Exeter)**

Mrs Barbara Lacey, Whitemoor Farm, EX6 7PU. ☎ (01647) 252423 • Map 191/861866 • BB **B** • S2 D1 T1 • 1-12 NX • Ⓥ Ⓑ Ⓓ Ⓢ Ⓣ 🛏 • ◆

■ EXETER

☆ Park View Hotel, 8 Howell Road, EX4 4LG.
☎ (01392) 271772 • Map 192/917933 • BB **B/C** • S1
D8 T3 F2 • 1-12 NX • Ⓑ Ⓓ Ⓡ Ⓟ Ⓣ • ◆◆◆ •
near city centre. www.parkviewhotel.freeserve.co.uk

☆ Mrs Sally Glanvill, Rydon Farm, Woodbury, EX5
1LB. ☎ (01395) 232341 • Map 192/002872 • BB **C/D**
• D1 T1 F1 • 1-12 • Ⓑ Ⓓ Ⓢ Ⓡ Ⓣ 🐾 • ◆◆◆◆ •
www.devonbandb.co.uk

Barbara & Donald Bligh, Hillcrest Corner, 1 Hillcrest
Park, EX4 4SH. ☎ (01392) 277443 • Map
192/923944 • BB **B** • EM book first £8 • S1 D1 T1 • 1-
12 NX • Ⓥ Ⓓ Ⓢ Ⓡ Ⓟ Ⓣ • Vegetarian food only.
SC also • dalbligh@ex.ac.uk

■ EXMOUTH
SOUTH WEST COAST PATH

Ann Jones, Sholton Guest House, 29 Morton Road,
EX8 1BA. ☎ (01395) 277318 • Map 192/999807 • BB
B/C • EM book first £9, 6.30pm • S1 D3 T2 F1 • 1-12
• Ⓥ Ⓑ Ⓓ Ⓢ Ⓡ Ⓟ Ⓣ 🐾

■ HARTLAND (Bideford)
SOUTH WEST COAST PATH

Mrs Y Heard, West Titchberry Farm, Hartland Point,
EX39 6AU. ☎ (01237) 441287 • Map 190/242272 •
BB **B** • EM book first £(if poss.), 6.30pm • D1 T1 F1 •
1-12 NX • Ⓥ Ⓓ Ⓢ Ⓟ Ⓣ • Easy access to coastal
footpath. SC also, Parking & pickups

Mrs G Johns, Hartland Quay Hotel, EX39 6DU.
☎ (01237) 441218 • Map 190/223247 • BB **C** • EM
£9, 7-8pm plus bar food • S2 D4 T4 F4 • 3-10 • Ⓥ Ⓑ
Ⓓ Ⓟ Ⓣ 🐾 • 2Cr • SC also

☆ Mrs Thirza Goaman, Elmscott Farm, EX39 6ES.
☎ (01237) 441276 • Map 190/231215 • BB **C** • EM
book first £8.50, 6pm • D1 T1 F1 • 3-10 • Ⓥ Ⓑ Ⓓ
Ⓢ Ⓟ Ⓣ • ◆◆◆◆

Mrs Jill George, Gawlish Farm, EX39 6AT.
☎/Fax 01237 441320 • Map 190/256263 • BB **B** • EM
book first £10, 6.30pm • D1 T2 • 1-12 NX • Ⓥ Ⓑ Ⓓ
Ⓢ Ⓟ Ⓣ 🐾

John Borrett, Docton Mill, Lymebridge, EX39 6EA.
☎ (01237) 441369 • Map 190/232226 • BB **E** • EM
book first £25.50, 8pm • D1 T1 • 1-12 • Ⓥ Ⓑ Ⓓ Ⓢ
Ⓟ Ⓣ • doctonmill.co.uk

■ HOLNE (Ashburton)
TWO MOORS WAY

Colin & Sue Gifford, Wellpritton Farm, TQ13 7RX.
☎ (01364) 631273 • Map 202/717705 • BB **C** • EM
book first £10, 7pm • D1 T2 F2 • 1-12 • Ⓥ Ⓑ Ⓓ Ⓢ
Ⓟ Ⓣ 🐾 • ◆◆◆◆

Colin & Sue Gifford, Wellpritton Farm, TQ13 7RX.
☎ (01364) 631273 • Map 202/716704 • BB **C** • EM
book first £9, 7pm • S1 D1 T1 F2 • 1-12 • Ⓥ Ⓑ Ⓓ
Ⓢ Ⓟ Ⓣ 🐾 • ◆◆◆◆

■ HONITON

Molly Bennett, Lane End Farm, Broadhembury, EX14
3LU. ☎ (01404) 841563 • Map 192,193/109050 • BB
B/C • EM book first £10, 6.30pm • T1 F2 • 1-12 • Ⓥ
Ⓑ Ⓓ Ⓟ Ⓣ 🐾 • ◆◆◆ •
www.farm-holidays.co.uk/cgi/details?sub_ref=908

■ HOPE COVE (Kingsbridge)
SOUTH WEST COAST PATH

☆ The Cottage Hotel, TQ7 3HJ. ☎ (01548) 561555 •
Map 202/676401 • BB **D/E** • EM book first £18.55,
7.30-8.30pm • S10 D/T20 F5 • 2-12 • Ⓥ Ⓑ Ⓓ Ⓢ
Ⓟ Ⓣ 🐾 • ★★ • B&B price inc. dinner. Open New
Year. www.hopecove.com • Display ad on next page.

■ IDEFORD COMBE (Newton Abbot)

Mary & Tom Morris, The Mount, TQ12 3GR.
☎ (01626) 331418 • Map 191/868752 • BB **C** • D2 T1
• 1-12 • Ⓑ Ⓓ Ⓢ Ⓟ Ⓣ • ◆◆◆ •
marytom1@aol.com

☆ See Display Advertisement

■ **ILFRACOMBE**
SOUTH WEST COAST PATH & TARKA TRAIL

☆ David & Marianna Holdsworth, Lyncott Guest House, 56 St Brannock's Road, EX34 8EQ. ☎/Fax (01271) 862425 • Map 180/515469 • BB **B** • EM book first £12.00, 6.30pm • S1 D3 F2 • 1-12 • Ⓥ Ⓑ Ⓓ Ⓢ Ⓣ • ◆◆◆◆ • www.s-h-systems.co.uk/hotels/lyncott.html

☆ The Ilfracombe Carlton Hotel, Runnacleave Road, EX34 8AR. ☎ (01271) 862446 • Map 180/515477 • BB **D** • EM £13.50, 7-8.30pm • S8 D20 T12 F8 • 3-12 • Ⓥ Ⓑ Ⓓ Ⓢ Ⓟ Ⓣ • ★★

Warren & Kirsten Millington, Sherborne Lodge Hotel, Torrs Park, EX34 8AY. ☎ (01271) 862297 • Map 180/514476 • BB **C** • EM book first £10, 6.30pm • S1 D8 T2 F2 • 1-12 • Ⓥ Ⓑ Ⓓ Ⓢ Ⓟ Ⓣ ⏱ • ◆◆◆ • www.smoothhound.co.uk/hotels/sherborne.html

Mr & Mrs P Wileman, Combe Lodge Hotel, Chambercombe Park Road, EX34 9QW. ☎ (01271) 864518 • Map 180/530473 • BB **B/C** • EM £9.50, 6.30pm • S2 D3 T1 F2 • 1-12 • Ⓥ Ⓑ Ⓓ Ⓢ Ⓟ Ⓣ ⏱

■ **IPPLEPEN (Newton Abbot)**
Colin & Joanne Bell, June Cottage, Dornafield Road, TQ12 5SH. ☎ (01803) 813081 • Map 202/839670 • BB **B/C** • EM book first £12.50, 6.30pm • D2 T1 • 1-12 • Ⓥ Ⓑ Ⓓ Ⓢ Ⓟ Ⓣ • ◆◆◆

■ **IVYBRIDGE**
TWO MOORS WAY

Mr and Mrs Hancox, The Toll House, Exeter Road, PL21 0DE. ☎ (01752) 893522 • Map 202/643563 • BB **B** • D1 T2 • 1-12 • Ⓑ Ⓓ Ⓢ Ⓡ Ⓟ Ⓣ ⏱ • info@thetollhouse.co.uk

■ **KING'S NYMPTON (Umberleigh)**
Edward & Suzanne Hazelden, Sampson Barton, EX37 9TG. ☎ 01769 572466 • Map 180/689219 • BB **C** • EM £12.00, 7-8pm • S1 T1 F1 • 1-12 • Ⓥ Ⓑ Ⓓ Ⓢ Ⓡ Ⓟ Ⓣ ⏱ • sb@jambo2u.freeserve.co.uk

■ **KINGSBRIDGE**
SOUTH WEST COAST PATH

Mrs S Nunnington, 3 Manor Gardens, TQ7 1BJ. ☎ (01548) 853859 • Map 202/735448 • BB **B/C** • S1 D1 • 1-12 NX • Ⓑ Ⓓ Ⓢ Ⓟ Ⓣ ⏱ Ⓜ • mike@kingsbridgesouthdevon.co.uk

Don & Paula Wolstenholme, 'Widget', TQ7 2EX. ☎ (01548) 511110 • Map 202/818385 • BB **C** • D2 T1 • 1-12 NX • Ⓑ Ⓓ Ⓢ Ⓟ Ⓣ • Food nearby. SW path 50yds.

Sally & Lynton Witts, Dair House, 9 Linhey Close, Waterside Park, TQ7 1LL. ☎ (01548) 853376 • Map 202/735445 • BB **B** • D1 T1 • 1-12 NX • Ⓑ Ⓓ Ⓢ Ⓟ

■ **KINGSWEAR (Dartmouth)**
SOUTH WEST COAST PATH

L Congdon, Carlton House, Higher Street, TQ6 0AG. ☎ (01803) 752244 • Map 202/880510 • BB **B** • EM book first £7.50, 6-7pm • S2 D2 T1 F1 • 1-12 • Ⓓ Ⓡ Ⓟ Ⓣ ⏱

■ **KNOWSTONE (South Molton)**
TWO MOORS WAY

Mrs J Bray, West Bowden Farm, EX36 4RP. ☎ (01398) 341224 • Map 181/833224 • BB **B/C** • EM £7.50, 6.30pm • S1 D3 T2 F2 • 1-12 • Ⓥ Ⓑ Ⓓ Ⓟ Ⓣ ⏱ • ◆◆◆

■ **LANGTREE (Great Torrington)**
Mrs Shelia Mears, Tor View, 28 Fore Street, EX38 8NG. ☎ (01805) 601140 • Map 190,180/451156 • BB **B** • EM book first £7.50, 7.30pm • S1 D1 T1 • 1-12 NX • Ⓥ Ⓑ Ⓓ Ⓢ Ⓟ Ⓣ ⏱ Ⓜ • bandbdevon@talk21.com

■ **LUSTLEIGH (Bovey Tracey, Newton Abbot)**
Judy & John Halsey, Brookside, TQ13 9TJ. ☎ (01647) 277310 • Map 191/785813 • BB **C** • D2 T1 • 1-12 NX • Ⓓ Ⓢ Ⓟ Ⓣ ⏱

■ **LYNMOUTH**
SOUTH WEST COAST PATH & TWO MOORS WAY

☆ Mrs J Pile, Oakleigh, 4 Tors Road, EX35 6ET.
☎ (01598) 752220 • Map 180/727494 • BB **C** • EM
book first £10.50, 6.45pm • S2 D3 T2 F2 • 2-11 • Ⓓ
Ⓟ Ⓣ 🛁

OAKLEIGH

Lynmouth, North Devon

Small comfortable guesthouse. Central, sunny
position at entrance to famous Watersmeet
Valley. Close to coastal footpath and Two
Moors Way, sea and cliff railway. All rooms
with tea/coffee-making facilities. Own car park
adjoining. B&B with dinner optional.

Tel. (01598) 752220

☆ Mr & Mrs C & J Parker, Tregonwell Riverside
Guesthouse, 1 Tors Road, EX35 6ET. ☎ (01598)
753369 • Map 180/727494 • BB **B/C/D** • S1 D3 T1 F2
• 2-12 NX • Ⓑ Ⓓ Ⓢ Ⓟ Ⓣ 🛁 • ◆◆◆ •
www.smoothhound.co.uk/hotels/tregonwl.html

Tregonwell Riverside Guest House
1 Tors Road, Lynmouth
Exmoor National Park

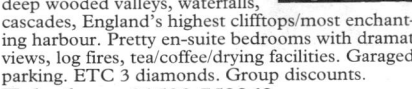

Warm welcomes guaranteed at
the best place to be for you
Exmoor ramblers. Our elegant
award-winning Victorian riverside
guesthouse is snuggled alongside
deep wooded valleys, waterfalls,
cascades, England's highest clifftops/most enchanting harbour. Pretty en-suite bedrooms with dramatic
views, log fires, tea/coffee/drying facilities. Garaged
parking. ETC 3 diamonds. Group discounts.
Telephone 01598 753369

☆ Tricia & Alan Francis, Glenville House, 2 Tors
Road, EX35 6ET. ☎ (01598) 752202 • Map
180/727494 • BB **C** • S1 D4 T1 • 2-11 NX • Ⓥ Ⓑ Ⓓ
Ⓢ Ⓟ Ⓣ Ⓜ • ◆◆◆◆ •
www.northdevon.co.uk/glenvillehouse

GLENVILLE
HOUSE

Lynmouth, Devon
☎ 01598 752202

Delightful licensed Victorian house in idyllic riverside setting. Tastefully decorated bedrooms and
pretty en-suites. Picturesque harbour and village.
Dramatic Exmoor scenery and
spectacular valley/coastal walks. Peaceful,
tranquil, romantic – a very special place. **AA** ◆◆◆◆

☆ Mrs S L Hobbs, The Bath Hotel, EX35 6EL.
☎ (01598) 752238 • Map 180/723496 • BB **E** • EM
£16, 7-8.30pm • S1 D8 T12 F3 • 2-11 • Ⓥ Ⓑ Ⓓ
Ⓢ Ⓟ Ⓣ 🛁 • ★★ • www.torslynmouth.co.uk

The Bath Hotel

Lynmouth, North Devon EX35 6EL
Friendly family run 2 star establishment with
good facilities and excellent food. 24
bedrooms all ensuite with TV, tea and coffee.
Situated on the edge of Exmoor an ideal
location for a walking holiday.
SPECIAL GROUP RATES AVAILABLE –
Please ring for details
Tel 01598 752238

■ **LYNTON**
SOUTH WEST COAST PATH & TWO MOORS WAY & TARKA TRAIL

☆ Sandrock Hotel, Longmead, EX35 6DH. ☎ (01598)
753307 • Map 180/715495 • BB **C** • EM £15, 7pm •
S1 D4 T3 • 2-11 NX • Ⓥ Ⓑ Ⓓ Ⓟ Ⓣ 🛁 • 3Cr/C

AA ★★ **SANDROCK HOTEL** RAC ★★

LONGMEAD, LYNTON
DEVON EX35 6DH
You will be made very welcome at Sandrock—a
family run hotel with 8 comfortable bedrooms with
colour TV, radio, tea/coffee-making facilities,
telephone. 7 private bathrooms. Fully licensed. CH.
Car park. B&B from £22, weekly BBE from £250.
Off season breaks. Colour brochure.
Mrs R Harrison ☎ **(01598) 753307**

Mrs V A Ashby, Rodwell, 21 Lee Road, EX35 6BP.
☎ (01598) 753324 • Map 180/717495 • BB **C** • EM
book first £10, 6.30pm • D4 T1 • 3-10 • Ⓑ Ⓓ Ⓢ
Ⓟ Ⓣ 🛁 • ◆◆◆

Marion Kirk, Meadhaven, 12 Crossmead, EX35 6DG.
☎ (01598) 753288 • Map 180/716493 • BB **B** • EM
book first £8.50, from 6.30pm • S2 D1 T1 • 1-12 • Ⓥ
Ⓓ Ⓢ Ⓟ Ⓣ 🛁

☆ Mr & Mrs D Hillier, Brendon House, Brendon,
EX35 6PS. ☎ (01598) 741206 • Map 180/770482 •
BB **C** • EM book first £15, 7.30pm • S1 D2 T1 F1 • 1-
12 NX • Ⓥ Ⓑ Ⓢ Ⓟ Ⓣ 🛁 • 3Cr/C •
brendonvalley.co.uk/Brendon_House.htm

EXMOOR
BRENDON
HOUSE
BRENDON
Nr Lynton

Enjoy Exmoor from an 18thC former farmhouse set
in the beautiful Lyn Valley. En-suite rooms with
tea/coffee, TV and enjoy superb Exmoor views.
Delicious home cooking – Licensed – Packed lunches.
David & Laura Hillier   Tel. 01598 741206
👑👑👑 Commended

☆ See Display Advertisement

☆ John McGowan, The Denes, 15 Longmead, EX35 6DQ. ☎ (01598) 753573 • Map 180/715495 • BB **B/C** • EM y, 6.30-8pm • D2 F3 • 1-12 • Ⓥ Ⓑ Ⓓ Ⓢ Ⓟ Ⓣ • ◆◆◆ • www.thedenes.com

☆ J & T Woolnough, Croft House Hotel, Lydiate Lane, EX35 6HE. ☎ (01598) 752391 • Map 180/717492 • BB **B/D** • EM book first £12, 7-8pm • D5 T2 • 2-11 • Ⓥ Ⓑ Ⓓ Ⓢ Ⓟ Ⓣ • ◆◆◆◆ • www.smoothhound.co.uk/hotels/crofthou.html

☆ John & Pauline Bathgate, Ingleside Hotel, Lee Road, EX35 6HW. ☎ (01598) 752223 • Map 180/720495 • BB **C** • EM £12, 7pm • D5 F2 • 1-12 NX • Ⓥ Ⓑ Ⓓ Ⓢ Ⓟ Ⓣ 🐾 • ◆◆◆◆ • johnpauldevon@aol.com

Longread, EX35 6DQ. ☎ (01598) 752361 • Map 180/715495 • BB **B/C** • EM book first £12, 7pm • S2 D3 T1 • 1-12 • Ⓥ Ⓑ Ⓓ Ⓢ Ⓟ Ⓣ 🐾 • ◆◆◆◆ • kingfordhousehotel@compuserve.co.uk

■ **MARTINHOE (Parracombe)**
SOUTH WEST COAST PATH

Mrs M Dallyn, Mannacott Farm, EX31 4QS. ☎ (01598) 763227 • Map 180/662481 • BB **B** • D1 T1 • 5-10 • Ⓑ Ⓓ Ⓢ Ⓟ

■ **MESHAW (South Molton)**

Fern Tor Vegetarian & Vegan Guest House, EX36 4NA. ☎ (01769) 550339 • Map 180/741207 • BB **B** • EM book first £11, 7pm • D2 T1 • 1-12 NX • Ⓥ Ⓑ Ⓓ Ⓢ Ⓟ Ⓣ 🐾 • www.ferntor.co.uk

■ **MORETONHAMPSTEAD (Newton Abbot)**

Mrs Trudie Merchant, Great Slon Combe Farm, TQ13 8QF. ☎ (01647) 440595 • Map 191/736862 • BB **C** • EM book first £12-£13, 6.30-7pm • D2 T1 • 1-12 • Ⓥ Ⓑ Ⓓ Ⓢ Ⓟ Ⓣ 🐾 • ◆◆◆◆Ⓢ • hmerchant@sloncombe.freeserve.co.uk

☆ Ken & Sue Harrison, The Old Post House, 18 Court Street, TQ13 8LG. ☎ (01647) 440900 • Map 191/753860 • BB **B/C** • S1 D4 T2 • 1-12 • Ⓑ Ⓓ Ⓢ Ⓟ Ⓣ • walking@theoldposthouse.com

■ **MORTEHOE (Woolacombe)**
SOUTH WEST COAST PATH & TARKA TRAIL

☆ The Lundy House Hotel, Chapel Hill, EX34 7DZ. ☎ (01271) 870372 • Map 180/455448 • BB **C/D/E** • EM £9.95, 7.30pm • D4 T1 F3 • 2-12 • Ⓥ Ⓑ Ⓓ Ⓢ Ⓟ Ⓣ 🐾 • ★★★ • www.lundyhousehotel.co.uk • See display box advert opposite.

■ **NORTH TAWTON**
TARKA TRAIL

Nicholas & Amanda Waldron, Kayden House Hotel, High Street, EX20 2HF. ☎ (01837) 82242 • Map 191/664016 • BB **C** • EM £10 • S2 D2 T2 F1 • 1-12 • Ⓥ Ⓑ Ⓓ Ⓟ Ⓣ 🐾 • ◆◆◆

■ **NORTHAM (Bideford)**
SOUTH WEST COAST PATH & TARKA TRAIL

Jill Drury, Tadworthy House, Tadworthy Road, EX39 1JN. ☎ (01237) 477501 • Map 180/445293 • BB **B** • S1 T1 F1 • 1-12 • Ⓑ Ⓓ Ⓢ Ⓟ Ⓣ 🐾 •

■ OKEHAMPTON
TARKA TRAIL

Mrs I Courtney, Ifold House, 27 New Road, EX20 1JE. ☎ (01837) 52712 • Map 191/586950 • BB **A/B** • D2 T1 • 1-12 NX • Ⓥ Ⓓ 🐾

Audrey & Tim Gibbons, Heathfield House, EX20 1EW. ☎ (01837) 54211 • Map 191/589946 • BB **B/C/D/E** • EM book first £20, 7.30-8pm • S1 D3 T1 F1 • 2-1 • Ⓥ Ⓑ Ⓓ Ⓢ Ⓟ Ⓣ 🐾 • ◆◆◆◆ • www.tgibbins.freeserve.co.uk

Mrs Susan Doubtfire, Meadowlea Guest House, 65 Station Road, EX20 1EA. ☎ (01837) 53200 • Map 191/588948 • BB **B** • EM book first £7.50, 6pm • S2 D1 T3 F1 • 1-12 • Ⓥ Ⓑ Ⓓ Ⓟ Ⓣ • ◆◆◆

Viv Kirkland, Penare, 2 Church Path, EX20 1LW. ☎ (01837) 55842 • Map 191/584954 • BB **C** • S1 T2 • 4-9 • Ⓑ Ⓓ Ⓢ Ⓡ Ⓟ Ⓣ 🐾 • penare.bb@virgin.net

☆ Lizzie St. George, Kerslake Farm, Meldon, EX20 4LU. ☎ (01837) 54892 • Map 191/558918 • BB **B/C** • EM book first £8, Any • D2 T2 F1 • 1-12 • Ⓥ Ⓑ Ⓓ Ⓢ Ⓡ Ⓟ Ⓣ 🐾 Ⓜ • Lizzie@cantabds.demon.co.uk

---

Kerslake Farm
Meldon, Okehampton, Devon EX20 4LU
Beautifully renovated farmhouse near high moorland tors and West Devon Way. Ideal centre for walking, cycling and touring. EM option; packed lunches; drying facilities; gardens; ample parking; some enauite rooms. Groups welcome. Also self-catering cottage.
Lizzie St George 01837 54892
lizzie@cantabds.demon.co.uk

The Lundy House Hotel
Friendly and comfortable licensed hotel. Vegetarian specialities. Magnificent sea-views across to Lundy Island. Hotel gardens lead directly onto the South West Coast Path. The National Trust Land surrounding the hotel makes an excellent base for walking and rambling. Pets welcome, free of charge.
Tel: 01271 870372 Fax 01271 871001
www.lundyhousehotel.co.uk

■ OTTERY ST MARY

Mrs E A Forth, Fluxton Farm, EX11 1RJ. ☎ (01404) 812818 • Map 192/086934 • BB **C** • EM book first £10, 6.45pm • S3 D3 T4 F2 • 1-12 • Ⓥ Ⓑ Ⓓ Ⓢ Ⓣ 🐾 • ◆◆ • Must be cat lovers!

■ PAIGNTON
SOUTH WEST COAST PATH

☆ Mr Booth, Torbay Holiday Motel, Totnes Road,

TQ4 7PP. ☎ (01803) 558226 • Map 202/854598 • BB **D** • EM £7, 6.30-9.00pm • D11 T5 • 1-12 NX • Ⓥ Ⓑ Ⓟ Ⓣ 🐾 • ★★ • enquiries@thm.co.uk

■ PLYMOUTH
SOUTH WEST COAST PATH

Mrs L Hallam, The Staymor, 66 North Road East, PL4 6AL. ☎ (01752) 660801 • Map 201/480553 • BB **B** • S2 D2 T2 F1 • 1-12 NX • Ⓑ Ⓓ Ⓡ Ⓟ Ⓣ • All rooms have private showers.

Jackie Moulds, Berkeley's of St James, 4 St James Place East, The Hoe, PL1 3AS. ☎ (01752) 221654 • Map 201/474541 • BB **C/D** • S1 D2 T1 F1 • 1-12 NX • Ⓑ Ⓓ Ⓢ Ⓡ Ⓟ Ⓣ • ◆◆◆◆ • www.smooth-hound.co.uk.hotels/berkely2.html

■ PONSWORTHY (Newton Abbot)
TWO MOORS WAY

Mrs E Fursdon, Old Walls Farm, TQ13 7PN. ☎ (01364) 631222 • Map 191/701747 • BB **C** • EM book first £8, 7pm • S1 D1 T1 • 1-12 NX • Ⓥ Ⓑ Ⓓ Ⓢ Ⓟ Ⓣ 🐾

■ POSTBRIDGE (High Dartmoor)
TWO MOORS WAY

Mr & Mrs J L Bishop, Hartyland, PL20 6SZ. ☎ (01822) 880210 • Map 191/644795 • BB **C** • EM book first £9.50, 6.00-9.00pm • S2 T2 F1 • 1-12 NX • Ⓥ Ⓓ Ⓟ Ⓣ 🐾 • andybishop@compuserve.com

TORBAY Holiday Motel
Totnes Road, Paignton TG4 7PP
Tel: 01803 558226   Fax 01803 663375
www.thm.co.uk   enquiries@thm.co.uk

Ideal for holidays, mini-breaks or overnight accommodation. Set in peaceful rural surroundings yet very close to all of Torbay's attractions – an ideal centre for touring South Devon.

Studio apartments, family suites or motel rooms available. Discounts for OAPs and children. Indoor and outdoor pool, sauna, solarium, bar, restaurant and shop. 35-acre picnic are with beautiful views over Torbay. Arrive and depart any day. Open all year.

Phone or write for brochure or enquiries.

VEGETARIANS
Many establishments do a veggie breakfast even if they don't do an evening meal

■ **POUNDSGATE (Ashburton, Newton Abbot)**
TWO MOORS WAY

Mrs Margaret Phipps, New Cott Farm, Poundsgate, TQ13 7PD. ☎ (01364) 631421 • Map 202/703727 • BB **C** • EM book first £12, 6pm • D2 T1 F1 • 1-12 NX • Ⓥ Ⓑ Ⓓ Ⓢ Ⓟ Ⓣ • ◆◆◆◆ • newcott@ruralink.co.uk

■ **RACKENFORD (Tiverton)**
TWO MOORS WAY

Mrs C Poole, Creacombe Parsonage Farm, Creacombe, EX16 8EL. ☎ (01884) 881441 • Map 181/820185 • BB **B** • EM book first £7.50, 6-9pm • T2 F1 • 1-12 • Ⓥ Ⓑ Ⓓ Ⓢ Ⓟ Ⓣ ⅋ • transport avail. Campsite & SC. creaky.parson@dialpipex.com

■ **SALCOMBE**
SOUTH WEST COAST PATH

Julie & Arthur Bouttle, Torre View Hotel, Devon Road, TQ8 8HJ. ☎ (01548) 842633 • Map 202/735385 • BB **D** • EM book first £14, 7pm • S1 D4 T2 F1 • 3-10 • Ⓥ Ⓑ Ⓓ Ⓢ Ⓟ Ⓣ • ◆◆◆◆ • bouttle@torreview.eurobell.co.uk

Janice Collins, Limericks B&B, Raleigh Road, TQ8 8AY. ☎ (01548) 842350 • Map 202/735389 • BB **B/C** • D2 T1 • 1-12 NX • Ⓑ Ⓓ Ⓢ Ⓣ

■ **SAMPFORD COURTENAY (Okehampton)**
TARKA TRAIL

Mrs R G Townsend Green, Southey Farm, Sampford Courtenay, EX20 2TE. ☎ (01837) 82446 • Map 191/633003 • BB **B** • S1 T1 • 1-12 • Ⓓ Ⓟ Ⓣ ⅋ • tg@southeyfarm.freeserve.co.uk

■ **SAMPFORD SPINEY (Yelverton)**

Linda Landick, Eggworthy Farm, PL20 6LJ. ☎ (01822) 852142 • Map 201/544719 • BB **C** • S1 D2 • 1-12 NX • Ⓑ Ⓓ Ⓢ ⅋ • ◆◆◆

■ **SCORRITON (Buckfastleigh)**
TWO MOORS WAY

John & Val Lunday, The Tradesman's Arms, TQ11 0JB. ☎ (01364) 631026 • Map 202/704685 • BB **C** • EM £6.50, up to 9.30pm • D2 • 1-12 NX • Ⓥ Ⓓ Ⓢ Ⓟ Ⓣ ⅋ • www.thetradesmansarms.com

■ **SEATON (Torpoint)**
SOUTH WEST COAST PATH

Mr & Mrs Webber, Tor's Guest House, 55 Harbour Rd, EX12 2LX. ☎ (01297) 20531 • Map 192/249899 • BB **B** • S1 D2 T1 F1 • 1-12 • Ⓑ Ⓟ Ⓣ

■ **SHALDON (Teignmouth)**
SOUTH WEST COAST PATH

K & P Underwood, Glenside Hotel, Ringmore Road, TQ14 0EP. ☎ (01626) 872448 • Map 192/926723 • BB **C** • EM book first £15, 7pm • S1 D3 T4 F2 • 3-10 • Ⓑ Ⓓ Ⓢ Ⓡ Ⓟ ⅋ • 3Cr/C • www.smoothhound.co.uk/hotels/glensideho.html

M & J Britton, Virginia Cottage, Brook Lane, TQ14 0HL. ☎ (01626) 872634 • Map 192, 202/926722 • BB **C** • D2 T1 • 4-11 • Ⓑ Ⓓ Ⓢ Ⓡ

■ **SHIRWELL (Barnstaple)**

Mrs Janet Pelling, The Spinney Guest House, EX31 4JR. ☎ (01271) 850282 • Map 180/590370 • BB **B/C** • EM book first £10, 7pm • S1 D2 T1 • 1-12 • Ⓥ Ⓑ Ⓓ Ⓢ Ⓣ ⅋ • ◆◆◆◆ • B&B only at Xmas

■ **SIDMOUTH**
SOUTH WEST COAST PATH

Mrs & Mrs M C Penaluna, Canterbury House, Salcombe Road, EX10 8PR. ☎ (01395) 513373/Freephone (0800) 328 1775 • Map 192/127878 • BB **B/C** • EM book first £8.50, 6pm • D3 T2 F3 • 1-12 • Ⓥ Ⓑ Ⓓ Ⓢ Ⓟ Ⓣ ⅋ • ◆◆◆ • cgh@eclipse.co.uk

Mrs E Tancock, Lower Pinn Farm, Peak Hill, EX10 0NN. ☎ (01395) 513733 • Map 192/102868 • BB **C/D** • D1 T1 F1 • 1-12 • Ⓑ Ⓓ Ⓣ ⅋ • ◆◆◆◆ • www.lowerpinnfarm.co.uk

P J Scorey, Cranmere House, 2 Fortfield Place, Station Road, EX10 8NX. ☎ (01395) 513933 • Map 192/123874 • BB **B** • S2 D2 T1 F1 • 1-12 • Ⓑ Ⓓ Ⓢ Ⓟ Ⓣ • ◆◆◆

■ **SLAPTON (Kingsbridge)**
SOUTH WEST COAST PATH

V J Mercer, Old Walls, TQ7 2QN. ☎ (01548) 580516 • Map 202/823449 • BB **B/C** • D2/F2 T1 • 1-12 • Ⓥ Ⓑ Ⓓ Ⓢ Ⓟ Ⓣ ⅋ Ⓜ • No disabled access (steps)

■ **STOKENHAM (Kingsbridge)**
SOUTH WEST COAST PATH

Mrs Esme Heath, Brookfield, TQ7 2SL. ☎ (01548) 580615 • Map 202/802428 • BB **B/C/D** • D1 T1 • 1-12 NX • Ⓑ Ⓓ Ⓢ Ⓟ Ⓣ Ⓜ • ◆◆◆◆ • heath@brookfield37.freeserve.co.uk

■ **TIVERTON**

Bridge Guest House, 23 Angel Hill, EX16 6PE. ☎ (01884) 252804 • Map 181/953125 • BB **C** • EM book first £14.00, 6.30-7pm • S5 D2 T1 F2 • 1-12 • Ⓥ Ⓑ Ⓓ Ⓣ • ◆◆◆

Angel Guest House, 13 St Peter Street, EX16 6NU. ☎ (01884) 253392 • Map 181/954126 • BB **B** • S1 D3 T1 F2 • 1-12 • Ⓑ Ⓓ Ⓢ Ⓟ Ⓣ • s cerimar@globalnet.co.uk

■ **TORQUAY**
SOUTH WEST COAST PATH

Swiss Court, 68 Vane Hill Road, TQ1 2BZ. ☎ (01803) 215564 • Map 202/920632 • BB **B/C** • S5 D3 • 1-12 NX • Ⓑ Ⓓ Ⓡ Ⓟ Ⓣ ⅋ Ⓜ • SC also

■ **UGBOROUGH (Ivybridge)**

Mrs Jane Johns, Hillhead Farm, PL21 0HQ. ☎ (01752) 892674 • Map 202/674564 • BB **C** • EM book first £12.50, 7ish • D2 T1 • 1-12 NX • Ⓑ Ⓓ Ⓢ Ⓟ Ⓣ ⅋ • ◆◆◆◆ • Transport av. from rail.

WEMBURY (Plymouth)
SOUTH WEST COAST PATH

Bay Cottage, 150 Church Road, PL9 0HR. ☎ 01752 862559 • Map 201/519487 • BB **D** • S1 D2 T2 • 1-12 NX • V B D S P T 🐾 • ◆◆◆ • TheFairies@aol.com

WEST ANSTEY (South Molton)
TWO MOORS WAY

☆ Mrs H Milton, Partridge Arms Farm, Yeo Mill, EX36 3NU. ☎ (01398) 341217 • Map 181/842263 • BB **C** • EM book first £10, 7pm • S1 D3 T1 F2 • 1-12 NX • V B D P T 🐾 • ◆◆◆

Exmoor
Partridge Arms Farm
Yeo Mill, West Anstey, S Molton
Olde Worlde farmhouse set within established family farm off A361, four miles west of Dulverton. We offer genuine hospitality and traditional farmhouse fare. Many of the bedrooms have en suite facilities. Licensed. Pets and children welcome.
Mrs H J Milton Tel. Anstey Mills (01398) 341217

WEST BUCKLAND (Barnstaple)
TARKA TRAIL

Jackie & Antony Payne, Huxtable Farm, EX32 0SR. ☎ (01598) 760254 • Map 180/665308 • BB **D** • EM £15, 7.30pm • D3 T1 F2 • 2-11 • V B D S P T • ◆◆◆◆ • Camping also. www.huxtablefarm.co.uk

WESTWARD HO! (Bideford)
SOUTH WEST COAST PATH & TARKA TRAIL

Mrs Catherine Pile, Culloden House Guest House, Fosketh Hill, EX39 1JA. ☎ 01237 479421 • Map 180/433290 • BB **D** • EM book first £14.00 (Apr-Sept only), 7-8pm • D5 T9 F2 • 1-12 • V B D S P T 🐾 • ◆◆◆◆ • culloden.house@ukgateway.net

WIDECOMBE-IN-THE-MOOR (Newton Abbot)
TWO MOORS WAY

The Old Rectory, TQ13 7TB. ☎ (01364) 621231 • Map 191/717767 • BB **C** • D2 T/F1 • 3-10 • B D S P T 🐾 • Food nearby • singles av. rachel.belgrave@care4free.net

Debbie Parkin, Littlecott Farm, TQ13 7UB. ☎ (01364) 621245 • Map 191/694779 • BB **C** • EM book first £8.50, 8-8.30pm • D2 • 4-10 NX • V B D S P T 🐾 • Debbie.Parkin@care4free.net

WINKLEIGH (Torrington)
TARKA TRAIL

Mrs Angela Lovell, Sunset View, 5 Ashplants Close, EX19 8HE. ☎ (01837) 83005 • Map 191/612081 • BB **B** • EM book first £6, 6-7pm • T1 • 3-10 • V S P T

YARCOMBE (Honiton)

Ann Stockwell, The Old Vicarage, EX14 9BD. ☎ 01404 861594 • Map 192,193/246082 • BB **C** • EM book first £12, 7.30pm • S1 D2 T1 • 2-11 • V D S P T • ◆◆◆◆ • jonannstockwell@aol.com

YELVERTON

Waverley Guest House, 5 Greenbank Terrace, PL20 6DR. ☎ (01822) 854617 • Map 201/521679 • BB **C** • S1 D2 T1 F1 • 1-12NX • B D S T 🐾 • 2Cr/C

Tricia Leavey, Rattery Bank, Harrowbeer Lane, PL20 6EA. ☎ (01822) 855088 • Map 201/519683 • BB **B** • EM book first £10, 7-10pm • D1 T1 • 1-12 NX • V B D P T • bandt@leavey.fsbusiness.co.uk

---

DORSET

ABBOTSBURY (Weymouth)
SOUTH WEST COAST PATH

Swan Lodge, DT3 4JL. ☎ (01305) 871249 • Map 194/578852 • BB **C** • EM £6, 6-10pm • D3 T2 F1 • 1-12 • V B D S T 🐾 • ◆◆◆

Mrs Pat Arnold, Chesil House, DT3 4JT. ☎ (01305) 871324 • Map 194/570853 • BB **C** • D1 T2 • 1-12 NX • B D S T

BLANDFORD FORUM

Mr & Mrs J Atkins, Park Lodge Bungalow, White Cliff Mill Street, DT11 7BN. ☎ (01258) 452834 • Map 194/884067 • BB **B** • D/S1 T/S1 • 1-12 NX • B D S P T 🐾 • gamesatkins@ukonline.co.uk

Sue Busst, South Pasture, St Leonard Avenue, DT11 7PD. ☎ (01258) 452804 • Map 195/890065 • BB **C** • EM book first £6.30 • T1 • 1-12 NX • V B D S P T • southpasture@aol.com

BOURNEMOUTH

Mrs E Davies, St Michaels Guest House, 42 St Michaels Road, Westcliff, BH2 5DY. ☎ (01202) 557386 • Map 195/082910 • BB **B** • EM £6, 6pm • S1 D2 T2 F1 • 1-12 • V D R T 🐾

Mrs E Rising, "Victoria", 120 Parkwood Road, Southbourne, BH5 2BN. ☎ (01202) 423179 • Map 195/127919 • BB **A** • D1 T1 • 5-10 • D R T 🐾 • Vegetarian breakfast if reqd.

Mr & Mrs Burrell, Westcotes House Hotel, 9 Southbourne Overcliff Drive, BH6 3TE. ☎ (01202) 428512 • Map 195/131914 • BB **C/D** • EM book first £11, 6.30pm • D3 T3 • 1-12 • V B S R T 🐾

BRIANTSPUDDLE (Dorchester)

☆ Longacre Barn, The Old Dairy, DT2 7HT. ☎ 01929 472531 • Map 194/818932 • BB **D** • EM book first £15, 7pm • D2 T1 F1 • 1-12 NX • V B D S P T • Groups also • derek@longacre-barn.freeserve.co.uk • See start of next page for display box advert.

■ BRIDPORT
SOUTH WEST COAST PATH

☆ Britmead House, West Bay Road, DT6 4EG. ☎ (01308) 422941 • Map 193/465912 • BB **C/D** • EM book first £16, 7pm • D3 T2 F2 • 1-12 NX • Ⓥ Ⓑ Ⓓ Ⓢ Ⓟ Ⓣ 🛁 • ◆◆◆◆ • SC also britmead@talk21.com

Mikki & Robert Hansowitz, Cranston, 27 Church Street, DT6 3PS. ☎ (01308) 456240 • Map 193/467927 • BB **B** • S3 D3 T3 F1 • 1-12 • Ⓑ Ⓓ Ⓢ Ⓟ Ⓣ 🛁 • ◆◆◆◆ • SC also

☆ Eypes Mouth Country Hotel, Eype, DT6 6AL. ☎ (01308) 423300 • Map 193/448914 • BB **D/E** • EM £16.00, 7-9pm • S2 D12 T3 F1 • 1-12 • Ⓥ Ⓑ Ⓓ Ⓢ Ⓟ Ⓣ 🛁 • ★★ • eypehotel@aol.com

Janice Warburton, Fleet Cottage, 152 West Bay Road, DT6 4AZ. ☎ (01308) 458698 • Map 193/465915 • BB **C** • EM book first £7, 6.30pm • S1 D2 T1 F1 • 1-12 • Ⓥ Ⓑ Ⓓ Ⓣ 🛁

Sue Boize, Fourfoot House, Eype, DT6 6AL. ☎ (01308) 425600 • Map 193/448914 • BB **C** • EM book first £ • D1 • 1-12 • Ⓑ Ⓓ Ⓢ Ⓟ Ⓣ 🛁

■ BURTON BRADSTOCK (Bridport)
SOUTH WEST COAST PATH

Mrs Andrea Gisborne, Burton Lodge, DT6 4PU. ☎ (01308) 897378 • Map 193/483901 • BB **C** • D1 T1 F1 • 3-12NX • Ⓑ Ⓓ Ⓢ Ⓣ 🛁 • Food nearby

■ CERNE ABBAS (Dorchester)
WESSEX RIDGEWAY

Terry and Pat Dean, The Singing Kettle, 7 Long Street, DT2 7JF. ☎ (01300) 341349 • Map 194/664011 • BB **C** • T2 F0 • 1-12 NX • Ⓑ Ⓓ Ⓢ Ⓟ Ⓣ 🛁 • Food nearby
www.users.globalnet.co.uk/~singingk

■ CHIDEOCK (Bridport)
SOUTH WEST COAST PATH

Mrs S Norman, Frogmore Farm, DT6 6HT. ☎ (01308) 456159 • Map 193/434925 • BB **B** • EM book first £10, 7pm • D1 T1 F1 • 1-12 • Ⓥ Ⓑ Ⓓ Ⓢ Ⓟ Ⓣ 🛁

☆ Eric & Denise Tweddle, Warren House, DT6 6JW. ☎ 01297 489704 • Map 193/420929 • BB **C/D** • D1 T1 F2 • 1-12 NX • Ⓑ Ⓓ Ⓢ Ⓟ Ⓣ • ◆◆◆◆

■ DORCHESTER

☆ Churchview Guest House, Winterbourne Abbas, DT2 9LS. ☎ (01305) 889296 • Map 194/618905 • BB **C/D** • EM £14, 7pm • S1 D4 T3 F1 • 1-12 NX • Ⓥ Ⓑ Ⓓ Ⓢ Ⓟ Ⓣ 🛁 • ◆◆◆ • www.churchview.co.uk • Groups also • See display box advert on next page

B&B ACCOMMODATION ENGLAND DORSET

Marian Tomblin, Lower Lewell Farmhouse, West Stafford, DT2 8AP. ☎ (01305) 267169 • Map 194/743897 • BB **C** • D1 T1 F1 • 1-12 NX • Ⓓ Ⓡ Ⓣ 🍴

■ EAST STOKE (Wareham)

Sarah Lowman, Long Coppice, Bindon Lane, BH20 6AS. ☎ (01929) 463123 • Map 194/855865 • BB **C** • T1 F1 • 1-12 NX • Ⓑ Ⓓ Ⓢ Ⓡ Ⓟ Ⓣ 🍴 Ⓜ • sarah@long-coppice.freeserve.co.uk

■ IBBERTON (Blandford Forum)
WESSEX RIDGEWAY

Mrs C Old, Manor House Farm, DT11 0EN. ☎ (01258) 817349 • Map 194/788077 • BB **B** • D2 T1 • 1-12 • Ⓑ Ⓢ Ⓟ Ⓣ 🍴 • SC also. Food nearby.

■ IWERNE MINSTER (Blandford Forum)

Mark Richardson, The Talbot Hotel, DT11 8QN. ☎ (01747) 811269 • Map 194/859128 • BB **B** • EM £6, 7-9.30pm • S1 D2 T1 F2 • 1-12 • Ⓥ Ⓑ Ⓓ Ⓟ Ⓣ

■ LULWORTH COVE (Wareham)
SOUTH WEST COAST PATH

☆ Mrs Catriona Miller, Cromwell House Hotel, BH20 5RJ. ☎ (01929) 400253/400332 • Map 194/822802 • BB **E** • EM £14, 7-8.30pm • S2 D7 T5 F3 • 1-12 NX • Ⓥ Ⓑ Ⓓ 🍴 • ★★ • lulworthcove.co.uk

■ LYME REGIS
SOUTH WEST COAST PATH

Keith Owen Lovell, Lucerne, View Road, DT7 3AL. ☎ (01297) 443752 • Map 193/339925 • BB **B/C** • S1 D3 T1 • 1-12 NX • Ⓑ Ⓓ Ⓢ Ⓣ • ◆◆◆ • SC also • lucerne@lineone.net

Lydwell House, Lyme Road, Uplyme, DT7 3TJ. ☎ (01297) 443522 • Map 193/330930 • BB **C/D** • EM book first £15, 6-8pm • S1 D1 T1 F2 • 1-12 • Ⓥ Ⓑ Ⓓ Ⓢ Ⓟ Ⓣ • ◆◆◆ • lydwell@brittain16.fsbusiness.co.uk

David & Anita Endersby, Rotherfield Guest House, View Road, DT7 3AA. ☎ (01297) 445585 • Map 193/338924 • BB **C** • S1 D2 T3 • 1-12 NX • Ⓑ Ⓢ Ⓟ Ⓣ 🍴 • ◆◆◆ • rotherfield@lymeregis.com

☆ Rachel Pike, The Orchard Country Hotel, Rousdon, DT7 3XW. ☎ (01297) 442972 • Map 193/296916 • BB **E** • EM book first £16, 7.15-7.45pm • S2 D6 T4 • 3-11 • Ⓥ Ⓑ Ⓓ Ⓢ Ⓟ Ⓣ • ★★ • Groups also the.orchard@btinternet.com

Wayne & Ann Bradbury, Charnwood Guest House, 21 Woodmead Road, DT7 3AD. ☎ (01297) 445281 • Map 193/339924 • BB **B/C** • S1 D4 T2 F1 • 1-12 • Ⓑ Ⓓ Ⓢ Ⓟ Ⓣ Ⓜ • ◆◆◆ • Groups also www.lymeregis.co./charnwood

Old Monmouth Hotel, 12 Church Street, DT7 3BS. ☎ (01297) 442456 • Map 193/344922 • BB **B/C** • EM book first £, 7-9.30pm • D4 T1 F1 • 1-12 NX • Ⓥ Ⓑ Ⓓ Ⓢ Ⓟ Ⓣ • oldmonhotel@btinternet.com

■ MILTON ABBAS (Blandford Forum)

Mrs O Moore, Gorse Hill Bungalow, DT11 0LH. ☎ (01258) 880660 • Map 194/806002 • BB **B/C** • D1 F2 • 1-12 • Ⓑ Ⓓ Ⓢ Ⓟ Ⓣ 🍴

■ OSMINGTON (Weymouth)
SOUTH WEST COAST PATH

K Legg, Rosedale, Church Lane, DT3 6EW. ☎ (01305) 832056 • Map 194/725830 • BB **B** • D1 T1 F1 • EASTER-11 • Ⓑ Ⓓ Ⓢ Ⓣ • ◆◆ • SC and bunkhouse also

■ POOLE
SOUTH WEST COAST PATH

Mrs North, The Laurels, 60 Britannia Road, BH14 8BB. ☎ (01202) 265861 • Map 195/033913 • BB **B** • S1 D1 T1 F1 • 1-12 NX • Ⓑ Ⓓ Ⓢ Ⓡ Ⓣ • www.smoothhound.co.uk/hotels/laurels.html

DORSET ENGLAND

B&B ACCOMMODATION

☆ See Display Advertisement

■ **POWERSTOCK (Bridport)**

Elaine Marsh, Powerstock Mill Farm, DT6 3SL.
☎ (01308) 485213 • Map 194/501967 • BB **C** • EM
book first £12.50, 7-7.30pm • S2 T1 • 1-12 NX • Ⓓ
Ⓟ • 1Cr/C

■ **PUDDLETOWN (Dorchester)**

Mrs J Stephens, Zoar House, DT2 8SR. ☎ (01305)
848498 • Map 194/762942 • BB **B** • D† T1 F1 • 1-12 •
Ⓥ Ⓑ Ⓓ Ⓢ Ⓟ Ⓣ 🐾 • SC also

■ **SHERBORNE**
MACMILLAN WAY

Mrs D Bower, Honeycombe View, Lower Clatcombe,
DT9 4RH. ☎ (01935) 814644 • Map 183/637179 •
BB **B** • T1 • 1-11 • Ⓑ Ⓓ Ⓢ Ⓡ Ⓣ

■ **SHILLINGSTONE (Blandford Forum)**
WESSEX RIDGEWAY

Mrs Rosemary Watts, Pennhills Farm, Sandy Lane,
Off Lanchards Lane, DT11 0TF. ☎ (01258) 860491 •
Map 194/821104 • BB **B** • D/F1 T/S1 • 1-12 • Ⓑ Ⓓ
Ⓢ Ⓟ Ⓣ🐾

■ **STOBOROUGH (Wareham)**

D & J Bryer, Hyde Cottage, Furzebrooke Rd, BH20
5AX. ☎ 01929 553344 • Map 195/927853 • BB **B/C** •
EM book first £8, 6.30-7.30pm • S1 D1 T1 F2 • 1-12
NX • Ⓥ Ⓑ Ⓓ Ⓢ Ⓡ Ⓟ Ⓣ🐾 •
hydecottbb@yahoo.co.uk

■ **STURMINSTER NEWTON**

Margie Fraser, Newton House, DT10 2DQ. ☎ (01258)
472783 • Map 194/783135 • BB **C** • S2 D2 T1 • 1-12
NX • Ⓑ Ⓓ Ⓢ Ⓟ • C • Nr Blackmore Vale Ring.
Parking avail.

■ **SUTTON POYNTZ (Weymouth)**
SOUTH WEST COAST PATH

Chris & Christine Galpin, Brookfield, White Horse
Lane, DT3 6LU. ☎ (01305) 833674 • Map
194/707838 • BB **B** • S1 D1 T1 • 2-9 • Ⓓ Ⓢ Ⓡ Ⓣ
• ◆◆◆ • Food nearby

■ **SWANAGE**
SOUTH WEST COAST PATH

☆ White Lodge Hotel, Grosvenor Road, BH19 2DD.
☎ (01929) 422696 Fax 425510 • Map 195/032783 •
BB **D** • EM book first £14.50, 6.30-7pm • S1 D5 T4
F3 • 1-12 NX • Ⓥ Ⓑ Ⓓ Ⓢ Ⓟ Ⓣ • ◆◆◆◆ •
Groups also • whitelodgehotel.co.uk

Susan Pickering, Hermitage Guesthouse, 1 Manor
Road, BH19 2BH. ☎ (01929) 423014 • Map
195/031785 • BB **B** • D2 T1 F4 • 3-11 NX • Ⓓ Ⓢ Ⓣ
🐾 Ⓜ

☆ Sunny South Bed & Breakfast, 118 Kings Road
West, BH19 1HS. ☎ (01929) 422665 • Map
195/023790 • BB **A/B** • S1 D/T/S1 F/T/D1 • 1-12 NX •
Ⓑ Ⓓ Ⓢ Ⓡ Ⓟ Ⓣ Ⓜ •
www.sunnysouth.btinternet.co.uk

☆ The Limes Hotel, 48 Park Road, BH19 2AE.
☎ 01929 422664 • Map 195/033783 • BB **C** • S3 D2
T4 F3 • 1-12 NX • Ⓑ Ⓓ Ⓢ Ⓡ Ⓟ Ⓣ🐾 • ◆◆◆ •
www.limeshotel.demon.co.uk

Janet Foran, Sandhaven, 5 Ulwell Rd, BH19 1LE.
☎ (01929) 422322 • Map 195/030798 • BB **B/C** • S1
D4 T2 F2 • 1-12 NX • Ⓥ Ⓑ Ⓓ Ⓢ Ⓡ Ⓟ Ⓣ🐾

■ **SYDLING ST NICHOLAS (Dorchester)**
WESSEX RIDGEWAY

Mrs J Wareham, City Cottage, DT2 9NX. ☎ (01300)
341300 • Map 194/632994 • BB **B** • S1 D1 • 1-12 NX
• Ⓓ Ⓟ

Mrs Barraclough, Magiston Farm, DT2 9NR.
☎ (01300) 320295 • Map 194/637967 • BB **B** • EM
book first £12.00, 7pm • S1/2 D1 T3 • 1-12 NX • Ⓥ
Ⓑ Ⓓ Ⓢ Ⓟ Ⓣ🐾 • ◆◆◆

■ THORNCOMBE (Chard)
WESSEX RIDGEWAY

Mr & Mrs Fortescue-Thomas, Rose Cottage, Holway, TA20 4PZ. ☎ (01460) 30578 (& Fax) • Map 193/381034 • BB **C** • D1 T1 • 1-12 NX • ⓑ ⓓ ⓢ ⓟ ⓣ • Transport to pub • a.fortesue-t@amserve.net

■ TOLLER PORCORUM (Dorchester)
☆ Nigel Spring, The Kingcombe Centre, DT2 0EQ. ☎ (01300) 320684 • Map 194/554991 • BB **B** • EM book first £12, 7.30pm • S5 D2 T5 F4 • 1-12 • ⓥ ⓓ ⓢ ⓟ ⓖ • ◆◆ • SC also • nspring@kingcombe-centre.demon.co.uk

Mrs Rachael Geddes, Colesmoor Farm, DT2 0DU. ☎ (01300) 320812 • Map 194/556971 • BB **C** • EM book first £9.50, 8pm • D2 T1 • 1-2 & 5-11 • ⓥ ⓑ ⓓ ⓢ ⓡ ⓟ ⓣ • ◆◆◆◆ • geddes.colesmoor@eclipse.co.uk

■ WAREHAM
Mr & Mrs Cake, Ashcroft, 64 Furzebrook Road, Stoborough, BH20 5AX. ☎ (01929) 552392 • Map 195/929850 • BB **B/C** • EM book first £8.5, 6.30pm • S1 D1 T1 F1 • 1-12NX • ⓥ ⓑ ⓓ ⓢ ⓡ ⓟ ⓣ ⓖ • www.ashcroft-b-and-b.freeserve.co.uk

Mrs I K Gegg, Glen Ness, 1 The Merrows, Off St Helens Road, Sandford, BH20 7AX. ☎ (01929) 552313 • Map 195/931896 • BB **B** • S3 D3 • 1-12 NX • ⓑ ⓓ ⓢ ⓡ ⓣ ⓖ

Jackie Laing, Tewkesbury Cottage, 28 Main Rd, BH20 5RL. ☎ (01929) 400561 • Map 194/822802 • BB **B/C** • D2 T1 • 1-12 NX • ⓑ ⓓ ⓟ ⓣ ⓖ • Single bookings taken.

■ WEST LULWORTH (Wareham)
SOUTH WEST COAST PATH

Val & Barry Burrill, Graybank B&B, Main Road, BH20 5RL. ☎ (01929) 400256 • Map 194/822802 • BB **B/C** • S1 D2 T3 F1 • 2-11 • ⓓ ⓢ ⓟ ⓣ ⓖ • ◆◆◆ • Food nearby. 450yds to path.

Mr & Mrs S Lance, The Old Barn, BH20 5RL. ☎ (01929) 400305 • Map 194/822802 • BB **C/D/E** • S2 D/F1 T1 F1 • 1-12 • ⓓ ⓢ ⓟ ⓣ ⓖ • ◆◆◆ • Food nearby • groups also • microwave available

☆ Shirley Hotel, BH20 5RL. ☎ (01929) 400358 • Map 194/822802 • BB **E** • EM £15, 6.45-8pm • S1 D9 T4 F1 • 2-11 NX • ⓥ ⓑ ⓓ ⓢ ⓟ ⓖ • ★★Ⓢ • www.shirleyhotel.co.uk

Mrs Jan Ravensdale, Elads-Nevar, West Road, BH20 5RZ. ☎ (01929) 400467 • Map 194/825805 • BB **B** • D1 T1 F1 • 1-12 NX • ⓑ ⓓ ⓢ ⓟ ⓣ ⓖ • Vegans/Veggies catered for.

■ WESTHOLME (Wareham)
Mr Dudley Bennett, Westholme Farmhouse, BH20 6AQ. ☎ (01929) 551154 • Map 194/887858 • BB **C/D/E** • T2 • 1-12 • ⓑ ⓓ ⓢ ⓣ

■ WEYMOUTH (Dorchester)
SOUTH WEST COAST PATH

☆ Gail Blackshaw, Pebbles Guest House, 18 Kirtleton Ave, DT4 7PT. ☎ (01305) 784331 • Map 194/679802 • BB **B** • EM £7, 6.00pm • S1 D3 T2 F2 • 1-12 • ⓥ ⓓ ⓢ ⓡ ⓟ ⓣ ⓖ • ◆ • steve.blackshaw@virgin.net

Ken & Ann Jones, Kimberley Guest House, 16 Kirtleton Avenue, DT4 7PT. ☎ (01305) 783333 • Map 194/679802 • BB **B/C** • EM book first £7.50, 6pm • S2 D6 T1 F2 • 1-12 • Ⓥ Ⓑ Ⓓ Ⓢ Ⓡ Ⓟ Ⓣ • ◆◆◆

☆ The Crown Hotel, 51-53 St Thomas St, DT4 8EQ. ☎ (01305) 760800 • Map 194/678788 • BB **D** • EM £8, 5-7.30pm • S18 D19 T34 F15 • 1-12 NX • Ⓥ Ⓑ Ⓓ Ⓡ Ⓟ Ⓣ • ★★ • crown@kingshotels.co.uk

■ **WIMBORNE**

Heather Jewitt, 'Melrose' 16 Charborough Way, Sturminster Marshall, BH21 4DH. ☎ (01258) 858359 • Map 195/945995 • BB **C** • EM book first £8, 6pm+ • D1 T1 • 1-12 • Ⓑ Ⓓ Ⓟ Ⓣ • ◆◆◆ • hjewitt@lineone.net

■ **WINTERBORNE KINGSTON**

Mr & Mrs Jenkins, West Acres, West Street, DT11 9AT. ☎ (01929) 471293 • Map 194/854976 • BB **B** • EM book first £9, 7.30pm • D1 T1 F1 • 1-12 • Ⓥ Ⓑ Ⓓ Ⓢ Ⓟ Ⓣ 🐾

■ **WORTH MATRAVERS (Swanage)**
SOUTH WEST COAST PATH

Frances & Ian Taylor, The Haven, BH19 3LF. ☎ (01929) 439388 • Map 195/975777 • BB **C/D** • EM book first £10 • D/F1 T1 • 1-12 NX • Ⓥ Ⓑ Ⓓ Ⓢ Ⓟ Ⓣ 🐾 • Transport to local pubs for food.

COUNTY DURHAM

■ **BISHOP AUCKLAND**

Miss M Gordon, Albion Cottage Guest House, Albion Terrace, Cockton Hill, DL14 6EL. ☎ (01388) 602217 • Map 93/210290 • BB **B** • S2 D1 T1 • 1-12 • Ⓓ Ⓡ Ⓣ 🐾 • ◆◆◆

■ **CASTLESIDE (Consett)**

☆ Liz Lawson, Bee Cottage Farm, DH8 9HW. ☎ (01207) 508224 • Map 87/070453 • BB **C/D/E** • EM book first £14.50, 7-8pm • S1 D3 T2 F5 • 1-12 • Ⓥ Ⓑ Ⓢ Ⓟ 🐾 • ◆◆◆ • Groups also

■ **COWSHILL (Wearhead)**

Janet Elliott, Alston & Killhope Riding Centre, Low Cornriggs Farm, DL13 1AQ. ☎ (01388) 537600 • Map 86,87/845413 • BB **C** • EM book first £11, 6-9.30pm • S1 D2 T1 F1 • 1-12 NX • Ⓥ Ⓑ Ⓓ Ⓢ Ⓟ Ⓣ 🐾 • ◆◆◆◆ • SSSI, riding school, bird watching

■ **DURHAM**

Mark Nimmins, 14 Gilesgate (Top of Claypath), DH1 1QW. ☎ 0191-384 6485 • Map 88/278427 • BB **B** • S1 D1 T1 F1 • 1-12 NX • Ⓓ Ⓢ Ⓡ Ⓣ 🐾 • ◆◆ • Close to city centre. www.nimmins.co.uk

Mrs Janie Milne, Lothlorien Guest House, Front Street, Witton Gilbert , DH7 6SY. ☎ 0191-371 0067 • Map 88/233456 • BB **C** • S1 D1 T1 • 1-12 NX • Ⓓ Ⓟ Ⓣ • ◆◆◆ • milnes-lothorien@talk21.com

Yvonne Bland, Hillrise Guest House, 13 Durham Road West, Bowburn, DH6 5AU. ☎ (0191) 377 0302 • Map 93/306376 • BB **C** • S1 D1 T2 F1 • 1-12 • Ⓑ Ⓓ Ⓢ Ⓟ Ⓣ • ◆◆◆◆

■ **FROSTERLEY (Weardale)**

Cliff & Susan Bell, 'Bellsview', 1 Whitfield Brow, DL13 2SZ. ☎ (01388) 528487 • Map 92/005347 • BB **B/C** • S1 D2 T0 • 1-12 NX • Ⓑ Ⓓ Ⓢ Ⓟ Ⓣ

**Do you know your rights when you're out walking in the countryside?
See pages 32-39**

B&B ACCOMMODATION

■ MIDDLETON-IN-TEESDALE (Barnard Castle)
PENNINE WAY

Andrew & Sheila Milnes, Brunswick House, 55 Market Place, DL12 0QH. ☎ (01833) 640393 • Map 91,92/946255 • BB **C** • EM book first £17, 7.30pm • D3 T2 • 1-12 NX • V B D S P T • ◆◆◆◆ • www.brunswickhouse.net

Maria Northey, Bluebell House, Market Place, DL12 0QG. ☎ (01833) 640584 • Map 91/947255 • BB **B/D** • D2 T1 F1 • 1-12 NX • B D S P T • M • ◆◆◆

Mr F Bennett, Market Place Guest House, 16 Market Place, DL12 0QG. ☎ (01833) 640300 • Map 91,92/947255 • BB **B** • D2 T1 • 1-12 NX • B D S P • ◆◆◆

Mrs I Watson, Lonton South Farm, DL12 0PL. ☎ (01833) 640409 • Map 91,92/943233 • BB **B/C** • S1 D1 T1 • 2-11 • B D S P T • ★★★

Mrs J A Finn, Belvedere House, 54 Market Place, DL12 0QA. ☎ (01833) 640884 • Map 91,92/947254 • BB **B** • D2 T1 • 1-12 NX • B S P T • SC also belvedere@thecoachhouse.net

Irene Stoddart, Wemmergill Hall Farm, Lunedale, DL12 0PA. ☎ (01833) 640379 • Map 91,92/901218 • BB **C** • EM book first £10, 6.30pm • D1 F1 • 1-12 • V B D S P T • ◆◆◆

■ SPENNYMOOR

10 South View, Middlestone Moor, DL16 7DF. ☎ (01388) 817544 • Map 93/252328 • BB **B/D** • EM book first £7.50, 6.30-7pm • S1 D2 T4 • 1-12 • V B D S P T • ◆◆◆ • thegablesghouse@aol.com

ESSEX

■ BOXTED (Colchester)
ESSEX WAY & STOUR VALLEY PATH

Mary Carter, Round Hill House, Parsonage Hill, CO4 5ST. ☎ (01206) 272392 • Map 168/002334 • BB **C/D/E** • EM book first £20, 7pm • D1 T1 F1 • 1-12 NX • V B D S P T • ◆◆◆◆ • Transport for elderly av • jermar@appleonline.net

■ BRADFIELD (Manningtree)
ESSEX WAY

EMSWORTH HOUSE
Ship Hill, Bradfield, Essex CO11 2UP

Stunning view of the river and countryside on the Essex Way. Comfort and hospitality my speciality!

Penny Linton 01255 870860
emsworthhouse@hotmail.coma

☆ Penny Linton, Emsworth House, Ship Hill, CO11 2UP. ☎ (01255) 870860 • Map 168,169/142310 • BB **C** • EM book first £10-20, Up to 8.00pm • S3 D2 T1 F1 • 1-12 NX • V B D P T • **C** • emsworth-house@hotmail.com

■ COGGESHALL (Colchester)
ESSEX WAY

Mr & Mrs Shaw, White Heather Guest House, 19 Colchester Road, CO6 1RP. ☎ (01376) 563004 • Map 168/861228 • BB **C** • S3 D2 • 1-11 • B D S R T • List/App

■ COLCHESTER

S F & J Powell, Scheregate Hotel, 36 Osborne Street, CO2 7DB. ☎ (01206) 573034 • Map 168/996250 • BB **C** • S15 D6 T8 F1 • 1-12 NX • B D R • 1Cr/App

Wendy Anderson, The Old Manse, 15 Roman Road, CO1 1UR. ☎ (01206) 545154 • Map 168/001254 • BB **C** • D/S1 T/S2 • 1-12 NX • B D S R P T • ◆◆◆ • www.doveuk.com/oldmanse

■ GREAT CHESTERFORD (Nr Saffron Walden)
ICKNIELD WAY

Mrs Christine King, Mill House, CB10 1NS. ☎ (01799) 530493 • Map 154/504431 • BB **B** • S1 D4 T1 • 1-12 • D S R P T

■ MARGARET RODING (Nr Great Dunmow)
ESSEX WAY

Mrs Joyce Matthews, "Greys", Ongar Road, CM6 1QR. ☎ (01245) 231509 • Map 167/605112 • BB **C** • D2 T1 • 1-12 NX • D S • ◆◆◆

■ PEBMARSH (Halstead)
STOUR VALLEY PATH

Mrs C Rice, Timbers, Cross End, CO9 2NT. ☎ (01787) 269330 • Map 168/859337 • BB **B** • EM N • T1 F1 • 3-10 • V B D S P T • ◆◆◆ • 1st night £37, subsequently £32

■ PLESHEY
ESSEX WAY

Fitzjohns Farmhouse, Mashbury Rd, Great Waltham, Cheltenham, CM3 1EJ. ☎ (01245) 360204/361224 • Map 167/676137 • BB **D/E** • EM book first £17.50 • D1 T1 • 1-12 NX • V B D S P • RosRenwick@aol.com

■ PURLEIGH (Chelmsford)

Mr & Mrs K Ascott, Purleigh Law, Walton Hall Lane, CM3 6TR. ☎ (01621) 828682 • Map 168/827023 • BB **B** • S1 D1 T1 • 1-12 NX • D S P T • M • St. Peters Way kevin.ascott@tesco.net

■ WIMBISH (Thaxted)

Linda Scanlan, 'Field View', Howlett End, CB10 2XW. ☎ (01799) 599616 • Map 154/585346 • BB **C/D** • S1 D2 • 1-12 NX • B S P T

☆ See Display Advertisement

■ WIX (Manningtree)
ESSEX WAY

New Farm House, Spinnels Lane, CO11 2UJ.
☎ (01255) 870365 • Map 168,169/164293 • BB **C/E** • EM book first £13.50, 7.30pm • S2 D4 T3 F2 • 1-11 • Ⓥ Ⓑ Ⓓ Ⓢ Ⓟ Ⓣ 🛁 • ◆◆◆ • newfarmhouse@which.net

---

GLOUCESTERSHIRE

■ BIRDLIP (Gloucester)
COTSWOLD WAY

P M Carter, Beechmount, GL4 8JH. ☎ (01452) 862262 • Map 163/925143 • BB **B/C** • EM book first £8, 7pm • D2 T2 F2 • 1-12 • Ⓥ Ⓑ Ⓓ Ⓢ Ⓟ Ⓣ 🛁 • ◆◆◆ • thebeechmount@breathemail.net

■ BLOCKLEY (Moreton-in-Marsh)
NORTH COTSWOLD DIAMOND WAY

Martin & Joan Dee, Park Farm, GL56 9TA. ☎ 01386 700266 • Map 151/165336 • BB **B** • S2 D1 T1 • 1-12 NX • Ⓓ Ⓢ Ⓡ Ⓟ Ⓣ 🛁

Mrs Sue Harrison, Greystone Farm, GL56 9LN.
☎ (01386) 700482 • Map 151/172375 • BB **C** • T1 • 1-12 • Ⓑ Ⓓ Ⓢ Ⓟ Ⓣ • susanharrison@farmer-sweekly.net

■ BOURTON-ON-THE-WATER (Cheltenham)
OXFORDSHIRE WAY & HEART OF ENGLAND WAY & NORTH COTSWOLD DIAMOND WAY

Mrs Joan Mustoe, 6 Moore Road, GL54 2AZ.
☎ (01451) 820767 • Map 163/169210 • BB **B** • S1 D1 T1 • 1-11 NX • Ⓑ Ⓓ Ⓢ Ⓣ 🛁

Jackie Morris, Fairlie, Riverside, GL54 2DP.
☎ (01451) 821842 • Map 163/168206 • BB **B** • D2 T1 • 1-12 NX • Ⓓ Ⓢ Ⓣ • ◆◆◆ • shower room/jacuzzi

■ BRISTOL

Arches Hotel, 132 Cotham Brow, Cotham, BS6 6AE.
☎ 0117 924 7398 • Map 172/588745 • BB **C** • S3 D2 T1 F3 • 1-12 NX • Ⓥ Ⓑ Ⓓ Ⓢ Ⓡ 🛁 • ◆◆◆ • Special diets catered. www.arches-hotel.co.uk

■ BROOKTHORPE (Gloucester)
COTSWOLD WAY

Brookthorpe Lodge
LICENSED GUEST HOUSE
Stroud Road, Brookthorpe, Gloucester GL4 0UQ
Tel/Fax 01452 812645
Elegant Georgian house set in lovely countryside at the foot of the Cotswold escarpment between Gloucester and Stroud.

ETC
◆◆◆
Visit our website at
www.brookthorpelodge.demon.co.uk

☆ Robert & Diana Bailey, Brookthorpe Lodge, Stroud Road, GL4 0UQ. ☎ (01452) 812645 • Map 162/835128 • BB **C** • EM book first £10.50, up to 9pm • S3 D2 T3 F2 • 1-12 • Ⓥ Ⓑ Ⓓ Ⓢ Ⓟ Ⓣ 🛁 • ◆◆◆ • enq@brookthorpelodge.demon.co.uk

■ CAM (Dursley)
COTSWOLD WAY

☆ Mrs Victoria Jennings, The Foresters Arms, 31 Chapel Street, GL11 5NX. ☎ 01453 549996 • Map 162/750002 • BB **B/C** • EM book first £10-14, 6-8.30pm • S1 D1 T1 F1 • 1-12 • Ⓥ Ⓑ Ⓓ Ⓢ Ⓟ Ⓣ 🛁 • ◆◆◆ • Groups also

Beautiful South Cotswolds
'FORESTERS'
(Formerly The Foresters Arms Inn, c.1800)
31 Chapel Street, Cam, Dursley, Glos GL11 5NX

Our luxury beamed four-poster room

Stay awhile and enjoy warm hospitality at our spacious home with *such a cosy atmosphere.*

The large oak-beamed guest lounge has a log fire and daily newspapers. Spacious oak beamed bedrooms with lovely Laura Ashley superior quality furnishings, remote control colour TVs and tea/coffee making facilities ensure a very comfortable stay. All rooms have ensuite or private bathrooms with showers and baths.

The Cotswold Way and Cam Peak and excellent walking country is on our doorstep and 150 attractions are within easy reach as are pretty, unspoilt villages and Cotswold market towns with antiques and gift shops. *We can supply maps and touring/walking leaflets to help you enjoy the area to the full.*

- Three excellent golf clubs with spectacular views nearby.
- Close to Westonbirt Arboretum & Slimbridge Wildfowl Trust
- Transport given to friendly real-ale inns.
- Off road parking
- Mainline station halt 5 minutes away to Gloucester and Cheltenham
- Dogs welcome by arrangement
- Very reasonable prices, with special discounts, from £20pp. Evening meals also.
- Walled sunny garden with hillview

10% off 7-night stays, 5% off 4–6 night stays (Sun–Fri inc.)

Quote *Details on request:* **Victoria Jennings**
Ref R1 *Tel:* **01453 549996** *Fax:* **01453 548200**
email: **vacationsbritain@hotmail.com**

■ CHARLTON KINGS (Cheltenham)
COTSWOLD WAY

☆ Charlton Kings Hotel, London Road, GL52 6UU.
☎ (01242) 231061 • Map 163/977201 • BB **E** • EM £18.75, 7-9pm • S2 D8 T2 F2 • 1-12 • Ⓥ Ⓑ Ⓓ Ⓢ Ⓟ Ⓣ 🛁 • ★★★Ⓢ • See display advert on next page.

174

CHARLTON KINGS HOTEL
CHELTENHAM

English Tourism Council ★★★ Silver Award
Welcomes Walkers. Ideally situated, on
edge of town just half a mile from
Cotswold Way. All rooms have

Geraldine White, 22 Ledmore Road, GL53 8RA.
☎ (01242) 526957 • Map 163/967207 • BB **A** • EM
book first £10, 7.30pm • S1 D1 T1 • 1-12 NX • Ⓥ Ⓑ
Ⓓ Ⓢ Ⓟ Ⓣ Ⓜ

■ CHELTENHAM
COTSWOLD WAY

North Hall Hotel, Pittville Circus Road, GL52 2PZ.
☎ (01242) 520589 • Map 163/958227 • BB **E** • EM
£12.50, 6.30-8pm • S10 D10 T6 • 1-12 NX • Ⓥ Ⓑ Ⓓ
Ⓡ Ⓟ Ⓣ 🐾 • ★★ • Northhallhotel@btinternet.com

Pauline Lyons, 374 Old Bath Road, Leckhampton,
GL53 9AD. ☎ (01242) 513313 • Map 163/949193 •
BB **C** • EM book first £12, 8pm • D1 • 2-11 NX • Ⓥ
Ⓑ Ⓓ Ⓢ Ⓟ Ⓣ

Ruth Jennings, "St Cloud", 97 Leckhampton Road,
GL53 0BZ. ☎ (01242) 575245 • Map 163/946202 •
BB **C** • D1 T2 F1 • 1-12 NX • Ⓥ Ⓓ Ⓢ Ⓡ Ⓟ Ⓣ •
◆◆◆

■ CHIPPING CAMPDEN
COTSWOLD WAY & HEART OF ENGLAND WAY & NORTH
COTSWOLD DIAMOND WAY

☆ Mrs D Bendall, Sandalwood House, Back-Ends,
GL55 6AU. ☎ /Fax (01386) 840091 • Map
151/143387 • BB **C/D** • D/F1 T1 • 1-12 NX • Ⓑ Ⓓ Ⓢ
Ⓣ • ◆◆◆◆ • Food nearby • cars can be left

Mrs Sinclair, Volunteer Inn, Lower High Street, GL55
6DY. ☎ (01386) 840688 • Map 151/150392 • BB **D** •
EM £4.50-8.50, 7-9pm • S1 D3 T2 F1 • 1-12 • Ⓥ Ⓑ
Ⓓ Ⓟ Ⓣ 🐾 • SC also • Camra recommended.
saravol@aol.com

Mrs J Whitehouse, Weston Park Farm, Dovers Hill,
GL55 6UW. ☎ (01386) 840835 • Map 151/130390 •
BB **D** • D1 F1 • 1-12 • Ⓑ Ⓓ Ⓟ Ⓣ • 2Cr • SC also

Mrs Janet Rawlings, Marnic House B&B, Broad
Campden, GL55 6UR. ☎ (01386) 840014/841473 •
Map 151/159378 • BB **C** • D2 T1 • 1-12 NX • Ⓑ Ⓓ
Ⓢ Ⓣ • ◆◆◆◆ • Food nearby marnic@zoom.co.uk

Mrs June Wadey, "Wyldlands", Broad Campden,
GL55 6UR. ☎ (01386) 840478 • Map 151/159378 •
BB **C** • S1 D1 T1 • 1-12 NX • Ⓑ Ⓓ Ⓢ Ⓣ Ⓜ •
◆◆◆◆ • Food nearby

Lygon Arms Hotel, High Street, GL55 6HB.
☎ (01386) 840318 • Map 151/153394 • BB **D** • EM
£6-£20, 6-10pm • D3 T1 F2 • 1-12 NX • Ⓥ Ⓑ Ⓓ Ⓢ
Ⓟ Ⓣ 🐾 • www.lygonarms.co.uk

☆ Sarah Drinkwater, The Old Bakehouse, Lower High
Street, GL55 6DZ. ☎ (01386) 840979 • Map
151/150392 • BB **D** • D3 T1 F1 • 1-12 NX • Ⓑ Ⓓ Ⓢ
Ⓟ Ⓣ

Mrs Benfield, Lower High Street, GL55 6DZ.
☎ 01386 840163 • Map 151/150392 • BB **C** • D1 T1 •
2-10 • Ⓑ Ⓓ Ⓟ Ⓣ 🐾

■ CLEEVE HILL (Cheltenham)
COTSWOLD WAY

Malvern View, GL52 3PR. ☎ (01242) 672017 • Map
163/983270 • BB **D** • D2 T2 • 1-12 NX • Ⓑ Ⓓ Ⓢ Ⓟ
Ⓣ • ◆◆◆ • vchoak@hotmail.com

Edward Saunders, Heron Haye, Petty Lane, GL52
3PW. ☎ (01242) 672516 • Map 163/987273 • BB **C** •
S1 D2 • 1-12 • Ⓓ Ⓢ Ⓟ 🐾 • List • 400 yds from
Cotswold Way • dick.whittamore@virgin.net

■ COLD ASHTON (Bath)
COTSWOLD WAY

Mrs J Bishop, Toghill House Farm, BS30 5RT.
☎ (01225) 891261 • Map 172/731724 • BB **D** • S1
D4 T3 F3 • 1-12 • Ⓑ Ⓓ Ⓢ Ⓟ Ⓣ 🐾 • C/3Q • SC
also, food nearby

☆ See Display Advertisement

☆ Dave & Carol Watts, The Chestnuts, SN14 8JT. ☎ (01225) 892020 • Map 172/749726 • BB **B/C** • EM book first £8, 7pm • D1 T1 • 1-12 NX • Ⓥ Ⓑ Ⓓ Ⓢ Ⓟ Ⓣ • dave@davecarol.freeserve.co.uk

■ COLEFORD
OFFA'S DYKE

D J & J M Atherley, "Westlands House", 20 Grove Road, Berry Hill, GL16 8QY. ☎ (01594) 837143 • Map 162/573122 • BB **B** • D1 T1 • 1-12 NX • Ⓢ Ⓣ 🐾

■ CRANHAM (Gloucester)
COTSWOLD WAY

Milly Dann, Pound Cottage, GL4 8HP. ☎ (01452) 812581 • Map 163/897130 • BB **C** • D1 T1 • 1-12 NX • Ⓓ Ⓢ Ⓟ Ⓣ • ddann@globalnet.co.uk

■ DOYNTON (Bristol)
COTSWOLD WAY

Mr & Mrs K Dinham, Wilkes Farm, BS30 5TJ. ☎/fax(0117 937) 2381 • Map 172/715745 • BB **C/D** • S1 D1 T1 F1 • 1-12 NX • Ⓑ Ⓓ Ⓢ 🐾 • www.country-retreats.com/wilkes-farm

■ DURSLEY
COTSWOLD WAY

Mr & Mrs P G Roberts, "Ingleside", 26 The Slade, GL11 4JX. ☎ (01453) 542735 • Map 162/755981 • BB **B** • T2 • 1-12 • Ⓥ Ⓓ Ⓢ Ⓣ Ⓜ • Food nearby • pete.ang@cwcom.net

Mrs Cecilia Boyle, 7 Prospect Place, GL11 4JL. ☎ (01453) 543445 • Map 162/755980 • BB **B** • EM book first £9.50, 8pm • D1 T1 • 1-12 NX • Ⓥ Ⓑ Ⓓ Ⓢ Ⓡ Ⓟ Ⓣ 🐾

■ EDGE (Stroud)
COTSWOLD WAY

Mrs A Sanders, Wild Acre, Back Edge Lane, GL6 6PE. ☎ (01452) 813077 • Map 162/849099 • BB **B/C** • D1 T1 • 4-10 • Ⓑ Ⓢ Ⓟ Ⓣ 🐾 • ◆◆◆ • Food nearby

■ ELKSTONE (Cheltenham)

Mrs L Eyre, High Beech, GL53 9PA. ☎ (01242) 870375 • Map 163/967131 • BB **C** • EM book first £7.50, 6-7pm • D2 • 1-12 • Ⓥ Ⓑ Ⓓ Ⓢ Ⓟ Ⓣ 🐾

■ FRAMPTON-ON-SEVERN
SEVERN WAY

The Bell Inn, The Green, GL2 7EP. ☎ (01452) 740346 • Map 162/748080 • BB **C** • EM £12, 7-9.30pm • D2 T2 • 1-12 • Ⓥ Ⓑ Ⓓ Ⓢ Ⓟ Ⓣ 🐾

■ GLOUCESTER
SEVERN WAY

☆ Messrs Hutton, Harescombe Grange, Painswick, GL4 0UY. ☎ (01452) 812683 • Map 162/844105 • BB **E** • EM book first £8, 7.30pm • D1 T2 • 1-12 • Ⓥ Ⓑ Ⓓ Ⓢ Ⓟ Ⓣ 🐾

■ GOTHERINGTON (Cheltenham)
COTSWOLD WAY

Mr & Mrs C J McMullen, Woods Cottage, Manor Lane, GL52 4QX. ☎ (01242) 673083 • Map 150/163/970293 • BB **B** • S1 T2 • 1-12 NX • Ⓓ Ⓢ Ⓟ Ⓣ 🐾

■ GREAT RISSINGTON
NORTH COTSWOLD DIAMOND WAY

Roger & Sandra Freeman, Stepping Stone, Rectory Lane, GL54 2LL. ☎ (01451) 821385 • Map 163/198173 • BB **D** • EM book first £15, 7.30pm • S1 D3 T1 • 1-12 NX • Ⓥ Ⓑ Ⓓ Ⓢ Ⓟ Ⓣ 🐾 • ◆◆◆ • Transport from rail av.

■ HAWKESBURY UPTON (South Glos)
COTSWOLD WAY

Anna, Ivy Cottage, Inglestone Common, GL9 1BX. ☎ (01454) 294237 • Map 172,162/754887 • BB **B/C** • EM book first £13-14.50, 6.30-8.30pm • S1 D3 T3 F1 • 1-12 NX • Ⓥ Ⓑ Ⓓ Ⓢ Ⓟ Ⓣ 🐾 • Transport back to Cotswold Way

■ KING'S STANLEY (Stonehouse)
COTSWOLD WAY

Jean Hanna, Old Chapel House, Broad Street, GL10 3PN. ☎ (01453) 826289 • Map 162/813033 • BB **C** • EM book first £6 upwards, 6.30-7.30pm • S1 D1 T2 F1 • 1-11 • Ⓥ Ⓑ Ⓓ Ⓡ Ⓟ Ⓣ • List

Mrs Louise Walker, "Stantone", Coldwell Lane, Middleyard, GL10 3PR. ☎ (01453) 822204 • Map 162/816030 • BB **B** • T1 • 1-11 • Ⓓ Ⓢ Ⓡ Ⓟ Ⓣ • Food nearby. Transport avail.

■ LECHLADE ON THAMES
THAMES PATH

Mr John Titchener, Cambrai Lodge, Oak Street, GL7 3AY. ☎ (01367) 253173 • Map 163/214998 • BB **C** • S1 D1 T1 F/D1 • 1-12 • B D S P T 🛁 • ◆◆◆◆⑤

■ LITTLE COMPTON (Moreton-in-Marsh)
NORTH COTSWOLD DIAMOND WAY

Susan Cox, Rigside, GL56 0RR. ☎ (01608) 674128 • Map 151/252307 • BB **C** • S1 D2 T1 • 1-12 • B D S P T 🛁 Ⓜ • ◆◆◆◆ • rigside@lineone.net

■ LITTLE SODBURY (Chipping Sodbury)
COTSWOLD WAY

Pauline Herbert, Crosshands Farm, BS37 6RJ. ☎ (01454) 324729 • Map 172/760828 • BB **C** • EM book first £15, 7-8pm • S1 D1 T1 • 1-12 • V B D S P T • crosshands.farm@virgin.net

■ LITTLE WITCOMBE (Gloucester)
COTSWOLD WAY

Miss J Bickell, Springfields Farm, GL3 4TU. ☎ (01452) 863532 • Map 163/924160 • BB **B** • EM book first £6-£7 (Oct-Feb only), 6.30-7pm • S1 D2 F/T1 • 1-12 NX • V D S P T 🛁 • ◆◆ • Food nearby

■ LONGHOPE (Forest Of Dean)

The Old Farm, Barrel Lane, GL17 0LR. ☎ (01452) 830252 • Map 162/683207 • BB **B/C** • D2 T1 • 1-12 NX • B D S P T 🛁 • ◆◆◆◆ • www.the-old-farm.co.uk

■ NEWENT

Cherry Grove B&B, Mill Lane, Kilcot, GL18 1NY. ☎ (01989) 720126 • Map 162/689253 • BB **A** • D1 F1 • 1-12 NX • B S T

■ NORTH NIBLEY (Dursley)
COTSWOLD WAY

☆ Diana A Eley, Nibley House, GL11 6DL. ☎ (01453) 543108 • Map 162/737958 • BB **D** • EM book first £10-£12, 7.30pm • D3 T2 F1 • 1-12 • V B D S P T 🛁 • Camping also. Luggage transport

☆ Mr P Rackley, Burrows Court, Nibley Green, GL11 6AZ. ☎ (01453) 546230 • Map 162/732967 • BB **D** • EM • D3 T2 F1 • 2-11 • B D S P T 🛁 • ◆◆◆ • Food nearby • www.burrowscourt.co.uk

■ NORTHLEACH (Cheltenham)
NORTH COTSWOLD DIAMOND WAY

Graham & Elaine Whent, Cotteswold House, Market Place, GL54 3EG. ☎ (01451) 860493 • Map 163/113145 • BB **D** • EM book first £20, 6.30-8pm • D2 T1 • 1-12 NX • V B D S T • ◆◆◆◆

■ OLD SODBURY (Bristol)
COTSWOLD WAY

John & Daphne Paz, Dornden, Church Lane, BS37 6NB. ☎ (01454) 313325 • Map 172/756814 • BB **D** • EM book first £11, 6.45pm • S2 T2 F5 • 1-12 NX • V B D S P T • ◆◆◆◆

■ PAINSWICK (Gloucester)
COTSWOLD WAY

Alison Bancroft-Livingston, Beaconsfield House, New Street, GL6 6UN. ☎ (01452) 813001 • Map 162/866097 • BB **D** • D1 T1 • 1-12 NX • B D S 🛁 Ⓜ

Jean Hernen, Brookhouse Mill Cottage, Tibbiwell Lane, GL6 6YA. ☎ (01452) 812854 • Map 162/869096 • BB **C** • D1 T1 F1 • 1-12 NX • B D S P T • List

Michele Burdett, Damsels Farm, GL6 6UD. ☎ (01452) 812148 • Map 162/875114 • BB **D** • D0 T1 F2 • 1-12 NX • B D S P T 🛁 Ⓜ • michele-burdett@aol.com

Wendy Hodgson, Skyrack, The Highlands, GL6 6SL. ☎ (01452) 812029 • Map 162/868105 • BB **C** • S1 D/F1 T/F1 • 1-12 NX • B D S P T 🛁 • ◆◆◆ • Baggage transfer • 3 night discount wendyskyrack@hotmail.com

Mrs Barbara Harley, Orchard House, 4 Court Orchard, GL6 6UU. ☎ (01452) 813150 • Map 162/866095 • BB **C** • S0 D1 T1 • 1-12 NX • B S T • harleydy@btinternet.com

☆ See Display Advertisement

Fiona Johnston, The Falcon Inn, New Street, GL6 6UN. ☎ (01452) 814222 • Map 162/866097 • BB **D** • EM £8.50, 7-9.30pm • D6 T3 F3 • 1-12 • Ⓥ Ⓑ Ⓓ Ⓢ Ⓟ Ⓣ ⚑ • ★★ • blennins@clara.net

■ **RANDWICK (Stroud)**
COTSWOLD WAY

Mr & Mrs J Taylor, Court Farm, GL6 6HH. ☎ (01453) 764210 • Map 162/827065 • BB **C** • EM book first £10-12, 7-7.30pm • S1 D1 T2 F1 • 1-12 NX • Ⓥ Ⓑ Ⓓ Ⓢ Ⓡ Ⓟ Ⓣ ⚑ • Luggage transfer av. johnetaylor@courtfarm.freeserve.co.uk

Mrs M Parish, Laurel Cottage, GL6 6HL. ☎ (01453) 763942 • Map 162/830066 • BB **B** • EM book first £8.00, from 6pm • D2 • 1-12 NX • Ⓥ Ⓓ Ⓢ Ⓡ Ⓟ ⚑

■ **REDBROOK (Monmouth)**
OFFA'S DYKE & WYE VALLEY WALK

Mrs M Evans, Tresco, NP5 4LY. ☎ (01600) 712325 • Map 162/536101 • BB **B** • EM book first £8.50, 6-6.30 (snacks till 8pm) • S2 D1 T1 • 1-12 • Ⓥ Ⓑ Ⓟ Ⓣ ⚑ Ⓜ • Mobile home sleeps 6 (B&B). £7pp bed only.

■ **RODBOROUGH (Stroud)**
COTSWOLD WAY

Stan Pound, The Laye-Bye, 7 Castlemead Road, GL5 3SF. ☎ (01453) 751514 • Map 162/847046 • BB **C** • EM book first £10.50, 6.30-7.00pm • S2 D2 T1 • 1-12 NX • Ⓥ Ⓑ Ⓓ Ⓢ Ⓡ Ⓟ Ⓣ Ⓜ • ◆◆◆◆

■ **ST BRIAVELS (Lydney)**
OFFA'S DYKE & WYE VALLEY WALK

Keith & Marion Allen, Woodcroft, Lower Meend, GL15 6RW. ☎ (01594) 530083 • Map 162/552042 • BB **C** • T1 F2 • 1-12 • Ⓑ Ⓓ Ⓢ Ⓟ Ⓣ ⚑ • Can use sign language • www.woodcroft.freeserve.co.uk

Ann Sabin, The Florence Country Hotel, Bigsweir, GL15 6QQ. ☎ (01594) 530830 • Map 162/544063 • BB **D** • EM book first £13, 7.30pm • S1 D4 T3 • 1-12 NX • Ⓥ Ⓑ Ⓓ Ⓢ Ⓟ Ⓣ ⚑ • ★★ • English/Welsh border • www.florencehotel.co.uk

Alan & May Ward, Oak Cottage, The Common, GL15 6SJ. ☎ (01594) 530440 • Map 162/538035 • BB **B** • EM £7.50 • D2 • 1-12 • Ⓥ Ⓑ Ⓓ Ⓢ Ⓟ ⚑ Ⓜ • Veg. food. 4 acres of own grounds. Transport av.

■ **STANTON (Broadway, Hereford & Worcs)**
COTSWOLD WAY

Mrs Angela Neilan, Shenberrow Hill, WR12 7NE. ☎ (01386) 584468 • Map 150/071342 • BB **D** • EM book first £11.50, from 6.30pm • S1 D2 T2 F2 • 1-12 NX • Ⓥ Ⓑ Ⓓ Ⓢ Ⓟ Ⓣ ⚑ • ◆◆◆◆

■ **STONEHOUSE**
COTSWOLD WAY

Mrs D Hodge, Merton Lodge, 8 Ebley Road, GL10 2LQ. ☎ (01453) 822018 • Map 162/815047 • BB **C** • D3 • 1-12 NX • Ⓑ Ⓢ Ⓡ ⚑ • 2Cr • Food nearby

■ **STOW-ON-THE-WOLD (Cheltenham)**
HEART OF ENGLAND WAY & NORTH COTSWOLD DIAMOND WAY

Helen & Graham Keyte, The Limes, Evesham Road, GL54 1EJ. ☎ (01451) 830034 • Map 163/181264 • BB **C** • D3 T1 F1 • 1-12 NX • Ⓑ Ⓓ Ⓣ ⚑

Robert & Dawn Smith, Corsham Field Farm House, Bledington Road, GL54 1JH. ☎ (01451) 831750 • Map 163/211259 • BB **B/C** • D2 T2 F3 • 1-12 • Ⓑ Ⓓ Ⓣ ⚑ • ◆◆◆ • Food nearby

Valerie Keyte, Fifield Cottage, Fosse Lane, GL54 1EH. ☎ (01451) 831056 • Map 163/189258 • BB **C** • D1 T1 F1 • 1-12 NX • Ⓑ Ⓓ Ⓣ ⚑

■ **STROUD**

☆ The Downfield Hotel, 134 Cainscross Road, GL5 4HN. ☎ (01453) 764496 • Map 162/841051 • BB **C** • EM £10, 6.30-8.15pm • S4 D8 T7 F2 • 1-12 • Ⓥ Ⓑ Ⓓ Ⓢ Ⓡ Ⓟ Ⓣ ⚑ • 3Cr/C • Groups also • www.downfieldotel.demon.co.uk

Mrs Glynis Solomon, Pretoria Villa, Wells Road, Eastcombe, GL6 7EE. ☎ (01452) 770435 • Map 163/891044 • BB **C** • EM book first £12, 7-8.30pm • S1 D1 T1 • 1-12 NX • Ⓥ Ⓑ Ⓓ Ⓢ Ⓟ Ⓣ • ◆◆◆◆

☆ Mrs Carol Walsh, The Firs, Selsley Road, North Woodchester, GL5 5NQ. ☎ (01453) 873088 • Map 162/840028 • BB **D** • D1 F1 • 1-12 NX • Ⓑ Ⓓ Ⓢ Ⓟ Ⓣ • ◆◆◆◆◆ • SC also • cwalsh3088@aol.com

■ **TEWKESBURY**
SEVERN WAY

Ms Lorraine J Bishop, Carrant Brook House, Rope Walk, GL20 5DS. ☎ (01684) 290355 • Map 150/896329 • BB **D** • EM book first £7, 5:30-7:00pm • S1 D1 T1 • 1-12 • Ⓑ Ⓓ Ⓢ Ⓡ Ⓟ Ⓣ Ⓜ • ◆◆◆

ENGLAND GLOUCESTERSHIRE

B&B ACCOMMODATION

■ TORMARTON (Badminton)
COTSWOLD WAY

The Compass Inn, GL9 1JB. ☎ (01454) 218242/218577 • Map 172/760780 • BB **E** • EM £5-£16.95, up to 10.30pm • S1 D11 T7 F5 • 1-12 NX • Ⓥ Ⓑ Ⓓ Ⓢ Ⓟ Ⓣ ♨ • 4Cr/C • Charge for dogs
www.compass-inn.co.uk

Heather Cadei, Chestnut Farm, GL9 1HS. ☎ (01454) 218563 also fax no. • Map 172/769791 • BB **C** • EM £10, 8.30pm • D3 T2 • 1-12 • Ⓥ Ⓑ Ⓓ Ⓟ ♨

■ ULEY (Dursley)
COTSWOLD WAY

G & N Kent, Hill House, Crawley Hill, GL11 5BH. ☎ (01453) 860267 • Map 162/788996 • BB **B/C** • EM book first £10.50, 6.30pm • S1 D1 T1 F1 • 1-12 NX • Ⓥ Ⓑ Ⓓ Ⓢ Ⓣ • SC also

Mrs Susan Strain, Cotswold House, 57 The Street, GL11 5SL. ☎ (01453) 860305 • Map 162/790985 • BB **C** • S1 D2 T1 • 1-11 • Ⓑ Ⓓ Ⓢ Ⓟ Ⓣ • Food nrby. Trans to Cots/way.
strain@uley.fsbusiness.co.uk

Mrs Catherine Bevan, Hodgecombe Farm, GL11 5AN. ☎ (01453) 860365 • Map 162/ • BB **B/C** • EM book first £10, 7pm • D2 T1 F0 • 4-10 • Ⓥ Ⓑ Ⓓ Ⓢ Ⓟ Ⓣ • ♦♦♦♦♦

■ UPPER COBERLEY (Cheltenham)
COTSWOLD WAY

Anne Allen, Upper Coberley Farm, GL53 9RB. ☎ (01242) 870306 • Map 163/980158 • BB **B** • EM book first £10, 7pm • D1 T1 • 2-11 • Ⓑ Ⓓ Ⓢ Ⓟ Ⓣ • ♦♦♦♦ • SC also

■ WESTONBIRT (Tetbury)

Sonja King, Avenue Farm, Knockdown, GL8 8QS. ☎ (01454) 238207 • Map 162,173/864903 • BB **C** • D1 T2 F1 • 1-12 NX • Ⓑ Ⓓ Ⓢ Ⓟ Ⓣ Ⓜ • ♦♦♦ • sonjames@breathemail.net

■ WINCHCOMBE (Cheltenham)
COTSWOLD WAY

Mrs J G Saunders, Great House, Castle Street, GL54 5JA. ☎ (01242) 602490 • Map 150,163/026282 • BB **C** • D1 T1 • 1-12 NX • Ⓑ Ⓓ Ⓢ Ⓣ

Mrs S Simmonds, Gower House, 16 North Street, GL54 5LH. ☎ (01242) 602616 • Map 150,163/025284 • BB **C** • D1 T2 • 1-12 NX • Ⓑ Ⓓ Ⓟ Ⓣ Ⓜ • ♦♦♦

Mrs J E Upton, Mercia, Hailes Street, GL54 5HU. ☎ (01242) 602251 • Map 150,163/026285 • BB **C** • D3 T1 • 1-12 NX • Ⓑ Ⓓ Ⓢ Ⓟ Ⓣ ♨ • ♦♦♦♦Ⓢ

Mrs Janet Cooper, Pilgrim House, Hailes, GL54 5PB. ☎ (01242) 603011 • Map 150/047304 • BB **C** • EM book first £10-£12, 7.30pm • D1 T2 • 1-12 NX • Ⓥ Ⓑ Ⓓ Ⓢ Ⓟ ♨ •

☆ Mrs C M Rand, Clevely Cottage, Wadfield Farm, Corndean Lane, GL54 5AL. ☎ (01242) 602059 • Map 150/163/025263 • BB **B/C** • EM book first £10, 6.30pm • D1 T1 F1 • 1-12 NX • Ⓥ Ⓑ Ⓓ Ⓟ Ⓣ • ♦♦♦ • Luggage forwarded.

Mrs M Robins, 1 Stancombe View, GL54 5LE. ☎ (01242) 603654 • Map 150,163/023285 • BB **B** • S1 D1 • 3-10 • Ⓑ Ⓓ Ⓢ Ⓟ Ⓣ • ♦♦♦ • Special diets by arrangement

Mrs S Chisholm, Blair House, 41 Gretton Road, GL54 5EG. ☎ (01242) 603626 • Map 150,163/023287 • BB **C** • S2 D1 T1 • 1-12 • Ⓑ Ⓓ Ⓢ Ⓟ Ⓣ • ♦♦♦

Ms Adeline Rucklidge, Rutland Court, Cowl Lane, GL54 5RA. ☎ (01242) 603101 • Map 150,163/024284 • BB **B/C** • S1 D2 • 2-11 NX • Ⓓ Ⓢ Ⓣ • ♦♦ • Special diets by arrangement

Mrs C Cozens, 5 Kenulf Road, GL54 5JL. ☎ (01242) 602581 • Map 150/030289 • BB **B** • T1 • 1-12 NX • Ⓓ Ⓢ ♨

Dora Wigg, Greenhyde, Langley Road, GL54 5QP. ☎ (01242) 602569 • Map 150, 163/015282 • BB **C** • EM book first £9, 7pm • T1/S1 F1 • 1-12 NX • Ⓥ Ⓑ Ⓓ Ⓢ Ⓟ Ⓣ Ⓜ • ♦♦♦♦ • Pub nearby

Ann Pratley, Glebe Farm, Wood-Stanway, GL54 5PG. ☎ (01386) 584404 • Map 150/065313 • BB **C** • EM book first £15, 6.30pm • D1 T2 • 1-12 NX • Ⓥ Ⓑ Ⓓ Ⓟ ♨

Wendy Cooke, Yorklands, 127 Gretton Road, GL54 5EL. ☎ (01242) 602102 • Map 150,163/022291 • BB **C** • S1 D1 T1 • 1-12 NX • Ⓑ Ⓓ Ⓢ Ⓣ Ⓜ

■ WOTTON-UNDER-EDGE
COTSWOLD WAY

Mrs K P Forster, Under-the-Hill House, Adey's Lane, GL12 7LY. ☎ (01453) 842557 • Map 172,162/758937 • BB **B/C** • D1 T1 • 3-10 • Ⓓ Ⓢ Ⓣ • Baggage transfer

Mrs Sandra Nixon, The Coffee Shop, 31a Long Street, GL12 7BX. ☎ (01453) 843158 • Map 172,162/757933 • BB **C** • S2 D3 T2 F1 • 1-12 • Ⓑ Ⓓ Ⓢ Ⓟ Ⓣ ♨ • wottongh@aol.com

GLOUCESTERSHIRE   ENGLAND   B&B ACCOMMODATION

Mrs April Haddrell, Falcon Cottage, 15 Station Road, Charfield, GL12 8SY. ☎ (01453) 843528 • Map 172,162/724922 • BB **C** • T2 • 1-12 NX • ⒹⓈⓉ • ◆◆◆◆

Mrs Julie James, Hillesley Mill, Alderley, GL12 7QT. ☎ (01453) 843258 • Map 172,162/770905 • BB **B/C** • S1 D1 T/F1 • 1-12 NX • ⒷⒹⓅⓉ🛁 • 2Cr/C • Food nearby

Mrs P A Gallop, Warren Farm, Blackquarries Hill, GL12 7QE. ☎ (01453) 842212 • Map 172,162/772935 • BB **C** • EM book first £7.50, 7.30-8.30pm • S1 D1 T3 • 1-12 NX • ⓋⒷⒹⓈⓅⓉ

■ **YORKLEY (Forest of Dean)**

Glenview, Lower Road, GL15 4TH. ☎ 01594 562966 • Map 162/635074 • BB **B** • D2 F1 • 1-12 NX • ⒹⓈ ⓅⓉ🛁

HAMPSHIRE

■ **ANDOVER**

Mr & Mrs Norton, Staggs, Windmill Hill, Ibthorpe, Hurstbourne Tarrant, SP11 0BP. ☎ (01264) 736235 • Map 185/374536 • BB **B** • EM book first £7.50, 6-9pm • S1 D1 T1 • 1-12 NX • ⓋⒹⓅⓉ • ◆◆ • staggscottage@aol.com

■ **BARTON-ON-SEA (Christchurch)**

The Old Coastguard, 53 Marine Drive East, BH25 7DX. ☎ /Fax (01425) 612987 • Map 195/241929 • BB **C/D/E** • EM £15, 7pm • D4 T2 • 1-12 • ⓋⒷⒹⓈ ⓇⓅⓉ🛁 • ◆◆◆ • www.theoldcoastguard.fsnet.co.uk

■ **BROCKENHURST**

Pauline Harris, Little Heathers, 13 Whitemoor Road, SO42 7QG. ☎ (01590) 623512 • Map 196/287026 • BB **C/D** • D/S/T1 F1 • 1-12 NX • ⒷⒹⓈⓇⓅ Ⓣ🛁 • ◆◆◆Ⓢ • little_heathers@hotmail.com

■ **BURITON (Petersfield)**
SOUTH DOWNS WAY

Mrs M Bray, Nursted Farm, GU31 5RW. ☎ (01730) 264278 • Map 197/754214 • BB **B** • T3 F1 • 5-2 • Ⓑ ⒹⓈⓇⓅ

■ **BURLEY (Ringwood)**

Mrs G Russell, Charlwood, Longmead Road, BH24 4BY. ☎ (01425) 403242 • Map 195/205037 • BB **C** • D1 T1 • 1-11 • ⒹⓈ Ⓣ🛁 • ◆◆◆◆

■ **CADNAM (New Forest)**

Simon & Elaine Wright, Bushfriers, Winsor Road, Winsor, SO40 2HF. ☎ 023 80 812552 • Map 196/314144 • BB **C** • D1 T1 • 1-12 NX • ⒷⒹⓈ ⓅⓉ🛁 • Transport available.

■ **CHERITON (Alresford)**
SOUTH DOWNS WAY

Margaret Hoskings, Brandy Lea, SO24 0QQ. ☎ (01962) 771534 • Map 185/581283 • BB **A** • S1 T1 • 1-12 • Ⓑ Ⓓ🛁

Mrs Caroline Smith, Old Kennetts Cottage, SO24 0PX. ☎ (01962) 771863 • Map 185/583285 • BB **D** • D1 T1 • 1-12 NX • ⒷⒹⓈⓅⓉ

■ **DUMMER (Basingstoke)**

☆ Mrs E Hutton, Oakdown Farm, RG23 7LR. ☎ (01256) 397218 • Map 185/587472 • BB **B** • D1 T2 • 1-12 • ⒷⒹⓈⓅⓉ🛁Ⓜ • ◆◆◆

OAKDOWN FARM

Dummer, Basingstoke
Wayfarers Walk 200m
North of Junction 7 M3. Secluded position.
Evening meal locally.
Lifts available. Car parking.
Tel. Basingstoke (01256) 397218
ETC 3 diamonds.

■ **EAST MEON (Petersfield)**
SOUTH DOWNS WAY

Jenny d'Amato, Dunvegan Cottage, Frogmore Lane, GU32 1QJ. ☎ (01730) 823213 • Map 185/688217 • BB **B/C** • D2 T3 F1 • 1-12 NX • ⒷⒹⓈⓅⓉ🛁 • ◆◆◆ • dunvegan@btinternet.com

■ **FORDINGBRIDGE**

Mr & Mrs R Harte, Alderholt Mill, Sandleheath Road, SP6 1PU. ☎ (01425) 653130 • Map 195/119143 • BB **C** • EM book first £15, 7-8.30pm • S1 D3 T1 • 1-12 NX • ⒷⒹⓈⓅⓉ🛁 • ◆◆◆◆ • www.alderholtmill.co.uk

■ **HAMBLEDON (Waterlooville)**

Mr & Mrs Lutyens, Mornington House, PO7 4RU. ☎ 023 9263 2704 • Map 196/644149 • BB **B/C** • T2 • 1-12 NX • ⒹⓈⓉ🛁 • ◆◆◆ • Food nearby. On the Wayfarers Walk.

■ **HIGHCLERE (Newbury, Berks)**

Westridge Open Centre, Andover Road, RG20 9PJ. ☎ (01635) 253322 • Map 174/436604 • BB **A** • S3 T1 • 1-12 NX • ⒹⓈⓉ • Extra for cooked breakfast. Closed public holidays

■ **KILMESTON**
SOUTH DOWNS WAY

Mrs J Cassey, Pond Cottage, SO24 0NL. ☎ 01962 771428 • Map 185/594257 • BB **B/C** • EM book first £12 • T1 • 1-12 NX • ⒷⓈⓅⓉ🛁

■ **KINGSCLERE (Newbury, Berks)**

Mrs S A Salm, Cleremede, Fox's Lane, RG20 5SL.
☎ (01635) 297298 • Map 174/521587 • BB **C** • D1 T2
• 1-12 • Ⓑ Ⓓ Ⓢ Ⓟ Ⓣ 🐾 • ◆◆◆◆ •
www.cleremede.co.uk

■ **LYMINGTON**

☆ Our Bench, Lodge Road, Pennington, SO41 8HH.
☎ (01590) 673141 • Map 196/307953 • BB **C** • EM
book first £10, 6.30pm • S1 D1 T1 • 1-12 NX • Ⓥ Ⓑ
Ⓓ Ⓢ Ⓡ Ⓟ Ⓣ • ◆◆◆◆ • www.ourbench.co.uk

Mrs Paula Farrell, Honeysuckle House, 24 Clinton
Road, SO41 9EA. ☎ (01590) 6766355 • Map
196/321962 • BB **C** • D1 • 3-10 • Ⓑ Ⓢ Ⓡ Ⓟ Ⓣ🐾 •
skyblue@beeb.net

■ **LYNDHURST (New Forest)**

☆ Paul Ames, Ormonde House Hotel, Southampton
Road, SO43 7BT. ☎ 023 8028 2806 • Map
196/305083 • BB **D** • EM £13-£16, 6.30-8pm • S1
D10 T8 F1 • 1-12 NX • Ⓥ Ⓑ Ⓓ Ⓢ Ⓡ Ⓟ Ⓣ🐾 •
◆◆◆◆ • www.ormondehouse.co.uk

William & Mary Dibben, Stable End, Emery Down,
SO43 7FJ. ☎ 023 8028 2504 • Map 196/290089 • BB
D • D1 T1 • 1-12 • Ⓑ Ⓓ Ⓢ Ⓣ • ◆◆◆ • dibben-
fam@aol.com

The Penny Farthing Hotel, Romsey Road, SO43 7AA.
☎ 023 8028 4422 • Map 196/298082 • BB **E** • S1 D9
T3 F2 • 1-12 NX • Ⓑ Ⓓ Ⓢ Ⓣ🐾 • ◆◆◆◆ •
www.pennyfarthinghotel.co.uk

■ **MEDSTEAD (Alton)**
THREE CASTLES WALK

Mrs Gill Siddall, Peachings, South Town Road, GU34
5ES. ☎ (01420) 564339 • Map 185,186/658360 • BB
C • EM book first £10, 7pm • S2 T1 • 1-12 NX • Ⓑ
Ⓓ Ⓢ Ⓟ Ⓣ Ⓜ • Pilgrims Way close by.

■ **NEW MILTON**

Mr & Mrs M Pearce, St Ursula, 30 Hobart Road,
BH25 6EG. ☎ (01425) 613515 • Map 195/239947 •
BB **C** • EM N • S2 D1 T2 F1 • 1-12 • Ⓑ Ⓓ Ⓢ Ⓡ ..
Ⓟ Ⓣ🐾 • ◆◆◆ • Access Cat 3.

■ **PETERSFIELD**
SOUTH DOWNS WAY

Mrs B West, Ridgefield, Station Road, GU32 3DE.
☎ (01730) 261402 • Map 197/743237 • BB **C** • D1 T2
• 1-12 NX • Ⓓ Ⓢ Ⓡ • ◆◆ • ymcokw@hants.gov.uk

Mrs P Scurfield, Heath Farmhouse, GU31 4HU. ☎
(01730) 264709 • Map 197/757224 • BB **B/C** • EM
book first £10, 7.30-8pm • D1 T1 F1 • 1-12 NX • Ⓥ
Ⓑ Ⓓ Ⓢ Ⓡ Ⓣ🐾 • ◆◆◆ • pruesc@waitrose.com

■ **RINGWOOD**

Mrs M Burt, Fraser House, Salisbury Road,
Blashford, BH24 3PB. ☎ /Fax (01425) 473958 • Map
195/149068 • BB **C/D** • D2 T2 • 1-12 • Ⓑ Ⓓ Ⓢ Ⓟ
Ⓣ🐾 • ◆◆◆

■ **ROMSEY (New Forest)**

☆ Mr & Mrs Hilsley, Abbey Hotel, 11 Church Street,
SO51 8BT. ☎ (01794) 513360 • Map 185/351212 •
BB **D/E** • EM £13, 6.30-9.30pm • S2 D3 T1 F1 • 1-12
NX • Ⓥ Ⓑ Ⓓ Ⓡ Ⓟ Ⓣ🐾 • ◆◆◆ •
di@abbeyhotelromsey.co.uk

☆ See Display Advertisement

■ ROMSEY (continued)

Mrs Christina Pybus, Pyesmead Farm, Plaitford, SO51 6EE. ☎ (01794) 323386 • Map 184/280193 • BB **B/C** • D2 T1 • 1-12 NX • Ⓑ Ⓓ Ⓢ Ⓣ 🐾 • ◆◆◆ • pyesmead@talk21.com

■ SELBORNE (Alton)

Mrs Judy Thompstone, Thatched Barn House, Grange Farm, Gracious Street, GU34 3JG. ☎ (01420) 511007 • Map 186/738339 • BB **C** • D1 T1 • 1-12 NX • Ⓓ Ⓢ Ⓟ 🐾 • ◆◆◆◆ • www.bobt.dircon.co.uk

■ SOBERTON (Droxford, Southampton)

Rosemary Taylor, Moortown Farm, Station Road, SO32 3QU. ☎ (01489) 877256 • Map 185/612179 • BB **C** • T1 F1 • 1-12 NX • Ⓑ Ⓓ Ⓢ Ⓣ • List/C

■ SOUTHSEA

Glenroy Guest House, 28 Waverley Road, PO5 2PW. ☎ 023 9281 4922 • Map 196/650985 • BB **B** • S2 D2 T2 F2 • 1-12 • Ⓑ Ⓓ Ⓡ Ⓣ • ◆◆

■ STOCKBRIDGE

Carbery Guest House, Salisbury Hill, SO20 6EZ. ☎ (01264) 810771 • Map 185/350351 • BB **D** • EM book first £14, 7pm • S4 D3 T2 F2 • 1-11 NX • Ⓥ Ⓓ Ⓟ Ⓣ • ◆◆◆

■ WINCHESTER
THREE CASTLES WALK & SOUTH DOWNS WAY

Mrs A Farrell, 5 Ranelagh Road, SO23 9TA. ☎ (01962) 869555 • Map 185/476286 • BB **C** • S1 D1 T1 F1 • 1-12 NX • Ⓑ Ⓓ Ⓢ Ⓡ Ⓣ Ⓜ • 2Cr/C • thefarrells@easicom.com

Mrs S Pell, The Lilacs, 1 Harestock Close, off Andover Road North, SO22 6NP. ☎ (01962) 884122 • Map 185/468321 • BB **B** • D/F1 T1 • 1-12 NX • Ⓑ Ⓓ Ⓢ Ⓡ Ⓟ Ⓣ • www.smoothhound.co.uk/hotels/lilacs.html

Mrs S Tisdall, 32 Hyde Street, SO23 7DX. ☎ (01962) 851621 • Map 185/480300 • BB **B** • D1 F1 • 1-12 NX • Ⓢ Ⓡ Ⓣ • Secure cycle storage

The Wessex Centre, Sparsholt College, Sparsholt, SO21 2NF. ☎ (01962) 797259 • Map 185/424320 • BB **C** • EM book first £10.50, 6-7.30pm • S295 D1 T20 • 4, 6-9 • Ⓥ Ⓑ Ⓓ Ⓢ Ⓟ Ⓣ • ★★Ⓢ • Groups of 10 or more • www.thewessexcentre.co.uk

☆ Mrs Kathy Pollock, Shawlands, 46 Kilham Lane, SO22 5QD. ☎ (01962) 861166 • Map 185/456288 • BB **C** • D1 T2 F1 • 1-12 NX • Ⓑ Ⓓ Ⓢ Ⓡ Ⓣ 🐾 • ◆◆◆◆

HEREFORD & WORCESTER

■ ALMELEY (Kington)

☆ Gwenda Hames, Almeley House, Almeley, HR3 6LB. ☎ (01544) 327269 • Map 148,149/332515 • BB **C/D** • D2 T1 • 1-12 NX • Ⓑ Ⓓ Ⓟ Ⓣ 🐾 • gwenda@hamesg.freeserve.co.uk

■ ASHTON UNDER HILL (Evesham)

M Sanger-Davies, Holloway Farm House, WR11 6SN. ☎ (01386) 881910 • Map 150/998382 • BB **C** • EM book first £12, 7.30pm • D1 T1 • 1-12 NX • Ⓑ Ⓓ Ⓟ Ⓣ 🐾 • mike.sangerdavies@btinternet.com

■ BEWDLEY (Worcestershire)

Mrs P A Grainger, Lightmarsh Farm, Crundalls Lane, DY12 1NE. ☎ (01299) 404027 • Map 138/788768 • BB **C/E** • D1 T1 • 1-12 NX • Ⓑ Ⓓ Ⓢ Ⓡ Ⓟ Ⓣ • ◆◆◆◆ • Steam railway - seasonal

Fleur Nightingale, Bank House, 14 Lower Park, DY12 2DP. ☎ (01299) 402652 • Map 138/789754 • BB **C** • EM N • S1 T1 F1 • 1-12 NX • Ⓓ Ⓢ Ⓟ Ⓣ • ◆◆◆

Mrs T Beves, Tarn, Longbank, DY12 2QT. ☎ (01299) 402243 • Map 138/764749 • BB **C** • S2 T2 • 2-11 • Ⓓ Ⓢ Ⓟ ♨ • Transport available.

■ BISHOPSTONE
WYE VALLEY WALK

Maggie Reohorn, Fairlands, HR4 7HX. ☎ 01981 590374 • Map 161,148,149/422430 • BB **B** • EM book first £12, 7pm • D2 • 1-12 • Ⓥ Ⓑ Ⓓ Ⓢ Ⓟ Ⓣ Ⓜ

■ BREDWARDINE (Hereford)
WYE VALLEY WALK

Mrs Sue Whittall, Old Court Farm, HR3 6BT. ☎ (01981) 500375 • Map 161,148,149/335445 • BB **C** • EM book first £18, 7-7.30pm • D2 T1 F1 • 1-12 NX • Ⓥ Ⓑ Ⓓ Ⓢ Ⓟ Ⓣ • ◆◆◆ • SC also. On River Wye

■ BROADWAY
COTSWOLD WAY

Olive Branch Guest House, 78 High Street, WR12 7AJ. ☎ (01386) 853440 • Map 150/098375 • BB **D/E** • EM book first £ • S1 D2 T3 F2 • -12 • Ⓑ Ⓢ Ⓟ Ⓣ ♨ • 3Cr/C • SC also • broadway@theolive-branch.co.uk

Southwold House, Station Road, WR12 7DE. ☎ (01386) 853681 • Map 150/091378 • BB **D** • S1 D4 T2 F1 • 1-12 NX • Ⓥ Ⓑ Ⓓ Ⓢ Ⓣ ♨ • ◆◆◆◆ • sueandnick.southwold@talk21.com

Adrian & Sandy, Pathlow House, 82 High Street, WR12 7AJ. ☎ (01386) 853444 • Map 150/101376 • BB **C** • EM £10, 6.30-7.30pm • D5 T3 F2 • 1-12 • Ⓥ Ⓑ Ⓓ Ⓢ Ⓟ Ⓣ ♨ • ◆◆◆ • pathlow@aol.com

☆ Mr Andrew Scott, Crown & Trumpet Inn, Church Street, WR12 7AE. ☎ (01386) 853202 • Map 150/095374 • BB **D** • EM £5-£8, 6.15pm • D3 T1 • 1-12 • Ⓥ Ⓑ Ⓣ ♨ • ◆◆◆ • www.cotswoldholidays.co.uk

Frank Allen, Whiteacres, Station Road, WR12 7DE. ☎ (01386) 852320 • Map 150/099374 • BB **D** • D4 T1 • 1-12 NX • Ⓑ Ⓓ Ⓢ Ⓣ ♨ • ◆◆◆◆ • whiteacres@btinternet.com

S & R Pinder, Windrush House, Station Road, WR12 7DE. ☎ (01386) 853577 • Map 150/090380 • BB **C** • EM book first £12.00, 7-8pm • D4 T1 • 1-12 • Ⓥ Ⓑ Ⓓ Ⓢ Ⓟ Ⓣ ♨ • ◆◆◆◆ • www.broadway-windrush.co.uk

■ BROMYARD

Simon & Penny Gardiner, Parkhouse, 28 Sherford Street, HR7 4DL. ☎ (01885) 482294 • Map 149/656545 • BB **C** • EM book first £12, 7-9pm • T3 F1 • 1-12 • Ⓥ Ⓑ Ⓓ Ⓢ Ⓟ Ⓣ ♨ • www.bromyard.co.uk/parkhouse

■ BYFORD (Hereford)
WYE VALLEY WALK

Mrs Audrey Mayson, Old Rectory, HR4 7LD. ☎ (01981) 590218 • Map 161,148,149/396429 • BB **C** • EM book first £, 7pm • D2 T1 • 3-10 • Ⓥ Ⓑ Ⓓ Ⓢ Ⓟ Ⓣ ♨ • www.smoothhound.co.uk/hotels/oldrectory2.html

■ COLWALL (Malvern)

Mrs Claire Adams, Brockhill Farm, Mathon Road, WR13 6EP. ☎ (01684) 540275 • Map 150/756437 • BB **B** • EM book first £12, until 8pm • D2 T1 • 1-12 • Ⓥ Ⓑ Ⓓ Ⓢ Ⓟ Ⓣ ♨ • www.brockhill.net

■ CROPTHORNE (Pershore)

Andrea & Malcolm Ward, The Cedars Guest House, Evesham Road (A44), WR10 3JU. ☎ (01386) 860219 • Map 150/997443 • BB **C** • D2 T2 F1 • 1-12 • Ⓑ Ⓓ Ⓢ Ⓣ • cedarsguesthouse@ukonline.co.uk

■ DILWYN (Leominster)

N J Perry, Conifers, 6 Orchard Close, HR4 8HQ. ☎ 01544 318125 • Map 148,149/416539 • BB **C** • EM book first £10, 7pm • S1 D1 • 2-12 • Ⓥ Ⓓ Ⓢ Ⓟ Ⓣ ♨ • national "Village of the Year 1999"

■ EVESHAM

Park View Hotel, Waterside, WR11 6BS. ☎ (01386) 442639 • Map 150/038433 • BB **C** • EM book first £10.75 (groups only) • S10 D5 T11 • 1-12 NX • Ⓥ Ⓓ Ⓢ Ⓡ Ⓟ ♨ • ◆◆◆ • superstay/co/uk

Mrs M W Addy, "Whitening Close", Arrow Lane, North Littleton, WR11 5QR. ☎ (01386) 832095 • Map 150/080473 • BB **B** • D2 T1 • 1-12 • Ⓑ Ⓓ Ⓢ Ⓣ Ⓜ • Cotswold walks arranged • overlooks Tythebarn (NT)

■ FOWNHOPE (Hereford)
WYE VALLEY WALK

Ann Corby, Pippins, Capler Lane, HR1 4PJ. ☎ (01432) 860677 • Map 149/581340 • BB **B** • T2 • 1-12 NX • Ⓑ Ⓓ Ⓢ Ⓟ Ⓣ

■ HEREFORD

Mrs Doreen Horne, Hopbine Hotel, Roman Road, HR1 1LE. ☎ (01432) 268722 • Map 149/512420 • BB **C** • S4 D6 T6 F4 • 1-12 • Ⓓ Ⓢ Ⓡ Ⓟ Ⓣ ♨ • ◆◆

☆ See Display Advertisement

■ **HERGEST (Kington)**
OFFA'S DYKE

Mrs E Protheroe, Bucks Head House, School Farm, HR5 3EW. ☎ (01544) 231063 • Map 148/262550 • BB **C** • EM £9-£9.50, 6.30-7pm • S2 D2 T1 F1 • 1-12 • Ⓥ Ⓓ Ⓟ Ⓣ 🐾 • SC also • clare@kc3.net

■ **HOARWITHY (Hereford)**
WYE VALLEY WALK

Val Gardner, Aspen House, HR2 6QP. ☎ (01432) 840353 • Map 149/543295 • BB **C** • D2 T1 • 1-12 • Ⓑ Ⓓ Ⓟ Ⓣ 🐾 • ◆◆◆◆ • hoarwithy@aol.com

■ **HUNTINGTON (Kington)**

Grace Watson, Hall's Mill House, HR5 3QA. ☎ (01497) 831409 • Map 148/255518 • BB **B/C** • EM book first £12, 7-8pm • D2 T1 • 1-12 NX • Ⓥ Ⓑ Ⓓ Ⓢ Ⓟ • ◆◆◆

■ **KINGSLAND (Leominster)**

☆ The Corners Inn, HR6 9RY. ☎ (01568) 708385 • Map 148,137,149/444615 • BB **E** • EM £7-12, 7-10pm • S3 D3 • 1-12 • Ⓥ Ⓑ Ⓓ Ⓢ Ⓟ Ⓣ • www.cornersinn.co.uk

The Corners Inn, Kingsland

Traditional black and white village inn dating back to early 16th century offering beautifully appointed en-suite accommodation, quality homemade food and traditional local beers and ciders.

Tel 01568 708385 Fax 01568 709033
www.cornersinn.co.uk
enq@cornersinn.co.uk

■ **KINGTON**
OFFA'S DYKE

☆ Burton Hotel, Mill Street, HR5 3BQ. ☎ (01544) 230323 • Map 148/296565 • BB **D** • EM £7.70-£15, from 7.30pm • S1 D6 T5 F3 • 1-12 • Ⓥ Ⓑ Ⓓ Ⓟ 🐾 • 4Cr/App • burton@hotelherefordshire.co.uk

BURTON HOTEL
Mill Street, Kington
Herefordshire HR5 3BQ

Fifteen large comfortable bedrooms, all with private bathroom, colour television, tea/coffee. Rambler's bar, lounge bar. Real Ales, real food in bars and restaurant. Packed lunches. Afternoon teas. Laundry services. Families welcomed. Special weekend breaks and group rates.

Tel Kington (01544) 230323
email burton@hotelherefordshire.co.uk

Mr & Mrs Darwin, Church House, Church Road, HR5 3AG. ☎ (01544) 230534 • Map 148/291567 • BB **C** • D1 T1 • 1-12 NX • Ⓓ Ⓢ Ⓟ 🐾 • darwin@kc3.co.uk

George & Barbara Johnston, The Swan Hotel, Church Street, HR5 3AZ. ☎ (01544) 230510 • Map 148/295567 • BB **C** • EM £7, 7-9pm • S6 D2 T1 F2 • 1-12 NX • Ⓥ Ⓑ Ⓓ Ⓢ Ⓟ Ⓣ 🐾 • Single lets available • rob.swan@talk21.com

Geoff & Patsy Cooper, Southbourne, Newton Lane, HR5 3NF. ☎ (01544) 231706 • Map 148/290570 • BB **B** • EM book first £9, 7pm • S1 D1 T1 • 1-12 NX • Ⓥ Ⓓ Ⓢ Ⓟ Ⓣ • Luggage transfer • Walking guide

■ **LEDBURY**

☆ Mrs Jane West, Church Farm, Coddington, HR8 1JJ. ☎ (01531) 640271 • Map 149/719426 • BB **C** • EM £13.00, 7pm • S1 D2 T1 • 2-12 NX • Ⓥ Ⓓ Ⓟ Ⓣ 🐾 • **C** • churchfarm1@hotmail.com

Church Farm
Coddington
☎ **01531 640271**
Share our lovely
16ᵗʰC listed home.

Working farm with quiet happy relaxed atmosphere • Evening meals, all home cooking by Aga • Log fires • Great walks • Malvern Hills • 20 years experience.

■ **LEOMINSTER**

Mrs J Ruell, Ladymeadow Farm, Luston, HR6 0AS. ☎ (01568) 780262 • Map 148,137,149,138/483645 • BB **B/C** • S1 D1 T1 F1 • 3-10 NX • Ⓑ Ⓓ Ⓢ Ⓣ • ◆◆◆ • Mortimer Trail & NT nearby

☆ Talbot Hotel, West Street, HR6 8EP. ☎ (01568) 616347 • Map 148,149/495590 • BB **C** • EM £6-18, 6.30-9.30pm • S2 D11 T7/11 F2 • 2-11+X • Ⓥ Ⓑ Ⓢ Ⓡ Ⓟ Ⓣ 🐾 • ★★★

The Talbot Hotel
Leominster - Herefordshire - HR6 8EP
3 Star AA/RAC/ETC Market Town Hotel.

Originally a 15th century coaching house sympathetically updated with ensuite bedrooms. Ideal location for ramblers visiting Herefordshire. Designated Black & White Trail through picturesque villages and beautiful countryside. Group rates offered for rambling club block bookings.

Enquiries & brochure telephone 01568 616347

Sylvia Davies, Chesfield, 112 South Street, HR6 8JF. ☎ (01568) 613204 • Map 148,149/495584 • BB **B/C** • D2 T1 F1 • 1-12 NX • Ⓑ Ⓓ Ⓢ Ⓡ Ⓟ Ⓣ 🐾 • ◆◆◆

■ **MALVERN**

☆ Sidney House, 40 Worcester Road, WR14 4AA. ☎ (01684) 574994 • Map 150/775463 • BB **C/D/E** • S1 D4 T2 F1 • 1-12 NX • Ⓑ Ⓓ Ⓢ Ⓡ Ⓟ 🐾 • ◆◆◆

Sue Reeves, Bredon House Hotel, 34 Worcester Road, WR14 4AA. ☎ (01684) 566990 • Map 150/775463 • BB **E** • EM book first £groups only • S2 D4 T2 F1 • 2-12 NX • Ⓥ Ⓑ Ⓓ Ⓡ Ⓟ Ⓣ ᴁ • ◆◆◆◆ • suereeves@bredonhousehotel.co.uk

Russeldene Hotel, 40 Priory Road, WR14 3DN. ☎ (01684) 562121 • Map 150/777454 • BB **D/E** • EM book first £18 (min 6), 7.30pm • S6 D3 T3 F2 • 1-12 • Ⓥ Ⓑ Ⓓ Ⓢ Ⓡ Ⓟ Ⓣ ᴁ • ◆◆◆ • Russeldene@aol.com

Oswald & Karen Dockery, The Malvern Hills Hotel, Wynds Point, WR13 6DW. ☎ (01684) 540690 • Map 150/765404 • BB **E** • EM £13.50, 6.30-9.30pm • S2 D7 T4 F2 • 1-12 • Ⓥ Ⓑ Ⓓ Ⓢ Ⓟ Ⓣ ᴁ • ★★★ • malhilhotl@aol.com

■ MUCH MARCLE (Ledbury)
WYE VALLEY WALK

Mrs Ann Jordan, New House Farm, HR8 2PH. ☎ (01531) 660604/674 • Map 149/640321 • BB **B** • EM book first £10 • D1 T1 F1 • 1-12 NX • Ⓥ Ⓑ Ⓓ Ⓟ Ⓣ • ◆◆◆ • Transport avail.

■ OMBERSLEY (Nr Droitwich)

Margaret Peters, Tytchney Gables, Boreley, WR9 0HZ. ☎ (01905) 620185 • Map 138, 150/825658 • BB **B** • S3 D1 T1 F1 • 1-12 • Ⓑ Ⓓ Ⓢ Ⓟ Ⓣ ᴁ

■ ROSS-ON-WYE

☆ Denise & Bob Robertson, Sunnymount Hotel, Ryefield Road, HR9 5LU. ☎ (01989) 563880 • Map 162/606242 • BB **D** • EM £12.50, 7pm • S1 D4 T2 • 1-12 • Ⓥ Ⓑ Ⓓ Ⓟ Ⓣ • ◆◆◆◆ • sunnymount@tinyworld.co.uk

☆ Vaga House, Wye Street, HR9 7BS. ☎ (01989) 563024 • Map 162/596241 • BB **B/C** • EM book first £4.25, 7pm • S1 D3 T2 F1 • 1-12 • Ⓥ Ⓑ Ⓓ Ⓟ Ⓣ ᴁ Ⓜ • ◆◆◆ • vagahouse@hotmail.com

Mrs Josephine Baker, Brookfield House, Overross Street, HR9 7AT. ☎ (01989) 562188 • Map 162/603246 • BB **C** • S2 D3 T3 • 1-12 NX • Ⓑ Ⓓ Ⓟ Ⓣ ᴁ • ◆◆◆ • www.brookfieldhouse.co.uk

Mrs S Bishop, Jollys, Goodrich, HR9 6HX. ☎ (01600) 890135 • Map 162/574194 • BB **C** • D2 T1 • 1-12 NX • Ⓑ Ⓓ Ⓢ Ⓟ Ⓣ ᴁ

■ STRETTON SUGWAS (Hereford)

New Priory Hotel, HR4 7AR. ☎ (01432) 760264 • Map 161,148,149/465429 • BB **D/E** • EM £7-10, 7-9pm • S2 D6 T1 F1 • 1-12 • Ⓥ Ⓓ Ⓡ Ⓟ Ⓣ ᴁ • ★ • newprioryhotel@ukonline.co.uk

■ TRUMPET (Ledbury)

Mrs Sally Lewis, Mainstone House, HR8 2RA. ☎ (01531) 670230 • Map 149/656396 • BB **B** • D1 T1 F1 • 1-12 NX • Ⓑ Ⓓ Ⓢ Ⓟ Ⓣ ᴁ • ◆◆◆

■ UPTON-UPON-SEVERN (Worcester)

E Denley, 1 Elm Villas, Holly Green, WR8 0PD. ☎ (01684) 592182 • Map 150/860410 • BB **B** • S1 D1 T1 F1 • 1-12 • Ⓥ Ⓑ Ⓢ Ⓣ ᴁ Ⓜ

■ VOWCHURCH

☆ Mrs Joyce Powell, The Old Vicarage, HR2 0QD. ☎ /fax (01981) 550357 • Map 161/370365 • BB **C/D** • EM book first £15, 7pm • S1 D2 T/F1 • 1-12 NX • Ⓥ Ⓑ Ⓓ Ⓢ Ⓟ Ⓣ ᴁ • ◆◆◆◆Ⓢ • www.golden-valley.co.uk/vicarage

■ WALTERSTONE
OFFA'S DYKE

☆ Howard Williams, Allt yr Ynys Country Hotel, HR2 0DU. ☎ (01873) 890307 • Map 161/335234 • BB **E** • EM £15-20, 7-10pm • D11 T6 F2 • 1-12 • Ⓥ Ⓑ Ⓓ Ⓢ Ⓟ Ⓣ 🐾 • ★★★★ • allthotel@compuserve.com

❋ Stunning 16th century manor in secluded Welsh border countryside, close to Offa's Dyke Path, in the shadow of the Black Mountains.
❋ WTB 4-Star Country Hotel (nominated as WTB Welsh Hotel of the Year) and Les Routiers Welsh Hotel of the Year.
❋ Award winning restaurant, indoor pool, sauna, jacuzzi, shooting and fishing, golf, cycling, horse riding, and stunning scenery. Perfect base for excellent walking.
❋ Lifts arranged. Easy access from Hereford (20 min) and the M4 motorway (25 min).
❋ Warm welcome assured from Howard and Elaine Williams

Allt Yr Ynys Country Hotel
near Abergavenny, Walterstone, Herefordshire HR2 0DU
Tel: (01873) 890307 Fax: (01873) 890539
allhotel@compuserve.com   www.allhotel.co.uk

HERTFORDSHIRE

■ BISHOP'S STORTFORD (HERTS)
Pearse House, Parsonage Lane, CM23 5BQ. ☎ (01279) 757400 • Map 167/502217 • BB **E** • EM book first £9, 7-8.30pm • S23 D7 T5 F2 • 1-12 NX • Ⓥ Ⓑ Ⓓ Ⓢ Ⓡ Ⓟ Ⓣ • ◆◆◆ • pearsehouse@route56.co.uk

■ HEMEL HEMPSTEAD
GRAND UNION CANAL WALK & CHILTERN WAY

Southville Private Hotel, 9 Charles Street, HP1 1JH. ☎ (01442) 251387 • Map 166/053066 • BB **C/D** • S10 D2 T6 F1 • 1-12 • Ⓡ 🐾 Ⓜ • List

ISLE OF WIGHT

■ BEMBRIDGE (Ryde)
ISLE OF WIGHT COAST PATH

Vi & Richard Beet, 'Sea Change', 22 Beachfield Rd, PO35 5TN. ☎ (01983) 878888 • Map 196/654875 • BB **C** • D2 T1 • 3-10 • Ⓑ Ⓢ Ⓟ Ⓣ • curzon@compuserve.com

■ BINSTEAD (Ryde)
ISLE OF WIGHT COAST PATH

Mrs Christine Hall, Elm Close Cottage, Ladies Walk, PO33 3SY. ☎ 01983 567161/0771 3540134 • Map 196/576928 • BB **B** • D2 T1 • 1-12 NX • Ⓑ Ⓓ Ⓢ Ⓡ Ⓟ Ⓣ • ◆◆◆◆ • elm_cottage@hotmail.com

■ BONCHURCH (Ventnor)
☆ The Lake Hotel, Shore Road, PO38 1RF. ☎ (01983) 852613 • Map 196/572778 • BB **D** • EM £8, 6.30-7pm • S2 D8 T6 F4 • 3-10 • Ⓥ Ⓑ Ⓓ Ⓢ Ⓟ Ⓣ 🐾 • ◆◆◆◆ • www.lakehotel.co.uk

VISITING BEAUTIFUL BONCHURCH?

THE LAKE HOTEL *offers comfortable double en-suite accommodation in charming country House Hotel in two acre garden. Residential bar and private car park. Run by the same family for the last 35 years. First class food and service assured.* ETC/RAC ◆◆◆◆

Bonchurch,
Isle of Wight PO38 1RF
Tel: (01983) 852613
www.lakehotel.co.uk
rambler@lakehotel.co.uk

4 NIGHT BREAK
INCLUDING CAR FERRY,
BREAKFAST & DINNER
(March/April/May).
£150.00 incl

■ BRIGHSTONE
ISLE OF WIGHT COAST PATH

Buddlebrook Guest House, Moortown Lane, PO30 4AN. ☎ (01983) 740381 • Map 196/426832 • BB **C** • D2 T1 • 1-12 • Ⓑ Ⓓ Ⓢ Ⓟ Ⓣ 🐾 • ◆◆◆ • SC also

■ CHALE (Ventnor)
ISLE OF WIGHT COAST PATH

Wendy Hardy, Yew Tree Cottage, PO38 2HL. ☎ (01983) 730660 • Map 196/482772 • BB **B** • S1 D2 • 3-10 • Ⓓ Ⓣ

Mrs E L Whittington, Cortina, Gotten Lane, PO38 2HQ. ☎ (01983) 551292 • Map 196/487791 • BB **B** • EM book first £6.50, 6.30pm • D1 T1 • 1-11 NX • Ⓥ Ⓓ Ⓢ • ◆◆◆

■ COWES
ISLE OF WIGHT COAST PATH

Mrs J Finch, Caledon Guest House, 59 Mill Hill Road, PO31 7EG. ☎ (01983) 293599 • Map 196/495956 • BB **B** • S2 D1 T1 F2 • 1-12 NX • Ⓓ Ⓢ Ⓣ 🐾

■ FRESHWATER
ISLE OF WIGHT COAST PATH

Brookside Forge Hotel, Brookside Road, PO40 9ER. ☎ (01983) 754644 • Map 196/336870 • BB **C** • EM book first £12, 7pm • S1 D2 T2 F2 • 1-12NX • Ⓑ Ⓢ 🐾 • ◆◆◆

Mr & Mrs C Murphy, The Traidcraft Shop, 119 School Green Road, PO40 9AZ. ☎ (01983) 752451 • Map 196/340870 • BB **B** • D1 T1 • 1-11 • Ⓓ Ⓢ Ⓣ Ⓜ • chris.murphy@freshwater20008.freeserve.co.uk

☆ Wendy & Peter Tayler, Rockstone Cottage Hotel, Colwell Chine Road, PO40 9NR. ☎ (01983) 753723 • Map 196/329876 • BB **C** • EM book first £14, 6.30-7pm • S1 D5 F1 • 1-12 • ⓥ Ⓑ Ⓓ Ⓢ Ⓟ Ⓣ • ◆◆◆◆ • www.rockstonecottage.co.uk

Farringford Hotel, Bedbury Lane, PO40 9PE. ☎ (01983) 752500 • Map 196/337861 • BB **E** • EM £19.95, 7.30-9.30pm • S3 D8 T4 F4 • 1-12 • ⓥ Ⓑ Ⓓ Ⓟ Ⓣ ⛤ • ★★★ • enquiries@farringford.co.uk

■ FRESHWATER BAY (Freshwater)
ISLE OF WIGHT COAST PATH

Karen Clements, The Firs, The Square, PO40 9QH. ☎ (01983) 756365 • Map 196/343860 • BB **D** • D2 T2 • 3-1 NX • Ⓑ Ⓢ Ⓟ Ⓣ ⛤

■ RYDE
ISLE OF WIGHT COAST PATH

Rowantrees, 63 Spencer Road, PO33 3AF. ☎ (01983) 568081 • Map 196/585926 • BB **B** • S2 D1 F1 • 1-12 NX • Ⓓ Ⓡ ⛤ Ⓜ • SC also

■ SHALFLEET (Newport)
ISLE OF WIGHT COASTAL PATH

M Young, The Old Malthouse, 1 Mill Road, PO30 4NE. ☎ (01983) 531329 • Map 196/414892 • BB **B** • D1 F1 • 1-12 NX • Ⓑ Ⓓ Ⓢ • ◆◆ • Food nearby

■ SHANKLIN
ISLE OF WIGHT COAST PATH

☆ Mrs P Metcalf, Culham Lodge, 31 Landguard Manor Road, PO37 7HZ. ☎ (01983) 862880 • Map 196/580820 • BB **C** • EM book first £7, 6pm • S1 D4 T5 • 1-12 NX • ⓥ Ⓑ Ⓓ Ⓢ Ⓡ Ⓟ Ⓣ Ⓜ • ◆◆◆◆ • metcalf@culham99.freeserve.co.uk

☆ John Sewell, Hambledon Hotel, Queens Road, PO37 6AW. ☎ (01983) 862403 • Map 196/584814 • BB **C** • EM book first £11, 6.30-7.00pm • S1 D5 T2 F2 • 1-11 • ⓥ Ⓑ Ⓓ Ⓢ Ⓡ ⛤ • ★★Ⓢ • Walking hols also • www.hambledon-hotel.co.uk

Chris & Molly Bland, Atholl Court, 1 Atherley Road, PO37 7AT. ☎ (01983) 862414 • Map 196/582818 • BB **B** • EM book first £6, 6pm • S3 D3 T3 • 3-10 • ⓥ Ⓑ Ⓓ Ⓢ Ⓡ Ⓟ Ⓣ • ◆◆◆ • info@antoll-court.co.uk

☆ Barry & Alison O'Sullivan, The Edgecliffe Hotel, Clarence Gardens, PO37 6HA. ☎ 01983 866199 • Map 196/585820 • BB **C** • EM book first £9.95, 6.30pm • S2 D7 T3 F3 • 1-12 • ⓥ Ⓑ Ⓓ Ⓢ Ⓡ Ⓟ Ⓣ • ◆◆◆◆ • edgeliffe-hotel@nationwide.sp-net • See next page for display advert.

Jonathan & Cheryl Rome, Farringford Hotel, 19 Hope Road, PO37 6EA. ☎ 01983 862176 • Map 196/585818 • BB **C** • EM book first £8, 6pm • S1 D4 T1 F1 • 1-12 NX • ⓥ Ⓑ Ⓓ Ⓢ Ⓡ Ⓟ Ⓣ ⛤ • ◆◆◆◆ • Groups also • www.netguides.co.uk/wight/farr-shanklin

☆ Rita & Les Burrows, St Leonards Hotel, 22 Queens Road, PO37 6AW. ☎ (01983) 862121 • Map 196/584814 • BB **C** • EM £8, 18pm • S1 D2 T1 F3 • 1-12 NX • ⓥ Ⓑ Ⓓ Ⓡ Ⓟ Ⓣ • ◆◆◆◆ • www.wight-breaks.co.uk • See next page for display advert.

■ TOTLAND BAY
ISLE OF WIGHT COAST PATH

Jacquie Simmonds, Norton Lodge, Granville Road, PO39 0AZ. ☎ (01983) 752772 • Map 196/325871 • BB **A/B** • D1 T1 F1 • 1-12 • B D T • 1Cr

■ VENTNOR
ISLE OF WIGHT COAST PATH

☆ Mick & Nava Young, St Andrew's Hotel, Belgrave Road, PO38 1JH. ☎ (01983) 852680 • Map 196/560773 • BB **C** • EM book first £10, 6.30-7.15pm • D5 T3 F2 • 1-10+X • V B D S P T • ◆◆◆ • Groups also

■ YARMOUTH
ISLE OF WIGHT COAST PATH

Mrs J Manfield, St Hilda, Victoria Road, PO41 0QW. ☎ (01983) 760814 • Map 196/356895 • BB **B** • D1 T1 • 3-10 • V D T 🐾 • SC also

Wavells B&B, Wavells Fine Foods, The Square, PO41 0NP. ☎ 01983 760738 • Map 196/355896 • BB **B/C/D** • D1 T1 F1 • 1-12 • B D S P T • No children under 8. Credit cards accepted

KENT

■ APPLEDORE
SAXON SHORE WAY

Mrs Belinda Massey, Horne's Place, TN26 2BS. ☎ (01233) 758305 • Map 189/957307 • BB **C** • EM book first £17.50, 7.30pm • D1 T1 • 1-12 NX • V B D S P T 🐾 • ◆◆◆

■ ASH (Canterbury)

Mrs J Smith, 55 Guilton, CT3 2HR. ☎ (01304) 812809 • Map 179/279582 • BB **B** • EM book first £7.50, 7pm • D2 • 1-12 NX • B S R T

■ ASHFORD
GREENSAND WAY

Mrs A Tucker, Quantock House, Quantock Drive, TN24 8QH. ☎ (01233) 638921 • Map 189/006434 • BB **C** • S1 D1 T1 • 1-12 NX • B D S R T • ◆◆◆

Warren Cottage Hotel, 136 The Street, Willesborough, TN24 0NB. ☎ (01233) 621905 • Map 189,179/034422 • BB **D** • EM book first £12, 6-7.30pm • S1 D3 T1 F1 • 1-12 • V B S R P T 🐾 • ◆◆◆ • www.warrencottage.co.uk

■ ASHURST (Tunbridge Wells)
WEALDWAY

Mrs J Soyke , Manor Court Farm, Stonecross, TN3 9TB. ☎ (01892) 740279 • Map 188/520390 • BB **C** • D1 T2 • 1-12 NX • B D S R P T 🐾 • ◆◆◆ • Camping also • jsoyke@jsoyke.freeserve.co.uk

■ BEARSTED (Maidstone)
NORTH DOWNS WAY

Carol & Ian Buse, The Hazels, 13 Yeoman Way, ME15 8PQ. ☎ (01622) 737943 • Map 188/795549 • BB **C** • T1 • 1-12 • B D S R P T • ◆◆◆◆ • dbuse@totalise.co.uk

■ BILSINGTON (Ashford)
SAXON SHORE WAY & GREENSAND WAY

Mrs Hopper, Willow Farm, Stone Cross, TN25 7JJ. ☎ (01233) 720484 • Map 189/028366 • BB **C/D** • EM book first £7.50 • S1 D1 T1 F1 • 1-12 NX • Ⓥ Ⓓ Ⓢ Ⓟ • ◆◆ • renee@willow-farm.freeserve.co.uk

■ BLADBEAN (Dover)

Mrs Min Barham, Molehills, CT4 6LU. ☎ (01303) 840051 • Map 189,179/179471 • BB **C** • EM book first £7, 7pm • D1 T1 • 1-12 NX • Ⓥ Ⓑ Ⓓ Ⓢ Ⓟ Ⓣ 🐾 • ◆◆◆◆ • molehills84@hotmail.com

■ CANTERBURY

Mr & Mrs Cabrini, London Guest House, 14 London Road, CT2 8LR. ☎ (01227) 765860 • Map 179/142584 • BB **C** • S2 D1 T2 F1 • 1-12 • Ⓓ Ⓡ Ⓣ • ◆◆◆ • londonguesthousecabnkz@supanet.com

Castle Court Guest House, 8 Castle Street, CT1 2QF. ☎ (01227) 463441 • Map 179/148576 • BB **C** • S2 D3 T3 F2 • 1-12 • Ⓑ Ⓓ Ⓢ Ⓡ Ⓟ Ⓣ 🐾 • ◆◆ • guesthouse@castlecourt.fsnet.co.uk

Mrs J Wright, Milton House, 9 South Canterbury Road, CT1 3LH. ☎ (01227) 765531 • Map 179/150567 • BB **B** • D1 T1 • 1-12 NX • Ⓓ Ⓢ Ⓡ Ⓣ 🐾 • List

Cathedral Gate Hotel, 36 Burgate, CT1 2HA. ☎ (01227) 464381 • Map 179/150578 • BB **C/D/E** • EM £7.25-£12.50, 7-9pm • S6 D9 T7 F5 • 1-12 • Ⓥ Ⓑ Ⓓ Ⓢ Ⓡ Ⓟ Ⓣ 🐾 • ◆◆◆ • cgate@cgate.demon.co.uk

Michelle & John Mercer, Little Courtney, 5 Whitstable Rd, St Dunstans, CT2 8DG. ☎ (01227) 454207 • Map 179/142584 • BB **B/C** • S1 T2 • 1-12 • Ⓓ Ⓡ Ⓟ Ⓣ 🐾

Keith & Anthea Rishworth, Oriel Lodge, 3 Queen's Avenue, CT2 8AY. ☎ (01227) 462845 • Map 179/143580 • BB **C/D** • S1 D3 T1 F1 • 1-12 • Ⓑ Ⓢ Ⓣ • ◆◆◆◆Ⓢ • www.oriel-lodge.co.uk

■ CAPEL-LE-FERNE (Folkstone)
NORTH DOWNS WAY

Mrs D Strutt, Xaipe, 18 Alexandra Road, CT18 7LD. ☎ (01303) 257956 • Map 179/252385 • BB **B** • D1 T1 • 3-10 • Ⓓ Ⓢ Ⓟ Ⓜ

■ CHALLOCK (Ashford)
NORTH DOWNS WAY

Mrs Frieda Nightingale, 'Orchards', Pested Lane, TN25 4BD. ☎ (01233) 740423 • Map 189/009516 • BB **C** • S1 D1 T1 • 1-12 NX • Ⓑ Ⓓ Ⓟ Ⓣ • ◆◆◆

■ CHARING (Ashford)
NORTH DOWNS WAY

E & R Bigwood, Timber Lodge, Charing Hill, TN27 0NG. ☎ (01233) 712822 • Map 189/959499 • BB **C** • EM book first £5-£10, 7.15pm • S/ D1 F1 • 1-12 NX • Ⓥ Ⓑ Ⓓ Ⓢ Ⓡ Ⓟ Ⓣ • ◆◆◆◆

Mrs Margaret Micklewright, 23 The Moat, TN27 0JH. ☎ (01233) 713141 • Map 189/955492 • BB **C** • T1 • 4-10 • Ⓑ Ⓓ Ⓢ Ⓡ Ⓣ Ⓜ

■ CHILHAM (Canterbury)
NORTH DOWNS WAY

Mrs J Dodd, Bagham Cross Cottages B&B, CT4 8DU. ☎ (01227) 730264 • Map 189,179/070536 • BB **C** • D1 T2 F1 • 4-10 • Ⓓ Ⓢ Ⓡ Ⓟ Ⓣ Ⓜ • cft-jdodds@supanet.com

Elisabeth Dyke, Folly House, CT4 8DU. ☎ 01227 738669 • Map 179/189/070536 • BB **E** • EM book first £12, 7pm • S1 D2 T1 • 1-12 NX • Ⓥ Ⓑ Ⓓ Ⓢ Ⓡ Ⓟ Ⓣ 🐾 • ◆◆◆◆

■ CLIFTONVILLE

Mr N A Shilling, 8 Gloucester Avenue, CT9 3NW. ☎ 01843 221220 • Map 179/375707 • BB **B** • EM £12, 7-8.30pm • S2 D2 T0 F0 • 1-12 • Ⓥ Ⓑ Ⓓ Ⓡ Ⓟ Ⓣ

■ CRANBROOK

Mrs D M Waddoup, The Hollies, Old Angley Road, TN17 2PN. ☎ (01580) 713106 • Map 188/775367 • BB **C** • EM book first £10, 7.00pm • S1 T1 F1 • 1-12 NX • Ⓑ Ⓓ Ⓢ Ⓟ Ⓣ 🐾

■ DEAL
SAXON SHORE WAY

Mrs Stobie, Ilex Cottage, Temple Way, Worth, CT14 0DA. ☎ (01304) 617026 • Map 179/335560 • BB **C** • D1 T1 F1 • 1-12 NX • Ⓑ Ⓓ Ⓢ Ⓡ Ⓟ 🐾 • ◆◆◆◆ • info@ilexcottage.com

■ DOVER
NORTH DOWNS WAY & SAXON SHORE WAY

Amanda Guest House, 4 Harold Street, CT16 1SF. ☎ (01304) 201711 • Map 179/320418 • BB **B** • D1 T2 F2 • 1-12 NX • Ⓑ Ⓓ Ⓢ Ⓡ • ◆◆◆ • pageant@port-of-dover.com

M J Casey, Bleriot's, 47 Park Avenue, CT16 1HE. ☎ (01304) 211394 • Map 179/316422 • BB **B/C** • S1 D3 T2 F2 • 1-12 NX • Ⓑ Ⓢ Ⓡ Ⓣ • ◆◆

☆ Alistair & Betty Dimech, Cleveland Guest House, 2 Laureston Place, CT16 1QX. ☎ (01304) 204622 • Map 179/322416 • BB **C** • EM book first £12.50, 7-8.30pm • D3 T1 F2 • 1-12 NX • Ⓥ Ⓑ Ⓓ Ⓡ 🐾 • ◆◆◆ • albetcleve@aol.com • See next page for display advert.

■ DYMCHURCH (Romney Marsh)

Waterside Guest House, 15 Hythe Road, TN29 0LN. ☎ (01303) 872253 • Map 189/105298 • BB **C/D** • EM £4.50, 5.30-8pm • D2 T2 F1 • 1-12 • Ⓥ Ⓑ Ⓓ Ⓟ Ⓣ • ◆◆◆◆ • www.smoothhound.co.uk/hotels/waterside.html

☆ See Display Advertisement

KENT

ENGLAND

B&B ACCOMMODATION

■ **FAVERSHAM**
SAXON SHORE WAY

Alan & Catherine Turner, Preston Lea, Canterbury Road, ME13 8XA. ☎ (01795) 535266 • Map 178/021604 • BB **D** • D1 T2 • 1-12 • Ⓑ Ⓓ Ⓢ Ⓡ Ⓟ Ⓣ • ◆◆◆◆Ⓢ • homepages.which.net/~alan.turner10

■ **FOLKESTONE**
NORTH DOWNS WAY

Normandie Guest House, 39 Cheriton Road, CT20 1DD. ☎ (01303) 256233 • Map 189,179/225360 • BB **B** • S1 D1 T2 F2 • 1-12 NX • Ⓢ Ⓡ Ⓣ

Abbey House Hotel, 5-6 Westbourne Gardens, (off Sandgate Road), CT20 2JA. ☎ (01303) 255514 • Map 189,179/217355 • BB **C** • EM book first £7, 6-7pm • S3 D3 T4 F4 • 1-12 • Ⓥ Ⓑ Ⓓ Ⓢ Ⓡ 🐾 • Groups also

Wycliffe Hotel, Mr & Mrs Shorland, 63 Bouverie Road West, CT20 2RN. ☎ (01303) 252186 • Map 189,179/219357 • BB **B** • EM book first £9, 6.30pm • S2 D5 T4 F2 • 1-12 • Ⓥ Ⓑ Ⓓ Ⓢ Ⓡ Ⓟ Ⓣ 🐾 • visitus.co.uk/bnbhtm/wycliffe

■ **GODMERSHAM (Canterbury)**
NORTH DOWNS WAY

☆ Maud Long, Waggoners Lodge, Eggarton Lane, CT4 7DY. ☎ (01227) 731118 • Map 189,179/072508 • BB **C** • EM book first £15, 7.30pm • D2 T1 • 1-12 • Ⓥ Ⓓ Ⓡ Ⓟ Ⓣ 🐾 • ◆◆◆ • maud@waggoners.freeserve.co.uk

■ **HARRIETSHAM (Maidstone)**
NORTH DOWNS WAY

Mrs Barbara Beveridge, 14 Chippendayle Drive, ME17 1AD. ☎ (01622) 858698 • Map 189/870527 • BB **C** • S1 D1 T2 • 1-12 NX • Ⓑ Ⓓ Ⓢ Ⓡ Ⓣ • johnbtaylor@homestay14.freeserve.co.uk

■ **HERNE BAY**
SAXON SHORE WAY

☆ Foxden, 5 Landon Road, off Beltinge Road, CT6 6HP. ☎ (01227) 363514 • Map 179/190680 • BB **C** • S2 D2 • 1-12 • Ⓑ Ⓓ Ⓢ Ⓡ Ⓣ 🐾 • ◆◆◆◆

Hobbit Hole, 41a Pigeon Lane, Herne, CT6 7ES. ☎ (01227) 368155 • Map 179/185669 • BB **C** • S1 D1 T1 F1 • 1-12 • Ⓥ Ⓑ Ⓓ Ⓢ Ⓡ Ⓜ • ◆◆◆ • Food nearby • hobhole@aol.com

■ **OTFORD (Sevenoaks)**
NORTH DOWNS WAY

Mr G A Levien, Moat Bungalow, Station Road, TN14 5QU. ☎ (01959) 524165 • Map 188/530590 • BB **B** • S1 T1 • 1-12 NX • Ⓓ Ⓢ Ⓡ 🐾 • Food nearby

Mrs C M Hord, 24a Pilgrims Way East, TN14 5QN. ☎ (01959) 523743 • Map 188/536593 • BB **C** • S2 T1 • 1-11 • Ⓥ Ⓑ Ⓓ Ⓢ Ⓡ Ⓟ Ⓣ • List • 100 yards from North Downs Way path • hord@globalnet.co.uk

Mrs Patricia Smith, 9 Warham Road, TN14 5PF. ☎ (01959) 523596 • Map 188/526590 • BB **C** • S1 D1 T1 • 1-12 NX • Ⓓ Ⓢ Ⓡ Ⓟ Ⓣ 🐾 • ◆◆ • Food nearby

■ **PLUCKLEY (Ashford)**
GREENSAND WAY

Jean Johnson, Miller's Mount, TN27 0SL. ☎ (01233) 840683 • Map 189/924454 • BB **B** • T1 • 1-12 NX • Ⓑ Ⓓ Ⓢ Ⓡ Ⓣ 🐾 Ⓜ • SC also

Veronica Johnson, Yew Tree Cottage, TN27 0QT. ☎ 01233 840547 • Map 189/926454 • BB **B** • EM book first £12, by arrangement • D1 F1 • 4-9 • Ⓥ Ⓑ Ⓓ Ⓢ Ⓡ Ⓟ Ⓣ

■ **RYARSH (West Malling)**
WEALDWAY & NORTH DOWNS WAY

Mrs J Edwards, Heavers Farm, Chapel Lane, ME19 5JU. ☎ (01732) 842074 • Map 177/665603 • BB **B** • EM book first £8-£15, 7.30pm • D1 T2 • 1-12 NX • Ⓥ Ⓓ Ⓢ Ⓟ Ⓣ🐾 • www.kentbedandbreakfast.co.uk

■ **SANDWICH**
SAXON SHORE WAY

Mrs R A Pettican, Le Trayas, Poulders Road, CT13 0BB. ☎ (01304) 611056 • Map 179/322576 • BB **B/C/D** • D1 T2 • 1-12 • Ⓑ Ⓓ Ⓢ Ⓡ Ⓟ Ⓣ • www.freespace.virgin.net/le.trayas

■ **SHEPHERDSWELL (Dover)**
NORTH DOWNS WAY

B & L Popple, Sunshine Cottage, The Green, Mill Lane, CT15 7LQ. ☎ (01304) 831359/831218/(0589) 572676 • Map 179/261478 • BB **C** • EM book first £9 (light suppers), 6-8.30pm • D4 T1 F1 • 1-12 • Ⓥ Ⓑ Ⓓ Ⓢ Ⓡ Ⓟ Ⓣ • ◆◆◆◆Ⓢ • sunshinecottage@shepherdswell.fsnet.co.uk

■ **SOUTHBOROUGH (Tunbridge Wells)**
WEALDWAY

Anneke Leemhuis, 10 Modest Corner, TN4 0LS. ☎/Fax (01892) 522450 • Map 188/571423 • BB **C** • EM book first £12.50, 7-8pm • D1 T2 • 1-12 • Ⓥ Ⓑ Ⓓ Ⓢ Ⓡ Ⓟ Ⓣ🐾 • modestanneke@lineone.net

■ **STELLING MINNIS (Canterbury)**

Mrs L Castle, Greatfield Farm, Misling Lane, CT4 6DE. ☎ (01227) 709223 • Map 189,179/134452 • BB **C** • D2 T1 • 1-12 • Ⓑ Ⓓ Ⓢ Ⓣ • ◆◆◆◆Ⓢ • SC also

Mrs F Anne Hunt, Bower Farm House, CT4 6BB. ☎ (01227) 709430 • Map 189,179/146475 • BB **C** • D1 T1 • 1-12 NX • Ⓑ Ⓓ Ⓣ🐾 • ◆◆◆◆Ⓢ • book@bowerbb.freeserve.co.uk

■ **STOWTING (Ashford)**
NORTH DOWNS WAY

Mrs Carole Cole, Water Farm, TN25 6BA. ☎ (01303) 862401 • Map 189,179/121412 • BB **C** • S1 T1 F1 • 1-12 NX • Ⓑ Ⓓ Ⓢ Ⓟ Ⓣ • SC also. Food nearby.

Caroline & Paul Boucher, Hillside Farm, Stowting Hill, TN25 6BE. ☎ (01303) 863520 • Map 189,179/124423 • BB **B** • D2 T1 • 1-12 NX • Ⓑ Ⓓ Ⓣ🐾 • Food nearby

Mrs A J Taylor, Boldens Wood, Fiddling Lane, TN25 6AP. ☎ (01303) 812011 • Map 189,179/111403 • BB **B** • EM book first £7.50, 7.30pm • S1 D/T1 • 1-12 NX • Ⓓ Ⓢ Ⓟ Ⓣ • duncantaylor_mulberry@compuserve.com

■ **TROTTISCLIFFE (West Malling)**
NORTH DOWNS WAY & WEALDWAY

Bramble Park, Church Lane, ME19 5EB. ☎ (01732) 822397 • Map 177/644604 • BB **C** • S1 T1 F1 • 1-12 • Ⓓ Ⓟ • Food nearby

■ **ULCOMBE (Maidstone)**
GREENSAND WAY

Mrs Diane Leat, Bramley Knowle Farm, Eastwood Road, ME17 1ET. ☎ 01622 858878 • Map 189/863485 • BB **B/C** • S1 D2 • 1-12 NX • Ⓑ Ⓓ Ⓢ Ⓣ • ◆◆◆ • Food nearby

■ **WESTWELL (Ashford)**
NORTH DOWNS WAY

Anna Graham, Berries Mount, Gold Hill, TN25 4LD. ☎ (01233) 712812 • Map 189/991476 • BB **C** • D1 T1 • 1-12 NX • Ⓓ Ⓢ Ⓟ

■ **WINGHAM (Canterbury)**

☆ N J Ellen, Crockshard Farmhouse, CT3 1NY. ☎ (01227) 720464 • Map 179/248559 • BB **C** • D2 T1 F4 • 1-12 • Ⓑ Ⓓ Ⓢ Ⓟ Ⓣ🐾 • p-e-crockshard@yahoo.co.uk

Crockshard Farmhouse
Wingham, Canterbury,
Kent CT3 1NY
Tel: 01227 720464

Situated in a peaceful hamlet a mile from the village of Wingham, most bedrooms are family rooms, some ensuite all with tea/coffee facilities. Home-produce for breakfast. Good choice of restaurants/pubs locally. Your host can advise on wealth of attractions in the area.

■ **WOULDHAM (Nr Rochester)**
NORTH DOWNS WAY

Mrs A Parnell, Wouldham Court Farmhouse, 246 High Street, ME1 3TY. ☎ (01634) 683271 • Map 188,178/714643 • BB **B/C** • EM £4, 7-9pm • S1 D1 F1 • 1-12 NX • Ⓥ Ⓓ Ⓢ Ⓟ Ⓣ🐾 • ◆◆◆ • wouldham.b-b@virgin.net

LANCASHIRE

■ **ARKHOLME (Carnforth)**

Michael & Elizabeth Mailer, Tithe Barn, Main Street, LA6 1AU. ☎ (015242) 22236 • Map 97/586720 • BB **C/D** • S1 D1 T1 • 1-12 • Ⓑ Ⓓ Ⓢ Ⓟ Ⓣ🐾 • ◆◆◆◆ • enquiries@tithe-barn.com

☆ See Display Advertisement

■ **BACUP**

Ann Isherwood, Pasture Bottom Farm, OL13 9UZ.
☎ (01706) 873790 • Map 103/878237 • BB **B** • EM
book first £8, 7pm • D1 T2 • 1-12 NX • Ⓥ Ⓑ Ⓓ Ⓢ
Ⓟ Ⓣ 🐾 • ◆◆◆ • haisherwood@zen.co.uk

■ **BARNOLDSWICK**
PENNINE WAY

Jackie & Allan Edwards, Fosters House, 203 Gisburn
Road, BB18 5JU. ☎ (01282) 850718 • Map
103/874475 • BB **C** • D1 T2 F1 • 1-12 NX • Ⓑ Ⓓ Ⓢ
Ⓟ Ⓣ • ◆◆ • Food nearby • jacalex@talk21.com

■ **BASHALL EAVES (Clitheroe)**

☆ Mrs Heather Nowell, Hodder House B&B, Hodder
House Farm, BB7 3LZ. ☎ 01254 826328 • Map
103/699416 • BB **B** • EM £10 • S1 D2 • 1-12 NX • Ⓥ
Ⓑ Ⓓ Ⓢ Ⓟ Ⓣ 🐾 •
www.hodderhousebb.freeserve.co.uk

HODDER HOUSE B&B
Farmhouse Bed & Breakfast

Near Ribble Way/Pendle
Hill/Trough of Bowland on the
banks of the Hodder, in beautiful
lush countryside, Hodder House
Farm awaits. En-suites available.

www.hodderhousebb.freeserve.co.uk
email-heather@hodderhousebb.freeserve.co.uk

01254 826328 OS Map 103 699416

■ **BOLTON-BY-BOWLAND (Clitheroe)**
RIBBLE WAY

☆ Middle Flass Lodge, Settle Road, BB7 4NY.
☎ (01200) 447259 • Map 103/790520 • BB **C/D** • EM
book first £16-18, 6-7pm • D2 T2 F1 • 1-12 NX • Ⓥ
Ⓑ Ⓓ Ⓢ Ⓟ Ⓣ • ◆◆◆◆ •
mflodge.freesevers.com/

**MIDDLE FLASS LODGE, SETTLE ROAD,
BOLTON-BY-BOWLAND,
CLITHEROE BB7 4NY**

Unrivalled Views across Forest of Bowland. Ideal base
for Dales, Lakes & Walking. Chef prepared cuisine,
Bedrooms En-suite, Drying Room, Ample Parking,
Gardens. Non-Smoking. Phone for details.
AA ◆◆◆◆ ETC ◆◆◆
Credit Cards Accepted (Switch/Delta pref., Visa accepted)
Tel: 01200 447259

■ **BURNLEY**

Julie Whitehead, 121/123 Ormerod Road, BB11 3QW.
☎ (01282) 423255 • Map 103/846331 • BB **C** • S4
D2 T3 F1 • 1-12 • Ⓑ Ⓓ Ⓡ Ⓟ Ⓣ 🐾 • ◆◆◆

■ **CARNFORTH**

☆ Mrs Melanie Smith, Capernwray House,
Capernwray, LA6 1AE. ☎ (01524) 732363 • Map
97/534718 • BB **C** • EM book first £9, 6-9pm • S1 D2
T1 • 1-12 NX • Ⓥ Ⓑ Ⓓ Ⓢ Ⓟ Ⓣ • ◆◆◆◆Ⓢ •
www.capernwrayhouse.com

Capernwray House
Capernwray Nr. Carnforth Lancashire

Beautifully Country House in
18 acres in Lune Valley.
Panoramic Views, Guest
Lounge. Close to Lakes, Dales,
Lancaster, Canal 5 mins walk.
No smoking. From £21 p.p.
En-suite available. Warm welcome. Phone for brochure.
Tel/Fax Roy & Melanie Smith 01524 732363
www.capernwrayhouse.com
English Tourist Council ◆◆◆◆

■ **CHIPPING (Nr Clitheroe)**

☆ Mrs Pat Gifford, Rakefoot Farm, Chaigley, BB7 3LY.
☎ (01995) 61332/(07889) 279063 • Map 103/663416
• BB **B/C** • EM book first £10-£12, 5-7pm • S1 D4 T2
F3 • 1-12 • Ⓥ Ⓑ Ⓓ Ⓟ Ⓣ 🐾 • ◆◆◆◆ • SC also •
transport av • Doubles let as singles.

Rakefoot Farm
B&B/self-catering
ETC ◆◆◆◆

17th century farmhouse and traditional stone barn
conversion. Original features, woodburners, home-cooked
meals, laundry, ensuite and ground floor available.
Longridge Fell/Forest of Bowland/AONB/Panoramic views.
Chipping ☎ 01995 61332

■ **CLITHEROE**
RIBBLE WAY

Mr & Mrs R E Berry, Lower Standen Farm, Whalley
Road, BB7 1PP. ☎ (01200) 424176 • Map
103/739400 • BB **B** • D2 T1 • 1-12 NX • Ⓑ Ⓓ Ⓡ
Ⓟ Ⓣ 🐾

Jean & Ken Lord, Brooklands, 9 Pendle Road, BB7
1JQ. ☎ /Fax 01200 422797 • Map 103/750414 • BB
B • D1 T2 • 1-12 • Ⓑ Ⓓ Ⓡ Ⓟ Ⓣ 🐾 • ◆◆◆ •
Transport avail. kenandjean@tesco.net

■ **COLNE**

Mrs Etherington, Wickets, 148 Keighley Road, BB8
0PJ. ☎ (01282) 862002 • Map 103/897402 • BB **B/C**
• S1 D1 T1 • 3-12 NX • Ⓑ Ⓓ Ⓢ Ⓡ Ⓟ Ⓣ •
◆◆◆◆ • wickets@colne.fsnet.co.uk

Mrs Carole Mitson, Higher Wanless Farm, Red Lane,
BB8 7JP. ☎ (01282) 865301 • Map 103/871413 • BB
C • EM book first £11, 7pm • S1 T/S1 F1 • 2-11 • Ⓥ
Ⓑ Ⓓ Ⓢ Ⓡ Ⓟ Ⓣ • ◆◆◆◆ • Transport from/to
Pendle Way • wanlessfarm@bun.com

■ **ECCLESTON (Chorley)**

Mrs K Motley, Parr Hall Farm, Parr Lane, PR7 5SL.
☎ (01257) 451917 • Map 108/518174 • BB **C** • D4 •
1-12 • ⒷⒹⓈⓅⓉ • ◆◆◆◆ • Food nearby
parrhall@talk21.com

■ **GARSTANG (Preston)**

Esther Heaton, Castleview, Bonds Lane, PR3 1ZB.
☎ (01995) 602022 • Map 102/493448 • BB **C** • S1 T4
• 1-12 NX • ⒷⒹⓉ🐾 • 2Cr

Tom M. Wilkinson, Sandbriggs, Lancaster Road, PR3
1JA. ☎ (01995) 603080 • Map 102/492459 • BB **B** •
S1 D2 T1 F1 • 1-12 • ⒷⒹⓉ🐾 • SC also

■ **SCORTON (Nr Preston)**

Christine Whitaker, Woodacre Hall Farm, PR3 1BN.
☎ 01995 602253 • Map 102/502470 • BB **B** • EM
book first £8 • D2 • 3-11 • ⒷⒹⓅⓉ🐾 • ◆◆◆

■ **SLAIDBURN (Clitheroe)**

Mary & Peter Cowking, Pages Farm, Woodhouse
Lane, BB7 3AH. ☎ (01200) 446205 • Map
103/704528 • BB **B** • EM book first £11.50, 6-8.30pm
• D2 T1 • 1-12 NX • ⓋⒷⒹⓈⓅⓉ • ◆◆

■ **WYCOLLER (Nr Colne)**

Pat Hodgson, Parson Lee Farm, BB8 8SU. ☎ (01282)
864747 • Map 103/937385 • BB **B** • EM book first £7,
6.30-8pm • D1 T1 F1 • 1-12 NX • ⓋⒷⒹⓈⓅ
Ⓣ🐾 • ◆◆◆ • pathodgson@hotmail.com

LEICESTERSHIRE & RUTLAND

■ **BELTON IN RUTLAND (Oakham)**
MACMILLAN WAY

☆ The Old Rectory, LE15 9LE. ☎ (01572) 717279 •
Map 141/814010 • BB **B/C/D** • S1 D2 T3 F2 • 1-12 • Ⓑ
ⒹⓈⓅⓉ🐾 • ◆◆◆ • SC/groups also • food nearby

The Old Rectory
Belton in Rutland, Oakham LE15 9LE
(01572) 717279
Macmillan Way,
Leicestershire
Round, Rutland
Water, Barnsdale
gardens.
Comfortable B&B
accommodation in conservation village.
Shop/pub 200 yards. SC also available.
RAC
◆◆◆

■ **BROOKE (Oakham)**
MACMILLAN WAY

Barbara Clemence, Old Rectory, LE15 8DE. ☎ (01572)
770558 • Map 141/850058 • BB **C** • EM book first £8 •
S1 D1 T1 • 1-12 NX • ⒷⒹⓈⓇⓅⓉ🐾

■ **GREAT DALBY (Melton Mowbray)**

Mrs Lynn Parker, Dairy Farm, LE14 2EW. ☎ (01664)
562783 • Map 129/743143 • BB **B** • D2 T1 • 1-12 • Ⓑ
ⒹⓈⓅⓉ🐾 • ◆◆◆ • Food nearby

■ **LOUGHBOROUGH**

Valerie Wood, Peachnook Guest House, 154 Ashby
Road, LE11 3AG. ☎ (01509) 264390 • Map
129/529196 • BB **A/C** • S1 D1 T1 F2 • 1-12 • ⒷⓇ
Ⓟ • List • Vegan breakfasts available.

■ **MARKET HARBOROUGH**
JURASSIC WAY

Mrs M J Hart, The Wrongs, Sibbertoft, LE16 9UJ.
☎ (01858) 880886 • Map 141/666829 • BB **B** • S1
D1 • 1-12 • ⒹⓈⓅⓉ🐾 • SC, Caravan, Camping
also • jasper.h.hart@farmline.com

■ **MOUNTSORREL (Loughborough)**

Mrs M A Pegg, The Barleyloft Guest House, 33A
Hawcliffe Road, LE12 7AQ. ☎ (01509) 413514 • Map
129/574156 • BB **B** • S1 D2 T1 F2 • 1-12 • Ⓓ Ⓡ Ⓟ
Ⓣ🐾 Ⓜ • Supermarket, pubs & restaurant nearby.

■ **NORTH LUFFENHAM (Rutland)**
JURASSIC WAY

Mrs Joan Cook, Pinfold House, 6 Pinfold Lane, LE15
8LE. ☎ (01780) 720175 • Map 141/934034 • BB **B** •
S3 D2 T1 F1 • 2-11 • ⒹⓈⓅⓉ🐾

■ **OAKS IN CHARNWOOD (Coalville)**

Kay Newcombe, Lubcloud Farm, LE12 9YA.
☎ (01509) 503204 • Map 129/479147 • BB **C** • D2 F1
• 1-12 • ⒷⒹⓈⓅⓉ

■ **REDMILE (Nottingham)**

P & M Need, Peacock Farm Guesthouse & Country
Restaurant, NG13 0GQ. ☎ (01949) 842475 • Map
129/790359 • BB **D** • EM £14.50, 7-9pm • S1 D2 T2
F4 • 1-12 • ⓋⒷⒹⓈⓇ🐾 • 3Cr • Group
discount. Bunkhouse and SC also

LINCOLNSHIRE

■ **BARNETBY (South Humberside)**
VIKING WAY

☆ Mrs Angela Vora, Holcombe House, Victoria Road,
DN38 6JR. ☎ (07850) 764002 • Map 112/059097 •
BB **C** • EM £9, 6-8pm • S4 D1 T2 F2 • 1-12 • Ⓥ Ⓑ
Ⓓ Ⓢ Ⓡ🐾 • 3Cr/C • See display advert on next
page • www.holcombeguesthouse.co.uk

Ramblers' Association members are covered
by a public liability insurance policy
further details from central office

☆ See Display Advertisement   **193**

Holcombe Guest House
34 Victoria Road
Barnetby, Lincolnshire
(VIKING WAY)

ETB ♛♛♛ **Commended**

Comfortable homely accommodation to rest your feet. Centrally heated, TV, beverage-making facilities, residents lounge with video. £20/person. Evening meals (inc. vegetarian) by arrangement.
Call Angela on 07850 764002

■ CAISTOR
VIKING WAY

Margaret Lundy, Moorland View, North Kelsey Road, LN7 6SF. ☎ (01472) 851613 • Map 113/104014 • BB **B** • D1 T2 F1 • 1-12 NX • D S P T

■ CRANWELL (Sleaford)
VIKING WAY

Mrs A Wood, Byards Leap Cottage, NG34 8EY. ☎ (01400) 261537 • Map 130/011498 • BB **B** • EM book first £7.50, 6.30pm • D1 T1 • 1-12 NX • V D S P T • ◆◆

■ CROXTON KERRIAL (Grantham)
VIKING WAY

Finola Delamere, The Pottery, Saltby Road, NG32 1QG. ☎ (01476) 870744 • Map 130/837291 • BB **B** • EM book first £8 • D2 • 1-12 • V D S P T Ⓜ • Transport av • fandf@thepottery.freeserve.co.uk

■ GRIMSBY

3 Victoria Road, Keelby, DN41 8EH. ☎ (01469) 561399 • Map 113/163099 • BB **A** • EM book first £5, 7pm • S1 T5 • 1-12 NX • D S P T • sparker3@talk21.com

■ LINCOLN
VIKING WAY

Mr & Mrs T Cain, ABC Guest House, 126 Yarborough Road, LN1 1HP. ☎ (01522) 543560 • Map 121/969723 • BB **C** • S2 D6 T2 F1 • 1-12 NX • B D S R T

Tony Downes, Old Rectory Guest House, 19 Newport, LN1 3DQ. ☎ (01522) 514774 • Map 121/975722 • BB **B** • S1 D3 T1 F1 • 1-12 NX • B D S R T

Alex Adkins, Edward King House, The Old Palace, Minster Yard, LN2 1PU. ☎ (01522) 528778 • Map 121/976718 • BB **B** • EM book first £9.20, (groups 6+) • S5 T11 F1 • 1-12 NX • V S R P T • ◆◆ • Groups also ekh@oden.org.uk

Jeff Longmuir, 7 South Park, LN5 8EN. ☎ (01522) 521624 • Map 121/973697 • BB **D** • S2 D4 T2 • 1-12 NX • B D R P T • ◆◆◆◆ • tennyson.hotel@virgin.net

■ MARKET RASEN
VIKING WAY

Mrs J Bridger, Waveney Cottage Guest House, Willingham Road, LN8 3DN. ☎ (01673) 843236 • Map 121,113/111890 • BB **B/C** • EM book first £8.50, 6.30pm • D/F1 T2 • 1-12 • V B D S R P T • ◆◆◆ • Transport av • www.waveneycottage.co.uk

■ SKEGNESS

Andy & Glenys Malcolm, Mayfair Hotel, PE25 3JZ. ☎ (01754) 764687 • Map 122/567626 • BB **B** • EM £7, 5.30pm • D2 T5 F1 • 2-12 NX • V B D S R P T Ⓜ

■ SKILLINGTON (Grantham)
VIKING WAY

Mrs E M Whatton, Sproxton Lodge Farm, NG33 5HJ. ☎ (01476) 860307 • Map 130/881252 • BB **B** • EM book first £8, 6-6.30pm • S1 D1 F1 • 1-12 NX • V B D S P T • ◆◆

■ SOUTH WITHAM (Grantham)
VIKING WAY

Margaret Lambert, Barn Own House, 20 High Street, NG33 5QB. ☎ 01572 767688 • Map 130/926196 • BB **C** • D2 T1 • 1-12 • B D S P T • ◆◆◆◆ • margaret@mcclambert.fsnet.co.uk

■ STAMFORD
JURASSIC WAY & MACMILLAN WAY

Mrs J Headland, Birch House, 4 Lonsdale Road, PE9 2RW. ☎ (01780) 754876 • Map 141/015067 • BB **C** • S2 D2 • 1-12 NX • D S R T • ◆◆◆

Mrs Sue Olver, The Mill, Mill Lane, Tallington, PE9 4RR. ☎ (01780) 740815 • Map 142/094081 • BB **D** • D2 T2 F2 • 1-12 • B D S T • ◆◆◆◆

■ WOODHALL SPA
VIKING WAY

Claire Brennan, Claremont Guest House, 9/11 Witham Road, LN10 6RW. ☎ (01526) 352000 • Map 122/191630 • BB **A-E** • S3 D2 T1 F4 • 1-12 • B D S P T • ◆◆ • Food nearby • small groups & camping also

Barry & Beryl Tonkinson, Pitchaway Guest House, The Broadway, LN10 6SQ. ☎ (01526) 352969 • Map 122/198632 • BB **C** • EM book first £8.50, 5-7.30pm • S2 D1 T3 F1 • 1-12 • V B D S T • ◆◆◆ • Near Spa Trail

GREATER LONDON

■ CENTRAL LONDON
THAMES PATH

St Athan's Hotel, 20 Tavistock Place, WC1H 9RE. ☎ 020 7837 9140 • Map 176,177/300823 • BB **C/D/E** • S16 D20 T10 F8 • 1-12 • B D R • List

■ PUTNEY
THAMES PATH

☆ Pip & Robert Taylor, bbputney, One Fanthorpe Street, SW15 1DZ. ☎ 020 8785 7609 • Map 176/233758 • BB **C/D** • EM book first £14, 8pm • D1 T1 • 1-12 NX • Ⓥ Ⓑ Ⓓ Ⓢ Ⓡ Ⓟ Ⓜ • bbputney@btinternet.com

■ SYDENHAM (London)

P. Robinson, 5 Whittell Gardens, SE26 4LN. ☎ 020 8699 3335 • Map 177/352722 • BB **B** • T2 • 1-12 NX • Ⓓ Ⓢ Ⓡ Ⓣ 🐾 Ⓜ

■ WIMBLEDON PARK (London)
THAMES PATH

☆ "Crossways", 61 Augustus Road, SW19 6LX. ☎ /Fax 0208 788 9913 • Map 176/245734 • BB **D** • EM book first £15, 7-730pm • S2 T2 • 1-12 NX • Ⓥ Ⓑ Ⓓ Ⓢ Ⓡ Ⓟ Ⓣ Ⓜ

GREATER MANCHESTER

■ SALFORD
CHESHIRE RING CANAL

White Lodge Hotel, 89 Great Cheetham Street West, M7 2JA. ☎ 0161 792 3047 • Map 109/823004 • BB **C/E** • S3 D3 T3 • 1-12 NX • Ⓓ Ⓡ 🐾 • 1Cr

MERSEYSIDE

■ NEW BRIGHTON (Wallasey, Wirral)

Mrs S Brereton, Sherwood Guest House, 55 Wellington Road, CH45 2ND. ☎ 0151-639 5198 • Map 108/307941 • BB **B** • EM book first £5, 6.30pm • S2 D2 T2 F2 • 1-12 NX • Ⓥ Ⓑ Ⓓ Ⓢ Ⓡ Ⓟ Ⓣ 🐾 • ◆◆◆ • frankbrereton@hotmail.com

■ SOUTHPORT

Penny Barker, The Sidbrook Hotel, 14 Talbot Street, PR8 1HP. ☎ (01704) 530608 • Map 108/334167 • BB **C** • D5 T2 F1 • 1-12 NX • Ⓑ Ⓓ Ⓢ Ⓡ Ⓟ Ⓣ • ◆◆◆

NORFOLK

■ ACLE
WEAVERS WAY

Joan & Malcolm Wallis, The Old Police House, Reedham Road, NR13 3DE. ☎ (01493) 751846 • Map 134/401101 • BB **B** • D1 T1 • 4-11 • Ⓢ Ⓡ Ⓣ Ⓜ

■ ALDBOROUGH
WEAVERS WAY

Mrs Janet Davison, Butterfly Cottage, The Green, NR11 7AA. ☎ (01263) 768198 • Map 133/184343 • BB **C** • S1 D1 F1 • 1-12 • Ⓑ Ⓓ Ⓢ Ⓟ Ⓣ 🐾 • ◆◆◆ • SC also

■ AYLSHAM (Norwich)
WEAVERS WAY

☆ The Old Pump House, Holman Road, NR11 6BY. ☎ (01263) 733789 • Map 133,134/190269 • BB **B/C/D** • EM book first £14.50 (APR-OCT), 6.30-7pm • S1 D2 T2 F1 • 1-12 NX • Ⓥ Ⓑ Ⓓ Ⓢ Ⓟ Ⓣ 🐾 • ◆◆◆◆

☆ Mr & Mrs Parry, The Old Bank House, 3 Norwich Road, NR11 6BN. ☎ 01263 733843/768606 • Map 133,134/194267 • BB **C** • EM book first £13.50, 7pm • D1 T1 F1 • 1-12 • Ⓥ Ⓑ Ⓓ Ⓢ Ⓟ Ⓣ 🐾 • SC also • bankhouse.beechwood@talk21.com • See display advert on next page.

☆ See Display Advertisement

NORFOLK

ENGLAND

ACCOMMODATION

B&B

■ BURNHAM OVERY STAITHE (King's Lynn)

Domville Guest House, Glebe Lane, PE31 8JQ. ☎ (01328) 738298 • Map 132/846440 • BB **C** • EM book first £9.50, 7pm • S3 D2 T2 • 1-12 NX • Ⓥ Ⓑ Ⓓ Ⓢ Ⓟ Ⓣ Ⓜ • ◆◆◆ • SC also

■ CASTLE ACRE (King's Lynn)
PEDDARS WAY & NORFOLK COAST PATH

Pam Gray , Willow Cottage Tea Rooms, Stocks Green, PE32 2AE. ☎ (01760) 755551 • Map 132/816151 • BB **B** • D2 T1 F/T1 • 2-11 • Ⓓ Ⓢ Ⓟ Ⓣ ⅏ • Food nearby. gv33@dialpipex.com

Gillian Clarke, Gemini House, Pyes Lane, PE32 2XB. ☎ (01760) 755375 • Map 132/815148 • BB **B** • D2 T2 • 1-12 • Ⓑ Ⓓ Ⓟ Ⓣ ⅏

■ CLEY-NEXT-THE-SEA
PEDDARS WAY & NORFOLK COAST PATH

Kalba Meadows & John Curtis, Whalebone House, High Street, NR25 7RN. ☎ (01263) 740336 • Map 133/045438 • BB **C** • EM (As part of Winter breaks) • D1 T1 • 1-12 • Ⓑ Ⓓ Ⓢ Ⓣ • 2 nights min stay, Easter-Oct. Winter breaks

■ CROMER
PEDDARS WAY & NORFOLK COAST PATH & WEAVERS WAY

T Jackson, Birch House, 34 Cabbell Road, NR27 9HX. ☎ (01263) 512521 • Map 133/216421 • BB **B/C** • EM book first £10, 6.30pm • S1 D4 T3 • 11 Jan - 13 Dec • Ⓥ Ⓑ Ⓓ Ⓢ Ⓡ Ⓟ Ⓣ • ◆◆◆

■ DOCKING (King's Lynn)
PEDDARS WAY & NORFOLK COAST PATH

Roger Roberts, North Farmhouse, Station Road, PE31 8LS. ☎ (01485) 518493 • Map 132/765372 • BB **B** • D1 T1 • 2-11 • Ⓑ Ⓓ Ⓢ Ⓟ Ⓣ ⅏ • ◆◆◆ • Food nearby • northfarmhouse@aol.com

■ GREAT BIRCHAM (Nr Hunstanton)
PEDDARS WAY & NORFOLK COAST PATH

Mr & Mrs I L Verrando, Kings Head Hotel, PE31 6RJ. ☎ 01485 578265 • Map 132/768322 • BB **D/E** • EM £15, 7-9pm • S1 D2 T2 F1 • 1-12 • Ⓥ Ⓑ Ⓓ Ⓟ Ⓣ ⅏

■ GREAT CRESSINGHAM
PEDDARS WAY & NORFOLK COAST PATH

Mike & Vanessa Woolnough, The Vines, IP25 6NL. ☎ 01760 756303 • Map 144/84900159 • BB **B** • D2 T1 • 1-12 NX • Ⓑ Ⓓ Ⓢ Ⓟ Ⓣ ⅏ • Transport av • the.vines@eidosnet.co.uk

■ GREAT HOCKHAM (Thetford)
PEDDARS WAY & NORFOLK COAST PATH

☆ Miriam Thomas, Manor Farm, Vicarage Road, IP24 1PE. ☎ 01953 498204 • Map 144/951926 • BB **B/C** • EM book first £12.00, 7pm • S1 D1 T1 • 1-12 NX • Ⓥ Ⓑ Ⓓ Ⓢ Ⓟ Ⓣ ⅏ • ◆◆◆ • manorfarm@ukf.net

■ HAPPISBURGH

Cliff House Teashop/Guesthouse, Beach Road, NR12 0PP. ☎ (01692) 650775 • Map 133/384309 • BB **B** • EM £6, up to 6pm • S2 D1 T1 • 1-12 NX • Ⓥ Ⓓ Ⓢ Ⓟ Ⓣ • ◆◆◆ • SC also

■ HINGHAM (Wymondham)

Mrs Melissa Sheldrake, The Watermill, Deopham Road, NR9 4NL. ☎ (01953) 850300 • Map 144/032007 • BB **C** • EM book first £12 • S2 D2 • 1-12 • Ⓥ Ⓑ Ⓓ Ⓢ Ⓟ

■ HUNSTANTON
PEDDARS WAY & NORFOLK COAST PATH

Robert Sturgess, Garganey House, 46 Northgate, PE36 6DR. ☎ (01485) 533269 • Map 132/674413 • BB **B** • EM £10.00, 7.15pm • S1 D2 T2 F1 • 1-12 NX • Ⓥ Ⓑ Ⓓ Ⓢ Ⓟ • ◆◆◆

Mrs Barbara Bamfield, The Gables, 28 Austin Street, PE36 6AW. ☎ (01485) 532514 • Map 132/674411 • BB **B/C** • EM book first £10.99, 6.30pm • D1 T1 F3 • 1-12 • Ⓥ Ⓑ Ⓓ Ⓢ Ⓟ Ⓣ • ◆◆◆◆

Bob & Sandy Duff-Dick, Rosamaly Guest House, 14 Glebe Avenue, PE36 6BS. ☎ (01485) 534187 • Map 132/675413 • BB **C** • EM book first £10, 5.30pm • S1 D3 T1 F2 • 1-12 NX • Ⓥ Ⓑ Ⓓ Ⓢ Ⓟ Ⓣ ⅏ • ◆◆◆

■ KING'S LYNN

Mrs J Bastone, Maranatha/Havana Guest House, 115 Gaywood Road, PE30 2PU. ☎ (01553) 774596 • Map 132/627204 • BB **B** • EM 6pm • S3 D1 T4 F3 • 1-12 • Ⓥ Ⓑ Ⓓ Ⓢ Ⓡ Ⓟ Ⓣ ⅏ Ⓜ • ◆◆◆ • Groups also

■ KNAPTON (North Walsham)

☆ Colin & Fiona Goodhead, White House Farm, NR28 0RX. ☎ 01263 721344 • Map 133/302341 • BB **C** • EM book first £8, 6-8pm • D1 T1 F1 • 1-12 • Ⓥ Ⓑ Ⓓ Ⓢ Ⓟ Ⓣ 🕭 • ◆◆◆◆ • goodhead@whfarm.swinternet.co.uk

WHITE HOUSE FARM
Knapton North Walsham

18th Century Listed Farmhouse Quiet village location, ideal for North **AA** ◆◆◆◆ Norfolk and Broads.
* En-suite B&B or S/C (groups welcome)
* Meals feature home-made/local produce
* Log fires and a warm welcome
℃: **01263 721344**
E-mail: GOODHEAD@whfarm.swinternet.co.uk

■ LITTLE CRESSINGHAM (Thetford)
PEDDARS WAY & NORFOLK COAST PATH

Mr J Wittridge, Sycamore House B&B, IP25 6NE. ☎ (01953) 881887 • Map 144/872001 • BB **C** • S2 D2 T1 • 1-12 • Ⓑ Ⓓ Ⓢ Ⓟ Ⓣ • Good food nearby, peaceful location.

■ MUNDFORD (Thetford)

Mrs Marion Ford, Old Bottle House, Cranwich, IP26 5JL. ☎ (01842) 878012 • Map 144/782948 • BB **C** • EM book first £12, 7.30pm • D1 T2 F1 • 1-12 NX • Ⓥ Ⓑ Ⓓ Ⓢ Ⓟ Ⓣ

■ MUNDHAM (Norwich)

Mr & Mrs K Southgate, Grange Farm Cottage, Grange Rd, NR14 6EP. ☎ (01508) 550027 • Map 134/324964 • BB **C/D** • D/F1 • 1-12 • Ⓑ Ⓓ Ⓢ Ⓟ Ⓣ

■ NARBOROUGH (King's Lynn)

Mrs C Green, "Paget", Lynn Road, PE32 1TE. ☎ (01760) 337734 • Map 143,132/750126 • BB **B** • S1 D1 T1 • 1-12 NX • Ⓑ Ⓓ Ⓢ 🕭

■ NEATISHEAD (Norwich)

Sue Wrigley, Regency Guest House, The Street, NR12 8AD. ☎ (01692) 630233 • Map 133,134/340210 • BB **C** • EM book first £Light meals • D2 T2 F1 • 1-12 • Ⓥ Ⓑ Ⓓ Ⓢ Ⓟ Ⓣ 🕭 • ◆◆◆◆ • SC also www.norfolkbroads.co.uk/regency

Jeremy Smerdon, Allens Farmhouse, Three Hammer Common, NR12 8XW. ☎ (01692) 630080 • Map 133/134/341202 • BB **B/C** • D2 T1 • 1-12 • Ⓑ Ⓓ Ⓢ Ⓟ Ⓣ 🕭 • ◆◆◆

■ NORTH PICKENHAM (Swaffham)
PEDDARS WAY & NORFOLK COAST PATH

Mrs B J Norris, Riverside House, Meadow Lane, PE37 8LE. ☎ (01760) 440219 • Map 144/865065 • BB **B** • D1 T2 • 1-12 NX • Ⓓ Ⓟ 🕭 • Food nearby

■ NORWICH

Mrs D Solomon, The Old Rectory, Crostwick, NR12 7BG. ☎ (01603) 738513 • Map 133,134/256159 • BB **D** • EM book first £9.50, 6.30-8.30pm (not Mon) • S1 D5 T5 F2 • 1-12 • Ⓥ Ⓑ Ⓓ Ⓢ Ⓟ Ⓣ 🕭 • ★★ • info@therectoryhotel.fsnet.co.uk

☆ University of East Anglia, Earlham Road, NR4 7TJ. ☎ 01603 593271 • Map 134/191080 • BB **B/C/D/E** • EM book first £5.10, 5.10pm • S52 D4 T6 • 1-12 NX • Ⓥ Ⓑ Ⓟ Ⓣ • SC also • Groups also conference.services@ula.ac.uk

■ SCOLE (Diss)
ANGLES WAY

Mr N Timmons, White Lodge, Diss Road, IP21 4DH. ☎ (01379) 740226 • Map 144,156/143790 • BB **C** • S1 D1 T1 F/D1 • Ⓑ Ⓓ Ⓢ Ⓡ Ⓣ 🕭

■ SEDGEFORD (Hunstanton)

Mrs J Frost, Park View, PE36 5LU. ☎ (01485) 571352 • Map 132/720357 • BB **B** • EM book first £8 • S1 D1 T1 • 3-11 • Ⓥ Ⓑ Ⓓ Ⓢ 🕭 • 1Cr

■ SHERINGHAM

Mrs E Meakin, Wykeham Guest House, Morley Road North, NR26 8JB. ☎ (01263) 823818 • Map 133/158427 • BB **C** • S1 D2 T1 • 4-10 • Ⓑ Ⓓ Ⓢ Ⓡ Ⓟ Ⓣ Ⓜ

Achimota, 31 North Street, NR26 8LW. ☎ (01263) 822379 • Map 133/154432 • BB **B/C** • EM book first £10, 6.30pm • D2 T1 • 1-12 NX • Ⓥ Ⓑ Ⓓ Ⓢ Ⓡ Ⓣ 🕭 Ⓜ • ◆◆◆ • www.broadland.com/achimota

Christine Perkins, Holly Cottage, 14a The Rise, NR26 8QB. ☎ (01263) 822807 • Map 133/161426 • BB **C** • D1 T1 F0 • 1-12 • B D S R P T • ◆◆◆◆ • hollyperks@aol.com 3nights Nov-Mar £45

Mr P Pigott, Bayleaf Guest House, 10 Saint Peters Road, NR26 8QY. ☎ (01263) 823779 • Map 133/156431 • BB **C** • D6 T3 F3 • 1-12 NX • B S R P T 🐾 • ◆◆◆

☆ Gillian Caldwell, Highfield Guest House, Montague Road, NR26 8LN. ☎ (01263) 825524 • Map 133/154431 • BB **B/C** • S1 D3 T2 F2 • 1-12 • B D S R P T • ◆◆◆◆

■ STALHAM (Norwich)
WEAVERS WAY

Mrs S Durrell-Walsh, The Old Surgery, High Street, NR12 9BB. ☎ (01692) 581248 • Map 133,134/372252 • BB **B** • EM book first £15, 7-9pm • S1 D1 T1 • 1-12 NX • V D S P • walsh01@globalnet.co.uk

☆ Mrs Barbara Mixer, Landell, Brick Kiln Lane, Ingham, NR12 9SX. ☎ 01692 582349 • Map 133,134/385255 • BB **B/C** • EM book first £10 • D1 T1 • 2-10 • B D S P T M

Gary & Beryl Holmes, Chapelfield Cottage B&B, Chapelfield, NR12 9EN. ☎ 01692 582173 • Map 133,134/369243 • BB **C** • D1 T1 • 1-12 NX • B D S P T 🐾 • ◆◆◆ • www.norfolkbroads.com/chapelfield

■ SWAFFHAM
PEDDARS WAY & NORFOLK COAST PATH

Mrs C Webster, Purbeck House, Whitsands Road, PE37 7BJ. ☎ (01760) 721805/725345 • Map 144/815090 • BB **B** • S2 D2 T2 F2 • 1-12 NX • B D P T 🐾

Mrs Doreen Harvey, Glebe Bungalow, 8a Princes Street, PE37 7BP. ☎ (01760) 722764 • Map 144/815090 • BB **B/C** • D1 T1 F1 • 1-12 • V B D S P T 🐾 • ◆◆◆◆ • Cat.3 Disabled

■ TAVERHAM (Norwich)

Foxwood Guest House, Fakenham Road, NR8 6HR. ☎ (01603) 868474 • Map 133/154152 • BB **C** • EM book first £7.50, 6.30pm • D1 T2 • 1-12 NX • V B D S P T • yvonne@foxwood7.fsnet.co.uk

■ THOMPSON (Thetford)
PEDDARS WAY & NORFOLK COAST PATH

Lavender Garnier, College Farm, IP24 1QG. ☎ (01953) 483318 • Map 144/933966 • BB **C** • D1 T2 • 1-12 • B D P

Brenda Mills, Thatched House, Pockthorpe Corner, IP24 1PJ. ☎ (01953) 483577 • Map 144/917967 • BB **C** • EM book first £7.50, 7pm • D1 T2 • 1-12 • V B D S T 🐾 M • List

■ THORPE MARKET (Cromer)

Barbara Reid, Manorwood, Church Road, NR11 8UA. ☎ (01263) 834938 • Map 133/245354 • BB **B/C** • T2 F1 • 1-12 • B D R P T 🐾 • ◆◆◆

■ WELLS-NEXT-THE-SEA
PEDDARS WAY & NORFOLK COAST PATH

Mrs J Court, Eastdene, Northfield Lane, NR23 1LH. ☎ (01328) 710381 • Map 132/919435 • BB **B** • EM Y, 7.30-8.45pm • S1 D2 T1 • 1-12 NX • B D S P T 🐾

C & L Shayes, Meadowside, Two Furlong Hill, NR23 1HQ. ☎ (01328) 710470 • Map 132/913433 • BB **C** • D1 T1 • 1-12 • B D S T

Mr & Mrs D Bramley, Brambledene, Warham Road, NR23 1NE. ☎ (01328) 711143 • Map 132/922429 • BB **B** • D2 • 11-9 • D S P

■ WROXHAM

Jean & Geoff Kimberley, The Dragon Flies, 5 The Avenue, NR12 8TN. ☎ (01603) 783822 • Map 133,134/302176 • BB **C** • D1 • 1-12 NX • B S R P T M • ◆◆◆◆ⓢ • geoff.kimberley@talk21.com Food nearby

NORTHAMPTONSHIRE

■ BRAUNSTON (Daventry)
GRAND UNION CANAL WALK & JURASSIC WAY

The Old Castle, London Road, NN11 7HB. ☎ (01788) 890887 • Map 152/533660 • BB **B/C** • S/T/D1 D2 T1 F1 • 1-12 NX • B D T 🐾

CRANFORD ST ANDREW (Kettering)

Audrey E Clarke, Dairy Farm, NN14 4AQ. ☎ (01536) 330273 • Map 141/923773 • BB **C/D** • EM book first £.14-15, 7pm • D2 T2 F1 • 1-12 NX • Ⓥ Ⓑ Ⓓ Ⓢ Ⓡ Ⓟ Ⓣ 🐾 • ◆◆◆◆Ⓢ

DAVENTRY
GRAND UNION CANAL WALK & JURASSIC WAY

Ann Spicer, Drayton Lodge, NN11 4NL. ☎ (01327) 702449 • Map 152/577620 • BB **D** • EM book first £15, 6.30pm • S1 D1 T3 • 1-12 NX • Ⓑ Ⓓ Ⓢ Ⓣ • ◆◆◆

KETTERING

Pennels Guest House, 175 Beatrice Road, NN16 9QR. ☎ (01536) 481940 • Map 141/868801 • BB **C** • EM £10.50, 6-7pm • S3 D1 T2 F1 • 1-12 • Ⓥ Ⓑ Ⓓ Ⓡ Ⓟ Ⓣ 🐾 • ◆◆◆ • pennels@aol.com

MOULTON (Northampton)

Poplars Hotel, Cross Street, NN3 7RZ. ☎ (01604) 643983 • Map 152/782661 • BB **D** • EM £13, 6.30-7.45pm • S4 D6 T5 F7 • 1-12 NX • Ⓥ Ⓑ Ⓓ Ⓢ Ⓟ Ⓣ 🐾 • 3Cr/C • poplars@btclick.com

NETHER HEYFORD (Northampton)
GRAND UNION CANAL WALK

Pam Clements, Heyford B&B, 27 Church Street, NN7 3LH. ☎ (01327) 340872 • Map 152/659586 • BB **B** • T3 • 1-12 • Ⓑ Ⓓ Ⓟ Ⓣ • ◆◆ • Food nearby.

SIBBERTOFT (Market Harborough, Leics)
JURASSIC WAY

Mrs M J Hart, The Wrongs, LE16 9UJ. ☎ (01858) 880886 • Map 141/666829 • BB **B** • S1 D1 • 1-12 • Ⓓ Ⓢ Ⓟ Ⓣ 🐾 • SC, Camping, Caravan also • jasper.h.hartT@farmline.com

SLAPTON (Nr Towcester)

Slapton Manor Farm, Chapel Lane, NN12 8PF. ☎ (01327) 860344 • Map 152/641467 • BB **C/D** • D1 T1 F1 • 1-12 NX • Ⓑ Ⓓ Ⓢ Ⓟ Ⓣ

STOKE BRUERNE (Towcester)
GRAND UNION CANAL WALK

Pam Hart, Beam End, Stoke Park, NN12 7RZ. ☎ (01604) 864802/864638 • Map 152/740489 • BB **D** • EM book first £10, 6-9pm • D2 T1 • 1-12 NX • Ⓥ Ⓑ Ⓓ Ⓢ Ⓟ Ⓣ • ◆◆◆◆Ⓢ • beamend@bun.com

NORTHUMBERLAND

ALNWICK

☆ D Turnbull & S Branson, Rock Farmhouse, Rock Village, NE66 3SE. ☎ (01665) 579235 • Map 81/192189 • BB **C** • EM book first £12.50, 6.45pm • D1 T1 F1 • 1-12 • Ⓥ Ⓑ Ⓓ Ⓢ Ⓟ Ⓣ 🐾 • ◆◆◆ • SC also. www.rockfarmhouse.freeserve.co.uk/

BAMBURGH

Mary Dixon, 'Broome', 22 Ingram Road, NE69 7BT. ☎ (01668) 214287 • Map 75/180347 • BB **D** • EM book first £17.50 • D1 T1 • 1-12 NX • Ⓓ Ⓢ Ⓟ Ⓣ • ◆◆◆◆ • mdixon4394@aol.com

BARDON MILL (Hexham)
PENNINE WAY

Mrs J Davidson, Crindledykes Farm, House Steads, NE47 7AF. ☎ (01434) 344316 • Map 86/782672 • BB **B** • EM book first £11-£12, 6.30-7pm • D1 T1 • 3-11 • Ⓓ Ⓢ Ⓡ Ⓟ • ◆◆◆◆

Mrs Valerie Gibson, Gibbs Hill Farm, Once Brewed, NE47 7AP. ☎ (01434) 344030 • Map 86,87/750691 • BB **C** • EM book first £12, 7pm • D2 T1 • 3-10 • Ⓥ Ⓑ Ⓓ Ⓢ Ⓟ Ⓣ • ◆◆◆ • Hadrians Wall • www.gibbshillfarm.co.uk

BARRASFORD (Hexham)

Joyce Milburn, Barrasford Arms Hotel, NE48 4AA. ☎ (01434) 681237 • Map 87/919733 • BB **D** • EM £8.50, 7.30-9pm • D2 T3 F1 • 1-12 NX • Ⓥ Ⓑ Ⓓ Ⓟ Ⓣ 🐾 • ◆◆◆ • SC and bk/house. www.smoothhound.co.uk/hotels/barrasfd.html

BEAL (Berwick on Tweed)
ST CUTHBERT'S WAY

Brockmill Farmhouse, TD15 2PB. ☎ 01289 381283 • Map 75/060436 • BB **B** • S1 D1 T1 F1 • 2-11 • Ⓓ Ⓢ Ⓟ Ⓣ 🐾 • ◆◆◆ •
www.lindisfarne.org.uk/brock-mill-farmhouse

BELFORD

Mr & Mrs Wood, The Farmhouse Guest House, 24 West Street, NE70 7QE. ☎ (01668) 213083 • Map 75/107339 • BB **B** • EM book first £6.95 • D2 F1 • 1-12 • Ⓥ Ⓑ Ⓓ Ⓢ Ⓟ Ⓣ • ◆◆◆

BELLINGHAM (Hexham)
PENNINE WAY

Ken & Joy Gaskin, Lyndale Guest House & Holiday Cottage, NE48 2AW. ☎ (01434) 220361 • Map 80/839833 • BB **C** • EM book first £12.50, 7pm • S1 D2 T1 F1 • 1-12 NX • Ⓥ Ⓑ Ⓓ Ⓢ Ⓟ Ⓣ • ◆◆◆◆ • Washing & Baggage Transfer

☆ See Display Advertisement

NORTHUMBERLAND   ENGLAND   B&B ACCOMMODATION

■ BERWICK-UPON-TWEED

Nick & Gail Maycock, The Friendly Hound, Ford Common, TD15 2QD. ☎ (01289) 388554 • Map 75/964389 • BB **C** • EM book first £8.50, 6.30-7.30pm • D3 F1 • 1-12 • Ⓥ Ⓑ Ⓓ Ⓢ Ⓟ Ⓣ • ◆◆◆◆ • friendlyhound.b.b.@talk.com

■ CORBRIDGE

☆ Mrs M J Matthews, The Hayes, Newcastle Road, NE45 5LP. ☎ (01434) 632010 • Map 87/996643 • BB **C** • S1 D0 T1 F1 • 1-11.5 NX • Ⓑ Ⓓ Ⓢ Ⓡ Ⓟ Ⓣ Ⓖ • ◆◆ • SC also • mjctmatthews@talk21.com

The Hayes
Bed & Breakfast and Self-catering
Newcastle Road, Corbridge NE45 5LP
RAMBLERS WELCOMED

Highly recommended accommodation in 7½ acres of gardens, paddocks and woodland. BB £20–£24.50. H&C and TV all rooms, most en-suite. Stair lift for disabled. Two self-catering cottages, plus one near Keswick. Large secluded caravan also available. Packed lunches by request.

Tel 01434 632010

■ CORNHILL ON TWEED

The Coach House at Crookham, TD12 4TD. ☎ (01890) 820293 • Map 74,75/911382 • BB **D/E** • EM £17.50, 7.30pm • S2 D2 T5 • 5-10 • Ⓥ Ⓑ Ⓓ Ⓢ Ⓟ Ⓣ Ⓖ • ◆◆◆◆ • www.coachhousecrookham.com

■ COTTONSHOPEBURNFOOT (Otterburn)

Mrs Bell, Border Forest Caravan Park, NE19 1TF. ☎ (01830) 520259 • Map 80/779014 • BB **B** • F2 • 1-12 NX • Ⓑ Ⓓ Ⓢ Ⓟ Ⓣ Ⓖ • Bunkhouse also

■ FALSTONE (Nr Kielder Water)
ALTERNATIVE PENNINE WAY

Mrs M Grimwood, Woodside, Yarrow, NE48 1BG. ☎ (01434) 240443 • Map 80/714874 • BB **B** • EM book first £8.50-9 -9-10.50, 6.30pm • D1 T1 • 4-10 NX • Ⓥ Ⓓ Ⓢ Ⓟ • ◆◆◆◆

Peter Laws, The Blackcock Inn, NE48 1AA. ☎ (01434) 240200 • Map 80/724875 • BB **C** • EM book first £5-10, 6.30-9pm • D/S2 T/S2 F1 • 1-12 • Ⓥ Ⓑ Ⓓ Ⓢ Ⓟ Ⓣ Ⓖ • ◆◆◆ • blackcock@falstone.fsbusiness.co.uk

■ FENWICK (Berwick-upon-Tweed)
ST CUTHBERT'S WAY

Cherry Trees, Fenwick Village, TD15 2PJ. ☎ (01289) 381437 • Map 75/066400 • BB **B** • EM book first £10, 7pm • S1 D1 T1 F1 • 5-9 • Ⓥ Ⓓ Ⓟ Ⓣ Ⓖ

VEGETARIANS
Many establishments do a veggie breakfast even if they don't do an evening meal

---

■ GREENHEAD VIA BRAMPTON
(nr Carlisle, Cumbria)
PENNINE WAY

Mrs P Staff, Holmhead Farm, Hadrians Wall/PW, CA6 7HY. ☎ (016977) 47402 • Map 86/661659 • BB **D** • EM book first £19.95, 7.30pm • D1 T2 F1 • 1-12 NX • Ⓥ Ⓑ Ⓓ Ⓢ Ⓟ Ⓣ • ◆◆◆◆ • Stone Tent available. bandbhadrianswall.com

■ HADRIAN'S WALL (Haydon Bridge)

☆ Mrs Lyn Murray, Hadrian Lodge, Hindshield Moss, North Road, NE47 6NF. ☎ (01434) 688688 • Map 87/830675 • BB **B** • EM £5, 6-8pm • S1 D3 T1 F4 • 1-12 • Ⓥ Ⓑ Ⓓ Ⓡ Ⓟ Ⓖ • ◆◆◆ • SC, hostel,+ groups • hadrianlodge@hadrianswall.co.uk

Hadrian Lodge
B&B ensuite • Bunks • Self-catering cottages • Fishing
Attractively converted former hunting lodge. Tranquil setting overlooking lakes in 18 acres of pasture bordered by pine forest. Great walking country near Hadrian's Wall/Housesteads and Vindolanda Roman forts. Warm welcome, enviable reputation for delicious home cooked meals. Licensed bar. Ring/write for brochure.   ETC ◆◆◆

Tel: Lyn Murray (01434) 688688
email hadrianlodge@hadrianswall.co.uk

■ HALTWHISTLE
PENNINE WAY

Mrs Heather Humes, Hall Meadows, Main Street, NE49 0AZ. ☎ (01434) 321021 • Map 86,87/708641 • BB **B** • S1 D1 T1 • 1-12 NX • Ⓓ Ⓡ Ⓟ Ⓣ • ◆◆◆

The Old School House, Fair Hill, NE49 9EE. ☎ (01434) 322595 • Map 86,87/706642 • BB **B/C** • S2 D1 T1 • 2-12 NX • Ⓑ Ⓓ Ⓢ Ⓡ Ⓟ Ⓣ • ◆◆◆◆ • www.oshouse.freeserve.co.uk/

■ HARBOTTLE (Rothbury)

Rosemary, The Byre Vegetarian B&B, NE65 7DG. ☎ 01669 650476 • Map 80/936047 • BB **B/C** • EM book first £8, 6-8pm • D1 T1 • 1-12 • Ⓥ Ⓓ Ⓢ Ⓟ Ⓣ • ◆◆◆◆ • www.the-byre.co.uk

■ HEXHAM

Mrs Joan Liddle, Peth Head Cottage, Juniper, Steel, NE47 0LA. ☎ (01434) 673286 • Map 87/938587 • BB **C** • S1 D2 • 1-12 NX • Ⓑ Ⓓ Ⓢ Ⓟ • ◆◆◆◆ • tedliddle@compuserve.com

Pat & Jim Mattinson, Ingarth, Leazes Lane, NE46 3AE. ☎ (01434) 603625 • Map 87/925642 • BB **C** • T1 • 1-12 NX • Ⓑ Ⓓ Ⓢ Ⓡ Ⓣ • ◆◆◆◆ • Library for maps/guides • mattinson@clara.co.uk

Philly Hutchinson, Ventnor House, 23 Elvaston Rd, NE46 2HA. ☎ (01434) 607814 • Map 87/934637 • BB **B** • EM book first £15, 7-8pm • D/T 1 • 1-12 NX • Ⓑ Ⓓ Ⓢ Ⓡ Ⓣ • ◆◆◆

■ HOLY ISLAND (Berwick-upon-Tweed)

Castle View, TD15 2SG. ☎ (01289) 389272 • Map 75/128422 • BB **D** • EM book first £8-12, 6.00-8.30pm • S2 D2 T1 F1 • 1-12 BOOK WELL ADVANCE APRIL • Ⓥ Ⓑ Ⓓ Ⓟ Ⓣ • john@viking-island.demon.co.uk

■ HORSLEY (Newcastle upon Tyne)

Mrs Pat Carr, Belvedere, Harlow Hill, , NE15 0QD. ☎ (01661) 853689 • Map 88/077683 • BB **B** • D1 T1 • 2-10 • Ⓑ Ⓓ Ⓢ Ⓡ Ⓟ Ⓣ 🐾 • On Hadrian's Wall

■ ROCHESTER (Nr Otterburn)
PENNINE WAY

Miss Debbie Cranston, Low Byrness, NE19 1TF. ☎ (01830) 520648 • Map 80/779012 • BB **C** • EM book first £12, 7pm • S1 D2 F1 • 1-12 NX • Ⓥ Ⓑ Ⓓ Ⓢ Ⓟ 🐾 • ◆◆◆◆ • 4 miles north of Rochester Village • pdq@globalnet.co.uk

■ ROTHBURY (Morpeth)

☆ Mrs J Pickard, Orchard Guest House, High Street, NE65 7TL. ☎ (01669) 620684 • Map 81/056017 • BB **C** • D2 T2 F1 • 1-12 NX • Ⓑ Ⓓ Ⓢ Ⓣ • ◆◆◆◆ • jpickard@orchardguesthouse.co.uk

Helen & David Edes, Well Strand, NE65 7UD. ☎ (01669) 620794 • Map 81/056016 • BB **B** • S1 D1 T1 • 1-12 NX • Ⓓ Ⓢ 🐾

Mrs June Taylor, Wagtail Farm, NE65 7PL. ☎ (01669) 620367 • Map 81/073008 • BB **B** • D2 • 5-10 • Ⓓ Ⓢ Ⓟ Ⓣ • ◆◆◆

■ STANNERSBURN (Falstone, Kielder Water)

☆ The Pheasant Inn, NE48 1DD. ☎ (01434) 240382 • Map 80/721866 • BB **E** • EM £6.95-£15, 7-9pm • D4 T3 F1 • 1-12 NX • Ⓥ Ⓑ Ⓢ Ⓟ Ⓣ 🐾 • ◆◆◆◆ • thepheasantinn@kielderwater.demon.co.uk

■ WARK (Hexham)
PENNINE WAY

Mrs Ann Bell, Woodpark Farm, NE48 3PZ. ☎ (01434) 230259 • Map 86/847798 • BB **B** • D1 F1 • 4-10 • Ⓓ Ⓢ Ⓟ Ⓣ

■ WARKWORTH (Morpeth)

Mrs D Graham, Bide a While, 4 Beal Croft, NE65 0XL. ☎ (01665) 711753 • Map 81/249053 • BB **B** • D1 F1 • 1-12 • Ⓑ Ⓓ Ⓢ Ⓣ 🐾 • ◆◆◆

■ WEST WOODBURN (Hexham)
PENNINE WAY

☆ Avril A Walton, Yellow House Farm, NE48 2RA. ☎ (01434) 270070 • Map 80/897860 • BB **B** • D1 T1 F1 • 1-12 • Ⓑ Ⓓ Ⓢ Ⓟ Ⓣ 🐾 • ◆◆◆ • Transport to rail.

■ WHITLEY BAY

Allen & Hilary Thompson, Marlborough Hotel, 20-21 East Parade, Central Promenade, NE26 1AP. ☎ (0191) 251 3628 • Map 88/356724 • BB **C/D** • EM book first £11.95, 6.30-7.30pm • S6 D3 T5 F3 • 1-12 NX • Ⓥ Ⓑ Ⓓ Ⓢ Ⓟ Ⓣ 🐾 • ◆◆◆◆ • reception@marlborough-hotel.com

■ WOOLER
ST CUTHBERT'S WAY

Mrs M Hugall, St Hilliers, 6 Church Street, NE71 6DA. ☎ (01668) 281340 • Map 75/990280 • BB **C** • S1 D1 T2 F1 • 1-12 NX • Ⓓ Ⓢ Ⓟ Ⓣ 🐾 • ◆◆◆ • SC also

Terry & Veronica Gilbert, Winton House, 39 Glendale Road, NE71 6DL. ☎ (01668) 281362 • Map 75/991283 • BB **B/C** • D2 T1 • 3-10 • Ⓑ Ⓓ Ⓢ Ⓟ Ⓣ • ◆◆◆ • Transport avail. • winton.house@virgin.net

☆ Tankerville Arms Hotel, 22 Cottage Road, NE71 6AD. ☎ (01668) 281581 • Map 75/990285 • BB **D/E** • EM Y • S2 D6 T6 F2 • 1-12 NX • Ⓥ Ⓑ Ⓓ Ⓢ Ⓟ Ⓣ 🐾 • ★★★ • www.tankervillehotel.co.uk • See also the display advert at the start of the next page

☆ See Display Advertisement

■ WOOLER (continued)
ST CUTHBERT'S WAY

Tankerville Arms Hotel

Charming 17th century coaching inn with superb en-suite accommodation in beautiful unspoilt Northumberland. Ideal for walking, touring, National Trust, coast and Scottish borders. Real ales, log fires, lovely gardens and excellent food.

Special rate from November to March.

WOOLER
NORTHUMBERLAND • NE71 6AD
Telephone: (01668) 281581
www.tankervillehotel.co.uk

☆ J Devenport, Tilldale House, 34/40 High Street, NE71 6BG. ☎ (01668) 281450 • Map 75/990281 • BB **B/C** • EM book first £8, 6-7.30pm • S3 D3 T3 F3 • 1-12 NX • Ⓥ Ⓑ Ⓓ Ⓢ Ⓟ Ⓣ 🛁 • ◆◆◆◆ • www.tilldalehouse.com

---

Tilldale House
Wooler, Northumberland
Charming stone built house, all bedrooms are comfortable, spacious and en-suite. home cooking with good choice of menu. Ideal for the beautiful Northumberland countryside, and St Cuthbert's Way.
B&B £17-£20, EM £8, ETC 4 diamonds
Further details 01668 281450
enquiries@tilldalehouse.com
www.tilldalehouse.com

Mrs J Allam, 1 Ryecroft Way, NE71 6BW. ☎ (01668) 281358 • Map 75/990283 • BB **C** • EM £6.50, 6-7pm • S2 T4 • 1-12 • Ⓥ Ⓑ Ⓟ Ⓣ 🛁 Ⓜ

NOTTINGHAMSHIRE

■ LAXTON (Newark)
ROBIN HOOD'S WAY

Mrs Pat Haigh, Manor Farm, Moorhouse Road, NG22 0NU. ☎ (01777) 870417 • Map 120/724666 • BB **B** • D1 F2 • 1-12 NX • Ⓓ Ⓢ Ⓟ Ⓣ 🛁 • ◆◆

■ SOUTHWELL (Newark)
ROBIN HOOD'S WAY

I S Wright, 56 Church Street, NG25 0HG. ☎ (01636) 812004 • Map 120/700539 • BB **C** • D2 T1 • 1-12 • Ⓑ Ⓓ Ⓢ Ⓡ Ⓟ Ⓣ • ianwright5@btinternet.com

---

OXFORDSHIRE

■ ABINGDON
THAMES PATH

Susie Howard, 22 East Saint Helen Street, OX14 5EB. ☎ (01235) 550979 • Map 164/497969 • BB **D** • S2 D1 T1 • 1-12 NX • Ⓑ Ⓓ Ⓢ Ⓟ Ⓣ • srhoward@talk21.com

■ ASCOTT-UNDER-WYCHWOOD (Chipping Norton)
OXFORDSHIRE WAY

Anne & Nigel Braithwaite, The Mill, OX7 6AP. ☎ (01993) 831282 • Map 164/309194 • BB **C** • S1 D/T2 • 1-12 • Ⓓ Ⓢ Ⓡ Ⓟ Ⓣ • ◆◆◆ • mill@auwoxon32.freeserve.co.uk

■ BAMPTON (Oxford)
THAMES PATH

Serena Fry-Ferretti, 9 Glebelands, OX18 2LH. ☎ (01993) 852715 • Map 164/312036 • BB **B** • EM book first £7.5, 8-9pm • S1 D1 • 1-12 NX • Ⓥ Ⓓ Ⓢ Ⓟ

■ BUSCOT (Faringdon)
THAMES PATH

Mrs E Reay, Apple Tree House, SN7 8DA. ☎ (01367) 252592 • Map 163/228981 • BB **C** • D2 T1 • 1-12 • Ⓑ Ⓓ Ⓢ Ⓣ • ◆◆◆ • emreay@aol.com

■ CASSINGTON (Oxford)
THAMES PATH

Barbara Newcombe-Jones, St Margaret's Lodge, The Green, OX8 1DN. ☎ (01865) 880361 • Map 164/453107 • BB **C** • D2 • 1-12 NX • Ⓑ Ⓢ Ⓟ Ⓣ

■ CHARLBURY

Ms Angela Widdows, Banbury Hill Farm, OX7 3JH. ☎ (01608) 810314 • Map 164/363209 • BB **B/C/E** • S1 D2 T2 F7 • 1-12 NX • Ⓑ Ⓓ Ⓢ Ⓡ Ⓣ • ◆◆◆◆ • www.charlburyoxfordaccom.co.uk

■ CHIMNEY-ON-THAMES (Bampton)
THAMES PATH

Mrs Jean Kinch, Chimney Farmhouse, OX18 2EH. ☎ 01367 870279 • Map 164/358008 • BB **D** • S1 D1 T1 • 2-11 • Ⓑ Ⓓ Ⓢ Ⓣ • ◆◆◆◆

■ DEDDINGTON (Oxford)

Joan White, Hill Barn, Milton Gated Road, OX15 0TS. ☎ (01869) 338631 • Map 151/466328 • BB **C** • D1 T2 F1 • 1-12 NX • Ⓑ Ⓢ Ⓟ Ⓣ 🛁 • ◆◆ • hillbarn-bb@supanet.com

■ EAST HENDRED (Wantage)

Mrs Iris Newman, Ridgeway Lodge Hotel, Skeats Bush, OX12 8LH. ☎ (01235) 833360 • Map 174/457884 • BB **E** • EM £8, 6-8.30pm • S4 D2 T4 F1 • 1-12 • Ⓥ Ⓑ Ⓓ Ⓟ Ⓣ 🕭

■ FARINGDON
THAMES PATH

☆ Andrew Ibbotson, Sudbury House Hotel, London Street, SN7 8AA. ☎ (01367) 241272 • Map 164/294954 • BB **E** • EM £19.95, 7-9.30pm • D39 T10 • 1-12 NX • Ⓥ Ⓑ Ⓓ Ⓢ Ⓟ Ⓣ 🕭 • Ⓜ • 4Cr • www.sudburyhouse.co.uk

■ HENLEY-ON-THAMES
OXFORDSHIRE WAY & THAMES PATH

Mrs J Williams, Lenwade, 3 Western Road, RG9 1JL. ☎ (01491) 573468/(0374) 941629 • Map 175/760817 • BB **D** • D2 T1 • 1-12 • Ⓑ Ⓓ Ⓢ Ⓡ Ⓟ Ⓣ 🕭 • ◆◆◆◆◆ • www.w36-ink.com/lenwade

Mr & Mrs E G Willis, Avalon, 36 Queen Street, RG9 1AP. ☎ (01491) 577829 • Map 175/762824 • BB **D** • S1 D1 T1 • 1-12 • Ⓑ Ⓓ Ⓢ Ⓡ Ⓣ • List/C • avalon@henleybb.fsnet.co.uk

Mr & Mrs Brooks, Jacksons Farm, Fawley Bottom, RG9 6JJ. ☎ (01491) 575330 • Map 175/747879 • BB **C** • EM book first £from £7.50, from 7pm • D/F1 T1 • 1-12 NX • Ⓥ Ⓑ Ⓓ Ⓟ Ⓣ 🕭

■ HOOK NORTON (Banbury)

Valerie & Donald Cornelius, Symnel, High Street, OX15 5NH. ☎ (01608) 737547 • Map 151/352331 • BB **B** • EM book first £8 • D1 T2 • 1-12 NX • Ⓥ Ⓓ Ⓢ Ⓟ Ⓣ 🕭 • ◆◆

Marcus & Judy Hughes, Manor Farm, OX15 5LU. ☎ (01608) 737204 • Map 151/372333 • BB **C** • 1-12 NX • Ⓓ Ⓢ Ⓟ Ⓣ • ◆◆◆ • 2 all-purpose rooms • jdyhughes@aol.com

■ LONG HANBOROUGH (WOODSTOCK) (Witney)

Tom & Carol Ellis, Wynford House, 79 Main Road, OX8 8JX. ☎ (01993) 881402 • Map 164/425143 • BB **C** • EM book first £10, 7pm • D1 T1 F1 • 1-12NX • Ⓥ Ⓑ Ⓓ Ⓢ Ⓡ Ⓣ 🕭

■ LONG WITTENHAM (Abingdon)
THAMES PATH

Mrs Jill Mellor, Witta's Ham Cottage, High Street, OX14 4QH. ☎ (01865) 407686 • Map 174,164/546937 • BB **C** • EM N • S1 D1 T1 • 1-12 NX • Ⓓ Ⓢ Ⓡ Ⓟ Ⓣ 🕭 • Food nearby

■ MOULSFORD-ON-THAMES (Wallingford)
THAMES PATH & RIDGEWAY

Mrs Maria Watsham, White House, OX10 9JD. ☎ (01491) 651397 • Map 174/591837 • BB **D/E** • EM book first £15 • S1 D1 T1 • 1-12 NX • Ⓥ Ⓓ Ⓢ Ⓡ Ⓟ Ⓣ • ◆◆◆◆◆

■ NORTH LEIGH (Witney)

☆ Mr & Mrs Hamilton, Gorselands Hall, Boddington Lane, OX8 6PU. ☎ (01993) 882292 • Map 164/399135 • BB **C** • D4 T1 F1 • 1-12 NX • Ⓥ Ⓑ Ⓓ Ⓢ Ⓡ Ⓣ 🕭 • ◆◆◆ • SC also • hamilton@gorselandshall.com

■ NORTH STOKE (Wallingford)
RIDGEWAY

Mrs Tanner, Footpath Cottage, The Street, OX10 6BJ. ☎ (01491) 839763 • Map 175/610863 • BB **C** • EM book first £9 • S1 D1 • 1-12 • Ⓥ Ⓑ Ⓓ Ⓢ Ⓟ Ⓣ 🕭 • List

■ OXFORD
THAMES PATH & THREE CASTLES WALK

Nest Lewis, Acorn Guest House, 260/262 Iffley Road, OX4 1SE. ☎ (01865) 247998 • Map 164/527049 • BB **C/D** • S4 D2 T1 F5 • 1-12 NX • Ⓑ Ⓓ Ⓢ Ⓣ • ◆◆ • Passenger lift to half of BB.

■ PISHILL (Henley-on-Thames)
OXFORDSHIRE WAY

Mrs E Lakey, Bank Farm, RG9 6HJ. ☎ (01491) 638601 • Map 175/723898 • BB **C** • S1 F1 • 1-12 • Ⓑ Ⓓ Ⓢ Ⓟ Ⓣ 🕭 • ◆◆ • bankfarm@compuserve.com

Joan Connolly, Orchard House, RG9 6HJ. ☎/Fax (01491) 638351 • Map 175/723898 • BB **C** • EM book first £, 7-9pm • S/D3 D2 T1 F3 • 1-12 NX • Ⓥ Ⓑ Ⓓ Ⓢ Ⓟ 🕭 • ◆◆◆

☆ See Display Advertisement

■ **SHILLINGFORD (Wallingford)**
Hilary Warburton, North Farm, Shillingford Hill, OX10 8NB. ☎ (01865) 858406 • Map 174,164/586924 • BB **D** • D2 T1 • 1-12 NX • Ⓑ Ⓓ Ⓢ Ⓟ Ⓣ 🐾 Ⓜ •
◆◆◆◆Ⓢ • www.country-accom.co.uk/northfarm/

■ **SPARSHOLT**
RIDGEWAY
The Star Inn, Watery Lane, OX12 9PL. ☎ (01235) 751001 • Map 174/347877 • BB **E** • EM £8, 7-9pm • D2 T5 F1 • 1-12 • Ⓥ Ⓑ Ⓢ Ⓣ • ◆◆◆◆

■ **TACKLEY (Woodstock)**
OXFORDSHIRE WAY
June Collier, 55 Nethercote Road, OX5 3AT. ☎ (01869) 331255 • Map 164/482206 • BB **C/D** • D1 T1 • 1-12 • Ⓑ Ⓓ Ⓢ Ⓡ Ⓟ Ⓣ • Baggage transfer.

■ **UFFINGTON (Faringdon)**
RIDGEWAY & JURASSIC WAY
C Wadsworth, The Craven, Fernham Road, SN7 7RD. ☎ (01367) 820449 • Map 174/303895 • BB **D** • EM £20, 7-8pm • S3 D3 T1 F1 • 1-12 • Ⓥ Ⓑ Ⓓ Ⓢ Ⓟ • www.thecraven.co.uk

■ **WALLINGFORD**
THAMES PATH & RIDGEWAY & CHILTERN WAY
Mrs J Standbridge, Dormer Cottage, High Street, Ewelme, OX10 6HQ. ☎ (01491) 833987 • Map 164,175/643916 • BB **B/C** • T1 F1 • 3-10 NX • Ⓓ Ⓢ Ⓟ Ⓣ

Jill & Tony Reeves, Little Gables, 166 Crowmarsh Hill, OX10 8BG. ☎ 01491 837834 • Map 175/627887 • BB **D** • S1 D/S2 T/S3 F/S2 • 1-12 NX • Ⓑ Ⓓ Ⓢ Ⓟ Ⓣ • ◆◆◆ • www.stayingaway.com

■ **WANTAGE**
RIDGEWAY
Mrs Stella Cowan, Lockinge Kiln Farm, The Ridgeway, OX12 8PA. ☎ 01235 763308 • Map 174/423833 • BB **B** • EM book first £8.50, 7pm • D1 T2 • 1-12 NX • Ⓥ Ⓓ Ⓢ Ⓟ Ⓣ 🐾

■ **WATLINGTON (Wallingford)**
OXFORDSHIRE WAY & RIDGEWAY
Mrs R Roberts, Woodgate Orchard Cottage, Howe Road, OX49 5EL. ☎ (01491) 612675 • Map 175/691937 • BB **C/D** • EM book first £ • D1 T1 F1 • 1-12 • Ⓑ Ⓓ Ⓢ Ⓟ •
mailbox@wochr.freeserve.co.uk

■ **WESTON-ON-THE-GREEN (Bicester)**
OXFORDSHIRE WAY
Mr & Mrs Godwin, Manor Farm, OX6 8QL. ☎ (01869) 350354 • Map 164/536183 • BB **D** • S1 D3 T1 F1 • 1-12 • Ⓑ Ⓓ Ⓢ Ⓡ Ⓟ • Food nearby

■ **WOOTTON (Woodstock)**
OXFORDSHIRE WAY
Mrs Nancy Fletcher, 8 Manor Court, OX20 1EU. ☎ (01993) 811186 • Map 164/438199 • BB **B** • S2 T1 • 1-11 • Ⓑ Ⓓ Ⓢ Ⓟ Ⓣ • App • Food nearby

SHROPSHIRE

■ **ABDON (Craven Arms)**
SHROPSHIRE WAY
☆ Mrs Jill Scurfield, Earnstrey Hill House, SY7 9HU. ☎ 01746 712579 • Map 137/587873 • BB **C/D** • EM book first £15.50 • D1 T2 • 1-12 NX • Ⓑ Ⓓ Ⓢ Ⓟ Ⓣ 🐾 • ◆◆◆◆ • hugh.scurfield@smwh.org.uk

■ **ASTON-ON-CLUN (Craven Arms)**
SHROPSHIRE WAY
Sue Reeves, Mill Stream Cottage, SY7 8EP. ☎ (01588) 660699 • Map 137/384816 • BB **C** • D1 T1 • 1-12 • Ⓓ Ⓢ Ⓡ Ⓟ Ⓣ 🐾 • ◆◆◆

■ **BISHOPS CASTLE (Montgomery, Powys)**
OFFA'S DYKE & SHROPSHIRE WAY
Peter & Phyllis Hutton, The Old Brick Guesthouse, 7 Church Street, SY9 5AA. ☎ (01588) 638471 • Map 137/323885 • BB **D** • EM book first £12, 7-7.30pm • S1 D2 T1 F1 • 1-12 NX • Ⓥ Ⓑ Ⓓ Ⓟ Ⓣ 🐾 • ◆◆◆ • Credit Cards accepted • oldBrick@beeb.net

Boars Head Hotel, Church Street, SY9 5AE. ☎ (01588) 638521 • Map 137/322884 • BB **E** • EM £8.5, 6.30-9.30pm • D1 T2 F1 • 1-12 • Ⓥ Ⓑ Ⓓ Ⓢ Ⓟ Ⓣ 🐾 • www.boarsheadhotel.co.uk

■ **BROSELEY**
Diane Kaiser, Orchard House, 40 King Street, TF12 5NA. ☎ (01952) 882684 • Map 127/671022 • BB **C** • EM book first £10, 6.30pm • D1 T1 F1 • 1-12 NX • Ⓥ Ⓑ Ⓓ Ⓣ 🐾 • ◆◆◆

■ **CARDINGTON (Church Stretton)**
Mrs O Pennington, Grove Farm, SY6 7JZ. ☎ (01694) 771451 • Map 137,138/505952 • BB **B** • EM book first £5 • T1 F1 • 1-12 • Ⓥ Ⓓ Ⓢ Ⓟ 🐾 • ◆◆

■ CHURCH STRETTON

☆ Belvedere Guest House, Burway Road, SY6 6DP.
☎ (01694) 722232 • Map 137/451941 • BB **D** • EM
• S3 D4 T3 F2 • 1-12 NX • Ⓥ Ⓑ Ⓓ Ⓢ Ⓡ Ⓟ Ⓣ
🐾 • 3Cr/C • Groups also • belv@bigfoot.com

Belvedere Guest House
BURWAY ROAD
CHURCH STRETTON

English Tourism Council, AA and RAC ◆◆◆◆

In superb walking country, a comfortable house on slopes of Long Mynd, minutes from Church Stretton. Bedroom tea-making facilities. Two lounges (one with TV). Packed lunches. 10% reduction for weekly or party bookings. Well-behaved pets and children welcome.

Tel. 01694 722232 • Fax. 01694 722232

☆ Joanna Brereton, Woolston Farm, Woolston, SY6 6QD. ☎ (01694) 781201 • Map 137/424871 • BB **B/C** • EM book first £10, 6.30pm • D2 T1 • 2-11 • Ⓥ Ⓓ Ⓢ Ⓟ Ⓣ 🐾 • ◆◆◆ • jbrereton@crosswinds.net

---

Woolston Farm
Church Stretton

Victorian farmhouse situated above Wistanstow. Long Mynd and Stiperstones nearby. Friendly atmosphere and good home cooking. ETC ◆◆◆◆

Contact Joanna Brereton
Marshbrook (01694) 781201

Mrs Margaret Knight, Rheingold, 9 The Bridleways, SY6 7AN. ☎ (01694) 723969 • Map 137,138/462934 • BB **C** • EM book first £10, 7.15pm • D2 T1 • 1-12 NX • Ⓑ Ⓢ Ⓡ Ⓟ Ⓣ • ◆◆

☆ Mr & Mrs E Webb, Brookfields Guest House, Watling Street Nth, SY6 7AR. ☎ (01694) 722314 • Map 137,138/459937 • BB **C/D** • EM £8.50, 6.30pm • D2 T1 F1 • 1-12 NX • Ⓥ Ⓑ Ⓓ Ⓢ Ⓡ Ⓟ Ⓣ • ◆◆◆

'Little Switzerland'
Church Stretton, Shropshire
Centre for Walking
Large comfortable Edwardian house and grounds. Panoramic views of the hills and the Long Mynd. Near to town and train station. Luxury en-suite bedrooms. home cooking. Evening meals. Licenced. Non-smoking. Drying room. Special breaks.   ETC
Mr & Mrs E Webb   ◆◆◆
Brookfields Guest House 01694 722314

☆ The Longmynd Hotel, Cunnery Road, SY6 6AG.
☎ (01694) 722244 • Map 137/449935 • BB **E** • EM £14.95+, 6.45-9pm • S6 D22 T13 F9 • 1-12 • Ⓥ Ⓑ Ⓓ Ⓢ Ⓡ Ⓟ Ⓣ 🐾 • ★★★★ •
reservations@longmynd.co.uk

The Longmynd Hotel
Church Stretton
Shropshire SY6 6AG
Tel 01694 722244
www.longmynd.co.uk
info@longmynd.co.uk

Breathtaking views, fine restaurant and bar facilities. Ideal location for walking the Shropshire hills and touring the area. Special interest packages and many amenities ETC
(incl. gym, pool, solarium) available.   ★★★

Patrick & Madeline Egan, Sayang House, SY6 7DD.
☎ (01694) 723981 • Map 137,138/476924 • BB **D** • EM book first £15, 7pm • T1 F/D2 • 1-12 NX • Ⓥ Ⓑ Ⓓ Ⓢ Ⓡ Ⓟ Ⓣ 🐾 • ◆◆◆◆ •
www.sayanghouse.co.uk

■ CLEEDOWNTON (Ludlow)
SHROPSHIRE WAY

Lower House Farm Guest House, SY8 3EH.
☎ (01584) 823648 • Map 138/582806 • BB **D** • EM book first £14.90, 7.30pm • S1 D1 T2 • 1-12 • Ⓑ Ⓓ Ⓢ Ⓟ Ⓣ 🐾 • ◆◆◆◆ • gsblack@talk21.com

■ CLEOBURY MORTIMER (Kidderminster)

Dinah M Thompson, Cox's Barn, Bagginswood, DY14 8LS. ☎ (01746) 718415/(0411) 355727 • Map 138/682805 • BB **C** • EM book first £8-£12, 6.30-8.30pm • D3 • 1-12 • Ⓥ Ⓑ Ⓓ Ⓢ Ⓟ Ⓣ 🐾 • ◆◆◆◆

■ CLUN (Craven Arms)
SHROPSHIRE WAY

M Ellison, New House Farm, SY7 8NJ. ☎ (01588) 638314 • Map 137/275863 • BB **D** • T1 F1 • 4-10 • Ⓑ Ⓓ Ⓢ Ⓟ Ⓣ 🐾 • ◆◆◆◆◆Ⓖ

Anthony & Sue Whitfield, Clun Farm House, High Street, SY7 8JB. ☎ (01588) 640432 • Map 137/302808 • BB **B** • EM book first £12-16 • D/F1 T/D1 F1 • 1-12 NX • Ⓥ Ⓑ Ⓓ Ⓢ Ⓟ 🐾 • List • Transport avail.

Mrs J Williams, Hurst Mill Farm, SY7 0JA.
☎ (01588) 640224 • Map 137/323811 • BB **C** • EM book first £8, 6-8pm • D1 T1 F1 • 1-12 NX • Ⓥ Ⓑ Ⓓ Ⓢ Ⓟ Ⓣ 🐾 Ⓜ • ◆◆◆ • SC also

Gill Dellacasa, Birches Mill, SY7 8NL. ☎ (01588) 640409 • Map 137/280820 • BB **D** • EM book first £17, 7.30pm • D2 T1 F1 • 4-10 • Ⓥ Ⓑ Ⓓ Ⓢ Ⓟ Ⓣ 🐾 Ⓜ • ◆◆◆◆ • SC also

☆ See Display Advertisement

■ **CLUN (Craven Arms) (continued)**
SHROPSHIRE WAY

☆ Reg Maund & Judy Bailey, Crown House, Church Street, SY8 8JW. ☎ (01588) 640780 • Map 137/300805 • BB **B/C** • S1 D1 T1 • 1-12 • B D S P T 🐾 Ⓜ • ◆◆◆◆

The Old Stables & Saddlery Crown House, Clun

We welcome muddy boots, happy people and friendly dogs, give free lifts to and from Offa's Dyke and are on the Shropshire Way. We have superb accommodation with ensuite and private facilities. A haven after a days walking.

☎ *01588 640780*

☆ Sun Inn, 10 High Street, SY7 8JB. ☎ (01538) 640559 • Map 137/312817 • BB **D** • EM £5.75, 6-9pm • D4 T1 F1 • 1-12 • V B D P T 🐾 • ◆◆◆

SUN INN CLUN
(E.T.B. THREE DIAMONDS)

XVth Century village Inn on Shropshire Way near Offas Dyke, en-suite accommodation (well behaved dogs welcome). Evening meals, drying facilities, packed lunches available, private parking, Bed & Breakfast **£25** per person. Special rates for 3 nights or more

01588 640559

John & Judy Adamson, Glebelands, 25 Knighton Road, SY7 8JH. ☎ 01588 640442 • Map 137/299805 • BB **B** • T2 • 4-12 NX • B D S P T • ◆◆◆ • Food nearby • tourism@clun25.freeserve.co.uk

■ **CRAVEN ARMS**
SHROPSHIRE WAY

☆ Roger & Sheila Davies, Hesterworth Holidays, Hopesay, SY7 8EX. ☎ (01588) 660487 • Map 137/391817 • BB **C** • EM £8.50-£12.50, 6-7.30pm • S3 D6 T10 F2 • 1-12 • V B D R P T 🐾 • ★★★★★ • www.go2.co.uk/hesterworth • SC and groups also

---

The symbols used in the Accommodation Guide are explained on page 287, just before the MAPS

HESTERWORTH HOLIDAYS
HOPESAY, CRAVEN ARMS, SHROPSHIRE SY7 8EX

On Shropshire Way – ETC ★★–★★★

Comfortable homely accommodation in country-house apartments and cottages surrounded by 12 acres of beautiful gardens and grounds. Large communal/dining room, good home-cooked meals, ideal for families or groups. Ludlow 10 miles. Private bathroom, CTV, pay phone, tea/coffee, licenced. B&B from £22. Evening meals £9.25–£12.50. Packed lunch by arrangement. Self-catering also.

Tel. Roger & Sheila Davies 01588 660487
Fax 01588 660153
www.go2.co.uk/hesterworth

■ **EASTHOPE (Much Wenlock)**
SHROPSHIRE WAY

Isobel & John Bushell, Madam's Hill, Hilltop, TF13 6DJ. ☎ (01746) 785269 • Map 138/565962 • BB **C** • D1 T1 F1 • 1-12 NX • D S P T 🐾 • ◆◆◆ • Food nearby

■ **ELLESMERE**

Mrs H Rodenhurst, Hordley Hall, Hordley, SY12 9BB. ☎ (01691) 622772 • Map 126/381308 • BB **C** • EM book first £12, 7-8pm • S1 D2 F1 • 1-12 • V B D S P T 🐾 • List/App

■ **GOBOWEN (Oswestry)**

Miss O Powell, Clevelands, Station Road, SY11 3JS. ☎ (01691) 661359 • Map 126/302334 • BB **B** • S2 D1 • 1-12 • D S R 🐾 • Food nearby

■ **HIGH ERCALL (Telford)**
SHROPSHIRE WAY

Judy Yates, The Mill House, Shrewsbury Road, TF6 6BE. ☎ 01952 770394 • Map 126/584163 • BB **D** • D1 F1 • 1-12 NX • D S P T 🐾 • ◆◆◆◆ • mill-house@talk21.com

■ **IRONBRIDGE (Telford)**

Janet Hunter, Post Office House, 6 The Square, TF8 7AQ. ☎ (01952) 433201 • Map 127/673034 • BB **C/E** • SO D2 F1 • 1-12 • B D P T 🐾 • ◆◆◆ • www.pohouse-ironbridge.fsnet.co.uk

■ **LUDLOW**
SHROPSHIRE WAY

☆ Cecil Guest House, Sheet Road, SY8 1LR.
☎ (01584) 872442 • Map 137,138/525742 • BB **C/D** •
EM book first £14.50, 7pm • S2 D2 T4 F1 • 1-12 NX •
Ⓥ Ⓑ Ⓓ Ⓢ Ⓡ Ⓟ Ⓣ ⬥ • ◆◆◆ • Groups also

CECIL GUEST HOUSE
Sheet Road, Ludlow, Shropshire SY8 1LR
Comfortable guest house offers a relaxing atmosphere,
freshly cooked food and spotlessly clean surroundings.
CH. Nine bedrooms with H&C, TV and tea-making
facilities, four en suite. Residents bar and lounge.
Parking. B&B from £20.00, EM £14.50.
Parties welcome. Mid week bookings taken.
Smoking only in bar.   English
AA   ☎ /Fax 01584 872442   Tourism
        SUE AND RON GREEN   Council
◆◆◆   ◆◆◆

Mrs J Bowen, Arran House, 42 Gravel Hill, SY8 1QR.
☎ (01584) 873764 • Map 148,137/313749 • BB **B** •
EM book first £10, 6pm • S2 D1 T1 • 1-12 NX • Ⓓ
Ⓢ Ⓡ Ⓟ Ⓣ ⬥ • ◆◆◆

Henwick House, Gravel Hill, SY8 1QU. ☎ (01584)
873338 • Map 137,138/515751 • BB **C** • S1 D1 T2 •
3-12 NX • Ⓑ Ⓓ Ⓢ Ⓡ Ⓟ Ⓣ ⬥ • ◆◆◆

■ **MINSTERLEY (Shrewsbury)**
Phil & June Breeze, Mandalay B&B, The Grove, SY5
0AG. ☎ (01743) 791758 • Map 126/373055 • BB **C** •
EM book first £ • D1 F1 • 1-12 • Ⓥ Ⓑ Ⓓ Ⓟ Ⓣ •
◆◆◆◆

■ **MONTFORD BRIDGE (Shrewsbury)**
Maureen Everall, Broomfields Farm, SY4 1HN.
☎ (01743) 850310 • Map 126/425176 • BB **C** •
EM book first £11, 7pm • D1 T2 • 1-12 NX • Ⓑ Ⓓ Ⓢ
Ⓟ ⬥

■ **MUCH WENLOCK**
Gaskell Arms Hotel, TF13 6AQ. ☎ (01952) 727212 •
Map 138/622998 • BB **E** • EM £7, 7-9.30pm • S4 D9
T5 F2 • 1-12 • Ⓥ Ⓑ Ⓓ Ⓟ Ⓣ • ◆◆◆ •
maxine@gaskellarms.co.uk

■ **MYDDLE (Shrewsbury)**
Mrs Gwen Frost, Oakfields, Baschurch Road, SY4
3RX. ☎ (01939) 290823 • Map 126/465235 • BB **B** •
D1 T1 F1 • 1-12 • Ⓓ Ⓢ Ⓡ Ⓣ ⬥ • ◆◆◆

■ **NORBURY (Bishops Castle, Shropshire)**
SHROPSHIRE WAY
Ann Williams, Shuttocks Wood, SY9 5EA. ☎ (01588)
650433 • Map 137/367924 • BB **C** • EM book first
£12.50, 7pm • D1 T2 • 1-12 NX • Ⓥ Ⓑ Ⓓ Ⓢ Ⓟ
Ⓣ • ◆◆◆◆ • shuttockswood@barclays.net

HIRING MAPS FROM THE RA MAP LIBRARY?
GIVE PLENTY OF NOTICE — MAPS OF
POPULAR AREAS RUN OUT IN HIGH SEASON

■ **OSWESTRY**
OFFA'S DYKE
The Bear Hotel and Bear's Paw Restaurant, Salop
Road, SY11 2NR. ☎ (01691) 652093 • Map
126/292295 • BB **C** • EM £8, 7-9.30pm • S3 D4 T2 F1
• 1-11 NX • Ⓥ Ⓑ Ⓓ Ⓟ Ⓣ ⬥ • ◆◆◆◆ • Groups
also • www.bearhotel.net

David & Sharon Atkinson, The Old Mill Inn, SY10
9AZ. ☎ (01691) 657058 • Map 126/252285 • BB **B** •
EM £6, 6-9.30pm • S2 D1 T2 • 1-12 • Ⓥ Ⓓ Ⓢ Ⓟ
Ⓣ • theoldmill.inn@virgin.net

■ **RATLINGHOPE (Shrewsbury)**
SHROPSHIRE WAY
Stuart & Carol Buxton, Marehay Farm, Ratlinghope,
Pontesbury, SY5 0SJ. ☎ (01588) 650289 • Map
137/381983 • BB **C** • T2 • 1-12 NX • Ⓑ Ⓓ Ⓢ Ⓟ Ⓣ
• ◆◆◆◆

■ **SHREWSBURY**
SHROPSHIRE WAY
Abbey Court House, 134 Abbey Foregate, SY2 6AU.
☎ (01743) 364416 • Map 126/506122 • BB **B/C** • S2
D3 T3 F2 • 1-12 NX • Ⓑ Ⓓ Ⓢ Ⓡ Ⓣ • ◆◆

☆ Sydney House Hotel, Coton Crescent, Coton Hill,
SY1 2LJ. ☎ (01743) 354681/Freecall (0800)
2981243 • Map 126/490135 • BB **D** • EM book first
£11-£14, 7.30pm • S2 D3 T2 • 1-12 NX • Ⓥ Ⓑ Ⓓ
Ⓢ Ⓡ Ⓟ Ⓣ • 3Cr/C

AA   VISA   ETB Commended
SYDNEY HOUSE HOTEL
Shrewsbury SY1 2LJ
Ideally situated within 10 mins walk of town centre,
railway station & castle. All rooms en-suite with
TV/teletext, clock radio/alarm, telephone, hairdryer,
tea/coffee making. Residents bar. Dinner available
£27.50-£30 pp. Private car park.
For brochure Phone/Fax 01743 354681
Freecall 0800 2981243

Pia Widen & John Brookes, Lucroft Hotel,
Castlegates, SY1 2AD. ☎ (01743) 362421 • Map
126/492128 • BB **B** • S6 D2 T2 F2 • 1-12 • Ⓓ Ⓡ Ⓣ
⬥ • 1Cr • piawiden@lineone.net

Gill Oldham-Malcolm, The Bancroft, Coton Crescent,
SY1 2NY. ☎ (01743) 231746 • Map 126/490135 • BB
B • S2 D1 T1 • 1-12 NX • Ⓑ Ⓓ Ⓢ Ⓡ Ⓟ Ⓣ ⬥ •
◆◆◆ • bancroft01@aol.com

■ **STIPERSTONES (Minsterley, Shrewsbury)**
SHROPSHIRE WAY
Mrs Jean Lees, The Old Chapel, Perkinsbeach Dingle,
SY5 0PE. ☎ (01743) 791449 • Map 126/363003 • BB
B • S1 T1 • 1-12 NX • Ⓓ Ⓢ Ⓟ Ⓣ • ◆◆◆◆ •
jean@a-lees.freeserve.co.uk

☆ See Display Advertisement

Alison Symons, 'Mulberry Cottage', 41 Snailbeach, SY5 0NX. ☎ (07855) 109538 • Map 126/372020 • BB **A** • EM book first £9, 7pm • S1 D1 • 1-12 • V̄ D̄ S̄ P̄ T̄ ♿

■ TREFONEN (Oswestry)

Helen & Stephen, The Pentre, SY10 9EE. ☎ (01691) 653952 • Map 126/238260 • BB **C** • EM book first £12, 7.30pm • F2 • 1-12 NX • V̄ B̄ D̄ S̄ P̄ T̄ ♿ • ♦♦♦♦ • thepentre@micro-plus-web.net

■ WEM (Shrewsbury)
SHROPSHIRE WAY

Mrs Anne James, Forncet, Soulton Road, SY4 5HR. ☎ (01939) 232996 • Map 126/521292 • BB **B** • EM book first £10, 6.30-8pm • S1 T1 F1 • 1-12 NX • V̄ D̄ S̄ R̄ P̄ • ♦♦

SOMERSET

■ ALLERFORD, NR PORLOCK (Minehead)
SOUTH WEST COAST PATH

Cathy Powell, Exmoor Falconry & Animal Farm, TA24 8HJ. ☎ 01643 862816 • Map 181/900477 • BB **B/C** • D2 T1 • 1-12 NX • V̄ D̄ S̄ P̄ T̄ ♿ • ♦♦♦ • www.exmoorfalconry.co.uk

■ AXBRIDGE
WEST MENDIP WAY

Gillian Aldridge, Waterside, Cheddar Road, BS26 2DP. ☎ (01934) 743182 • Map 182/438545 • BB **B** • EM book first £10, 7pm • D2 T1 • 1-11 • V̄ B̄ D̄ S̄ P̄ T̄ ♿ • ♦♦♦

■ BATH
COTSWOLD WAY

Mrs P J Rowe, Abode, 7 Widcombe Crescent, Widcombe Hill, BA2 6AH. ☎ (01225) 422726 • Map 172/757641 • BB **C** • S2 D/S2 T1 • 1-11 NX • B̄ D̄ S̄ R̄ T̄ • 2Cr

Mrs M Gould, 3 Pulteney Terrace, BA2 4HJ. ☎ (01225) 316578 • Map 172/756645 • BB **B** • D1 T1 F1 • 1-12 NX • D̄ R̄ T̄

☆ Cranleigh, 159 Newbridge Hill, BA1 3PX. ☎ (01225) 310197 • Map 172/724656 • BB **E** • D4 T2 F2 • 1-12 NX • B̄ D̄ S̄ R̄ P̄ T̄ • ♦♦♦♦ • cranleigh@btinternet.com

CRANLEIGH, BATH

The Cotswold Way goes close to our door—this is the perfect spot to begin or end your walk! Lovely Victorian house with beautiful views, 8 spacious ensuite bedrooms and generous breakfasts. Non-smoking, private parking.

Tel (01225) 310197
Fax (01225) 423143
E-mail: Cranleigh@btinternet.com

Jenny Bennett, Kinlet Guest House, 99 Wellsway, BA2 4RX. ☎ (01225) 420268 • Map 172/746635 • BB **C** • S1 D1 T1 F1 • 1-12 • B̄ D̄ S̄ R̄ T̄ • ♦♦♦ • kinlet@inbath.freeserve.co.uk

Marion Dodd, Brocks, 32 Brock Street, BA1 2LN. ☎ (01225) 338374 • Map 172/746652 • BB **D/E** • D2 T2 F2 • 1-12 NX • B̄ D̄ S̄ R̄ • ♦♦♦♦ • marion@brocksguesthouse.co.uk

M A Cooper, Flaxley Villa, 9 Newbridge Hill, BA1 3PW. ☎ (01225) 313237 • Map 172/731651 • BB **C** • S1 D1 T2 F1 • 1-12 • B̄ R̄ • ♦♦♦

☆ Mrs Theresa Boyle, Wentworth House Hotel, 106 Bloomfield Road, BA2 2AP. ☎ (01225) 339193 • Map 172/745635 • BB **E** • EM £12 (£5 snack), until 8pm • D10 T6 F2 • 1-12 NX • V̄ B̄ D̄ S̄ R̄ P̄ T̄ • ♦♦♦♦ • stay@wentworthhouse.co.uk

Janet Cross, Clearbrook Farm, Midford, BA2 7DE. ☎ (01225) 723227 • Map 172/765603 • BB **C** • S2 D2 T/F1 • 1-12 • D̄ S̄ P̄ T̄ • Food nearby

Lou Gay, Rainbow Wood Farm, Claverton Down, BA2 7AR. ☎ /fax (01225) 466366 • Map 172/754645 • BB **D** • D2 T/F1 • 1-12 NX • B̄ D̄ S̄ R̄ P̄ T̄

■ BATHFORD (Bath)

Beverley Smart, Garston Cottage, 28 Ashley Road, BA1 7TT. ☎ (01225) 852510 • Map 172/792668 • BB **C** • D2 T/D2 F1 • 1-12 NX • B̄ D̄ S̄ T̄ ♿ • ♦♦♦ • Groups also. garstoncot@aol.com

■ BECKINGTON (Frome)
MACMILLAN WAY

Mrs Angela Pritchard, Pickford House, Bath Road, BA3 6SJ. ☎ (01373) 830329 • Map 183/799523 • BB **B** • EM £14, 7pm • S1 D2 T2 • 1-12 • V̄ B̄ D̄ S̄ P̄ T̄ ♿ • ♦♦♦♦ • AmPritchar@aol.com

■ BICKNOLLER (Taunton)

Mrs M Summers, Warrescote, 2 Trendle Lane, TA4 4EG. ☎ (01984) 656257 • Map 181/118392 • BB **B** • T2 • 10 JAN TO 10 DEC • B̄ D̄ S̄ R̄ T̄ ♿

■ BISHOPS LYDEARD (Taunton)

☆ Jane & David Hinton, The Mount, Mount Street, TA4 3AN. ☎ (01823) 432208 • Map 181,193/168296 • BB **C** • S1 T3 • 1-12 NX • D̄ S̄ P̄ T̄ • ♦♦♦♦

■ BRIDGWATER

Mrs D Chappell, Cokerhurst Farm, 87 Wembdon Hill, TA6 7QA. ☎ (01278) 422330 • Map 182/280378 • BB **D** • D1 T1 F1 • 1-12 NX • Ⓑ Ⓓ Ⓢ Ⓡ Ⓟ Ⓣ • ◆◆◆◆ • www.cokerhurst.clara.net

■ BURNHAM-ON-SEA

☆ David Cox, Laburnum House Lodge Hotel, TA9 3RJ. ☎ (01278) 781830 • Map 182/302448 • BB **C/D** • EM £8-10, 7-9pm • S5 D20 T20 F15 • 1-12 • Ⓥ Ⓑ Ⓓ Ⓡ Ⓟ Ⓣ ⬧ • ★★Ⓢ • www.laburnmhh.co.uk

SOMERSET

Sedgemoor, Burnham-on-Sea

Rural, coastal, situated on edge of nature reserve. Flat land walking along miles of the Bristol Channel estuary, Quantocks nearby. Log fires, sauna, solarium, indoor pool and good home cooking.

Laburnham House 01278 781830

■ CHARLTON HORETHORNE (Sherborne, Dorset)

Susan Stretton, Beech Farm, Sigwells, DT9 4LN. ☎ (01963) 220524 • Map 183/642231 • BB **B** • EM book first £8, 6.30-9pm • S1 D1 T1 F1 • 1-12 NX • Ⓑ Ⓓ Ⓟ Ⓣ ⬧

■ CHEW STOKE (Bristol)

Mrs Ann Hollomon, Orchard House, Bristol Road, BS40 8UB. ☎ (01275) 333143 • Map 182, 172/561618 • BB **C** • EM book first £10, 6.45pm • S1 D2 T3 F1 • 1-12 • Ⓥ Ⓑ Ⓓ Ⓟ Ⓣ • ◆◆◆ • orchardhse.ukgateway.net

■ CLEVEDON

Mrs E Potter, 'Bibury', 5 Sunnyside Road, BS21 7TE. ☎ (01275) 873315 • Map 171,172/405713 • BB **B** • D1 F1 • 1-12 NX • Ⓓ Ⓢ

Do you know your rights when you're out walking in the countryside? See pages 32-39

■ CREWKERNE

Frank E Joyce MHCIMA, George Hotel and Courtyard Restaurant, Market Square, TA18 7LP. ☎ (01460) 73650 • Map 193/441098 • BB **D** • EM £5-£15, 6.30-9.30pm • S3 D5 T2 F3 • 1-12 • Ⓥ Ⓑ Ⓓ Ⓢ Ⓡ Ⓟ Ⓣ ⬧ • ◆◆◆

■ CULBONE (Minehead)

Mrs E J Richards, Silcombe Farm, TA24 8JN. ☎ (01643) 862248 • Map 181/833482 • BB **B** • EM book first £10, 7.30pm • S1 D1 T2 • 1-12 NX • Ⓥ Ⓑ Ⓓ Ⓢ Ⓟ Ⓣ ⬧

■ DULVERTON

TWO MOORS WAY

Mrs Jane Buckingham, Town Mills, TA22 9HB. ☎ (01398) 323124 • Map 181/914279 • BB **C/D** • D4 T1 • 1-12 NX • Ⓑ Ⓓ Ⓟ Ⓣ ⬧ • ◆◆◆◆Ⓢ

☆ Exton House Hotel, Exton, TA22 9JT. ☎ (01643) 851365 • Map 181/926336 • BB **C/D/E** • EM book first £15.50, 7.30pm • S1 D3 T2 F3 • 1-12 • Ⓥ Ⓑ Ⓓ Ⓢ Ⓟ Ⓣ ⬧ Ⓜ • ◆◆◆◆ • Discounts for RA members

Mrs C Nurcombe, Marsh Bridge Cottage, TA22 9QG. ☎ (01398) 323197 • Map 181/904288 • BB **B/C** • EM book first £12.50, 7pm • D1 T1 F1 • 1-12 • Ⓥ Ⓑ Ⓓ Ⓢ Ⓟ Ⓣ ⬧ • Riverside location

■ DUNSTER (Minehead)

SOUTH WEST COAST PATH

☆ Catherine Carter, The Yarn Market Hotel, High Street, TA24 6SF. ☎ (01643) 821425 • Map 181/992437 • BB **D** • EM book first £15, 7.30pm • S2 D12 T3 F3 • 1-12 • Ⓥ Ⓑ Ⓓ Ⓢ Ⓡ Ⓟ Ⓣ ⬧ • ★★★ • Totally non-smoking • yarnmarket.hotel@virgin.net

B&B ACCOMMODATION   ENGLAND   SOMERSET

SOMERSET · ENGLAND

B&B ACCOMMODATION

■ EXFORD (Minehead)
TWO MOORS WAY

Gillian Lamble, Edgcott House, TA24 7QG.
☎ (01643) 831495 • Map 181/847387 • BB **C** • EM
book first £15, 7.30pm • S2 D1 T1 • 1-12 • Ⓥ Ⓑ
Ⓓ Ⓣ 🌃 • ◆◆◆

☆ Nigel Winter, Exmoor Lodge, Chapel Street, TA24
7PY. ☎ (01643) 831694 • Map 181/853384 • BB **B/C**
• EM book first £12, 7-8pm • S1 D3 T1 • 1-12 • Ⓥ Ⓑ
Ⓓ Ⓢ Ⓣ🌃 • Veg. food only

EXMOOR LODGE
01643 831694
Chapel Street, Exford, Somerset TA24 7PY.

Get away from it all in the beautiful
countryside of Exmoor National Park, ideal for
walking.
Freshly prepared vegetarian and vegan food.
(Advanced booking required).
Non smoking. Most rooms en-suite.
Telephone Nigel for colour brochure.

☆ Mike & Myra Ellicott, Stockleigh Lodge, TA24 7PZ.
☎ (01643) 831500 • Map 181/853385 • BB **C** • EM
book first £12.50, 6.30-7pm • S2 D3 T2 F2 • 1-12 •
Ⓥ Ⓑ Ⓓ Ⓢ Ⓟ Ⓣ🌃 • ◆◆◆

Stockleigh Lodge
Exford, Exmoor, Somerset TA24 7PZ
Licensed, Bed & Breakfast Accommodation
Friendly atmosphere in large country house in
centre of Exmoor National Park.
En-suite accommodation.
Groups welcome.
Ring for full colour brochure:
Tel 01643 831500 · Fax 01643 831595

■ HINTON ST GEORGE
Mrs B Hudspith, "Rookwood", West Street, TA17
8SA. ☎ (01460) 73450 • Map 193/417126 • BB **B** •
S1 T1 • 1-12 NX • Ⓑ Ⓓ Ⓢ Ⓟ Ⓣ

■ HOLFORD (Bridgwater)
Mrs Susan Ayshford, Forge Cottage, TA5 1RY.
☎ (01278) 741215 • Map 181/158413 • BB **B** • EM
book first £8, 6-7pm • D2 T1 • 1-12 NX • Ⓥ Ⓓ Ⓟ
Ⓣ🌃 • List

Mrs V Stone, Glenstone Farm, TA5 1RY. ☎ (01278)
741526 • Map 181/158413 • BB **B** • EM £8, 7:30pm •
D2 T1 F1 • 1-12NX • Ⓥ Ⓑ Ⓓ Ⓢ Ⓟ Ⓣ🌃

Ramblers' Association members are covered
by a public liability insurance policy
further details from central office

☆ John & Denice Page, Combe House Hotel, TA5 1RZ.
☎ (01278) 741382 • Map 181/151416 • BB **D** • EM
£19.75, 7.30-8.30pm • S4 D5 T7 F1 • 2-12 • Ⓥ Ⓑ Ⓓ
Ⓢ Ⓟ Ⓣ🌃 • ★★Ⓢ • enquiries@combehouse.co.uk

Combe House Hotel
Holford Somerset
TA5 1RZ

Combe House, a 17th century country hotel
is situated at the foot of the Quantock hills,
a designated Area of Outstanding Natural
Beauty. The hotel is an ideal base for
ramblers to explore the countryside from
the Quantocks to Exmoor.

◆ Relax in total peace and quiet away
from all traffic noise.

◆ Enjoy good food, well-equipped comfortable bedrooms, cosy bar and
lounge and the welcoming and
friendly ambience.

◆ Leave your car at the hotel and start
your ramble from the front door.

◆ Ideal for groups, special rates available upon request.

Phone now 01278 741382
or email enquiries@combehouse.co.uk
for colour brochure

AA 2 Star with Rosette
ETC 2 Star Silver Award

■ KILVE (Bridgwater)
Ian & Jackie Perrior, Kilve PO & Stores, TA5 1EA.
☎ (01278) 741214 • Map 181/148428 • BB **B** • S1
D2 T2 F1 • 1-12 NX • Ⓓ Ⓢ Ⓟ Ⓣ🌃

■ KINGSTON-ST-MARY (Taunton)
Lower Marsh Farm, TA2 8AB. ☎ (01823) 451331 •
Map 193/224279 • BB **C** • EM book first £14, 7.30-
9.00pm • D1 T1 F1 • 1-12 • Ⓥ Ⓑ Ⓓ Ⓢ Ⓡ Ⓟ
Ⓣ • ◆◆◆ • Singles lets av • mail@lowermarshfarm.co.uk

■ MINEHEAD
Colin & Maureen Smith, Fernside, The Holloway,
TA24 5PB. ☎ (01643) 707594/708995 • Map
181/966464 • BB **B** • EM book first £7.50, 6-6.30pm •
D2 F1 • 1-12 NX • Ⓥ Ⓑ Ⓓ Ⓢ Ⓡ Ⓟ Ⓣ • 2Cr/C
• colin.cjs@btinternet.com

210

☆ Mr & Mrs M Pretty, Lyn Valley Guest House, 3 Tregonwell Road, TA24 5DT. ☎ /fax 01643 703748 • Map 181/973463 • BB **B** • S2 D4 T2 F1 • 3-10 • Ⓑ Ⓓ Ⓢ Ⓡ Ⓟ Ⓣ • ◆◆◆

Mrs Susan Sanders, 1 Glenmore Road, TA24 5BQ. ☎ 01643 706225 • Map 181/974462 • BB **B** • S2 D2 T1 F1 • 3-12 • Ⓥ Ⓑ Ⓢ Ⓟ Ⓣ

John & Jenny Allaway, Marshfield Hotel, Tregonwell Road, TA24 5DU. ☎ (01643) 702517 • Map 181/973461 • BB **C** • EM book first £12.50, 6.30-7.00pm • S1 D4 T7 F1 • 3-10 • Ⓥ Ⓑ Ⓓ Ⓢ Ⓡ Ⓟ Ⓣ 🦮 • ◆◆◆◆ • marshfield.hotel@minehead18.freeserve.co.uk

Jannine Bakker, 'Beverleigh', Beacon Road, TA24 5SE. ☎ (01643) 708450 • Map 181/966469 • BB **B/C** • D2 T1 • 1-12 • Ⓑ Ⓓ Ⓢ Ⓡ Ⓟ Ⓣ • beverleigh@talk21.com

■ MUDFORD (Yeovil)

Mrs E Tavener, The Old Kiln, Higher Brickyard, Main Street, BA21 5TG. ☎ (01935) 850958 • Map 183/572195 • BB **B** • EM book first £8, 6.30-8.30pm • S2 D1 T1 F1 • 1-12 • Ⓥ Ⓑ Ⓓ Ⓢ • List/C

■ NETHER STOWEY (Bridgwater)

☆ Susan Lilienthal, Parsonage Farm, TA5 1HA. ☎ (01278) 733237 • Map 181/185387 • BB **C** • EM book first £14, 7.30pm • D1 T1 F1 • 1-12 NX • Ⓥ Ⓑ Ⓓ Ⓢ Ⓟ Ⓣ 🦮 Ⓜ

M A Morse, 18 Castle Street, TA5 1LN. ☎ (01278) 733686 • Map 181/192397 • BB **C** • D2 F1 • 1-12 NX • Ⓑ Ⓓ Ⓢ Ⓟ Ⓣ

■ NORTH CADBURY
MACMILLAN WAY

Mr & Mrs J Wade, Ashlea House, High Street, BA22 7DP. ☎ (01963) 440891 • Map 183/635274 • BB **C/D** • EM book first £11.50, 7.30-8pm • D1 T1 • 1-10 • Ⓥ Ⓑ Ⓓ Ⓢ Ⓟ Ⓣ • ◆◆◆◆ • Transport available • www.ashlea.btinternet.com

☆ Mr & Mrs Robinson, The Catash Inn, BA22 7DH. ☎ 01963 440248 • Map 183/635274 • BB **E** • EM £4-£14, 7-9pm • D1 T1 F1 • 1-12 NX • Ⓥ Ⓑ Ⓢ Ⓟ Ⓣ • www.catash.demon.co.uk

■ PORLOCK (Minehead)
SOUTH WEST COAST PATH

Mrs J Stiles-Cox, Leys - The Ridge, Off Bossington Lane, TA24 8HA. ☎ /Fax (01643) 862477 • Map 181/892469 • BB **B** • S2 D/T1 • 1-12 NX • Ⓑ Ⓢ Ⓟ Ⓣ

Mr & Mrs D Urry, Overstream Hotel, TA24 8QJ. ☎ (01643) 862421 • Map 181/886466 • BB **C/D** • EM book first £10.50, 7pm • S2 D2 T3 F2 • 3-10 NX • Ⓥ Ⓑ Ⓓ Ⓢ Ⓣ • ◆◆◆ • Guided walks also

R G Thornton, The Lorna Doone Hotel, High Street, TA24 8PS. ☎ (01643) 862404 • Map 181/887469 • BB **C/D** • EM book first £14, 6.15-8.30pm • S3 D4 T4 F2 • 1-12 NX • Ⓥ Ⓑ Ⓓ Ⓢ Ⓟ Ⓣ 🦮 • ◆◆◆ • Group rates • lorna@doone99.freeserve.co.uk

☆ Doverhay Place, Minehead Rd, TA24 8EX. ☎ (01643) 862996 • Map 181/888468 • BB **D** • EM book first £10, 7pm • S6 D4 T12 F1 • 1-12 • Ⓥ Ⓑ Ⓓ Ⓢ Ⓟ Ⓣ 🦮 • ◆◆◆◆ • Groups also, Mini breaks. Doverhay@aol.com • See display on next page.

☆ See Display Advertisement

■ PORLOCK (Minehead) (continued)
SOUTH WEST COAST PATH

AA ◆◆◆◆
DOVERHAY PLACE
Minehead Road,
Porlock TA24 8EX

100 year old country house with beautiful garden.
Ideal Exmoor centre. Drying facilities, excellent
meals, packed lunches. Log fire, en-suite rooms, TV,
tea making and phone. B&B rates or half/full board.
Special group rates. Brochure available.
Tel/Fax: 01643 862996   Doverhay@aol.com
www.smoothound.co.uk/hotels/Doverhay

Mrs S Coombs, Hurlstone, Sparkhayes Lane, TA24
8NE. ☎ (01643) 862650 • Map 181/887489 • BB **B** •
D1 T1 • 1-12 NX • Ⓓ Ⓟ Ⓣ ⚲

☆ Richard Crowden, Burley Cottage Guest House,
Parsons Street, TA24 8QJ. ☎ (01643) 862563 • Map
181/886466 • BB **C** • D3 T1 • 1-12 • Ⓑ Ⓓ Ⓢ Ⓟ Ⓣ

Tel
01643
862563

Parsons St,
Porlock
TA24 8QJ

Situated in the village of Porlock in
Exmoor National Park
in deepest Somerset
Car parking • Ensuite facilities • open all year
round • Non-smoking • Full central heating •
Packed meals on request • Private Guest
lounge • Radio, TV, Tea/Coffee facilities in all
rooms • Ideal base for visiting Exmoor.

■ SHIPHAM (Winscombe)
WEST MENDIP WAY

Mrs Helen Stickland, Herongates, Horseleaze Lane,
BS25 1UQ. ☎ (01934) 843280 • Map 182/437579 •
BB **B** • EM book first £12, 7-7.30pm • D1 T1 F1 • 1-
12 NX • Ⓥ Ⓑ Ⓓ Ⓢ Ⓟ Ⓣ • ◆◆◆

■ TAUNTON

Mrs D C Besley, Prockters Farm, West Monkton, TA2
8QN. ☎ (01823) 412269 • Map 193/262285 • BB **C** •
S2 D2 T2 • 1-12 • Ⓑ Ⓓ Ⓡ Ⓟ Ⓣ ⚲ • ◆◆◆

■ TIMBERSCOMBE (Minehead)

John & Linda Lowe, Wanneroo Farm, TA24 7TU.
☎ (01643) 841493 • Map 181/973446 • BB **B/C** • D1
T1 F1 • 1-12 NX • Ⓑ Ⓓ Ⓢ Ⓟ Ⓣ ⚲ • ◆◆◆ •
www.smoothhound.co.uk/hotels/wanneroo.html

■ TIMSBURY (Bath)

Old Malt House Hotel, Radford, BA3 1QF. ☎ (01761)
470106 • Map 172/672578 • BB **E** • EM £9-18, 7-
8.30pm • S2 D3 T5 F2 • 1-12 NX • Ⓥ Ⓑ Ⓓ Ⓢ Ⓟ
Ⓣ ⚲ • ★★ • www.oldmalthouse.co.uk

■ WELLS
WEST MENDIP WAY

Robert & Margaret Pletts, Cadgwith, Hawkers Lane,
BA5 3JH. ☎ (01749) 677799 • Map 182/559462 • BB
B • S1 D1 T1 F1 • 1-12 NX • Ⓑ Ⓓ Ⓢ Ⓟ Ⓣ ⚲ •
◆◆◆◆

☆ John Howard, Furlong House, Lorne Place, St
Thomas Street, BA5 2XF. ☎ (01749) 674064 • Map
182,183/554460 • BB **C** • S0 D2 T1 • 1-12 NX • Ⓑ
Ⓓ Ⓢ Ⓣ • ◆◆◆◆ • Johnhowardwells@cs.com

AA ◆◆◆◆
Furlong House
Lorne Place
St Thomas Street
Wells BA5 2XF
01749 674064

Enjoy our peaceful garden, near the Mendip
Way and the cathedral. We offer en-suite
accommodation, off-street parking, bicycle
lock-up, drying facilities and a warm welcome.
John Howard

■ WEST QUANTOXHEAD (Taunton)

Miss A Kennard, Blakes Farmhouse, Lower
Weacombe, TA4 4ED. ☎ (01984) 632588 • Map
181/111408 • BB **B/D** • D2 T1 • 4-9 • Ⓓ Ⓢ Ⓟ Ⓣ
⚲ • Food nearby.

■ WESTON-SUPER-MARE

☆ Braeside Hotel, 2 Victoria Park, BS23 2HZ.
☎ (01934) 626642 • Map 182/317621 • BB **C** • S2 D5
T1 F1 • 1-12 NX • Ⓑ Ⓓ Ⓢ Ⓡ Ⓣ ⚲ Ⓜ • ◆◆◆◆ •
3rd night free Nov-Apr • braeside@tesco.net

Braeside
Hotel
2 Victoria Park
Weston-Super-Mare
Somerset BS23 2HZ
braeside@tesco.net
Tel/Fax:
(01934) 626642

Delightful, family-run hotel, close to the sea
front. All rooms en suite; colour TV; coffee/tea
making. Some sea views. Ideal centre for
walking the Quantock and Mendip Hills.
English Tourism Council   AA
◆◆◆◆   ◆◆◆◆

J F Taylor, Baymead Hotel, Longton Grove Road,
BS23 1LS. ☎ (01934) 622951 • Map 182/320618 •
BB **D** • EM book first £7.50, 6.15pm • S11 D8 T11 F3
• 3-12 • Ⓥ Ⓑ Ⓢ Ⓡ Ⓟ Ⓣ ⚲ • 3Cr/C • Groups also

■ WINSCOMBE (Cheddar)

Christine Marlow, Home Farm, Barton, BS25 1DX.
☎ 01934 842078 • Map 182/397567 • BB **C** • D2 F1 •
1-12 • Ⓑ Ⓓ Ⓢ Ⓟ Ⓣ ⚲ • ◆◆◆◆Ⓢ • www.home-
farmcottages.co.uk

■ WIVELISCOMBE (Taunton)

☆ Jenny Blackshaw, North Down Farm, Pyncombe Lane, TA4 2BL. ☎ /fax 01984 623730 • Map 181/069265 • BB **C** • EM book first £12, 6-8pm • D1 F1 • 1-11 • Ⓥ Ⓑ Ⓓ Ⓢ Ⓟ Ⓣ ⓑ • ◆◆◆

NORTH DOWN FARM
WIVELISCOMBE
SOMERSET
TA4 2BL
TEL/FAX 01984 623730

Exmoor Somerset Devon border. Traditional working farm. Panoramic views over beautiful countryside. Central for walking Exmoor and Quantocks. Home produced food. Log fires, comfortable and friendly atmosphere. All rooms en-suite, TV, Tea/coffee
ETB 3 Diamonds

■ YEOVIL

☆ The Cavern, Stoke Cross, Stoke High Street, Stoke-sub-Hamdon, TA14 6PP. ☎ (09065) 534567 • Map 193/474174 • BB **B** • EM from £1.90, 10am-10pm • S4 D4 T2 F2 • 1-12 • Ⓥ Ⓑ Ⓓ Ⓢ Ⓡ Ⓟ Ⓣ ⓑ • uk-techology@ukonline.co.uk

The Cavern at Somerset

1 hour 30 minutes from London. Warm comfy 16th century atmosphere. Ham Hill country has over 200 different walks to suit all. Log fire, beer, wine and a soft bed await you after a healthy stroll
(by the famous Parrott trail and historic remains)

09065 534567 or 01935 826826
Fax 01935 826565 Email info@caverncafe.com
Website www.caverncafe.com

Paterson & Sue Weir, Slipper Cottage, 41 Bishopston, Montacute, TA15 6UX. ☎ (01935) 823073 • Map 193,183/496170 • BB **B/D** • D1 T1 • 1-12 NX • Ⓓ Ⓢ Ⓣ • ◆◆◆ • www.slippercottage.co.uk

■ YEOVILTON (Yeovil)

Mrs Susie Crang, Cary Fitzpaine Farmhouse, Cary Fitzpaine, BA22 8JB. ☎ (01458) 223250 • Map 183/548270 • BB **C** • EM book first £12, 7pm • S1 D1 T1 F1 • 1-12 NX • Ⓥ Ⓑ Ⓓ Ⓢ Ⓟ Ⓣ ⓑ • ◆◆◆◆ • acrang@aol.com

STAFFORDSHIRE

■ ARMITAGE (Rugeley)
HEART OF ENGLAND WAY

Mrs M Lewis, Park Farm, Hawkesyard, Armitage Lane, WS15 1ED. ☎ (01889) 583477 • Map 128/061161 • BB **B** • S1 T1 F1 • 1-12 NX • Ⓑ Ⓓ Ⓡ Ⓟ Ⓣ ⓑ • ◆◆◆

■ CHEADLE (Stoke-on-Trent)
STAFFORDSHIRE WAY

Dave & Kate Scorey, The Old Convent, Bank Street, ST10 1NR. ☎ (01538) 756356 • Map 119/008432 • BB **A** • EM book first £6.50 • S2 D1 T1 • 1-12 NX • Ⓥ Ⓓ Ⓟ Ⓣ ⓑ • Alton Towers 5 miles.

■ CHEDDLETON (Leek)
STAFFORDSHIRE WAY

Nancy Sherratt, Little Brookhouse Farm, ST13 7DF. ☎ (01538) 360350 • Map 118/964508 • BB **C** • S1 D2 T1 • 1-12 NX • Ⓑ Ⓓ Ⓢ Ⓣ • ◆◆◆◆

Mrs Margaret Heath, The Outlook, 111 Basford Bridge Lane, ST13 7EQ. ☎ (01538) 360752 • Map 118/973512 • BB **C** • EM book first £12, 6pm • D1 T1 • 1-12 NX • Ⓥ Ⓓ Ⓢ Ⓣ • List/C • Baggage transfer

Prospect House Guest House, 334 Cheadle Road, ST13 7BW. ☎ (01782) 550639 • Map 118/967506 • BB **C** • EM book first £12.50 • S1 D1 T1 F2 • 1-12 • Ⓥ Ⓑ Ⓢ Ⓟ Ⓣ ⓑ • ◆◆◆◆ • prospect@talk21.com

■ CHORLEY (Farewell, Lichfield)
HEART OF ENGLAND WAY

Mrs E Clewley, Little Pipe Farm, WS13 8BS. ☎ (01543) 683066 • Map 128/078105 • BB **B** • EM book first £8, 6.30-7pm • S1 D1 T1 F1 • 1-12 • Ⓥ Ⓓ Ⓟ • ◆◆◆

■ FOXT (Stoke-on-Trent)

Ken & Gill Morris, Shawgate Farm Guest House, Shay Lane, ST10 2HN. ☎ /Fax (01538) 266590 • Map 119/035483 • BB **C** • EM book first £12, 7pm • D5 T5 F5 • 1-12 NX • Ⓥ Ⓑ Ⓢ Ⓟ Ⓣ • ◆◆◆ • ken_morris@lineone.net

■ GRINDON (Leek)
WHITE PEAK WAY

☆ Mrs P Simpson, Summerhill Farm, ST13 7TT. ☎ (01538) 304264 • Map 119/083534 • BB **B** • EM book first £12, 6.30-7pm • D2 T/D1 F1 • 1-12 • Ⓥ Ⓑ Ⓓ Ⓢ Ⓟ ⓑ • ◆◆◆◆ • SC also

PEAK DISTRICT FARMHOUSE B&B
Summerhill Farm
Grindon, Leek
☎ 01538 304264

Tastefully furnished, ensuite facilities, tea/coffee, colour TV. Amid rolling countryside overlooking the Dove and Manifold Valleys. *English Tourism Council*
AA "Wonderful for Walkers".
◆◆◆ Ideally situated for Buxton, ◆◆◆◆
Chatsworth House, Potteries, Alton Towers.

☆ See Display Advertisement

■ **HORTON (Leek)**
STAFFORDSHIRE WAY

Mrs Irene Harrison, Croft Meadows Farm, ST13 8QE.
☎ (01782) 513039 • Map 118/921577 • BB **B** • S3
D1 T1 • 1-12 • Ⓑ Ⓓ Ⓢ Ⓟ Ⓣ • ◆◆◆ • SC also

■ **LEEK**
STAFFORDSHIRE WAY

Judith Rider, Beechfields, Park Road, ST13 8JS.
☎ (01538) 372825 • Map 118/982572 • BB **C** • D2 F1
• 1-12 • Ⓑ Ⓓ Ⓢ Ⓟ Ⓣ 🐾 • ◆◆◆◆

■ **THREAPWOOD (Nr Cheadle, Stoke-on-Trent)**
STAFFORDSHIRE WAY

Bradley Elms Farm, ST10 4RA. ☎ (01538) 753135 •
Map 128,119/010430 • BB **C** • EM book first £10,
6.30-7.30pm • D4 T3 F2 • 2-10 • Ⓥ Ⓑ Ⓟ Ⓣ •
◆◆◆◆

■ **WOOTTON (Ashbourne, Derbyshire)**
STAFFORDSHIRE WAY

Liz & Frank Burslem, Chapel House, DE6 2GW.
☎ (01335) 324554 • Map 128,119/109454 • BB **B** •
S1 D1 T1 • 1-12 NX • Ⓑ Ⓓ Ⓢ Ⓟ Ⓣ Ⓜ

SUFFOLK

■ **ALDEBURGH**

Mrs Colchester, Plomesgate, Warren Hill Lane, IP15
5QB. ☎ /Fax (01728) 454370 • Map 156/458581 • BB
B/C • D1 T1 • 1-12 NX • Ⓑ Ⓓ Ⓢ Ⓟ Ⓣ •
vandi.alde@faxvia.net

■ **BECCLES**
ANGLES WAY

Mr & Mrs W T Renilson, Catherine House, 2
Ringsfield Road, NR34 9PQ. ☎ (01502) 716428 •
Map 156/418897 • BB **C** • D3 • 1-12 • Ⓥ Ⓑ Ⓓ Ⓢ
Ⓡ Ⓟ Ⓣ • ◆◆◆◆

■ **BLYTHBURGH (Halesworth)**

Mrs S E Harris, Little Thorbyns, The Street, IP19 9LS.
☎ (01502) 478664 • Map 156/452752 • BB **C** • EM
book first £10, 6.30pm • S1 D1 T1 F1 • 1-12 NX • Ⓥ
Ⓑ Ⓓ Ⓢ Ⓟ Ⓣ • 2Cr/C • SC also

■ **DARSHAM (Saxmundham)**

Mrs Bloomfield, Priory Farm, IP17 3QD. ☎ (01728)
668459 • Map 156/416700 • BB **C** • D1 T1 • 3-10 • Ⓑ
Ⓓ Ⓢ Ⓡ Ⓣ • ◆◆◆ • SC also

■ **DUNWICH (SAXMUNDHAM)**

The Red House, St James Street, IP17 3DT.
☎ (01728) 648411 • Map 156/477705 • BB **B** • S1
D1 • 1-12 NX • Ⓓ Ⓢ Ⓟ Ⓣ

■ **EAST BERGHOLT (Colchester, Essex)**
ESSEX WAY

Mrs Natalie Finch, Rosemary, Rectory Hill, CO7 6TH.
☎ (01206) 298241 • Map 155,169/073344 • BB **C** •
S1 T2 • 1-12 • Ⓓ Ⓢ Ⓡ Ⓟ 🐾 • ◆◆◆ • Food
nearby

■ **FRAMLINGHAM (Woodbridge)**

Brian & Phyllis Collett, Shimmens Pightle,
Dennington Road, IP13 9JT. ☎ (01728) 724036 •
Map 156/277643 • BB **C** • S1 D1 T1 F1 • EASTER-10
• Ⓓ Ⓢ • ◆◆◆ • Beverages served to rooms

■ **HORRINGER-CUM-ICKWORTH (Bury St Edmunds)**

☆ Rose Cottage & Laurels Stables, IP29 5SN.
☎ (01284) 735281 • Map 155/825613 • BB **B** • EM
book first £7, Up to 8pm • D1 T2 • 1-12 NX • Ⓥ Ⓑ
Ⓓ Ⓢ Ⓡ Ⓟ Ⓣ 🐾 • Disabled access 1 twin

■ **KNODISHALL (Saxmundham)**

Joan Gadsby, Sun Cottage, Snape Road, IP17 1UT.
☎ (01728) 833892 • Map 156/432607 • BB **C** • D1 T1
• 3-10 • Ⓑ Ⓓ Ⓢ Ⓟ Ⓣ • ◆◆◆◆ • suncot-
tage@supanet.com

■ **LAVENHAM (Sudbury)**

Mrs Hazel Rhodes, Weaners Farm, Bears Lane, CO10
9RX. ☎ (01787) 247310 • Map 155/917481 • BB **C** •
D1 T2 • 1-12 NX • Ⓓ Ⓢ Ⓣ

B & H Massey, The Island House, Lower Road, CO10
9QJ. ☎ (01787) 248181 • Map 155/918493 • BB **D** •
D1 T1 • 1-12 • Ⓑ Ⓓ Ⓢ Ⓟ Ⓣ • ◆◆◆◆ •
www.lavenham.co.uk/islandhouse/

■ **LOWESTOFT**

Mr Geoff Ward, The Albany Hotel, 400 London Road
South, NR33 0BQ. ☎ (01502) 574394 • Map
134/541914 • BB **C** • EM book first £8.50, 6pm • S2
D2 T/D2 F1 • 1-12 • Ⓥ Ⓑ Ⓓ Ⓢ Ⓡ Ⓟ Ⓣ 🐾 •
◆◆◆ • albanyhotel-lowestoft.co.uk

■ **MIDDLETON (Saxmundham)**

Mrs D Crowden, Rose Villa, The Street, IP17 3NJ.
☎ (01728) 648489 • Map 156/429678 • BB **B** • S1
D1 T1 • 1-12 • Ⓡ Ⓣ

■ **NAYLAND (Colchester)**
ESSEX WAY & STOUR VALLEY PATH

Mrs P Heigham, Hill House, Gravel Hill, CO6 4JB.
☎ (01206) 262782 • Map 155/976345 • BB **C** • S1
D1 T1 F1 • 1-12 NX • Ⓑ Ⓓ Ⓢ Ⓟ Ⓣ • HC • Food
nearby • heigham.hillhouse@rdplus.net

■ **REYDON (Southwold)**

Mardale, 54 Halesworth Road, IP18 6NR. ☎ (01502)
724850 • Map 156/496770 • BB **C** • EM book first £8,
7.30pm • S1 D1 • 3-10 • Ⓥ Ⓓ Ⓢ Ⓟ Ⓣ

■ SOUTHWOLD

Mrs L Whiting, Saxon House, 86 Pier Avenue, IP18 6BL. ☎ (01502) 723651 • Map 156/510767 • BB **D** • D4 T3 F1 • 1-12 NX • B D S P T 🛁 • ◆◆◆

■ STEEPLE BUMPSTEAD (Haverhill)

Mrs S J Stirling, Yew Tree House, 15 Chapel Street, CB9 7DQ. ☎ (01440) 730364 • Map 154/680411 • BB **C/D** • EM £12, 6-8pm • S1 D1 T1 • 3-12 NX • V B S T • ◆◆◆

■ STOKE-BY-NAYLAND (Colchester, Essex)
ESSEX WAY & STOUR VALLEY PATH

Deirdre Wollaston, Thorington Hall, CO6 4SS. ☎ (01206) 337329 • Map 155/004357 • BB **C** • S1 D1 T1 • 4-9 • B D S P 🛁 • C

■ STOWMARKET

Mrs Mary Noy, Red House Farm, Station Road, Haughley, IP14 3QP. ☎ (01449) 673323 • Map 155/041623 • BB **D** • S2 D1 T1 • 1-11 • B D S P T • ◆◆◆◆ • SC also

■ SUDBOURNE (Woodbridge)

Mrs A Wood, Long Meadows, Gorse Lane, IP12 2BD. ☎ (01394) 450269 • Map 156/412532 • BB **B** • EM book first £10 (Oct-Mar only), 7.30pm • S1 D1 T1 • 1-12 NX • B D S P T 🛁 • ◆◆◆

■ WESTLETON (Dunwich)

Mrs Molly Catchpole, 21 Grange View, IP17 3EJ. ☎ (01728) 648481 • Map 156/438689 • BB **B** • D1 • 1-12 NX • D S P T M

SURREY

■ BOWLHEAD GREEN (Godalming)
GREENSAND WAY

Mrs Susanna Langdale, Heath Hall Farm, Bowlhead Green, GU8 6NW. ☎ (01428) 682808 • Map 186/918388 • BB **D** • S1 D1 T1 F1 • 1-12 NX • B D S P T 🛁 • ◆◆◆ • Food nearby sukey.langdale@talk21.com

■ CRANLEIGH

The White Hart, Ewhurst Road, GU6 7AE. ☎ (01483) 268647 • Map 187/060390 • BB **C/E** • EM £5-£10, 6-9pm • S2 D7 T3 F2 • 1-12 • V B D T 🛁 • List/App • pasilver@netcomuk.co.uk

■ DORKING
NORTH DOWNS WAY

The Waltons, 5 Rose Hill, RH4 2EG. ☎ (01306) 883127 • Map 187/166491 • BB **B/C** • EM book first £10-£15, 7-8.30pm • S1 D2 T1 F2 • 1-12 • V D S R T 🛁 • thewaltons@rosehill5.demon.co.uk

Fairdene Guest House, Moores Road, RH4 2BG. ☎ (01306) 888337 • Map 187/169496 • BB **C/D** • D2 T2 F1 • 1-12 • D S R P T 🛁 • ◆◆◆ • zoe@fairdene5.freeserve.co.uk

Mrs Z Richardson, Fairdene Guest House, Moores Road, RH4 2BG. ☎ (01306) 888337 • Map 187/169496 • BB **C/D** • D2 T2 F1 • 1-12 • D S R P T 🛁 • ◆◆◆ • zoe@fairdene5.freeserve.co.uk

■ GATWICK (Horley)

Averill Yeo, Logans Guest House, 93 Povey Cross Road, RH6 0AE. ☎ (01293) 783363 • Map 187/272423 • BB **D** • EM £4, 6-9pm • S2 D3 T3 F2 • 1-12 • V B S R P T 🛁 • 2Cr

☆ The Turret Guest House, 48 Massetts Road, RH6 7DS. ☎ (01293) 782490 • Map 187/286426 • BB **C/E** • S2 D3 T2 F3 • 1-12 NX • B S R P T M • ◆◆◆ • www.theturret.com 1 triple room available

■ GUILDFORD
NORTH DOWNS WAY

Mr & Mrs Bourne, Weybrook House, 113 Stoke Road, GU1 1ET. ☎ (01483) 302394 • Map 186/998504 • BB **C** • S1 D1 F1 • 1-12 NX • D S R P T 🛁 • www.geocities.com/guildford_surrey/weybrook.html

■ HOLMBURY ST MARY (Dorking)
GREENSAND WAY

Gill Hill, Bulmer Farm, Pasturewood Road, RH5 6LG. ☎ (01306) 730210 • Map 187/114441 • BB **C** • D3 T5 • 1-12 • B D S T • ◆◆◆◆ • SC also, food nearby

Francesca McCann, Woodhill Cottage, RH5 6NL. ☎ 01306 730498 • Map 187/107452 • BB **B/C/D** • D1 T1 F1 • 1-12 • B D S T 🛁

■ HORLEY (Nr Gatwick)

Prinsted Guest House, Oldfield Road, RH6 7EP. ☎ (01293) 785233 • Map 187/277424 • BB **E** • S2 D2 T2 F2 • 1-12 NX • B D S R T • ◆◆◆◆ • www.networkclub.co.uk/prinsted

Mrs Moira Palmer, Oakdene Guest House, 32 Massetts Road, RH6 7DS. ☎ (01293) 772047 • Map 187/286426 • BB **E** • S3 D2 T2 F2 • 1-12 • B D R T • List • lentonoakdene.co.uk

☆ See Display Advertisement

SURREY – EAST SUSSEX *(ENGLAND — B&B ACCOMMODATION)*

■ OXTED
NORTH DOWNS WAY & VANGUARD WAY & GREENSAND WAY

Rosehaven, 12 Hoskins Road, RH8 9HT. ☎ (01883) 712700 • Map 187/392527 • BB **C** • T2 • 3-12 NX • Ⓓ Ⓢ Ⓡ Ⓟ Ⓣ

Laurie Rodgers, Pinehurst Grange Guesthouse, East Hill (A25), RH8 9AE. ☎ (01883) 716413 • Map 187/392525 • BB **C/D** • S1 D1 T1 • 1-12 NX • Ⓓ Ⓢ Ⓡ Ⓟ Ⓣ

■ REDHILL
NORTH DOWNS WAY

Lynwood Guest House, 50 London Road, RH1 1LN. ☎ (01737) 766894 • Map 187/280511 • BB **E** • S2 D2 T2 F3 • 1-12 NX • Ⓑ Ⓓ Ⓡ Ⓣ • lynwoodguesthouse@yahoo.co.uk

■ SHALFORD (Guildford)
NORTH DOWNS WAY

Mrs M J Deeks, The Laurels, 23 Dagden Road, GU4 8DD. ☎ (01483) 565753 • Map 186/000475 • BB **C** • EM book first £7, 7-8pm • D1 T1 • 1-12 NX • Ⓥ Ⓓ Ⓢ Ⓡ Ⓟ Ⓣ ♨ Ⓜ • By Pilgrims Way. 'G' Award from Guildford Tourist Board

Norah Morden, 2 Northfield, GU4 8JN. ☎ (01483) 570431 • Map 186/003462 • BB **C** • T1 • 1-12 • Ⓑ Ⓓ Ⓢ Ⓡ Ⓟ Ⓣ • tonymorden@freeuk.com

■ SHERE (Guildford)
NORTH DOWNS WAY

Mrs M James, Manor Cottage, GU5 9JE. ☎ (01483) 202979 • Map 187/072479 • BB **C** • S1 D1 • 4-10 NX • Ⓓ Ⓢ Ⓡ Ⓣ

■ SOUTH GODSTONE
GREENSAND WAY

Mr D I Nunn, The New Bungalow, Old Hall Farm, Tandridge Lane, RH8 9NS. ☎ (01342) 892508 • Map 187/376483 • BB **B/C** • D2 T1 F0 • 1-12 NX • Ⓑ Ⓓ Ⓢ Ⓡ Ⓟ Ⓣ ♨ • ♦♦♦ • Transport also • donnunn@compuserve.com

■ WESTCOTT (Dorking)
NORTH DOWNS WAY

Mr & Mrs Nyman, Corner House, Guildford Road, RH4 3QE. ☎ (01306) 888798 • Map 187/143486 • BB **B** • S1 D1 T1 F1 • 1-12 • Ⓓ Ⓢ Ⓡ Ⓟ Ⓣ ♨

EAST SUSSEX

■ ALFRISTON (Polegate)
SOUTH DOWNS WAY & VANGUARD WAY

Dilys & Alex Bayes, Winton Lee, The Broadway, BN26 5XH. ☎ (01323) 870593 • Map 199/514031 • BB **C** • D1 T1 • 1-12NX • Ⓑ Ⓓ Ⓢ Ⓡ Ⓟ Ⓣ • arbayes@netscapeonline.co.uk

☆ Elizabeth & David Brown, Riverdale House, Seaford Road, BN26 5TR. ☎ (01323) 871038 • Map 199/516024 • BB **D/E** • D3 T2 F1 • 1-12 NX • Ⓑ Ⓓ Ⓡ Ⓣ • ♦♦♦♦ • www.cuckmere-valley.co.uk/riverdale/

Elizabeth & Alan Foulkes, Merebank, Seaford Road, BN26 5TP. ☎ (01323) 870477 • Map 199/518026 • BB **C** • D1 T1 F1 • 1-12 NX • Ⓓ Ⓢ Ⓣ ♨

Mrs Patsy Embry, 'Dacres', BN26 5TP. ☎ (01323) 870447 • Map 199/518028 • BB **D** • T1 • 1-12 NX • Ⓑ Ⓓ Ⓢ Ⓣ Ⓜ

■ BATTLE (Hastings)
Chris & Janet Whiteman, Abbey View, Caldbec Hill, TN33 0JS. ☎ (01424) 775513 • Map 199/747166 • BB **D/E** • D2 T1 • 1-12 • Ⓑ Ⓓ Ⓢ Ⓡ Ⓟ Ⓣ • ♦♦♦♦

■ BOREHAM STREET (Bexhill)
Mrs Daphne Griffin, Baldocks, BN27 4SQ. ☎ (01323) 832107 • Map 199/667112 • BB **C** • EM book first £10, 7.30pm • D1 T1 • 1-12 NX • Ⓥ Ⓢ Ⓟ Ⓣ ♨

■ BRIGHTON
SOUTH DOWNS WAY

☆ Brighton Marina House Hotel, 8 Charlotte Street, BN2 1AG. ☎ (01273) 605349/679484 • Map 198/319038 • BB **B/C/D** • EM book first £12 upwards, 6.30-7.30pm • S3 D7 T4 F3 • 1-12 • Ⓥ Ⓑ Ⓡ Ⓣ • ◆◆◆ • Groups also • See display on previous page.

■ BUXTED (Uckfield)
WEALDWAY & VANGUARD WAY

Mr & Mrs Bailey, Buxted Inn, High Street, TN22 4LA. ☎ (01825) 733510 • Map 199/498234 • BB **C** • EM book first £country inn/restaurant, 6pm till late • SO D2 T0 F1 • 1-12 NX • Ⓥ Ⓓ Ⓢ Ⓡ Ⓟ Ⓣ ♿ Ⓜ

■ CHELWOOD GATE (Ashdown Forest)

Mrs D A Birchell, Holly House, Beaconsfield Road, RH17 7LF. ☎ (01825) 740484 • Map 187/419297 • BB **C** • EM book first £12, By arrangement • S1 D2 T2 • 1-12 • Ⓥ Ⓑ Ⓓ Ⓡ Ⓟ Ⓣ ♿ • ◆◆◆◆ • db@hollyhousebnb.demon.co.uk

■ COLEMANS HATCH (Hartfield)
VANGUARD WAY & WEALDWAY

Mrs L Hawker, Gospel Oak, TN7 4ER. ☎ (01342) 823840 • Map 187/447327 • BB **C** • EM book first £10, 8pm • D1 T1 • 1-12 • Ⓥ Ⓑ Ⓓ Ⓢ Ⓟ Ⓣ ♿ Ⓜ • ◆◆◆

■ DANEHILL (Haywards Heath, West Sussex)

Mrs J M Jennings, Greenacres, Horsted Lane, RH17 7HP. ☎ (01825) 790863 • Map 187,198/397278 • BB **A** • EM book first £6.50, 6-8.30pm • D1 T1 • 1-11 NX • Ⓥ Ⓑ Ⓓ Ⓢ Ⓟ Ⓣ Ⓜ

■ EASTBOURNE
SOUTH DOWNS WAY & WEALDWAY

J Pattenden, Ambleside Hotel, 24 Elms Avenue, BN21 3DN. ☎ (01323) 724991 • Map 199/616989 • BB **B/D** • EM book first £7, 6pm • S2 D6 T6 • 1-12 • Ⓥ Ⓓ Ⓢ Ⓡ Ⓣ ♿

Mrs Doreen Sisley, 29 Manvers Road, BN20 8HH. ☎ (01323) 726645 • Map 199/588992 • BB **B** • EM £5 • S1 T1 • 2-12 NX • Ⓥ Ⓓ Ⓡ Ⓟ Ⓣ

Brayscroft Hotel, 13 South Cliff Avenue, BN20 7AH. ☎ (01323) 647005 • Map 199/609980 • BB **D** • EM book first £12, 6.00pm • S1 D2 T2 • 1-12 • Ⓥ Ⓑ Ⓓ Ⓢ Ⓡ Ⓟ Ⓣ ♿ • ◆◆◆◆ • brayscroft@hotmail.com

Hanburies Hotel, 4 Hardwick Road, BN21 4NY. ☎ (01323) 730698 • Map 199/611987 • BB **C** • EM £8, 6.30pm • S3 D4 T5 F1 • 1-12 • Ⓥ Ⓑ Ⓓ Ⓢ Ⓡ Ⓟ Ⓣ ♿ • ◆◆◆ • Groups also

Anne & John Walker, The Manse, 7 Dittons Road, BN21 1DW. ☎ 01323 737851 • Map 199/605992 • BB **B** • D1 T2 • 1-12 NX • Ⓑ Ⓓ Ⓡ Ⓟ Ⓣ ♿

Princes Hotel, Lascelles Terrace, BN21 4BL. ☎ (01323) 722056 • Map 199/613984 • BB **D/E** • EM £10, 6.45-8.15pm • S16 D13 T17 F2 • 2-12 • Ⓥ Ⓓ Ⓡ Ⓟ Ⓣ ♿ • ★★★ • princes-hotel@btconnect.com

Trevor & Brenda Gomersall, Alfriston Hotel, Lushington Road, BN21 4LL. ☎ (01323) 725640 • Map 199/611988 • BB **C** • EM book first £10, 6pm • S5 D3 T2 F2 • 3-10 • Ⓥ Ⓑ Ⓓ Ⓢ Ⓡ Ⓣ • ◆◆◆ • alfristonhotel@fsbdial.co.uk

■ FAIRWARP (Uckfield)
WEALDWAY & VANGUARD WAY

Jane Rattray, Broom Cottage, Browns Brook, TN22 3BY. ☎ (01825) 712942 • Map 198/472272 • BB **C** • D1 T1 • 1-12 • Ⓑ Ⓓ Ⓢ Ⓟ Ⓣ ♿ • ◆◆◆◆

■ FRAMFIELD (Uckfield)
WEALDWAY

☆ Caroline Penny, Beggars Barn, Barn Lane, TN22 5RX. ☎ (01825) 890868 • Map 199/510215 • BB **C** • EM book first £7 • S1 D2 F1 • 1-11 • Ⓥ Ⓑ Ⓓ Ⓡ Ⓟ Ⓣ ♿ • ◆◆◆◆Ⓢ • www.beggarbarn.co.uk

■ GLYNDE (Lewes)
SOUTH DOWNS WAY

Mr & Mrs B Tolton, Ranscombe House, Ranscombe Lane, BN8 6AA. ☎ (01273) 858538 • Map 198/439086 • BB **C** • D2 T1 F1 • 1-12 NX • Ⓑ Ⓓ Ⓡ Ⓣ ♿

■ GROOMBRIDGE (Tunbridge Wells)
WEALDWAY

Brenda Horner, Ventura, The Ridge, Withyam Road, TN3 9QU. ☎ (01892) 864711 • Map 188/521369 • BB **B/E** • EM book first £10, 6.30-7pm • S1 D1 T1 • 1-12 NX • Ⓥ Ⓑ Ⓓ Ⓢ Ⓟ Ⓣ ♿

■ HAILSHAM
WEALDWAY

David & Jill Hook, Longleys Farm Cottage, Harebeating Lane, BN27 1ER. ☎ (01323) 841227 • Map 199/598105 • BB **B** • EM book first £8 • D1 T1 F1 • 1-12 • Ⓑ Ⓓ Ⓢ Ⓟ Ⓣ ♿ • ◆◆◆

Brenda & Harold Barrow, Batchelors, Cowbeech Hill, BN27 4JB. ☎ (01323) 832215 • Map 199/617135 • BB **E** • D1 T2 • 1-12 NX • Ⓑ Ⓓ Ⓢ Ⓣ • ◆◆◆

EAST SUSSEX ENGLAND B&B ACCOMMODATION

217

Kathryn Webster, Little Marshfoot Farmhouse, Mill Road, BN27 2SJ. ☎ (01323) 844690 • Map 199/602092 • BB **D** • EM book first £8 • D1 T1 • 1-12 • Ⓥ Ⓑ Ⓓ Ⓢ Ⓟ Ⓣ Ⓜ • ★★★★ • kathryn.webster@which.net

■ HASTINGS

John & June Dyer, White Cottage, Battery Hill, Fairlight, TN35 4AP. ☎ (01424) 812528 • Map 199/873123 • BB **C** • D2 T1 • 2-10 • Ⓑ Ⓓ Ⓢ Ⓣ • ◆◆◆

Mike & Sandra Power, West Hill Cottage, Exmouth Place, TN34 3JA. ☎ (01424) 716021 • Map 199/823095 • BB **B** • D1 T2 • 1-12 • Ⓑ Ⓓ Ⓢ Ⓡ Ⓟ Ⓣ ⏃ • ◆◆◆

John & Angela Gilbey, Mount Pleasant Farm, Whitehart Hill, Guestling, TN35 4LR. ☎ (01424) 813108 • Map 199/852137 • BB **C/E** • D4 T1 • Mid/8-Mid/9+X • Ⓑ Ⓓ Ⓢ Ⓟ Ⓣ ⏃ • ◆◆◆◆ • Transport available

■ HORAM (Heathfield)
WEALDWAY & VANGUARD WAY

Mrs Barbara Curtis, Oak Mead Nursery, TN21 9ED. ☎ (01435) 812962 • Map 199/592171 • BB **B** • S1 D1 T1 • 1-11 • Ⓑ Ⓓ Ⓢ Ⓟ Ⓣ • ◆◆◆

■ KINGSTON (Lewes)
SOUTH DOWNS WAY

Jean Hudson, "Nightingales", The Avenue, BN7 3LL. ☎ (01273) 475673 • Map 198/389083 • BB **D** • S1 D1 T1 F0 • 1-12 NX • Ⓑ Ⓓ Ⓢ Ⓡ Ⓟ Ⓣ • ◆◆◆◆◆ • SC also. Food nearby

Mrs Diana Artlett, Settlands, Wellgreen Lane, BN7 3NP. ☎ (01273) 472295 • Map 198/398082 • BB **D** • D1 T1 • 1-12 NX • Ⓓ Ⓢ Ⓡ Ⓟ Ⓣ • ◆◆◆◆

■ LEWES

Vic,Veronica & Declan Newman, The Black Horse Inn, Western Road, BN7 1RS. ☎ (01273) 473653 • Map 198/409100 • BB **C/D** • D/S3 T/S1 • MID JAN-MID DEC • Ⓓ Ⓢ Ⓡ Ⓟ Ⓣ ⏃ • veronica@blackhorse.uk.com

Berkeley House Hotel, 2 Albion Street, BN7 2ND. ☎ (01273) 476057 • Map 198/417102 • BB **E** • D4 T/F1 • 1-12 NX • Ⓑ Ⓓ Ⓢ Ⓡ Ⓟ Ⓣ • ◆◆◆◆ • www.berkeleyhousehotel.co.uk

Lesley Gorski, Pump Cottage, 6 St Nicholas Lane, BN7 2JY. ☎ 01273 473765 • Map 198/416099 • BB **C** • T1 • 1-12 • Ⓓ Ⓢ Ⓡ Ⓟ Ⓣ

Mrs V Chapman, The Old Coach House, BN7 1UA. ☎ (01273) 483138 • Map 198/413099 • BB **D** • T1 • 1-12 NX • Ⓑ Ⓢ Ⓡ Ⓟ Ⓣ ⏃

Mrs Charlotte Greene, Phoenix House, 23 Gundreda Road, BN7 1PT. ☎ (01273) 473250 • Map 198/407104 • BB **C** • S1 D1 T1 • 1-12 NX • Ⓑ Ⓓ Ⓢ Ⓡ Ⓟ Ⓣ • charg55@yahoo.com

Penny Martin, Innesmore, Brighton Road, BN7 1EB. ☎ (01273) 474177 • Map 198/402097 • BB **D** • T3 • 1-12 • Ⓓ Ⓢ Ⓡ Ⓟ Ⓣ

■ MAYFIELD

B Powner, April Cottage Guest House and Tearoom, West Street, TN20 6BA. ☎ (01435) 872160 • Map 188,199/585269 • BB **C** • S1 D/S1 T/S1 • 1-12 • Ⓑ Ⓓ Ⓢ Ⓟ ⏃ • 16th century building - centre of village.

■ OVINGDEAN (Brighton)

Geraldine Hynam, Ashdown House, Ovingdean Road, BN2 7BB. ☎ 01273 309689 • Map 198/356037 • BB **C** • EM book first £8, 7pm • S1 T1 • 1-12 NX • Ⓑ Ⓢ Ⓟ Ⓣ • gerrie50@hotmail.com

■ PEASMARSH (Rye)

Flackley Ash Hotel, TN31 6YH. ☎ (01797) 230651 • Map 199,189/881233 • BB **E** • EM £22.50, 7-9.30pm • T1 F6 • 1-12 • Ⓥ Ⓑ Ⓓ Ⓢ Ⓡ Ⓟ Ⓣ ⏃ • ★★★ • flackleyash@marstonhotels.co.uk

■ PLUMPTON GREEN (Lewes)
SOUTH DOWNS WAY

Mrs M Baker, Farthings, Station Road, BN7 3BY. ☎ (01273) 890415 • Map 198/360162 • BB **D** • EM book first £5-£7, 7pm • D2 T1 F1 • 1-12 • Ⓥ Ⓑ Ⓓ Ⓢ Ⓡ Ⓟ Ⓣ ⏃

■ RYE
SAXON SHORE WAY

☆ Mrs J Hadfield, Jeake's House, Mermaid Street, TN31 7ET. ☎ (01797) 222828 • Map 189/919203 • BB **D/E** • S1 D7 T1 F2 • 1-12 • Ⓑ Ⓓ Ⓢ Ⓡ Ⓣ ⏃ • ◆◆◆◆◆ Ⓢ

Tel. Rye (01797) 222828 Fax (01797)222623
Beautiful listed building built in 1689. Set in medieval cobblestoned street, renowned for its smuggling associations. Breakfast—served in eighteenth century galleried former chapel—is traditional or vegetarian. Oak beamed and panelled bedrooms overlook the marsh and roof-tops to the sea. Brass or mahogany bedsteads, linen sheets and lace, En-suite bathrooms, hot drink trays, direct dial telephones and televisions. Four poster honeymoon suite available. Residential license. Wonderful walking country. Private car park. Bike hire nearby. Brochure on request.
AA 5 diamonds, premier selected
ETC 5 sparkling diamonds
RAC 5 sparkling diamonds & warm welcome awards

Barbara & Denys Martin, Little Saltcote, 22 Military Rd, TN31 7NY. ☎ (01797) 223210 • Map 189/923212 • BB **B/C** • D2 F3 • 1-12 NX • Ⓑ Ⓓ Ⓢ Ⓡ Ⓟ Ⓣ 🌣 • ◆◆◆ • littlesaltcote.rye@virgin.net

■ SEAFORD
SOUTH DOWNS WAY & VANGUARD WAY

Mrs Kay L Tullett, Bentley Guest House, 23 Pelham Road, BN25 1ES. ☎ (01323) 893171 • Map 198/481988 • BB **B** • S2 D2 T1 • 1-12 NX • Ⓑ Ⓓ Ⓢ Ⓡ Ⓣ

Exceat Farmhouse Restaurant, Seven Sisters Country Park, BN25 4AD. ☎ 01323 870218 • Map 199/519995 • BB **C/D** • D2 T1 • 1-12 NX • Ⓑ Ⓓ Ⓢ Ⓟ Ⓣ 🌣

■ STREAT (Hassocks)
SOUTH DOWNS WAY

Valerie & John Eastwood, North Acres, BN6 8RX. ☎ (01273) 890278 • Map 198/353154 • BB **C** • S1 T3 F1 • 1-12 NX • Ⓓ Ⓢ Ⓡ Ⓟ Ⓣ • Groups also. Transport available. eastwood_streat@yahoo.com

■ WILMINGTON (Polegate)
SOUTH DOWNS WAY & WEALDWAY & VANGUARD WAY

David Stott, Crossways Hotel, BN26 5SG. ☎ (01323) 482455 • Map 199/547048 • BB **E** • EM book first £28.95, 7.30-8.45pm • S2 D3 T2 • 2-12 NX • Ⓥ Ⓑ Ⓓ Ⓢ Ⓡ Ⓣ • ◆◆◆◆◆ • crossways@fastnet.co.uk

■ WINCHELSEA
SAXON SHORE WAY

☆ Strand House, Tanyards Lane, TN36 4JT. ☎ (01797) 226276 • Map 189/907175 • BB **C/D/E** • S4 D8 T2 F2 • 1-12 NX • Ⓑ Ⓓ Ⓢ Ⓡ Ⓟ Ⓣ • ◆◆◆◆ • smoothhound.co.uk/hotels/strand.html

The Strand House
Winchelsea, East Sussex
TN36 4JT
Tel 01797 226276
Fax 01797 224806

15th century – 10 individually decorated en-suite bedrooms, residents lounge/bar, inglenooks, oak beams, gardens. Farmhouse breakfasts. Close to footpaths, buses and trains
strandhouse@winchelsea98.fsnet.co.uk

Sally Palmer, Wickham Manor Farm, Pannel Lane, TN36 4AG. ☎ (01797) 226216 • Map 189/898165 • BB **D** • EM book first £15, 7.30pm • S1 D2 T1 F1 • 1-12 NX • Ⓥ Ⓑ Ⓢ Ⓡ Ⓟ Ⓣ 🌣 • ★★★

VEGETARIANS
Many establishments do a veggie breakfast even if they don't do an evening meal

---

WEST SUSSEX

■ AMBERLEY (Arundel)
SOUTH DOWNS WAY

Mrs Bridget Jollands, Bacons, BN18 9NJ. ☎ (01798) 831234 • Map 197/031131 • BB **B** • T2 • 1-12 NX • Ⓓ Ⓡ 🌣

Mr & Mrs G Hardy, "Woodybanks", Crossgates, BN18 9NR. ☎ (01798) 831295 • Map 197/041136 • BB **B** • D1 T1 • 1-12 NX • Ⓓ Ⓢ Ⓡ Ⓟ Ⓣ • Some facilities for disabled

■ ARUNDEL
SOUTH DOWNS WAY

Arden Guest House, 4 Queen's Lane, BN18 9JN. ☎ (01903) 882544 • Map 197/019068 • BB **B/C** • D5 T3 • 1-12 • Ⓑ Ⓢ Ⓡ Ⓣ • ◆◆◆

Peter & Sarah Fuente, Mill Lane House, Slindon, BN18 0RP. ☎ (01243) 814440 • Map 197/964084 • BB **C** • EM book first £11.50, 7pm • S1 D3 T2 F1 • 1-12 • Ⓥ Ⓑ Ⓓ Ⓟ Ⓣ 🌣 • 2Cr/C • SC also

☆ Mrs Faggetter, Woodpeckers, 15 Dalloway Road, BN18 9HJ. ☎ (01903) 883948 • Map 197/006064 • BB **C** • EM book first £8, 6.30-7pm • D3 • 1-12 • Ⓥ Ⓑ Ⓓ Ⓢ Ⓡ Ⓟ Ⓣ • ◆◆◆◆ • Off-season singles discount

Walk the South Downs from Woodpeckers
15 Dalloway Road, Arundel, West Sussex BN18 9HW
Our country retreat, overlooking the Arun Valley, is ideal for walks on the Sussex Downs or ambling along the banks of the River Arun. Accommodation offers double en-suite rooms, TV, tea/coffee and hairdryer facilities. Big home cooked breakfast and evening meals by prior arrangement. A high standard of comfort and friendliness. Non-smoking rooms. Single walkers can be accommodated by arrangement from £35pppn. **OPEN ALL YEAR. Tel: 01903 883948**

Mrs J Carter, 9 Dalloway Road, BN18 9HJ. ☎ (01903) 882253 • Map 197/006064 • BB **B** • S1 T1 • 1-11 • Ⓓ Ⓡ Ⓟ Ⓣ

■ BURGESS HILL

☆ Sue & Mike Mundy, The Homestead, Homestead Lane, Valebridge Road, RH15 0RQ. ☎ (01444) 246899 • Map 198/323208 • BB **C** • S1 D3 T2 • 1-12 • Ⓑ Ⓓ Ⓢ Ⓡ Ⓟ Ⓣ • ◆◆◆◆ • Kennels nearby www.burgess-hill.co.uk • Display box on next page.

■ BURY (Pulborough)
SOUTH DOWNS WAY

Mrs Carol Clarke, Harkaway, 8 Houghton Lane, RH20 1PD. ☎ (01798) 831843 • Map 197/012130 • BB **B** • S2 D1 T1 • 1-12 • Ⓑ Ⓓ Ⓢ Ⓡ Ⓟ Ⓣ

☆ See Display Advertisement

The Homestead
Burgess Hill

Quiet, comfortable, friendly home in peaceful setting of 7.5 acres at the end of a private lane.Handy for Glyndebourne, South Downs Way, Nat. Trust locations etc.

Tel/Fax 01444 246899   ETC ◆◆◆◆

■ BURY (Pulborough) (continued)
SOUTH DOWNS WAY

Jane & Peter House, Tanglewood, Houghton Lane, RH20 1PD. ☎ (01798) 831606 • Map 197/012130 • BB **B/C** • S1 D1 • 1-12 • Ⓓ Ⓢ Ⓡ Ⓟ Ⓣ

■ CHICHESTER

Ethel & Tony Hosking, "Hedgehogs", 45 Whyke Lane, PO19 2JT. ☎ (01243) 780022 • Map 197/867044 • BB **B/C** • S1 D1 • 1-12 • Ⓓ Ⓢ Ⓡ Ⓟ Ⓣ 🐾 • ◆◆◆

■ CLAYTON (Hassocks)
SOUTH DOWNS WAY

Mrs C Bailey, Dower Cottage, Underhill Lane, BN6 9PL. ☎ (01273) 843363 • Map 198/309136 • BB **C** • S1 D3 T1 F1 • 1-12 NX • Ⓑ Ⓓ Ⓢ Ⓡ Ⓟ • SC also. www.smoothhound.co.uk/hotels/dower.html

■ COCKING (Midhurst)
SOUTH DOWNS WAY

Josephine Longland, Moonlight Cottage Tea Rooms, GU29 0HN. ☎ 01730 813336 • Map 197/877176 • BB **C** • D2 T1 • 1-12 • Ⓓ Ⓢ Ⓟ Ⓣ • moonlightcottage.net

Ruth Higgins, Cinque Port House, Bell Lane, GU29 0HU. ☎ (01730) 813594 • Map 197/877176 • BB **C** • S1 T2 • 1-12 NX • Ⓓ Ⓢ Ⓟ 🐾 • Food nearby • www.cinqueporthouse.com

■ COPSALE (Horsham)

P & A Churcher, Copsale Farm, RH13 6QU. ☎ (01403) 732237 • Map 187,198/172248 • BB **C** • D2 T1 F1 • 1-12 • Ⓑ Ⓓ Ⓢ Ⓣ 🐾 • On Downs Link

■ COPTHORNE (Nr Gatwick)

☆ The Smyth Family, Linchens, New Domewood, RH10 3HF. ☎ (01342) 713085 • Map 187/345402 • BB **D** • EM book first £10 • S4 D3 T2 F3 • 1-12 NX • Ⓥ Ⓑ Ⓓ Ⓢ Ⓟ Ⓣ 🐾 Ⓜ • www.linchens.com

■ DUNCTON (Petworth)
SOUTH DOWNS WAY

Mrs Phyl Folkes, Drifters, GU28 0JZ. ☎ (01798) 342706 • Map 197/961173 • BB **C** • S1 D1 T2 • 1-12 NX • Ⓑ Ⓓ Ⓢ Ⓟ Ⓣ • ◆◆◆ • Food nearby

■ EAST ASHLING (Chichester)

Sylvia Jones, Englewood, PO18 9AS. ☎ (01243) 575407 • Map 197/820075 • BB **C** • D2 • 1-12 NX • Ⓑ Ⓓ Ⓡ Ⓟ Ⓣ • ◆◆◆◆ • Food nearby

■ EAST GRINSTEAD
VANGUARD WAY

Susie & Ian Forbes, Moat House, Moat Road, RH19 3JZ. ☎ (01342) 326785 • Map 187/391385 • BB **C** • EM book first £9, 7-7.30pm • S1 D2 T3 F1 • 1-12 • Ⓥ Ⓑ Ⓓ Ⓢ Ⓡ Ⓟ Ⓣ 🐾 • Groups also

■ GRAFFHAM (Petworth)
SOUTH DOWNS WAY

Mr & Mrs S A Jollands, Brook Barn, GU28 0PU. ☎ (01798) 867356 • Map 197/929180 • BB **D** • D1 • 1-12 NX • Ⓑ Ⓓ Ⓢ Ⓟ Ⓣ 🐾 • ◆◆◆◆ⓢ

■ HEYSHOTT (Midhurst)
SOUTH DOWNS WAY

Robert & Judith Ralph, Little Hoyle, Hoyle Lane, GU29 0DX. ☎ /Fax (01798) 867359 • Map 197/906187 • BB **C** • D1 • 1-12 NX • Ⓑ Ⓓ Ⓢ Ⓟ Ⓣ • ◆◆◆◆

■ MIDHURST
SOUTH DOWNS WAY

Joanna Whitmore-Jones, Oakhurst Cottage, Carron Lane, GU29 9LF. ☎ (01730) 813523 • Map 197/877214 • BB **D** • S1 D1 T1 • 1-12 • Ⓑ Ⓓ Ⓢ Ⓟ Ⓣ • ◆◆◆

■ POYNINGS (Brighton, East Sussex)
SOUTH DOWNS WAY

Mrs Carol Revell, Manor Farm, BN45 7AG. ☎ (01273) 857371 • Map 198/262122 • BB **C** • D1 T2 • 3-12 NX • Ⓑ Ⓓ Ⓢ Ⓟ Ⓣ • ◆◆◆◆ • manor_farm@hotmail.com

■ STEYNING
SOUTH DOWNS WAY

Mrs J Morrow, 5 Coxham Lane, BN44 3LG. ☎ (01903) 812286 • Map 198/176116 • BB **B** • S1 T2 • 1-12 • Ⓑ Ⓓ Ⓟ Ⓣ 🐾

☆ Springwells Hotel, 9 High Street, BN44 3GG. ☎ (01903) 812446/812043 • Map 198/177112 • BB **E** • S2 D3 T4 F1 • 1-12 NX • Ⓑ Ⓓ Ⓟ Ⓣ 🐾

Mrs Shapland, Wappingthorn Farmhouse, Horsham Road, BN44 3AA. ☎ (01903) 813236 • Map 198/176144 • BB **C/D** • S2 D2 T1 • 1-12 • Ⓑ Ⓓ Ⓢ Ⓟ Ⓣ • ◆◆◆◆ • SC also • www.wappingthorn.demon.co.uk

■ STORRINGTON (Pulborough)
SOUTH DOWNS WAY

☆ Mrs M Smith, Willow Tree Cottage, Washington Road, RH20 4AF. ☎ (01903) 740835 • Map 198/101138 • BB **C** • D2 T1 F1 • 1-12 NX • Ⓑ Ⓓ Ⓢ Ⓟ Ⓣ 🐾

■ WASHINGTON (Pulborough)
SOUTH DOWNS WAY

Barry & Mary Sturgess, Long Island, School Lane, RH20 4AP. ☎ (01903) 892237 • Map 198/120129 • BB **C** • D1 T1 F1 • 1-12 • Ⓓ Ⓢ Ⓟ Ⓣ 🐾

WARWICKSHIRE

■ ALCESTER
HEART OF ENGLAND WAY

John & Margaret Canning, Glebe Farm, Exhall, B49 6EA. ☎ (01789) 772202 • Map 150/102550 • BB **C** • S2 D1 T1 • 1-12 NX • Ⓓ Ⓢ Ⓣ 🐾 • ◆◆◆ • SC also

■ BIDFORD-ON-AVON
HEART OF ENGLAND WAY

Don & Lin Newbury, Fosbroke House, 4 High Street, B50 4BU. ☎ 01789 772327 • Map 150/101519 • BB **C** • EM book first £10, 7pm • S1 D2 T1 F1 • 1-12 NX • Ⓥ Ⓑ Ⓓ Ⓢ Ⓟ Ⓣ 🐾 • ◆◆◆◆ • www.smoothhound.co.uk/hotels/fosbroke.html

■ BLACKWELL (Shipston-on-Stour)

Blackwell Grange, CV36 4PF. ☎ 01608 682357 • Map 151/239435 • BB **D** • EM book first £14-£15.50 • S1 D1 T1 • 1-12 NX • Ⓑ Ⓓ Ⓢ Ⓟ Ⓣ • SC also • some disabled access

■ BURTON DASSETT (Southam)

☆ Lisa Woodward, The White House Bed & Breakfast, CV47 2AB. ☎ (01295) 770143 • Map 151/416498 • BB **C** • EM book first £15, 6-9pm • D2 T1 • 1-12 • Ⓥ Ⓑ Ⓓ Ⓢ Ⓟ Ⓣ • ◆◆◆◆ • lisa@whitehouse10.freeserve.co.uk

■ HASELEY KNOB (Warwick)
GRAND UNION CANAL WALK

Mrs Pat Clapp, The Croft, CV35 7NL. ☎ (01926) 484447 • Map 139/233711 • BB **C** • S1 D1 T1 F2 • 1-12 NX • Ⓑ Ⓓ Ⓢ Ⓣ 🐾 • ◆◆◆◆ • www.croftguesthouse.co.uk

■ ILMINGTON (Stratford-upon-Avon)

Mrs Radford, Crab Mill, Grump Street, CV36 4LE. ☎ (01608) 682233 • Map 151/209433 • BB **C** • D1 T1 F1 • 9-7 NX • Ⓑ Ⓓ Ⓣ • luke.hodgkin@kcl.ac.uk

☆ See Display Advertisement

■ KENILWORTH

Trevor & Angela Jefferies, The Abbey Guest House, 41 Station Road, CV8 1JD. ☎ (01926) 512707 • Map 140/290717 • BB **C** • S2 D2 T3 • 1-12 NX • Ⓑ Ⓢ Ⓟ Ⓣ Ⓜ • ◆◆◆◆ • abbeyguesthouse.com

Mrs Patricia Snelson, Banner Hill Farmhouse Accom., Rouncil Lane, CV8 1NN. ☎ (01926) 852850 • Map 140/268708 • BB **B** • EM £7.50 • S2 D2 T4 F2 • 1-12 NX • Ⓥ Ⓑ Ⓓ Ⓢ Ⓟ Ⓣ ⛪ • 1Cr • Groups also

Trudi & Ken Wheat, The Hollyhurst Guest House, 47 Priory Road, CV8 1LL. ☎ (01926) 853882 • Map 140/289720 • BB **C** • EM book first £ • S1 D1 T4 F1 • 1-12 NX • Ⓑ Ⓓ Ⓢ Ⓣ • ◆◆◆ • www.hollyhurstguesthouse.co.uk

■ LONG MARSTON (Stratford-upon-Avon)
HEART OF ENGLAND WAY

Mrs Taylor, Church Farm, CV37 8RH. ☎ (01789) 720275 • Map 151/153484 • BB **C** • T1 F/D1 • 1-12 NX • Ⓑ Ⓓ Ⓢ Ⓟ Ⓣ ⛪ • 2Cr/C • Food nearby wiggychurchfarm@hotmail.com

■ MERIDEN (Coventry)
HEART OF ENGLAND WAY

☆ Cooperage Farm B&B, Old Road, CV7 7JP. ☎ (01676) 523493 • Map 140/251820 • BB **D** • EM £8, 6-9pm • D2 T2 F2 • 2-12 NX • Ⓥ Ⓑ Ⓡ Ⓣ ⛪ • ◆◆

Cooperage Farm
Meriden, Warwickshire

B&B in the attractive village of Meriden on the Heart of England Way. Tea/coffee facilities and a good English breakfast. Ample car parking. Cooperage Farm is a 300-year-old Listed farmhouse.

Tel. 01676 523493
www.cooperagefarm.co.uk
lucy@cooperagefarm.co.uk

■ PAILTON (Rugby)

The White Lion Inn, Coventry Road, CV23 0QD. ☎ (01788) 832359 • Map 140/470820 • BB **D** • EM £6.95, 6.30-10.00pm • T9 • 1-12 • Ⓥ Ⓑ Ⓓ Ⓢ Ⓟ Ⓣ ⛪ • ★★★

■ SOUTHAM (Leamington Spa)
GRAND UNION CANAL WALK

Mrs E Bishop, "Briarwood", 34 Warwick Road, CV47 0HN. ☎ (01926) 814756 • Map 151/414615 • BB **C** • S1 D1 • 1-12 NX • Ⓑ Ⓓ Ⓢ Ⓟ Ⓣ • 2Cr/C

■ STRATFORD-UPON-AVON
HEART OF ENGLAND WAY

The Hunter's Moon Guesthouse, 150 Alcester Road, CV37 9DR. ☎ (01789) 292888 • Map 151/186552 • BB **C/D** • S2 D4 T3 F3 • 1-12 NX • Ⓥ Ⓑ Ⓓ Ⓢ Ⓡ Ⓣ ⛪ • ◆◆◆ • thehuntersmoon@NTLworld.com

Nando's, 18/19 Evesham Place, CV37 6HT. ☎ (01789) 204907 • Map 151/197547 • BB **B/C** • EM £8 (groups only), 6pm • S3 D10 T6 F3 • 1-12NX • Ⓥ Ⓑ Ⓢ Ⓡ Ⓟ Ⓣ ⛪ • ◆◆

☆ Jo & Roger Pettitt, Parkfield Guest House, 3 Broad Walk, CV37 6HS. ☎ (01789) 293313 • Map 151/197546 • BB **C** • S1 D3 T2 F1 • 1-12 • Ⓑ Ⓓ Ⓢ Ⓡ Ⓟ Ⓣ ⛪ • ◆◆◆ • parkfield@btinternet.com

---

STRATFORD-UPON-AVON
Parkfield Guest House, 3 Broad Walk CV37 6HS

An attractive Victorian house in a quiet location, 5 minutes' walk to town centre & Royal Shakespeare Theatre and one minute from start of Greenway leading to Heart of England Way. Rooms have colour TV and tea/coffee-making facilities. Most rooms en suite. Full English or vegetarian breakfast. Brochure on request. Large private car park. A no-smoking house.

AA RAC ☎ **01789 293313** ETB ◆◆◆
Email: parkfield@btinternet.com

Travellers Rest Guest House, Joan & Clive Horton, 146 Alcester Road, CV37 9DR. ☎ /Fax (01789) 266589 • Map 151/186553 • BB **B/C** • S/D1 T1 F/D/T1 • 1-12 NX • Ⓑ Ⓓ Ⓢ Ⓡ Ⓟ Ⓣ • ◆◆◆ • hortontr@hotmail.com

■ WARWICK
GRAND UNION CANAL WALK

☆ Elizabeth Hughes, Hither Barn, Star Lane, Claverdon, CV35 8LW. ☎ (01926) 842839 • Map 151/203652 • BB **E** • EM book first £13-£15, 6.30-7pm (gluten free av.) • D/S2 T/S/F1 • 1-12 • Ⓥ Ⓑ Ⓢ Ⓡ Ⓟ Ⓣ ⛪ • ◆◆◆

Hither Barn

Bed and full English breakfast, vegetarians welcome. Peaceful countryside with excellent pubs/restaurants within walking distance. Adjacent country club, fishing/golf. Easy run to NEC, NAC, Stratford-upon-Avon and Cotswolds. Prices from £22.50, ensuite rooms. Star Lane, Claverdon, Warwick CV35 8LW **Tel: 01926 842839**

■ WIMPSTONE (Stratford-Upon-Avon)

Joan James, Whitchurch Farm, CV37 8NS. ☎ (01789) 450275 • Map 151/215488 • BB **B** • D2 T1 • 1-12 NX • Ⓥ Ⓑ Ⓓ Ⓢ Ⓟ Ⓣ • ◆◆◆

■ WIXFORD (Alcester)
HEART OF ENGLAND WAY

Mrs Margaret Kember, Orchard Lawns, B49 6DA. ☎ (01789) 772668 • Map 150/087547 • BB **C** • S1 D1 T1 • 1-12 NX • Ⓑ Ⓓ Ⓢ Ⓟ Ⓣ ⛪ • ◆◆◆◆Ⓢ • Food nearby • margaret.orchardlawns@farmersweekly.net

WEST MIDLANDS

■ HAMPTON-IN-ARDEN (Solihull)
GRAND UNION CANAL WALK

Miss Victoria Dickenson, The Hollies, Kenilworth Road, B92 0LW. ☎ (01675) 442681 • Map 139/226792 • BB **D** • EM book first £2-£5 (sandwiches), up till 9pm • S1 D/S4 T/S4 F/S2 • 1-12 NX • ⒝ ⒟ ⒮ ⓡ ⓟ ⓣ ⌂ • ◆◆◆ • m_hardwick@hotmail.com

■ SOLIHULL
GRAND UNION CANAL WALK

Mr & Mrs J Townsend, Ivy House, Warwick Road, Heronfield Knowle, B93 0EB. ☎ (01564) 770247 • Map 139/194750 • BB **E** • S3 D2 T2 F1 • 1-12 • ⒝ ⒮ ⓡ ⓣ ⌂ • ◆◆◆ • john@ivy-guest-house.freeserve.co.uk

WILTSHIRE

■ ASHTON KEYNES (Swindon)
THAMES PATH

Valerie Threlfall, 1 Cove House, SN6 6NS. ☎ (01285) 861226 • Map 173,163/046940 • BB **D** • D2 T1 • 1-12 NX • ⒝ ⒟ ⒮ ⓟ ⓣ ⌂ • 2Cr/HC

■ BRADFORD-ON-AVON
MACMILLAN WAY

Mr & Mrs J Benjamin, The Locks, 265 Trowbridge Road, BA15 1UA. ☎ (01225) 863358 • Map 173/833597 • BB **C** • S1 D1 T1 F1 • 1-12 • ⒝ ⒟ ⒮ ⓡ ⓟ ⓣ

■ BREMHILL (Calne)

Elizabeth Sinden, Lowbridge Farm, SN11 9HE. ☎ (01249) 815889 • Map 173/987737 • BB **C** • EM £10.50, 7-9pm • T1 F1 • 1-12 • ⓥ ⒟ ⒮ ⓟ ⓣ ⌂ • Camping & Caravan also. Horses welcome.

■ CALNE

G Brandani, White Hart Hotel, 2 London Road, SN11 0AB. ☎ (01249) 812413 • Map 173/999706 • BB **C** • EM £9, 6-10pm • S3 D4 T4 F3 • 1-12 • ⓥ ⒝ ⒟ ⓟ ⓣ ⌂ • 1Cr • Groups also

■ CHICKLADE (Hindon, Salisbury)
WESSEX RIDGEWAY

Mrs W A Jerram, Chicklade Lodge, SP3 5SU. ☎ (01747) 820389 • Map 184/910345 • BB **C** • EM book first £10, 7.30pm • T2 • 1-12 NX • ⓥ ⒟ ⒮ ⓟ ⓣ ⌂ • aud.jerram@virgin.net

■ CRICKLADE (Swindon)
THAMES PATH

Mrs J Rumming, Waterhay Farm, Leigh, SN6 6QY. ☎ (01285) 861253 • Map 173, 163/061931 • BB **C** • D1 T1 • 1-12 NX • ⒝ ⒟ ⒮ ⓣ • ◆◆◆

Jemma Maraffi, Dolls House, Latton, SN6 6DJ. ☎ (01793) 750384 • Map 163/092953 • BB **D** • EM book first £9, 6.30pm • S1 D1 T2 • 1-12 • ⒝ ⒟ ⒮ ⓟ ⓣ • ◆◆◆ • gemma-maraffi@bbdollshouse.freeserve.co.uk

■ CRUDWELL (Malmesbury)

☆ Chris Marston, Mayfield House Hotel, Crudwell, SN16 9EW. ☎ (01666) 577409 • Map 173,163/954929 • BB **D** • EM £15, 6.30-8.45pm • S3 D11 T10 • 1-12 • ⓥ ⒝ ⒟ ⒮ ⓟ ⓣ ⌂ • 3Cr • mayfield@callnetuk.com

■ EASTON ROYAL (Pewsey)

Mrs Margaret Landless, Follets, SN9 5LZ. ☎ (01672) 810619/0468 560302 • Map 174/208606 • BB **C/D** • EM book first £10 • D2 T1 • 1-12 NX • ⒝ ⒟ ⒮ ⓟ ⓣ • ◆◆◆◆ • margaretlandless@talk21.com

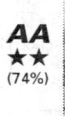

■ LACOCK (Chippenham)

Mrs S McDowell, Lacock Pottery B&B, The Tanyard, SN15 2LB. ☎ (01249) 730266 • Map 173/916686 • BB **D** • D2 T1 • 1-12 NX • ⒝ ⒟ ⒮ ⓟ ⓣ ⌂ • ◆◆◆◆ • simonemcdowell@lacockbedandbreakfast.com

Mrs Elaine Sexton, The Old Rectory, Cantax Hill, SN15 2JZ. ☎ (01249) 730335 • Map 173/914687 • BB **C** • D1 T1 F1 • 1-12 • ⒝ ⒟ ⒮ ⓣ ⌂ • ◆◆◆◆ • Food nearby • www.rectorylacock.freeserve.co.uk

■ LITTLETON PANELL (West Lavington, Devizes)
WESSEX RIDGEWAY

May & Philip Linton, Littleton Lodge (A360), SN10 4ES. ☎ (01380) 813131 • Map 184/997543 • BB **D** • D2 T1 • 1-12 • ⒝ ⒟ ⒮ ⓣ • ◆◆◆◆ • Transport avail • stay@littletonlodge.co.uk

☆ See Display Advertisement

■ **LUDWELL (Shaftesbury, Dorset)**
WESSEX RIDGEWAY

Mrs Ann Rossiter, Birdbush Farm, SP7 9HH.
☎ (01747) 828252 • Map 184/913229 • BB **B** • S1
D1 • 3-10 NX • D S P T

Mrs Christine Dieppe, Ye Olde Wheelwrights,
Birdbush, SP7 9NH. ☎ 01747 828955 • Map
184/913230 • BB **B** • D1 T1 • 3-10 NX • S P T ⬥
• charles@cdieppe.freeserve.co.uk

■ **MANTON (Marlborough)**

Mrs Barbara Couzens, Sunrise, SN8 4HL. ☎ /Fax
(01672) 512878 • Map 173/170670 • BB **C** • D1 T2 •
2-11 • B S T • ◆◆◆

■ **OGBOURNE ST GEORGE (Marlborough)**
RIDGEWAY

Mr G H Edwins, Foxlynch, Bytham Road, SN8 1TD.
☎ (01672) 841307 • Map 173/190740 • BB **B** • 1-12
• V B D P T ⬥ • Bunkroom only, camping
also

Parklands Hotel & Restaurant, High Street, SN8 1SL.
☎ (01672) 841555 • Map 174/200744 • BB **E** • EM
book first £14.85, 7-9.30pm • S2 D2 T6 • 1-12 • V B
D S P T ⬥ • ◆◆◆◆ • m.a.r.b@btinternet.com

■ **PEWSEY**

Mrs Margot Andrews, Huntleys Farm, Manningford
Abbotts, SN9 6HZ. ☎ (01672) 563663 • Map
173/145593 • BB **B** • EM book first £12 • S1 D1 T/S1
• 1-12 • V B D S R P T ⬥ • ★★★

■ **REDLYNCH (New Forest Heritage Village)**

Mr & Mrs J Churchill, Yew Tree Cottage, Grove Lane,
SP5 2NR. ☎ (01725) 511730 • Map 184/202212 •
BB **B** • S1 D1 T1 • 1-12 NX • D S T • Food near-
bysthechurchills@freeserve.co.uk

■ **SALISBURY**

Mrs Gill Rodwell, Farthings, 9 Swaynes Close, SP1
3AE. ☎ (01722) 330749 • Map 184/145306 • BB **C** •
S2 D1 T1 • 1-12 NX • B D S R T Ⓜ • ◆◆◆ •
farthings@shammer.freeserve.co.uk

Mrs Kay Bugden, Avon View House, 287 Castle Road,
SP1 3SB. ☎ (01722) 333723 • Map 184/141319 • BB
B • D2 T1 • 1-12 NX • B D S R T

Hayburn Wyke Guest House, 72 Castle Road, SP1
3RL. ☎ (01722) 412627 • Map 184/142309 • BB **C** •
D3 T2 F2 • 1-12 • B D S R T ⬥ • ◆◆◆ •
www.hotels.uk.com/HAYBURNWYKE.htm

Jaqueline Lawrence, Stratford Lodge, 4 Park Lane,
SP1 3NP. ☎ 01722 325177 • Map 184/142315 • BB **E**
• EM £18, 7-8pm • D4 T2 F2 • 1-12 NX • V B D S
R P T • ◆◆◆◆ • enquiries@stratfordlodge.co.uk

WATCH THIS SPACE
The Ramblers website at www.ramblers.org.uk will be
expanding to include accommodation for walkers
in the near future.

Trish Smith, The Old Rectory B&B, 75 Belle Vue
Road, SP1 3YE. ☎ (01722) 502702 • Map
184/145305 • BB **B/C/D** • D1 T2 • 1-12 • B D S
R P T • ◆◆◆◆ • theoldrectory-bb.co.uk

Ann & Peter Arthey, Byways House, 31 Fowler's Rd,
SP1 2QP. ☎ (01722) 328364 • Map 184/149299 • BB
C/D/E • S4 D7 T7 F5 • 1-12 NX • V B D S R P
T ⬥ • ◆◆◆ • www.bed-breakfast-stonehenge.co.uk

■ **SEMINGTON (Trowbridge)**

Mrs M Bruges, Brook House, BA14 6JR. ☎ (01380)
870232 • Map 173/898607 • BB **C** • D1 T1 F1 • 2-11 •
B D S T ⬥

■ **WARMINSTER**
WESSEX RIDGEWAY

Farmers' Hotel, 1 Silver Street, BA12 8PS. ☎ (01985)
213815 • Map 183/871451 • BB **B** • EM £8.50, 6-
10pm • S9 D4 T7 F3 • 1-12 • V B D R P T
⬥ • ◆ • Groups also

■ **WINTERBOURNE MONKTON (Swindon)**
RIDGEWAY & WESSEX RIDGEWAY

Kevin & Doreen Murrin, The New Inn, SN4 9NW.
☎ (01672) 539240 • Map 173/100720 • BB **C/E** • EM
£6, 7-9.30pm • D2 T3 • 1-12 • V B D S P T
⬥ • ◆◆◆

■ **ZEALS (Longcross)**

Irene & John Snook, Corner Ways Cottage, BA12
6LL. ☎ (01747) 840477 • Map 183/787320 • BB **C** •
D2 T1 • 1-12 NX • V B D S T • ◆◆◆◆ •
www.smoothhound.co.uk/a13331.html

EAST YORKSHIRE

■ **BAINTON**

Mrs Jill Byass, Bainton Burrows Farm, YO25 9BS.
☎ (01377) 217202 • Map 106/945533 • BB **B/C** • S1
T2 • 1-12 NX • B D S P T ⬥ • ◆◆◆

■ **BEVERLEY**

☆ Miss Julie Anderson, Eastgate Guest House, 7
Eastgate, HU17 0DR. ☎ (01482) 868464 • Map
107/036394 • BB **C** • S5 D6 T2 F3 • 1-12 • B D S
R T ⬥ • ◆◆◆

WILTSHIRE – EAST YORKSHIRE
ENGLAND B&B ACCOMMODATION

Sarah King, 1 Woodlands, HU17 8BT. ☎ (01482) 862752 • Map 106,107/029395 • BB **B/C** • EM book first £12, 7pm • S1 D1 T2 • 1-12 NX • Ⓥ Ⓑ Ⓓ Ⓢ Ⓡ 🏃 • neilandsarah@mansle.karoo.co.uk

■ BRIDLINGTON

☆ Helen Gallagher, Rosebery House, 1 Belle View, Tennyson Avenue, YO15 2ET. ☎ (01262) 670336 • Map 101/186671 • BB **B** • D3 T1 F3 • 1-12 NX • Ⓑ Ⓓ Ⓢ Ⓡ Ⓟ Ⓣ🏃 • ◆◆◆

Rosebery House

A Grade II listed Georgian house with a long garden and sea view. Amenities close by. Ideal for walking and touring. Near Flamborough Head and Bempton bird reserve. High standard of comfort and friendliness. All rooms ensuite, CH, TV, tea/coffee facilities. Vegetarians welcome, pack lunches available.

Helen Gallagher 01262 670336 or fax 608381 Rosebery House, 1 Belle Vue, Tennyson Av., Bridlington, East Yorkshire YO15 2ET

■ FLAMBOROUGH

Flaneburgh Hotel, North Marine Road, YO15 1LF. ☎ (01262) 850284 • Map 101/229709 • BB **D** • EM £8, 6.30-8.30pm • D10 T5 F3 • 1-12 NX • Ⓥ Ⓑ Ⓓ Ⓢ Ⓟ Ⓣ🏃 • ★★ • www.flaneburghotel.co.uk

■ HUGGATE

Peter & Patricia Elliott, The Wolds Inn, Driffield Road, YO42 1YH. ☎ (01377) 288217 • Map 106/882550 • BB **B/C** • EM £9, 7-9.30pm • D2 T1 • 1-12 • Ⓥ Ⓑ Ⓟ Ⓣ🏃 • huggate@woldsinn.freeserve.co.uk

■ LONDESBOROUGH (York)
WOLDS WAY

Mrs P Rowlands, Towthorpe Grange, YO43 3LB. ☎ (01430) 873814 • Map 106/876438 • BB **B** • EM book first £5 • D2 T1 F0 • 1-12 NX • Ⓥ Ⓓ Ⓢ Ⓣ 🏃 • SC also • all rooms available for single use

■ MILLINGTON (York)
WOLDS WAY

Mrs M Dykes, Laburnum Cottage, YO42 1TX. ☎ (01759) 303055 • Map 106/830517 • BB **B/C** • EM book first £7, 7pm • S T1 F1 • 2-10 • Ⓥ Ⓑ Ⓓ Ⓢ Ⓟ Ⓣ🏃

■ POCKLINGTON (York)
WOLDS WAY

Kay & David West, Ashfield Farm, Canal Head, YO42 1NW. ☎ (01759) 305238 • Map 106/800474 • BB **B/C** • D1 T2 F1 • 1-12 • Ⓑ Ⓓ Ⓢ Ⓟ Ⓣ🏃

■ SOUTH CAVE (Brough)
WOLDS WAY

Mrs Laura Greenwood, Rudstone Walk Country Accommodation, HU15 2AH. ☎ (01430) 422230 • Map 106/917342 • BB **E** • EM book first £17, from 7.30pm • S7 D7 T7 F3 • 1-12 • Ⓥ Ⓑ Ⓓ Ⓢ Ⓟ Ⓣ🏃 • ◆◆◆◆ • SC also • www.rudstone-walk.co.uk

NORTH YORKSHIRE

■ AMPLEFORTH (York)

P. Gill & A. van der Horst, Shallowdale House, West End, YO62 4DY. ☎ (01439) 788325 • Map 100/579786 • BB **E** • EM book first £21, 7.30pm • D1 T/D2 • 1-12 NX • Ⓥ Ⓑ Ⓓ Ⓢ Ⓟ Ⓣ • ◆◆◆◆◆Ⓢ • Fax 01439 788885

■ ASKRIGG (Leyburn)

Mr & Mrs B Bowe, Syke's House, DL8 3HT. ☎ (01969) 650535 • Map 98/947910 • BB **C** • EM book first £11, 7pm • D1 T1 F1 • 1-12 NX • Ⓥ Ⓓ Ⓟ Ⓣ🏃 • SC also

Mrs B Percival, Milton House, DL8 3HJ. ☎ (01969) 650217 • Map 98/948910 • BB **B/C** • D3 • 1-12 NX • Ⓑ Ⓓ Ⓢ Ⓟ Ⓣ🏃 • ◆◆◆ • Food nearby

Mrs Kate Empsall, Whitfield Helm, DL8 3JF. ☎ (01969) 650565 • Map 98/934916 • BB **C** • D1 T1 • 1-12 NX • Ⓑ Ⓓ Ⓢ Ⓟ Ⓣ🏃 • ◆◆◆◆ • SC also • empsall@askrigg.yorks.net

■ AYSGARTH (Nr Leyburn)

☆ Stow House Hotel, Aysgarth Falls, DL8 3SR. ☎ (01969) 663635 • Map 98/014883 • BB **E** • EM book first £16, 7.30pm • D5 T4 • 1-12 • Ⓥ Ⓑ Ⓓ Ⓢ Ⓟ Ⓣ🏃 • ◆◆◆◆

■ BEDALE

Mrs Jill Welham, Rowan Rise, Mill Lane, Well, DL8 2RX. ☎ (01677) 470394 • Map 99/266818 • BB **B** • D1 T1 • 1-12 NX • Ⓓ Ⓢ Ⓟ Ⓣ

■ BLAKEY (Kirkbymoorside)
COAST TO COAST WALK

The Lion Inn, YO62 7LQ. ☎ (01751) 417320 • Map 100,94/678997 • BB **B/C/D** • EM £5.75, upto 10pm • D6 T1 F3 • 1-12 • Ⓥ Ⓑ Ⓓ Ⓟ Ⓣ🏃Ⓜ • ◆◆◆

☆ See Display Advertisement

■ BLAKEY RIDGE (nr Kirkbymoorside)
COAST TO COAST WALK

Roy Atherton, High Blakey House, YO62 7LQ.
☎ (01751) 417186 • Map 100,94/678997 • BB **C/D**
• S/D1 D/T/F1 T/F/D1 • 1-12 NX • B D S P T
⚬ • ◆◆◆◆ • Food nearby •
highblakey.house@virginnet.co.uk

■ BUCKDEN (Skipton)
DALES WAY

Tim & Gwen Berry, Romany Cottage, BD23 5JA.
☎ (01756) 760365 • Map 98/942772 • BB **B** • S1 D1
T2 • 1-12 NX • D S P T ⚬ M •
romany.cottage@totalise.co.uk

Mrs M E Wood, East House Farm, Beckermonds,
BD23 5JL. ☎ (01756) 760816 • Map 98/873802 • BB
C • EM book first £12 • T2 • 3-12 • V D S P T

Lynn Thornborrow, West Winds Cottage, BD23 5JA.
☎ (01756) 760883 • Map 98/942772 • BB **B** • D2 T1
• 1-12 NX • D S P T

Mrs Anne Close, Longbarn Cottage, BD23 5JA.
☎ (01756) 760866 • Map 98/942772 • BB **B** • D1 • 1-
12 NX • B D S P T

Mrs A Huck, Birks View, BD23 5JA. ☎ 01756 760873
• Map 98/943772 • BB **B** • D1 T1 • 1-12 NX • D S
P T

Jack & Shirley Leach, Rose Cottage, BD23 5JA.
☎ 01756 760340 • Map 98/943772 • BB **B** • D1 T1 •
1-11 • B D S P T

■ BURNSALL (Skipton)
DALES WAY

☆ Mr J E Lodge, Burnsall Manor House Hotel, BD23
6BW. ☎ 01756 720231 • Map 98/032614 • BB **D** •
EM book first £10, 7-8pm • D5 T3 • 1-12 • V B D
S P T ⚬ • ◆◆◆ • www.manorhouseuk.co.uk

■ CARPERBY (Leyburn)

Mrs D Mason, Cross House, DL8 4DQ. ☎ (01969)
663457 • Map 98/006898 • BB **B** • D1 T1 • 1-12 NX •
B D S P T M

■ CASTLETON (Whitby)

Mrs Della Wedgwood, Greystones, 30 High Street,
YO21 2DA. ☎ (01287) 660744 • Map 94/684079 •
BB **B** • D3 • 1-12 • B D S R P T • ◆◆◆

■ CATTERICK VILLAGE (Richmond)
COAST TO COAST WALK

Carol Archer, Rose Cottage Guest House, 26 High
Street, DL10 7LJ. ☎ (01748) 811164 • Map
99/249979 • BB **C** • EM book first £9.50, 6.30pm • S1
D1 T2 • 1-12 NX • V B S P T ⚬ M • ◆◆◆

■ CLOUGHTON (Scarborough)
CLEVELAND WAY

Mr D P Martin, Gowland Farm, Gowland Lane, YO13
0DU. ☎ (01723) 870924 • Map 94,101/991961 • BB
B • EM book first £9 (exclu. Jul-Aug), 6pm • S1 D1
T1 • 4-10 • D P M • SC also
www.gowlandfarm.co.uk

■ CONISTON COLD (Skipton)
PENNINE WAY

☆ Porch House, BD23 4EA. ☎ (01756) 749685 •
Map 103/903550 • BB **B** • EM book first £8, 6-7pm •
S1 D1 • 1-12 NX • D S P T

■ DANBY (Whitby)
COAST TO COAST WALK

Mrs B Tindall, Rowantree Farm, YO21 2LE.
☎ (01287) 660396 • Map 94/704073 • BB **B** • EM
book first £8, 6.30pm • S1 T1 • 1-12 NX • V D S
R P T • ◆◆◆ • Transport av.

Jack & Mary Lowson, Sycamore House, YO21 2NW.
☎ (01287) 660125 • Map 94/688058 • BB **C** • EM
book first £12, 6-8pm • S1 D1 T1 F1 • 1-12NX • V
B D S P T • ◆◆◆ • Transport av •
sycamore-danby@btinternet.com

■ EASINGWOLD (York)

Rachel Ritchie, The Old Rectory, Thormanby, YO6 3NN.
☎ (01845) 501417 • Map 100/527698 • BB **B** • D1 T1
F1 • 1-12 NX • B D S P • SC also. Food nearby

■ EAST MARTON (Skipton)
PENNINE WAY

Joan Pilling, Sawley House, BD23 3LP. ☎ (01282)
843207 • Map 103/909515 • BB **C** • S1 T3 • 1-12 NX
• D R P T ⚬ • Food nearby •
jon@pilling16.fsnet.co.uk

■ **EGTON BRIDGE (Whitby)**

☆ Mr & Mrs D White, Broom House, Broom House Lane, YO21 1XD. ☎ (01947) 895279 • Map 94/796054 • BB **C** • EM book first £11.95, 7pm • D3 T1 F2 • 1-12 NX • Ⓥ Ⓑ Ⓓ Ⓢ Ⓡ Ⓟ • ◆◆◆◆ • SC also • welcome@broomhouseegtonbridge.freeserve.co.uk

An excellent place to stay. We provide comfortable en-suite rooms, first-class meals, and an idyllic setting with views over the Esk valley. En-route Coast-to-Coast and Esk Valley Walks.

☎ **01947 895279**

Mr & Mrs White
Egton Bridge
English Tourism Council ◆◆◆◆

■ **ELLINGSTRING (Masham)**

Mrs Celia Wright, Holybreen, HG4 4PW. ☎ (01677) 460216 • Map 99/174838 • BB **B** • EM book first £6, 7pm • D1 F1 • 1-12 NX • Ⓥ Ⓓ Ⓢ Ⓟ Ⓣ ☕ • ◆◆◆ • anne.wright@virgin.net

■ **FARNDALE (York)**

Mrs M Featherstone, Keysbeck Farm, YO62 7UZ. ☎ (01751) 433221 • Map 100/665950 • BB **A** • EM book first £6, 6-7pm • D2 T1 • 1-12 NX • Ⓥ Ⓢ ☕

■ **FILEY**
WOLDS WAY

Seafield Hotel, 9/11 Rutland Street, YO14 9JA. ☎ (01723) 513715 • Map 101/117804 • BB **B** • EM £5.50, 6pm • S2 D4 T1 F7 • 1-12 NX • Ⓥ Ⓑ Ⓓ Ⓢ Ⓡ Ⓟ Ⓣ • ◆◆◆ • Groups also

☆ Kate & Roger Broome, Gables Guest House, Rutland St, YO14 9JB. ☎ (01723) 514750 • Map 101/116804 • BB **B** • EM £10, 7pm • D/S2 T/D/F2 F1 • 1-12 • Ⓥ Ⓑ Ⓓ Ⓡ Ⓟ Ⓣ ☕ • ◆◆◆ • kate_gables@yahoo.com

The Gables Filey

Rutland Street, Filey North Yorkshire YO14 9JB

Unspoiled Edwardian Seaside resort The Gables is a family run Guest House with all rooms en-suite close to town and beach. Cleveland Way, Wolds Way. Excellent area for walking and bird watching

Phone Kate:

01723 514750

for brochure

C Cullen & B Illingworth, 7 Rutland Street, Abbot's Leigh, YO14 9JA. ☎ (01723) 513334 • Map 101/117804 • BB **B** • EM book first £10, 6-8.30pm • S/D3 D3 T2 F1 • 1-12 • Ⓥ Ⓑ Ⓓ Ⓢ Ⓡ Ⓟ Ⓣ • ◆◆◆ • barbara-abbots@yahoo.co.uk

■ **GANTON (Scarborough)**
WOLDS WAY

Mrs Iris Hallaways, Cherry Tree Cottage, 23 Main Street, YO12 4NR. ☎ (01944) 710507 • Map 101/988776 • BB **B/C** • S1 T1 F1 • 3-11 • Ⓑ Ⓓ Ⓢ Ⓟ Ⓣ ☕ Ⓜ • ◆◆◆

■ **GARGRAVE (Skipton)**
PENNINE WAY

Mrs Denise Haynes, Old Hall Cottage, 41 West Street, BD23 3RJ. ☎ (01756) 749412. Fax 01756 748123 • Map 103/931542 • BB **C** • D1 T1 • 1-12 NX • Ⓑ Ⓓ Ⓢ Ⓡ Ⓣ • ◆◆◆ • e-mail oldhallcot@aol.com

■ **GIGGLESWICK (Settle)**
RIBBLE WAY

☆ Harts Head Hotel, Belle Hill, BD24 0BA. ☎ (01729) 822086 • Map /812640 • BB **B/C/D** • EM £7.50, 5.30-9pm • S2 D5 T2 F1 • 1-12 NX • Ⓥ Ⓑ Ⓓ Ⓢ Ⓡ Ⓟ Ⓣ • ◆◆◆ • hartshead@hotel52.freeserve.co.uk

■ **GLAISDALE (WHITBY, YORKSHIRE)**
COAST TO COAST WALK

☆ T J & S K Spashett, Red House Farm, YO21 2PZ. ☎ (01947) 897242 • Map 94/772049 • BB **D** • S1 D2 T1 F1 • 1-12 NX • Ⓑ Ⓓ Ⓢ Ⓡ Ⓟ Ⓣ ☕ • SC also • dogs OK in kennels spashettredhouse@talk21.com

Mrs A Mortimer, Hollins Farm, YO21 2PZ. ☎ (01947) 897516 • Map 94/753042 • BB **B** • D1 T1 F1 • 1-12 NX • Ⓓ Ⓢ Ⓡ Ⓟ Ⓣ ☕ • ◆◆◆ • Camping also. Food nearby (transport available)

☆ See Display Advertisement

Mr & Mrs Danaher, London House Farm, Dale Head, YO21 2PZ. ☎ 01947 897166 • Map 94/744031 • BB **C/D** • EM book first £13, 7pm • D1 T1 F1 • 4-10 • Ⓥ Ⓑ Ⓓ Ⓢ Ⓟ Ⓣ ♨ Ⓜ • SC also • marydanaher@hotmail.com

Mrs Julie Lake, Lanes Farm, YO21 2PU. ☎ (01947) 897577 • Map 94/771058 • BB **B** • EM book first £8.50 • D1 T1 • 1-12 NX • Ⓥ Ⓑ Ⓓ Ⓢ Ⓡ Ⓟ Ⓣ • lanesfarm@msn.com

■ GOATHLAND (Whitby)
COAST TO COAST WALK

Mr & Mrs R Ellis, Fairhaven Hotel, The Common, YO22 5AN. ☎ (01947) 896361 • Map 94/830099 • BB **C/D** • EM book first £14, 7pm • S2 D2 T2 F3 • 1-12 • Ⓥ Ⓑ Ⓓ Ⓢ Ⓡ Ⓟ Ⓣ ♨ • ♦♦♦ • www.thefairhavenhotel.co.uk

■ GRASSINGTON (Skipton)
DALES WAY

Mrs P Robertshaw, Springroyd House, 8a Station Road, BD23 5NQ. ☎ (01756) 752473 • Map 98/001639 • BB **C** • D1 T2 • 1-12 NX • Ⓑ Ⓓ Ⓢ Ⓟ Ⓣ ♨ • ♦♦♦ • springroyd.house@btinternet.com

Mrs Trewartha, Mayfield, Low Mill Lane, BD23 5BX. ☎ (01756) 753052 • Map 98/007633 • BB **C** • S1 D2 T1 F1 • 1-12 • Ⓑ Ⓓ Ⓢ Ⓟ Ⓣ ♨ • www.yorkshirenet.co.uk/stayat/mayfield.com

☆ R M Richardson, Foresters Arms, Main Street, BD23 5AA. ☎ (01756) 752349 • Map 98/003642 • BB **D** • EM £7, 6-8.30pm (-9.30pm w/e) • D4 T1 F2 • 1-12 NX • Ⓥ Ⓑ Ⓟ Ⓣ ♨ • ♦♦♦

☆ Mrs I Wallace, Craiglands, 1 Brooklyn, Threshfield, BD23 5ER. ☎ (01756) 752093 • Map 98/998639 • BB

C/D • S1 D2 T1 • 1-12 NX • Ⓑ Ⓓ Ⓢ Ⓟ Ⓣ • ♦♦♦♦ • www.craiglands.yorks.net

Andrew & Cynthia Colley, Lythe End, Wood Lane, BD23 5DF. ☎ 01756 753196 • Map 98/000647 • BB **C** • D1 F1 • 1-12 NX • Ⓑ Ⓓ Ⓢ Ⓟ Ⓣ • SC also colley@grassington.fsnet.co.uk

■ GREAT AYTON (Middlesbrough)
CLEVELAND WAY

Mr & Mrs Houghton, Eskdale Cottage, 31 Newton Road, TS9 6DT. ☎ (01642) 724306 • Map 93/563112 • BB **B/C** • EM book first £12, 6.30ish • S1 T2 • 1-12 NX • Ⓥ Ⓓ Ⓢ Ⓡ Ⓟ Ⓣ • malcolm.houghton@talk21.com

■ GREAT BROUGHTON (Stokesley)

☆ Mrs M Sutcliffe, Ingle Hill, Great Broughton, Stokesley, TS9 7ER. ☎ (01642) 712449 • Map 93/548063 • BB **B** • D1 T1 F1 • 1-12 NX • Ⓑ Ⓓ Ⓢ Ⓟ Ⓣ ♨

Don Robinson, Holme Farm, 12 The Holme, TS9 7HF. ☎ (01642) 712345 • Map 93/546062 • BB **B** • D2 T2 • 1-12 • Ⓓ Ⓢ Ⓟ • donshome.demon.co.uk

■ GRINTON (Richmond)
COAST TO COAST WALK

Mrs K Brown, Scarr House, DL11 6JA. ☎ (01748) 884479 • Map 98/047985 • BB **B** • D1 T1 • 5-3 • Ⓓ Ⓟ Ⓣ ♨

■ GROSMONT (Whitby)
COAST TO COAST WALK

C & J Williamson, Grosmont Farm, YO22 5QJ. ☎ (01947) 895367 • Map 94/832063 • BB **B** • EM £7, 7.30pm • S1 D1 F1 • 1-12 • Ⓥ Ⓓ Ⓢ Ⓡ Ⓟ Ⓣ ♨ • williamson.grosmont@virgin.net

■ GUNNERSIDE (Richmond)
COAST TO COAST WALK & PENNINE WAY

Mrs A I Porter, Oxnop Hall, DL11 6JJ. ☎ (01748) 886253 • Map 98/931973 • BB **C/D** • EM book first £15, 6.30pm • S1 D2 T3 F2 • 1-12 NX • Ⓥ Ⓑ Ⓓ Ⓢ Ⓟ Ⓣ • ♦♦♦♦

■ HARROGATE

Mrs E Barker, Barker's Guest House, 202/204 Kings Road, HG1 5JG. ☎ (01423) 568494 • Map 104/304563 • BB **B/C** • S1 D1 F/T/D1 • 1-12 NX • Ⓑ Ⓓ Ⓢ Ⓡ Ⓣ • ♦♦♦ • Food nearby eebarkeruk@yahoo.co.uk

Janet Frankland, Amadeus Hotel, 115 Franklin Road, HG1 5EN. ☎ (01423) 505151 • Map 104/303560 • BB **D** • S2 D1 T2 • 1-12 NX • Ⓑ Ⓓ Ⓢ Ⓡ Ⓟ Ⓣ Ⓜ • ◆◆◆◆ • www.acartha.com/amadeushotel

☆ Charles & Gill Richardson, The Coppice, 9 Studley Road, HG1 5JU. ☎ (01423) 569626 • Map 104/302559 • BB **C** • EM book first £15, 6-7.30pm • S1 D2 T1 F1 • 1-12 NX • Ⓥ Ⓑ Ⓓ Ⓢ Ⓡ Ⓟ Ⓣ • 3Cr/C

■ HARWOOD DALE (Scarborough)
CLEVELAND WAY

Burgate Farm, YO13 0DS. ☎ (01723) 870333 • Map 94,101/971951 • BB **C** • EM book first £10, 7.30-8.30pm • S1 F1 • 3-11 • Ⓥ Ⓓ Ⓢ Ⓟ Ⓣ 🐾 • ◆◆◆

■ HAWES
PENNINE WAY

Mrs L Ward, East House, Gayle Lane, DL8 3RZ. ☎ (01969) 667405 • Map 98/871892 • BB **B/C** • S1 D1 T1 • 2-11 • Ⓑ Ⓓ Ⓢ Ⓟ Ⓣ • ◆◆◆◆ • lornaward@lineone.net

Mrs S McGregor, Gayle Laithe, Gayle, DL8 3RR. ☎ (01969) 667397 • Map 98/869896 • BB **B** • S1 D1 T1 • 3-11 • Ⓓ Ⓟ Ⓣ

Mrs Gwen Clark, Ebor Guest House, Burtersett Road, DL8 3NT. ☎ (01969) 667337 • Map 98/876897 • BB **B** • D2 T1 • 1-12 NX • Ⓑ Ⓓ Ⓢ Ⓟ Ⓣ 🐾 • 2Cr/C • gwen@eborhouse.freeserve.co.uk

☆ Gordon Sleightholm, White Hart Inn, Main Street, DL8 3QL. ☎ (01969) 667259 • Map 98/875897 • BB **C** • EM book first £7.50, 7-8.30pm • S1 D4 T2 • 2-11 • Ⓥ Ⓓ Ⓢ Ⓟ Ⓣ 🐾 • ◆◆◆

☆ Mrs S Turner, Thorney Mire House, Appersett, DL8 3LU. ☎ (01969) 667159 • Map 98/852899 • BB **B/C** • S1 D2 • 2-10 • Ⓑ Ⓓ Ⓢ Ⓟ Ⓣ Ⓜ • ◆◆◆◆ • sylvia@thorneymire.yorks.net

■ HAWNBY (Helmsley)

Sarah Wood, Easterside Farm, Hawnby, York, YO62 5QT. ☎ (01439) 798277 • Map 100/552895 • BB **C** • EM book first £13, 6.30pm • D2 T1 F2 • 1-12 NX • Ⓑ Ⓓ Ⓢ Ⓟ Ⓣ • ◆◆◆ • eastersidefarm.co.uk

☆ Dave Young, The Hawnby Hotel, Hilltop, Hawnby, YO62 5QS. ☎ (01439) 798202 • Map 100/542898 • BB **E** • EM book first £6.50, 7-10pm • D2 T4 • 1-12 • Ⓥ Ⓑ Ⓓ Ⓢ Ⓟ Ⓣ 🐾 • ◆◆◆◆ • Groups also • www.hawnbyhotel.co.uk

■ HEBDEN (Grassington, Skipton)
DALES WAY

Mrs P J Kitching, Court Croft, Church Lane, BD23 5DX. ☎ (01756) 753406 • Map 98/026630 • BB **B** • T2 • 1-12 • Ⓓ Ⓟ Ⓣ 🐾 • ◆◆◆

■ HELMSLEY (York)

Mrs H O'Neil, Ashberry, 41 Ashdale Road, YO62 5DE. ☎ (01439) 770488 • Map 100/616838 • BB **B** • S1 D1 T1 • 1-12 NX • Ⓓ Ⓢ Ⓟ Ⓣ 🐾 • oneil@ashberry.totalserve.co.uk

■ HIGH BENTHAM (Lancaster)

Jean Newhouse, Newbutts Farm, LA2 7AN. ☎ (01524) 241238 • Map 98/696695 • BB **B** • EM book first £ • S2 D2 T2 F2 • 1-12 NX • Ⓥ Ⓑ Ⓓ Ⓢ Ⓟ Ⓣ 🐾 • ◆◆◆

☆ See Display Advertisement

■ HORTON-IN-RIBBLESDALE (Settle)
PENNINE WAY & RIBBLE WAY

Frank & Margaret Lane, The Rowe House, BD24 0HT. ☎ (01729) 860212 • Map 98/804728 • BB **B/C/D** • D2 T3 • 3-10 NX • B D R P T • ◆◆◆ • therowehouse@lineone.net

Margaret Kenyon, South House Farm, BD24 0HU. ☎ (01729) 860271 • Map 98/786741 • BB **C** • EM book first £9, 6.30pm • D2 T1 F1 • 3-10 • V D S R P T

Colin & Joan Horsfall, Studfold House, BD24 0ER. ☎ (01729) 860200 • Map 98/812701 • BB **B/C** • EM £6, 6.30pm • D2 T1 F1 • 1-12 NX • V B D R P T

Michael & Tricia Johnson, The Golden Lion Hotel, BD24 0HB. ☎ (01729) 860206 • Map 98/807721 • BB **B/C** • EM £8, 7-9.30pm • S1 D2 T2 • 1-12 NX • V B D R P T • Bunkhouse also

Mrs J Barker, The Willows, BD24 0HT. ☎ /Fax (01729) 860373 • Map 98/802729 • BB **B** • EM book first £9, 6-7.30pm • D1 T1 F1 • 3-11 • V B D R P T • 3 Peaks Walk

Hikers Guest House, 3 & 4 Pen-y-Ghent View, BD24 0HE. ☎ (01729) 860300 • Map 98/810725 • BB **B** • S1 D1 T1 F1 • 1-11 • D R P T • www.hikers.fsbusiness.co.uk

■ HUBBERHOLME (Skipton)
DALES WAY

Mrs S M Middleton, Low Raisgill, BD23 5JQ. ☎ (01756) 760351 • Map 98/906786 • BB **C** • S1 D1 T1 • 1-12 NX • B D S P T • ◆◆◆◆

■ HUTTON-LE-HOLE (York)

The Barn Hotel, YO62 6UA. ☎ (01751) 417311 • Map 100,94/705900 • BB **D/E** • EM £14, 7.30pm • S1 D4 T1 F1 • 1-12 NX • V B D S P T • ◆◆◆ • fairhurst@lineone.net

■ INGLEBY CROSS (Northallerton)
COAST TO COAST WALK

North York Moors Adventure Centre, Park House, DL6 3PE. ☎ (01609) 882571 • Map 99/453995 • BB **B** • S3 T3 F2 • 1-12 NX • D P T • Groups also • www.coast-to-coast.org.uk

■ INGLETON (Via Carnforth)

Mrs Anne Brown, Ingleborough View Guest House, Main Street, LA6 3HH. ☎ (015242) 41523 • Map 98/695732 • BB **C** • D3 T2 F1 • 1-12 NX • B D P T • ◆◆◆◆

Mrs P A Garner, Bridge End Guest House, Mill Lane, LA6 3EP. ☎ (015242) 41413 • Map 98/695733 • BB **C** • EM book first £10, 6.30pm • D3 • 1-12 • V B D P T • garner01@tinyworld.co.uk

Mrs Mollie Bell, Langber Country Guest House, Tatterthorne Road, LA6 3DT. ☎ (015242) 41587 • Map 98/689709 • BB **B** • EM book first £7.50, 6.30pm • S1 D2 T2 F2 • 1-12 NX • V B D S R P T • 2Cr

☆ Ferncliffe Country Guest House, 55 Main Street,, LA6 3HJ. ☎ (015242) 42405 • Map 98/695732 • BB **C** • D1 T4 • 1-12 NX • B D S P T • ◆◆◆◆ • ferncliffe@hotmail.com

Phil & Carolyn Smith, Inglenook Guest House, 20 Main Street, LA6 3HJ. ☎ (015242) 41270 • Map 98/695732 • BB **C** • EM book first £10, 6.30pm • D3 T2 • 1-12 NX • V B S P T • ◆◆◆ • www.nebsweb.co.uk/inglenook

Mrs C Brennand, Nutstile Farm, LA6 3DT. ☎ (015242) 41752 • Map 98/694712 • BB **B** • D2 T1 F1 • 1-12 • B D S R P T

☆ Penny & Paol Weaire, The Dales Guest House, Main Street, LA6 3HH. ☎ 015242 41401 • Map 98/692727 • BB **C** • EM book first £10, 6.30pm • S1 D3 T1 • 1-12 NX • V B D S P T Ⓜ • ◆◆◆ • dalesgh@hotmail.com

Mrs E A Neale, Bank House, Westhouse, LA6 3NP. ☎ 015242 41155 • Map 98/677742 • BB **A** • EM book first £6, 6-7pm • D1 F1 • 1-12 NX • V D S P T

■ KELD (Richmond)
PENNINE WAY & COAST TO COAST WALK

☆ Ernest & Doreen Whitehead, Butt House , DL11 6LJ. ☎ (01748) 886374 • Map 91/893009 • BB **B** • EM book first £10, 7.30pm • S1 D2 T1 F1 • 3-9 NX • V B D S P T

■ KETTLEWELL (Skipton)
DALES WAY

Mrs Lorna Thornborrow, Lynburn, BD23 5RF.
☎ (01756) 760803 • Map 98/970720 • BB **B** • D1 T1
• 2-11 • Ⓓ Ⓢ Ⓟ Ⓣ • ◆◆◆

Mr & Mrs R Elliott, Langcliffe Country House, BD23
5RJ. ☎ (01756) 760243 • Map 98/969723 • BB **E** •
EM book first £18, 7pm • D3 T2 F1 • 1-12 NX • Ⓥ Ⓑ
Ⓢ Ⓟ • ◆◆◆◆

Sheila Lofthouse, Chestnut Cottage, BD23 5RL.
☎ 01756 760804 • Map 98/969723 • BB **C** • D1 T2 •
1-12 • Ⓓ Ⓢ Ⓟ Ⓣ • ◆◆◆

■ KILBURN (York)
CLEVELAND WAY

Mrs C Thompson, Church Farm, YO61 4AH.
☎ (01347) 868318 • Map 100/516796 • BB **B** • EM
book first £8 • D1 F1 • 1-12 NX • Ⓥ Ⓑ Ⓓ Ⓢ Ⓟ
Ⓣ ⬜ • ◆◆

■ KIRKBYMOORSIDE (York)

Mary Clarke, Mount Pleasant, Rudland, Fadmoor,
YO62 7JJ. ☎ 01751 431579 • Map 100/657917 • BB
B • EM book first £6.50, 6.30-8pm • T1 F1 • 1-12 NX
• Ⓥ Ⓓ Ⓢ Ⓟ Ⓣ • ◆◆◆
www.mountpleasantbedandbreakfast.co.uk

■ LANGCLIFFE (SETTLE)
RIBBLE WAY

☆ Bowerley Country Hotel, BD24 9LY. ☎ (01729)
823811 • Map 98/820648 • BB **C/D** • EM £10, 6.30-
8.30pm • S2 D4 T8 F4 • 1-12 • Ⓥ Ⓑ Ⓓ Ⓢ Ⓡ
Ⓟ Ⓣ ⬜ • ★★ • Groups also

■ LOTHERSDALE
PENNINE WAY

☆ Mrs M Foster, Lynmouth, Dale End, BD20 8EH.
☎ (01535) 632744 • Map 103/960460 • BB **B** • D1 F2
• 1-12NX • Ⓑ Ⓓ Ⓢ Ⓡ Ⓟ Ⓣ • Hostel also •
gfoster488@aol.com

■ MALHAM (Skipton)
PENNINE WAY

River House Hotel, BD23 4DA. ☎ (01729) 830315 •
Map 98/901628 • BB **E** • EM book first £15 • S1 D6
T3 • 1-12 • Ⓥ Ⓑ Ⓓ Ⓢ Ⓟ Ⓣ • ◆◆◆ • Groups
also www.riverhousehotel.co.uk

R Boatwright, Beck Hall Guest House, BD23 4DJ.
☎ (01729) 830332 • Map 98/898631 • BB **B/C** • EM
£7.50 • S1 D7 T4 F2 • 1-12 NX • Ⓥ Ⓑ Ⓓ ⬜ • 1Cr

Vera Sharp, Miresfield Farm Guesthouse, BD23 4DA.
☎ (01729) 830414 • Map 98/901628 • BB **C** • EM
book first £12, 6.30pm • S1 D5 T5 F2 • 1-12 • Ⓥ Ⓑ
Ⓓ Ⓢ ⬜ • ◆◆◆ • Groups also •
chris@miresfield.freeserve.co.uk

G & H J Boocock, The Buck Inn, BD23 4DA.
☎ (01729) 830317 • Map 98/901628 • BB **D/E** • EM
£10-£12, 7-9pm • D6 T2 F2 • 1-12 • Ⓥ Ⓑ Ⓓ Ⓢ
Ⓟ Ⓣ • ★★ • SC also

■ MASHAM (Ripon)

☆ Bank Villa Guest House, HG4 4DB. ☎ (01765)
689605 • Map 99/224810 • BB **C** • EM book first £18,
7.30pm • D3 T2 F1 • 1-12 NX • Ⓥ Ⓑ Ⓓ Ⓢ Ⓟ
Ⓣ • ◆◆◆◆

☆ See Display Advertisement

B&B ACCOMMODATION ENGLAND NORTH YORKSHIRE

■ **MIDDLEHAM (Leyburn)**

☆ Mrs Elizabeth Frisby, The Priory, DL8 4QG. ☎ (01969) 623279 • Map 99/127877 • BB **C** • EM book first £13, 6.30pm • S1 D3 T3 F1 • 3-11 • Ⓥ Ⓑ Ⓓ Ⓢ Ⓟ Ⓣ ⛾ • ♦♦♦

THE PRIORY

MIDDLEHAM, NORTH YORKSHIRE

TEL 01969 623279

A tastefully restored Georgian house, close to castle. Comfortable lounge with fireplace. En-suite rooms with TV. Secure parking. Home cooking. Drying room.

■ **NEWTON-ON-OUSE (York)**

Mr & Mrs E Huck, Village Farm Holidays, Cherry Tree Avenue, YO30 2BN. ☎ (01347) 848064 • Map 100/511600 • BB **C** • S1 D1 T2 • 1-12 • Ⓑ Ⓓ Ⓢ Ⓟ Ⓣ ⛾ • ♦♦♦♦ • yorkshirenet.co.uk/stayat/villagefarm

■ **NORTHALLERTON**
COAST TO COAST WALK

Mrs M M Pearson, Lovesome Hill Farm, Lovesome Hill, DL6 2PB. ☎ (01609) 772311 • Map 99/361998 • BB **C/D** • EM book first £15, 7-7.30pm • S1 D1 T1 F1 • 3-10 NX • Ⓥ Ⓑ Ⓓ Ⓢ Ⓟ • ♦♦♦♦ • Camping Barn also

Mrs M Longley, Alverton Guest House, 26 South Parade, DL7 8SG. ☎ (01609) 776207 • Map 99/367934 • BB **B** • S2 D1 T1 F1 • 1-12 NX • Ⓑ Ⓓ Ⓢ Ⓡ Ⓟ Ⓣ • ♦♦♦ • alverton.26@talk21.com

■ **OLD MALTON (Malton)**

Mrs P M Hemesley, Applebye House, 99 Town Street, YO17 7HD. ☎ (01653) 696370 • Map 100/800729 • BB **B** • EM book first £10, 7.30pm • D1 T1 • 1-12 NX • Ⓓ Ⓢ Ⓡ Ⓟ ⛾

■ **OSMOTHERLEY (Northallerton)**
CLEVELAND WAY & COAST TO COAST WALK

Marion Wood, Oak Garth Farm, North End, DL6 3BH. ☎ (01609) 883314 • Map 99/456976 • BB **C** • D1 T1 • 1-11 • Ⓓ Ⓢ Ⓟ Ⓣ • ♦♦

■ **OVER SILTON (Thirsk)**
CLEVELAND WAY

Sian Goodwin, Moorfields Farm, YO7 2LJ. ☎ (01609) 883351 • Map 99/452933 • BB **B** • EM book first £7.50 • S2 D1 • 1-12 NX • Ⓥ Ⓓ Ⓟ Ⓣ ⛾

■ **PATELEY BRIDGE (Harrogate)**
NIDDERDALE WAY

☆ Peter & Rita Briggs, Roslyn Hotel, 9 King Street, HG3 5AT. ☎ (01423) 711374 • Map 99/157656 • BB **C/D** • EM book first £11, 7pm • D3 T1 F2 • 1-12 • Ⓥ Ⓑ Ⓓ Ⓟ Ⓣ • ♦♦♦ • roslynhotelatpateley@talk21.com

Mrs C E Nelson, Nidderdale Lodge Farm, Fellbeck, HG3 5DR. ☎ (01423) 711677 • Map 99/179653 • BB **C** • D2 T1 • 3-10 • Ⓑ Ⓓ Ⓢ Ⓟ Ⓣ • ♦♦♦

Mrs Joan Ravilious, Greengarth, Greenwood Road, HG3 5LR. ☎ (01423) 711688 • Map 99/156657 • BB **B** • S1 D2 T1 • 1-12 NX • Ⓑ Ⓓ Ⓢ Ⓟ Ⓣ ⛾ • ♦♦♦

Mrs Vivienne Simpson, Dale View, Old Church Lane, HG3 5LY. ☎ (01423) 711506 • Map 99/162655 • BB **B/C** • EM book first £8, 6-7pm • S1 D2 F1 • 1-12 • Ⓥ Ⓑ Ⓓ Ⓢ Ⓟ Ⓣ ⛾ • ♦♦♦

■ **PICKERING**

Mrs R Metcalf, 103 Westgate, YO18 8BB. ☎ (01751) 472500 • Map 100/793840 • BB **B** • D2 T1 • 1-12 NX • Ⓡ

Mrs M Rayner, Kirkham Garth, Whitby Road, YO18 7AT. ☎ (01751) 474931 • Map 100/800840 • BB **C** • S1 D1 T1 F1 • 1-12 • Ⓓ Ⓢ Ⓡ Ⓣ

☆ Mr & Mrs C Gardner, The Old Manse Guest House, Middleton Road, YO18 8AL. ☎ (01751) 476484 • Map 100/792841 • BB **C** • EM book first £12.50, 7pm • D5 T2 F1 • 1-12 • Ⓥ Ⓑ Ⓓ Ⓢ Ⓡ Ⓟ Ⓣ ⛾ • ♦♦♦♦

☆ Joan & Rod Lovejoy, Heathcote House, 100 Eastgate, YO18 7DW. ☎ (01751) 476991 • Map 100/802836 • BB **C** • EM book first £10, 7pm • D3 T2 • 2-12 NX • Ⓥ Ⓑ Ⓓ Ⓢ Ⓡ Ⓣ • ♦♦♦♦ • joanlovejoy@lineone.net

Jackie Heaton, Swan Cottage, Newton upon Rawcliffe, YO18 8QA. ☎ (01751) 472502 • Map 100,94/812907 • BB **B** • EM book first £10.50, 7-8pm • S1 D1 T/F1 • 1-12NX • Ⓥ Ⓓ Ⓢ Ⓡ Ⓟ Ⓣ 🐾 Ⓜ • ◆◆◆ • No EM Easter-Oct

Mrs Diana Wardle, Rosebank, 61 Ruffa Lane, YO18 7HN. ☎ 01751 472531 • Map 100/801839 • BB **B** • D2 F1 • 3-10 • Ⓑ Ⓓ Ⓢ Ⓣ • ◆◆◆◆

■ PIERCEBRIDGE (Darlington)
Anne Graham, Holme House, DL2 3SY. ☎ /Fax (01325) 374280 • Map 93/221151 • BB **C** • S2 T1 F1 • 1-12 NX • Ⓑ Ⓓ Ⓢ Ⓣ 🐾 • ◆◆◆ • graham@holmehouse22.freeserve.co.uk

■ RAVENSCAR (Scarborough)
CLEVELAND WAY & COAST TO COAST WALK

☆ Mrs B Leach, Bide-a-While, 3 Lorings Road, YO13 0LY. ☎ (01723) 870643 • Map 94/984011 • BB **B** • EM book first £6, 5-6.30pm • D2 T1 F1 • 1-12 NX • Ⓥ Ⓑ Ⓓ Ⓢ Ⓟ • ◆◆◆

■ REETH (Richmond)
COAST TO COAST WALK

Mrs Denise Guy, Springfield House, Quaker Close, DL11 6UY. ☎ (01748) 884634 • Map 98/039993 • BB **B** • S1 D1 T1 • 1-12 • Ⓓ Ⓢ Ⓟ Ⓣ • ◆◆ • springfield.house@breathemail.net

The Buck Hotel, DL11 6SW. ☎ (01748) 884210 • Map 98/038993 • BB **D** • EM £9, 6-9pm • S1 D6 T2 F1 • 1-12 • Ⓥ Ⓑ Ⓓ Ⓟ Ⓣ 🐾 • ◆◆◆ • www.buckhotel.co.uk

Mrs M G Kenyon, Sunnybrow, DL11 6TJ. ☎ (01748) 884800 • Map 98/039992 • BB **A** • T1 • 1-12 • Ⓑ Ⓓ 🐾

Jenny Davies, 2 Bridge Terrace, DL11 6TP. ☎ (01748) 884572 • Map 98/040991 • BB **B** • D1 T1 • 3-10 • Ⓓ Ⓢ Ⓟ • ★ • www.coast2coast.co.uk/2bridgeterrace

Arkle House, Mill Lane, DL11 6SJ. ☎ (01748) 884815 • Map 98/040994 • BB **C** • D1 F1 • 1-12 NX • Ⓑ Ⓓ Ⓢ Ⓟ Ⓣ • ◆◆◆◆ • www.arklehouse.com

Ann Bain, 'Walpardoe', Anvil Square, DL11 6TE. ☎ (01748) 884626 • Map 98/038992 • BB **B** • S1 T1 • 2-10 • Ⓓ Ⓟ Ⓣ

■ RICHMOND
COAST TO COAST WALK

Mrs S M Lee, 27 Hurgill Road, DL10 4AR. ☎ (01748) 824092 • Map 92/169011 • BB **B** • S1 D1 T2 • 1-12 NX • Ⓓ Ⓢ Ⓟ Ⓣ • ◆◆

☆ Thelma Jackson, Willance House Guest House, 24 Frenchgate, DL10 7AG. ☎ (01748) 824467 (and fax) • Map 92/174012 • BB **C** • EM £12.50, from 6.30pm • S1 D1 T1 F1 • 1-12 • Ⓥ Ⓑ Ⓓ Ⓢ Ⓟ Ⓣ 🐾 • ◆◆◆◆

Sue Adams, Windsor House, 9 Castle Hill, DL10 4QP. ☎ (01748) 823285 • Map 92/171008 • BB **B** • EM £5.50, until 9pm • S1 D/F7 T2 F1 • 1-12 • Ⓥ Ⓑ Ⓓ Ⓢ Ⓟ Ⓣ 🐾 • jamesandsueadams@comp.com

Mrs S Woodward, 66 Frenchgate, DL10 7AG. ☎ (01748) 823421 • Map 92/174012 • BB **C** • D2 T1 • 1-12 NX • Ⓑ Ⓓ Ⓟ Ⓣ 🐾 • ◆◆◆ • paul@66frenchfreeserve.co.uk

☆ See Display Advertisement

NORTH YORKSHIRE ENGLAND B&B ACCOMMODATION

233

K & T Teeley, West End Guest House & Cottages, 45 Reeth Road, DL10 4EX. ☎ 01748 824783 • Map 92/161011 • BB **C** • S1 D2 T1 F1 • 1-12 NX • 🅱 🅳 🆂 🆃 🛁 • ◆◆◆◆Ⓢ • SC also • Groups also. westend@skillsline.org

☆ The Kings Head Hotel, Market Place, DL10 4HS. ☎ (01748) 850220 • Map 92/172007 • BB **E** • EM £19.50, 7-9.15pm • S5 D18 T7 • 1-12 • 🆅 🅱 🅳 🆂 🅿 🆃 🛁 • ★★ • res@kingsheadrichmond.co.uk

Kings Head Hotel
Market Place, Richmond, North Yorks DL10 4HS
Tel 01748 850220
Beautiful Georgian hotel ideally situated for Coast to Coast walkers. All rooms en-suite with beverage making facilities, satelite TV, hairdryer, radio alarm, telephone.
Excellent dinners and bar meals available.
Free packed lunch when booking a 2 night short break

■ RIPON

☆ Irene Foster, Limetree Farm, Hutts Lane, Grewelthorpe, HG4 3DA. ☎ (01765) 658450 • Map 99/212773 • BB **C** • EM book first £12, 6.30pm • D2 T1 • 1-12 NX • 🅱 🅳 🅿 🆃 🛁 • ◆◆◆◆

LIME TREE FARM
Grewelthorpe, Nr Ripon
Yorkshire Dales near Masham Old farmhouse in secluded wooded countryside. Open fires, beams, oak panelling. Private facilities all bedrooms. Excellent walking country. Good home-cooked food. B&B from £20. DB&B £32. Ring for brochure.
01765 658450   ETC 4 diamonds

Susi Wimpress, Bishopton Grove House, HG4 2QL. ☎ 01765 600888 • Map 99/301711 • BB **C** • EM book first £12.50, 6-7.30pm • D1 T1 F1 • 1-12 • 🅱 🅳 🅿 🆃 🛁 • ◆◆◆◆ • wimpress@bronco.co.uk

■ ROBIN HOOD'S BAY
CLEVELAND WAY & COAST TO COAST WALK

Mrs G Luker, Meadowfield, Mount Pleasant North, YO22 4RE. ☎ (01947) 880564 • Map 94/951054 • BB **B** • S2 D2 T1 • 1-12 NX • 🅱 🅳 🆂 🅿 🆃 • Vegan breakfasts avail.

Mrs Reynolds, South View, Sledgates, Fylingthorpe, YO22 4TZ. ☎ 01947 880025 • Map 94/940048 • BB **B** • D2 • 1-12 NX • 🅳 🅿 🛁

☆ Mike Parry, Orchard House, The Bolts, YO22 4SG. ☎ (01947) 880912 • Map 94/952050 • BB **C** • D2 T1 F1 • 1-12 NX • 🅱 🆃

Orchard House
The Bolts, Robin Hood's Bay, North Yorkshire YO22 4SG
Accommodation in Robin Hood's Bay is competitive, but Orchard House is amongst the best. Standing in its own grounds in the centre of the village only a few hundred yards from the sea all rooms are en-suite, furnished to a high standard and have views over open countryside.
Mr Mike Parry   **Tel: 01947 880912**

■ ROSEDALE ABBEY (Pickering)

Mrs S Smith, Low Bell End Farm, YO18 8RE. ☎ (01751) 417127 • Map 100,94/717970 • BB **B** • EM book first £7, 7pm • D1 T1 F1 • 1-12 NX • 🅳 🆂 🅿 🛁

☆ Mrs Linda Sugars, Sevenford House, Thorgill, YO18 8SE. ☎ (01751) 417283 • Map 100,94/724949 • BB **C** • D1 T1 F1 • 1-12 • 🅱 🅳 🆂 🅿 🆃 • ◆◆◆◆ • SC also. Food nearby

Sevenford House
Rosedale Abbey
Nr. Pickering N. Yorks
Tel. (01751) 417283
Fax (01751) 417505
Email sevenford@aol.com
ETC and AA
◆◆◆◆
Lovely country house standing in 4 acres of beautiful gardens. Tastefully furnished en-suite bedrooms, with TV, radio & tea/coffee facilities. Wonderful views overlooking valley and moorland. A relaxing guests' lounge/ library with open fire. Drying room. Brochure.

■ RUNSWICK BAY (Saltburn-by-the-Sea)
CLEVELAND WAY

☆ Jennifer Smith, Cockpit House, The Old Village, TS13 5HU. ☎ (01947) 840504/603047 • Map 94/810161 • BB **B** • S0 D1 T2 • 3-10 • 🅳 🅿 🆃 🛁 • ◆◆

RUNSWICK BAY, NEAR WHITBY
On the Cleveland Way/North York Moors
COCKPIT HOUSE
Seafront position near beach/pub/café. All sea views. Double or twin rooms. Visitors bathroom and lounge. TV. Drinks/drying facilities. B&B £17. Children less.
Tel. 01947 840504   ETC
(603047 out of season)   ◆◆

'The Firs', 26 Hinderwell Lane, TS13 5HR. ☎ (01947) 840433 • Map 94/791168 • BB **C** • EM £12.50, 6-7.30pm • S1 D4 T2 F4 • 3-12 • 🆅 🅱 🅳 🆂 🅿 🆃 🛁 • ◆◆◆ • www.the-firs.co.uk

■ **SANDSEND (Whitby)**
CLEVELAND WAY

Bungalow Hotel, YO21 3TG. ☎ (01947) 893272 •
Map 94/859128 • BB **D** • EM book first £14 • S6 D5
T3 F4 • 3-11 • Ⓥ Ⓑ Ⓓ Ⓡ Ⓟ Ⓣ ♨ • Groups also

■ **SCARBOROUGH**
CLEVELAND WAY

Brincliffe Edge Private Hotel, 105 Queens Parade,
YO12 7HY. ☎ (01723) 364834 • Map 101/039895 •
BB **C** • S1 D6 F3 • 3-10 • Ⓑ Ⓓ Ⓢ Ⓡ Ⓟ Ⓣ •
www.spiderweb.co.uk/brincliffeedge

Ms P M Carley, Lylac Dene Guest House, 52 West
Street, South Cliff, YO11 2QP. ☎ (01723) 363973 •
Map 101/043874 • BB **B** • EM £4, 5.30pm • S1 D3 T1
F2 • 1-11 NX • Ⓥ Ⓓ Ⓡ Ⓟ Ⓣ

■ **SCOTCH CORNER (RICHMOND)**

☆ Quality Scotch Corner Hotel, Junction A1/A66,
DL10 6NR. ☎ (01748) 850900 • Map 93/213052 •
BB **E** • EM £10.95, 7-9.45pm • S14 D28 T48 F2 • 1-
12 • Ⓥ Ⓑ Ⓓ Ⓟ Ⓣ ♨ • 4Cr •
www.qualityinn.com/hotel/gb609

QUALITY HOTEL
SCOTCH CORNER

With 90 fully en-suite bedrooms,
full restaurant and bar facilities the
Quality Hotel is ideal for any type of
weekend break or holiday.
Giving excellent access to all areas
of interest such as The Yorkshire
Dales, Moors, Richmondshire and the
North Pennines.
Weekend and short breaks available.
To make a reservation or for further
information, give us a call on
01748 850900

■ **SETTLE**
PENNINE WAY & RIBBLE WAY

☆ The Oast Guest House, 5 Pen-y-Ghent View, BD24
9JJ. ☎ (01729) 822989 • Map 98/817639 • BB **B/C** •
EM £12, 6.30-7pm • S1 D2 T2 F1 • 1-12 • Ⓥ Ⓑ Ⓓ
Ⓢ Ⓡ Ⓟ Ⓣ • ◆◆◆ • Vegan EM av •
www.yorkshirenet.co.uk/stayat/theoast

☆ See Display Advertisement

☆ Whitefriars Country Guest House, Church Street,
BD24 9JD. ☎ (01729) 823753 • Map 98/819637 • BB
B/C • EM book first £12, 7-8pm • S1 D3 T2 F3 • 1-12
NX • Ⓥ Ⓑ Ⓓ Ⓢ Ⓡ Ⓟ Ⓣ • ◆◆◆ •
www.whitefriars-settle.co.uk

Greta & Robert Duerden, Liverpool House Guest
House, Chapel Square, BD24 9HR. ☎ (01729)
822247 • Map 98/822635 • BB **C** • S2 D3 T2 • 1-12 •
Ⓑ Ⓓ Ⓢ Ⓡ Ⓟ Ⓣ • ◆◆◆ • Food nearby

☆ Golden Lion Hotel, Duke Street, BD24 9DU. ☎
(01729) 822203 • Map 98/819635 • BB **C/E** • EM
£8.50, 6-10pm • S1 D7 T4 F2 • 1-12 • Ⓥ Ⓑ Ⓓ Ⓡ
Ⓟ Ⓣ ♨ • ◆◆◆ • Groups also •
bookings@goldenlion.yorks.net

Teona & Paul Raistrick, Yorkshire Rose Guest House,
Duke Street, BD24 9AW. ☎ (01729) 822032 • Map
98/817632 • BB **B/C** • S1 D2 T1 F1 • 1-12 • Ⓥ Ⓑ Ⓓ
Ⓢ Ⓡ Ⓟ Ⓣ • ◆◆◆ • yorkshirerose@tinyonline.co.uk

NORTH YORKSHIRE ENGLAND

B&B ACCOMMODATION

235

■ SHERBURN (Malton)
WOLDS WAY

Dee Dwyer, Cherry Tree Cottage, YO17 8PG.
☎ (01944) 710851 • Map 101/959771 • BB **B** • EM
book first £7.50, 7pm • T1 F1 • 1-12 NX • Ⓥ Ⓓ Ⓢ Ⓟ Ⓣ

■ SHERIFF HUTTON (York)

Mrs Elaine Hemingway, Hall Farm, High Stittenham,
YO60 7TW. ☎ (01347) 878461 • Map 100/678676 •
BB **B** • EM book first £7, 5-7.30pm • D1 T1 F1 • 1-12
• Ⓥ Ⓑ Ⓓ Ⓟ Ⓣ • ♦♦♦♦

■ SKELTON (Saltburn-by-the-Sea)
CLEVELAND WAY

B Bull, Westerland's Guest House, 27 East Parade,
TS12 2BJ. ☎ (01287) 650690 • Map 94/655185 • BB
B • EM book first £6, 6.30-7pm • S2 D3 F1 • 3-10 •
Ⓥ Ⓑ Ⓓ Ⓢ Ⓡ Ⓟ Ⓣ

■ SKIPTON

Highfield Hotel, 58 Keighley Road, BD23 2NB.
☎ (01756) 793182 • Map 103/988512 • BB **B** • EM
book first £7, 7.30-8pm • S2 D6 T1 F2 • 1-12NX • Ⓥ
Ⓑ Ⓡ Ⓟ Ⓣ • ★★

Phillis Sapsford, Alton House, 5 Salisbury St, BD23
1NQ. ☎ (01756) 794780 • Map 103/984519 • BB **C** • S1
D2 T2 F2 • 1-12 NX • Ⓑ Ⓓ Ⓢ Ⓡ Ⓟ Ⓣ Ⓜ • ♦♦♦

Mrs Heather Simpson, Low Skibeden Farmhouse,
Skibeden Road, BD23 6AB. ☎ (01756) 793849 • Map
104/012524 • BB **C/D** • D1 T1 F3 • 1-12 NX • Ⓑ Ⓓ
Ⓢ Ⓡ Ⓟ Ⓣ • ♦♦♦♦
skibhols.yorksdales@talk21.com

■ SLEIGHTS (nr Whitby)
COAST TO COAST WALK

☆ Pat Beale, Ryedale House, 156 Coach Road, YO22
5EQ. ☎ /Fax (01947) 810534 • Map 94/866070 • BB
B/C • S2 D2 • 4-10 • Ⓑ Ⓓ Ⓢ Ⓡ Ⓟ Ⓣ •
♦♦♦♦ • SC also

North York Moors National Park
ETC ♦♦♦♦   **Near Whitby**
"Heartbeat" country 3fi
miles Whiby, magnificent
for walking. Relaxing house
exclusive to non-smokers,
high standards, comfort-
able beds, private facilities,
landscaped gardens.
Extensive breakfast menu (traditional/vegetarian). Regret
no pets or young children. Minimum stay 2 nights.
**Pat Beale, Rydale House, Coach Road, Sleights,
N.Yorks YO22 5EQ   Tel/Fax: (01947) 810534**

■ STAINFORTH

Jean Leftwich, Bridge End Cottage, BD24 9PG.
☎ (01729) 822149 • Map 98/822672 • BB **B** • EM
book first £7 • S1 D1 • 1-12 NX • Ⓥ Ⓑ Ⓓ Ⓢ Ⓡ
Ⓟ Ⓣ • ♦♦♦

■ STAITHES (Saltburn-by-the-Sea)
CLEVELAND WAY

☆ Betty & Trevor Readman, Captain Cook Inn, 60
Staithes Lane, TS13 5AD. ☎ (01947) 840200 • Map
94/781184 • BB **B/C** • EM £3.50-£9.50, till 9pm • D2
T1 F1 • 1-12 • Ⓥ Ⓑ Ⓓ Ⓟ Ⓣ

THE CAPTAIN COOK INN
Staithes, North York Moors National Park
Tel. 01947 840200

**Friendly family inn in scenic fishing village.
H&C, colour TV, tea & coffee making
facilities in all rooms.**

✳

**We have a 7-seat minibus to assist small
parties on the Cleveland Way or any other
walk in the whole National Park area.**

Florence Verrill, Springfields, 42 Staithes Lane, TS13
5AD. ☎ 01947 841011 • Map 94/780183 • BB **B** • S1
D1 • 1-12 • Ⓑ Ⓢ Ⓜ • ♦♦♦

■ SUMMERBRIDGE (Harrogate)
NIDDERDALE WAY

Mrs J E Smith, Dalriada, Cabin Lane, Dacre Banks,
HG3 4EE. ☎ (01423) 780512 • Map 99/196621 • BB
B/C • EM book first £9.50, 6-7pm • S1 D1 T1 • 1-12
NX • Ⓑ Ⓓ Ⓢ Ⓟ Ⓣ • ♦♦

■ SUTTON BANK (Thirsk)
CLEVELAND WAY

Mrs K M Hope, High House Farm, YO7 2HA.
☎ (01845) 597557 • Map 100/523830 • BB **C** • EM
book first £10, 1-12pm • S1 D1 T1 F1 • 1-12 NX • Ⓥ
Ⓓ Ⓟ Ⓣ • ♦♦♦

Mrs J Jeffray, Cote Faw, YO7 2EZ. ☎ (01845)
597363 • Map 100/522829 • BB **B** • S1 D1 F1 • 1-12
NX • Ⓓ Ⓢ Ⓟ • SC also

■ THIRSK

Mrs Anne Lee, The Conifers, 8a Ingramgate, YO7
1DD. ☎ (01845) 522179 • Map 99/432821 • BB **A** •
S1 D1 T/F1 • 1-12 • Ⓓ Ⓢ Ⓡ Ⓟ

☆ See Display Advertisement

Sharon & David Barker, Fourways Guest House, Town End, YO7 1PY. ☎ (01845) 522601 • Map 99/427818 • BB **B** • EM book first £8, 6.30pm • S3 D2 T2 F1 • 1-12 • Ⓥ Ⓑ Ⓓ Ⓢ Ⓡ Ⓟ Ⓣ 🐾 • ★★
• fourways@nyorks.fsbusiness.co.uk

■ THORALBY (Leyburn)

Mrs A Bailey, Penview Farmhouse, DL8 3SU.
☎ (01969) 663319 • Map 98/002868 • BB **C** • EM book first £14.50, 6-8.30pm • D/S1 T/S1 F/S1 • 1-12 NX • Ⓑ Ⓓ Ⓢ Ⓟ Ⓣ 🐾 • ◆◆◆

■ THORPE BASSETT (Malton)

Anne Baron, The Old School House, YO17 8LU.
☎ (01944) 758797 • Map 110/862733 • BB **B** • EM book first £5-6, by arrangement • S1 D1 T1 • 4-10 • Ⓥ Ⓓ Ⓢ Ⓟ Ⓣ 🐾 Ⓜ • Only take walkers

■ THRESHFIELD (Skipton)
DALES WAY

Rebecca Huff, Station House, BD23 5ES. ☎ (01756) 752667 • Map 98/996638 • BB **B** • T1 • 1-11 • Ⓑ Ⓓ Ⓟ Ⓣ 🐾 • ◆◆◆•
www.yorkshirenet.co.uk/stayat/stationhouse/

Janette Kitching, Grisedale Farmhouse B&B, BD23 5NT. ☎ (01756) 752516 • Map 98/979634 • BB **B** • D1 T1 • 4-12 NX • Ⓓ Ⓟ Ⓣ 🐾

■ THWAITE (Richmond)
PENNINE WAY

I & J Danton, Kearton Country Hotel, DL11 6DR.
☎ (01748) 886277 • Map 98/892982 • BB **D** • EM book first £7, 6.30pm • S1 D3 T7 F2 • 1-12 • Ⓥ Ⓑ Ⓓ Ⓟ Ⓣ 🐾 • ◆◆◆ •
www.keartoncountryhotel.co.uk

■ WALDEN (West Burton)

Mr & Mrs P Mort, Grange House, Walden Head, DL8 4LF. ☎ (01969) 663641 • Map 98/988808 • BB **C** • EM book first £10.50, 6-7pm • S1 D1 T1 • 1-12 NX • Ⓥ Ⓑ Ⓓ Ⓢ Ⓟ Ⓣ • ◆◆◆◆ • SC also

■ WEST BURTON (Leyburn)

Ann Stanley, West Burton House, DL8 4JY.
☎ (01969) 663582 • Map 98/015865 • BB **B** • D1 F1 • 6-9 • Ⓑ Ⓓ Ⓢ Ⓟ Ⓣ

■ WEST HESLERTON (Malton)
WOLDS WAY

Andree & Brian Hillas, The Old Rectory, YO17 8RE.
☎ (01944) 728285 • Map 101/912760 • BB **C** • D1 T1 F1 • 1-12 NX • Ⓑ Ⓓ Ⓢ Ⓟ Ⓣ 🐾 Ⓜ • ◆◆◆◆ •
www.oldrectoryny.fsnet.co.uk

■ WHITBY
CLEVELAND WAY & COAST TO COAST WALK

☆ Flora & Harry Collett, Ashford, 8 Royal Crescent, YO21 3EJ. ☎ (01947) 602138 • Map 94/894113 • BB **C** • D5 T1 F3 • 1-12 NX • Ⓑ Ⓓ Ⓢ Ⓡ Ⓣ •
www.ashfordguesthouse.com

Falcon Guest House, 29 Falcon Terrace, YO21 1EH.
☎ (01947) 603507 • Map 94/896106 • BB **B** • D/T/F2 • 1-12 • Ⓓ Ⓢ Ⓡ Ⓣ • Can accommodate 7

☆ J & C Gledhill, Prospect Villa, 13 Prospect Hill, YO21 1QE. ☎ (01947) 603118 • Map 94/894105 • BB **B/C** • EM book first £9.75, 6.30pm • S2 D2 T1 F2 • 1-12 NX • Ⓥ Ⓑ Ⓓ Ⓢ Ⓡ Ⓟ Ⓣ • ◆◆◆ • Caravan also

Storrbeck Guest House, 9 Crescent Avenue, YO21 3ED. ☎ (01947) 605468 • Map 94/894110 • BB **B** • EM book first £7.50, 6.30pm • S1 D2 T2 • 1-12 NX • Ⓥ Ⓑ Ⓓ Ⓢ Ⓡ Ⓟ Ⓣ 🐾 • ◆◆◆ •
storrbeck@bigfoot.com

■ WIGGLESWORTH (Skipton)

☆ Steve & Susan Amphlett, The Plough Inn, BD23 4RJ. ☎ (01729) 840243 • Map 98/809569 • BB **D/E** • EM £12.95, 7-9.15pm • D7 T2 F3 • 1-12 • Ⓥ Ⓑ Ⓢ Ⓡ Ⓟ Ⓣ Ⓜ • ★★ •
www.the-plough-wigglesworth.freeserve.co.uk

YORK

Dairy Wholefood Guest House, 3 Scarcroft Road, YO23 1ND. ☎ (01904) 639367 • Map 105/601509 • BB **C** • S1 D2 T1 F2 • 2-11 • Ⓑ Ⓢ Ⓡ Ⓣ 🛆 • ◆◆◆ • www.dairyguesthouse.freeserve.co.uk

☆ Priory Hotel, 126/128 Fulford Road, YO10 4BE. ☎ (01904) 625280 • Map 105/607508 • BB **E** • EM £10.50, 6.30-9.30pm • S1 D6 T2 F6 • 1-12 NX • Ⓥ Ⓑ Ⓓ Ⓡ Ⓣ🛆 • 3Cr • www.priory-hotelyork.co.uk

PRIORY HOTEL
126-128 FULFORD ROAD
YORK YO10 4BE
TEL (01904) 625280
FAX (01904) 637330
All rooms with private facilities.
Restaurant and bar available. AA and
RAC listed. Private car park. Ten
minutes riverside walk to city centre.
www.priory-hotelyork.co.uk

Mr Arthur Farrell, Bank House, 9 Southlands Road, YO2 1NP. ☎ (01904) 627803 • Map 105/600507 • BB **B/C** • S1 D3 T1 F2 • 1-12 • Ⓑ Ⓓ Ⓢ Ⓡ Ⓟ Ⓣ 🛆 • ◆◆◆

☆ Bill Pitts & Rosie Blanksby, Holmwood House, 114 Holgate Road, YO2 4BB. ☎ (01904) 626183 • Map 105/590512 • BB **E** • D10 T3 F1 • 1-12 • Ⓑ Ⓓ Ⓢ Ⓡ Ⓣ Ⓜ • ◆◆◆◆ • holmwood.house@dial.pipex.com

HOLMWOOD HOUSE YORK
We offer luxury en-suite rooms (14) with excellent
breakfasts, close to the city centre and railway
station. Dales and Moors are close and we can
organise a minibus for groups. Special breaks.
Tel: 01904 626183 • Fax: 01904 670899
holmwood.house@dial.pipex.com
Bill Pitts & Rosie Blanksby

WEST YORKSHIRE

BIRSTALL (Batley)

Oakwell Motel, Low Lane, WF17 9HD. ☎ (01924) 441514 • Map 104/221262 • BB **A/B/C** • S6 D1 T4 F1 • 1-12 • Ⓑ Ⓓ Ⓡ Ⓟ Ⓣ 🛆

BLACKSHAWHEAD (Hebden Bridge)
PENNINE WAY & CALDERDALE WAY

Mrs Miriam Whitaker, Badger Fields Farm, Badger Lane, HX7 7JX. ☎ (01422) 845161 • Map 103/968277 • BB **B** • D1 F1 • 1-12NX • Ⓓ Ⓢ Ⓡ Ⓟ Ⓣ 🛆 • ◆◆◆

BRADFORD

Ivy Guest House, 3 Melbourne Place, BD5 0HZ. ☎ (01274) 727060 • Map 104/159324 • BB **B** • S3 D3 T4 • 1-12 • Ⓥ Ⓓ Ⓡ Ⓣ • ◆◆• 101524.3725@compuserve.com

GREETLAND (Halifax)
CALDERDALE WAY

Mrs Sylvia Shackleton, Crawstone Knowl Farm, Rochdale Road, Upper Greetland, Calderdale, HX4 8PX. ☎ (01422) 370470 • Map 104/081213 • BB **B** • EM book first £8.50, 7pm • S1 D1 T1 F1 • 1-12 • Ⓥ Ⓑ Ⓓ Ⓢ Ⓡ Ⓟ Ⓣ 🛆 • ◆◆◆

HAWORTH (Keighley)

Mr & Mrs D Bell, Ebor House, Lees Lane, BD22 8RA. ☎ (01535) 645869 • Map 104/039376 • BB **B** • T3/S3 • 1-12 NX • Ⓑ Ⓓ Ⓢ Ⓡ Ⓣ 🛆 • ◆◆◆ • derekbelle@aol.com

HEBDEN BRIDGE
PENNINE WAY & CALDERDALE WAY

Ann Anthon, Prospect End, 8 Prospect Terrace, Savile Road, HX6 6NA. ☎ (01422) 843586 • Map 103/982272 • BB **B/C** • D/S1 T/S1 • 1-12 • Ⓑ Ⓓ Ⓢ Ⓡ • ◆◆◆

☆ Mrs M J Audsley, Myrtle Grove, Old Lees Road, HX7 8HL. ☎ (01422) 846078 • Map 103/994278 • BB **C** • D1 F1 • 1-12 • Ⓥ Ⓑ Ⓓ Ⓢ Ⓡ Ⓟ Ⓣ 🛆 Ⓜ • ◆◆◆◆ • Home grown produce • vegetarian

HEBDEN BRIDGE — MYRTLE GROVE
Calderdale & Pennine Way

Homely & comfortable stone cottage in scenic location. Moors and riverside walking. En suite, tea/coffee, TV, radio. Specialise in vegetarian food. Price band C/D. One double and one family room. Single bookings accepted. Pick-up service

Myrtle Grove, Old Lees Road, Hebden Bridge HX7 8HL
Tel. 01422 846078

Hebden Lodge Hotel, 6-10 New Road, HX7 8AD. ☎ 01422 845272 • Map 103/994270 • BB **D** • EM £15, 6-10pm • S2 D6 T4 F1 • 1-12 • Ⓥ Ⓑ Ⓓ Ⓢ Ⓡ Ⓟ Ⓣ 🛆 • ★★

A Barrs, 1 St John's Close, HX7 8PD. ☎ (01422) 843321 • Map 104/007265 • BB **A/B** • T1 • 3-10 • Ⓓ Ⓢ Ⓡ Ⓟ Ⓣ Ⓜ • ◆◆◆ • angela.barrs@lineone.net

HOLME VILLAGE (Holmfirth, Huddersfield)
PENNINE WAY

Ms J Hayfield & J Sandford, Holme Castle Country Hotel, HD7 1QG. ☎ (01484) 680680 • Map 110/107058 • BB **D/E** • EM book first £15 & £22, 7.30pm • S1 D3 T2 F2 • 1-12 • Ⓥ Ⓑ Ⓓ Ⓢ Ⓟ Ⓣ 🛆 • ◆◆◆◆ • www.holmecastle.com

■ HOLMFIRTH

☆ Market Walk, HD7 1DA. ☎ (01484) 681212 • Map 110/142081 • BB **C/E** • EM £8, 4-9pm • S7 D11 T2 • 1-12 • Ⓥ Ⓑ Ⓓ Ⓟ 🛏 • ★★★★ • oldbridgehotel@enterprise.net

Mrs Alison Booth, Uppergate Farm, Hepworth, HD7 1TG. ☎ (01484) 681369 • Map 110/162068 • BB **C** • EM book first £10, 7-9pm • T1 F1 • 1-12 • Ⓑ Ⓓ Ⓢ Ⓟ 🛏 • ◆◆◆◆

■ ILKLEY
DALES WAY

Summerhill Guest House, 24 Crossbeck Road, LS29 9JN. ☎ (01943) 607067 • Map 104/119471 • BB **B** • S2 D1 T2 • 1-12 NX • Ⓑ Ⓓ Ⓢ Ⓡ Ⓟ Ⓣ • ◆◆◆

Petra Roberts, Roberts Family B&B, 63 Skipton Road, LS29 9HF. ☎ (01943) 817542 • Map 104/110479 • BB **B** • EM N • D2 T1 • 1-12 • Ⓑ Ⓓ Ⓢ Ⓡ Ⓟ 🛏 • ◆◆

■ MARSDEN (Huddersfield)
PENNINE WAY

Mr & Mrs T Fussey, Forest Farm Guest House, Mount Road, HD7 6NN. ☎ (01484) 842687 • Map 110/042105 • BB **B** • EM book first £7, 7pm • D1 T1 F1 • 1-12 NX • Ⓥ Ⓓ Ⓡ Ⓟ Ⓣ 🛏 • Bunkhouse also www.pennine-yorkshire.com

Ms Joan Hayes, Throstle Nest Cottage, 3 Old Mount Road, HD7 6DU. ☎ /Fax 01484 846371 • Map 110/045115 • BB **B** • T1 F1 • 1-12 NX • Ⓥ Ⓓ Ⓡ Ⓟ Ⓣ 🛏 Ⓜ • ◆◆◆ • www.pennine-yorkshire.com

■ MIDGLEY (Hebden Bridge)
CALDERDALE WAY

Mrs Sandra Scott, 2 Lane Ends, HX2 6TU. ☎ (01422) 883388 • Map 104/035262 • BB **B** • EM book first £8 • D1 T1 • 1-12 NX • Ⓥ Ⓑ Ⓓ Ⓢ Ⓡ Ⓟ Ⓣ • ◆◆◆◆ • www.lane_ends_b&b@hutton.worldonline.co.uk

■ OAKWORTH (Keighley)

☆ Railway Cottage, 59 Station Road, BD22 0DZ. ☎ (01535) 642693 • Map 104/038383 • BB **B** • S2 D3 • 1-12 • Ⓑ Ⓓ Ⓢ Ⓡ Ⓟ Ⓣ • ◆◆◆

■ OTLEY

Mrs P M Davison, 11 Newall Mount, LS21 2DY. ☎ (01943) 462898 • Map 104/200460 • BB **B** • S1 D1 T1 F1 • 1-12 • Ⓓ Ⓢ Ⓡ Ⓟ Ⓣ 🛏 • ◆◆◆

■ STANBURY (NR HAWORTH) (Keighley)
PENNINE WAY

☆ Mrs Taylor, Ponden House, BD22 0HR. ☎ (01535) 644154 • Map 103/992371 • BB **C** • EM book first £11.50, 7pm • D1 T1 F1 • 1-12 • Ⓥ Ⓑ Ⓓ Ⓢ Ⓟ Ⓣ 🛏 Ⓜ • ◆◆◆◆

■ TODMORDEN (Lancashire)
PENNINE WAY & CALDERDALE WAY

Jean Butterworth, Cherry Tree Cottage, Woodhouse Road, OL14 5RJ. ☎ (01706) 817492 • Map 103/955244 • BB **B/C** • EM book first £10, 5.30-7pm • S1 D1 T2 • 1-12 NX • Ⓥ Ⓑ Ⓓ Ⓢ Ⓡ Ⓟ Ⓣ 🛏 • ◆◆◆◆

Isle of Man

■ **DOUGLAS**
ISLE OF MAN COASTAL PATH

☆ Mrs Betty Quirk, Rangemore Guest House, 12 Derby Square, IM1 3LS. ☎ (01624) 674892 • Map 95/375765 • BB **B** • EM book first £9, 6pm • S2 D4 T3 F1 • 3-12 NX • Ⓥ Ⓑ Ⓓ Ⓢ Ⓡ Ⓟ Ⓣ 🌲 • 3Cr/C • Ferry nearby. Travel arranged (sea or air) • See previous page for display advert.

St Heliers Hotel, Central Promenade, IM2 4LU. ☎ (01624) 624355 • BB **B/C** • EM book first £7.50, 6-6.30pm • S2 D13 T2 F4 • 1-12 NX • Ⓥ Ⓑ Ⓢ Ⓟ Ⓣ 🌲 • 1Cr/C

■ **RAMSEY**
ISLE OF MAN COASTAL PATH

Mrs J G Dent, Thorncliffe, Ballure Road, IM8 1NE. ☎ (01624) 813885 • Map 95/455940 • BB **C** • S2 D2 T2 F1 • 1-12 NX • Ⓓ Ⓢ Ⓡ Ⓟ Ⓣ 🌲 • 1Cr/C

Scotland

ARGYLL & BUTE

■ **ARROCHAR**

Mr & Mrs Chandler, Rowantree Cottage, Main Street, G83 7AA. ☎ (01301) 702540 • Map 56/299045 • BB **C** • EM £10, 6.30pm • D2 T1 • 1-12 • Ⓥ Ⓑ Ⓓ Ⓡ Ⓟ Ⓣ 🌲 • ★★★★ • rowantreecottage@cs.com

Ursula Craig, Lochside Guest House, Main Street, G83 7AA. ☎ (01301) 702467 • Map 56/299045 • BB **C** • EM book first £10, 7-8pm • S2 D3 T1 F1 • 1-12 • Ⓥ Ⓑ Ⓓ Ⓢ Ⓡ Ⓟ Ⓣ 🌲 • ★★★★ • lochsidegh@aol.com

■ **BRIDGE OF ORCHY (Argyll)**
WEST HIGHLAND WAY

Mrs F Aitken, Achallader, PA36 4AG. ☎ (01838) 400253 • Map 50/323444 • BB **B** • EM £9, 5-9pm • S3 D1 T1 F1 • 2-11 • Ⓥ Ⓓ Ⓟ 🌲

■ **DALMALLY (Argyll)**

A W Cressey, Craig Villa Guest House, PA33 1AX. ☎ (01838) 200255 • Map 50/168273 • BB **C** • EM book first £12, 7pm • D2 T2 F2 • 3-10 • Ⓑ Ⓓ Ⓢ Ⓡ Ⓟ Ⓣ • 3Cr/C • www.smoothhound.co.uk/hotels/craigvilla.html

John Burke, Orchy Bank, PA33 1AS. ☎ (01838) 200370 • Map 50/152279 • BB **B** • S2 D2 T2 F2 • 1-12 NX • Ⓓ Ⓢ Ⓡ Ⓟ Ⓣ 🌲 • ★★ • Food nearby aj.burke@talk21.com

■ **HELENSBURGH (Nr Loch Lomond)**

Anne & John Urquhart, Thorndean, 64 Colquhoun Street, G84 9JP. ☎ (01436) 674922 • Map 56/297830 • BB **C/D** • D1 T1 F1 • 1-12 • Ⓑ Ⓓ Ⓢ Ⓡ Ⓟ Ⓣ • ★★★★ • www.sol.co.uk/t/theurquhartsSS

■ **OBAN (Argyll)**

Mrs M Wardhaugh, Kathmore, Soroba Road, PA34 4JF. ☎ (01631) 562104 • Map 49/860292 • BB **B/C** • EM N • D3 T1 F1 • 1-12 NX • Ⓑ Ⓓ Ⓢ Ⓡ Ⓟ Ⓣ 🌲 • ★★★★ • www.morvenwardhaugh@hotmail.com

Christine MacDonald, Bracker, Polvinister Road, PA34 5TN. ☎ (01631) 564302 • Map 49/866300 • BB **B** • D2 T1 • 3-11 • Ⓑ Ⓓ Ⓢ Ⓡ Ⓣ • ★★★★ • cmacdonald@connectfree.co.uk

■ **TARBERT (Kintyre)**

Elizabeth Tinney, Dunivaig, Pier Road, PA29 6UG. ☎ (01880) 820896 • Map 62/879685 • BB **B** • D2 F1 • 1-12 • Ⓑ Ⓓ Ⓟ Ⓣ 🌲

CENTRAL BELT

AYRSHIRE (E, N & S), CLACKMANNANSHIRE, DUMBARTONSHIRE (E & W), DUNDEE, EDINBURGH, FALKIRK, FIFE, GLASGOW, INVER-CLYDE, LANARKSHIRE (N & S), LOTHIAN (E & W), MIDLOTHIAN, RENFREWSHIRE & EAST RENFREWSHIRE

■ **ANSTRUTHER (Fife)**

The Hermitage, Ladywalk, KY10 3EX. ☎ (01333) 310909 • Map 59/567036 • BB **C/D** • D3 T1 • 1-12 NX • Ⓓ Ⓢ Ⓟ Ⓣ • b&b@thehermitage.co.uk

■ **BIGGAR**

☆ Tinto Hotel, Biggar Road, Symington, ML12 6FT. ☎ (01899) 308454 • Map 72/990357 • BB **E** • EM £12.85, 4.30-9pm • S5 D13 T7 F2 • 1-12 • Ⓥ Ⓑ Ⓓ Ⓟ Ⓣ 🌲 • ★★★

■ **CRAIL (FIFE)**

Caiplie House, 53 High Street, KY10 3RA. ☎ (01333) 450564 • Map 59/615075 • BB **B/C** • EM book first £8, 7pm • S1 D3 T2 F1 • 3-11 • Ⓥ Ⓑ Ⓓ Ⓢ Ⓟ Ⓣ 🌲 • ★★★★ • caipliehouse@talk21.com

■ **DOUGLAS**

Mrs Shirley Irvine, Dallmartin Cottage, 2 Cairnhouse Road, ML11 0RS. ☎ (01555) 851433 • Map 71/843355 • BB **B** • EM book first £8 • S3 D1 T3 F1 • 1-12 • Ⓥ Ⓓ Ⓢ Ⓟ 🌲

■ EDINBURGH

Mrs Y Pretty, Barrosa Guest House, 21 Pilrig Street, EH6 5AN. ☎ (0131) 554 3700 • Map 66/264753 • BB **C/D** • D3 T3 F2 • 1-12 NX • Ⓑ Ⓢ Ⓡ Ⓣ 🖱 • ★★

Mrs H Donaldson, Invermark, 60 Polwarth Terrace, EH11 1NJ. ☎ 0131-337 1066 • Map 66/235717 • BB **B** • S1 T1 F1 • 1-12 NX • Ⓓ Ⓢ Ⓡ Ⓟ Ⓣ 🖱 • ★★ • SC also

Mrs C A Darlington, Borodale, 7 Argyle Place, (off Melville Drive), EH9 1JU. ☎ 0131-667 5578 • Map 66/256724 • BB **C** • S1 D1 T1 F1 • 1-12 NX • Ⓑ Ⓓ Ⓢ Ⓡ • ★★★ • Food nearby

■ HADDINGTON (East Lothian)

Barbara Williams, Eaglescairnie Mains, Gifford , EH41 4HN. ☎ (01620) 810491 • Map 66/516689 • BB **C/D** • S2 D1 T1 • 1-12 NX • Ⓑ Ⓓ Ⓢ Ⓟ Ⓣ 🖱 • ★★★★ • williams.eagles@btinternet.com

■ LARGS (Ayrshire)

Mrs M Watson, South Whittlieburn Farm, Brisbane Glen, KA30 8SN. ☎ (01475) 675881 • Map 63/218632 • BB **C** • D1 T1 F1 • 1-12 NX • Ⓑ Ⓓ Ⓢ Ⓡ Ⓟ Ⓣ • ★★★★

■ LESMAHAGOW (Douglas)

Mrs Shirley Irvine, Dallmartin Cottage, 2 Cairnhouse Road, ML11 0RS. ☎ 01555 851433 • Map 71/843355 • BB **B** • EM £8 • S3 D1 T3 F1 • 1-12 • Ⓥ Ⓓ Ⓢ Ⓟ 🖱

■ LEUCHARS (Fife)

Pinewood Country House, Tayport Road, St Michaels, KY16 0DU. ☎ (01334) 839860 • Map 59/572328 • BB **C** • EM book first £12, 7pm • D3 T2 • 1-12NX • Ⓥ Ⓑ Ⓓ Ⓢ Ⓡ Ⓟ Ⓣ • ★★★ • www.pinewood-house.com

■ MILNGAVIE (Glasgow)
WEST HIGHLAND WAY

Mrs Heather Ogilvie, 13 Craigdhu Avenue, G62 6DX. ☎ 0141-956 3439 • Map 64/547742 • BB **B** • T1 F1 • 3-10 • Ⓓ Ⓢ Ⓡ Ⓟ Ⓣ 🖱 • ★★★ • Food nearby

John & Barbara Adam, 96 Strathblane Road, G62 8HD. ☎ 0141 584 9400 • Map 64/559749 • BB **C** • T2 • 1-12 NX • Ⓑ Ⓓ Ⓢ Ⓡ Ⓟ Ⓣ

Julie Fell, Barloch Guest House, 82-84 Strathblane Road, G62 8DH. ☎ (0141) 956 1432 • Map 64/558746 • BB **C** • S3 D2 T1 • 1-12 • Ⓑ Ⓓ Ⓢ Ⓡ Ⓟ Ⓣ • www.barlochguesthouse.co.uk

■ MUIRKIRK (Cumnock)

Mr & Mrs D Peebles, Coach House Inn, 1 Furnace Road, KA18 3RE. ☎ (01290) 661257 • Map 71/695271 • BB **C** • EM £7-£11, 7-9pm • S1 T2 • 1-12 • Ⓥ Ⓢ Ⓟ Ⓣ 🖱 • ★★

DUMFRIES & GALLOWAY

■ CASTLE DOUGLAS (Kirkcudbright)

☆ Celia Pickup, Craigadam, DG7 3HU. ☎ (01556) 650233 • Map 84/797728 • BB **D** • EM book first £15, 6-8pm • D2 T4 • 1-12 NX • Ⓥ Ⓑ Ⓓ Ⓢ Ⓣ 🖱 • ★★★★ • SC also craigadam.com

Craigadam
Castle Douglas
DG7 3HU

Craigadam is an elegant 18th century farmhouse with antique furnishings. All rooms en-suite. Dine in our oak-panelled diningroom where we specialise in venison, duck and salmon etc. All home cooking using local produce.

TASTE OF SCOTLAND MEMBER

☎ **01556 650233**
www.craigadam.com

■ GLENLUCE (Newton Stewart, Wigtownshire)

☆ Kelvin House Hotel, 53 Main Street, DG8 0PP. ☎ (01581) 300303 • Map 82/198574 • BB **C** • EM £5, 6-9.30pm • D3 T3 • 1-12 • Ⓥ Ⓑ Ⓓ Ⓟ 🖱 • ★★★

KELVIN HOUSE HOTEL

Built c.1770, an unpretentious, recently renovated hotel situated on the village main street. Excellent reputation for food and noted for its real ales and malt whiskies.

Family run, with the emphasis on relaxation ... enabling our guests to enjoy some of Scotland's most enjoyable unspoilt countryside and allowing them to unwind from the pressures of life.

53 Main Street, Glenluce, Wigtownshire DG8 0PP. Tel/Fax 01581 300303 Concessionary rates for parties

Mr J Thomas, Rowan Tree Guest House, 38 Main Street, DG8 0PS. ☎ (01581) 300244 • Map 82/198574 • BB **B/C** • D1 T2 F2 • 1-12 • Ⓑ Ⓓ Ⓢ Ⓟ Ⓣ 🖱 • 2 Cr • rowangh@totalise.co.uk

■ KIRKGUNZEON (Dumfries)

Ms L Harrison & N Robinson, Cowans Farm Guesthouse, DG2 8JY. ☎ (01387) 760284 • Map 84/872673 • BB **B/C** • EM book first £10, 6.15pm • S1 D1 T/D2 F2 • 1-12 • Ⓥ Ⓑ Ⓢ Ⓟ Ⓣ 🖱 • ★★★ • SC also (Mobile home)

■ LANGHOLM

☆ Langholm & Eskdale Accommodation Providers. See Langholm Walks Initiative advert ove rthe next two pages for full details of this project.

☆ See Display Advertisement

Langholm Walks

The Langholm Walks are part of a project to way mark two hundred miles of walking routes based on a set of articles that have appeared over the years written by a local man under the pseudonym of "Wanderer" in our local paper.

The first stage of this project, comprising of 50 miles of way marked routes, was opened by Magnus Magnusson on 22nd August 2000 and Langholm Accommodation providers are geared up to provide a warm welcome to all walkers when they visit this wonderful corner of the Scottish Border country. Langholm is a small mill town in Dumfriesshire, 22 miles north of Carlisle on the A7 and is easily accessible by car from North (A7 and M74) and South (M6) and by public transport through the Borders Bus and Rail Link from Carlisle Station or Galashiels.

The country round Langholm offers some of the most wonderful views imaginable over the Solway Plain and the Border hills. A walk from the town opens up vistas on all sides and rewards the visitor with changing prospects as the walks unfold. The walks opened in August range from 3 to 9 miles in length and from track and path to rough country in terrain.

Walk to your heart's content

For further details write to Langholm Walks, 98 High Street, Langholm DG13 0DH or visit our web site on www.langholmwalks.co.uk

SCOTLAND   DUMFRIES & GALLOWAY

B&B ACCOMMODATION

WALK IN THE FOOTSTEPS OF THE BORDER REIVER, RELAX IN THE COMFORT OF
THE REIVERS REST

A 240 year old inn, centre of historic Langholm, personally managed by Paul and Betty Hayhoe. There is always a warm welcome and the promise of the very best in borders cuisine and hospitality. 5 en suite twin/double rooms
STB 3 star Inn STB Walkers welcome scheme. Real ale, log fire,drying facilities.
NO SMOKING
High Street Langholm Dumfriesshire DG13 0DJ
Telephone / Fax: 013873 81343
Visit us at www.reivers-rest.demon.co.uk/

Burnfoot House

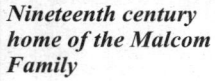

Nineteenth century home of the Malcom Family

Now home to Rosemary and Stephen Laverack who assure you of a warm welcome, whether you choose bed and breakfast in one of the three large, newly refurbished, double, en-suite bedrooms or self catering in one of the five cottages in 19 acres of beautiful grounds.

Burnfoot House, Langholm, Dumfriesshire, DG13 0NG
Telephone: 013873 70611
Fax:013873 70616
e-mail sg.laverack@burnft.co.uk
Web site http:// www.burnft.co.uk

DUMFRIES & GALLOWAY   SCOTLAND   B&B ACCOMMODATION

MOFFAT
SOUTHERN UPLAND WAY

Mrs M Struthers, Wykeham Lodge, Old Well Road, DG10 9AW. ☎ (01683) 220188 • Map 78/086054 • BB **B** • S1 D1 T1 • 3-10 • ⊤ 🐾

Joan & John Marchington, Seamore House, Academy Road, DG10 9HW. ☎ (01683) 220404 • Map 78/083055 • BB **B** • D1 T3 F1 • 1-12 NX • Ⓥ Ⓑ Ⓓ Ⓢ Ⓟ ⊤ 🐾 • ★★★ • www.seamorehouse.co.uk

Mrs L Taylor, Morag, 19 Old Carlisle Road, DG10 9QJ. ☎ (01683) 220690 • Map 78/093046 • BB **B** • EM book first £9, 5.30-7pm • S1 D1 T1 • 1-12 • Ⓥ Ⓓ Ⓢ Ⓟ ⊤ 🐾 • ★★★

John Muirhead, Marvig Guest House, Academy Road, DG10 9HW. ☎ (01683) 220628 • Map 78/084055 • BB **B** • S1 D2 T2 F1 • 1-12 • Ⓑ Ⓓ Ⓢ Ⓟ ⊤ • ★★★ • marvig.moffat@tesco.net

Heather Quigley, North Nethermiln, Old Carlisle Road, DG10 9QJ. ☎ (01683) 220325 • Map 78/093046 • BB **B** • EM £7, 7pm • S/T1 D1 F1 • 1-12 • Ⓥ Ⓓ Ⓢ Ⓟ ⊤

Mrs D McIntyre, Cruachan, Old Carlisle Road, DG10 9QN. ☎ 01683 220800 • Map 78/093040 • BB **B** • EM book first £8.50, 6.30-7.30pm • D1 • 1-12 • Ⓥ Ⓑ Ⓓ Ⓢ Ⓟ ⊤ Ⓜ

☆ Annandale Arms Hotel, High Street, DG10 9HF. ☎ 01683 220013 • Map 78/084053 • BB **E** • EM £8, 5-9pm • S1 D4 T4 F2 • 1-12 NX • Ⓥ Ⓑ Ⓓ Ⓟ ⊤ 🐾 • ★★ • Reception@AnnandaleArmsHotel.co.uk

---

ANNANDALE ARMS HOTEL
High Street, Moffat, DG10 9HF
Situated on the A701, one mile off Junction 15 A74/M6. In the middle of the Moffat Hills and the Southern Upland Way. Owner a keen walker and can provide plenty of local knowledge. Rooms offer high standard of comfort. Delicious home-cooked menu. Drying facilities. One hour from Carlisle to the South or Edinburgh/Glasgow to the North. Excellent rates for walking parties. Dogs Welcome.

01683-220013
Email: Reception@AnnandaleArmsHotel.co.uk
Web site: www.AnnandaleArmsHotel.co.uk

Derek Watkins, Kirkland House, Well Road, DG10 9AR. ☎ (01683) 221133 • Map 78/086053 • BB **B/C** • S1 D2 T1 F1 • 1-12 • Ⓑ Ⓓ Ⓢ Ⓟ ⊤ 🐾 • ★★★★ • derekwatkins@kirklandhouse.freeserve.co.uk

NEWTON STEWART

Mrs Hazel Dickson, Kilwarlin, 4 Corvisel Road, DG8 6LN. ☎ (01671) 403047 • Map 83/409650 • BB **B** • S1 D1 F1 • 3-10 • Ⓓ Ⓢ Ⓟ ⊤ • ★★★Ⓦ

PORTPATRICK (Stranraer)
SOUTHERN UPLAND WAY

Michael & Eileen Pinder, Melvin Lodge, South Crescent, DG9 8LE. ☎ (01776) 810238 • Map 82/000538 • BB **C** • S2 D3 T1 F/T4 • 1-12 NX • Ⓑ Ⓓ Ⓢ Ⓟ ⊤ 🐾 • ★★

STRANRAER
SOUTHERN UPLAND WAY

Mrs Helen Ross, Rawer Farm Cottage, South Glenstockdale, DG9 8TS. ☎ 01776 810328 • Map 82/008599 • BB **B** • EM £6.50 • S1 D1 T1 F1 • 1-12 • Ⓥ Ⓓ Ⓢ Ⓟ ⊤ 🐾 • www.rawer.co.uk Transport available.

WANLOCKHEAD (Sanquhar)
SOUTHERN UPLAND WAY

Sue & Sandy Jenkins, Millennium Cottage, Garden Dyke, ML12 6UZ. ☎ (01659) 74577 • Map 78/872128 • BB **B** • EM book first £4.50, 7.30pm • D2 T2 F4 • 1-12 • Ⓥ Ⓓ Ⓟ • SC also • charlesajenkins@talk21.com

---

HIGHLAND

AVIEMORE

Jonathan Gatenby, Ravenscraig Guest House, Grampian House, PH22 1RP. ☎ (01479) 810278 • Map 35,36/895131 • BB **C** • S1 D5 T4 F2 • 1-12 • Ⓓ Ⓢ Ⓡ Ⓟ ⊤ 🐾 • ★★★ • www.aviemore.co.uk/ravenscraig

BADACHRO (Wester Ross)

Mrs Diana Vaughan, Harbour View, IV21 2AA. ☎ 01445 741316 • Map 19/780735 • BB **B** • S1 D2 T1 F1 • 4-10 • Ⓑ Ⓓ Ⓟ ⊤ 🐾 • business.virgin.net/harbour.view/index.htm

BALLACHULISH (Argyll)

Mrs Jeanette Watt, Riverside House, PA39 4JE. ☎ (01855) 811473 • Map 41/081580 • BB **B** • D2 T1 • 3-10 NX • Ⓑ Ⓓ Ⓢ Ⓟ ⊤ • ★★★

Mrs Diana Macaskill, Park View, 18 Park Road, PA39 4JS. ☎ (01855) 811560 • Map 41/080582 • BB **A/B** • D3 T1 • 1-12 NX • Ⓓ Ⓢ Ⓟ ⊤ 🐾 • ★★Ⓦ • db.macaskill@talk21.com

G Castles, Inverlaroch, Albert Road, PH49 4JR. ☎ 01855 811726 • Map 41/078586 • BB **B/C** • D1 T1 F1 • 2-10 • Ⓑ Ⓢ Ⓟ ⊤ • inverlaroch@talk21.com

BALMACARA (Kyle, Wester Ross)

Mrs Anne Porter, "Feorlig", Kirkton, IV40 8EG. ☎ (01599) 566281 • Map 33/832273 • BB **B** • EM book first £10, 7pm • S1 D2 T1 • 2-11 • Ⓥ Ⓓ Ⓟ ⊤ 🐾 • Twin room is bunks

BANAVIE (Fort William)
WEST HIGHLAND WAY

Kay Gretton, Rhiw Goch, PH33 7LX. ☎ (01397) 772373 • Map 41/116744 • BB **C** • T3 • 1-12 NX • Ⓑ Ⓓ Ⓢ Ⓡ Ⓟ ⊤ • ★★★★ • kay@rhiwgoch.prestel.co.uk

BEAULY (Inverness-shire)

Elizabeth Brown, Ardgowan Lodge, Wester Phoiness, IV4 7BA. ☎ (01463) 741745 • Map 26/525432 • BB **C** • EM book first £15, 7pm • D2 T1 • 3-10 • Ⓥ Ⓑ Ⓓ Ⓢ ⊤ • ★★★★ • www.ardgowanlodge.co.uk

■ BERRIEDALE (Caithness)

Mrs S Steven, Mulberry Croft, 2 East Newport, KW7 6HA. ☎ (01593) 751245 • Map 17/131246 • BB **B** • EM book first £8, 6-8pm • D/F1 T1 • 1-12 NX • Ⓥ Ⓓ Ⓢ Ⓟ 🏂

■ BOAT OF GARTEN (Inverness-shire)

☆ Claire Johnston, Craigard House Hotel, Kinchurdy Road, PH24 3BP. ☎ 01479 831206 • Map 36/942185 • BB **C/D** • EM £5-£20, 6-9pm • S4 D6 T5 F2 • 1-12 • Ⓥ Ⓑ Ⓓ Ⓢ Ⓡ Ⓟ Ⓣ 🏂 • ★★★★ • craigard@zetnet.co.uk

Craigard House Hotel

200 year old Victorian hunting lodge, now a three star hotel, perfectly situated for the Speyside Way and all 32,000 acres of the Loch Morlich nature reserve. Walk, climb, or cycle while exploring some of Britain's most ancient natural forest. Twenty well-equipped ensuite rooms, award winning food, well stocked bar and real log fires.
Tel: (01479) 831206 www.craigard-house-hotel.co.uk

■ BONAR BRIDGE

Ralph & Diane Tapper, Gneiss House, Invershin, IV27 4ET. ☎ (01549) 421282 • Map 21/578955 • BB **B** • D1 T2 • 5-9 • Ⓑ Ⓓ Ⓢ Ⓡ Ⓣ • dianetapper@onetel.net.uk

■ DIABAIG (Achnasheen, Ross-shire)

Mrs I Ross, Ben Bhraggie, IV22 2HE. ☎ (01445) 790268 • Map 24,19/802605 • BB **A** • EM book first £9, 7.30pm • D1 T1 • 3-10 • Ⓥ Ⓑ Ⓢ Ⓟ • SC also

Ms Anne Ross, Croft No 3, Torridon, IV22 2HE. ☎ (01445) 790240 • Map 24, 19/802605 • BB **B** • EM book first £13, 7.30pm • S1 D1 T1 • 1-12 NX • Ⓥ Ⓑ Ⓓ Ⓢ Ⓟ • List/C • SC also. Postbus from station.

■ DRUMNADROCHIT (Inverness-shire)

Sandra Silke, Westwood, Lower Balmacaan, IV63 6WU. ☎ (01456) 450826 • Map 26, 35/503285 • BB **B/C** • EM book first £13, 6-8pm • S1 D1 T1 • 1-12 • Ⓥ Ⓑ Ⓓ Ⓢ Ⓟ Ⓣ 🏂 Ⓜ • ★★★ • sandra@west-woodbb.freeserve.co.uk

■ FORT AUGUSTUS (Inverness-shire)

Bob & June Burnett, Kettle House, Golf Course Road, PH32 4BY. ☎ (01320) 366408 • Map 34/373083 • BB **B** • S2 D1 T1 • 1-11 • Ⓑ Ⓓ Ⓢ Ⓟ Ⓣ 🏂 Ⓜ • ★★★

■ FORT WILLIAM (Inverness-shire)
WEST HIGHLAND WAY

Rhu Mhor Guest House, Alma Road, PH33 6BP. ☎ (01397) 702213 • Map 41/107740 • BB **B** • S2 D3 T1 F1 • 4-10 • Ⓑ Ⓓ Ⓢ Ⓡ Ⓣ 🏂 • ★★ • www.rhumhor.co.uk

Craig Nevis Guest House, Belford Road, PH33 6BU. ☎ (01397) 702023 • Map 41/108741 • BB **B** • S2 D3 T3 F2 • 1-12 NX • Ⓑ Ⓓ Ⓡ Ⓣ • 2Cr/C

☆ Mrs D Macbeth, Glenlochy Guest House, Nevis Bridge, PH33 6PF. ☎ (01397) 702909 • Map 41/114742 • BB **B/C** • D5 T4 F2 • 1-12 NX • Ⓑ Ⓓ Ⓢ Ⓡ Ⓟ Ⓣ 🏂 • ★★★ • SC also

Abrach House, Caithness Place, PH33 6JP. ☎ (01397) 702535 • Map 41/097729 • BB **C** • S1 D2 T1 • 1-12 NX • Ⓑ Ⓓ Ⓢ Ⓡ Ⓟ Ⓣ 🏂 • ★★★ • SC also • transport av. cmoore3050@aol.com

☆ Catherine Henderson, Distillery House, Nevis Bridge, PH33 6LR. ☎ (01397) 700103, Fax (01397)702980 • Map 41/113744 • BB **C/D/E** • S1 D3 T2 F1 • 1-12 NX • Ⓑ Ⓓ Ⓢ Ⓡ Ⓟ 🏂 • ★★★★

☆ Elizabeth Ann Allton, Alltonside Guest House, Achintore Road, PH33 6RW. ☎ (01397) 703542 • Map 41/085718 • BB **B/C** • D3 T1 F2 • 1-12 • Ⓑ Ⓓ Ⓢ Ⓡ Ⓣ 🏂 • ★★★ • alltonside@aol.com

■ FORT WILLIAM (Inverness-shire) (continued)
WEST HIGHLAND WAY

Mrs A Grant, Glen Shiel Guest House, Achintore Road, PH33 6RW. ☎ (01397) 702271 • Map 41/085718 • BB **B** • D3 T1 F1 • 3-10 • B D S R T • ★★ • Groups also

Ossian's Hotel, High Street, PH33 6DH. ☎ (01397) 700857 • Map 41/102739 • BB **B/C** • EM £8, 6.30-9pm • S5 D10 T10 F10 • 1-12 NX • V B D R P T 🐾 • ossiansfw@aol.com

■ GAIRLOCH (Ross-shire)

Mike & Shirley Powley, Oakwood, 1 Braeside Road, IV21 2BG. ☎ (01445) 712069 • Map 19/808753 • BB **B** • D1 T1 • 4-9 • B D S P T

■ GLENCOE (Ballachulish, Argyll)

☆ The Glencoe Hotel, PH49 4HW. ☎ (01855) 811245 • Map 41/097587 • BB **D** • EM £10, 6-9pm • S3 D9 T3 • 1-12 NX • V B D S P T 🐾 • ★★ • Groups also glencoehotel@hotmail.com

■ INVERNESS

Ian & Mary Jamieson, Glencairn Guest House, 19 Ardross Street, IV3 5NS. ☎ (01463) 232965 • Map 26/662449 • BB **B/C** • S4 D4 T4 • 1-12 • B S R T • glencairnguesthouse@u.genie.co.uk

Hazeldean House, 125 Lochalsh Road, IV3 5QS. ☎ 01463 241338 • Map 26/657453 • BB **B** • S2 D5 T3 F1 • 1-12 • B S R T 🐾 • ★★★ • www.hazeldeanhouse.co.uk

■ KINCRAIG (Kingussie, Inverness-shire)

Nick & Patsy Thompson, Insh House, PH21 1NU. ☎ (01540) 651377 • Map 35/836038 • BB **B** • EM book first £10, 7pm • S2 D1 T1 F1 • 1-12 NX • V B D S P T 🐾 • ★★★ • SC also www.kincraig.com/inshhouse.htm

■ KINGUSSIE (Inverness-shire)

The Osprey Hotel, Ruthven Road, PH21 1EN. ☎ (01540) 661510 • Map 35/756005 • BB **C/D** • EM book first £19.95, 7.30-8pm • S2 D4 T3 • 1-12 • V B D S R P T 🐾 • ★★★ • Group discount • www.ospreyhotel.co.uk

Bhuna Monadh, 85 High Street, PH21 1HX. ☎ (01540) 661186/(0385) 931345 • Map 35/759007 • BB **B** • D1 T1 • 1-12 • V B D S R P T 🐾 • joan@bhunamonadh.demon.co.uk

■ KINLOCHLEVEN (Argyll, Lochaber)
WEST HIGHLAND WAY

Miss MacAngus, "Hermon", PH50 4RA. ☎ (01855) 831383 • Map 41/189622 • BB **B** • D1 T2 • 3-10 • B D S P T

Elsie Robertson, Edencoille Guest House, PA40 4SE. ☎ (01855 831) 358 • Map 41/180617 • BB **B/C** • EM £12, 6-9.30pm • D1 T3 F2 • 1-12 • V B D S P T • ★★★

Martin & Margaret Reece, MacDonald Hotel, Fort William Road, PH50 4QL. ☎ (01855) 831539 • Map 41/182622 • BB **D/E** • EM £8, 5.30-9pm • D4 T5 F1 • 3-12 • V B D S P T 🐾 • ★★★ • www.macdonaldhotel.co.uk

■ KYLE OF LOCHALSH

Kyle Hotel, Main Street, IV40 8AB. ☎ (01599) 534204 • Map 33/761273 • BB **E** • EM book first £15, 6-9.30pm • S9 D7 T15 • 1-12 NX • V B D S R P T 🐾 • ★★★ • Group discounts • thekylehotel@btinternet.com

■ LOCHCARRON (Strathcarron, Ross-shire)

Ms M Innes, Aultsigh, Croft Road, IV54 8YA. ☎ (01520) 722558 • Map 25/905400 • BB **B** • D1 T1 F1 • 1-12 NX • D S P T 🐾 • moyra.innes@talk21.com

■ MALLAIG (Inverness-shire)

J & T Smith, Springbank Guest House, East Bay, PH41 4QF. ☎ (01687) 462459 • Map 40/678967 • BB **B** • EM book first £8.50, 7pm • S2 D2 T3 F1 • 1-12 NX • V D S R P T 🐾 • 1Cr/App

■ MELVAIG (Gairloch)

Rua Reidh Lighthouse, IV21 2EA. ☎ (01445) 771263 • Map 19/740919 • BB **B** • EM book first £12, 7pm • D2 T2 F2 • 2-12 • Ⓥ Ⓑ Ⓓ Ⓢ Ⓟ ♨ • ★★ • see Hols/Hostel • www.scotland-info.co.uk/ruareidh.htm

■ MORAR BY MALLAIG (Inverness-shire)

Mrs U Clulow, Sunset Guest House, PH40 4PA. ☎ (01687) 462259 • Map 40/677933 • BB **B** • EM £7, 6.30-9pm • S1 D1 T1 F2 • 1-12 • Ⓥ Ⓑ Ⓓ Ⓢ Ⓡ Ⓟ Ⓣ • 1Cr/App • Thai food. members.aol-com/sunsetgh

■ NETHY BRIDGE
SPEYSIDE WAY

David & Cathy Mordaunt, Mondhuie, PH25 3DF. ☎ (01479) 821062 • Map 36/991207 • BB **B** • EM book first £6, 7.30pm • D1 T1 • 1-10 • Ⓥ Ⓓ Ⓢ Ⓟ Ⓣ ♨ • cathy.mordaunt@virgin.net

Linda Renton, Aspen Lodge, PH25 3DA. ☎ (01479) 821042 • Map 36/000205 • BB **B** • D1 T1 • 1-12 NX • Ⓑ Ⓓ Ⓢ Ⓟ Ⓣ • ★★★ Ⓦ • www.nethybridge.com/aspenlodge.htm

■ SHIELDAIG (Strathcarron)

Trevor Bradley, Rowan Bank, IV54 8XN. ☎ (01520) 755246 • Map 24/817542 • BB **B/C** • EM book first £14-17 • D1 T2/F1 • 1-12 NX • Ⓥ Ⓑ Ⓢ

■ SPEAN BRIDGE (Inverness-shire)

Lynn MacFarlane, Coire Glas Guest House, Roy Bridge Road, PH34 4EU. ☎ (01397) 712272 • Map 41/227819 • BB **B** • EM book first £12, 7-8.30pm • S1 D4 T4 F2 • 1-10 • Ⓥ Ⓑ Ⓓ Ⓢ Ⓡ Ⓟ Ⓣ • ★★ • enquiry@coireglas.co.uk

Isabel Muir, Mahaar, Corriechoille Road , PH34 4EP. ☎ (01397) 712365 • Map 41,34/220816 • BB **B** • EM book first £9, 6-8pm • S2 D1 T1 F1 • 1-12 • Ⓥ Ⓓ Ⓡ Ⓟ Ⓣ ♨ • ★★ • mahaar.bnb@btinternet.com

☆ Helen Maclean, Dreamweavers, Earendil, Mucomir, PH34 4EQ. ☎ 01397 712548 • Map 41,34/186838 • BB **C** • EM book first £10 • D1 T1 F1 • 1-12 • Ⓥ Ⓑ Ⓓ Ⓢ Ⓟ Ⓣ ♨ • ★★ • helen@dreamweavers.co.uk Suitable for disabled & children

Mr & Mrs Stewart, Lesanne, PH34 4EP. ☎ (01397) 712231 • Map 41,34/221815 • BB **A/B** • D1 T2 F1 • 1-12 NX • Ⓑ Ⓓ Ⓢ Ⓡ Ⓟ Ⓣ

■ STRATHPEFFER (Ross-shire)

Mrs Janet Greathead, Hideaway, Craigdarroch Drive, Contin, IV14 9EL. ☎ (01997) 421127 • Map 26/447573 • BB **B** • D2 T/S1 • 1-12 NX • Ⓑ Ⓓ Ⓢ Ⓟ Ⓣ • ★★★

■ THURSO (Caithness)

Barbara MacIvor, "Ivordene", Janetstown, KW14 7XF. ☎ (01847) 894760 • Map 11,12/089656 • BB **B** • EM book first £7, 6-7.30pm • S1 D1 T2 F1 • 1-12 • Ⓥ Ⓓ Ⓢ Ⓡ Ⓟ ♨

■ TOMICH, NR CANNICH (Beauly)

☆ The Tomich Hotel, IV4 7LY. ☎ (01456) 415399 • Map 25/283243 • BB **D** • EM £12, 6.30-9.30pm • D4 T4 • 1-12 NX • Ⓥ Ⓔ Ⓓ Ⓢ Ⓟ Ⓣ ♨ • ★★★ • tomich@tomich.freewire.co.uk

■ TONGUE (Lairg, Sutherland)

Mrs J B MacIntosh, 77 Dalcharn, IV27 4XU. ☎ (01847) 611251 • Map 10/622587 • BB **A/B** • EM book first £7, 6.30-7pm • S1 D1 T1 F1 • 1-12 NX • Ⓥ Ⓑ Ⓓ Ⓢ Ⓟ Ⓣ • ★★

■ TORRIDON (by Achnasheen, Ross-shire)

Mrs Mary Mackay, "Benview", Inver Alligin, Loch Torridon, IV22 2HB. ☎ (01445) 791333 • Map 24/845577 • BB **B** • D2 T1 • 1-12 NX • Ⓓ Ⓢ • SC also

■ ULLAPOOL (Ross-shire)

The Ceilidh Place Clubhouse, West Argyle Street, IV26 2TY. ☎ (01854) 612103 • Map 19/126939 • BB **B** • EM £12-£15 • S4 T3 F4 • 1-12 • Ⓥ Ⓓ Ⓟ ♨ • Bunkhouse accommodation, groups also

B&B ACCOMMODATION SCOTLAND HIGHLAND

☆ See Display Advertisement

ISLE OF ARRAN

■ BLACKWATERFOOT (Brodick)

Marjorie Bannatyne, Lochside , KA27 8EY.
☎ (01770) 860276 • Map 68,69/903268 • BB **C** • EM
book first £7, 6.30pm • S1 D2 T1 F1 • 1-12 NX • Ⓥ
Ⓑ Ⓓ Ⓟ Ⓣ 🦮 • sc also

■ BRODICK

☆ Glencloy Farm Guesthouse, Glencloy, KA27 8DA.
☎ (01770) 302351 • Map 69/008361 • BB **C/D** • S1
D2 T2 • 1-12 • Ⓑ Ⓓ Ⓢ Ⓟ Ⓣ 🦮 • ★★★

Glencloy Farmhouse
Brodick, Isle of Arran

Set in a peaceful glen close
to Brodick, this is the ideal
base for exploring Arran. Cosy rooms, sumptuous
breakfasts using local produce and our own hen's eggs,
delicious farmouse teas and packed lunches. Close to
Brodick Castle, museum, mountains and golf.

Tel. 01770 302351
www.smoothhound.co.uk/hotels/glencloy.html

■ CORRIE (Brodick, Isle of Arran)

☆ Celia & Nigel, Blackrock Guest House, KA27 8JP.
☎ (01770) 810 282 • Map 69,63/023439 • BB **C** • EM
for groups £15, 6.30pm • S2 D2 T1 F4 • 1-11 NX • Ⓥ
Ⓑ Ⓓ Ⓢ Ⓟ Ⓣ 🦮 Ⓜ • ★★ •
www.arran.uk.com/corrie/blackrock

BLACKROCK HOUSE
Corrie, Isle of Arran

Nestling in the foot of Greatfell, on the outskirts of
"the prettiest village in Europe" (Asquith). Come
and enjoy our traditional Scottish guest house,
established on the shore-edge in the 1930s.
Ensuite; panoramic island views; natural garden;
abundant wildlife!! Groups of up to 16. Back all
together? Constant hot water!

Proprietors Celia & Nigel
Tel. 01770 810282

Barbara Langley, Felmemris, KA27 8JP. ☎ 01770
810216 • Map 69,63/019441 • BB **B** • S1 D2 T1 • 1-
12 NX • Ⓑ Ⓓ Ⓢ Ⓟ Ⓣ 🦮

ISLE OF MULL

■ FIONNPHORT

J & E Wagstaff, Red Bay Cottage, Deargphort, PA66
6BP. ☎ (01681) 700396 • Map 48/312242 • BB **B** •
EM book first £10, 7.30-9.30pm • D1 T2 • 1-12 • Ⓥ
Ⓓ Ⓢ Ⓟ Ⓣ 🦮

■ PENNYGHAEL

Fiona Brown & Norman Salkeld, Tigh Na H-Abhann,
PA70 6HB. ☎ (01681) 704229 • Map 48/534282 • BB
B • D2 T1 • 4-10 • Ⓓ Ⓢ Ⓟ Ⓣ 🦮

■ TOBERMORY (Isle of Mull)

T V & B M Bettley, The Cedars, Dervaig Road, PA75
6PY. ☎ (01688) 302096 • Map 47/501553 • BB **B** •
D1 T1 • 1-12 NX • Ⓓ Ⓟ Ⓣ • ★★

ISLE OF SKYE

■ CARBOST (Glen Eynort)

Mr Robert Van Der Vliet, "The Blue Lobster", IV47
8SG. ☎ (01478) 640320 • Map 32/376264 • BB **B** •
EM book first £8-15, 6-9pm • T6 • 3-12 • Ⓥ Ⓓ Ⓟ
Ⓣ 🦮 • ★★ • SC also

■ PORTREE

David Watson, Old Forestry Cottage B&B, Manse
Lane, IV51 9QB. ☎ (01478) 612389 • Map
23/485435 • BB **B** • EM book first £9.50 • D2 T1 F1 •
1-12 • Ⓥ Ⓓ Ⓢ Ⓟ Ⓣ • ◆◆ • david.vip@virgin.net
Catherine McCleod, Cuag, 7 Kitson Crescent, IV51
9DP. ☎ 01478 612273 • Map 23/483483 • BB **B** • S1
D1 • 5-10 • Ⓢ • ★★★

■ STRUAN

Mrs M Mackinnon, "Seaforth", Coillore, IV56 8FX.
☎ (01470) 572230 • Map 23,32/354376 • BB **B** • D1
T2 • 4-10 • Ⓓ Ⓟ Ⓣ • ★★

Mr M Mackay, Ard-Bhealaidh, Balgown, IV56 8FA.
☎ (01470) 572334 • Map 23,32/352387 • BB **B** • S1
D1 F1 • 4-10 • Ⓑ Ⓢ Ⓣ 🦮 • ★★★ • ard-
bhealaidh@uk-bedandbreakfasts.com

NORTH EAST SCOTLAND

ABERDEEN, ABERDEENSHIRE, ANGUS AND MORAY

■ ABERDEEN

☆ Colin & Frances Moore, Roselea Hotel, 12
Springbank Terrace, AB11 6LS. ☎ (01224) 583060 •
Map 38/938055 • BB **B/C** • D3 T1 F2 • 1-12 • Ⓑ Ⓓ
Ⓢ Ⓡ Ⓟ Ⓣ 🦮 • ★★

ROSELEA HOTEL
12 Springbank Terrace,
ABERDEEN
Tel/Fax: 01224 583060
Email:
candfmoore@roseleahotel.demon.co.uk
Family-run city centre hotel, convenient for bus/railway
stations and P & O ferry terminal • Commended by STB •
Vegetarian breakfasts available • TV and tea/coffee making
facilities in all rooms • Ideal base for coastal and country
walks in North East Scotland • Drying facilities • B&B
from £16 (standard) £20 (en-suite).

■ **BALLATER (Aberdeenshire)**

Gairnshiel Lodge, Glengairn, AB35 5UQ. ☎ (013397) 55582 • Map 37/277014 • BB **C** • EM book first £16, 7.30pm • D2 F6 • 1-12 • B D S P T ♿

Ravenswood Hotel, Braemar Road, AB35 5RQ. ☎ (013397) 55539 • Map 44,37/365960 • BB **C** • EM £16.95, 6.30-8.30pm • S2 D3 T5 • 12-10 NX • V B D S P T ♿ • ★★★ • cathy.fyfe@virginnet.co.uk

■ **BRAEMAR (Aberdeenshire)**

Mrs I C McKellar, Morningside, Kindrochit Drive, AB35 5YQ. ☎ (013397) 41370 • Map 43/153914 • BB **B** • EM book first £6-£10, 6.30-8pm • D/S1 T/S1 • 1-10 • V D P ♿ • List/C

☆ Callater Lodge, 9 Glenshee Road, AB35 5YQ. ☎ (013397) 41275 • Map 43/153914 • BB **D** • EM book first £15, 7.30pm • S1 D3 T3 • 1-12 NX • V B D S P T ♿ • ★★★★ • www.hotel-braemar.co.uk

---

Royal Deeside, Aberdeenshire
Callater Lodge
Small, friendly, comfortable family-run hotel in large grounds close to the centre of Braemar. Surrounded by superb hill country, it is an ideal base for walking and other country holidays. Licensed, Lounge, Drying Room, Parking etc. **B&B £23–£29, Dinner £15.**
Self-catering also available. *Contact Maria Franklin*
9 Glenshee Road, Braemar, Aberdeenshire AB35 5YQ
tel 013397 41275, fax 013397 41345 or email
maria@hotel-braemar.co.uk http://www.hotel-braemar.co.uk

■ **DUFFTOWN (Morayshire)**
SPEYSIDE WAY

Mrs J Smart, Errolbank, 134 Fife Street, AB55 4AQ. ☎ (01340) 820229 • Map 28/327397 • BB **B** • EM book first £8, 6-8pm • S1 D1 F3 • 1-12 • V D P T ♿

Mr & Mrs Donald, Gowanbrae, 19 Church Street, AB55 4AR. ☎ (01340) 820461 • Map 28/324397 • BB **B** • EM book first £10, 7pm • D2 T1 F3 • 1-12 NX • V B D S P T • ★★★ • www.gowanbrae-dufftown.co.uk

■ **GLAMIS (Angus)**

Mrs Jean Ruffhead, Arndean, Linross, PH12 8QT. ☎ (01307) 840535 • Map 54/353493 • BB **B** • EM book first £7 • T1 F1 • 1-12 NX • V D P T ♿ • ★★Ⓦ • arndean@btinternet.com

■ **LETHAM (Angus, Tayside)**

Jean Stewart, Woodville, Heathercroft, Guthrie Street, DD8 2PS. ☎ (01307) 818090 • Map 54/526488 • BB **C** • EM £10-12, 6-8pm • T2 • 1-12 • V B D S P T • ★★★

■ **STRATHDON (Aberdeenshire)**

Mrs Elizabeth Ogg, Buchaam Farm, AB36 8TN. ☎ (019756) 51238 • Map 37/393134 • BB **B** • D1 T1 F1 • 5-10 • D S P • ★★ • SC also • e.ogg@talk21.com

■ **TOMINTOUL (Banffshire)**
SPEYSIDE WAY

Anne Shearer, Croughly Farm, AB37 9EN. ☎ (01807) 580476 • Map 36/174213 • BB **B** • D1 F1 • 5-10 • S P T • ★★ • johnannecroughly@tinyworld.co.uk

Bracam House, 32 Main Street, AB37 9EX. ☎ (01807) 580278 • Map 36/170185 • BB **A** • S1 D1 T1 • 1-12 • B D S P T ♿ • ★★★ • cameron-tomintoul@compuserve.com

ORKNEY ISLANDS

■ **BURRAY**

Mrs Murray & Mrs Woodward, Vestleybanks, KW17 2SX. ☎ (01856) 731305 • Map 7,6/451968 • BB **C** • EM book first £10.50, 7.00pm • D1 T1 • 3-10 • V D S • ★★★★ • SC also vestleybanks@btinternet.com Overlooks Scapa Flow.

PERTH & KINROSS

■ **BIRNAM (Dunkeld)**

Caroline Neil, Waterbury Guest House, Murthly Ter, PH8 0BG. ☎ 01350 727324 • Map 52,53/032418 • BB **C** • EM £11, 7pm • S2 D3 T1 F2 • 1-12 • V B D S R P T ♿ • ★★★ • bneil@waterbury.demon.co.uk

■ **BLAIR ATHOLL (Perthshire)**

Dalgreine Guest House, Off St Andrew's Crescent, PH18 5SX. ☎ (01796) 481276/481627 • Map 43/878653 • BB **B** • EM book first £9-£11.50, 6.30-7.30pm • S1 D2 T2 F1 • 1-12 • V B D S R P T • ★★★

E Mackenzie, Moraybank, St Andrews Crescent, Bridge of Tilt, PH18 5TA. ☎ (01796) 481612 • Map 43/878653 • BB **B** • EM book first £7, 6pm • D1 T1 • 3-11 • V D S R P T

■ **PERTH**

Pat & Brian Smith, Beeches, 2 Comelybank, PH2 7HU. ☎ (01738) 624486 • Map 53, 58/124245 • BB **B** • EM book first £8, 6.00pm • S2 D1 T1 • 1-12 • V B D S R P T ♿ • ★★★ • enquiries@beeches-guest-house.co.uk

Hazel Harward-Taylor, Greenacres, Chapelhill, Logiealmond, PH1 3TQ. ☎ (01738) 880302 • Map 52,58,53/005300 • BB **C** • D1 T1 • 1-12 • B D S P T ♿ • ★★★ • Food nearby www.logiealmond.co.uk

■ **PITLOCHRY**

The Poplars, 27 Lower Oakfield, PH16 5DS. ☎ (01796) 472129 • Map 52/945580 • BB **D/E** • EM £15, 7pm • D4 T4 F3 • 1-12 NX • V B D S R P T ♿ • www.poplars-hotel.co.uk

☆ See Display Advertisement

■ **STANLEY (Perth)**

Glensanda House, Six Acres, Station Road, PH1 4NS. ☎ (01738) 827016 • Map 53/108334 • BB **B** • S1 D1 T1 • 1-12 • Ⓑ Ⓢ Ⓟ Ⓣ

SCOTTISH BORDERS

■ **ANCRUM (Jedburgh, Roxburghshire)**
ST CUTHBERT'S WAY

☆ Michael O'Sullivan, Cheviot View, The Green, Ancrum, TD8 6XA. ☎ 01835 830563 • Map 74/626243 • BB **B** • D2 T1 • 1-12 • Ⓑ Ⓓ Ⓢ Ⓟ Ⓣ ⌕ • ★★★ • Food nearby mickjo.osullivan@eggconnect.net

CHEVIOT VIEW
The Green, Ancrum, TD8 6XA
Comfortable village green house with fantastic views. Friendly welcome for ST. CUTHBERT'S WAY walkers and tourers. Creature comforts include: lounge, drying facilities, and packed lunches. Michael is also happy to book your pub supper across the green.

© **01835 830563**

Mary Anderson, Lilliard B&B, Harrietsfield, TD8 6TZ. ☎ (01835) 830593 • Map 74/626263 • BB **C** • EM book first £12, 7pm • D1 T2 • 3-10 • Ⓥ Ⓑ Ⓓ Ⓢ Ⓟ Ⓣ • ★★★ • alexander@lilliard.freeserve.co.uk

■ **AYTON (Eyemouth, Berwickshire)**

Mrs S Riach, Ayton Mains Farmhouse, TD14 5RE. ☎ 018907 81336 • Map 67/934621 • BB **B** • S2 D1 T1 • 4-10 • Ⓓ Ⓢ Ⓟ Ⓣ • ★★ • Evening meal possible.

■ **ECKFORD (Kelso)**
ST CUTHBERT'S WAY

David Butterfield, The Old Joiners Cottage, TD5 8LG. ☎ (01835) 850323 • Map 74/710263 • BB **C** • EM book first £8 upwards, 6.30-7pm • D1 F1 • 1-12 NX • Ⓥ Ⓑ Ⓓ Ⓢ Ⓟ Ⓣ ⌕ • ★★★Ⓦ • Lift to/from St Cuthbert's Way joiners.cottage@virgin.net

■ **GALASHIELS (Selkirkshire)**
SOUTHERN UPLAND WAY

Mrs S Field, Ettrickvale, 33 Abbotsford Road, TD1 3HW. ☎ (01896) 755224 • Map 73/499352 • BB **B** • EM book first £6, 6-8pm • D1 T2 • 1-12 NX • Ⓥ Ⓓ Ⓢ Ⓟ Ⓣ ⌕ • ★★

■ **HAWICK (Roxburghshire)**

☆ Mr L & Mr N Neish, Elm House Hotel, 17 North Bridge Street, TD9 9RD. ☎ (01450) 372866 • Map 79/503149 • BB **C** • EM £12, 5-9.30pm • S2 D4 T6 F3 • 1-12 NX • Ⓥ Ⓑ Ⓓ Ⓢ Ⓟ Ⓣ ⌕ • ★★ • www.elmhouse-hawick.fisnet.co.uk

■ **JEDBURGH (Roxburghshire)**
ST CUTHBERT'S WAY

☆ Alan & Christine Swanston, Ferniehirst Mill Lodge, TD8 6PQ. ☎ (01835) 863279 • Map 80/654171 • BB **C** • EM book first £14, 7.30pm • S1 D3 T4 F1 • 1-12 • Ⓥ Ⓑ Ⓓ Ⓟ Ⓣ ⌕ • ★ • ferniemill@aol.com

Martin Arthur, Bridgehouse B&B, 5 Bridge Street, TD8 6DW. ☎ (01835) 863405 • Map 74/653208 • BB **B** • D1 T/D1 • 1-12 NX • Ⓑ Ⓢ Ⓟ Ⓣ ⌕ • ★★★
Elizabeth Kinghorn, Riverview, Newmill Farm, TD8 6TH. ☎ (01835) 862145/864607 • Map 74/659227 • BB **C** • D2 T1 • 4-10 • Ⓑ Ⓓ Ⓢ Ⓟ Ⓣ • ★★★

■ **KELSO (Roxburghshire)**

E Galbraith, Border Hotel, Woodmarket, TD5 7AX. ☎ (01573) 224791 • Map 74/728340 • BB **B** • EM book first £7-8, 5-6pm • S3 D2 T1 F3 • 1-12 NX • Ⓥ Ⓓ Ⓟ ⌕

■ **KIRK YETHOLM (Roxburghshire)**
PENNINE WAY

Gail Brooker, Blunty's Mill, TD5 8PG. ☎ (01573) 420288 • Map 74/825284 • BB **C** • EM book first £10-£14, 6-8pm • T2 • 1-12 • Ⓥ Ⓑ Ⓓ Ⓟ Ⓣ ⌕ • 2Cr/C • gail_rowan@hotmail.com

Mrs Margaret Campbell, Valleydene, High Street, TD5 8PH. ☎ (01573) 420286 • Map 74/828281 • BB **C/D** • EM £12, 7-8pm • D1 T2 F1 • 1-12 NX • Ⓥ Ⓑ Ⓓ Ⓢ Ⓟ Ⓣ ⌕ • ★★★

■ LAUDER (Berwickshire)
SOUTHERN UPLAND WAY

Mr & Mrs P Gilardi, The Grange, 6 Edinburgh Road, TD2 6TW. ☎ (01578) 722649 • Map 73/526479 • BB B • D1 T2 • 1-12 NX • Ⓓ Ⓢ Ⓟ Ⓣ • ★★★

■ MELROSE
ST CUTHBERT'S WAY & SOUTHERN UPLAND WAY

Mrs Susan Graham, Dunfermline House, Buccleuch Street, TD6 9LB. ☎ (01896) 822148 • Map 73/546340 • BB D • S1 D2 T2 • 1-12 • Ⓑ Ⓓ Ⓢ Ⓟ Ⓣ ♨ • ★★★★ • www.dunmel.freeserve.co.uk

Mrs Margaret Aitken, The Gables, Darnick, TD6 9AL. ☎ (01896) 822479 • Map 73/531342 • BB B • S1 D1 T1 • 1-12 NX • Ⓓ Ⓢ Ⓟ Ⓣ ♨ • ★★★

Mrs Julie John, Birch House, High Street, TD6 9PB. ☎ (01896) 822391 • Map 73/547342 • BB B • S1 D1 T1 • 1-12 NX • Ⓑ Ⓓ Ⓢ Ⓟ Ⓣ ♨ Ⓜ • ★★★

Mrs Ellen Haldane, Priory View, 15 Priors Walk, TD6 9RB. ☎ (01896) 822087 • Map 73/552340 • BB B • EM book first £10, 6pm • D2 T1 • 1-12 • Ⓥ Ⓓ Ⓢ Ⓟ Ⓣ • ★★★

■ PEEBLES (Tweeddale)

Carl & Catherine Lane, Lindores, 60 Old Town, EH45 8JE. ☎ /Fax 01721 720441 • Map 73/248404 • BB B • EM book first £9, 6-8pm • S1 D2 T1 F1 • 1-12 • Ⓥ Ⓑ Ⓓ Ⓢ Ⓟ Ⓣ ♨ Ⓜ • ★★★ • www.aboutscot-land.co.uk/peebles/lindores.html

■ SELKIRK

Mrs Janet MacKenzie, Ivy Bank, Hillside Terrace, TD7 4LT. ☎ (01750) 21270 • Map 73/473286 • BB B • S1 D1 T1 • 2-12 NX • Ⓑ Ⓓ Ⓢ Ⓟ Ⓣ ♨ • ★★ • nel-lamackenzie@ivybankselkirk.freeserve.co.uk

■ TEVIOTHEAD (Hawick)

Mrs Mary Jackson, Colterscleuch, TD9 0LF. ☎ (01450) 850247 • Map 79/419067 • BB B • EM £6, 7pm • S1 D/T1 T1 F1 • 1-12 • Ⓥ Ⓑ Ⓓ Ⓟ Ⓣ ♨ • 2Cr/C

■ TOWN YETHOLM (Kelso, Roxburghshire)
PENNINE WAY

Mrs L S Hurst, Lochside, TD5 8PD. ☎ 01573 420349 • Map 74/798282 • BB C • D1 T1 • EASTER-10 • Ⓑ Ⓓ Ⓢ Ⓣ ♨ • ★★★ • Bronze award for Green tourism

■ TRAQUAIR (Innerleithen, Peebles-shire)
SOUTHERN UPLAND WAY

Mrs J A Caird, The School House, EH44 6PR. ☎ (01896) 830425 • Map 73/331345 • BB B • EM book first £10, 6.30pm • D1 T1 F1 • 1-12 NX • Ⓥ Ⓓ Ⓢ Ⓟ ♨ • C

WATCH THIS SPACE
The Ramblers website at www.ramblers.org.uk will be expanding to include accommodation for walkers in the near future.

SHETLAND ISLANDS

■ PAPA STOUR

Andy & Sabina Holt-Brook, Northouse, ZE2 9PW. ☎ (01595) 873238 • Map 3/177606 • BB B • EM £7-£8, 6-7pm • S1 D1 T1 F1 • 1-12 • Ⓥ Ⓑ Ⓓ Ⓢ Ⓟ Ⓣ ♨ • ★

STIRLING

■ BALMAHA (Loch Lomond)
WEST HIGHLAND WAY

Elizabeth Bates, Bay Cottage, G63 0JQ. ☎ (01360) 870346 • Map 56/421908 • BB C • EM book first £12.50, 7pm • S1 D1 T1 F2 • 3-10 • Ⓥ Ⓑ Ⓓ Ⓢ Ⓟ Ⓣ ♨ • ★★★ Ⓦ • bb.12@btinternet.com

Fay MacLuskie, 'Critreoch', Rowardennan Rd, G63 0AW. ☎ (01360) 870309 • Map 56/403932 • BB C • D1 T1 • 5-9 • Ⓑ Ⓓ Ⓢ Ⓟ Ⓣ ♨ Ⓜ • ★★★

■ CALLANDER (Perthshire)

"Annfield", North Church Street, FK17 8EG. ☎ (01877) 330204 • Map 57/630079 • BB C • D4 T2 F1 • 2-11 NX • Ⓑ Ⓓ Ⓢ Ⓣ ♨ • ★★★

■ CRIANLARICH (Perthshire)
WEST HIGHLAND WAY

Glenardran Guest House, FK20 8QS. ☎ (01838) 300236 • Map 52/388253 • BB C • D2 T2 • 1-12 NX • Ⓑ Ⓓ Ⓢ Ⓡ Ⓟ Ⓣ ♨ • ★★★

☆ Suie Lodge Hotel, Glen Dochart, FK20 8QT. ☎ (01567) 820417 • Map 51/488278 • BB C • EM £6, until 9pm • S1 D4 T4 F2 • 1-12 NX • Ⓥ Ⓑ Ⓓ Ⓢ Ⓟ Ⓣ ♨ • 2Cr • SC also in winter JReillysuie@aol.com

☆ Ben More Lodge Hotel, FK20 8QS. ☎ (01838) 300210 • Map 51/445278 • BB D/E • EM £8, 6-8.45pm • D8 T1 F2 • 1-12 NX • Ⓥ Ⓑ Ⓓ Ⓢ Ⓡ Ⓟ ♨ • ★★ • john@ben-more.demon.co.uk • See next page for display advert.

☆ See Display Advertisement

■ DRYMEN (Loch Lomond)
WEST HIGHLAND WAY

Mrs D Reid, Croft Burn Cottage Bed & Breakfast, Croftamie, G63 0HA. ☎ (01360) 660796 • Map 57/484857 • BB **B/C** • EM book first £11, 6.30-7.30pm • D1 T1 F1 • 1-11 NX • Ⓥ Ⓑ Ⓓ Ⓢ Ⓟ Ⓣ ⁂ • ★★★★ • SC caravan also johnreid@croftburn.fsnet.co.uk

Frances Lander, 17 Stirling Road, G63 0BW. ☎ (01360) 660273 • Map 57/476886 • BB **B** • T1 F1 • 1-12 • Ⓓ Ⓢ Ⓟ Ⓣ ⁂ • ★ • david_lander@lineone.net

■ KILLIN (Perthshire)

Fairview House, Main Street, FK21 8UT. ☎ (01567) 820667 • Map 51/572328 • BB **C** • EM book first £15, 7pm • S1 D4 T2 • 1-12 NX • Ⓥ Ⓑ Ⓓ Ⓢ Ⓟ Ⓣ ⁂ • ★★★★ • info@fairview-killin.co.uk

☆ Isabel Carnochan, Breadalbane House, Main Street, FK21 8UT. ☎ (01567) 820135 • Map 51/572328 • BB **C** • EM book first £15, 7pm • D2 T2 F2 • 2-11 • Ⓥ Ⓑ Ⓓ Ⓢ Ⓟ Ⓣ • ★★★★ • stay@breadalbane48.freeserve.co.uk

■ STRATHYRE (Stirling)

Mr & Mrs W Harley, Coire Buidhe, Main Street, FK18 8NA. ☎ (01877) 384288 • Map 57/561170 • BB **B** • S1 T1 F4 • 1-12 NX • Ⓑ Ⓓ Ⓢ Ⓟ Ⓣ ⁂ • ★ • Food nearby

Terry & Lorna Hart, The Ben Sheann Hotel, Main Street, FK18 8NA. ☎ (01877) 384609 • Map 57/561170 • BB **B** • EM £5-£6, 12-9pm • S1 D5 T3 F1 • 1-12 • Ⓥ Ⓑ Ⓓ Ⓢ Ⓟ Ⓣ ⁂ • ★★ • Bike hire, wheelchair access • bensheann@freeuk.com

☆ Mr & Mrs Stewart, Munro Hotel, FK18 8NA. ☎ (01877) 384263 • Map 57/561170 • BB **A/B/C** • EM Y, 6-7pm • S3 D/F6 • 1-12 • Ⓥ Ⓑ Ⓓ Ⓟ Ⓣ ⁂ Ⓜ • 6 extra bunk spaces

■ TYNDRUM (By Crianlarich, Perthshire)
WEST HIGHLAND WAY

☆ Jim & Diane Mailer, Glengarry House, FK20 8RY. ☎ (01838) 400224 • Map 50/329302 • BB **B/C** • EM book first £12 • D1 T1 F1 • 1-12 NX • Ⓥ Ⓑ Ⓓ Ⓢ Ⓡ Ⓟ Ⓣ ⁂ • ★★ • www.glengarry.co.uk

Wales

ANGLESEY

■ CEMAES BAY

Frances & Bill O'Donnell, Treddolphin Guest House, LL67 0ET. ☎ (01407) 710388 • Map 114/373935 • BB **B** • EM £6.50, 6pm • S2 D2 T2 F2 • 1-12 NX • Ⓥ Ⓓ Ⓢ Ⓟ Ⓣ • ★★

■ HOLYHEAD

Mrs B Simms, 4 Walthew Avenue, LL65 1AF. ☎ (01407) 762941 • Map 114/244830 • BB **B** • EM book first £7.50, 6-6.30pm • S1 D1 T1 • 1-12 • Ⓓ Ⓡ Ⓟ Ⓣ ⁂

■ MENAI BRIDGE

☆ Ms Rosemary A Abas, Bwthyn, Brynafon, LL59 5HA. ☎ (01248) 713119 • Map 114, 115/557717 • BB **B** • EM book first £12.50, 6.30-7pm • D2 • 1-12 NX • Ⓥ Ⓑ Ⓢ Ⓡ Ⓟ Ⓣ • ★★★★

Bwthyn
Brynafon, Menai Bridge
Isle of Anglesey LL59 5HA

Warm, welcoming non-smoking B&B in
century-old Victorian terrace fi minute
from Menai Straits • WTB 4-star B&B
Award • 1fi miles A5/A55,
2 miles rail/coaches & North Wales
Coastal Footpath • 7 miles Snowdonia •
Limited private parking & cycle storage
• Beautifully fitted en suite double rooms,
power showers (1 + bath), CTVs, scrumptious
home cooking, traditional and vegetarian.
B&B £17.50, p/p double, 1 night
or £17 p/p 2 nights,
£17/£16 p/p 3 nights plus. Dinner £12.50.

**Discount offer for over 45s
3 nights DB&B £79 p/p (double).**
Come as guests — leave as friends.
Tel/Fax 01248 713119

■ **MOELFRE**

Chris & Neil, Deanfield House, LL72 8HD. ☎ (01248)
410899 • Map 114/512862 • BB **C** • EM book first
£9.95, 6.30-7pm • D2 T2 • 1-12 • Ⓥ Ⓑ Ⓓ Ⓟ Ⓣ
🛁 • ★★★★ • deanfield@lineone.net

■ **RHOSCOLYN (Holyhead)**

Carol Gough, Glan Towyn, LL65 2NJ. ☎ 01407
860380 • Map 114/272752 • BB **B/C** • D2 T2 • 1-12 •
Ⓑ Ⓢ Ⓟ Ⓣ • ★ • carol.glantowyn@talk21.com

Mrs Ann Chadwick, Gwynfryn House, LL65 2EQ. ☎
01407 861107 • Map 114/265766 • BB **B** • S2 D2 • 1-
12 NX • Ⓓ Ⓢ Ⓟ Ⓣ 🛁 • ★★★ •
ann_dennis@tesco.uk

CARMARTHENSHIRE

■ **BRECHFA (Carmarthen)**

☆ Glasfryn Guest House and Restaurant, SA32 7QY.
☎ (01267) 202306 • Map 146/526303 • BB **C** • EM
£10-£12, 7-9pm • D2 T1 • 1-12 • Ⓥ Ⓑ Ⓓ Ⓢ Ⓟ
Ⓣ 🛁 • ★★★★ • joyce.glasfryn@clara.co.uk

■ **CARMARTHEN**

Mrs Rosemary Jones, Trebersed Farm, St Peters,
Travellers Rest, SA31 3RR. ☎ (01267) 238182 • Map
145,159/381200 • BB **C** • D1 T1 F1 • 1-12 NX • Ⓑ Ⓓ
Ⓢ Ⓡ Ⓟ 🛁 • ★★★★ •
trebersed.farm@farmline.com

■ **LLANDEILO**

Mr & Mrs Samuel, 4 Bank Tce, SA19 6AY. ☎ 01558
824333 • Map 159/628221 • BB **B** • EM book first
£7.50 • S2 D1 T1 • 1-12 NX • Ⓥ Ⓓ Ⓢ Ⓡ Ⓟ Ⓣ

■ **LLANDOVERY**
CAMBRIAN WAY

Llwyncelyn Guest House, SA20 0EP. ☎ (01550)
720566 • Map 146/160/761347 • BB **B/D** • S1 D1 T3 •
1-12 NX • Ⓥ Ⓓ Ⓢ Ⓡ Ⓟ Ⓣ • ★★

■ **PENTRE-TY-GWYN (Llandovery)**

Wendy Joslin, Y Neuadd, SA20 0RN. ☎ (01550)
721005 • Map 160/818356 • BB **C** • EM book first £5-
£6.50 • D2 T1 • 1-12 NX • Ⓥ Ⓑ Ⓓ Ⓢ Ⓟ Ⓣ 🛁 •
★★

■ **RHANDIRMWYN (Llandovery)**
CAMBRIAN WAY

☆ Bryan & Pat Williams, Bwlch-y-Ffin, SA20 0PG.
☎ (01550) 760311, ring for exact location • Map
146,147/795481 • BB **B** • EM book first £13, 6.30-
7.30pm • S1 D1 T2 • 1-12 NX • Ⓥ Ⓓ Ⓢ Ⓟ Ⓣ 🛁
• Transport from station

☆ See Display Advertisement

■ **RHANDIRMWYN (Llandovery) (continued)**
CAMBRIAN WAY

Anthea Jones, Nantybai Mill, SA20 0PB. ☎ (01550) 760211 • Map 146,147/773445 • BB **B** • EM £12, 6.30pm • S1 D1 T1 • 1-12 NX • Ⓥ Ⓓ Ⓢ Ⓟ Ⓣ

CEREDIGION

■ **BOW STREET (Aberystwyth)**

Mrs A Edwards, Garreg Lwyd, Penygarn, SY24 5BE. ☎ (01970) 828830 • Map 135/625852 • BB **B** • S1 D1 T1 F1 • 1-12 NX • Ⓓ Ⓡ Ⓟ Ⓣ • ★★

■ **CARDIGAN**

P Williams, Norbury, Napier Street, SA43 1ED. ☎ (01239) 613160 • Map 145/179463 • BB **A** • EM book first £5-£7, 6-7pm • S1 D2 T2 • 1-12 • Ⓥ Ⓑ

■ **CWMYSTWYTH**
CAMBRIAN WAY

Mrs P Liford, Tainewyddion, SY23 4AF. ☎ (01974) 282672 • Map 135,147/790749 • BB **A/B** • EM book first £7, 7pm • S1 T2 • 3-10 • Ⓥ Ⓑ Ⓓ Ⓢ Ⓟ • Advance bookings only

■ **LLANDDEWI BREFI (Tregaron)**

Annie Zakiewicz, Brynheulog, SY25 6PE. ☎ (01570) 493615 • Map 146/659544 • BB **C** • EM book first £10, 7pm • D1 • 1-12 • Ⓥ Ⓑ Ⓓ Ⓢ Ⓟ Ⓣ • ★★★ • www.brynheulog.com

■ **NEW QUAY**

Mrs V Kelly, Ty Hen Farm Cottages & Leisure Centre, Llwyndafydd, SA44 6BZ. ☎ (01545) 560346 • Map 145/360558 • BB **D** • EM book first £12.50, 7pm • D1 T1 • 3-10 • Ⓥ Ⓑ Ⓓ Ⓢ Ⓣ 🛏 • SC also • tyhen@ouvip.com

☆ Ralph Jewess, Brynarfor Hotel, New Road, SA45 9SB. ☎ (01545) 560358 • Map 145/393593 • BB **D** • EM £8.50-15, 7-8pm • S1 D2 T1 F3 • 3-10 • Ⓥ Ⓑ Ⓓ Ⓢ Ⓟ Ⓣ • ★★ • www.brynarfor.co.uk

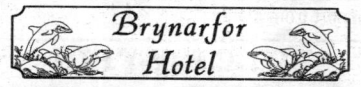
■ **PONTERWYD (Aberystwyth)**
CAMBRIAN WAY

☆ John & Jill Wall, The George Borrow Hotel, SY23 3AD. ☎ (01970) 890230 • Map 135/746805 • BB **D** • EM £5.25, 6.30-9.00pm • S2 D2 T3 F2 • 1-12 NX • Ⓥ Ⓑ Ⓓ Ⓟ 🛏 • ★★ • www.george-borrow.co.uk

■ **RHYDLEWIS**

Judith Russill, Rhydlewis House, SA44 5PE. ☎ (01239) 851748 • Map 145/347474 • BB **C** • EM book first £14, 7pm • D2 T1 • 1-12 NX • Ⓥ Ⓑ Ⓓ Ⓢ Ⓟ Ⓣ • ★★★★ • www.terradat.co.uk/rhydlewis

CONWY

■ **ABERGELE**

Paul & Jacqui James, Glan Llyn, Llanfair Road, LL22 8PD. ☎ (01745) 832742 • BB **B** • D1 T1 • 1-12 NX • Ⓓ Ⓟ Ⓣ 🛏 • www.glan-llyn.fsnet.co.uk

■ **BETWS-Y-COED**

☆ Mr & Mrs B Youe, Fairy Glen Hotel, LL24 0SH. ☎ (01690) 710269 • Map 115/798546 • BB **C** • EM book first £12.50, 7-7.30pm • S1 D3 T2 F2 • 2-10 • Ⓥ Ⓑ Ⓓ Ⓢ Ⓡ Ⓟ Ⓣ 🛏 • ★★

Graham & Jean Brayne, Glan Llugwy, LL24 0BN. ☎ (01690) 710592 • Map 115/784565 • BB **B** • S1 D2 T1 F1 • 1-12 NX • Ⓓ Ⓢ Ⓡ Ⓟ Ⓣ • ★★

☆ Deborah & Ian Baxter, The Ferns Non-Smokers Guest House, LL24 0AN. ☎ (01690) 710587 • Map 115/795562 • BB **C** • D6 T1 F2 • 1-12 • Ⓥ Ⓑ Ⓓ Ⓢ Ⓡ Ⓟ Ⓣ • ★★★★ • betws-y-coed.co.uk/accomodation/ferns/

The Ferns
Non-smokers' Guest House
HOLYHEAD ROAD
BETWS-Y-COED LL24 0AN
PHONE/FAX: 01690 710587

The Ferns is conveniently situated in the village of Betwys, all rooms en-suite, TV, beverage trays, clocks and hair dryers. *Ian and Deborah will make every effort to ensure that your stay is a comfortable one.*
WTB ★★★ Guest House

AA
QQQQ

Which?
recommended

☆ Marion Betteney, Bryn Afon, LL24 0BB. ☎ (01690) 710403 • Map 115/792566 • BB **C** • D5 T4 • 1-12 NX • Ⓑ Ⓓ Ⓢ Ⓡ Ⓟ Ⓣ • ★★★ • wbetteney@aol.com

Bryn Afon
Betws-y-Coed, Gwynedd
A comfortable, centrally situated guest house, with car park, by the river Llugwy.
Drying facilities. TV. Coffee/tea maker in all rooms, most ensuite.
Forest, mountain & lake walks at our doorstep.

Tel. 01690 710403   Fax 01690 710989
Email: wbetteney@aol.com

☆ Ray & Barbara Valadini, The Old Courthouse, Henllys, Old Church Rd, LL24 0AL. ☎ (01690) 710534 • Map 115/795568 • BB **D** • S1 D3 T3 F1 • 2-11 & XMAS • Ⓑ Ⓓ Ⓢ Ⓡ Ⓟ Ⓣ Ⓜ • ★★★ • Groups also • henllys@betws-y-coed.co.uk

SNOWDONIA
The Old Courthouse Hotel – Henllys
Unique • Elegant • Antique • Peaceful riverside garden setting • Spotless in suite rooms • Converted Victorian magistrates court.
Warm welcome • No smoking • No pets.
Tel/Fax 01690 710534

☆ Margaret Martin, Mairlys Guest House, Holyhead Road, LL24 0AN. ☎ (01690) 710190 • Map 115/795562 • BB **C** • S1 D3 T1 • 3-11 • Ⓑ Ⓓ Ⓢ Ⓡ Ⓣ • ★★★ •
www.betws-y-coed.co.uk/accomodation/mairlys

■ CAPEL CURIG (Betws-y-Coed)
☆ Ms Kristian & Ms Desborough , Bron Eryri Guest House, LL24 0EE. ☎ (01690) 720240 • Map 115/734573 • BB **C** • D2 T2 F1 • 1-12 • Ⓑ Ⓓ Ⓢ Ⓟ Ⓣ ⟁ • ★★ • Guided walks also •
betws-y-coed.co.uk/acc/Bron-Eryri

Mairlys Betws-y-Coed
Situated close to village centre. Ideal for walking or touring. Mairlys is a non-smoking establishment, full central heating, double rooms en-suite, twin and single rooms semi en-suite, colour TV, coffee/tea facilities in all bedrooms.
Telephone 01690 710190
www.betws-y-coed.co.uk/accommodation/mairlys

CAPEL CURIG
BRON ERYRI GUEST HOUSE
Snowdonia National Park
Spectacular mountain views.
En suite rooms with TV etc. Guest lounge – log fire.
Hearty breakfast, great hospitality. B&B from £21.
WTB Highly Commended. Non-smoking.

★★   **01690 720240**   ★★

Walking & art breaks by Jullie Desborough (MLC)
Tailor-made e.g. 50+, women only, small groups
www.betws-y-coed.co.uk/acc/Bron-Eryri/

Alison Cousins, Llugwy Guest House, LL24 0ES. ☎ (01690) 720218 • Map 115/719581 • BB **B** • S1 D2 T1 • 1-12 NX • Ⓓ Ⓢ Ⓟ Ⓣ • 1Cr/C

■ CONWY
CAMBRIAN WAY
Stan & Vivien Watson-Jones, Glan Heulog Guest House, Llanrwst Road, LL32 8LT. ☎ (01492) 593845 • Map 115/779772 • BB **B** • EM book first £9.50, 6.30pm • D2 T2 F2 • 1-12 • Ⓥ Ⓑ Ⓓ Ⓢ Ⓡ Ⓟ Ⓣ ⟁ • ★★ • glanheulog@no1guesthouse.freeserve.co.uk
☆ Bob & Liz Rubie, Llys Gwilym Guest House, 3 Mountain Road, Cadnant Park, LL32 8PU. ☎ (01492) 592351 • Map 115/775779 • BB **B** • S2 D2 T1 F2 • 1-12 NX • Ⓑ Ⓓ Ⓢ Ⓡ Ⓣ ⟁ • ★★ •
www.conwy-guesthouse.co.uk

Llys Gwilym
**Guest House
Mountain Road
Conwy**
Spoilt for walks? Try Conwy!
Conway Mountain, Sychnant Pass – Tal-y-Fan – The Carnedds. Perfect walking centre. All facilities. Small groups welcome. Special off season prices. Non-smoking - Pets welcome
Tel: 01492-592351 Bob or Liz
www.conwy-guesthouse.co.uk

Ever thought of taking a Ramblers Holiday?
Telephone 01707 331133 for a brochure

■ **LLANDUDNO**

☆ Mrs M Newberry, The Hotel Carmen, Carmen Sylva Rd, LL30 1LZ. ☎ (01492) 876361 • Map 115/783811 • BB **B** • EM book first £7.50-8, 6pm • S2 D11 T3 • 3-11+X • Ⓥ Ⓓ Ⓢ Ⓡ Ⓟ Ⓣ • ★★

■ **LLANFAIRFECHAN**

Mr & Mrs Colin Goodey, The Towers, Promenade, LL33 0DA. ☎ (01248) 680012 • Map 115/679753 • BB **C** • S3 D4 T2 F2 • 1-12 • Ⓑ Ⓓ Ⓢ Ⓡ Ⓟ Ⓣ 🏠 • SC & Studio Flat avail. for small grps 6-12.

■ **TREFRIW**

☆ Philip Booth, Argoed Guest House, LL27 0TX. ☎ (01492) 640091 • Map 115/780631 • BB **C** • EM book first £12.50, 7pm • S1 D2 T1 F1 • 1-12 NX • Ⓥ Ⓑ Ⓓ Ⓢ Ⓡ Ⓟ Ⓣ 🏠 Ⓜ • ★★★ • kath.argoed@btinternet.com

☆ Mike & Jan Bertenshaw, Crafnant Guest House, LL27 0JH. ☎ (01492) 640809 • Map 115/780631 • BB **B/C** • D3 T1 F1 • 2-11 • Ⓑ Ⓓ Ⓢ Ⓡ Ⓟ Ⓣ • ★★★ • www.trefriw.co.uk

GWYNEDD

■ **ABERDARON (Pwllheli)**

Vivien Bate, Bryn Mor, LL53 8BS. ☎ (01758) 760344 • Map 123/172265 • BB **B** • EM book first £10, 6pm • S1 D1 T1 F1 • 1-11 • Ⓥ Ⓓ Ⓢ Ⓟ Ⓣ

■ **ABERDYFI**
DYFI VALLEY WAY

Marion & Jim Billingham, Preswylfa, LL35 0LE. ☎ (01654) 767239 • Map 135/613962 • BB **D** • EM book first £16, 7-8.30pm • D2 T1 • 1-12 • Ⓥ Ⓑ Ⓓ Ⓢ Ⓡ Ⓟ Ⓣ • ★★★ • www.smoothhound.co.uk/hotels/preswylf.html

Shelia Mathias, Panteidal Nursery, LL35 0RG. ☎ (01654) 767322 • Map 135/661972 • BB **D/E** • EM £15-£20, 7-9pm • D2 T1 • 1-12 • Ⓥ Ⓑ Ⓓ Ⓢ Ⓟ Ⓣ 🏠 • www.panteidalorganics.co.uk

Mrs Jennifer Johnson, Awel Y Mor, 4 Bodfor Terrace, LL35 0EA. ☎ (01654) 767058 • Map 135/612959 • BB **B/C** • S1 D1 T2 F3 • 1-12 NX • Ⓑ Ⓓ Ⓢ Ⓡ Ⓟ Ⓣ 🏠 • ★★★ • website.lineone.net/~awelymor

■ **ABERGYNOLWYN (Tywyn)**

☆ Mr K Lycett, Dolgoch Falls Hotel, LL36 9UW. ☎ (01654) 782258 • Map 135/649046 • BB **D/E** • EM book first £15, 7pm • S1 D3 T2 • 3-12NX • Ⓥ Ⓑ Ⓓ Ⓢ Ⓡ Ⓟ Ⓣ 🏠 • ★★★ • dolgochfalls@tinyworld.co.uk

■ **ABERSOCH (Pwllheli)**

Mrs Chris Stanworth, Angorfa Guest House, Lon-Sarn-Bach, LL53 7EB. ☎ (01758) 712967 • Map 123/313279 • BB **C** • EM book first £12, from 6.30pm • D3 T2 F1 • 1-11 • Ⓥ Ⓑ Ⓓ Ⓢ Ⓟ Ⓣ • SC also

■ BALA

Mr & Mrs N S Jones, Frondderw, Stryd-y-fron, LL23 7YD. ☎ (01678) 520301 • Map 125/915368 • BB **C** • EM book first £13.50, 6.30pm • S1 D2 T2 F2 • 3-11 NX • Ⓥ Ⓑ Ⓓ Ⓢ • ◆◆◆ • also 2 stars • www.thefron.co.uk

☆ Mrs Lindsay Hind, Abercelyn, Llanycil, LL23 7YF. ☎ (01678) 521109 • Map 125/913352 • BB **C** • EM book first £13.50(only Oct-March), 7.30pm • D2 T1 F1 • 1-12 NX • Ⓥ Ⓑ Ⓓ Ⓢ Ⓟ Ⓣ • ★★★ • SC also • info@abercelyn.co.uk

BALA LAKE Southern Snowdonia

Former Rectory in own grounds, spacious bedrooms, log fires, home-produce cooking. Quiet walking in uncrowded mountain scenery away from popular routes. Guided walking. Visitors can be met by car. s/c garden cottage (sleeps 6) nearby.
Brochure Mrs Lindsay Hind, Abercelyn
Tel: 01678 521109 Fax 521109
Email: info@abercelyn.co.uk

■ BARMOUTH
CAMBRIAN WAY

Mrs D Lewis, The Gables, Mynach Rd, LL42 1RL. ☎ (01341) 280553 • Map 124/609166 • BB **B** • EM book first £12, 6.30-7.30pm • S1 D2 F1 • 2-11 • Ⓥ Ⓑ Ⓓ Ⓢ Ⓡ Ⓟ Ⓣ ♿ • ★★ • Guided walks also

■ BEDDGELERT (Caernarfon)
CAMBRIAN WAY

☆ Lynda Osmond, Plas Colwyn Guest House, LL55 4UY. ☎ (01766) 890458 • Map 115/589482 • BB **B/C** • EM book first £14 , 7.30-8.30pm • S1 D2 T1 F2 • 1-12 NX • Ⓥ Ⓑ Ⓓ Ⓢ Ⓟ Ⓣ ♿ • ★★★ • plascolwyn@hotmail.com

Plas Colwyn Guest House
Beddgelert

The ideal centre for exploring Snowdonia's beauty. Enjoy delicious home-cooked meals, including vegetarian, in our intimate licensed restaurant. All rooms H&C, some en-suite, with tea/coffee facilities. Private off-road parking.
Non-smoking throughout

Accommodation for the North section of the Cambrian Way
Lynda Osmond
☎ **01766 890458**

John & Rae Duffield, Gwesty Plas Tan-Y-Graig, LL55 4LT. ☎ (01766) 890310 • Map 115/587483 • BB **B/C** • EM book first £12.50, 7-8pm • D2 T2 F2 • 1-12 NX • Ⓥ Ⓑ Ⓓ Ⓢ Ⓟ Ⓣ • ay.b@virgin.net

Sygun Fawr Countryhouse, LL55 4NE. ☎ (01766) 890258 • Map 115/598485 • BB **D/E** • EM £16, 7-

8pm • D6 T2 F1 • 2-12 • Ⓥ Ⓑ Ⓓ Ⓢ Ⓟ Ⓣ ♿ • ★★★ • www.sygunfawr.co.uk

■ BLAENAU FFESTINIOG
CAMBRIAN WAY

Ann & Bob Cole, Bryn Elltyd, LL41 3TW. ☎ (01766) 831356 • Map 124/681448 • BB **B** • EM book first £8.50 inc. wine, 7.30pm • D1 T3 • 1-12 • Ⓥ Ⓑ Ⓓ Ⓢ Ⓡ Ⓟ Ⓣ ♿ Ⓜ • ★★ • SC and guided walks also • www.mtn.co.uk/bobcole

■ BRITHDIR (Dolgellau)

Mrs G D Evans, Y Goedlan, LL40 2RN. ☎ (01341) 423131 • Map 124/765184 • BB **B** • S1 D1 T1 F1 • 2-11 • Ⓓ Ⓢ Ⓣ • ★★★

■ CAERNARFON

☆ Tony & Liz Cox, The Menai Bank Hotel, North Road, LL55 1BD. ☎ (01286) 673297 • Map 114,115/482633 • BB **C/D** • EM £14.95, 7-9pm • S1 D8 T2 F5 • 1-12 • Ⓥ Ⓑ Ⓓ Ⓢ Ⓟ Ⓣ ♿ • ★★ • www.menaibankhotel.co.uk

SNOWDONIA
THE MENAI
BANK HOTEL
Tel: 01286 673297
North Road, Caernarfon,
Gwynedd LL55 1BD

Elegant Edwardian house with many period features. Magnificent views over the Menai Straits to Anglesey. Town centre and castle nearby. Close Snowdonia, Lleyn Peninsula and Anglesey. Delicious home cooking and well stocked bar. Warm welcome from proprietors Tony & Liz. Comfortably furnished rooms. Watch the magnificent sunset from our elegant lounge!

■ DOLGELLAU
CAMBRIAN WAY

Baron & Margaret Westwood, Esgair Wen Newydd, Garreg Feurig, Llanfachreth Road, LL40 2YA. ☎ (01341) 423952 • Map 124/736185 • BB **B** • EM book first £9, 7pm • D2 T1 • 3-11 • Ⓥ Ⓓ Ⓢ Ⓟ Ⓣ • ★★★ • Welcome host award

Mr & Mrs E P Rowlands, Tanyfron, Arran Road, LL40 2AA. ☎ (01341) 422638 • Map 124/735176 • BB **C** • D1 T1 F1 • 2-11 • Ⓑ Ⓓ Ⓢ Ⓣ • ★★★ • SC also.• Tanyfron@tesco.net

■ DOLGELLAU (continued)
CAMBRIAN WAY

☆ Mrs N Jones, Dwy Olwyn, Coed-y-Fronallt, LL40 2YG. ☎ (01341) 422822 • Map 124/734183 • BB **B/C** • EM £9, 7pm • D1 T2 F1 • 2-12 • V D S P T • ★★★ • Groups also

---

Mrs N. Jones

DWY OLWYN
DOLGELLAU, GWYNEDD
LL40 2YG

TEL. 01341 422822

A warm welcom awaits you in this comfortable guesthouse, set in an acre of landscaped gardens. Magnificent views of Cader Idris. Peaceful position yet only 10 minutes walk into town. Ideal base for touring, within Snowdonia National Park. Convenient for sandy beaches, narrow gauge railways, alternative technology centre, RSPB sanctuary, picturesque walks including famous Precipice Walk high above Mawddach estuary. Spacious bedrooms with colour TV, clock radio, hairdryer, tea/coffee facilities. Good home cooking. Lounge with good selection of maps, guide books and informative leaflets. Ample parking. Packed lunches if required. Cleanliness and personal attention assured. Brochure available.

WTB ★★★ Highly Commended

☆ J S & M Bamford, Ivy House, Finsbury Square, LL40 1RF. ☎ (01341) 422535 • Map 124/727177 • BB **B/C** • EM Menu, 6-8.00pm • D3 T2 F1 • 1-12 NX • V B D P T • ★★ • ivy.hse.dolgellau@ic24.net

---

IVY HOUSE
DOLGELLAU
WTB ★★

At the centre of an idyllic walking area, a country town guesthouse, offering good homemade food: big breakfasts, evening meals and packed lunches. Fully centrally heated and licenced, all bedrooms have TV hairdryers and tea/coffee making facilities, some en-suite.

Tel 01341 422535 Fax 01341 422689
ivy.hse.dolgellau@ic24.net

Ms Paddi Dunne, Penbryn Croft, Cader Road, LL40 1RN. ☎ (01341) 422815 • Map 124/725175 • BB **C** • EM book first £10, 6pm • D2 T4 • 1-12 • D S P T • paddi@penbryncroft.co.uk

R Gwyn Jones, Bryn Yr Odyn, LL40 1UG. ☎ (01341) 423470 • Map 124/720178 • BB **B** • D1 T2 • 1-12 • D S P T • ★★ • SC also Rgwynbrynyrodyn@aol.com

Mrs B Pick, Ar y Graig, Taicynhaeaf, LL40 2TU. ☎ (01341) 430242 • Map 124/690192 • BB **C** • F2 • 1-12 NX • B D S P T • ★★★ • ar-y-graig@talk21.com

■ DYFFRYN ARDUDWY

Val & Tom Bethell, Parc Yr Onnen, LL44 2DU. ☎ (01341) 247033 • Map 124/592242 • BB **B** • EM book first £10, 7pm • D1 T1 F1 • 1-12 NX • V B D S R P T • ★★★

■ FFESTINIOG
CAMBRIAN WAY

☆ Jenny Gardner, 'Hillcrest', Pant Llwyd, Bala Rd, LL41 4PW. ☎ (01766) 762787 • Map 124/707421 • BB **C** • EM £12.5, 7.30pm • S1 D1 T1 • 1-12 • V B D S P T • ★★★ • hillcrestjen@talk21.com

---

Hillcrest
Bed & Breakfast
Ffestiniog
A rural setting with a backdrop of mountains, centrally located in an area steeped in history and culture. Excellent accommodation with unrivalled panoramic views from all rooms. Landscaped garden, good food and a haven for relaxation, walking or sight-seeing, a warm welcome guaranteed.

Phone/Fax 01766 762787

■ HARLECH
CAMBRIAN WAY

Mrs J Jones, Tyddyn Gwynt, LL46 2TH. ☎ (01766) 780298 • Map 124/601302 • BB **B** • EM book first £10 • S1 D1 T1 F1 • 1-12 • V D R P T • ★★

Gweneth Evans, Glanygors, Llandanwg, LL46 2SD. ☎ (01341) 241410 • Map 124/570285 • BB **B** • EM book first £8, 6pm • D1 T1 F1 • 1-12 • V B D S R P T • ★★★

■ LLAN FFESTINIOG
CAMBRIAN WAY

Brian & Gwen Maddison, Morannedd, LL41 4LG. ☎ (01766) 762734 • Map 124/705423 • BB **B/C** • EM book first £10-£11, 7.30pm • S1 D2 T1 • 1-12 NX • V B D S P T • www.morannedd-guesthouse.co.uk

■ LLANABER (Barmouth)
CAMBRIAN WAY

Mrs P Thompson, Llwyndu Farmhouse, LL42 1RR. ☎ (01341) 280144 • Map 124/598195 • BB **D/E** • EM book first £16.95, 8pm • D4 T1 F2 • 1-12 NX • V B D S R P T • ★★★ • www.llwyndu-farmhouse.co.uk

---

■ **LLANBERIS (Caernarfon)**

Mount Pleasant Hotel, High Street, LL55 4HA.
☎ (01286) 870395 • Map 114,115/577602 • BB **B/C** •
EM £10, 6-9pm • S2 D2 T1 F2 • 1-12 • Ⓥ Ⓑ Ⓓ Ⓟ
Ⓣ 🛁 • ★ ★ Groups also mph@waterton.org.uk

Snowdon Cottage, Pentre Castell, LL55 4UB. ☎
(01286) 872015 • Map 115/585596 • BB **A/B** • EM
book first £14 • S1 D1 T1 • 1-12 • Ⓥ Ⓓ Ⓢ Ⓟ Ⓣ
• john.maggie@lineone.net

■ **LLANEGRYN (Tywyn)**

Anne & David Sylvester, Cefn Coch Country Guest
House, LL36 9SD. ☎ 01654 712193 • Map
124/596052 • BB **C** • EM £14, 7pm • D2 T3 • 2-11 •
Ⓥ Ⓑ Ⓓ Ⓢ Ⓟ Ⓣ 🛁 • ★★★★ •
www.cefncoch.force9.co.uk

■ **LLANFAIR (Harlech)**

☆ Ann Jones, Fron Deg, LL46 2RE. ☎ (01766) 780448
• Map 124/575295 • BB **B** • EM book first £9, 6-7.30pm
• S1 D1 T1 • 1-12 NX • Ⓥ Ⓑ Ⓓ Ⓡ Ⓟ Ⓣ 🛁

FRON DEG, LLANFAIR, HARLECH

18thC cottage above magnificent unspoilt beach.
Central for all Southern Snowdownia walks. Ensuite
available. Cottagey and comfortable with antique
furniture. Dinner by arrangement.

Tel. 017666 780448

■ **MAENTWROG (Blaenau Ffestiniog)**

Mrs E Jackson, Bron-y-Wern, LL41 4HN. ☎ (01766)
590210 • Map 124/665405 • BB **B** • S1 D1 T1 • 1-12
NX • Ⓓ Ⓢ Ⓟ Ⓣ

The Old Rectory Hotel, LL41 4HN. ☎ (01766)
590305 • Map 124/664404 • BB **C** • EM book first
£9.50-13.95, 6-7pm • D6 T2 F2 • 1-12 NX • Ⓥ Ⓑ
Ⓓ Ⓢ Ⓟ Ⓣ 🛁

■ **NANTGWYNANT (Caernarfon)**

Pen-y-Gwryd Hotel, Pen-y-Gwryd, LL55 4NT.
☎ (01286) 870211 + 870768 • Map 115/660558 • BB
C/D • EM book first £17, 7.30-8pm • S1 D8 T6 F1 • 1-
11 • Ⓥ Ⓑ Ⓓ Ⓢ Ⓟ 🛁 • ★★

■ **PANT GLAS (Gardolbenmaen)**

☆ Terry Gibbins, Hen Ysgol (Old School), Bwlch
Derwin, LL51 9EQ. ☎ (01286) 660701 • Map
123,115/456474 • BB **B** • EM book first £11, 7pm •
D1 T1 F1 • 1-12 • Ⓥ Ⓑ Ⓓ Ⓢ Ⓟ Ⓣ 🛁 • ★★Ⓦ •
www.portmadog.com/school.html

■ **PENRHYNDEUDRAETH (Porthmadog)**

☆ Hilary & Paul Davies, Talgarth, LL48 6DR. ☎ (01766)
770353 • Map 124/615398 • BB **B** • EM book first £8.50,
7pm • S3 D1 • 1-12 NX • Ⓥ Ⓓ Ⓢ Ⓡ Ⓟ

■ **TRAWSFYNYDD**
CAMBRIAN WAY

Mrs P A Osborne, Old Mill Farmhouse, Fron Oleu
Farm, LL41 4UN. ☎ (01766) 540397 • Map
124/710349 • BB **C** • EM book first £12, 7pm • D3 T2
F2 • 1-12 • Ⓥ Ⓑ Ⓓ Ⓢ Ⓟ Ⓣ 🛁 • ★★ •
penmar@oldmillfarm.spacomputers.com

■ **TYWYN**
CAMBRIAN WAY

Anne Lloyd-Jones, Hendy Farm, LL36 9RU.
☎ (01654) 710457 • Map 135/594013 • BB **C** • D2 T1
• 3-10 • Ⓑ Ⓓ Ⓢ Ⓡ Ⓟ Ⓣ 🛁 • ★★★ • SC also
jones@farmline.com

MONMOUTHSHIRE

■ **ABERGAVENNY**

Mr & Mrs B Cook, The Guest House & Mansel
Restaurant, 2 Oxford Street, NP7 5RP. ☎ (01873) 854823
• Map 161/303147 • BB **B** • EM £11.99, 5.30-8pm •
S3 D5 T5 F3 • 3-12NX • Ⓥ Ⓓ Ⓢ Ⓡ Ⓟ Ⓣ • ★★

Neil & Julia Herring, Park Guest House, 36 Hereford
Road, NP7 5RA. ☎ (01873) 853715 • Map
161/303146 • BB **B** • S1 D2 T2 F1 • 1-12 NX • Ⓓ Ⓡ
Ⓟ Ⓣ • ★★

☆ See Display Advertisement

Lynda Reardon Smith, Pentre House, Brecon Road, NP7 7EW. ☎ (01873) 853435 • Map 161/282150 • BB **B** • D2 T1 F1 • 1-12 NX • Ⓑ Ⓓ Ⓢ Ⓡ Ⓟ Ⓣ • ★★★ • Food nearby

■ **CHEPSTOW**
OFFA'S DYKE & WYE VALLEY WALK

Eileen Grassby, Lower Hardwick House, Hardwick Hill, NP16 5PT. ☎ (01291) 622162 • Map 172, 162/531935 • BB **B** • S2 D2 T2 F2 • 1-12 • Ⓑ Ⓓ Ⓡ Ⓣ 🛁 Ⓜ • Camping also

■ **LLANFIHANGEL CRUCORNEY (Abergavenny)**
OFFA'S DYKE

Ann Davies, Penyclawdd Farm, NP7 7LB. ☎ (01873) 890591 • Map 161/312200 • BB **B** • EM book first £10, 6.30-7pm • S/D/F2 • 1-12 • Ⓥ Ⓓ Ⓢ Ⓡ Ⓟ Ⓣ 🛁 • ★★★

■ **LLANGATTOCK-LINGOED (Abergavenny)**
OFFA'S DYKE

Karen Ball, The Old Rectory, NP7 8RR. ☎ (01873) 821326 • Map 161/362201 • BB **B** • EM book first £10, 6.30pm • S1 D2 T1 F1 • 1-12 • Ⓥ Ⓑ Ⓓ Ⓟ Ⓣ 🛁 • ★★ • Bunkhouse also

■ **MONMOUTH**
OFFA'S DYKE & WYE VALLEY WALK

☆ Church Farm Guest House, Mitchel Troy, NP5 4HZ. ☎ (01600) 712176 • Map 162/493104 • BB **C** • EM book first £13, 7-7.30pm • S1 D3 T2 F2 • 1-12 NX • Ⓥ Ⓑ Ⓓ Ⓢ Ⓟ Ⓣ 🛁 Ⓜ • ★★ • SC also. See also Walking Holidays section: Wysk Walks

---

CHURCH FARM GUEST HOUSE
Mitchel Troy, Monmouth

WTB ★★ Guest House   **AA** ♦♦♦

Set in large garden with stream, a 16th Century former farmhouse with oak beams and inglenook fireplaces. Excellent base for Wye Valley, Forest of Dean, Black Mountains. CH. Mainly en-suite bedrooms. Groups welcomed (discounts available). Also SC unit. Rosey and Derek Ringer.

Tel. 01600 712176
WYSK WALKS–See Walking Holidays section

Mrs Cantrell, Wye Avon, Dixton Road, NP25 3PR. ☎ (01600) 713322 • Map 162/512134 • BB **B** • S1 D1 T1 F1 • 1-12 NX • Ⓓ Ⓢ Ⓟ

The Riverside Hotel, Cinderhill Street, NP25 5EY. ☎ (01600) 715577/713236 • Map 162/504123 • BB **D/E** • EM £6-£14, 6.30-9.30pm • D6 T9 F2 • 1-12 • Ⓥ Ⓑ Ⓓ Ⓟ 🛁 • ★★ • No smoking restaurant

Yvonne Beale, Cherry Orchard Farm, Long Lane, Penallt , NP25 4AJ. ☎ (01600) 714447 • Map 162/526090 • BB **B** • EM book first £12, 7.30pm • D2 T1 • 1-12 NX • Ⓥ Ⓓ Ⓢ Ⓟ Ⓣ 🛁 • yvonne@janus.co.uk

■ **PANDY (Abergavenny)**
OFFA'S DYKE

Mrs Sandra Lyon, The Lancaster Arms, Old Hereford Road, NP7 8DW. ☎ (01873) 890699 • Map 161/334221 • BB **C** • EM £5, from 7pm • T2 • 1-12 • Ⓥ Ⓑ Ⓟ Ⓣ 🛁 • ★★ • free camping

■ **TINTERN (Chepstow)**
OFFA'S DYKE & WYE VALLEY WALK

Dereck & Vickie Stubbs, Parva Farmhouse Hotel, NP16 6SQ. ☎ (01291) 689411/689511 • Map 162/526009 • BB **E** • EM £19.50, 7-8.30pm • D3 T3 F3 • 1-12 • Ⓥ Ⓑ Ⓓ Ⓢ Ⓟ Ⓣ 🛁 • ★★★ • www.hoteltintern.co.uk

G T & M M Mark, Holmleigh, Monmouth Road, NP16 6SG. ☎ (01291) 689521 • Map 162/529008 • BB **B** • S1 D1 T1 • 1-12 • Ⓓ Ⓟ 🛁

NORTH EAST WALES

DENBIGHSHIRE, FLINTSHIRE & WREXHAM

■ **CAERWYS (Mold)**
OFFA'S DYKE

Mrs N Price, Plas Penucha, CH7 5BH. ☎ (01352) 720210 • Map 116/108733 • BB **C** • EM book first £11, 7pm • S4 D2 T2 • 1-12 • Ⓥ Ⓑ Ⓓ Ⓢ Ⓟ Ⓣ 🛁 • ★★★

■ **CORWEN (Denbighshire)**

Corwen Court Private Hotel, London Road, LL21 0DP. ☎ (01490) 412854 • Map 125/080434 • BB **B** • EM book first £9, 7pm • S6 D4 • 3-11 • Ⓥ Ⓑ Ⓓ Ⓟ 🛁

■ **DENBIGH**

Cayo Guest House, 74 Vale Street, LL16 3BW. ☎ (01745) 812686 • Map 116/055663 • BB **B** • EM book first £9, 6.30-7pm • S1 D2 T3 • 1-12 NX • Ⓥ Ⓑ Ⓢ Ⓟ Ⓣ 🛁 • ★★

The Bull Hotel, Hall Square , LL16 3NU. ☎ (01745) 812582 • Map 116/053660 • BB **B** • EM £3.50, 6.30-9pm • S2 D5 T5 F1 • 1-12 • Ⓥ Ⓑ Ⓟ Ⓣ

■ **LLANBEDR (Ruthin)**

Mrs Joyce O'Connor, The Clwyd Gate Hotel, Mold Road, LL15 1YF. ☎ 01824 704444 • Map 116/166581 • BB **D** • EM £5, 6-8.30pm • S7 D6 T4 F3 • 1-12 • Ⓥ Ⓑ Ⓓ Ⓟ Ⓣ 🛁 • 3Cr/HC • SC also

■ **LLANGOLLEN (Denbighshire)**
OFFA'S DYKE

☆ Mrs Eira Jeffreys, Hendy Isa, Horseshoe Pass Road, LL20 8DE. ☎ (01978) 861232 • Map 117/201444 • BB **B** • F4 • 1-12NX • Ⓑ Ⓢ Ⓟ Ⓜ • ★★★ • Food nearby members.aol.com/hendyisa/index.htm

Horseshoe Pass Road, Llangollen LL20 8DE
Distinctive country house set amongst beautiful scenery. Many varied prepared walks. Spacious bedrooms. Private parking. Website http://members.aol.com/hendyisa/index.htm lists fully updated information (68KB). Hosts keen walkers.

WTB 3 Stars ☎ (01978) 861232

Mrs B W Evans, The Grange, Grange Road, LL20 8AP. ☎ (01978) 860366 • Map 117/218413 • BB **C** • D2 T1 F2 • 1-12 NX • B D S P T • ★★★ • grange.llangollen@talk21.com

Mr D Roberts, Hillcrest Guest House, Hill Street, LL20 8EU. ☎ (01978) 860208 • Map 117/217418 • BB **C** • EM book first £12, 5.30-7.30pm • D3 T2 F2 • 1-12 • V B D S P T • ★★★ • david@hillcrest-llangollen.freeserve.co.uk

Robert Jaques, Bryn Derwen Hotel, Abbey Road, LL20 8EF. ☎ (01978) 860583 • Map 117/209431 • BB **C** • EM £10, 7-9pm • S4 D4 T6 F2 • 1-12 • V B D P T 🐕 • ★★ • Groups also robert@brynderwen.freeserve.co.uk

Mrs Anne Anderson, 'Plas Tegid', Abbey Road, LL20 8SP. ☎ (01978) 861013 • Map 117/212423 • BB **B** • S1 D1 T1 F1 • 1-12 NX • B D S P T 🐕 • ★★★

■ PRESTATYN (Denbighshire)
OFFA'S DYKE

Y Kubler, Roughsedge Guest House, 26-28 Marine Rd, LL19 7HD. ☎ (01745) 887359 • Map 116/066833 • BB **B** • EM book first £10.50, 7pm • S2 D4 T2 F2 • 1-12 NX • V B D S R P T • 2Cr/C • roughsedge@ykluber.fsnet.co.uk

■ RUTHIN (Denbighshire)

Mrs M Ranson, "Rhianfa", Ffordd Llanrhydd,, LL15 1PP. ☎ (01824) 702971 • Map 116/127581 • BB **C** • D2 T1 • 1-12 NX • B D S P T • 2Cr/HC

PEMBROKESHIRE

■ AMROTH (Narberth)
PEMBROKESHIRE COAST PATH & LANDSKER BORDERLANDS TRAIL

Roy & Edith Williamson, Ashdale Guest House, SA67 8NA. ☎ (01834) 813853 • Map 158/160071 • BB **B** • EM book first £7.50, 6pm • S1 D4 T3 F0 • 3-11 • V D S R P 🐕 • 2Cr

Beachhaven Guest House, Sea Front, SA67 8NG. ☎ (01834) 813310 • Map 158/165071 • BB **B** • EM £5, 6.30pm • S1 D1 T1 F1 • 1-12 NX • B D T 🐕 • ★★

■ BEGELLY (Tenby)
PEMBROKESHIRE COAST PATH

Margaret West, Manian Lodge Apart/Hotel, SA68 0XE. ☎ (01834) 813273 • Map 158/115079 • BB **B** • EM book first £9.99, 6.30-7.30pm • S2 D4 T1 F11 • 4-12 • B D S R P T 🐕 • ★★ • www.manianlodge.co.uk

■ BEREA (St David's)
PEMBROKESHIRE COAST PATH

Gill & Andrew Leese, Cwmwdig Water Guest House, SA62 6DW. ☎ (01348) 831434 • Map 157/805305 • BB **C/D** • EM book first £14, 7pm • S2 D3 T2 F3 • 1-12 NX • V B D S P T 🐕 • ★★★ • AndrewCwmwdig@aol.com

■ BOSHERSTON (Nr Pembroke)
PEMBROKESHIRE COAST PATH

Marcia & Lawrence Giardelli, Trefalen Farm, SA71 5DR. ☎ (01646) 661643 • Map 158/974939 • BB **B** • S3 D1 T2 F1 • 1-12 • D S P 🐕 • ★★⦾ • SC also, Groups also. trefalen@aol.com

■ BROAD HAVEN (Haverfordwest)
PEMBROKESHIRE COAST PATH

Mr & Mrs Main, Lion Rock, SA62 3JP. ☎ (01437) 781645 • Map 157/860143 • BB **C/D** • EM book first £15(NOT JUL/AUG), 7-9pm • S2 D2 T1 • 1-12 NX • V B D S P T 🐕 • ★★★

Mrs F Morgan, Anchor Guesthouse, Enfield Road, SA62 3JN. ☎ (01437) 781051 • Map 157/861138 • BB **B/C** • S1 D4 T2 F1 • 1-12 NX • B D P T 🐕 • 3Cr/HC • anch@bdhn.fsnet.co.uk

■ CASTLEMARTIN (Pembroke)
PEMBROKESHIRE COAST PATH

Mrs Ruth Smith, Chapel Farm, SA71 5HW. ☎ (01646) 661312 • Map 158/894989 • BB **C/D** • EM book first £10, 6.30pm • T1 F1 • 1-12 NX • V B D S P T • ★★★

■ DALE (Haverfordwest)
PEMBROKESHIRE COAST PATH

Elizabeth Webber, Allenbrook, SA62 3RN. ☎ (01646) 636254 • Map 157/811059 • BB **D** • S1 D1 T1 F1 • 1-11 NX • B D P T • ★★★★ • SC also • allenbrook@talk21.com

■ DINAS CROSS (Newport)
PEMBROKESHIRE COAST PATH

Len & Claire Urwin, Fron Isaf Farmhouse, SA42 0SW. ☎ (01348) 811339 • Map 157/018384 • BB **C** • EM book first £15 • T1 F1 • 4-10 NX • V D S P T 🐕 • ★★★ • Transport/Luggage transfer claire.len@cwcom.net

> **Even when you see 🐕 in an entry — ask first before bringing yours**

☆ See Display Advertisement

■ **DYFFRYN (Goodwick)**
PEMBROKESHIRE COAST PATH

Ivybridge, Drim Mill, SA64 0JT. ☎ (01348) 875366 • Map 157/943371 • BB **C** • EM book first £12.50, 6.30-8pm • S1 D3 T3 F4 • 1-12 NX • Ⓥ Ⓑ Ⓓ Ⓡ Ⓟ Ⓣ 🐾 • ★★ • www.ivybridge.cwc.net

■ **FISHGUARD**
PEMBROKESHIRE COAST PATH

Gillian Wheat, 55 West Street, SA65 9NG. ☎ (01348) 873592 • Map 157/955371 • BB **A** • EM book first £6, 7-8pm • D2 • 1-12 • Ⓥ Ⓓ Ⓡ Ⓟ Ⓣ

Abergwaun Hotel, Market Square, SA65 9HG. ☎ (01348) 872077 • Map 157/958370 • BB **D** • EM £10, 6-9pm • S3 D3 T2 F2 • 1-12 • Ⓥ Ⓑ Ⓓ Ⓡ Ⓟ Ⓣ 🐾 • ★★ • www.abergwaun.com

Mrs Kristiina Bjorkqvist, Cartref Hotel, 15-19 High Street, SA65 9AW. ☎ (01348) 872430 • Map 157/956369 • BB **D** • S4 D2 T2 F2 • 1-12 • Ⓑ Ⓓ Ⓡ Ⓟ Ⓣ 🐾 • ★★ • cartref@themail.co.uk

■ **FRESHWATER EAST (Pembroke)**

East Trewent Farm, SA71 5LR. ☎ (01646) 672127 • Map 158/007973 • BB **C** • S1 D2 T2 F1 • 1-12 • Ⓑ Ⓓ Ⓡ Ⓟ Ⓣ 🐾 • ◆◆

■ **GOODWICK (Fishguard)**
PEMBROKESHIRE COAST PATH

☆ Hope & Anchor Inn, SA64 0BP. ☎ (01348) 872314 • Map 157/945382 • BB **C** • EM £5, 7-9pm • S1 D1 T2 • 1-12 NX • Ⓥ Ⓑ Ⓓ Ⓡ Ⓟ Ⓣ 🐾 • 2Cr

---

HOPE & ANCHOR INN

GOODWICK, PEMBROKESHIRE SA64 0BP

Small friendly inn on Coastal Path overlooking Fishguard harbour. H&C, shaver points, tea-making facilities. Restaurant for snacks or evening dinner. Packed lunches. "Real ale". All rooms en-suite & TV's. WTB. B/B £21.00 p.p.

Tel. Terry or Mary McDonald
01348 872314

Bryntirion Guest House, Glanymor Road, SA64 0ER. ☎ (01348) 872189 • Map 157/940379 • BB **B** • S1 D1 T1 F1 • 1-12 NX • Ⓓ Ⓡ Ⓟ 🐾 • 2Cr

☆ Alastair T Hendrie, Stanley House, Quay Road, SA64 0BS. ☎ (01348) 873024 • Map 157/945383 • BB **B** • S1 D2 T2 F1 • 1-12 • Ⓑ Ⓓ Ⓢ Ⓡ Ⓣ • ◆◆◆

Maureen Miller, 2 Siriole, Quay Road, SA64 0BS. ☎ (01348) 872375 • Map 157/945383 • BB **B** • S1 D2 F3 • 1-12 • Ⓑ Ⓓ Ⓡ Ⓟ Ⓣ 🐾 • siriolequesthouse@hotmail.com

---

VEGETARIANS
Many establishments do a veggie breakfast even if they don't do an evening meal

---

Stanley House

Quay Road, Goodwick, Fishguard SA64 0BS

Guest house on coastal path (map ref 157/945383). Views of Fishguard Bay and the Preseli Hills convenient to shops, buses and trains. Backpack transfer arranged.

BB £16.50 Ensuite £19.50

Contact A T Hendrie 01348 873024
🦢🦢 Commended   *AA* ◆◆◆

■ **HAVERFORDWEST**
PEMBROKESHIRE COAST PATH

☆ Margaret Davies, Cuckoo Mill Farm, Pelcomb Bridge, SA62 6EA. ☎ (01437) 762139 • Map 157,158/933172 • BB **B/C** • EM £9-£11, 6-8.30pm • S1 D2 T1 F1 • 1-12 • Ⓥ Ⓑ Ⓓ Ⓢ Ⓡ Ⓟ Ⓣ 🐾 • ★★★

Cuckoo Mill Farm
Pelcomb Bridge
Haverfordwest   WTB ★★★

Mixed farm in central Pembrokeshire. Country walking. Six miles to coastal path. Meal times to suit guests. Excellent home cooking. Cosy farmhouse. Warm, well-appointed rooms. En-suite, TV, radio. Tea/coffee facilities.

Telephone 01437 762139

■ **LITTLE HAVEN (Haverfordwest)**
PEMBROKESHIRE COAST PATH

Whitegates, SA62 3LA. ☎ (01437) 781552 • Map 157/857129 • BB **C** • EM book first £16, 7pm • S1 D3 T1 F1 • 1-12 NX • Ⓥ Ⓑ Ⓓ 🐾 • ★★ • SC also

■ **MANORBIER (Tenby)**
PEMBROKESHIRE COAST PATH

Mrs Jill McHugh, The Old Vicarage, SA70 7TN. ☎ (01834) 871452 • Map 158/069979 • BB **C** • D1 T1 • 1-12 NX • Ⓑ Ⓓ Ⓢ Ⓡ Ⓟ Ⓣ • List • SC also oldvic@manorbier-tenby.fsnet.co.uk

Susan Robinson, Honeyhill, Warlows Meadow, SA70 7SX. ☎ (01834) 871906 • Map 158/064983 • BB **C** • EM book first £8, 7pm • D1 T1 • 1-12 NX • Ⓥ Ⓑ Ⓓ Ⓢ Ⓡ Ⓟ Ⓣ • ★★

■ **MARLOES (Haverfordwest)**
PEMBROKESHIRE COAST PATH

☆ Foxdale Guesthouse/Campsite, Glebe Lane, Marloes, SA62 3AY. ☎ (01646) 636243 • Map 157/795084 • BB **C** • D3 T1 • 3-11 • Ⓥ Ⓑ Ⓓ Ⓢ Ⓟ Ⓣ Ⓜ • ★★★ • foxdale.guest.house.8m.com

Foxdale
Guest House

Marloes   WTB ★★★

A friendly and warm welcome is extended to
all walkers. Spectacular scenery, varied land-
scapes, peace and tranquillity.
Ideal for Pembrokeshire Coast Path.
☎ 01646 636243
www.foxdale.guest.house.8m.com

Llysmeddyg Guest House
Newport
AN IDEAL WALKING/CYCLING HOLIDAY

Discover North Pembrokeshire, Preseli mountains
and Coast Path. Return to our Listed house with
large comfortable rooms, separate tables, log fires,
home cooking. Licensed. Packed lunches. Private
car park. Bike hire available.
Also self-catering flat. Brochure.

 Tel. 01239 820008 WTB ★★★
Grid Ref: SN059392

■ **MILFORD HAVEN**

Belhaven House Hotel, 29 Hamilton Terrace, SA73
3JJ. ☎ (01646) 695983 • Map 157,158/904058 • BB
B/C • EM £13.50, 6.30-9.30pm • S5 D2 F4 • 1-12 NX
• Ⓥ Ⓑ Ⓓ Ⓢ Ⓡ Ⓟ Ⓣ🐾 • ◆◆ •
www.westwaleshotels.com

■ **MOYLEGROVE (Cardigan)**
PEMBROKESHIRE COAST PATH

☆ Patricia & David Phillips, The Old Vicarage Country
Guest House, SA43 3BN. ☎ (01239) 881231 • Map
145/123446 • BB **C/D** • EM book first £16, 7pm • D2
T1 • 3-10 • Ⓥ Ⓑ Ⓓ Ⓢ Ⓟ Ⓣ • ★★★★ •
www.old-vic.co.uk

The Old Vicarage
Moylegrove
www.old-vic.co.uk

Idyllic haven in a walker's paradise

Relax in the timeless tranquility of Bluestone Country

Lifts to & from walks arranged

Imaginative cooking - licenced

No smoking   **01239 881231**   ★★★★
No children   stay@old-vic.co.uk   COUNTRY HOUSE

Mrs B Jones, Hillview, SA43 3BW. ☎ 01239 881219
• Map 145/113444 • BB **C** • EM book first £7.30, 7-
7.30pm • T1 • 1-12 • Ⓥ Ⓑ Ⓓ Ⓢ Ⓟ Ⓣ

Mrs Joy Bloss, 'Trewidwal', SA43 3BY. ☎ (01239)
881651 • Map 145/126452 • BB **B** • EM book first £8,
7pm • S1 D1 F1 • 1-11 • Ⓥ Ⓑ Ⓓ Ⓢ Ⓟ Ⓣ🐾 Ⓜ
• Alan.Bloss@btinternet.com

■ **NEWPORT**
PEMBROKESHIRE COAST PATH

Chris & Rosemary Joseph, Hafan Deg, Off Long
Street, SA42 0TN. ☎ (01239) 820301 • Map
145/057392 • BB **B/C** • S1 D1 T2 • 3-10 • Ⓑ Ⓓ Ⓢ
Ⓟ Ⓣ🐾 • ★★

☆ Ian & Penny Ross, Llysmeddyg Guest House, East
Street, SA42 0SY. ☎ (01239) 820008 • Map
145/059392 • BB **C** • EM book first £14.50, 7.45pm •
S1 D2 T2 F1 • 1-12 NX • Ⓥ Ⓑ Ⓓ Ⓢ Ⓟ Ⓣ •
★★★ • SC also • penny@ipross.freeserve.co.uk

Mr & Mrs N A Paul, Llys Dewi, Fishguard Road, SA42
0UF. ☎ (01239) 820177 • Map 157,145/039387 • BB
B • S1 D1 T1 F1 • 1-12 NX • Ⓑ Ⓓ Ⓢ Ⓟ Ⓣ🐾 •
2Cr • Transport available

Margaret Jean Dunham, Soar Hill, Cilgwyn Road,
SA42 0QG. ☎ (01239) 820506 • Map 145/065384 •
BB **B/C** • D1 T1 F1 • 1-12 • Ⓑ Ⓓ Ⓢ Ⓟ Ⓣ Ⓜ •
★★★ • sparhill@hotmail.com

■ **NEYLAND**
PEMBROKESHIRE COAST PATH

Julie & David Hawley, Y Ffynnon, 45 Honeyborough
Road, SA73 1RF. ☎ (01646) 601369 • Map
157/960061 • BB **B** • S1 D1 T1 • 1-12 NX • Ⓓ Ⓢ Ⓡ
Ⓟ Ⓣ • ★

■ **NOLTON HAVEN (Haverfordwest)**
PEMBROKESHIRE COAST PATH

Jim Canton, Nolton Haven Farm, SA62 7NH.
☎ (01437) 710263 • Map 157/860187 • BB **B** • S1
D2 T1 F3 • 1-12 NX • Ⓑ Ⓓ Ⓟ Ⓣ🐾 • ★ •
www.noltonhaven.com

■ **PEMBROKE**
PEMBROKESHIRE COAST PATH

The Barnikel Family, High Noon Guest House, Lower
Lamphey Road, SA71 4AB. ☎ (01646) 683736 • Map
157,158/990011 • BB **B/C** • EM book first £10.95, 7-
7.30pm • S3 D3 T1 F2 • 1-12 NX • Ⓥ Ⓑ Ⓓ Ⓢ Ⓡ
Ⓟ Ⓣ🐾 • ★★ • Groups also • www.highnoon.co.uk

Mrs Nannette Pearce, Merton Place House, 3 East
Back, SA71 4HL. ☎ (01646) 684796 • Map
157,158/986014 • BB **B** • S1 D2 T2 • 1-12 NX • Ⓓ
Ⓢ Ⓡ Ⓣ • ★★

■ **PUNCHESTON (Haverfordwest)**

Betty Devonald, Penygraig Farmhouse, SA62 5RJ.
☎ (01348) 881277 • Map 157,158,145/007297 • BB
B/C • D1 F1 • 4-10 • Ⓑ Ⓓ Ⓢ Ⓟ Ⓣ🐾 • ★★★ •
daviddevonald@farming.co.uk

☆ See Display Advertisement

B&B ACCOMMODATION   WALES   PEMBROKESHIRE

■ ST DAVID'S
PEMBROKESHIRE COAST PATH

☆ Mac & Sandra Thompson, Ramsey House, Lower Moor, SA62 6RP. ☎ (01437) 720321 • Map 157/747250 • BB **D/E** • EM £15–£16, 7pm • D4 T3 • 1-12 NX • Ⓥ Ⓑ Ⓓ Ⓢ Ⓟ Ⓣ 🐾 • ★★★★ • www.smoothhound.co.uk/hotels/ramsey.html

ST. DAVID'S
WTB ★★★★   AA/RAC ◆◆◆◆

Half mile from Pembrokeshire Coast Path

Superior non-smoking licensed guest
house catering exclusively for adults.
Ideally situated for daily walks on
Pembrokeshire Coast Path.
All rooms en-suite
Award-winning Welsh speciality menus
Dogs welcome   Private Parking
Dinner, bed & breakfast from £44–£48 p.p.p.n.
For Brochure call 01437 720321
ramseyho.stdavids@btinternet.com

☆ Mrs M Jones, Lochmeyler Farm Guest House, Llandeloy, Pen-y-Cwm, SA62 6LL. ☎ (01348) 837724 • Map 157/855275 • BB **C** • EM book first £12.50, 7pm • S2 D6 T6 F2 • 1-12 • Ⓥ Ⓑ Ⓓ Ⓢ Ⓟ Ⓣ 🐾 • ★★★★ • Groups also www.lochmeyler.co.uk

WTB ★★★★ Farm   AA/RAC ◆◆◆◆◆

GUEST HOUSE

16 en-suite non-smoking luxury bedrooms, TV and
refreshment facilities. Centre St David's peninsula.
Ideal for exploring Pembrokeshire Coastal Path and
countryside. B&B £20–£25pppn. Optional dinner
£12.50. Groups welcome. Colour brochure.
Tel: 01348 837724   Fax: 01348 837622
www.lochmeyler.co.uk

Rob & Gloria Pugh, Alandale Guest House, 43 Nun Street, SA62 6NU. ☎ (01437) 720404 • Map 157/754256 • BB **C** • S1 D3 T1 • 1-12 NX • Ⓑ Ⓓ Ⓢ Ⓟ Ⓣ • alandale@tinyworld.co.uk

■ ST ISHMAEL'S (Haverfordwest)
PEMBROKESHIRE COAST PATH

Mrs M Williams, Skerryback Farmhouse, Sandy Haven, SA62 3DN. ☎ (01646) 636598 • Map 157/852074 • BB **C** • EM book first £15 • D1 T1 F1 • 1-12 NX • Ⓥ Ⓑ Ⓓ Ⓢ Ⓣ • ★★★★ • www.pfh.co.uk/skerryback

■ TENBY
PEMBROKESHIRE COAST PATH

Sandra Milward, West Wales Walking, Glenholme Guest House, Picton Terrace, SA70 7DR. ☎ (01834) 843909 • Map 158/133001 • BB **B** • EM £12, 6pm • S1 D3 T1 F3 • 1-12 NX • Ⓥ Ⓑ Ⓓ Ⓢ Ⓡ Ⓟ Ⓣ 🐾 Ⓜ • ★★

Shirley Aston, Sunny Bank, Harding Street, SA70 7LL. ☎ (01834) 844034 • Map 158/131005 • BB **C** • EM book first £10, 6-6.30pm • D2 T1 F2 • 1-12 NX • Ⓥ Ⓑ Ⓢ Ⓡ Ⓣ • ★★★★ • www.sunny-bank.co.uk

Karen & Jeff Lapham, Glenthorne Guest House, 9 Deer Park, SA70 7LE. ☎ (01834) 842300 • Map 158/131005 • BB **B** • EM book first £9, 6pm • S1 D5 T1 F2 • 2-11 • Ⓥ Ⓑ Ⓓ Ⓢ Ⓡ Ⓟ Ⓣ 🐾 • ★★

■ TREFIN/TREVINE (St Davids, Haverfordwest)
PEMBROKESHIRE COAST PATH

Jill & Robin Moore, Awel-Mor Guest House, Pen Parc, SA62 5AG. ☎ (01348) 837865 • Map 157/845312 • BB **C/D** • EM book first £15, 6.30pm • D2 T1 • 3-10 • Ⓥ Ⓑ Ⓓ Ⓢ Ⓟ Ⓣ • ★★★★ • robin.jill@awel-mor.freeserve.co.uk

Anthony & Judith Johnson, Bryngarw, Abercastle Rd, SA62 5AR. ☎ (01348) 831211 • Map 157/842325 • BB **C/D** • EM book first £15, 7pm • D3 T2 F1 • 1-12 NX • Ⓥ Ⓑ Ⓓ Ⓢ Ⓟ Ⓣ 🐾 • ★★★★ • a.r.johnson@dial.pipex.com

Lynne Brodie, The Old Court House Vegetarian Guest House, SA62 5AX. ☎ (01348) 837095 • Map 157/838325 • BB **C** • EM book first £14.50, 7.30pm • D2 T1 • 1-12 • Ⓥ Ⓑ Ⓓ Ⓢ Ⓟ Ⓣ 🐾 • ★★★ • www.pembrokeshire-online.co.uk/courthouse

POWYS

■ ABERHAFESP (Newtown)
SEVERN WAY

Dave & Sue Jones, Dyffryn Farm Holidays, SY16 3JD. ☎ (01686) 688817 • Map 136/052954 • BB **D** • D1 T1 • 1-12 NX • Ⓑ Ⓓ Ⓟ Ⓣ • ★★★★ • www.daveandsue.clara.net

■ BOUGHROOD (Brecon)
WYE VALLEY WALK

M Brown, Balangia, Station Road, LD3 0YF. ☎ (01874) 754453 • Map 161/129387 • BB **B** • S1 D1 T1 • 4-10 • Ⓓ Ⓢ Ⓟ Ⓣ 🐾 • Food nearby

■ **BRECON**
TAFF TRAIL

☆ Mrs M Meredith, Lodge Farm, Talgarth, LD3 0DP.
☎ (01874) 711244 • Map 161/173344 • BB **C** • EM
book first £13, 7pm • S1 D1 T1 F1 • 1-12 NX • Ⓥ Ⓑ
Ⓓ Ⓢ Ⓣ 🚲 • ★★★ •
marionlodgefarm@hotmail.com

LODGE FARM
Talgarth, Brecon

Welcome to our 17th century farm house situated
in the Brecon Beacons National Park, well placed
for walking the Black Mountains and Brecon
Beacons. En suite bedrooms, tea-making facilities.
Good, freshly prepared food including vegetarian.
Non-smoking. FHB Members.

WTB ★★★

Tel 01874 711244

Mr & Mrs G Richards, Flag & Castle Guest House, 11
Orchard Street, LD3 8AN. ☎ (01874) 625860 • Map
160/040285 • BB **C** • S0 D1 T2 F0 • 1-12 • Ⓑ Ⓢ Ⓟ
• 3Cr/C

☆ The Beacons, 16 Bridge Street, LD3 8AH.
☎ (01874) 623339 • Map 160/042285 • BB **B/C/D** •
EM £9.95-£17.85, 6.30-9pm • S1 D4 T3 F6 • 1-12 NX
• Ⓥ Ⓑ Ⓢ Ⓟ Ⓣ 🚲 • ★★★ • Groups also.
www.beacons.brecon.co.uk

The Beacons, Brecon
Accommodation and Restaurant

Recently restored listed Georgian townhouse
offering standard, en-suite & luxury rooms all
beautifully appointed to suit all pockets.
Candlelit restaurant offering fine food & wines
(5 nights). Cosy cellar bar, elegant lounge,
private parking and bike store.

RAC
♦♦♦ **Tel/Fax 01874 623339** ♦♦♦ AA

beacons@brecon.co.uk   www.beacons.brecon.co.uk

☆ Mr & Mrs Smith, The Grange , The Watton, LD3
8ED. ☎ (01874) 624038 • Map 160/047283 • BB **B/C**
• D3 T1 F4 • 1-12 NX • Ⓑ Ⓓ Ⓢ 🚲

THE GRANGE GUEST HOUSE
Brecon

Detached Georgian guest house, standing in its
own grounds. We offer a totally non-smoking
establishment. All attractively decorated bedrooms
have colour TV and tea-making facilities. En suite
bedrooms available. Vegetarians catered for.
Private car park and gardens.
Safe garaging for cycles.
Margaret & Bob Smith
Telephone 01874 624038

☆ Mrs K E M Evans, Upper Cantref Farm, Cantref,
LD3 8LR. ☎ (01874) 665223 • Map 160/057258 • BB
B/C • D1 F1 • 4-11 • Ⓑ Ⓓ Ⓢ Ⓣ • 2Cr/C • SC also
• www.btinternet.com/~cantref/breconbeacons

BRECON BEACONS

Family run farmhouse
accommodation with
excellent views and within
walking distance of the
main peaks of the Brecon
Beacons. Comfortable
spacious bedrooms in a large traditional farmhouse.
Wholesome food. Set in a quiet rural location on a
working sheep and pony farm with on site riding. Ideal
centre for walking, biking etc.   **Tel/Fax 01874 665223**
Upper Cantref Farm, Cantref, Brecon LD3 8LR
www.btinternet.com/~cantref/breconbeacons

☆ The Old Mill, Felinfach, LD3 0UB. ☎ (01874)
625385 • Map 161/091332 • BB **B/C** • D1 T2 • 2-11 •
Ⓑ Ⓓ Ⓢ Ⓟ Ⓣ • ★★★Ⓦ • Food nearby

THE OLD MILL
FELINFACH, BRECON, POWYS

A 16th century converted corn mill, peacefully
situated in its own grounds. Inglenook fireplace,
exposed beams, TV lounge, beverage trays.
Ideally situated for walks and touring the Brecon
Beacons National Park and Black Mountains or
just relaxing. Local inn within walking distance.
Packed lunches by arrangement.
A friendly welcome awaits you.

Tel. 01874 625385

Mrs Marie Gray, Shiwa Lodge, Llangorse, LD3 7UG.
☎ (01874) 658631/712188 • Map 161/135275 • BB
C • S1 D1 T1 F1 • 1-12 NX • Ⓑ Ⓓ Ⓢ Ⓟ Ⓣ

☆ Mr & Mrs G Venner, 'Cherrypicker', 9 Orchard
Street, LD3 8AN. ☎ (01874) 624665 • Map
160/041285 • BB **B** • EM book first £7.50 • D2 T1 • 1-
12 NX • Ⓑ Ⓓ Ⓢ Ⓟ Ⓣ 🚲 •
www.cherrypickerhouse.co.uk

Cherrypicker House
Brecon

This war, and friendly Georgian town
house maintains many of its original
features yet is tastefully modernised to
include modern day ensuite comforts.
Ideally situated for exploring the National
Park and the old town of Brecon.
01874 624665
www.cherrypickerhouse.co.uk

VEGETARIANS
Many establishments do a veggie breakfast even if
they don't do an evening meal

☆ See Display Advertisement

B&B ACCOMMODATION WALES POWYS

■ BUILTH WELLS
WYE VALLEY WALK

☆ Biddy Williams, Dol-Llyn-Wydd Farm, LD2 3RZ.
☎ (01982) 553660 • Map 147/042488 • BB **B** • EM
book first £10, 7.30-8.30pm • S2 D1 T2 • 2-12 NX •
Ⓥ Ⓑ Ⓓ Ⓢ Ⓡ Ⓟ • ★★

DOL-LLYN WYDD FARM
BUILTH WELLS   WTB ♨♨

17th C farmhouse lying beneath the Eppynt Hills
• Superb area for walking-touring-birdwatching.
• Easy distance of Elan Valley, Brecon Beacons,
Black Mountains • Good home cooking,
comfortable rooms • One mile from Builth Wells
on B4520 signed Upper Chapel, first left down
quiet farm lane — 200 yards, house on left.

Tel. Mrs Williams 01982 553660

Mrs Joyce Shaw, Sunnybank, Newry Road, LD2 3LZ.
☎ (01982) 553814 • Map 147/046499 • BB **B/C** • EM
book first £10, 6.30-7pm • D2 F/T1 • 1-12 NX • Ⓥ
Ⓑ Ⓓ Ⓢ Ⓡ Ⓟ Ⓣ

Woodlands Guest House, Hay Road, LD2 3YL.
☎ (01982) 552354 • Map 147/045511 • BB **B/C** • T6 •
1-12 • Ⓑ Ⓓ Ⓢ Ⓟ Ⓣ • ◆◆◆◆ • heskethn@aol.com
Ros & Martin Wiltshire, Bron Wye, 5 Church St, LD2
3BS. ☎ (01982) 553587 • Map 147/039512 • BB **B** •
S1 D2 T1 F1 • 1-12 • Ⓑ Ⓓ Ⓢ Ⓡ Ⓟ Ⓣ 🐾 • ★★
Vic Morris, The Cedars, Hay Road, LD2 3BP. ☎
(01982) 553356 • Map 147/046511 • BB **C** • S2 D1
T3 F1 • 1-12 • Ⓥ Ⓑ Ⓓ Ⓡ Ⓟ Ⓣ 🐾 • ★★ •
www.cedars.ltd.co

■ BUTTINGTON (Welshpool)
GLYNDWR'S WAY & OFFA'S DYKE

M Broxton, 1 Plas Cefn Holding, Heldre Lane, SY21
8SX. ☎ (01938) 570225 • Map 126/266092 • BB **B** •
EM book first £6 upwards, 6-7pm • S1 D1 F1 • 1-12
NX • Ⓥ Ⓓ Ⓢ Ⓟ Ⓜ

■ CAPEL-Y-FFIN (Abergavenny, Monmouthshire)
CAMBRIAN WAY & OFFA'S DYKE

Griffiths Family, The Grange, NP7 7NP. ☎ (01873)
890215/157 • Map 161/251315 • BB **C** • EM book
first £12, 7.45pm • S1 D1 T2 F2 • 3-11 • Ⓥ Ⓑ Ⓓ
Ⓟ Ⓣ 🐾 • ★ • Camping also

■ DISCOED (Presteigne)
OFFA'S DYKE

Mrs Anne Owens, Gumma Farm, LD8 2NP.
☎ (01547) 560243 • Map 137, 148/288651 • BB **C** •
EM book first £12.50, 7-8pm • S1 D1 T1 • 4-11 • Ⓥ
Ⓑ Ⓓ Ⓟ Ⓣ 🐾 Ⓜ • ★★★

■ DYLIFE (Nr Staylittle, Llanbrynmair)
GLYNDWR'S WAY & CAMBRIAN WAY

☆ Star Inn , SY19 7BW. ☎ (01650) 521345 • Map
135/863940 • BB **B** • EM £5.95, 7pm • S2 D2 T2 F1 •
1-12 • Ⓥ Ⓑ Ⓓ Ⓟ 🐾

The Star Inn
Set in breathtaking countryside, superb food,
Real Ales, residents lounge, colour TV, H&C,
showers/bath. Full central heating, excellent
ambience, own tea and coffee making facilities, a warm and friendly welcome guaranteed.

AA QQ recommended.
Tel: 01650 521345

■ ERWOOD (Builth Wells)
WYE VALLEY WALK

Alistair Legge, Trericket Mill, LD2 3TQ. ☎ (01982)
560312 • Map 148, 161/112414 • BB **C** • EM book
first £5-£12.50 veg. only, 7-8pm • S1 D2 T1 F2 • 1-
12 NX • Ⓥ Ⓑ Ⓓ Ⓢ Ⓟ Ⓣ Ⓜ • 2Cr/C🌐 •
Bunkhouse & camping • www.trericket.co.uk
☆ David & Aly Beavins, Gromaine Cottage, LD2 3SZ.
☎ (01982) 560360 • Map 161,148/107423 • BB **B/C** •
EM book first £10, 7-8pm • S1 D1 T1 F1 • 1-12 • Ⓥ
Ⓑ Ⓓ Ⓢ Ⓟ Ⓣ 🐾 Ⓜ • B&B@beavins.fsnet.co.uk

B&B on the Wye Valley Way
Gromaine Cottage, Erwood, Builth Wells
We're in easy reach of the Brecon Beacons
Pets Welcome. Muddy boots/mountain bikes? There's
storage with drying facilities.
Ensuite rooms, comfortable and warm with tea and
coffee. Great home cooking.

Telephone Dave Beavins 01982 560360

Off season offers available!

■ FOEL, LLANGADFAN (Welshpool)
GLYNDWR'S WAY

Mandy Jones, Dyffryn, SY21 0NR. ☎ (01938)
820214 • Map 125/992114 • BB **B** • EM £5-£9 • D2 T1
• 1-12 NX • Ⓥ Ⓓ Ⓢ Ⓟ Ⓣ • Transport available

■ GLADESTRY (Powys)
OFFA'S DYKE

☆ Mrs M Hughes, Stonehouse Farm, HR5 3NU.
☎ (01544) 370651 • Map 148/236546 • BB **B** • EM
book first £6, 7pm • S1 D1 T1 • 1-12 NX • Ⓥ Ⓓ Ⓢ
Ⓟ Ⓣ 🐾

■ GUILSFIELD (Welshpool)
GLYNDWR'S WAY

Eve Pearce, Vine House, Oak Lane, SY21 9NH.
☎ 01938 554431 • Map 126/217116 • BB **B** • S1 D1
T1 F1 • 1-12 NX • Ⓑ Ⓓ Ⓢ Ⓟ Ⓣ • ★★★ • Transport
available • www.geocities.com/vinehouse2000

■ HAY-ON-WYE
OFFA'S DYKE & WYE VALLEY WALK

Linda Webb, The Old Post Office, Llanigon, HR3 5QA. ☎ (01497) 820008 • Map 161,148/213401 • BB **B/E** • D2 T1 • 1-12 • Ⓥ Ⓑ Ⓓ Ⓢ Ⓣ 🕭 • ★★★ • Veg. breakfast only hay-on-wye.co.uk/oldpost

John Evans, Tinto House, Broad Street, HR3 5DB. ☎ (01497) 820590 • Map 161,148/228423 • BB **C** • D2 T1 F1 • 1-12 NX • Ⓑ Ⓓ Ⓢ Ⓟ Ⓣ 🕭 • ★★★ • www.hay-on-wye.co.uk/tinto

Winnifred Hughes, Fernleigh, Hardwick Road, Cusop, HR3 5QX. ☎ (01497) 820459 • Map 161,148/235422 • BB **B** • EM £16.00 • D2 T1 • 3-10 • Ⓑ Ⓓ Ⓢ Ⓟ Ⓜ

Bob and Annabel Crook, La Fosse Guest House, Oxford Road, HR3 5AJ. ☎ (01497) 820613 • Map 161,142423 • BB **C** • D4 T1 • 1-12 NX • Ⓑ Ⓓ Ⓢ 🕭 • 2Cr

Jon Field, The Bear, Bear Street, HR3 5AN. ☎ 01497 821302 • Map 161,148/230424 • BB **C/D** • D2 T1 • 1-12 • Ⓥ Ⓑ Ⓓ Ⓢ Ⓟ Ⓣ 🕭 • Meals for groups • jon@thebear-hay-on-wye.co.uk

Brookfield Guest House, Brook Street, HR3 5BQ. ☎ 01497 820518 • Map 161,148/230425 • BB **B/C** • D3 T3 F2 • 1-12 • Ⓑ Ⓓ Ⓢ Ⓟ Ⓣ • www.brookfield-guesthouse.btinternet.co.uk

■ HEOL SENNI (Brecon)

Mrs M J Mayo, Maeswalter Farm, LD3 8SU. ☎ (01874) 636629 • Map 160/931236 • BB **C** • EM book first £10.50, 6.30-7pm • D3 T1 F1 • 1-12 • Ⓥ Ⓑ Ⓓ Ⓢ Ⓟ Ⓣ 🕭 • ◆◆◆ • maeswalter@talk21.com

THREE WELLS FARM
Chapel Road, Howey
Llandrindod Wells
Tel. 01597 824427 Fax. 822484

A country farm in idyllic setting. Ideally situated for rambling and touring the hear of Wales. En-suite rooms with TV, hospitality tray and telephone. Central heating. Drying room. B&B £19–£28 Oct–Apr.
GROUP BOOKINGS WELCOME

STONEHOUSE FARM
GLADESTRY, KINGTON, HEREFORDSHIRE
Listed building situated on Offa's Dyke Footpath

Ideal for touring mid-Wales. Perfect for ramblers. B&B, dinner by arrangement, vegetarian cooking on request. Packed lunches. Home produced food. Friendly atmosphere. H&C and tea/coffee facilities in bedrooms. Razor points. Sitting room, TV. Children and pets welcome.

Tel Gladestry (01544) 370651

■ HOWEY (Llandrindod Wells)

☆ MR & Mrs Keith Roobottom, Three Wells Country Hotel, Chapel Road, LD1 5PB. ☎ (01597) 824427 • Map 147/067586 • BB **B/C** • EM book first £10.50, 7pm • S1 D10 T5 • 1-12 • Ⓥ Ⓑ Ⓓ Ⓢ Ⓡ Ⓟ Ⓣ 🕭 • 4Cr/HC • k.roobottom@which.net

■ KNIGHTON
GLYNDWR'S WAY & OFFA'S DYKE

Mrs Dana Simmons, The Fleece House, Market Street, LD7 1BB. ☎ (01547) 520168 • Map 148,137/284723 • BB **C/D** • T6 • 1-12 • Ⓑ Ⓓ Ⓢ Ⓡ Ⓟ Ⓣ Ⓜ • ★★★ • Guided walks also

Milebrook House Hotel, LD7 1LT. ☎ (01547) 528632 • Map 148/315727 • BB **D** • EM £18.50, from 7pm • S2 D6 T4 F1 • 1-12 • Ⓥ Ⓑ Ⓓ Ⓢ Ⓡ Ⓟ Ⓣ • ★★★

☆ Sue Ashe, Offa's Dyke House, 4 High Street, LD7 1AT. ☎ 01547 528634/0780 8090549 • Map 148,137/285725 • BB **B** • EM book first £8 • S1 D3 T2 • 1-12 NX • Ⓥ Ⓓ Ⓢ Ⓡ Ⓟ Ⓣ 🕭 • ★★ • Groups also

■ LLANANNO (Llandrindod Wells)
GLYNDWR'S WAY

R & D Taylor, Bwlch Farm, Glyndwrs Way, LD1 6TT. ☎ (01597) 840366 • Map 147,136/085747 • BB **C** • EM book first £15, 7.30pm • D2 T1 • 4-10 • Ⓥ Ⓑ Ⓓ Ⓢ Ⓟ Ⓣ 🕭 • ★★★ • SC also. taylor@bwlch-farm.fsnet.co.uk

■ LLANBADARN FYNYDD (Llandrindod Wells)
GLYNDWR'S WAY

Mr W T & Mrs B Ainsworth, Hillside Lodge Guest House, LD1 6TU. ☎ (01597) 840364 • Map 136/085764 • BB **C** • EM book first £10 • T1 F2 • 1-12 • Ⓥ Ⓑ Ⓓ Ⓢ Ⓟ Ⓣ 🕭 • ★★★ • SC also

■ LLANDRINDOD WELLS

B W J Griffiths, Ty-Clyd Guest House, 4 Park Terrace, LD1 6AY. ☎ (01597) 822122 • Map 147/057609 • BB **B** • EM book first £8.50, Up to 9pm • S1 D2 T4 • 1-12 NX • Ⓥ Ⓓ Ⓢ Ⓡ Ⓟ Ⓣ • 1Cr/C • author@tydyd.demon.co.uk

☆ See Display Advertisement

☆ Llanerch 16th Century Inn, LD1 6BG. ☎ (01597) 822086 • Map 147/058613 • BB **D** • EM £5-£10, 6-9pm • S2 D6 T3 F2 • 1-12 NX • Ⓥ Ⓑ Ⓓ Ⓢ Ⓡ Ⓟ Ⓣ 🐾 • ★★ • Groups also llanerchinn@ic24.net

☆ Mrs C Nixon, Brynhir Farm, Chapel Road, Howey, LD1 5PB. ☎ (01597) 822425 • Map 147/067586 • BB **C** • EM book first £10, 7pm • S2 D2 T4 F1 • 1-12 • Ⓥ Ⓑ Ⓓ Ⓢ Ⓡ Ⓟ Ⓣ 🐾 • ★★★★

Mrs B J Jones, Rhydithon, Dyffryn Road, LD1 6AN. ☎ (01597) 822624 • Map 147/058613 • BB **B** • EM book first £8.50, 6-8pm • S1 D1 T1 • 1-12 NX • Ⓥ Ⓑ Ⓓ Ⓢ Ⓡ Ⓟ Ⓣ 🐾 • ★★

☆ Mrs Ruth Jones, Holly Farm, Howey, LD1 5PP. ☎ (01597) 822402 • Map 147/049589 • BB **C** • EM book first £10, 7pm • D2 T2 F1 • 1-12 • Ⓥ Ⓑ Ⓓ Ⓢ Ⓡ Ⓟ Ⓣ • ★★★

■ LLANGURIG (Llanidloes)
Margaret Hartey, The Old Vicarage, SY18 6RN. ☎ (01686) 440280 • Map 147/912799 • BB **B/C** • EM £11, 7pm • D2 T2 • 1-12 NX • Ⓥ Ⓑ Ⓓ Ⓢ Ⓟ Ⓣ 🐾 Ⓜ • ★★

■ LLANIDLOES
GLYNDWR'S WAY

Tom Lines, Lloyds Hotel & Restaurant, Cambrian Place, SY18 6BX. ☎ (01686) 412284 • Map 136/955844 • BB **B/C/D** • EM book first £20 • S4 D2 T3 • 3-12 • Ⓥ Ⓑ Ⓓ Ⓢ Ⓣ • ★★ • Groups also

■ LLANRHAEADR-YM-MOCHNANT (Oswestry, Shropshire)
☆ Mrs J Morgan, Llys Morgan, SY10 0JZ. ☎ (01691) 780345 • Map 125/123261 • BB **B** • EM book first £8, from 6.30pm • D1 T1 F1 • 1-12 NX • Ⓥ Ⓑ Ⓓ Ⓟ Ⓣ • 3Cr/HC • e.b.morgan@dial.pipex.com

B&B ACCOMMODATION   WALES   POWYS

Mike & Dot Scott, Powys House, Market Square, SY10 0JG. ☎ 01691 780201 • Map 125/123261 • BB **B** • EM book first £10, 7.30pm • D2 • 1-12 NX • Ⓥ Ⓓ Ⓟ Ⓣ • llanrhaeadrpo@gofornet.co.uk

■ LLANWDDYN (Oswestry, Shropshire)
GLYNDWR'S WAY

Jacqui Clark, Ty Uchaf, SY10 0ND. ☎ (01691) 870286 • Map 125/997216 • BB **C** • EM £5 • D1 F1 • 1-12 • Ⓥ Ⓑ Ⓓ Ⓢ Ⓟ Ⓣ 🏠 • ★★★ • users.breathemail.net/clarklakeview/clarklakeview/

■ LLANWRTYD WELLS

☆ Eileen & Bernie Dodd, Belle Vue Hotel, LD5 4RE. ☎ (01591) 610237 • Map 147/879467 • BB **A/B/C** • EM £4-£14, 6.30-9.30pm • S3 D2 T8 F2 • 1-12 • Ⓥ Ⓑ Ⓓ Ⓡ 🏠 • 2Cr/App • Groups also

Plasnewydd, Irfon Terrace, LD5 4RH. ☎ (01591) 610293 • Map 147/879466 • BB **B** • S2 D1 T1 • 2-11 • Ⓓ Ⓢ Ⓡ Ⓟ Ⓣ • ★★

David & Pam Dubock, 'Orleswell', Erw Haf, Ffos Rd, LD5 4RT. ☎ (01591) 610747 • Map 147/882467 • BB **B/C** • T1 • 1-12 NX • Ⓑ Ⓓ Ⓢ Ⓡ Ⓟ Ⓣ • ★★★★

■ MACHYNLLETH
GLYNDWR'S WAY

Mrs M Vince, Maenllwyd, Newtown Road, SY20 8EY. ☎ (01654) 702928 • Map 135/752008 • BB **C** • D4 T3 F1 • 1-12 NX • Ⓑ Ⓓ Ⓢ Ⓡ Ⓟ Ⓣ 🏠 • ★★★★ • www.cyber-space.co.uk/maenllwyd.htm

Mrs Lona Williams, Awelon, Heol Powys, SY20 8AY. ☎ (01654) 702047 • Map 135/747008 • BB **B** • S1 D1 T1 F0 • 1-12 NX • Ⓓ Ⓢ Ⓡ Ⓟ Ⓜ • ★★

Elaine Petrie, Pendre, Maengwyn Street, SY20 8EF. ☎ (01654) 702088 • Map 135/749008 • BB **B** • D2 T1 F2 • 1-11 • Ⓑ Ⓓ Ⓟ Ⓟ Ⓣ 🏠 • ★★

Wynnstay Hotel, Maengwyn Street, SY20 8AE. ☎ (01654) 702941 • Map 135/745007 • BB **E** • EM £6 upwards, 7-9pm • S8 D10 T6 F5 • 1-12 • Ⓥ Ⓑ Ⓓ Ⓢ Ⓡ Ⓟ 🏠 • ★★ • www.wynnstay-hotel.com

Gwelfryn B&B, 6 Greenfields Terrace, Bank Street, SY20 8DR. ☎ 01654 702532 • Map 135/746006 • BB **B** • S1 D1 T1 F1 • 3-11 • Ⓑ Ⓓ Ⓢ Ⓡ Ⓟ Ⓣ 🏠 • ★★ • www.gwelfryn.co.uk

■ MONTGOMERY
OFFA'S DYKE

Gaynor Bright, Little Brompton Farm, SY15 6HY. ☎ (01686) 668371 • Map 137/244941 • BB **C** • EM book first £10 (by prior arrangement), 6.30pm • S1 D1 T1 F1 • 1-12 • Ⓥ Ⓑ Ⓓ Ⓢ Ⓟ Ⓣ 🏠 • ★★★ • gaynor.brompton@virgin.net

Mark & Sue Michaels, Dragon Hotel, SY15 6PA. ☎ (01686) 668359 • Map 137/222964 • BB **E** • EM £7-£20, 7-9pm • S2 D9 T5 F4 • 1-12 • Ⓥ Ⓑ Ⓓ Ⓟ Ⓣ 🏠 • ★★★★ • reception@dragonhotel.com

■ NEWTOWN

David & Jean Burd, Plas Canol, New Road, SY16 1AS. ☎ (01686) 625598 • Map 136/108913 • BB **B** • EM book first £10, 6pm • S1 T1 F1 • 1-12 • Ⓥ Ⓑ Ⓓ Ⓢ Ⓡ Ⓟ Ⓣ • ★★★

■ PONTROBERT (Meifod)
GLYNDWR'S WAY

C E A Gilson, Pentre, SY22 6JL. ☎ (01691) 648348 • Map 125/108154 • BB **B/C** • EM book first £12, 7.30-9.30pm • S2 D1 T1 • 4-10 • Ⓥ Ⓑ Ⓓ Ⓢ Ⓟ Ⓣ • ★★ • pentre@btclick.com

■ PRESTEIGNE
OFFA'S DYKE

Mr & Mrs Rowlatt, 14 Hereford Street, LD8 2AR. ☎ (01544) 260466 • Map 148/316643 • BB **B** • EM book first £9, 7pm • D1 T1 • 1-12 NX • Ⓑ Ⓓ Ⓢ

☆ Marenee & Terry Monaghan, Carmel Court, King's Turning Road, LD8 2LD. ☎ (01544) 267986 • Map 148,137/320639 • BB **B** • S1 D5 T3 F2 • 1-12 NX • Ⓓ Ⓢ Ⓟ Ⓣ 🏠 • ★

WALES POWYS B&B ACCOMMODATION

☆ See Display Advertisement

■ **RHAYADER (Elan Valley)**

Mrs B Lawrence, Brynteg, East Street, LD6 5EA.
☎ (01597) 810052 • Map 147,136/972681 • BB **B** •
S1 D2 T1 • 1-12 NX • Ⓑ ⓓ Ⓟ Ⓣ Ⓜ • ★★ •
brynteg@hotmail.com

Mr & Mrs R Price, Downfield Farm, LD6 5PA.
☎ (01597) 810394 • Map 147,136/988684 • BB **B** •
D2 T1 • 3-10 • ⓓ Ⓢ Ⓣ • ★★

Mrs Ann Griffiths, Liverpool House, East Street, LD6
5EA. ☎ (01597) 810706 • Map 147,136/972681 • BB
B • EM book first £10, 6.30pm • S1 D5 F2 • 1-12 NX •
Ⓥ Ⓑ ⓓ Ⓢ Ⓟ Ⓣ 🛏 • ★★ • Groups also
ann@liverpoolhouse.net

☆ Elan Valley Hotel, Elan Valley, LD6 5HN.
☎ (01597) 810448 • Map 147,136/945665 • BB **D/E** •
EM £5.50-£20, 7-9pm • S2 D4 T2 F3 • 1-12 NX • Ⓥ
Ⓑ ⓓ Ⓟ 🛏 • ★★ • Groups also
www.elanvalleyhotel.co.uk

☆ The Horseshoe, Church Street, LD6 5AT. ☎ 01597
810982 • Map 147,136/969680 • BB **B** • EM £10,
7pm • S2 D2 T1 • 1-12 NX • Ⓥ Ⓑ ⓓ Ⓢ Ⓟ Ⓣ •
★★★ • horseshoe@easicom.com

Mrs A Edwards, Beili Neuadd, LD6 5NS. ☎ (01597)
810211 • Map 147/994698 • BB **C** • S1 D2 T1 • 1-12
NX • Ⓑ ⓓ Ⓢ Ⓟ Ⓣ Ⓜ Ⓜ • ★★★★ •
ann-carl@thebeili.freeserve.co.uk

Patricia Collard, Riverside Lodge, LD6 5HL.
☎ (01597) 810770 • Map 147,136/938659 • BB **B** •
EM £7.95, 7-8.30pm • S3 D4 T2 F2 • 1-12 • Ⓥ Ⓑ
ⓓ Ⓢ Ⓟ 🛏 • ★★ • www.riverside-lodge.com

■ **TALGARTH (Brecon)**

Mrs Megan Price, Craigend, The Bank, LD3 0BN.
☎ (01874) 711084 • Map 161/156336 • BB **B/C** • EM
book first £10, 7pm • S1 D2 T1 • 1-12 • Ⓥ Ⓑ
Ⓢ Ⓣ • 2Cr/C

■ **TALYBONT-ON-USK (Brecon)**
TAFF TRAIL

Laura Kostoris, Erw yr Danty, LD3 7YN. ☎ (01874)
676498 • Map 161/103231 • BB **B/C** • S1 D1 T1 • 1-
12 NX • ⓓ Ⓟ Ⓣ 🛏 • ★★★

■ **WELSHPOOL**
GLYNDWR'S WAY & OFFA'S DYKE

Mrs Freda Emberton, Tynllwyn Farm, SY21 9BW.
☎ (01938) 553175 + 553054 • Map 126/215086 • BB
B • S2 D/S2 T/S2 F/S2 • 1-12 NX • Ⓑ ⓓ Ⓡ Ⓟ Ⓣ
🛏 • ★★★

T & J Jones, Severn Farm, SY21 7BB. ☎ (01938)
553098 Fax 01938 553821 • Map 126/231070 • BB **B**
• EM book first £9, 6.30pm • S2 D1 T1 F2 • 1-12 NX •
Ⓥ ⓓ Ⓡ Ⓟ Ⓣ 🛏 • ★★★

SOUTH WALES

BLAENAU GWENT, BRIDGEND, CARDIFF, CAERPHILLY, MERTHYR
TYDFIL, NEWPORT, NEATH PORT TALBOT, RHONDDA CYNON TAFF,
SWANSEA & TORFAEN

■ **BISHOPSTON (The Mumbles)**

Mrs M Stringer, Barlands Cottage, 1 Old Kittle Rd ,
SA3 3JU. ☎ (01792) 232615 • Map 159/575892 • BB
B • D1 • 1-12 NX • ⓓ Ⓢ Ⓟ Ⓣ 🛏

■ **CARDIFF**
CAMBRIAN WAY & TAFF TRAIL

Rambler Court Hotel, Wendy Cronin, 188 Cathedral
Road, CF11 9JE. ☎ 029 2022 1187 • Map
171/167773 • BB **B** • S3 D4 T4 F3 • 1-12 NX • Ⓑ ⓓ
Ⓢ Ⓡ Ⓣ 🛏 • ★★

■ **CWMTAF (Merthyr Tydfil)**
TAFF TRAIL

Mrs M Evans, Llwyn Onn Guest House, CF48 2HT.
☎ (01685) 384384 • Map 160/012115 • BB **D** • S1
D2 T1 • 1-12NX • Ⓑ ⓓ Ⓢ Ⓟ Ⓣ • ★★★★ •
llwyn.onn@talk21.com

■ **LLANGENNITH (Gower)**

Mrs Philippa Poulton, Western House, SA3 1HU.
☎ (01792) 386620 • Map 159/426915 • BB **B** • D1 T1
F1 • 1-12 • Ⓑ ⓓ Ⓢ Ⓟ Ⓣ 🛏 •
stevepippa@llangennith.freeserve.co.uk

■ **LLANMADOC (Gower)**

Tallizmand, SA3 1HA. ☎ (01792) 386373 • Map
159/444933 • BB **C** • EM book first £12, 6.30-8pm •
S1 D1 T1 F1 • 1-12 NX • Ⓥ Ⓑ ⓓ Ⓢ Ⓟ Ⓣ 🛏 •
★★★Ⓦ

■ **MARGAM (Neath Port Talbot)**

Mrs Rhiannon Gaen, Ty'n-Y-Caeau, SA13 2NW. ☎ (01639) 883897 • Map 170/792863 • BB **C** • EM book first £9.50, 6-6.30pm • D1 T4 F2 • 2-11 • Ⓥ Ⓑ Ⓓ Ⓢ Ⓡ Ⓟ Ⓣ 🌄 • ★★ • SC also

■ **MERTHYR TYDFIL**
TAFF TRAIL

☆ Tregenna Hotel, Park Terrace, CF47 8RF. ☎ (01685) 723627/382055/723481 • Map 160/049066 • BB **D** • EM £10, 6.30-10pm • S5 D6 T7 F5 • 1-12 • Ⓥ Ⓑ Ⓓ Ⓢ Ⓡ Ⓟ Ⓣ 🌄 Ⓜ • ◆◆◆ • SC also • tregenna.co.uk

■ **PONTSTICILL (Merthyr Tydfil)**

☆ Penrhadw Farm, CF48 2TU. ☎ 01685 723481/723627 • Map 160/054109 • BB **D** • EM book first £10, 6.30-7.30pm • S1 D2 T2 • 1-12 NX • Ⓥ Ⓑ Ⓓ Ⓢ Ⓡ Ⓟ Ⓣ Ⓜ • ★★★★★ • tregenna.co.uk

■ **PORT EYNON (Gower)**

☆ Mark & Susan Cottell, Culver House Hotel, SA3 1NN. ☎ (01792) 390755 • Map 159/468853 • BB **D/E** • EM book first £12.50, 6.30-8.3pm • S4 D4 T2 F3 • 1-12 NX • Ⓥ Ⓑ Ⓓ Ⓢ Ⓟ Ⓣ 🌄 • ★★

■ **PORTHCAWL (Bridgend)**

Rockybank Bed & Breakfast, 15 De Breos Drive, CF36 3JP. ☎ (01656) 785823 • Map 170/819779 • BB **C** • D1 T1 F1 • 1-12 NX • Ⓑ Ⓓ Ⓢ Ⓟ Ⓣ • ★★★Ⓦ • Food nearby • jeanlewis.members.beeb.net

■ **ST BRIDES WENTLOOGE (Near Newport)**

Chapel Guest House, Church Road, St Brides Wentlooge, NP10 8SN. ☎ (01633) 681018 • Map 171/294822 • BB **C** • EM £8-£10, 6-10pm • S1 D1 T1 F1 • 1-12 • Ⓥ Ⓑ Ⓓ Ⓢ Ⓡ Ⓟ Ⓣ 🌄 • ★★

■ **UPPER CWMTWRCH (Swansea)**

☆ Judy & Trevor Goldfinch, Cwm Clyd Farm, SA9 2XY. ☎ (01639) 761135 • Map 160/761135 • BB **B** • EM £5 • S1 D1 T1 • 1-12 • Ⓥ Ⓑ Ⓓ Ⓢ Ⓟ Ⓣ • judy.goldfinch@ukonline.co.uk

■ **WELSH ST DONAT'S (Cowbridge)**

Mrs June Jenkins, Bryn-y-Ddafad, CF71 7ST. ☎ (01446) 774451 • Map 170/024768 • BB **C** • EM book first £5, 6-7.30pm • S2 D2 • 1-12 NX • Ⓥ Ⓑ Ⓓ Ⓢ Ⓟ Ⓣ • ★★★ • www.bydd.co.uk

Ireland

COUNTY ANTRIM

■ **CARRICKFERGUS**

Mrs B Barron, Beechgrove B&B, 412 Upper Road, Trooperslane, BT38 8PW. ☎ (02893) 363304 • BB **B** • EM book first £10, 6.30-7.30pm • S1 D2 T1 F2 • 1-12 • Ⓥ Ⓑ Ⓓ Ⓡ Ⓟ Ⓣ 🌄 • beechgrove@netni.co.uk

☆ See Display Advertisement

COUNTY DONEGAL

■ KINCASSLAGH

Richard Cannon & Agnes Lynch, Belcruit. ☎ 00 353 75 43146 • BB **B** • EM £10 • S1 D1 T0 F0 • 1-12 • Ⓥ Ⓑ Ⓓ Ⓟ Ⓣ 🐾 • SC also • transport avail.

DUBLIN

■ DUBLIN
WICKLOW WAY

☆ C Cassells, 24 Charleville Road, Phibsborough, Dublin 7. ☎ 00 353 1 838 9812 • BB **D** • S1 D1 T1 • 1-12 NX • Ⓓ Ⓢ Ⓡ

COUNTY KERRY

■ ANNASCAUL (Dingle Peninsula)

Mrs Kathleen O'Connor, "Four Winds". ☎ 00 353 66 9157168 • Map 70/ • BB **B** • D2 T2 F1 • 1-12 NX • Ⓑ Ⓓ Ⓟ Ⓣ • ITB/App • SC also

■ GLENCAR
KERRY WAY

☆ Mrs Mary O'Connor, "Rocklands", Cappantanvalley. ☎ 00 353 66 9760177 • Map 78/V721875 • BB **B** • EM £11 • D2 T1 • 4-9 • Ⓥ Ⓑ Ⓓ Ⓢ Ⓟ

Johnny Walsh, Climbers Inn. ☎ 00 353 66 9760101 • Map 78/841724 • BB **A/B/C/D** • EM book first £9.50, 6.30-9.30pm • D2 T7 F2 • 1-12 • Ⓥ Ⓑ Ⓓ Ⓢ 🐾 • ITB/App • www.climbersinn.com

■ TRALEE

Kathleen Daly, Finglas House, Camp Village, Camp. ☎ 00 357 66 7130125 • BB **B** • D2 T2 F1 • 4-10 • Ⓑ Ⓓ Ⓢ Ⓟ 🐾 Ⓜ • Food nearby

COUNTY WICKLOW

■ GLENDALOUGH

Carmel Hawkins, Carmels, Annamoe. ☎ 00 353 404 45297 • BB **B** • D2 T2 • 3-10 • Ⓑ Ⓓ Ⓢ • Bord Failte • carmelsbandb@eircom.net

■ GLENEALY (Ashford)

☆ Mrs Catherine Byrne Fulvio, Ballyknocken House. ☎ 00 353 404 44627 • BB **D** • EM book first £18.75, 7pm • S1 D3 T3 F1 • 3-12 NX • Ⓥ Ⓑ Ⓓ Ⓢ Ⓟ Ⓣ • ◆◆◆ • SC also cfulvio@ballyknocken.com

France

NORMANDY

■ COTE D'ARMOR

Rod & Vicky Ricketts, La Vielle Boulangerie, 22330 Langourla. ☎ 00 33 2 96 30 42 90 • BB **A/B** • EM book first £55 Francs • D2 F2 • 1-12 NX • Ⓑ Ⓓ Ⓢ Ⓟ Ⓣ • rodannvicky@aol.com

HAUT-SAVOIE (RHONE-ALPES)

■ VERCHAIX (Samoens)

Geoff Jordan, Chalet Les Adrets, La Balme 74440, Verchaix, France. ☎ (00 33) 450901486 • BB **A/B** • EM book first £9 • D2 F1 • 1-12 NX • Ⓑ Ⓓ Ⓢ Ⓟ Ⓣ • www.lesadrets.fsnet.co.uk

ORIENTALE

■ MAUREILLAS

☆ Gregor & Claire Penfold, Mas Dien Bach 66480. ☎ 00 33 4 68 83 04 10 • BB **B/C** • EM book first £12, 7.30pm • D3 T2 F1 • 1-11 • Ⓥ Ⓑ Ⓓ Ⓢ Ⓟ

PAS DE CALAIS

■ RAYE-SUR-AUTHIE (Hesdin)

Mike Potter, L'ancien presbytere, Raye-sur-Authie 62140, France. ☎ 0033 (0) 321 8632 25/(01227) 720464 • BB **C/D** • S2 D2 F2 • 1-12 • Ⓑ Ⓓ Ⓟ Ⓣ • Boulogne/Calais 1hr • Picardie area • sallelec@compuserve.com

PROVENCE

■ SAUZET

☆ Guy & Jane Eills, Chemin Les Eclozeaux. ☎ 00 33 475 518 663 • BB **C/E** • EM book first £7-£10, 8.30pm • D2 T4 • 1-12 • Ⓥ Ⓑ Ⓓ Ⓢ Ⓡ Ⓟ Ⓣ ⚑ • SC also • Groups also

☆ See Display Advertisement

Index to the Accommodation Guide

....

Any town which is only listed as a postal town and not in its own right is not included in this index. For example, for Highclere, Newbury, only Highclere is listed. If Newbury had entries of its own, it too would be listed, but as it appears only as a postal town in this Guide, it is not. Many small villages in this index are within the entries and it will be necessary to search for them once you get to the page.

H–L

ACCOMMODATION INDEX

277

P–S

ACCOMMODATION INDEX

279

Path Problem Report Form

WHERE WAS THE PROBLEM? Please give as much information as you can.

County_____District_____

Parish/Community_____

From (place) _____

_____ Gridref._____

To (place)_____

_____ Grid ref._____

Path number if known_____

Date problem encountered_____

WHAT WAS THE PROBLEM? Be precise and quote a grid reference for any specific point. Draw a sketch map if you think it will help. If anyone spoke to you, please give details, including their name and address if known.

WHAT TO DO NEXT? Give us your details

Name_____

Address_____

_____

Telephone_____ **Tick box for more Report Forms** ❏

Send this form to
Your local Ramblers representative (see Area & Group Contacts section in this Yearbook) or
Ramblers' Association, 2nd Floor, Camelford House, 87-90 Albert Embankment,
London SE1 7TW. Telephone 020 7339 8500. Fax 020 7339 8501.

Where have you been staying?

IF YOU LIKED IT AND IT ISN'T IN THIS BOOK, PLEASE GIVE
DETAILS HERE

Remove this page and send it to the Yearbook Editor, The
Ramblers' Association, 2nd Floor, Camelford House, 87-90
Albert Embankment, London SE1 7TW

Continue overleaf if necessary, the more the merrier!

Did they let you down?

Please indicate if you do not wished to be mentioned by name in any correspondence.

Continue overleaf if necessary.

285

Abbreviations and symbols used in the Accommodation Guide

☆	A display ad is either below or nearby
BB	Bed & Breakfast accommodation
SC	Self-catering accommodation
pppn	Per Person Per Night, some SC advertisers prefer this method
GA	Group accommodation
HSC	Hostels and Camping accommodation
A	Price per person per night under £14.99
B	Price per person per night £15–£19.99
C	Price per person per night £20–£24.99
D	Price per person per night £25–£29.99
E	Price per person per night £30 or over – n.b. the price could be considerably over £30
EM	Evening meal normally available (unless 'book first') with average price/time served. If there's not time stated, it is probably flexible, but worth checking.
S, D, T, F	Number of single, double, twin or family rooms available. A family room is usually understood as a double plus a single, but this will vary.
1-12	Months open (1 = January)
NX	Closed Christmas (may be open New Year, worth enquiring)
+X	Open Christmas (i.e. but not the rest of December)
Ⓓ	Drying facilities available, should usually be a separate room.
Ⓥ	Vegetarian evening meals available routinely. NB Many places not showing this symbol do provide a vegetarian cooked breakfast and often provide vegetarian evening meals
Ⓢ	Some smoking restrictions. Vary from no smoking in certain rooms to no smoking at all – enquire
Ⓑ	At least one room has private bath/shower and/or toilet
Ⓡ	A railway station is within 2 miles
Ⓟ	A packed lunch can be obtained, you may have to order when booking, and it would usually cost extra.
Ⓣ	Tea/coffee making facilities are available in the bedrooms. n.b. Proprietors may have 24 hours facilities elsewhere.
🐕	You may be able to take a dog having first consulted with the proprietor. Please note that some establishments only accept guide dogs.
Ⓜ	The advertiser is a member of the Ramblers' Association
Tourist board ratings.	
★	Star rating (Hotels)
◆	Diamond rating (Guest Accommodation) Note that some establishments will still have an older system due to the timing of inspections. Where this rating appears in an English establishment it may be an AA or RAC award instead, these organisations now have a common system of rating in England.
Ⓢ Ⓖ	Silver, or Gold award.
Ⓦ	Walkers & Cyclists Welcome scheme (Scotland).
k/Comm/HC	(for self-catering) k = keys, Comm = Commended, HC = Highly Commended

INDEX MAP

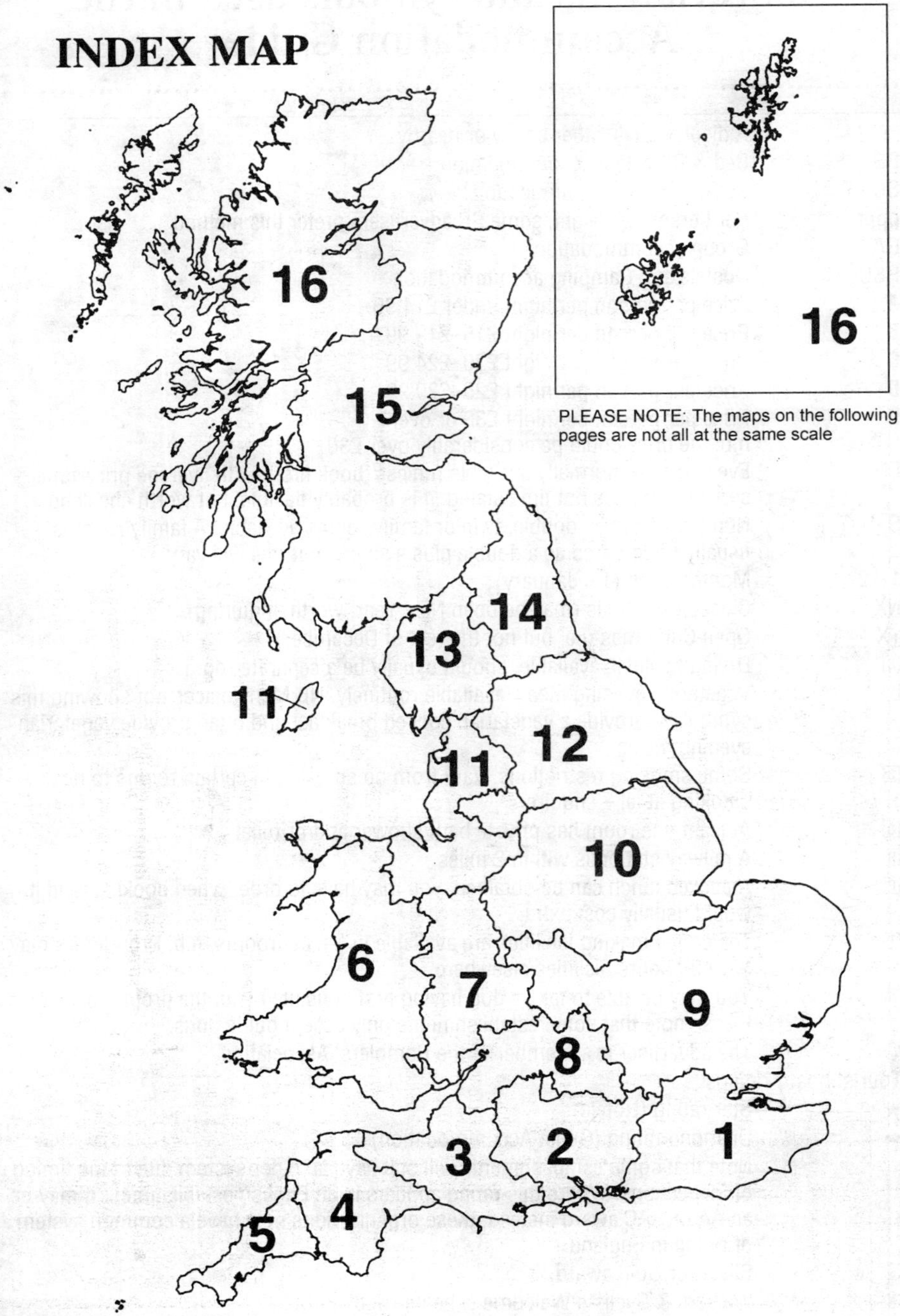

16

16

PLEASE NOTE: The maps on the following pages are not all at the same scale

15

14

13

11

12

11

10

6

7

9

8

3

2

1

4

5

MAP 1

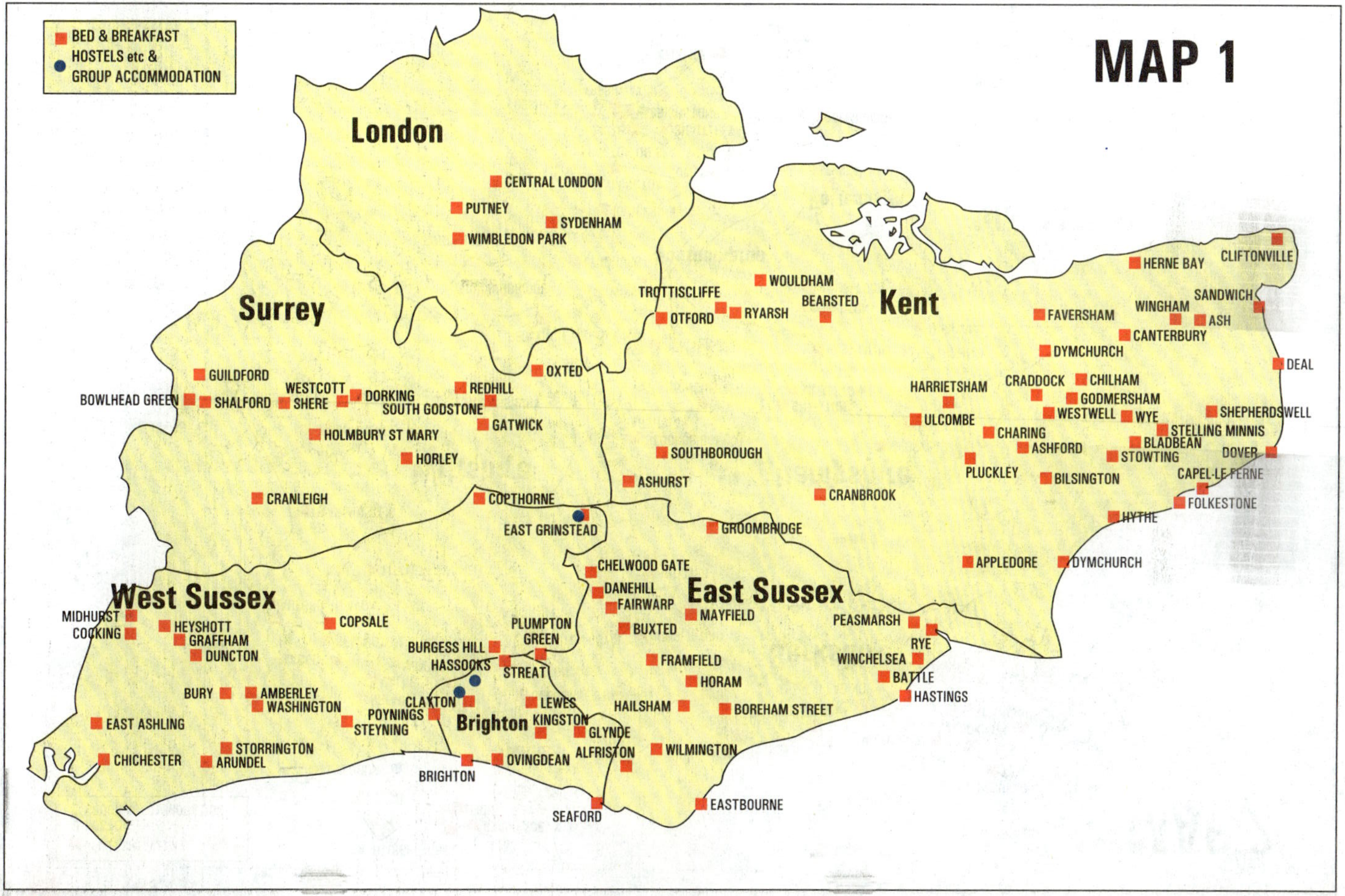

London

Kent

Surrey

East Sussex

West Sussex

BED & BREAKFAST
HOSTELS etc &
GROUP ACCOMMODATION

CLIFTONVILLE
DEAL
HERNE BAY
SANDWICH
WINGHAM
ASH
SHEPHERDSWELL
CANTERBURY
STELLING MINNIS
FAVERSHAM
CHILHAM
GODMERSHAM
WYE
DYMCHURCH
CRADDOCK
WESTWELL
BLADBEAN
STOWTING
DOVER
CAPEL-LE-FERNE
FOLKESTONE
HARRIETSHAM
CHARING
ASHFORD
BILSINGTON
HYTHE
ULCOMBE
PLUCKLEY
APPLEDORE
DYMCHURCH
WOULDHAM
BEARSTED
RYARSH
CRANBROOK
RYE
HASTINGS
WINCHELSEA
BATTLE
PEASMARSH
SOUTHBOROUGH
GROOMBRIDGE
MAYFIELD
WILMINGTON
TROTTISCLIFFE
OTFORD
ASHURST
CHELWOOD GATE
DANEHILL
FAIRWARP
BUXTED
FRAMFIELD
HORAM
BOREHAM STREET
EASTBOURNE
OXTED
COPTHORNE
EAST GRINSTEAD
PLUMPTON GREEN
STREAT
HAILSHAM
GLYNDE
ALFRISTON
CENTRAL LONDON
SYDENHAM
REDHILL
GATWICK
LEWES
KINGSTON
OVINGDEAN
SEAFORD
PUTNEY
WIMBLEDON PARK
SOUTH GODSTONE
DORKING
WESTCOTT
SHERE
HOLMBURY ST MARY
HORLEY
BURGESS HILL
HASSOCKS
CLAYTON
POYNINGS
Brighton
BRIGHTON
GUILDFORD
SHALFORD
CRANLEIGH
COPSALE
STEYNING
BOWLHEAD GREEN
HEYSHOTT
GRAFFHAM
DUNCTON
BURY
AMBERLEY
WASHINGTON
STORRINGTON
MIDHURST
COCKING
EAST ASHLING
CHICHESTER
ARUNDEL

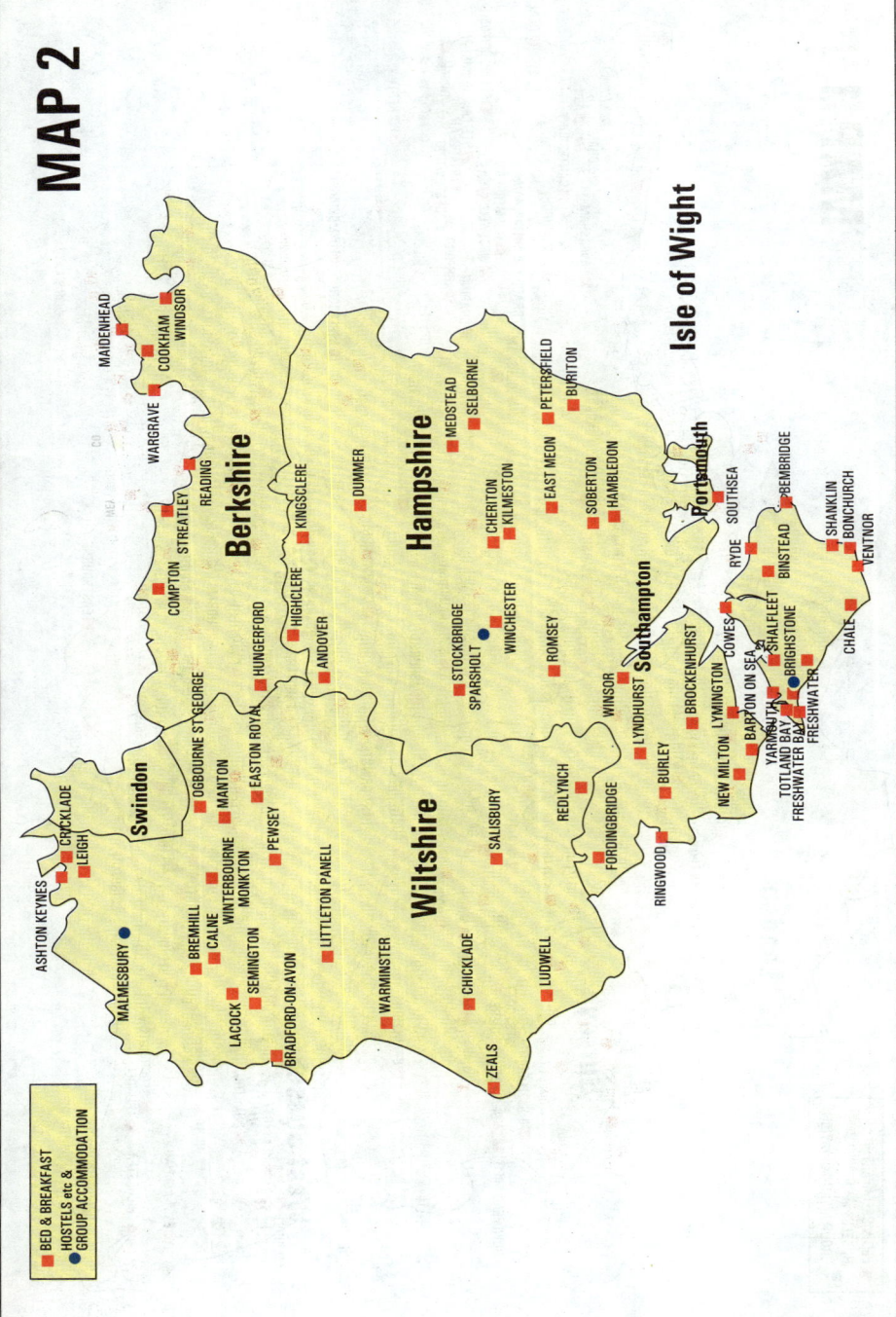

MAP 2

Isle of Wight

Berkshire

Hampshire

Portsmouth

Southampton

Swindon

Wiltshire

MAIDENHEAD
WINDSOR
COOKHAM
WARGRAVE
READING
STREATLEY
COMPTON
BERKSHIRE
KINGSCLERE
DUMMER
HIGHCLERE
HUNGERFORD
ANDOVER
OGBOURNE ST GEORGE
MANTON
EASTON ROYAL
PEWSEY
WINTERBOURNE MONKTON
CALNE
BREMHILL
SEMINGTON
LACOCK
BRADFORD-ON-AVON
LITTLETON PANELL
WARMINSTER
CHICKLADE
LUDWELL
ZEALS
SALISBURY
REDLYNCH
FORDINGBRIDGE
RINGWOOD
WINSOR
LYNDHURST
BROCKENHURST
BURLEY
NEW MILTON
LYMINGTON
BARTON ON SEA
COWES
YARMOUTH
FRESHWATER BAY
TOTLAND BAY
FRESHWATER
BRIGHSTONE
SHALFLEET
BINSTEAD
RYDE
SOUTHSEA
BEMBRIDGE
SHANKLIN
BONCHURCH
VENTNOR
CHALE
STOCKBRIDGE
SPARSHOLT
WINCHESTER
ROMSEY
MEDSTEAD
SELBORNE
PETERSFIELD
BURITON
EAST MEON
CHERITON
KILMESTON
SOBERTON
HAMBLEDON
ASHTON KEYNES
CRICKLADE
LEIGH
MALMESBURY

Legend:
- BED & BREAKFAST
- HOSTELS etc &
  GROUP ACCOMMODATION

MAP 3

Bath & NE Somerset
North Somerset
Somerset
Dorset
Poole
Bournemouth

BATHFORD
BATH
CHEW STOKE
TIMSBURY
BECKINGTON
NORTH CADBURY
YEOVILTON
CHARLTON HORETHORNE
WELLS
SHIPHAM
AXBRIDGE
WEDMORE
CLEVEDON
WINSCOMBE
WESTON-SUPER-MARE
BURNHAM-ON-SEA
WEST QUANTOXHEAD
HOLFORD
KILVE
NETHER STOWEY
BRIDGWATER
KINGSTON ST MARY
TAUNTON
BICKNOLLER
BISHOPS LYDEARD
WIVELISCOMBE
DUNSTER
MINEHEAD
ALLERFORD
PORLOCK
TIMBERSCOMBE
CULBONE
EXFORD
EXTON
DULVERTON
MUDFORD
HINTON ST GEORGE
CREWKERNE
THORNCOMBE
LYME REGIS
CHIDEOCK
BRIDPORT
EYPE
BURTON BRADSTOCK
WINTERBOURNE ABBAS
POWERSTOCK
SYDLING ST NICHOLAS
TOLLER PORCORUM
FRAMPTON
DORCHESTER
CERNE ABBAS
SHERBORNE
STURMINSTER NEWTON
SHILLINGSTON
IWERNE MINSTER
BLANDFORD FORUM
CRANBORNE
STURMINSTER MARSHALL
IBBERTON
MILTON ABBAS
WINTERBORNE KINGSTON
BRIANTSPUDDLE
PUDDLETOWN
SUTTON POYNTZ
WEYMOUTH
LULWORTH COVE
WEST LULWORTH
EAST STOKE
HOLME
WAREHAM
STOBOROUGH
KIMMERIDGE
WORTH MATRAVERS
SWANAGE
POOLE
BOURNEMOUTH
ABBOTSBURY

Legend:
- ■ BED & BREAKFAST
- ● HOSTELS etc & GROUP ACCOMMODATION

MAPS

291

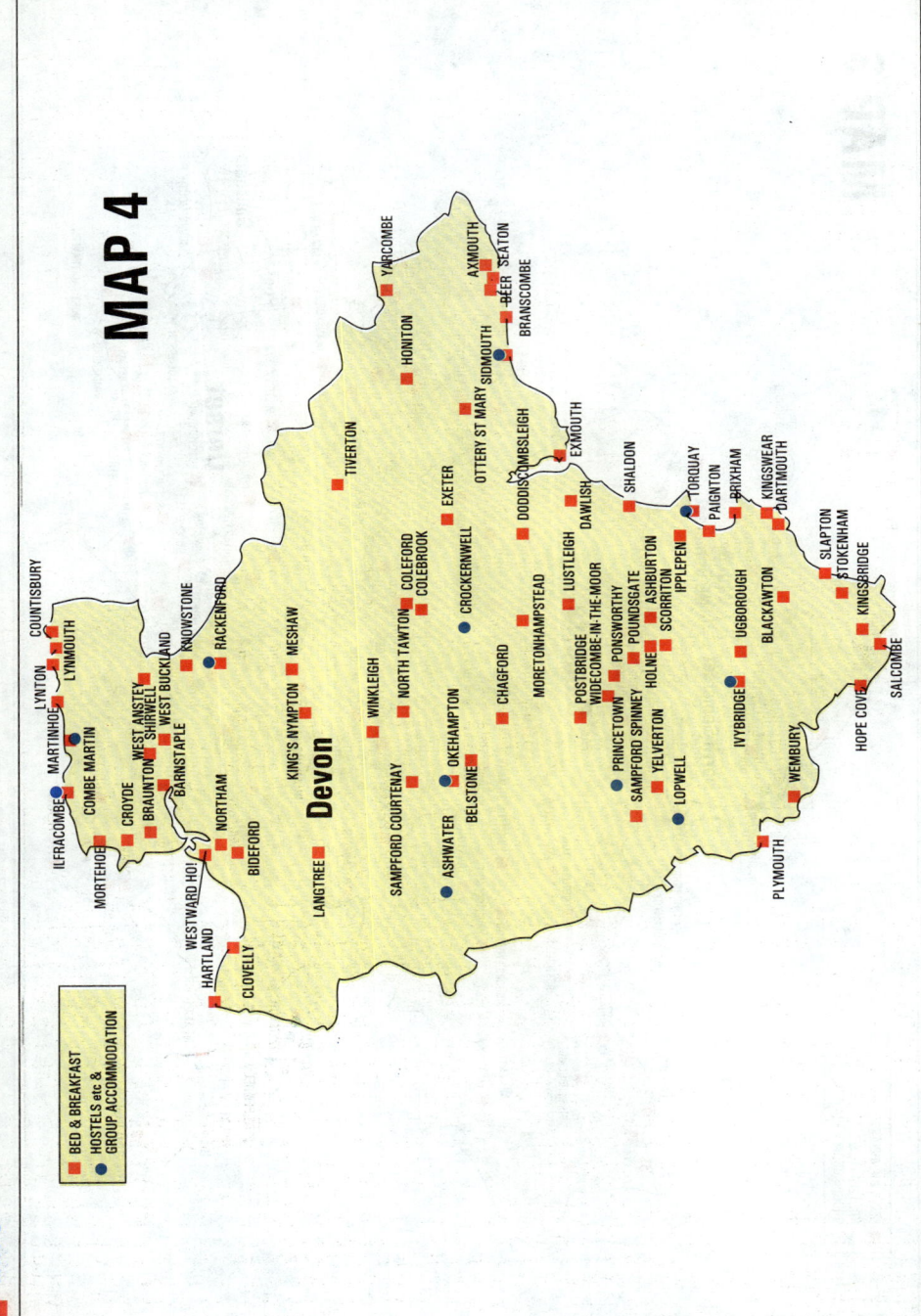

MAP 4

Devon

Legend:
- ■ BED & BREAKFAST
- ● HOSTELS etc. & GROUP ACCOMMODATION

Locations shown on map:

YARCOMBE, AXMOUTH, SEATON, BEER, BRANSCOMBE, HONITON, SIDMOUTH, OTTERY ST MARY, DUMBSLEIGH, DODDISCOMBSLEIGH, EXMOUTH, TIVERTON, EXETER, CROCKERNWELL, COLEFORD, COLEBROOK, DAWLISH, SHALDON, TORQUAY, PAIGNTON, BRIXHAM, KINGSWEAR, DARTMOUTH, NORTH TAWTON, MORETONHAMPSTEAD, LUSTLEIGH, WIDECOMBE-IN-THE-MOOR, PONSWORTHY, POSTBRIDGE, ASHBURTON, SCORRITON, HOLNE, IPPLEPEN, SLAPTON, STOKENHAM, KINGSBRIDGE, COUNTISBURY, LYNMOUTH, LYNTON, MARTINHOE, KNOWSTONE, RACKENFORD, MESHAW, ILFRACOMBE, COMBE MARTIN, WEST ANSTEY, SHIRWELL, WEST BUCKLAND, KING'S NYMPTON, WINKLEIGH, UGBOROUGH, BLACKAWTON, CROYDE, BRAUNTON, BARNSTAPLE, SAMPFORD COURTENAY, OKEHAMPTON, PRINCETOWN, SAMPFORD SPINNEY, YELVERTON, IVYBRIDGE, MORTEHOE, NORTHAM, BELSTONE, LOPWELL, WEMBURY, BIDEFORD, ASHWATER, HOPE COVE, SALCOMBE, WESTWARD HO!, LANGTREE, HARTLAND, CLOVELLY, PLYMOUTH, CHAGFORD

MAP 5

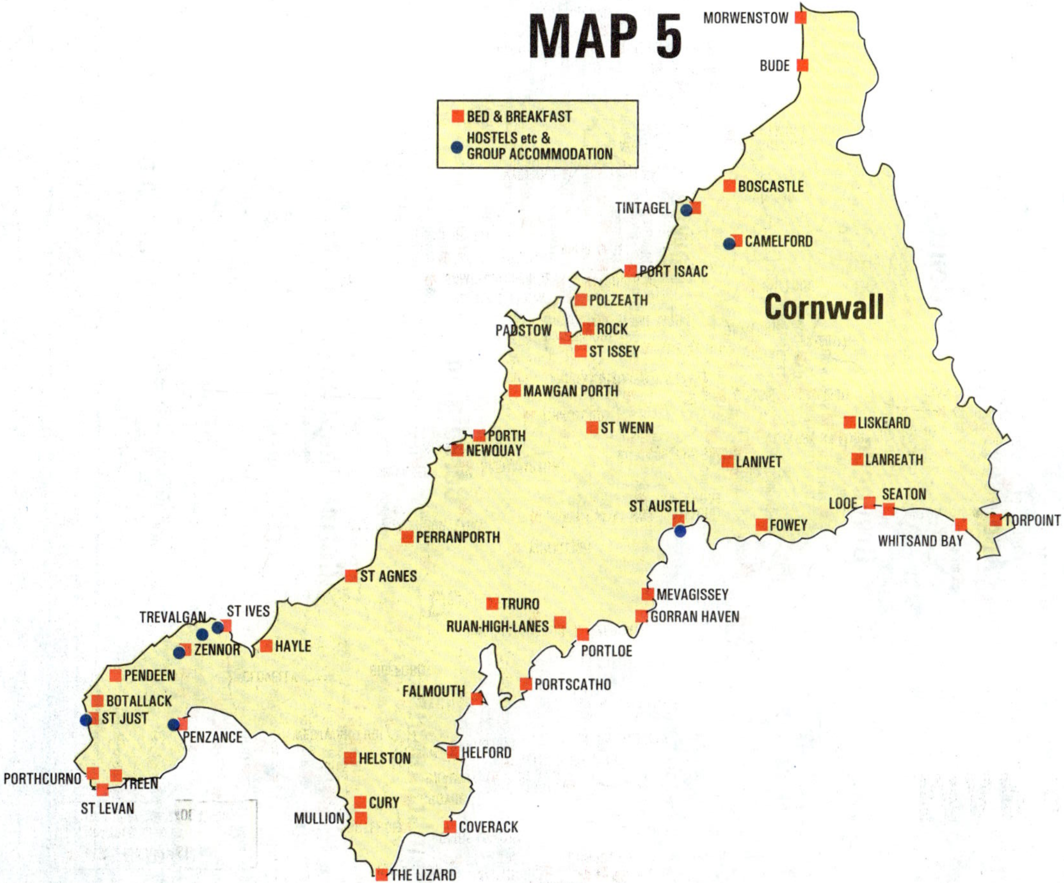

Cornwall

BED & BREAKFAST
HOSTELS etc &
GROUP ACCOMMODATION

MORWENSTOW
BUDE
BOSCASTLE
TINTAGEL
CAMELFORD
PORT ISAAC
POLZEATH
ROCK
ST ISSEY
PADSTOW
MAWGAN PORTH
ST WENN
PORTH
NEWQUAY
PERRANPORTH
ST AGNES
TREVALGAN
ST IVES
HAYLE
ZENNOR
PENDEEN
BOTALLACK
ST JUST
TREEN
PORTHCURNO
ST LEVAN
PENZANCE
TRURO
RUAN-HIGH-LANES
PORTSCATHO
PORTLOE
GORRAN HAVEN
MEVAGISSEY
ST AUSTELL
FOWEY
LANIVET
LANREATH
SEATON
LOOE
LISKEARD
TORPOINT
WHITSAND BAY
FALMOUTH
HELFORD
HELSTON
CURY
MULLION
COVERACK
THE LIZARD

MAP 6

BED & BREAKFAST
HOSTELS etc &
GROUP ACCOMMODATION

Anglesey

CEMAES BAY
MOELFRE
HOLYHEAD
LLANFAIRFECHAN
RHOSCOLYN
LLANDUDNO
ABERGELE
CONWY

Conwy

MENAI BRIDGE
CAERNARFON
TREFRIW
GWYTHERIN
LLANBERIS
CAPEL CURIG
BETWS-Y-COED
PENMACHNO

Gwynedd

BEDDGELERT
PANT GLAS
NANTGWYNANT
BLAENAU FFESTINIOG
LLANFFESTINIOG
TRAWSFYNYDD
BALA
PENRHYNDEUDRAETH
MAENTWROG
HARLECH
ABERSOCH
LLANFAIR
DYFFRYN ARDUDWY
ABERDARON
LLANABER
BRITHDIR
DOLGELLAU
BARMOUTH
LLANWDDYN
LLANRHAEADR -YM-MONCHNANT

Powys

ABERGYNOLWYN
FOEL
GUILSFIELD
LLANEGRYN
PONTROBERT
WELSHPOOL
BUTTINGTON
TYWYN
MONTGOMERY
ABERDYFI
MACHYNLLETH
ABERHAFESP
DYLIFE
NEWTOWN
LLANGURIG
BOW STREET
PONTERWYD
LLANIDLOES
CWMYSTWYTH
LLANANNO
LLANBADARN FYNYDD
KNIGHTON
DISCOED
PRESTEIGNE
RHAYADER

Ceredigion

LLANDRINDOD WELLS
HOWEY
NEW QUAY
NEWBRIDGE ON WYE
GLADESTRY
RHYDLEWIS
LLANDDEWI BREFI
LLANWRYTD WELLS
BUILTH WELLS
CARDIGAN
LLANWENOG
HAY-ON-WYE

Pembrokeshire

MOYLGROVE
GOODWICK
NEWPORT
RHANDIRMWYN
PENTRE-Y-GWYN
ERWOOD
BOUGHROOD
DYFFRYN
DINAS CROSS
LLANDOVERY
TALGARTH
FISHGUARD
PUNCHESTON
BRECON
ABEREIDDY
TREFIN
HEOL SENNI
BERE
LLANDELOY
CAPEL-Y-FFIN
ST DAVID'S
BRECHFA
LLANFRYNACH
TALBONT-
ON-USK
NOLTON HAVEN
HAVERFORDWEST
BROAD HAVEN
LITTLE HAVEN
CARMARTHEN
LLANDEILO
MARLOES
BEGELLY
DALE
MARTLETWY
CWMTAF
AMROTH
PONTSTICILL
PEMBROKE
TENBY
ST ISHMAILS
MERTHYR TYDFIL
MILFORD HAVEN
MANORBIER
UPPER CWMTWRCH
CASTLEMARTIN
BOSHERSTON
NEYLAND
LLANGENNITH
LLANMADOC
FRESHWATER EAST
BISHOPSTON
PORT EYNON
MARGAM
PORTHCAWL
CARDIFF
ST BRIDES WENTLOOGE
WELSH ST DONATS

Carmarthenshire

South Wales

MAPS

294

MAP 7

BED & BREAKFAST
HOSTELS etc &
GROUP ACCOMMODATION

ELLESMERE
GOBOWEN
TREFONEN
OSWESTRY
WEM
NANTMAWR QUARRY
MYDDLE
MONTFORD BRIDGE
HIGH ERCALL
SHREWSBURY
MINSTERLEY
Shropshire
IRONBRIDGE
BROSELEY
MUCH WENLOCK
STIPERSTONES
RATLINGHOPE
CARDINGTON
EASTHOPE
NORBURY
CHURCH STRETTON
BISHOPS CASTLE
ABDON
CRAVEN ARMS
CLUN
ASTON-ON-CLUN
CLEEDOWNTON
CLEOBURY MORTIMER
BEWDLEY
LUDLOW
BRAMPTON BRYAN
Hereford & Worcester
KINGSLAND
LEOMINSTER
OMBERSLEY
KINGTON
DILWYN
BROMYARD
HERGEST
ALMELEY
HUNTINGTON
COLWALL
CROPTHORNE
GT MALVERN
COLWALL
TRUMPET
EVESHAM
BREDWARDINE
UPTON-UPON-SEVERN
BISHOPSTONE
BROADWAY
BYFORD
HEREFORD
STRETTON SUGWAS
FOWNHOPE
LEDBURY
VOWCHURCH
ASHTON UNDER HILL
MUCH MARCLE
HOARWITHY
PANDY
ROSS-ON-WYE
LLANFIHANGEL
CRUCORNEY
LLANGATTOCK-LINGOED
ABERGAVENNY
MONMOUTH
Monmouthshire
TINTERN
CHEPSTOW

MAPS

295

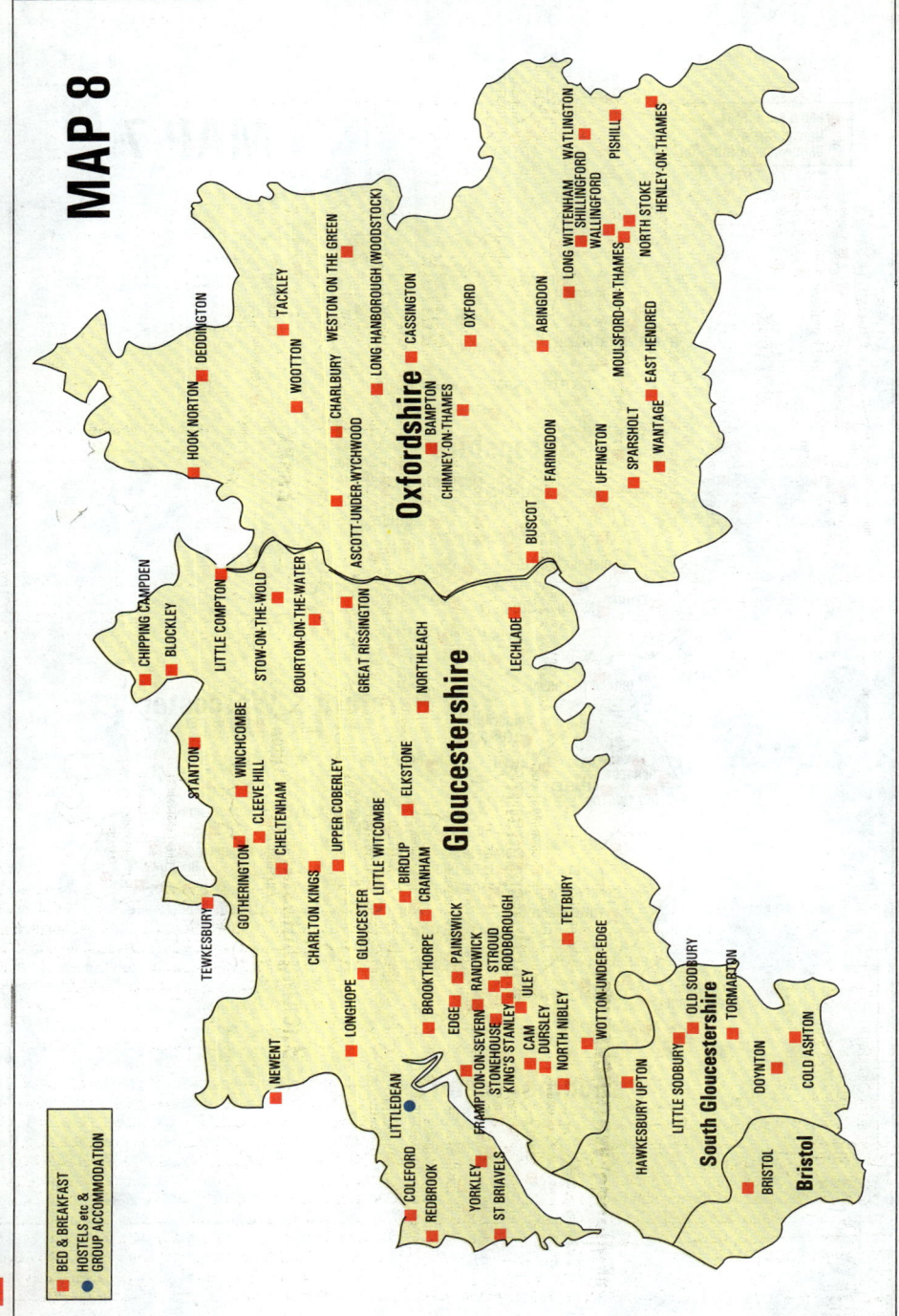

MAP 8

Oxfordshire

Gloucestershire

South Gloucestershire

Bristol

HOOK NORTON
DEDDINGTON
WOOTTON
TACKLEY
CHARLBURY
WESTON ON THE GREEN
LONG HANBOROUGH (WOODSTOCK)
CASSINGTON
OXFORD
ABINGDON
LONG WITTENHAM
WATLINGTON
SHILLINGFORD
PISHILL
WALLINGFORD
MOULSFORD-ON-THAMES
NORTH STOKE
HENLEY-ON-THAMES
EAST HENDRED
ASCOTT-UNDER-WYCHWOOD
BAMPTON
CHIMNEY-ON-THAMES
FARINGDON
UFFINGTON
SPARSHOLT
WANTAGE
BUSCOT
LECHLADE

CHIPPING CAMPDEN
BLOCKLEY
LITTLE COMPTON
STOW-ON-THE-WOLD
BOURTON-ON-THE-WATER
GREAT RISSINGTON
NORTHLEACH
STANTON
WINCHCOMBE
CLEEVE HILL
CHELTENHAM
UPPER COBERLEY
ELKSTONE
GOTHERINGTON
LITTLE WITCOMBE
BIRDLIP
CRANHAM
CHARLTON KINGS
GLOUCESTER
TEWKESBURY
LONGHOPE
BROOKTHORPE
PAINSWICK
EDGE
RANDWICK
STROUD
RODBOROUGH
ULEY
TETBURY
WOTTON-UNDER-EDGE
NEWENT
FRAMPTON-ON-SEVERN
STONEHOUSE
KING'S STANLEY
CAM
DURSLEY
NORTH NIBLEY
LITTLEDEAN
COLEFORD
REDBROOK
YORKLEY
ST BRIAVELS
HAWKESBURY UPTON
LITTLE SODBURY
OLD SODBURY
TORMARTON
DOYNTON
COLD ASHTON
BRISTOL

Legend

- ■ BED & BREAKFAST
- ● HOSTELS etc & GROUP ACCOMMODATION

MAP 9

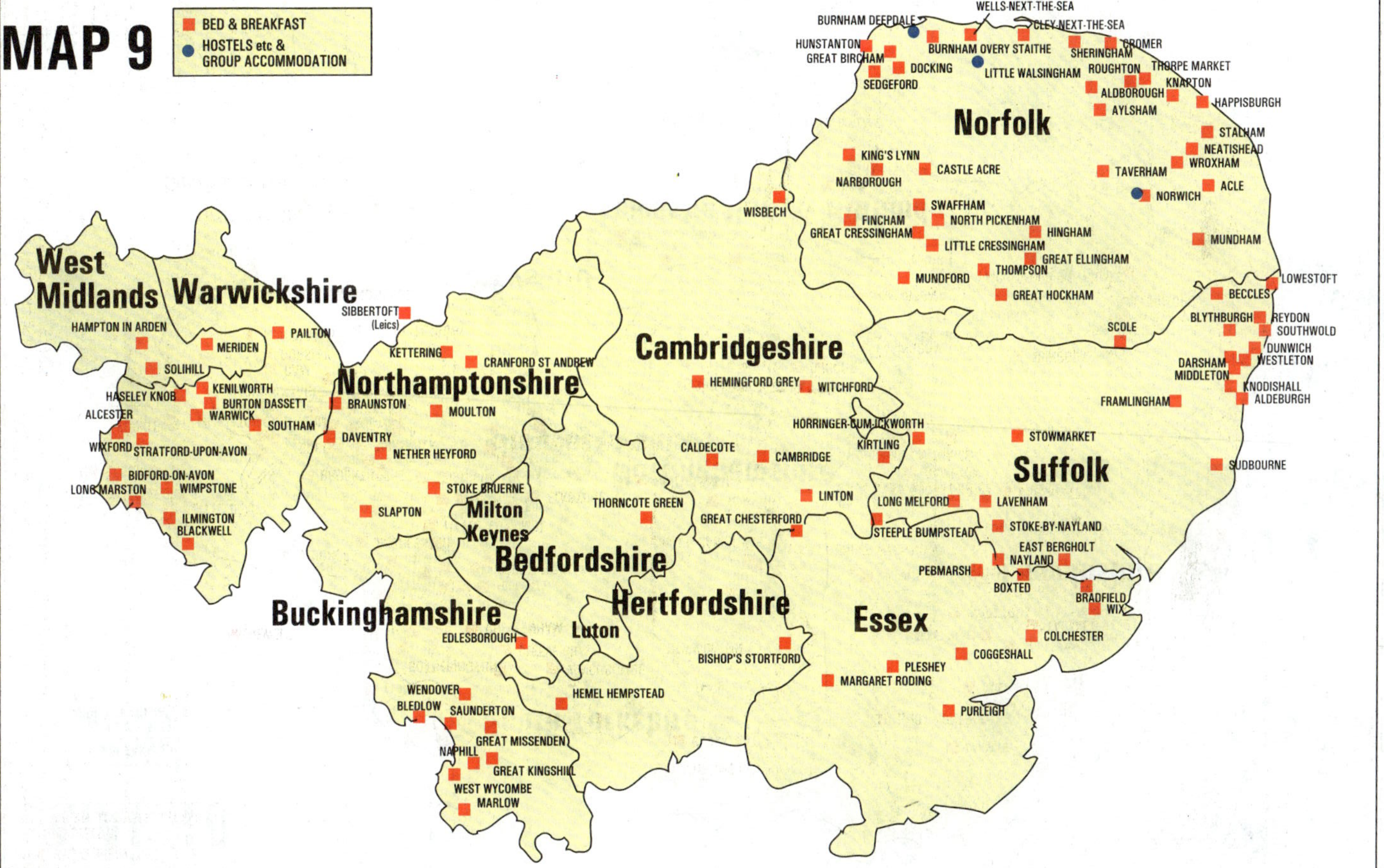
BED & BREAKFAST
HOSTELS etc & GROUP ACCOMMODATION
Norfolk
Suffolk
Cambridgeshire
Essex
Hertfordshire
Bedfordshire
Luton
Milton Keynes
Buckinghamshire
Northamptonshire
Warwickshire
West Midlands
BURNHAM DEEPDALE
WELLS-NEXT-THE-SEA
CLEY-NEXT-THE-SEA
HUNSTANTON
GREAT BIRCHAM
BURNHAM OVERY STAITHE
SHERINGHAM
CROMER
DOCKING
LITTLE WALSINGHAM
ROUGHTON
THORPE MARKET
SEDGEFORD
ALDBOROUGH
KNAPTON
HAPPISBURGH
AYLSHAM
STALHAM
NEATISHEAD
KING'S LYNN
CASTLE ACRE
WROXHAM
TAVERHAM
NARBOROUGH
ACLE
NORWICH
WISBECH
SWAFFHAM
FINCHAM
NORTH PICKENHAM
GREAT CRESSINGHAM
HINGHAM
MUNDHAM
LITTLE CRESSINGHAM
GREAT ELLINGHAM
THOMPSON
MUNDFORD
LOWESTOFT
GREAT HOCKHAM
BECCLES
SIBBERTOFT
(Leics)
BLYTHBURGH
REYDON
SOUTHWOLD
HAMPTON IN ARDEN
PAILTON
SCOLE
MERIDEN
KETTERING
CRANFORD ST ANDREW
DUNWICH
DARSHAM
WESTLETON
SOLIHILL
MIDDLETON
KNODISHALL
KENILWORTH
HEMINGFORD GREY
WITCHFORD
HASELEY KNOB
BRAUNSTON
BURTON DASSETT
ALDEBURGH
FRAMLINGHAM
ALCESTER
WARWICK
MOULTON
SOUTHAM
HORRINGER-CUM-ICKWORTH
DAVENTRY
KIRTLING
STOWMARKET
WIXFORD
STRATFORD-UPON-AVON
NETHER HEYFORD
CALDECOTE
CAMBRIDGE
SUDBOURNE
BIDFORD-ON-AVON
LONG MARSTON
WIMPSTONE
STOKE BRUERNE
LINTON
LONG MELFORD
LAVENHAM
ILMINGTON
BLACKWELL
SLAPTON
THORNCOTE GREEN
GREAT CHESTERFORD
STOKE-BY-NAYLAND
STEEPLE BUMPSTEAD
EAST BERGHOLT
NAYLAND
PEBMARSH
BOXTED
BRADFIELD
WIX
EDLESBOROUGH
BISHOP'S STORTFORD
COLCHESTER
COGGESHALL
PLESHEY
MARGARET RODING
WENDOVER
HEMEL HEMPSTEAD
BLEDLOW
SAUNDERTON
PURLEIGH
GREAT MISSENDEN
NAPHILL
GREAT KINGSHILL
WEST WYCOMBE
MARLOW

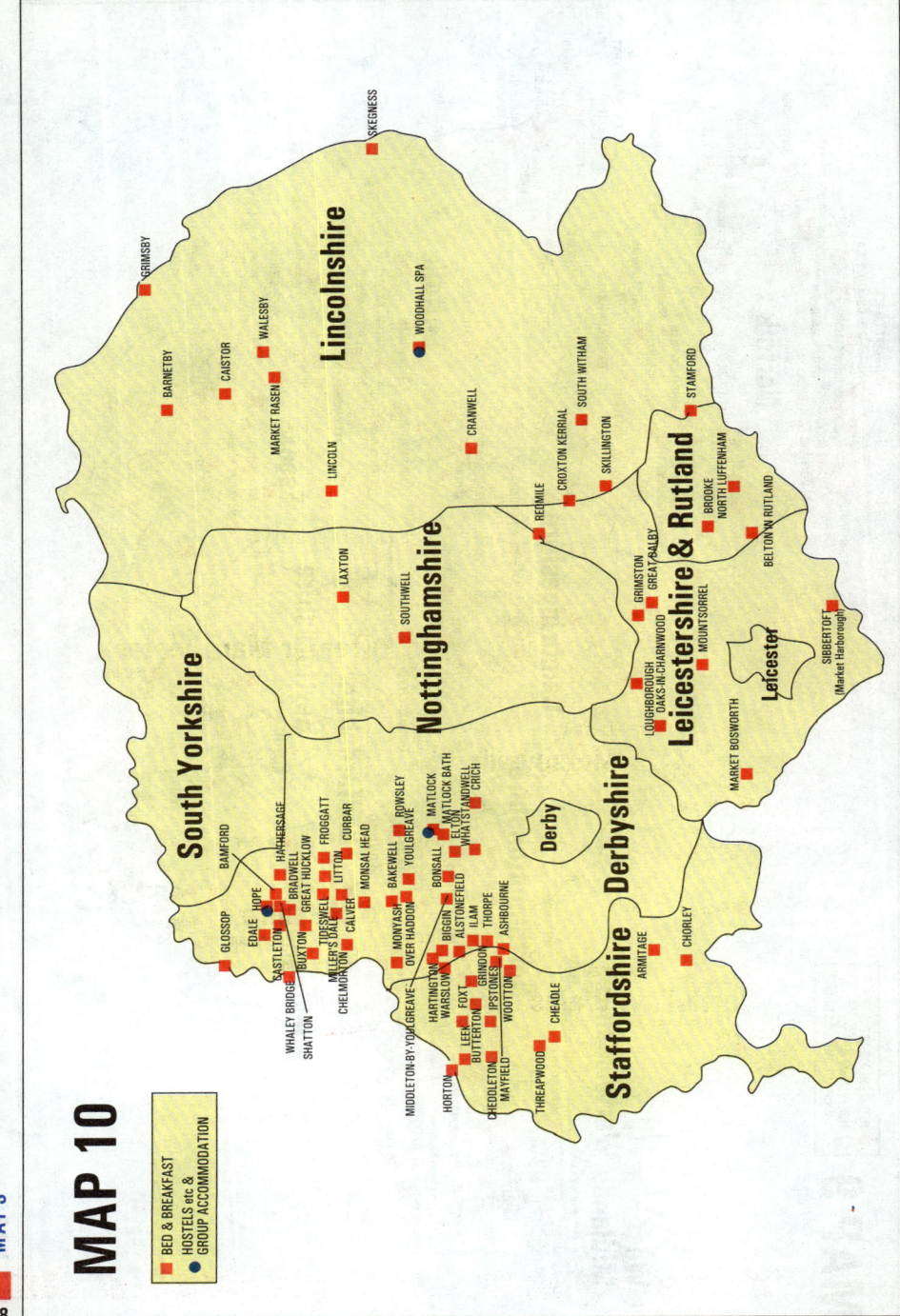

MAP 10

BED & BREAKFAST
HOSTELS etc &
GROUP ACCOMMODATION

South Yorkshire

Lincolnshire

SKEGNESS

GRIMSBY

BARNETBY

CAISTOR

WALESBY

MARKET RASEN

WOODHALL SPA

LINCOLN

CRANWELL

CROXTON KERRIAL

SOUTH WITHAM

SKILLINGTON

REDMILE

STAMFORD

Leicestershire & Rutland

NORTH LUFFENHAM

BROOKE

BELTON IN RUTLAND

GRIMSTON

GREAT DALBY

MOUNTSORREL

SIBBERTOFT
(Market Harborough)

LOUGHBOROUGH
OAKS-IN-CHARNWOOD

Leicester

MARKET BOSWORTH

LAXTON

SOUTHWELL

Nottinghamshire

Derby

Derbyshire

Staffordshire

BAMFORD

HATHERSAGE

FROGGATT

CURBAR

GREAT HUCKLOW

BRADWELL

BUXTON

TIDESWELL

LITTON

CALVER

MONSAL HEAD

BAKEWELL

ROWSLEY

YOULGREAVE

MATLOCK

MATLOCK BATH

CRICH

ELTON

WHATSTANDWELL

BONSALL

GLOSSOP

EDALE

HOPE

CASTLETON

MILLER'S DALE

CHELMORTON

WHALEY BRIDGE

SHATTON

MONYASH

OVER HADDON

BIGGIN

ALSTONEFIELD

ILAM

THORPE

ASHBOURNE

HARTINGTON

WARSLOW

GRINDON

WOOTTON

MIDDLETON-BY-YOULGREAVE

LEEK

FOX

BUTTERTON

IPSTONES

CHEADLE

HORTON

CHEDDLETON

MAYFIELD

THREAPWOOD

ARMITAGE

CHORLEY

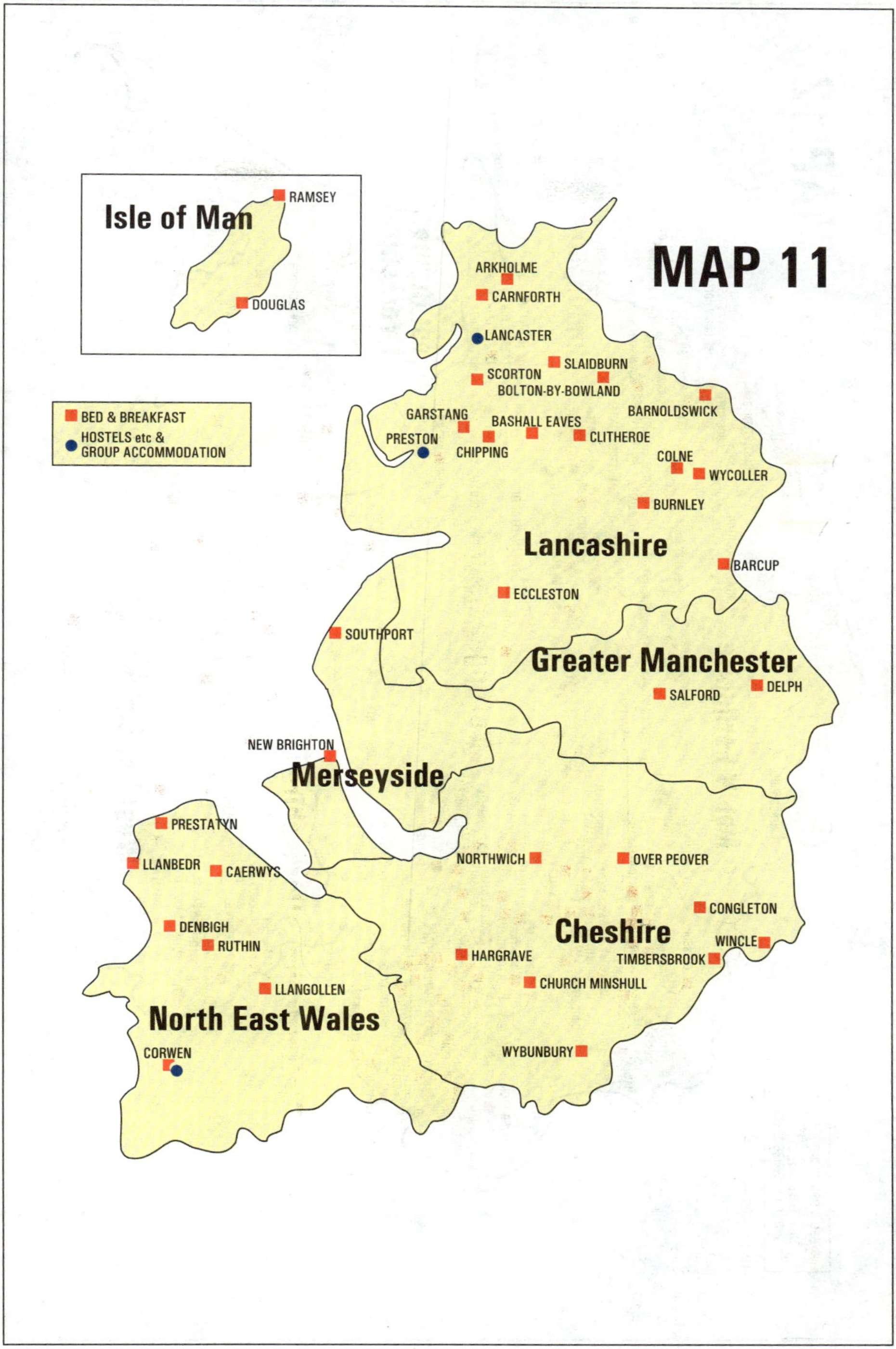

Isle of Man

RAMSEY

DOUGLAS

MAP 11

- ■ BED & BREAKFAST
- ● HOSTELS etc &
  GROUP ACCOMMODATION

ARKHOLME

CARNFORTH

● LANCASTER

SLAIDBURN

SCORTON

BOLTON-BY-BOWLAND

GARSTANG

BASHALL EAVES

BARNOLDSWICK

PRESTON

CHIPPING

CLITHEROE

COLNE

WYCOLLER

BURNLEY

Lancashire

BARCUP

ECCLESTON

SOUTHPORT

Greater Manchester

SALFORD

DELPH

NEW BRIGHTON

Merseyside

PRESTATYN

LLANBEDR

CAERWYS

NORTHWICH

OVER PEOVER

CONGLETON

DENBIGH

RUTHIN

Cheshire

WINCLE

HARGRAVE

TIMBERSBROOK

LLANGOLLEN

CHURCH MINSHULL

North East Wales

CORWEN

WYBUNBURY

MAP 12

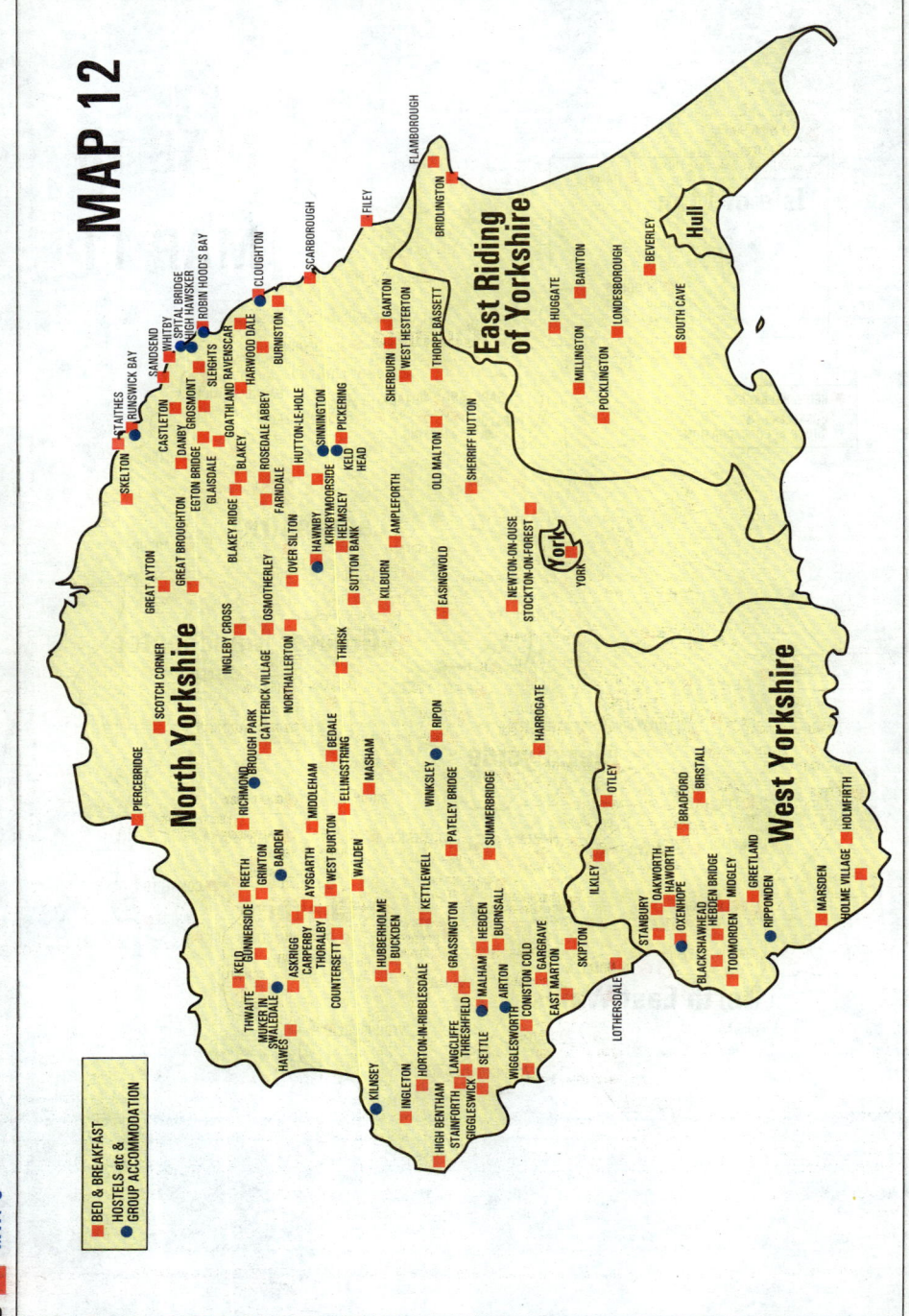

North Yorkshire

East Riding of Yorkshire

West Yorkshire

Hull

York

RUNSWICK BAY
STAITHES
SKELTON
CASTLETON
SANDSEND
WHITBY
SPITAL BRIDGE
HIGH HAWSKER
ROBIN HOOD'S BAY
SLEIGHTS
CLOUGHTON
GROSMONT
DANBY
EGTON BRIDGE
GLAISDALE
HARWOOD DALE
BURNISTON
SCARBOROUGH
FILEY
FLAMBOROUGH
BRIDLINGTON

GOATHLAND
RAVENSCAR
BLAKEY RIDGE
BLAKEY
ROSEDALE ABBEY
HUTTON-LE-HOLE
GUNNINGTON
PICKERING
GANTON
SHERBURN
WEST HESTERTON
THORPE BASSETT

GREAT AYTON
INGLEBY CROSS
OSMOTHERLEY
FARNDALE
OVER SILTON
HAWNBY
KIRKBYMOORSIDE
HELMSLEY
KELD HEAD
SUTTON BANK
KILBURN
AMPLEFORTH
OLD MALTON
SHERRIFF HUTTON

HUGGATE
BAINTON
LONDESBOROUGH
BEVERLEY
MILLINGTON
POCKLINGTON
SOUTH CAVE

SCOTCH CORNER
NORTHALLERTON
THIRSK
EASINGWOLD
NEWTON-ON-OUSE
STOCKTON-ON-FOREST

PIERCEBRIDGE
BROUGH PARK
CATTERICK VILLAGE
RICHMOND
BEDALE
ELLINGSTRING
MASHAM
WINKSLEY
RIPON
HARROGATE

GRINTON
REETH
BARDEN
MIDDLEHAM
WEST BURTON
WALDEN
KETTLEWELL
PATELEY BRIDGE
SUMMERBRIDGE

KELD
GUNNERSIDE
THWAITE
MUKER IN SWALEDALE
HAWES
ASKRIGG
CARPERBY
THORALBY
COUNTERSETT
HUBBERHOLME
BUCKDEN
GRASSINGTON
HEBDEN
BURNSALL

KILNSEY
INGLETON
HIGH BENTHAM
HORTON-IN-RIBBLESDALE
STAINFORTH
LANGCLIFFE
GIGGLESWICK
THRESHFIELD
SETTLE
MALHAM
AIRTON
WIGGLESWORTH
CONISTON COLD
EAST MARTON
GARGRAVE
SKIPTON
LOTHERSDALE

OTLEY
ILKLEY
BRADFORD
BIRSTALL
STANBURY
OAKWORTH
HAWORTH
OXENHOPE
BLACKSHAWHEAD
HEBDEN BRIDGE
TODMORDEN
MIDGLEY
GRETLAND
RIPPONDEN
MARSDEN
HOLME VILLAGE
HOLMFIRTH

KEY
- ■ BED & BREAKFAST
- ● HOSTELS etc & GROUP ACCOMMODATION

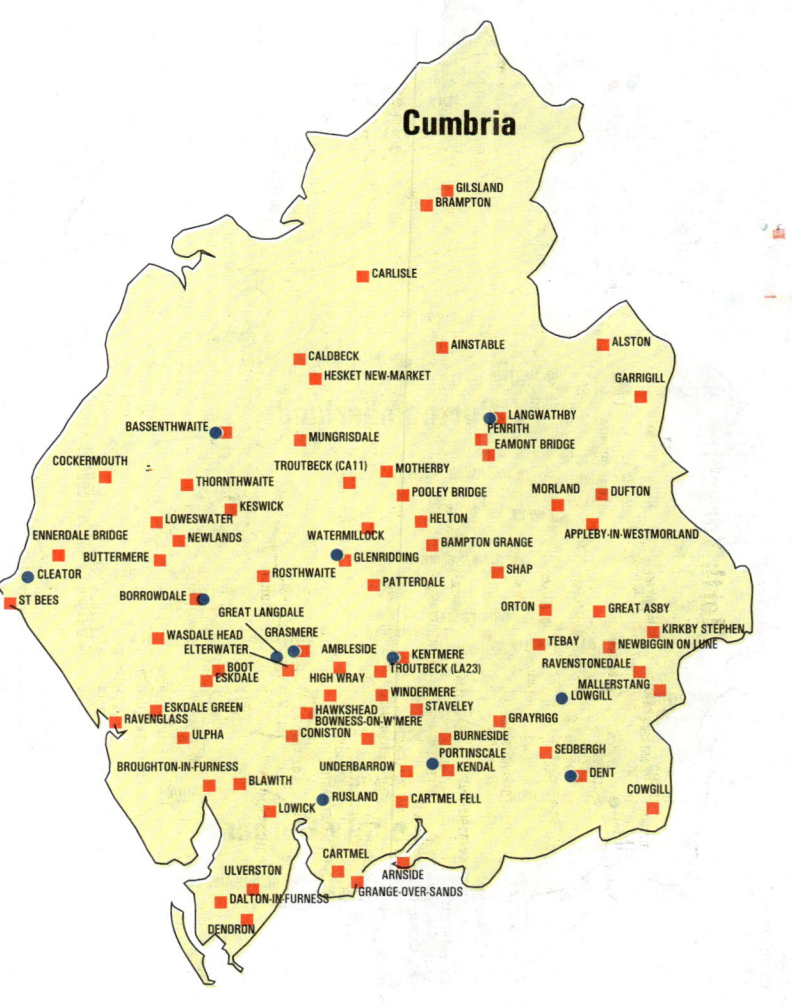

MAP 13

Cumbria

BED & BREAKFAST
HOSTELS etc &
GROUP ACCOMMODATION

GILSLAND
BRAMPTON

CARLISLE

AINSTABLE   ALSTON

CALDBECK   GARRIGILL
HESKET NEW-MARKET

LANGWATHBY
BASSENTHWAITE   MUNGRISDALE   PENRITH
                                              EAMONT BRIDGE
COCKERMOUTH   TROUTBECK (CA11)   MOTHERBY
                  THORNTHWAITE   POOLEY BRIDGE   MORLAND   DUFTON
                        KESWICK
            LOWESWATER   HELTON
ENNERDALE BRIDGE   NEWLANDS   WATERMILLOCK   BAMPTON GRANGE   APPLEBY-IN-WESTMORLAND
            BUTTERMERE
      CLEATOR   ROSTHWAITE   GLENRIDDING
St BEES   BORROWDALE   PATTERDALE   SHAP
                        GREAT LANGDALE   ORTON   GREAT ASBY
            WASDALE HEAD   GRASMERE   KIRKBY STEPHEN
            ELTERWATER   AMBLESIDE   KENTMERE   TEBAY   NEWBIGGIN ON LUNE
                  BOOT   TROUTBECK (LA23)   RAVENSTONEDALE
                  ESKDALE   HIGH WRAY   MALLERSTANG
            ESKDALE GREEN   WINDERMERE   LOWGILL
RAVENGLASS   HAWKSHEAD   STAVELEY   GRAYRIGG
                  ULPHA   BOWNESS-ON-W'MERE
                        CONISTON   BURNESIDE
      BROUGHTON-IN-FURNESS   UNDERBARROW   PORTINSCALE   SEDBERGH
                                                    KENDAL
                  BLAWITH   DENT
            LOWICK   RUSLAND   CARTMEL FELL   COWGILL

                  CARTMEL
      ULVERSTON   ARNSIDE
            DALTON-IN-FURNESS   GRANGE-OVER-SANDS
      DENDRON

MAPS

301

MAP 14

- ■ BED & BREAKFAST
- ● HOSTELS etc &
  GROUP ACCOMMODATION

Northumberland

Tyneside

County Durham

BERWICK-UPON-TWEED

CORNHILL ON TWEED

BEAL

HOLY ISLAND

FENWICK

BELFORD

BAMBURGH

WOOLER

ALNWICK

HARBOTTLE

WARKWORTH

ROCHESTER

ROTHBURY

COTTONHOPEBURNSFOOT

HORSLEY

FALSTONE

STANNERSBURN

WEST WOODBURN

BELLINGHAM

WARK

BARRASFORD

WHITLEY BAY

NEWCASTLE-UPON-TYNE

GREENHEAD

HADRIAN'S WALL

HALTWHISTLE

BARDON MILL

CORBRIDGE

HEXHAM

SLAGGYFORD

CASTLESIDE

COWSHILL

DURHAM

FROSTERLEY

SPENNYMOOR

MIDDLETON-IN-TEESDALE

BISHOP AUCKLAND

MAP 15

BED & BREAKFAST
HOSTELS etc &
GROUP ACCOMMODATION

North East
Scotland

DUFFTOWN
TOMINTOUL
STRATHDON
ABERDEEN
BALLATER
BRAEMAR

Perth &
Kinross

SPITTAL OF GLENSHEE
BLAIR ATHOLL
LETHAM
PITLOCHRY
GLAMIS
BIRNAM
STANLEY
TYNDRUM
KILLIN
PERTH
LEUCHARS

Stirling

STRATHYRE
CRAIL
ANSTRUCHER
CALLANDER
BALMAHA
DRYMEN
STIRLING
MILNGAVIE
EDINBURGH
HADDINGTON
LARGS
AYTON

Isle of
Arran

CORRIE
LAUDER
Scottish
Borders
Central Belt
BIGGAR
PEEBLES
GALASHIELS
LESMAHAGOW
MELROSE
KELSO
BRODICK
DOUGLAS
TRAQUAIR
TOWN YETHOLM
KIRK YETHOLM
BLACKWATERFOOT
SELKIRK
MUIRKIRK
ANCRUM
ECKFORD
WANLOCKHEAD
HAWICK
JEDBURGH
MOFFAT
TEVIOTHEAD
Dumfries &
Galloway
LANGHOLM
NEWCASTLETON

CASTLE DOUGLAS
STRANRAER
NEWTON STEWART
KIRKGUNZEON
PORTPATRICK
GLENLUCE

MAP 16

Shetland

PAPA STOUR

Orkney

BURRAY

SOUTH GALSON

Lewis

Western Islands

Highland

TONGUE

THURSO

BERRIEDALE

North Harris

South Harris

LEVERBURGH

BONAR BRIDGE

Raasay

MELVAIG

CAMUSNAGAUL

GAIRLOCH

ULLAPOOL

North Uist

STAFFIN

Rona

BADACHRO

DIABAIG

TORRIDON

SHIELDAIG

STRATHPEFFER

ACHNASHELLACH

PORTREE

South Uist

STRUAN

LOCHCARRON

INVERNESS

BEAULY

EAST LEWISTON

INVERNESS

CARRBRIDGE

GRANTOWN-ON-SPEY

Scalpey

KYLE OF LOCHALSH

BALMACARA

TOMICH

DRUMNADROCHIT

NETHY BRIDGE

Skye

CARBOST

BOAT OF GARTEN

AVIEMORE

Canna

Rhum

FORT AUGUSTUS

KINCRAIG

Barra

KIRKBEAG

GLENFESHIE

MALLAIG

FORT WILLIAM

INVERGARRY

KINGUSSIE

NEWTONMORE

Eigg

MORAR BY MALLAIG

BANAVIE

SPEAN BRIDGE

Coll

CORPACH

ROY BRIDGE

Tiree

TOBERMORY

ONICH

KINLOCHLEVEN

HYNISH

Mull

ARLE

APPIN

GLENCOE

OBAN

BALLACHULISH

PENNYGHAEL

FIONNPHORT

BRIDGE OF ORCHY

DALMALLY

Argyle & Bute

Collonsay

ARROCHAR

Jura

HELENSBURGH

Islay

TARBERT

PORT ELLEN

■ BED & BREAKFAST

● HOSTELS etc & GROUP ACCOMMODATION

MAPS

304